HUMAN RESOURCES
and the
LAW

HUMAN RESOURCES
and the
LAW

Mark A. Rothstein
Law Foundation Professor of Law
University of Houston
General Editor

Charles B. Craver
Merrifield Research Professor of Law
George Washington University

Elinor P. Schroeder
Professor of Law
University of Kansas

Elaine W. Shoben
Edward W. Cleary Professor of Law
University of Illinois

in collaboration with

Lea S. VanderVelde
Professor of Law
University of Iowa

The Bureau of National Affairs, Inc., Washington, D.C.

Library of Congress Cataloging-in-Publication Data

Human resources and the law / Mark A. Rothstein . . . [et al.]
    p.   cm.
  Includes index.
  ISBN 0-87179-845-X
  1. Labor laws and legislation—United States.   I. Rothstein, Mark A.
KF3319.H78 1994
344.73'01—dc20
[347.3041]

94-28896
CIP

Published by BNA Books, 1231 25th St., N.W.
Washington, D.C. 20037
Printed in the United States of America
International Standard Book Number 0-87179-845-X

Preface

The field of human resources has become increasingly subject to legal constraints. An ever-expanding series of laws regulate employee recruitment; preemployment testing; wages, hours, and fringe benefits; nondiscrimination; occupational safety and health; workers' compensation; discharge, unemployment insurance; pensions; and other matters. Human resource professionals simply cannot perform their jobs without a knowledge of the law.

This book is intended to aid knowledgeable nonlawyers to understand human resources law. As a book about law, it is not intended to explain administration, organization, or management techniques. It will not, for example, explain how to hire or fire employees. On the other hand, the book is not designed to substitute for legal advice in any particular case, which would require a thorough knowledge of the specific facts and would vary by jurisdiction. The book also does not contain an exhaustive, technical analysis for lawyers of the myriad legal issues. Our three-volume treatise, *Employment Law,* published by West Publishing Company, was written for that purpose.

Human resource professionals who read and refer to this book should learn, in a single, understandable volume, the legal framework regulating human resources. We hope this book will help human resource professionals to deal more effectively with their lawyers in legal disputes. More important, we hope that by informing human resource professionals about potential problem areas, they will be able to prevent disputes and lawsuits from arising in the first place.

The authors are indebted to Sam Bresler of Computer Sciences Corporation for his valuable suggestions about the contours of the book. We also thank Diana Huezo for her excellent job of word processing on the manuscript.

April, 1994

Introduction

American employment law traces its roots to feudal England. Servants lived on the property of their masters and often worked for a single master for their entire lives. The law regarded the relationships of household and agricultural servants to their masters as analogous to those of a child to a parent. Applying concepts from domestic relations law, masters were held to be responsible for the wrongful acts of their servants; they also owed to their servants a duty to provide them with competent fellow servants and to afford them reasonable protection from harm. These general principles of master and servant law still exist today, although many other aspects of their relationship have changed.

In general, English legal doctrine was adopted in colonial America, and later, the United States. As urbanization and industrialization expanded in the nineteenth century, workers were less dependent on their employers for food, shelter, clothing, medical care, and other necessities than they had been in feudal days. A new set of relationships began to emerge that was more closely related to commercial contracts.

A key legal issue surrounding the new contractual employment relationship was the duration of the employment contract when the parties did not expressly agree to this term. The answer for American law came from an unlikely source. In 1877, a lawyer and legal scholar from Albany, New York, named Horace G. Wood published the book, *A Treatise on Master and Servant*. In this legal text, Wood asserted that employment relationships without a specific duration were terminable "at will" by either party. This meant that the employee was free to quit at any time for any reason, and the employer was free to discharge the employee at any time for any reason. Although the legal basis for making such an assertion has been questioned by modern legal scholars, Wood's rule was quickly adopted and soon became the clearly acknowledged American rule of at-will employment.

Wood's rule went unchallenged for nearly 100 years. During the 1960s, however, the courts in many jurisdictions recognized the hardships that the rule often caused and began creating a number of exceptions to it. Today, although the rule is still recognized to some extent in virtually every jurisdiction, at least one or more exceptions to the rule also have been recognized in each jurisdiction.

Modern employment law also has been shaped increasingly by statutory enactments at the state and federal levels. At the state level, workers' compensation laws enacted in the early part of the twentieth century often were the first attempts to regulate working conditions in a comprehensive way. At the federal level, the first major wave of legislation was enacted during the New Deal. These laws include the National Labor Relations Act (1935), which gave workers the right to join unions and bargain collectively, and the Fair Labor Standards Act (1938), which set minimum wage rates, required higher pay for overtime, and prohibited the use of child labor in goods or services involved in interstate commerce.

Beginning in the 1960s, a new wave of federal and state civil rights laws were enacted to prohibit discrimination. These laws include the Equal Pay Act of 1963, which prohibits gender-based wage differentials; Title VII of the Civil Rights Act of 1964, which prohibits discrimination in employment on the basis of race, color, religion, sex, and national origin; the Age Discrimination in Employment Act of 1967, which prohibits discrimination against individuals age 40 and older; and the Rehabilitation Act of 1973 and the Americans with Disabilities Act of 1990, which prohibit discrimination on the basis of disability.

Beginning in 1970, Congress and state legislatures began enacting a variety of laws regulating conditions of employment. Among these federal laws are the Occupational Safety and Health Act (1970), the Employee Retirement Income Security Act (1974), the Federal Mine Safety and Health Act (1977), the Worker Adjustment and Retraining Notification Act (1988), the Employee Polygraph Protection Act (1988), and the Family and Medical Leave Act (1993).

Modern employment law considers three main legal sources: constitutional law, statutory law, and common law. Federal constitutional protections, such as First Amendment freedom of speech, only apply to governmental actions. Therefore, in the employment context, constitutional challenges may be brought only with respect to federal, state, or local governmental employment or employment actions undertaken by private sector employers because of a government requirement, such as government-mandated drug testing. Constitutional protections do not apply to the purely private dealings between private parties, including private sector employment. Some state constitutions, however, may be applicable to the private sector.

The second source of employment law is statutory law. This includes any applicable federal, state, or local law. For example, in addition to the federal statutes discussed above, employers may also have to comply with a state law that prohibits discrimination on the basis of sexual orientation or a local ordinance that regulates cigarette smoking in the workplace. Many laws also authorize administrative agencies to implement the laws by issuing certain standards or regulations. These administrative regulations, such as workplace safety and health standards issued by the Occupational Safety and Health Administration (OSHA), have the same binding legal effect as if they were statutorily enacted. A number of laws, such as those dealing with unemployment insurance and workers' compensation, also provide that initial determinations are made by administrative tribunals.

The third source of employment law, the common law, consists of court-made doctrine established over time by decisions of numerous courts. The employment at-will rule is a common law rule. So too are rules dealing with the construction of written contracts. Various tort cases, lawsuits seeking damages for harms caused by conduct the law recognizes as wrongful, also apply to employment law. Some examples are legal actions based on negligence, defamation, and invasion of privacy. The common law differs somewhat in each state and is constantly evolving.

Contents

2. Employment Discrimination

3. Wages, Hours, and Benefits

4. Conditions of Employment

6. Workers' Compensation

1

Establishing the Employment Relationship

INTRODUCTION

Modern employment law has limited the traditional freedom employers have enjoyed to hire, fire, and control terms and conditions of employment, but the law has operated essentially in a negative way. Especially in the private, nonunion sector, in which employment is regulated by neither civil service laws nor collective bargaining agreements, the law has been more proscriptive than prescriptive—prohibiting employers from behaving in certain ways rather than requiring that they behave in other ways.

The hiring process is an excellent illustration of this general principle. Employers still have fairly wide discretion in adopting hiring practices they deem valuable to the enterprise. For example, they may use want ads, employment agencies, or any other method of developing a pool of applicants; they may use application forms, interviews, references, or other methods of soliciting information from or about the individual; they may check an individual's credit record or criminal record; they may require aptitude tests, physical ability tests, or drug tests. The employer's selection method will run afoul of the law only if it violates a legal proscription.

There are four main categories of legal doctrines regulating the hiring process. First, for public sector employees and some governmentally regulated employees, constitutional protections apply. For example, the U.S. Constitution's Fourth Amendment ban on unreasonable search and seizure applies to the drug testing of both public employees and private sector employees whose drug testing is government mandated. Second, federal statutes regulate various aspects of the hiring process. For example, the federal Employee Polygraph Protection Act prohibits most polygraph testing in the private sector. Third, state constitutional law and state and local statutes regulate the hiring process. For example, several states have laws prohibiting employers from inquiring into an applicant's HIV status. Fourth, there may be common law, primarily tort, remedies available to applicants to redress defamation, invasion of privacy, intentional infliction of emotional distress, and other wrongs. Common law remedies also are available to third parties, such as individuals injured as a result of an employer's negligent hiring, to redress harms caused by the hiring process.

Although this chapter is concerned with the hiring process, a number of the cases cited in the chapter are actually discharge cases. This is because there are relatively few common law hiring cases brought by unsuccessful applicants for employment. One reason for this is that the law is less sympathetic to the claims of individuals who have been denied an opportunity to obtain employment as opposed to employees whose employment, perhaps after a long tenure, has been wrongfully ended. For example, there is a large body of case law on common law wrongful discharge actions in tort and contract, but there is little if any case law involving actions for wrongful refusal to hire. Second, unsuccessful job seekers are much less likely than discharged employees to file a lawsuit, because the loss of an employment opportunity to an applicant is less tangible and other employment options are usually being pursued concurrently. The other reason for including nonhiring cases in this chapter is simply that it is more efficient to discuss, for example, all of drug testing in one place.

Much of the controversy surrounding legal regulation of the hiring process has to do with the regulation of access to information. While employers still may not be told whom to hire or how to hire, if employers are limited in the types of information available to them to use in deciding employability, then the hiring process can be regulated indirectly and, perhaps, less pervasively. At the same time, this type of regulation also furthers other interests, such as protecting confidentiality and privacy.

The final part of this chapter deals with the contract and tort issues arising from hiring. It discusses the formation of employment contracts and their express and implied terms. It also focuses on the determinants and significance of the employment relationship for tort purposes, including the liability of employers for torts committed by their employees within the scope of employment.

WANT ADS

Section 704(b) of Title VII of the Civil Rights Act of 1964 (Title VII)[1] provides that it is an unlawful employment practice for an employer, labor union, or employment agency to publish any notice or advertisement indicating any preference, limitation, specification, or discrimination in employment based on race, color, religion, sex, or national origin. Most of the cases involving alleged violations of this provision have centered on gender-based preferences. According to guidelines issued by the Equal Employment Opportunity Commission (EEOC), the federal agency charged with enforcing Title VII, section 704(b) prohibits placing advertisements in gender-segregated newspaper columns.

Although the language of Title VII makes it clear that employers, unions, and employment agencies would violate the law by placing gender-segregated want ads, it is not clear from the statute and regulations whether newspapers can be held responsible under Title VII for running the discriminatory ads. Based on the legislative history of Title VII, however, the courts have been unanimous in holding that newspapers are not liable for these ads under Title VII.

To bring an action under section 704(b), an individual must be "aggrieved." In *Hailes v. United Airlines*,[2] the Fifth Circuit Court of Appeals held that for purposes of section 704(b), an aggrieved person is someone who is "able to demonstrate that he has a real, present interest in the type of employment advertised [and is] able to show he

---

[1] 42 U.S.C. §2000e (1993).
[2] 464 F.2d 1006, 4 FEP Cases 1022 (5th Cir. 1972).

was effectively deterred from applying for such employment." In *Hailes*, the court held that the plaintiff had met this test because, even though he did not apply for United's "stewardess" position under a "help wanted-female" column, he had been rejected because of gender when he had answered a similar ad run by another airline.

Section 4(e) of the Age Discrimination in Employment Act (ADEA)[3] contains a similar prohibition on age-based want ads. Although want ads traditionally have not been segregated by age, they often have contained language indicating a preference for younger applicants. In *Hodgson v. Approved Personnel Service, Inc.*,[4] the Fourth Circuit Court of Appeals rejected the government's guidelines, which indicated that certain "trigger" words, such as "young," "boy," and "recent college graduate," were per se illegal under the ADEA. Instead, the court held that the context must be considered. If the trigger words are used as part of a general invitation to prospective customers to use the employment agency's services, then they are legal; if they refer to qualifications for a specific job, then they are illegal.

Both Title VII and the ADEA provide for coordination with state fair employment acts and nearly every state has enacted legislation restricting the content of want ads similar to section 704(b) of Title VII and section 4(e) of the ADEA. Some of the state laws also prohibit discrimination based on other factors, such as marital status or sexual orientation, and want ad restrictions therefore are also broader. In addition, several states have enacted "aiding and abetting" laws, which have been used to charge newspapers with violations for running discriminatory want ads. In *Pittsburgh Press Co. v. Pittsburgh Commission on Human Relations*,[5] the Supreme Court held that the newspaper's First Amendment rights were not violated by finding that its gender-segregated want ad column violated the "aiding and abetting" provision of the city's fair employment ordinance.

EMPLOYMENT AGENCIES

Most states began licensing and regulating employment agencies during the Great Depression, when high unemployment led to some

---

[3] 29 U.S.C. §§621–34 (1993).
[4] 529 F.2d 760, 11 FEP Cases 688 (4th Cir. 1975).
[5] 413 U.S. 376, 5 FEP 1141 (1973).

exploitative and unscrupulous employment agency practices. These laws remain on the books, although many have been amended and updated. Today, about two-thirds of the states have laws that regulate employment agencies in some way.

Typically, these laws require employment agencies to be licensed and bonded, prohibit them from charging in advance, and set maximum fees. Some of the laws have been challenged on constitutional grounds, but without success. In upholding the validity of New York's law, the court wrote: "It seems quite incredible that a codification of a business practice, adopted largely in the interest of fair dealing, can be regarded as an unlawful usurpation of legislative power."[6]

In addition to state regulation of the business practices of employment agencies, discrimination in referrals is prohibited by section 703(b) of Title VII, which provides: "It shall be an unlawful employment practice for an employment agency to fail or refuse to refer for employment, or otherwise to discriminate against an individual because of his race, color, religion, sex, or national origin, or to classify or refer for employment on the basis of his race, color, religion, sex, or national origin."

Section 701(c) of Title VII defines the term "employment agency" as "[a]ny person regularly undertaking with or without compensation to procure employees for an employer or to procure for employees opportunities to work for an employer and includes an agent of such person." A law school placement office has been held to be an employment agency under this definition. A newspaper that runs want ads, however, has been held not to be an employment agency.

Every state has its own employment service, which attempts to find appropriate jobs for the unemployed. These state agencies, mandated by a provision of the Federal Unemployment Tax Act, also are responsible for the distribution of unemployment compensation benefits.

In addition to statutory duties, employment agencies owe a common law duty of reasonable care to both the individuals they attempt to place and the employers to which they refer potential employees. For example, in one case an employment agency received a telephone call from a man who asked the agency to send over someone to do routine office work at a motorcycle repair shop. Without making a check on the employer, the employment agency dispatched a woman to the caller's

---

[6]National Employment Exch. v. Geraghty, 60 F.2d 918, 921 (2d Cir. 1932).

"office," which turned out to be an empty room. The woman was abducted and sexually assaulted. In an action for negligence against the employment agency, the court held that the employment agency owed a duty of care to the woman to make sure that the referral was legitimate. This legal duty was based on the contractual relationship between the woman and the agency, the agency's ability to foresee some danger to her, and its ability to exercise some control over the employers to whom it made referrals.[7]

An employment agency also has a duty of reasonable care to employers in the referral of prospective employees. For example, an employment agency was held liable to an employer because a referred employee stole the employer's property. The court termed "perfunctory" the agency's compliance with the minimum statutory requirements of recording the name and address of the applicant, and contacting former employers. Because the employee was to be placed in a private home, reasonable care demanded a more thorough investigation.[8]

APPLICATION FORMS

The first direct contact between an applicant and an employer often involves the completion of an application form. Although forms vary widely, they customarily solicit personal information, such as name, address, telephone number, educational background, and work history. Application forms are lawful unless they have the purpose or effect of discriminating on the basis of one or more statutorily proscribed criteria.

Title VII does not specifically prohibit an employer from asking applicants to indicate their race, color, religion, sex, or national origin. Nevertheless, "inquiries which either directly or indirectly disclose such information, unless otherwise explained, may constitute evidence of discrimination prohibited by Title VII."[9] Moreover, because the *use* of such information in making decisions regarding hiring violates Title VII, virtually all employers exclude such questions from their application forms.

---

[7]Keck v. American Employment Agency, 652 S.W.2d 2 (Ark. 1983).

[8]Janof v. Newsom, 53 F.2d 149 (D.C. Cir. 1931).

[9]Office of Public Affairs, Equal Employment Opportunity Commission, Pre-Employment Inquiries (1981).

The fair employment laws of most states take the approach of Title VII. Several states, however, go beyond Title VII and expressly prohibit various preemployment questions on application forms. In fact, some states publish detailed preemployment inquiry guides, which indicate what questions are legal and what questions are illegal. **Commonly, questions that ask for the applicant's race, color, religion, sex, national origin, age, or disabilities are prohibited**. In addition, some states prohibit application forms from asking questions that indirectly reveal this information. Thus, questions such as hair color, eye color, height, weight, photograph, arrest record, marital status, birthplace, names and addresses of parents, ages of dependents, and reference of a religious leader are often prohibited as well. These additional provisions have been upheld in court.

Falsifications

There are a number of cases involving the falsification of application forms. Falsification of information will justify an employer's refusal to hire as well as the discharge of an employee who already has been hired. If the falsification involves the answer to a question that the employer was not lawfully permitted to ask, then the falsification may not justify the discharge.

The courts are divided on the issue of whether falsification of a lawful question will justify a discharge that was made for an unlawful reason before the employer learned of the falsification. This is sometimes referred to as the "after-acquired evidence doctrine." Most courts have upheld the discharge. In general, these courts hold that an employer is not liable for a discharge based solely on unlawful motives, such as a violation of Title VII, if the employer can prove that it would have discharged the plaintiff in any event if it had knowledge of the falsification. Similar results have been reached in cases involving resume fraud and the falsification of periodic forms after employment.

In *Wallace v. Dunn Construction Co.*,[10] the Eleventh Circuit Court of Appeals rejected the majority approach because "it excuses all liability based on what *hypothetically* would have occurred absent the alleged discriminatory motive *assuming the employer had knowledge*

---

[10]968 F.2d 1174, 1179, 59 FEP Cases 997 (11th Cir. 1992) (emphasis in original).

that it would not acquire until sometime during the litigation arising from the discharge." According to the court, the result is that the plaintiff is left in a worse position simply by being a member of a protected class or by having engaged in protected activity.

Disclaimers

Some employers place disclaimers of any job security in their application forms in order to minimize the risk of a breach of contract claim following termination of an employee. The disclaimers state that the employment is "at will," which means that the employee may be fired at any time for any reason. Most courts will consider the existence of such a disclaimer as a factor, although not necessarily dispositive, of the agreement of the parties regarding the duration of employment.

INTERVIEWS

The job interview is a well-established practice in U.S. employment. Although some civil service laws specify the particulars of job interviews, in the private sector the specifics of job interviews are left to the employer. Because the interview is often a crucial step in the process of deciding which applicant to hire, it is frequently a focus of applicants who believe they were denied employment unfairly. The courts have held, however, that it is lawful for an employer to refuse to hire an applicant who had a poor interview, which was caused by the applicant's abrasive personality or unresponsive and unassertive demeanor.

The most common lawsuits involving interviews are Title VII actions based on alleged gender discrimination. A variety of interview conduct has been held to violate Title VII, such as discouraging females from seeking traditionally male jobs and asking a female applicant whether she could wield a sledge hammer when this was not a part of the job. It also has been held to violate Title VII for employers to ask women about their childbearing plans. **Although some courts have held that it is not necessarily a violation of Title VII for an employer to ask only female applicants "family oriented" questions about marital status and child care arrangements, employers would be well advised to conduct gender-neutral interviews.**

Similar issues have arisen under state gender discrimination laws. Surprisingly, sexist comments, including asking an applicant how she felt about sleeping with her boss, have not automatically resulted in the finding of gender discrimination. Asking a woman applicant whether she would be afraid of loud machinery or working at night also did not necessarily establish gender discrimination. Such questions can be evidence of discrimination, however. In contrast, gender-neutral interviews leave no room for doubt about their legality.

Statements made to an applicant at a job interview also have been used in an attempt to establish an oral contract that, for example, precluded termination without just cause. In *Weiner v. McGraw-Hill*,[11] the applicant was assured in the initial employment interview that the employer terminated employees only for just cause. The application also specified that termination would be only for just cause. The New York Court of Appeals held that an action for breach of contract would lie based on a subsequent dismissal without just cause. Most courts, however, have held to the contrary and have refused to find that statements made at an interview establish an oral contract.

REFERENCES

Along with application forms and interviews, the use of references is a standard element of the hiring process. Despite a lack of empirical data about the efficacy of reference checks in employee selection and a growing reluctance of former employers to provide negative references for fear of liability, the use of references remains pervasive.

There is little direct regulation of references, except for an occasional statute conferring a good faith immunity from liability for defamation on employers that write letters of reference in good faith. More common are "service letter" statutes in effect in 11 states.[12] These laws generally provide that, upon the request of a former employee, the former employer must provide a letter indicating the former employee's job title, dates of employment, and, in some cases, the reason for leaving employment.

---

[11] 443 N.E.2d 441, 118 LRRM 2689 (N.Y. 1982).

[12] California, Indiana, Kansas, Missouri, Montana, Nebraska, North Carolina, Oklahoma, Texas, Washington, and Wisconsin.

Aside from service letter statutes, employers are not required to provide a reference. If they choose to do so, they will generally not be liable for a bad reference unless it was given in bad faith. If an employer provides a reference, it is unclear whether there is a duty to provide an *accurate* reference and, if so, to whom is the duty owed. One case considered the issue directly and found no duty. In *Moore v. St. Joseph Nursing Home*,[13] an employee of the defendant was discharged after 24 disciplinary warnings for violence and use of alcohol and drugs. The employee was later hired by another employer, in whose employ he savagely beat and murdered a co-worker. The estate of the deceased worker contended that the original employer had a duty to disclose the violent propensities of the employee to the second employer. The Michigan Court of Appeals, while noting that this type of information *should* be made known, nevertheless held that, in the absence of a special relationship between the former employer and the victim, there was no *duty* to disclose the information. "[W]e conclude that a former employer has no duty to disclose malefic information about a former employee to the former employee's prospective employer."

DEFAMATION

A variety of written and oral statements in the employment setting have given rise to lawsuits for defamation. These include statements made about current or former employees by employers, former employers, coemployees, and other parties. These legal actions may arise at any stage of the employment relationship, from preemployment to post-termination.

Defamation, the act of harming another person's reputation through the publication of an injurious falsehood, may be based on a written (libel) or verbal (slander) statement. It consists of a false, unprivileged, and defamatory statement made to another person with some degree of fault on the part of the person making the statement.

The first element of a defamation action is a showing that the statement is defamatory. "A communication is defamatory if it so tends to harm the reputation of another as to lower him in the estimation of the

---

[13]459 N.W.2d 100 (Mich. App. 1990).

community or to deter third persons from associating or dealing with him."[14] It is not necessary that the communication actually harm another person's reputation so long as it has a "general tendency to have such an effect." In addition, the statement need only prejudice the individual in the eyes of a "substantial and respectable minority" of members of the community.

It is important to distinguish defamatory statements from statements of opinion. Although this is a critical distinction in the law, it is often difficult to make this distinction. Derogatory assertions of fact are defamatory. Thus, saying that an employee was fired for stealing, that a former employee was unethical, that an employee was fired for falsifying time cards, and that an employee attempted to bribe a co-worker into engaging in unauthorized conduct have been held to be defamatory. Even less assertive or more equivocal statements have been held to be defamatory. For example, courts have found the following statements defamatory: saying that fellow physicians "lacked confidence" in a physician, declining to tell a customer why a former employee had been dismissed in an effort not to embarrass the former employee, and saying that "after what he did it is no wonder" a reference would not be given.

The mere statement of opinion, however, is not defamation. A former employer's referring to an employee as an "emotional problem," characterizing an employee as "unprofessional," "insubordinate," and "abusive," and even saying that he "would not trust the plaintiff as far as he could throw him" have been held to be mere opinion and thus not defamatory.

If an opinion also implies underlying factual assertions capable of a defamatory meaning, then it will be actionable. This has been referred to as "informational opinion." Statements that an individual did not properly perform job obligations and had poor rapport with other administrators, that an individual was too detail-oriented, and that an airline pilot was "paranoid" have been held to be defamatory.

Based on the doctrine of *New York Times Co. v. Sullivan*,[15] legal actions for defamation also must satisfy First Amendment considerations. The maker of a false and defamatory statement concerning a private person in relation to a purely private matter is only subject to

---

[14]*Restatement (Second) of Torts* §559 (1989).
[15]376 U.S. 254, 1 Media L. Rep. 1527 (1964).

liability if the maker of the statement knows that the statement is false, acts in reckless disregard for the falsity of the statement, or acts at least negligently in failing to ascertain the truth or falsity of the statement.

Because written statements have a greater degree of permanence, libel is actionable without a showing of special harm to the plaintiff. The harm is presumed. In an action for slander, however, there must be evidence of special harm unless the statement involves particular subjects that constitute slander per se. The imputation of misconduct involving an individual's business, trade, profession, or office has been held to be slander per se. Thus, a statement that an employee had been fired for drunkenness, an accusation of theft, and allegations about excessive absenteeism and misrepresentation of salary have been held to be slander per se.

Publication

An important element of the tort of defamation is publication, defined as the intentional or negligent communication of the defamatory matter to someone other than the person defamed. In the employment context there have been several issues. For example, some courts hold that communication among supervisory and managerial personnel is not publication, although others hold that there is publication, but there is a qualified privilege protecting speakers for liability for good faith communications. In addition, most courts hold that simply placing material in an individual's personnel file does not constitute publication.

Traditionally, the publication requirement means that the defamatory statement must be communicated directly to a third person. There was no publication if the statement was communicated only to the person defamed, even if the person defamed subsequently communicated what was said to another person. There is a trend in employment cases, however, to permit actions for defamation to be based on "self-publication" by the defamed party to a third person. Typically, these cases involve employees who were discharged by a prior employer, allegedly for some misconduct. When a subsequent, potential employer asks why the individual left the prior employer, if the applicant is truthful, he or she will repeat the defamatory reason that was given to the individual by the employer. Some courts hold that this self-publication of defamatory material is tantamount to a defamatory communication by the former employer to the potential employer and therefore should be actionable.

The jurisdictions are divided on the viability of defamation actions based on self-publication. The modern cases rejecting the theory generally adopt the position that self-publication fails to satisfy the traditional definition of publication. The cases adopting the theory of self-publication generally require either that the originator of the statement knew or had reason to know that the defamed party would repeat the statement to a third party or that it was foreseeable to the originator of the defamatory matter that the person defamed would be *compelled* to communicate the matter to a third person.

Because truth is an absolute defense in a defamation action, defendants in self-publication cases sometimes have asserted that the statement made to the former employee was not defamatory because it was truthful. For example, an employer could assert that the employee *was* discharged for stealing; that was the true reason for the discharge, regardless of whether the employee actually stole anything. Nevertheless, courts have not necessarily focused on the literal meaning of the words used, but their implication. According to one court: "Requiring that truth as a defense go to the underlying implication of the statement, at least where the statement involves more than a simple allegation, appears to be the better view."[16]

Privileges

Statements made in the employment context may be absolutely or conditionally privileged. If a communication is absolutely privileged, it is a complete bar to a defamation action, irrespective of whether the statement was known to be false and thus made maliciously or in bad faith. Consent to the publication of defamatory matter by the person defamed is a complete defense. There is also an absolute privilege for statements made in judicial or administrative proceedings so long as they are pertinent to the subject of the controversy. This includes statements to the EEOC, labor grievance hearings, and National Labor Relations Board hearings. Statements made during investigations prior to or in conjunction with judicial or administrative proceedings also are

---

[16]Lewis v. Equitable Life Assurance Soc'y, 389 N.W.2d 876, 899, 1 IER Cases 1269 (Minn. 1986).

absolutely privileged. Statements made in unemployment compensation proceedings may be absolutely or conditionally privileged, depending on the jurisdiction.

A publication may be subject to a conditional or qualified privilege if there is a reasonable belief that the recipient or a third party has an important interest in the information and there is either a legal duty to disclose it or it is within the bounds of decent conduct. For example, a defamatory statement may be conditionally privileged if there is a common interest between the publisher and the recipient and the publisher reasonably believes that the recipient has an interest and is entitled to know. The privilege arises from the social necessity of permitting and encouraging full and unrestricted disclosure. Unlike absolute privileges, however, conditional privileges will be lost if abused.

Generally, if an employer communicates the reason for firing an employee to other employees, it is qualifiedly privileged based on common interest. Thus, employers have been privileged to tell co-workers, individually or in groups, that an employee was discharged for being drunk and misbehaving, stealing, altering a time card, falsifying an employment application, selling drugs, or vandalism. Reports by and to supervisory and managerial personnel concerning an employee's work performance are generally held to be conditionally privileged based on interest and duty, as well as public policy. A former employer's supplying of a reference to a prospective employer also is protected by a conditional privilege. As mentioned earlier, a conditional privilege may be lost if it is abused. Abuse can occur when (1) the publisher has knowledge of the falsity of a statement or a reckless disregard for whether the statement is true or false; (2) a statement is published for a purpose other than the one for which the privilege applies; (3) the statement is published to a person not reasonably necessary to accomplish the purpose for which the material is privileged; (4) the publisher is motivated primarily by ill will; or (5) there is excessive publication. For example, posting notices on bulletin boards, making announcements over the public address system, or publishing information in a company newsletter could be viewed as excessive publication.

CRIMINAL RECORDS

Many employers attempt to discover whether applicants for employment have a criminal record, including both arrests and convictions. The legality of such inquiries varies widely, depending on the nature of the job, the method of inquiry, and the existence of a relevant state law. The three different types of criminal records laws are those that require, permit, or prohibit the use of criminal records.

A variety of state laws mandate that a preemployment criminal record review must be performed for all applicants seeking employment in certain particularly sensitive jobs. Examples include the following: child care employees, child welfare employees, youth detention employees, youth correction employees, school employees, home health employees, nursing home aides, police officers, security guards, corrections employees, nuclear workers, and lottery employees. At least one state, Utah, allows school districts and private schools to require job applicants to pay the costs of a criminal background check if the applicant passes an initial review.

An employer that investigates the applicant's criminal record must determine the extent to which the information will be used in the hiring process. State law may require that anyone convicted of a felony be rejected from certain jobs. The employer also may establish or may be required to establish a time period after convictions that will result in disqualification from certain jobs. If an employer fails to perform a state-mandated criminal record review, this fact may be introduced as evidence of negligence in a negligent hiring case.

The second category is comprised of state laws authorizing employers to gain access to criminal records, even though employers are not required to do so. Some of the laws grant a more general right of access to the records of certain types of crimes, such as sex crimes. A common statutory scheme is to permit access to criminal records only for specific jobs. In the public sector, the job categories include the following: school teachers, child care employees, employees of facilities for the mentally ill, employees of juvenile detention facilities, public housing employees, and employees of the state auditor general. In the private sector, the job categories include the following: private school employees, employees with disciplinary power over minors, public utilities employees, bank employees, credit union employees, nuclear employees, gaming employees, and higher education security employees.

The third category of state laws are those that restrict the access to or use of criminal records. Some states limit the availability of criminal records information to employers or allow individuals to apply for jobs without revealing their criminal records. Other states limit employer access to arrest records, limit access to arrest records more than one year old, or prohibit employers from asking about arrests not leading to conviction.

The purpose of the laws restricting access to and disclosure of criminal records is to prevent discrimination in employment against individuals with criminal records. Some specific statutes attempt to accomplish this end directly, by prohibiting unreasonable discrimination against individuals with prior criminal offenses. More frequently, however, challenges to employment discrimination on the basis of prior conviction or arrest are based on constitutional grounds or are alleged to violate Title VII.

In *Butts v. Nichols*,[17] a challenge was brought against an Iowa law that barred all convicted felons from civil service positions. The court held that the absolute prohibition on hiring for all positions constituted a violation of the U.S. Constitution's guarantee of equal protection of the laws. State constitutional law also has been used to challenge the refusal to hire individuals with arrest records.

Private sector challenges to refusal to hire based on criminal records have been brought under Title VII. The leading case is *Green v. Missouri Pacific Railroad*,[18] in which the Eighth Circuit Court of Appeals held that criminal convictions may be considered on an individual basis, but that blanket rejections of all convicted criminals may be an indirect form of race discrimination. The Ninth Circuit Court of Appeals has applied this principle with even greater force to the use of arrest records because members of racial and ethnic minorities are more likely to have an arrest record.[19]

FINGERPRINTING

Fingerprinting is used by employers to verify the identity of applicants and employees, often as part of a review of criminal records. As might be expected, fingerprinting is most often used in jobs where there is concern about possible criminal activity or public safety.

---

[17]381 F. Supp. 573, 8 FEP Cases 676 (S.D. Iowa 1974).
[18]523 F.2d 1290, 11 FEP Cases 658 (8th Cir. 1975).
[19]Gregory v. Litton Sys., 472 F.2d 631, 5 FEP Cases 267 (9th Cir. 1972).

A variety of federal statutes and regulations require the fingerprinting of applicants and employees. Numerous state laws also require the fingerprinting of certain employees, such as school employees, child care employees, juvenile services employees, gambling industry employees, police and security officers, and certain health care providers. Other laws permit the fingerprinting of gambling industry employees, lottery employees, museum and hospital employees, bar and restaurant employees, and bank employees.

Mandatory fingerprinting laws have been challenged under several federal and state constitutional theories. In *Iacobucci v. City of Newport*,[20] the plaintiff asserted that a municipal ordinance requiring the fingerprinting of employees serving alcoholic beverages violated the U.S. Constitution. The Sixth Circuit Court of Appeals upheld the ordinance and termed the fingerprinting requirement "only minimally intrusive."

In constitutional challenges, the governmental entities have asserted the need for criminal deterrence as the primary reason for the fingerprinting requirement. This claim has been well received by the courts. For example, in *Iacobucci* the court stated that "[b]ecause the ordinance bears a rational relationship to a legitimate governmental interest, we view it as a proper exercise of the City's police power." The courts also have relied on the minimal intrusion of fingerprinting. "The day is long past when fingerprinting carried with it a stigma of any implication of criminality. . . . The submission of one's fingerprints is no more an invasion of privacy than the submission of one's photograph or signature to a prospective employer."[21]

Fingerprinting requirements generally are imposed on public employees or private sector employees in regulated industries. For other private sector employees, although fingerprinting is not required by the government, it may be required by the employer. The only exception seems to be if there is a specific statute that prohibits private sector employers from requiring fingerprints as a condition of employment. For example, New York has an outright ban on fingerprinting. In Louisiana, it is unlawful for a public or private employer to pass on the cost of fingerprinting to a prospective employee.

---

[20]785 F.2d 1354 (6th Cir.), *rev'd and remanded on other grounds*, 479 U.S. 92 (1986).

[21]Thom v. New York Stock Exch., 306 F. Supp. 1002, 1007, 1009 (S.D.N.Y. 1969), *aff'd*, 425 F.2d 1074 (2d Cir.), *cert. denied*, 398 U.S. 905 (1970).

CREDIT RECORDS

Some employers use credit information about applicants and employees as an indication of whether the individual is responsible, trustworthy, and stable. Use of this information for an employment purpose, however, may implicate the federal Fair Credit Reporting Act, state credit reporting laws, common law, and the federal Bankruptcy Act.

The Fair Credit Reporting Act (FCRA)[22] is the principal federal law regulating the use of consumer credit information. The FCRA was designed to protect consumers from inaccurate or arbitrary information in a consumer report being used as a factor in determining an individual's eligibility for credit, insurance, or employment. The FCRA attempts to achieve this goal by limiting the types of information contained in consumer reports, restricting access to consumer files, requiring notice to the consumer when an adverse action is based on a consumer report, mandating consumer access to review credit files, and permitting the inclusion of consumer statements in disputed files. The FCRA is enforced by the Federal Trade Commission (FTC).

Under the FCRA, credit reporting agencies must maintain procedures to ensure that their consumer reports are accurate and that users of the reports are using them only for lawful purposes. The FCRA also provides for the exclusion of obsolete information. Consumer reports may not include bankruptcies more than 10 years old, nor any lawsuits, judgments, paid tax liens, accounts placed on collection or charged to profit or loss, information regarding the consumer's arrest, indictment or conviction of a crime or other adverse information more than seven years old. These restrictions, however, do not apply to reports used for employment in which the annual salary reasonably may be expected to exceed $20,000. The FCRA also requires that credit reporting agencies furnishing reports for employment purposes notify the consumer whenever any public record information is reported that could have an adverse effect on the consumer's ability to obtain employment.

If an employer takes adverse action based on a credit report, the employer is required to inform the applicant or employee of the reason for the decision and supply the individual with the name and

---

[22]15 U.S.C. §§1681–81t (1993).

address of the reporting agency from which the report was obtained. To obtain a more detailed "investigative consumer report" on an applicant or employee, the employer must disclose to the individual, within three days of the request, that it has ordered such a report. The notice must disclose that the report will include information about the applicant's character and reputation, and that the applicant has the right to request full disclosure of the report's contents. If the individual requests a full disclosure of the report, this information must be provided within five days of the request. These notice requirements do not apply if the individual is being considered for a position for which the individual has not applied.

Individuals may bring lawsuits under the FCRA against consumer reporting agencies, employees of reporting agencies, and users of consumer reports (including employers). In actions for both negligent and willful noncompliance with the FCRA, actual damages, costs, and attorney fees may be recovered. Punitive damages may be awarded in the court's discretion for willful noncompliance, even without proof of malice. Cases arising under the FCRA may be brought in any United States district court.

About one-third of the states also have laws regulating some aspect of the consumer reporting industry. The FCRA preempts state laws only to the extent they are inconsistent with the FCRA. For the most part, these state laws are patterned after the FCRA and some even provide additional protection.

Applicants and employees adversely affected in their employment opportunities by a credit report also may have state common law remedies available in the form of tort actions for defamation, negligence, or invasion of privacy. The FCRA provides a qualified immunity against such lawsuits, however, if there has been compliance with the procedures set forth in the FCRA and the disclosure was not done maliciously.

The federal Bankruptcy Code[23] also provides protection from employment discrimination against applicants and employees. Section 525 of the Bankruptcy Act prohibits public and private employers from denying or terminating employment solely because an individual has declared bankruptcy, discharged a debt, or not paid a discharged debt. Although most cases involving section 525 involve employees

---

[23] 11 U.S.C. §§1101–74 (1993).

being terminated subsequent to their filing for or being discharged in bankruptcy, the law also applies to an employer's preemployment inquiries.

Discrimination in employment because of outstanding debt also may be actionable under a state garnishment statute or under Title VII. Most states prohibit the discharge of employees for at least some aspect of garnishment, such as child support or wage assignment. Several of the statutes provide for back pay, reinstatement, or damages.

Employer policies providing for the discharge of employees after multiple wage garnishments has been held to violate Title VII because of the greater impact on minorities. Employer defenses of inconvenience, annoyance, and expense have been insufficient to justify the policies. Although garnishment-based discrimination has been applied to reprimands, the discipline for failure to pay "just debts" was held not to violate Title VII in the absence of clear evidence of the racial effects of the policy.

NEGLIGENT HIRING

Negligent hiring is a lawsuit against an employer for injuries to an employee or a third party caused by an employee's intentional or negligent acts. The basis of the action is that the employer was negligent in hiring the employee who caused the injury. A virtually identical type of lawsuit is one based on negligent retention. Here, the employee's conduct after hiring should have alerted the employer of the incompetence or dangerousness of the employee. Thus, the employer's breach of duty was the failure to discharge the employee. Similar actions also have been brought for the negligent hiring of an independent contractor, the negligent hiring of a former employee, negligent training, and negligent supervision.

The courts have tended to focus on two key questions. First, did the employer know or should it have known of the employee's incompetence or dangerous propensities and was it foreseeable that these propensities would create a risk of harm to other individuals? Second, did the employer's negligent hiring of the incompetent or dangerous employee cause the injury?

As in any negligence action, the starting point is the existence of a legal duty. A duty is an obligation to conform to a particular standard of conduct toward another. The duty to a third party or fellow employee is based on the foreseeability of harm. There can be no liability unless the court determines that the employer owed a duty of care to a particular plaintiff.

The courts have been fairly expansive in the relationships between an employer and a third party that will create a duty on the part of the employer to protect the third party from harm caused by the employee. The relationships include: a doctor and patient, a housing inspector and the tenants of the apartment complex he inspected, an armed security guard and the customers of a convenience store, and the resident manager and the tenants of an apartment complex. In some cases, however, the courts have been unwilling to find a duty of care from the employer to a party injured by the employee. For example, in one case the court held that an employer was not required to search the criminal record of an applicant for a cashier's position.

There also is generally no duty to a party whose relationship with the employee arose through casual contact unrelated to the employment. "[T]he mere existence of the employer-employee relationship does not entitle a third person to seek recovery for injuries inflicted by the employee on the theory of negligence in hiring."[24] For example, in one case the defendant's employee met the plaintiff at a cocktail lounge where she was a waitress. He then drove her to his employer's premises, where he raped her. In an action for negligent hiring, the court observed that the waitress was not a customer, patron, or invitee of the defendant-employer and therefore she was beyond the scope of duty owed by the defendant to the public.[25]

Another interesting question of duty was raised in the case of *Moore v. St. Joseph Nursing Home, Inc.*,[26] in which a security guard was savagely beaten and murdered by a co-worker. The decedent's estate brought an action against the co-worker's former employer, which failed to disclose to the subsequent employer that the employee had been discharged after 24 warnings about violence, alcohol use, and drug use. The court held that "a former employer has no duty to disclose malefic information about a former employee to the former employee's prospective employer."

---

[24]Lange v. B & P Motor Express, Inc., 257 F. Supp. 319, 323 (N.D. Ind. 1966).
[25]Baugher v. A. Hattersley & Sons, 436 N.E.2d 126, 128 (Ind. App. 1982).
[26]459 N.W.2d 100 (Mich. App. 1990).

After a duty has been established, the next step is to determine whether the employer has breached the duty by hiring or retaining the employee. The jury will consider whether the employer acted in a reasonable manner considering the type of position for which the individual was applying, the information available to the employer, the cost and availability of obtaining additional information, and the foreseeability of harm. Not surprisingly, liability is more likely to be found when the employee is responsible for transporting children or carrying a firearm, the employee has access to a master key or to customers' homes, the employee is working in a "highly volatile" atmosphere, or the employee had engaged in a prior incident of misconduct.

A common issue is the appropriate amount of weight to be given to the employer's failure to review an individual's criminal record. **The majority rule currently is that, absent special circumstances, the employer has no duty to investigate whether an individual has a criminal record.** Even with the existence of a special circumstance, however, "liability of an employer is not to be predicated solely on failure to investigate criminal history of an applicant, but rather, in the totality of the circumstances surrounding the hiring, whether the employer exercised reasonable care."[27]

The next step is to determine whether there is legal cause between the alleged negligence of the defendant and the harm suffered by the plaintiff. This involves a consideration of two factors: whether the negligent employment practices of the employer led to the individual being hired or retained and whether the employment of the individual set in motion or contributed to the chain of events that led to the injury of the plaintiff.

UNDOCUMENTED ALIENS

Under the Immigration Reform and Control Act of 1986 (IRCA),[28] it is unlawful for an employer knowingly to recruit, hire, or continue to employ individuals who are in the country illegally. The IRCA requires that employers verify employment eligibility upon filling a position.

---

[27]Ponticas v. K.M.S. Invs., 331 N.W.2d 907 (Minn. 1983).
[28]8 U.S.C. §1324a (1993).

Employers must gather proof of an employee's identity and employability and retain records of that verification for three years. Thus, employers have a duty to determine that a person is authorized to work in the United States. Employers must also complete an INS Form I-9 (Employment Eligibility Verification Form) for each new employee and retain those forms for three years. The Immigration and Naturalization Service (INS) is responsible for enforcing the IRCA.

The IRCA contains sanction provisions that penalize employers for two different types of conduct. The first type is knowingly hiring an alien who is unauthorized to work at the time of hiring or continuing to employ an alien who becomes unauthorized because of a change in immigration status.

The second type of violation is failing to verify new employees' work authorization. This type of violation occurs when the employer fails to fill out the INS Form I-9, or fails to keep the forms for the proper period of time, or fails to allow the INS or the Labor Department to inspect the forms. If an employer has notice that an employee's documentation is incorrect, the employer is in the same position as if the employee had failed to produce the documentation. The employer may be assessed civil penalties for this type of violation, ranging from $100 to $1,000.

Employers have a defense if they comply in good faith with the employment provisions. Complying with paperwork requirements establishes a good faith defense to an allegation of unlawful hiring. Nevertheless, following proper paperwork procedures will not protect an employer from sanctions for unlawfully continuing employment if the employer has the requisite knowledge. An employer fulfills its obligation to verify an employee's authorization by "examining a document which 'reasonably appears on its face to be genuine.'"[29] Thus, an employer that examines an employee's false Social Security card and valid driver's license, but fails to detect that the Social Security card is false is not liable for failing to verify the employee's authorization.

An "employer" is a person or entity, including an agent or anyone acting in the interest of the person or entity, who engages the services or labor of an employee. Liability under the IRCA stems from the act of hiring, not merely the state of being an employer. Thus, either an

---

[29]Collins Food Int'l, Inc. v. United States Immigration & Naturalization Serv., 948 F.2d 549 (9th Cir. 1991).

employer or its agent may be liable under the Act. A parent corporation also may be liable for a subsidiary's unlawful hiring practices. Nonetheless, a parent corporation and its subsidiary may obtain separate entity status if they can prove that they are physically distinct subdivisions which do their own hiring, so long as the two entities do not refer to the practices of the other and are not under common control.

If an employer discovers that its employees do not have the proper documentation, the employer does not have to suspend or fire the employees immediately so long as the employer takes immediate steps to investigate. Employers are exempted from the IRCA violations for current employees hired before November 6, 1986. If the employee quits or is terminated by the employer, then the employee loses this "grandfather" status.

RESIDENCY REQUIREMENTS

Many municipal governments and a few state governments have established residency requirements for eligibility for public employment. These requirements are of two main types: durational and continuing. Both types of requirements have been challenged on constitutional and other grounds.

Durational residency requirements, less commonly used, condition eligibility for employment on the individual having resided in the jurisdiction for a minimum period of time. In *Shapiro v. Thompson*,[30] the Supreme Court held that a one-year durational residency requirement for eligibility for welfare benefits was unconstitutional because it denied equal protection and infringed upon the fundamental right to travel. The Supreme Court stated that the right to travel encompassed the right to "migrate, resettle, find a job, and start a new life." This rationale has been used by the lower courts in invalidating durational residency requirements for state and local employment.

Continuing residency requirements are more common. They require residency within or near a specified government unit as a condition of obtaining or continuing employment. Unlike durational residency

---

[30]394 U.S. 618 (1969), *overruled in part on other grounds*, Edelman v. Jordan, 415 U.S. 651 (1974).

requirements, continuing residency requirements have been held not to implicate the fundamental constitutional right to travel.

Continuing residency requirements have been challenged on a variety of legal theories. In *McCarthy v. Philadelphia Civil Service Commission*,[31] a firefighter was discharged because he moved his permanent residence from Philadelphia to New Jersey, in violation of Philadelphia's continuing residency ordinance. The plaintiff challenged the ordinance as unconstitutionally abridging the right to travel. The Supreme Court rejected the claim, distinguishing *Shapiro* and similar cases on the ground that they involved durational residency requirements. According to the Court, because the ordinance was "appropriately defined and uniformly applied," it was constitutional.

Lower court decisions after *McCarthy* have found numerous factual bases to uphold residency requirements. For example, residency requirements for public school teachers and counselors have been upheld because residents have greater understanding of the urban problems faced by their students; have greater commitment to an urban education system; are more likely to vote for district taxes, less likely to engage in illegal strikes, and more likely to be involved in school and community activities; have a greater personal stake in the district; have reduced tardiness due to traffic delays; and have greater opportunity to become personally acquainted with students.

Lower court decisions upholding continuing residency requirements for police and firefighters have used similar reasoning: enhanced performance due to greater personal knowledge of the city, greater personal stake in the city's progress, reduced tardiness and absenteeism, and economic benefits to the city from local expenditure of salaries; availability in emergencies; crime deterrence due to the presence of off-duty police; and concern for ethnic balance and reduction of unemployment in the inner city.

CIVIL SERVICE

In 1881 President James A. Garfield was assassinated by Charles J. Guiteau, an insane and disappointed office seeker. As a direct consequence, Congress enacted the Pendleton Act to eliminate patronage in federal employment and to institute efficient and objective federal

---

[31]424 U.S. 645 (1976).

personnel practices. The Pendleton Act established the Civil Service Commission to implement merit selection, management, and adjudication of complaints by applicants and employees. Although the Pendleton Act was subject to a number of minor amendments over the years, a sweeping revision was made in 1978. In enacting the Civil Service Reform Act (CSRA),[32] Congress made major changes in the federal civil service. The current federal civil service system is extremely complicated and there may be adverse consequences from failing to comply with specific procedures. Accordingly, great care and expert assistance is recommended in handling federal civil service matters.

The CSRA abolished the Civil Service Commission, dividing its functions between two newly created agencies, the Office of Personnel Management (OPM) and the Merit Systems Protection Board (MSPB). The OPM was given responsibility for the administration and enforcement of the civil service, including maintaining the system of competitive examinations and position appointments. The MSPB was assigned the quasi-judicial role of protecting employees against unjust actions.

To be recognized as a federal employee, and therefore subject to protection under the CSRA, an individual must be appointed by a federal officer or employee, engage in the performance of a federal function, and be subject to the supervision of federal officers or employees. Court decisions have held that being hired as a subcontractor, being housed in a government building, or working at an Army commissary are not enough to establish civil service status.

In addition to the federal civil service laws, virtually every state has some version of a merit system applicable to all or most of its civil service and most states use some form of competitive testing. Many states afford their public employees statutory protections exceeding those applicable to federal employees and, for example, prohibit discrimination based on an expunged juvenile record, marital status, parenthood, sexual orientation, or weight.

POLYGRAPHS

Employers long have been eager to assess whether applicants and employees are honest, trustworthy, and law-abiding. Although no

---

[32]Pub. L. No. 95-454, 92 Stat. 1111 (codified in scattered sections of 5, 10, 15, 28, 31, 38, 39, and 42 U.S.C.).

device is capable of measuring whether someone is telling the truth, the polygraph is based on the theory that lying leads to conscious conflict, which induces fear or anxiety, which in turn produces measurable physiological changes. Polygraphs usually measure three different types of physiological responses. The rate and depth of respiration is measured by pneumographs strapped around the chest and abdomen. Cardiovascular activity is measured by a blood pressure cuff (sphygmomanometer) placed around the bicep. Electrodermal response (galvanic skin response) is measured by electrodes attached to the fingertips.

A number of states have regulated polygraphs for many years, but congressional interest in the subject is much more recent. In 1983 the Office of Technology Assessment of the United States Congress (OTA) undertook a detailed review of the scientific literature on the accuracy of polygraphs. OTA concluded that there are serious questions about the accuracy of polygraphs. "[T]here is very little research or scientific evidence to establish polygraph test validity in screening situations, whether they be preemployment, preclearance, periodic or aperiodic, random, or 'dragnet.'"[33] Overall, accuracy rates were estimated at 50 to 90 percent. When used as a preemployment screen, polygraphs may disqualify as many as 30 percent of applicants.[34]

Despite scientific evidence casting doubt on the accuracy of polygraphs, numerous employers have asserted that polygraphs are highly effective in screening out workers who steal or engage in other forms of misconduct. One reason may be that, because people taking the polygraphs believe the test will detect any lies they tell, while taking the polygraph they admit to various kinds of wrongdoing and they are not hired or are fired as a result. The polygraphs are then credited with ferreting out these people. By the mid-1980s, as many as two million polygraphs were performed in the private sector each year, most frequently by banks, jewelers, retail stores, and fast food outlets.

Based in part on the OTA study, Congress enacted the Employee Polygraph Protection Act of 1988 (EPPA).[35] The law prohibits about 85 percent of the polygraph use in the private sector. An employer may not "require, request, suggest or cause an employee or prospective

---

[33]Office of Technology Assessment, U.S. Congress, *Scientific Validity of Polygraph Testing* 8 (Washington, D.C.: OTA 1983).

[34]David Bruce Robbins, "Psychiatric Conditions in Worker Fitness and Risk Evaluation," 3 *Occup. Med.: State of the Art Revs.* 309, 314 (1988).

[35]29 U.S.C. §§2001–09 (1993).

employee to take or submit to any lie detector test" or "discharge, discipline, or discriminate" against an applicant or employee on the basis of or refusal to take a polygraph. The proscription applies not only to polygraphs, but also to the deceptograph, voice stress analyzer, psychological stress evaluator, or any other similar mechanical or electrical device used to determine honesty.

There are three exceptions to the ban on the private sector use of polygraphs. First, a polygraph may be given in connection with an ongoing investigation involving economic loss or injury to the employer's business. Second, polygraphs may be performed on prospective employees of an employer whose business consists of providing security services for the protection of nuclear power, electrical power, public water supply, radioactive or toxic waste, public transportation, or currency, negotiable securities, precious commodities or instruments, or proprietary information. Third, an employer that manufactures, distributes, or dispenses controlled substances may test prospective employees who will have access to such activities or current employees in connection with an investigation of misconduct involving controlled substances.

These private sector exceptions are qualified. An individual tested pursuant to the "investigation" exception must have had access to the property in question, the employer must have a reasonable suspicion that the employee was involved in the incident, and the employer must set forth in writing the specific incident involved and the basis for testing the particular employee. The employee may not be discharged on the basis of the polygraph without additional supporting evidence. An employer testing employees under the "security" or "controlled substance" exceptions also may not use the polygraph as the sole basis for discharge.

All polygraph testing in the private sector is subject to various procedural limitations. These include written notice of the test date, time, and place; written notice of the test characteristics; opportunity to review the questions to be asked; and the right to legal counsel. The polygraph examiner may not ask questions regarding religious, racial, or political beliefs, or about any matter relating to sexual behavior, nor may the examiner ask questions in a manner designed to "degrade or needlessly intrude on" the examinee.

Polygraph examiners are not permitted to make recommendations concerning employment decisions and they must have a current license if required by the state. Disclosure of the results of testing is limited to the examinee, the requesting employer, and a court ordering disclosure. An employer may disclose an admission of criminal conduct to an appropriate governmental agency.

The EPPA is enforced by the Secretary of Labor[36] and provides for the assessment of civil penalties of up to $10,000. The Secretary of Labor also is authorized to bring a legal action in federal court to get a court order mandating the cessation of violations of the EPPA. In addition, the EPPA provides for private lawsuits by an affected applicant or employee. The available remedies include employment, reinstatement, promotion, and the payment of lost wages and benefits.

While the EPPA applies to virtually all private sector employers, it does not apply to federal, state, or local government employers. There are also exemptions for national defense and security organizations and their consultants, and for contractors of the FBI. Judicial decisions have held that a polygraph examiner may not be held liable as an "employer" under the EPPA. In addition, the EPPA does not prohibit the arbitration of a polygraph grievance pursuant to a contract provision.

The EPPA does not preempt any state or local law or collective bargaining agreement that is more restrictive with respect to lie detector tests than any provision of the EPPA. About half the states[37] have antipolygraph statutes and 11 of these states[38] include state governments. The statutes often prohibit requesting as well as requiring the taking of a polygraph.

HONESTY TESTING

One of the consequences of enactment of the federal EPPA has been an increase in the use of other tests purporting to measure

---

[36]The Secretary's implementing regulations appear at 29 C.F.R. pt. 801, App. A. (1993).

[37]Alaska, California, Connecticut, Delaware, the District of Columbia, Hawaii, Idaho, Iowa, Maine, Maryland, Massachusetts, Michigan, Minnesota, Montana, Nebraska, Nevada, New Jersey, Oregon, Pennsylvania, Rhode Island, Tennessee, Vermont, Washington, West Virginia, and Wisconsin.

[38]Alaska, Connecticut, Delaware, the District of Columbia, Hawaii, Iowa, Maryland, Michigan, Nevada, Rhode Island, and Washington.

"honesty" or "integrity." Paper and pencil honesty tests are widely used by various companies, most frequently in retail, fast food, banking, and other service businesses. The tests attempt to screen out individuals who are likely to be dishonest on the job and thereby seek to reduce employee crimes such as theft and bribery.

Although there are several different honesty tests in common use, two main types of questions are used. First, overt questions ask whether the individual has been dishonest in the past, what the individual's attitude is toward theft by others, and similar direct questions. There also may be less direct overt questions, such as "Do you like to take chances?" The second type of honesty test is more personality based. It attempts to measure personality traits such as dependability, cooperation, drug avoidance, organizational delinquency, and "wayward impulse."

The accuracy of honesty tests remains a subject of great controversy. Critics argue, among other things, that individuals who honestly admit to prior indiscretions are often eliminated as dishonest while those who untruthfully assert that they have always been honest pass. Defenders of the tests claim that the tests are less intrusive than polygraphs, cheaper and easier to use than psychological tests, and are highly effective in reducing employee theft. Congress has not yet seen fit to legislate in this area, but it is continuing to study the issue of paper and pencil honesty tests.

The EPPA does not apply to paper and pencil honesty tests. Similarly, state polygraph laws do not prevent the use of these tests. For example, in one case, the Supreme Court of Minnesota construed language in the state's polygraph law prohibiting the use of "any test purporting to test honesty." The court held that the prohibition is limited to tests which "purport to measure physiological changes in the subject tested. . . ." Therefore, the statute did not apply to paper and pencil honesty tests. The court was concerned that without such a construction the statute would be unconstitutionally vague.[39]

Only two states so far have enacted legislation specifically directed at paper and pencil honesty tests. The use of the tests is completely prohibited in Massachusetts. In Rhode Island, they may be used so long as they are not the "primary basis for an employment decision."

---

[39]State v. Century Camera, 309 N.W.2d 735 (Minn. 1981).

PSYCHOLOGICAL AND PERSONALITY TESTING

Psychological testing has become an increasingly popular method of screening applicants and employees. Many employers use psychological testing to facilitate proper job placement to increase productivity; prevent violence, drug and alcohol abuse, and the legal liability that they can cause; reduce the number of workers' compensation claims for mental health disorders; and reduce health insurance claims for mental illness.

A wide variety of scientific (and pseudo-scientific) measures come under the heading of psychological testing. The tests in common usage include personality tests (both objective and projective), individual psychological assessments, vocational preference tests, and graphoanalysis (handwriting tests).

For the most part, psychological tests are largely unregulated. The only exceptions are the occasional cases in which the use of a test had the effect of discriminating on the basis of race, color, religion, sex, or national origin. In *Soroka v. Dayton Hudson Corp.*,[40] an applicant for the position of store security officer was required to take a "Psychscreen," a combination of the Minnesota Multiphasic Personality Inventory (MMPI) and the California Psychological Inventory. The test, consisting of 704 true-false questions, asked questions about, among other things, religious attitudes and sexual orientation. Despite being hired for the job, the plaintiff brought a legal action in which he claimed that the Psychscreen violated the California Constitution's right to privacy, as well as various state statutes. The trial court denied the plaintiff's motion for a court order banning the test, but the California Court of Appeal reversed. The appellate court held that, under California law, applicants have the same rights as employees and that the employer failed to prove that the test was job related.

Psychological testing also may be challenged as violating state and federal disability discrimination laws. Under the Americans with Disabilities Act (ADA),[41] psychological testing may be considered a medical examination. Therefore, these examinations may not be given until after a conditional offer of employment. In addition, in some

---

[40] 1 Cal. Rptr. 2d 77, 6 IER Cases 1491 (Cal. App. 1991), *review dismissed*, 862 P.2d 148 (Cal. 1993).

[41] 42 U.S.C. §§12101–12213 (1993).

states, all medical examinations must be job related. In such a state, the employer may have a difficult time in using any psychological tests for some jobs.

MEDICAL TESTING

Medical screening is the process by which a work force is selected by the application of medical criteria. It has been in wide use in the United States since the turn of the century when large companies began employing "factory surgeons" to determine whether applicants and employees were free of disease and had the necessary strength, stamina, vision, hearing, and other physical attributes to perform the job.[42]

The use of medical screening has increased greatly in the last quarter century as many companies realized that it was in their economic interests to employ workers who not only were in good health at the time they began work, but who were also likely to remain in good health in the future. Thus, medical screening became both diagnostic and predictive. It also was concerned with both occupationally related disorders and nonoccupationally related disorders.

The traditional time for medical screening was before the individual was hired—at the preemployment stage. By the early 1980s, 90 percent of applicants for jobs at large plants (more than 500 workers) and over 50 percent of applicants for jobs at smaller plants (fewer than 500 workers) were subject to preemployment medical examinations. Over time, preemployment medical examinations became increasingly detailed and sophisticated. One consequence of this trend was that individuals with disabilities became identified early on and, in many instances, experienced limitations on their employment opportunities.

When the ADA was enacted in 1990, section 102(d) was included, which mandated major changes in the way many companies traditionally evaluated the fitness for duty of job applicants. Under this section, all preemployment medical examinations and medical inquiries are illegal. "[A] covered entity shall not conduct a medical examination or make inquiries of a job applicant as to whether such applicant is an individual with a disability or as to the nature and severity of such disability."

---

[42]See M.A. Rothstein, *Medical Screening and the Employee Health Cost Crisis* (Washington, D.C.: BNA Books, 1989).

The ADA's prohibition on preemployment inquiries includes medical questionnaires, oral inquiries into disabilities, and medical examinations, whether conducted by human resources or medical personnel. The only exception is that "[a] covered entity may make preemployment inquiries into the ability of an applicant to perform job-related functions." These inquiries, however, must be narrowly tailored. The employer may describe or demonstrate a particular job function and inquire whether the applicant can perform the function with or without accommodation. The employer also may ask about the applicant's ability to perform specific job functions, such as lifting boxes or manipulating small parts.

Despite these limitations on preemployment examinations, employers are permitted to make the successful completion of a medical examination a valid condition of employment. The examination, however, may not take place until after the employer has made a conditional offer of employment. Section 102(d)(3) provides that "[a] covered entity may require a medical examination after an offer of employment has been made to a job applicant and prior to the commencement of the employment duties of such applicant, and may condition an offer of employment on the results of such examination. . . ."

These "employment entrance examinations" must satisfy three requirements. First, all entering employees in the same job category must be subject to an examination regardless of disability. Second, information obtained at an employment entrance examination must be collected and maintained on separate forms and in separate medical files. The information must be treated as confidential, except that supervisors and managers may be informed regarding necessary restrictions on the work or duties of the employee and necessary accommodations; first aid and safety personnel may be informed, when appropriate, if the disability might require emergency treatment; and government officials investigating compliance with the ADA must be provided with relevant information on request. Third, employers may not use medical criteria to screen out individuals with disabilities unless the medical criteria are job related.

The employment entrance examination is less clearly regulated by the actual language of the ADA than other types of medical examinations. Under the ADA, preemployment medical inquiries are prohibited entirely and medical examinations of current employees must be job related or voluntary. For employment entrance examinations, if a conditional offer is withdrawn because of a medical examination, the medical criteria for the decision must be job related. The key issue left unclear in the ADA is whether the actual examinations given to conditional offerees must be job related. According to the Equal Employment Opportunity Commission (EEOC), the agency charged with promulgating regulations under the ADA: "Medical examinations conducted in accordance with this Section do not have to be job-related and consistent with business necessity."

Although the ADA is the most important law regulating medical screening by employers, it is not the only one. For example, other disabilities laws may extend protections to individuals not covered by the ADA, such as federal government employees who are covered by section 501 of the Rehabilitation Act and employees of small employers in the private sector who may be covered under a state disabilities law.

Applicants for jobs with public sector employers also may challenge medical screening practices on constitutional grounds. An illustrative case is *Gargiul v. Tompkins*,[43] in which a tenured kindergarten teacher took an extended sick leave because of a back ailment. When she sought to return to work, she was told that she would have to be examined by the school district's physician, who was male. She refused to be examined by a male physician, citing her personal "creed," but offered to go at her own expense to any woman physician selected by the school board or recommended by the local medical society. The school board rejected this offer and denied her reinstatement. The Second Circuit Court of Appeals held that, as a tenured teacher, the woman had a property interest in her job that, under the Fourteenth Amendment to the U.S. Constitution, could not be denied her without due process of law. According to the court, the school board's action was so arbitrary that it violated due process.

If medical screening has the purpose or effect of discriminating against applicants on the basis of race, color, religion, sex, national origin, or age, then an employment discrimination action may lie. The most common allegation is gender discrimination. At least one significant age discrimination case also has been brought. In *EEOC v. Massachusetts*,[44] a Massachusetts statute requiring certain state

---

[43]704 F.2d 661 (2d Cir. 1983), *vacated and remanded on other grounds,* 465 U.S. 1016 (1984).
[44]987 F.2d 64, 61 FEP Cases 313 (1st Cir. 1993).

employees over the age of 70 to take at their own expense, and pass, an annual physical examination to continue employment was challenged as violating the ADEA. The court struck down the statute. "Here, the Commonwealth of Massachusetts allows age to be the determinant as to when an employee's deterioration will be so significant that it requires special treatment. Such a conception of and use of age as a criteria for decline and unfitness for employment strikes at the heart of the ADEA."

A variety of other laws require, prohibit, or regulate specific forms or aspects of medical screening of applicants and employees. The Occupational Safety and Health Act requires various medical examinations before individuals may be assigned to work in certain hazardous environments. Some state laws prohibit employers from charging applicants or employees for employer-mandated medical examinations or requiring preemployment pelvic examinations.

Another important set of legal issues related to medical screening involves an employer's or physician's potential liability for negligent medical screening. This may take one of at least five forms. First, a rejected applicant may allege that a physician's negligent assessment of the applicant resulted in the denial of employment. For example, in *Armstrong v. Morgan*,[45] an employee, upon being promoted, was required to have a physical examination performed by a company-retained physician. The physician's report indicated that the employee was in very poor health and, as a result, the employee lost his job. According to the Texas Court of Civil Appeals, a negligence action against the physician stated a valid claim. "Dr. Morgan owed Appellant Armstrong a duty not to injure him physically or otherwise. If Dr. Morgan negligently performed the examination and as a result gave an inaccurate report of the state of appellant's health, and appellant was injured as a proximate result thereof, actionable negligence would be shown."

A second potential source of liability involves injuries caused during the course of an examination or treatment. Not surprisingly, there are few cases in which injuries are alleged to have been caused during an examination. Negligent treatment cases, however, are more common. For example, in *Nolan v. Jefferson Downs, Inc.*,[46] a racetrack

---

[45]545 S.W.2d 45 (Tex. App. 1977).
[46]592 So. 2d 831 (La. App. 1991), *cert. denied*, 596 So.2d 558 (La. 1992).

physician was found partially at fault in the negligent treatment of a jockey's eye injury. The physician seldom went to the track himself and delegated his duties to a gynecologist who was a convicted felon. The gynecologist's negligent treatment and failure to refer the jockey to an ophthalmologist caused permanent injury. An important fact in *Nolan* was that the racetrack physician was an independent contractor. Most negligent treatment cases brought against company-salaried health care providers have been held to be barred by workers' compensation.

A third theory on which plaintiffs have sued is that a negligent medical assessment resulted in an improper job placement, which caused the individual to be injured on the job. Actions against employer-salaried physicians and employers for improper job placement will normally be found to be barred by workers' compensation, but actions against independent contractor physicians are more likely to be successful.

A fourth source of liability involves actions in which the plaintiff alleges that in conducting a medical examination the physician failed to diagnose a serious injury or illness. The resulting delay in treatment thus is alleged to have aggravated the individual's condition or reduced the likelihood of successful treatment. **Even though an employer may be under no duty to conduct an examination, once the duty is assumed, any negligence in performing the examination may be actionable**.

In *Green v. Walker*,[47] a physician contracted with an employer to perform an annual physical examination of an offshore cook. The physician then allegedly negligently failed to diagnose the early stages of lung cancer and the employee subsequently died. The man's widow brought a medical malpractice lawsuit. The Fifth Circuit Court of Appeals held that even in the absence of a traditional physician-patient relationship, a physician owes a duty to an employee undergoing an employer-mandated medical examination. The examining physician still has "a duty to conduct the requested tests and diagnose the results thereof, exercising the level of care consistent with the doctor's professional training and expertise, and to take reasonable steps to make information available timely to the examinee of any findings that pose an imminent danger to the examinee's physical or mental well-being."

Finally, a physician may be liable if a negligent medical assessment causes injuries to a third party. For example, in *Wharton Transport*

---

[47]910 F.2d 291 (5th Cir. 1990).

Corp. v. Bridges,[48] a truck driven by a Wharton employee struck the rear of an occupied car parked on the side of a road. The collision resulted in one death and three severe injuries to the occupants. Wharton paid $426,000 to settle the case brought by the occupants and then brought an action against the third-party physician it had retained to perform the DOT-mandated examination to determine whether the driver was physically fit to drive a truck in interstate commerce. Wharton alleged that the physician was negligent in certifying the driver as physically fit when subsequent examination indicated that he had a variety of severe impairments. The Tennessee Supreme Court held that the physician owed a duty to Wharton and that an action would lie. It further held that a jury could find that the injuries sustained by the occupants were reasonably foreseeable as a result of the physician's negligence.

HIV TESTING

In March 1985, the Food and Drug Administration (FDA) approved the first commercial tests to detect antibodies to the human immunodeficiency virus (HIV). Almost immediately, concerns were raised that these tests, designed to screen donated blood, might be used by employers to screen people. Although there have been some reports of screening being performed on applicants and employees, these incidents have been relatively isolated. Nevertheless, HIV testing by employers, particularly in settings such as the health care industry, continues to be an important topic that raises a variety of legal issues.

There are five main reasons why an employer would possibly consider the HIV testing of job applicants. They are to protect co-workers and customers from exposure to the virus, to protect the HIV-positive individual from exposure to an unhealthy work environment, to mollify customers and co-workers that the work force is "AIDS or HIV free," to reduce health insurance costs by excluding individuals who are likely to require expensive medical care in the near future, and to promote public health by identification of infected individuals. None of these reasons, however will serve as a defense to the exclusion of individuals who are HIV-positive.

---

[48]606 S.W.2d 521 (Tenn. 1980).

It is important to understand that HIV tests do not diagnose AIDS, do not indicate when an HIV-positive individual will develop AIDS, and do not even detect the HIV virus itself. The tests detect the nonneutralizing antibodies produced by the body after exposure to HIV. Development of antibodies usually occurs six to eight weeks after infection and thus an HIV test administered in this time period will be negative, even though the individual has been exposed to HIV and is presumably capable of transmitting the infection to others. It is also important to note that the Centers for Disease Control and Prevention (CDC) has indicated that HIV cannot be transmitted through casual contact in the workplace. **Similarly, the Presidential Commission on HIV has stated that "there is no justification for fear of transmission of the virus in the vast majority of workplace and public settings."[49]**

In July 1991, the CDC issued updated guidelines on HIV-infected health care workers. Its prior directives had emphasized the use of universal precautions against infection and experts agreed that the risk of transmission from a patient to a health care worker was greater than from a health care worker to a patient. Nevertheless, because of the much-publicized case of an AIDS-infected dentist transmitting the infection to some of his patients, the CDC seemed to modify its position. While continuing to support universal precautions as the primary technique for prevention of transmission of HIV, the CDC also suggested that health care workers performing certain "exposure prone" procedures determine their own HIV status and refrain from performing those procedures if they are HIV infected. These guidelines are quite controversial and could result in both state legislative proposals to implement them and legal challenges to prevent adoption by hospitals.

There are several different types of state laws that attempt to prevent the use of HIV testing by employers. For example, some states (Hawaii, Massachusetts, and Vermont) prohibit employers from performing HIV tests or requiring the disclosure of the results of an HIV test. North Carolina bans HIV testing of employees but not applicants. Other states ban only the HIV testing of current health care employees (Maine), or ban only the HIV testing of state applicants and employees (Pennsylvania). Another group of states permits HIV testing only if

---

[49]Report of the Presidential Commission on the Human Immunodeficiency Virus Epidemic 113 (Washington, D.C.: Presidential Commission, 1988).

being HIV negative is a bona fide occupational qualification, which is certified by the state epidemiologist (Iowa and Wisconsin) or proven by the employer (Florida, Kentucky, New Mexico, Texas, and Washington). In Nevada, where prostitution is legal, the Board of Health tests prostitutes for HIV once a month.

The next category consists of HIV legislation that does not prohibit the testing of individuals, but prohibits the use of HIV test results or HIV-based discrimination (California, Kansas, and Nebraska). A number of cities also have enacted ordinances that prohibit discrimination in employment on the basis of AIDS or HIV status.

Besides these HIV-specific laws, virtually every state and the federal government have enacted laws prohibiting discrimination in employment on the basis of disability. In several states (Alaska, California, Colorado, Kansas, Michigan, Minnesota, Missouri, Ohio, Pennsylvania, Rhode Island, and Utah), employers are prohibited from inquiring into non-job-related disabilities, which would include HIV. In other states and under the ADA, the use of HIV test results or other HIV status information is prohibited.

AIDS and HIV infection have been held to be handicapping conditions under the Rehabilitation Act. Cases decided under the Rehabilitation Act, however, have not always prohibited HIV testing in the workplace. For example, in *Leckelt v. Board of Commissioners*,[50] an employee was fired from his position as a licensed practical nurse when he refused to disclose the result of his HIV test. The nurse claimed that this action amounted to discrimination on the basis of a perceived handicap. The hospital argued that he was not fired because of an actual or perceived handicap, but because his refusal to provide the information prevented the hospital from taking any necessary steps to prevent the spread of infection. The Fifth Circuit Court of Appeals agreed with the hospital, in a decision that has been widely criticized. In another case,[51] a district court upheld the HIV testing of U.S. State Department employees on the grounds that medical care may be less available while serving at a foreign post.

HIV testing in the workplace also has been challenged on constitutional grounds. In *Glover v. Eastern Nebraska Community Office of*

---

[50]909 F.2d 820, 53 FEP Cases 1136 (5th Cir. 1990).
[51]Local 1812 v. United States Dep't of State, 662 F. Supp. 50, 2 IER Cases 47 (D.D.C. 1987).

Retardation,[52] the Eighth Circuit Court of Appeals held that a policy requiring the mandatory HIV testing of employees of a center for the mentally retarded violated the ban on unreasonable search and seizure of the Fourth Amendment of the U.S. Constitution. Because there was no risk of transmission of HIV from the kind of contact between the employees and their clients, the court held that the testing was an unreasonable search and seizure. On the other hand, mandatory HIV testing of all full-time firefighters and paramedics as a part of their annual physical examinations was upheld on the ground that they are at risk of contracting and transmitting HIV because of their exposure to blood and certain body fluids.

Another issue related to HIV testing is the problem of confidentiality. Indeed, a legitimate concern about protecting employee confidentiality is one of the main reasons why most employers would be reluctant to perform HIV testing even if it were legal. Some states have statutes specifically providing for criminal or civil liability for wrongfully disclosing an individual's HIV status. Even without such a law, however, common law actions for defamation, invasion of privacy, or other torts are possible. For example, in one case,[53] the defendant was found liable for slander for merely passing on a rumor that the plaintiff had AIDS. Similarly, actions have been based on company officials telling a large group of the plaintiff's co-workers that the plaintiff had AIDS and an insurance company physician's disclosure to parties in a workers' compensation case that the plaintiff was HIV positive.

CIGARETTE SMOKING

There is a growing trend among employers to restrict cigarette smoking in the workplace. Many of the restrictions are mandated by state and local laws, but the increased activism of nonsmokers and a desire to reduce health insurance and workers' compensation costs also have contributed to the proliferation of restrictions on workplace smoking.

Laws restricting workplace smoking may be viewed as a subset of laws restricting smoking in public places. Practically every state has

---

[52]867 F.2d 461, 4 IER Cases 65 (8th Cir.), *cert. denied*, 493 U.S. 932 (1989).
[53]McCune v. Neitzel, 457 N.W.2d 803 (Neb. 1990).

some kind of law restricting smoking in public places. Most of these states have laws that apply to smoking in the workplace. Twenty states[54] restrict smoking in public sector and private sector workplaces and 18 states[55] restrict smoking only in public sector workplaces. Public sector restrictions apply either to government workplaces or to any building owned or leased by the government. Private sector restrictions include allowing an employer to restrict smoking by posting a sign prohibiting smoking, requiring employers to establish or negotiate a smoking policy through collective bargaining, and banning smoking except in designated areas in any enclosed workplace. Colorado simply urges private businesses to designate nonsmoking work areas.

Besides these state laws, approximately 500 local smoking ordinances have been enacted, affecting over 57 million people. Thus, numerous employers are required to have policies on smoking, including separating smokers from nonsmokers. Many other employers have voluntary adopted strict smoking rules and policies. These policies are expressly permitted under the ADA, which provides: "Nothing in this chapter shall be construed to preclude the prohibition of, or the imposition of restrictions on, smoking in places of employment. . . ."

An increasing number of employers also have attempted to regulate off-the-job smoking in order to facilitate on-the-job restrictions to reduce health insurance costs, and because of synergistic effects of cigarette smoking and occupational exposures. In addition, some jurisdictions have "heart and lung" statutes, which presume that any cardiovascular or respiratory impairment in a firefighter, police officer, or other designated public employee is work related. Because the effect of these laws is to presume that smoking-induced impairments are "work related" for purposes of workers' compensation, some of these jurisdictions, either by statute or other mandate, prohibit certain public employees from smoking on or off the job.

Employers attempting to regulate off-the-job smoking have run up against a variety of challenges. In *Grusendorf v. City of Oklahoma*

---

[54]Alaska, Connecticut, District of Columbia, Florida, Hawaii, Illinois, Iowa, Maine, Minnesota, Montana, Nebraska, New Hampshire, New Jersey, New Mexico, New York, Pennsylvania, Rhode Island, Utah, Vermont, and Wisconsin.

[55]Arizona, Arkansas, Colorado, Delaware, Idaho, Indiana, Kansas, Maryland, Massachusetts, Michigan, Nevada, North Dakota, Ohio, Oklahoma, Oregon, South Carolina, Virginia, and Washington.

City,[56] a firefighter trainee was fired for violating an agreement that he would not smoke on or off duty for one year after being hired. He brought suit claiming his constitutional rights of liberty, privacy, property, and due process had been violated. The Tenth Circuit Court of Appeals held that the plaintiff failed to prove that the ban on smoking was irrational. "Good health and physical conditioning are essential requirements for firefighters."

About half the states[57] have recently enacted laws prohibiting discrimination in employment against an applicant or employee based on smoking off the job. The specifics of the laws vary. They may prohibit an employer from discriminating against an employee on the basis of the employee's participating in lawful activity or use of lawful products off the employer's premises during nonworking hours (Colorado, Illinois, Nevada, North Carolina, North Dakota, West Virginia, and Wisconsin), smoking or using tobacco products (Arizona, Connecticut, Indiana, Louisiana, Maine, Mississippi, Missouri, New Hampshire, New Jersey, Oklahoma, Oregon, Rhode Island, South Carolina, South Dakota, Virginia, West Virginia, and Wyoming), using an "agricultural product" off the job (Tennessee), using consumable products off the employer's premises during nonworking hours (Minnesota and New York), or because the employee is a smoker (Kentucky, Louisiana, and New Mexico). Seven of the states (Kentucky, Louisiana, Maine, Mississippi, New Hampshire, New Mexico, and Tennessee) link the antidiscrimination protection to the employee's following the employer's smoking policy at work, and seven states (Colorado, Illinois, Nevada, New Jersey, New Mexico, Oregon, and South Dakota) allow off-the-job restrictions if they have a rational relationship to the employment or nonsmoking is an occupational qualification. Oregon has an exception for collective bargaining agreements. Eighteen of the 22 state laws[58] specifically protect an applicant or prospective employee.

---

[56]816 F.2d 539, 2 IER Cases 51 (10th Cir. 1987).

[57]Arizona, Colorado, Connecticut, Illinois, Indiana, Kentucky, Louisiana, Maine, Mississippi, Nevada, New Hampshire, New Jersey, New Mexico, North Dakota, Oklahoma, Oregon, Rhode Island, South Carolina, South Dakota, Tennessee, Virginia, and Wisconsin.

[58]Arizona, Connecticut, Illinois, Indiana, Kentucky, Louisiana, Maine, Mississippi, Nevada, New Hampshire, New Jersey, New Mexico, North Dakota, Oklahoma, Oregon, Rhode Island, South Carolina, and Virginia.

GENETIC TESTING

The issue of genetic testing in employment first received public attention in the early 1980s when there was concern that genetic testing would be used to screen out individuals who were genetically predisposed to occupational illness. At that time, a few employers used biochemical genetic tests to measure the biological effects of genes, including proteins and enzymes. Because many of the genetic conditions suspected of predisposing workers to occupational diseases, such as sickle cell trait, were associated with particular racial or ethnic groups, there was a significant amount of adverse publicity and congressional attention. This fact, plus the failure to develop an adequate scientific justification for the testing, led most observers to believe that biochemical genetic testing in employment had virtually stopped by the mid-1980s.

At the end of the decade a new concern about possible genetic testing in employment came to the fore. New developments in molecular genetics associated with the Human Genome Project (a 15-year scientific undertaking to map and sequence all of the genes in humans) promised to be able to predict the genetic factors in each individual that could lead to illness years in the future. Although these new DNA-based screening techniques might be used to predict future occupational diseases, the main concern was that these tests could be used to screen out individuals who were thought to be at an increased risk of developing nonoccupationally related illnesses. The motivation for this genetic screening would be the desire to reduce the rapidly increasing cost of employer-provided employee health insurance.

Laws directed at genetic testing and discrimination in employment were first enacted in the 1970s to combat irrational sickle cell trait discrimination that arose out of government-sponsored sickle cell screening programs. Florida, Louisiana, and North Carolina enacted laws prohibiting discrimination in employment on the basis of sickle cell trait. These laws remain in effect today.

As the prospects increased for more broad based genetic discrimination in employment, other states enacted genetic discrimination laws. In 1981, New Jersey enacted a law prohibiting employment discrimination based on an individual's "atypical hereditary cellular or blood trait," defined to include sickle cell trait, hemoglobin C trait, thalassemia trait, Tay-Sachs trait, or cystic fibrosis trait. In 1989, Oregon amended its unlawful employment practices act to prohibit employers from requiring applicants or employees to undergo "genetic screening," although the term is not further defined. In 1990, New York enacted a law prohibiting discrimination based on sickle cell trait, Tay-Sachs trait, or Cooley's anemia (beta-thalassemia) trait. In 1992, Wisconsin enacted a law prohibiting employers from requiring applicants or employees to undergo genetic testing or from using the information from genetic tests in employment decisions. Also in 1992, Iowa made it unlawful for an employer to solicit or require genetic testing as a condition of employment or to discriminate against any person who obtains a genetic test. A 1992 Rhode Island law prohibits employers from requesting, requiring, or administering genetic tests to an individual as a condition of employment.

Besides these specific laws, genetic discrimination may constitute a violation of Title VII because it may have a disparate impact along the lines of race, color, religion, sex, or national origin. For example, discrimination based on sickle cell anemia has been alleged to be disparate impact race discrimination.

By far, the most likely source of protection for individuals claiming genetic discrimination in employment will be the federal and state laws prohibiting discrimination on the basis of disability. The federal Rehabilitation Act prohibits discrimination against otherwise qualified individuals with disabilities, but it applies only to the federal government (section 501), federal government contractors (section 503), and federal grantees (section 504). Virtually every state also has its own law prohibiting discrimination in employment on the basis of handicap or disability, but the coverage, rights, and remedies vary.

The newest and most important law prohibiting discrimination in employment on the basis of disability is the ADA. It is a complex and far-reaching law, but one that was not specifically drafted with the problems of genetic discrimination in mind. Although the ADA clearly prohibits discrimination against individuals who are currently affected with a genetic disease, it is not settled whether the ADA covers other individuals, such as currently unaffected individuals who carry the gene for a late-onset genetic disease, unaffected carriers of recessive and x-linked conditions, and individuals at an increased risk of a multifactorial disorder.

DRUG TESTING

During the 1970s, as a way of monitoring heroin use among people at drug treatment centers, automated and increasingly sophisticated tests were developed to measure the metabolites of drugs in urine. It was not long before these techniques were applied in other settings, such as the military, which began drug testing in 1981. By the mid-1980s drug testing was widely adopted in both public and private sector employment.

Although blood, hair, and other specimens have been used on occasion, urine testing is, by far, the most common. This raises a variety of privacy and other concerns. There is also a small but growing use of "impairment tests," largely computer programs and eye tests, which attempt to detect impairment from any source. These tests have not yet been widely adopted and have not been challenged in court.

More drug testing is performed at the preemployment stage than at any other time, but some employers use preplacement, periodic, random, for cause, postaccident, or return-to-work testing instead of, or in addition to, preemployment testing. Aside from the legal issues, there are a number of technical concerns about urine drug testing. These include the following:

- to ensure that the sample is not adulterated, indirect or direct observation of urination may be necessary;

- elaborate measures often are required to maintain the chain of custody of the specimen;

- laboratory quality often varies widely;

- to be accurate, more expensive confirmatory tests are necessary to augment the initial screening test;

- a medical review officer may be necessary to evaluate the result in light of possible cross-reacting prescription medications or other substances;

- drug tests, by revealing prescription medications taken, may reveal an underlying medical condition;

- the delay between testing and receipt of the results precludes their use to prevent impaired workers from starting on the job;

- the tests measure the inert metabolites of substances as they are being excreted and do not measure the tested-for substances themselves;

- the tests do not measure impairment (past or present), the amount of the substance originally ingested, or the length of time between ingestion and the test; and

- many testing programs are often limited to five or so illicit substances and do not attempt to measure alcohol or other lawful substances of abuse.

Most drug testing is performed by professional laboratories, although "on-site" tests have become an increasingly popular alternative. While on-site tests are less accurate (especially when not confirmed), they are faster, less expensive, and do not require trained personnel. In 1992, however, the Health Care Financing Administration promulgated final regulations implementing the Clinical Laboratory Improvements Act of 1988,[59] which subjects on-site drug testing by employers to the regulation of the Act.[60] Among other things, all regulated laboratories must use confirmatory tests, be supervised by a physician, have strict requirements for technicians, and use detailed proficiency testing and quality assurance measures. This regulation may have the effect of making on-site testing infeasible for many employers.

Federal Employees

In 1986, acting on a recommendation by his Commission on Organized Crime, President Reagan issued Executive Order 12,564. The Order requires the head of each executive agency to establish a program to test for illegal drug use by employees in sensitive positions. "Sensitive positions" is defined to include individuals handling classified information; serving as Presidential appointees; serving in positions related to national security; serving as law enforcement officers; serving in positions charged with protecting life, property, and public health and safety; and serving in jobs requiring a high degree of trust and confidence. In all, about half of the nation's two million federal employees are covered.

---

[59]42 U.S.C. §263a (1993).
[60]42 C.F.R. pt. 493 (1993).

The Executive Order authorizes drug testing under four circumstances: (1) where there is reasonable suspicion of illegal drug use; (2) in conjunction with the investigation of an accident; (3) as a part of an employee's counseling or rehabilitation for drug use through an employee assistance program (EAP); and (4) to screen any job applicant for illegal drug use. The Order mandates the use of confirmatory testing and allows the employee to provide a urine specimen in private unless there is reason to believe adulteration will occur.

The Executive Order also prescribes the action agencies must take when an employee's test is positive. Employees will be referred to an EAP and refusal to participate in the EAP will result in dismissal. Employees in sensitive positions are removed from duty pending successful completion of rehabilitation through the EAP. Agencies must initiate disciplinary action against any employee found to use illegal drugs unless the employee satisfies three criteria: (1) the employee must voluntarily identify himself or herself as a drug user before being identified through other means; (2) the employee must seek EAP rehabilitation; and (3) the employee must refrain from illegal drug use in the future. The employee must be dismissed if he or she is found continuing to use illegal drugs after initial identification.

Federal drug testing initiatives led directly and indirectly to increased use of drug testing by private sector employers. The direct effects center on two federal laws. First, the Drug-Free Workplace Act of 1988[61] is directed at federal government contractors and grant recipients. It requires all such entities to certify that they will provide a drug-free workplace. In addition, all holders of grants or contracts in excess of $25,000 must:

- notify employees that the unlawful manufacture, distribution, dispensation, possession, or use of a controlled substance is prohibited and indicate the sanctions for violations;

- establish a drug-free awareness program;

- sanction or require the participation in a drug rehabilitation program for an employee convicted under a criminal drug statute; and

- make a good faith effort to maintain a drug-free workplace.

---

[61]41 U.S.C. §§701–07 (1993).

Significantly, the Drug-Free Workplace Act does not require drug testing.

The second federal law directly affecting private sector drug testing is the Omnibus Transportation Employee Testing Act of 1991.[62] This law codifies earlier Department of Transportation regulations requiring the drug testing of employees in the transportation industry. It also adds the requirement of random alcohol testing for the six million covered employees. Besides these specific enactments, the federal government's lead role in encouraging drug testing has led to the voluntary adoption of drug testing by an increasing number of private sector employers as well as the enactment of drug testing laws and policies by numerous state and local government employers.

Government-mandated drug testing has been challenged on a variety of constitutional grounds. Without question, the most commonly asserted claim is that drug testing constitutes a violation of the Fourth Amendment's prohibition against unreasonable searches and seizures. In the companion cases of *National Treasury Employees Union v. Von Raab*[63] and *Skinner v. Railway Labor Executives' Association*[64] the Supreme Court addressed the constitutionality of government-ordered drug testing.

In *Von Raab*, a federal employees' union sought to enjoin the United States Customs Service from mandating drug tests of three groups of employees seeking promotions. The positions involved: (1) drug interdiction, (2) carrying firearms, or (3) handling classified materials. Although it held that a drug test is a search subject to the Fourth Amendment, the Supreme Court, five to four, held that the tests on the first two groups of employees could be conducted without a warrant, probable cause, or any individualized suspicion. Justice Kennedy's majority opinion noted that the government has a compelling interest in ensuring that front-line drug enforcement personnel are physically fit and have unimpeachable integrity and judgment. Because of the nature of the job, the Court concluded that the employees have a diminished expectation of privacy. The Court discounted the fact that only five of the first 3,600 people tested positive, by asserting that the testing program may well have a deterrent effect on the use of drugs by

---

[62]49 U.S.C. §§1618a, 2717 (1992).
[63]489 U.S. 656, 4 IER Cases 246 (1989).
[64]489 U.S. 602, 4 IER Cases 224 (1989).

employees. With regard to the employees seeking to handle classified material, however, the Court held that the category was too vague because it could result in the testing of mail clerks, attorneys, and other employees not on the front line in the fight against drugs.

In a pointed dissent, Justice Scalia asserted that the drug testing of Customs Service employees is entirely "symbolic" and that whatever value this symbolism may have, it is not enough to override important constitutional protections. He also complained that the government failed to cite any instances in which the "speculated horribles" of employing people who had not been subject to drug testing actually had occurred. He argued that the safety rationale was so broad that it could be used to justify the testing of automobile drivers, construction workers, and school crossing guards.

In the companion case of *Skinner,* the Supreme Court considered a challenge to the Federal Railroad Administration's drug and alcohol testing regulations requiring blood and urine tests for railroad employees involved in train accidents or who violate certain rules. The tests are administered automatically, without a warrant, probable cause, or individualized suspicion. With an analysis similar to *Von Raab,* Justice Kennedy's majority opinion held that the drug tests were permissible under the Fourth Amendment, and that the government had demonstrated a compelling interest due to the safety-sensitive nature of the positions involved.

Von Raab and *Skinner* established the validity of some drug tests of federal government employees and federally mandated tests of some private sector employees. To a large extent, the decisions are fact-sensitive. The Court was concerned in both cases with what it deemed to be persuasive evidence of the need to test to ensure public safety. The cases did not resolve the constitutionality of the drug testing of other categories of public and private employees.

Numerous lower court cases have considered the validity of federal drug testing programs as applied to various federal employees. **In general, the validity of drug testing depends on the degree to which the testing is essential to ensure public safety**. For example, the Navy's random drug testing of civilian employees required to hold top secret security clearances, the Defense Logistics Agency's random testing of employees with top secret security clearances, and police officers, firefighters, nurses, first line environmental protection specialists, motor vehicle operators, heavy equipment operators, and locomotive operators all have been upheld. On the other hand, the testing of postal workers without individualized suspicion and the testing of all federal prison employees regardless of their position were struck down.

Most of the federal sector cases challenging drug testing have been brought by current employees. In *Willner v. Thornburgh*,[65] however, applicants for the position of attorney with the Antitrust Division of the Department of Justice argued that the preemployment drug testing requirement was unconstitutional. Despite the absence of a safety rationale, the D.C. Circuit Court of Appeals upheld the drug testing requirement. The court, unreceptive to the privacy assertions of the applicants, stated: "If individuals view drug testing as an indignity to be avoided, they need only refrain from applying."

State and Local Government Employees

Challenges to the drug testing of state and local government employees often have paralleled the challenges brought by federal employees. If the employees are in safety-sensitive positions, drug testing is usually upheld. For example, in *Penny v. Kennedy*,[66] Chattanooga, Tennessee, police officers and firefighters challenged the city's mandatory, suspicionless urine drug testing program. The Sixth Circuit Court of Appeals upheld the program, noting the city's compelling interest in ensuring that there is no risk of impairment of these public safety officials. The court, however, remanded the case for consideration of whether the manner and means of the testing were reasonable. Similar results have been reached in other cases.

Drug testing of corrections officers and personnel has been upheld because of the government's compelling interests in avoiding the dangers of a drug-impaired prison work force and in preventing drug smuggling to prisoners. These justifications resulted in the Seventh Circuit Court of Appeals' upholding of the testing program in *Taylor v. O'Grady*,[67] but it also caused the court to limit testing to those officers with prisoner contact or the opportunity to smuggle drugs to prisoners.

---

[65]928 F.2d 1185, 6 IER Cases 498 (D.C. Cir.), *cert. denied*, 112 S. Ct. 669, 6 IER Cases 1696 (1991).
[66]915 F.2d 1065, 5 IER Cases 1290 (6th Cir. 1990).
[67]888 F.2d 1189, 4 IER Cases 1569 (7th Cir. 1989).

A number of cases have involved the drug testing of municipal transit employees. The courts generally have permitted the testing because of the dire results of a drug-induced accident, although there have been some distinctions drawn between the timing of the tests (e.g., preemployment, periodic) and the basis of the tests (e.g., random, reasonable suspicion, postaccident). For example, the Third Circuit Court of Appeals upheld the random drug testing of transportation workers in safety-sensitive positions, but it required a particularized suspicion to validate return-to-work testing.[68] Postaccident drug testing has been upheld, but the courts have struck down random drug testing of workers not in safety-sensitive positions.

Government-Regulated Private Sector Employees

With regard to the drug testing of private sector employees, the most important factor affecting legality is whether the testing is government mandated. If so, then this "state action" or "governmental action" will permit the employees to assert constitutional arguments similar to those raised by public sector employees. Again, the degree to which the job involves public safety is often controlling. For example, testing of applicants and employees in nuclear power plants has been upheld.

The largest group of private sector employees subject to federal drug testing mandates is transportation workers. The Department of Transportation's regulations have been challenged by various groups and with little success. Thus, the drug testing of railroad crews, airline pilots, airline ground employees in safety-sensitive positions, crews of private vessels, and pipeline workers all have been upheld on the basis of safety.

Challenges to state drug testing requirements brought by private sector employees have varied more widely, with the results depending on the nature of the position, the method of testing, and other factors. For example, New Jersey and Illinois laws mandating the drug testing of horse racing personnel were upheld by the Third and Seventh Circuit Courts of Appeals, but a similar Massachusetts law was struck down by the Supreme Judicial Court of Massachusetts.

---

[68]Transport Workers Union v. Southeastern Pa. Transp. Auth., 884 F.2d 709, 6 IER Cases 510 (3d Cir. 1989).

State Constitutions and Statutes

Because unregulated private sector employees cannot use federal constitutional grounds to challenge drug testing, they sometimes have asserted that the testing violates state law, either constitutional or statutory. The two principal claims have been unlawful search and seizure and invasion of privacy. Most of the state search and seizure cases involve state and local government employees. State courts have viewed state constitutional search and seizure arguments similar to search and seizure arguments based on the Fourth Amendment.

A variety of state drug testing laws also have been enacted. Many of the laws mandate or authorize drug testing for certain state and local employees (Arizona, Connecticut, Illinois, Kansas, and Tennessee). Some of them track the language of the federal Drug-Free Workplace Act and apply to state contractors and grantees (California, Florida, and South Carolina). In addition, many states have enacted laws related to drug testing in the private sector. These laws either limit drug testing, regulate the procedures for drug testing, or encourage or mandate the drug testing of certain employees in the private sector.

Seven states (Connecticut, Iowa, Maine, Minnesota, Montana, Rhode Island, and Vermont) have enacted laws that seek to limit, but not prohibit, drug testing in the private sector. All of the laws permit the preemployment testing of applicants and some permit the periodic testing of employees if advance notice is given. Exceptions are often made for public safety officers and employees in safety-sensitive jobs. "For cause" testing is generally permitted if there is "probable cause," "reasonable cause," or "reasonable suspicion" that an employee is impaired. Most of the laws require that the sample collection be performed in private and that drug testing records be kept confidential. Most of the laws require confirmatory testing. State drug testing laws, however, have been held to be preempted by federal law when they seek to restrict federally mandated testing.

Nine states (Florida, Hawaii, Illinois, Louisiana, Mississippi, Nebraska, Nevada, North Carolina, and Oregon) regulate various procedures used in private or public sector drug testing. For example, they specify that notices must be posted to advise employees of the testing, require the use of certified laboratories, or grant employees the right to have the sample retested.

Finally, the Utah Drug and Alcohol Testing Act permits drug testing as a condition of hiring or continued employment so long as employers and managers also submit to testing periodically. Employers performing drug testing must have a written policy and confirmatory tests must be used. Employers that satisfy these requirements are immune from liability for defamation or other torts based on the drug testing. The law also prohibits any action based on the failure to conduct a drug test.

Disabilities Laws

The ADA has several provisions dealing with illegal drugs and alcohol. Section 104(a) excludes from the definition of "qualified individual with a disability" "any employee or applicant who is currently engaging in the illegal use of drugs, when the covered entity acts on the basis of such use." Nevertheless, three categories of individuals are still considered "individuals with disabilities." These are an individual who (1) has successfully completed drug rehabilitation and is no longer engaging in the illegal use of drugs; (2) is participating in a rehabilitation program and is no longer using drugs; or (3) is erroneously regarded as engaging in such use but is not engaging in such use. The term "currently engaging" is not limited to a period of days or weeks, but applies to any recent use that indicates that the individual is actively engaged in such conduct.

The ADA gives employers wide discretion to combat the use of illegal drugs and alcohol in the workplace. Covered employers may prohibit the use of illegal drugs and alcohol in the workplace; require that employees not be under the influence of alcohol or illegal drugs at the workplace; require that employees behave in conformance with the federal Drug-Free Workplace Act; hold an employee who engages in the illegal use of drugs or who is an alcoholic to the same qualification and job performance standards as other employees; and require that employees comply with applicable Department of Defense, Nuclear Regulatory Commission, and Department of Transportation regulations.

The ADA is neutral on the issue of drug testing; the tests are not encouraged, prohibited, or authorized. In addition, the ADA provides that "a test to determine the illegal use of drugs shall not be considered a medical examination." This means that drug tests, unlike "medical examinations," may be performed at the preemployment stage. Nevertheless, employers that perform drug tests prior to a conditional offer of employment may have a problem. Employers subject to federal testing standards (as well as other employers using a good testing protocol or subject to the Clinical Laboratories Improvements Act) must use a medical review officer after testing to interview the subject of any initial positive result. The medical review officer is required to ask the individual about prescription medications that could have produced a false positive result. Under the ADA, however, it is illegal for an employer or any agent of the employer to inquire into the medications taken by an individual at the preemployment stage. This problem is avoided, however, by simply performing the drug testing after a conditional offer of employment.

Common Law

Workplace drug testing has given rise to a variety of common law actions, most frequently invasion of privacy, negligence, defamation, and wrongful discharge. The actions have been based on the acts of the employer and other third parties at all stages of the employment relationship, from preemployment to postemployment.

A wide range of employer conduct has been alleged to constitute an invasion of privacy and there has been a wide range of results. For example, one court rejected the argument that an employer's requirement that an employee divulge the medications she was taking established common law invasion of privacy. Similarly, the drug testing of all at-will employees did not amount to an invasion of privacy, even though the failure to consent was grounds for dismissal. The method of testing often is the key factor in establishing liability. In one case, damages for invasion of privacy and negligent infliction of emotional distress were affirmed where a drilling rig employee was "disgusted" by a drug testing procedure in which he was forced to submit a urine sample under direct observation.

Actions for negligence may be brought against an independent laboratory for failing to perform a drug test in a reasonable manner. Although at least one jurisdiction has recognized a duty running from the laboratory to an employee and from the laboratory to an applicant, it has refused to recognize an action by an employee against an employer for negligence due to the laboratory's error or an action against the laboratory for negligent interference with contract. Actions also may be brought by the employer for negligence against the laboratory, especially where laboratory errors led to liability by the employer to employees.

Actions for wrongful discharge also have been brought on several theories, mostly allegations that discharging an individual for refusing to take a drug test or because of the results of a drug test violates public policy. Although originally these arguments were uniformly rejected, and still often are, an increasing number of jurisdictions have been willing to entertain common law challenges to drug testing. For example, in West Virginia drug testing will violate public policy unless it is based on a "reasonable good faith objective suspicion" or it is to protect public safety or the safety of others. In Pennsylvania and New Jersey, the public policy exception also may be violated by drug testing, although the testing of employees in safety-sensitive jobs is still likely to be upheld. In Alaska, drug testing that focuses on a single employee without prior notice has been held to violate the implied covenant of good faith and fair dealing. In California, the discharge of an employee for refusing to submit to a drug test also is actionable.

FORMATION OF THE EMPLOYMENT RELATIONSHIP

The employer-employee relationship is a contractual relationship. The actual contract may be oral or written, express or implied by the conduct of the parties, bilateral or unilateral. Generally, however, employment contracts are deemed to be unilateral contracts requiring the traditional contract elements of offer, acceptance, and consideration.

The "American" rule is that oral contracts of indefinite duration (the most common form of employment contracts) are presumed to be "at-will" contracts. Essentially, this means that the employment relationship may be terminated by either the employer or the employee without notice and for any reason. This rule, of course, has spawned great controversy and numerous exceptions.

The terminability provisions which characterize at-will contracts may be altered in both written and oral contracts by an agreement of the parties that employment will not be terminated except for "cause," "good cause," or similar language.

Offer

An offer for employment need not be exceedingly formal. The offer may be oral or written. It may be made by telephone, by letter, by an employee manual or handbook, or by an advertisement. An offer also may be implied through the conduct of the employer. Most states do not have strict requirements and will uphold an offer unless the intent of the offering party cannot reasonably be inferred from the outward manifestations of the parties.

At a minimum, an offer of employment must be clear, definite, and explicit. An offer must be sufficiently certain to allow a court to determine the duties of each party. The mere possibility of future employment, expression of good will or good intentions, or a general expression of policy are not sufficient to constitute an offer. Thus, not every utterance by an employer is an offer. A statement indicating specific pay, hours, location, and responsibilities is generally required.

Acceptance

Acceptance of an offer need not be made in the same form as the offer. For example, an employee may accept a written offer orally or through action. If an employer and an employee fail to reduce their agreement to a final written version, but the parties act affirmatively upon their negotiations, the courts are free to find that an enforceable agreement exists because of the manifestation of the parties' intent to be bound. If the parties do not agree on material terms, however, then the employee cannot be deemed to have accepted any offer. Also, if an employee attempts to change the terms of the offer in an acceptance, the employee's actions constitute a counteroffer, not an acceptance.

Consideration

To be enforceable, an employment contract must be supported by consideration. The importance of the type consideration provided arises mostly in the context of determining whether employment is at will or terminable only for cause. At-will employment contracts usually are considered to be "unilateral" contracts. The employer makes an offer or a promise, which the employee accepts through performance. The employee's action in reliance upon the employer's promise is sufficient consideration to make the employer's promise binding.

Additional consideration may be necessary if a contract is not at will, but terminable only for cause. Even a contract that lacks a specific duration may be regarded as a termination for cause contract if the employee furnishes independent and additional consideration. If an employee provides consideration beyond performing duties under the employment contract, then the presumption of employment at will may be rebutted. Merely continuing to work in the same employment relationship is not sufficient. But, if the relationship changes through the addition of a new agreement, such as an agreement to pay severance wages or a new noncompetition clause, then continuing to work under the revised agreement is sufficient consideration to make the new provisions binding.

As a general rule, services and obligations associated with beginning new employment will not be considered sufficient additional consideration to override the presumption of at-will employment. Thus, moving to another city, resigning from a former position or job, or foregoing other employment or ceasing to search for other employment are not sufficient consideration to alter at-will status.

Probationary Periods

Many private and public sector employees must successfully complete a probationary period before becoming a permanent employee. Whether a special probationary period exists depends on the agreement of the parties, and this agreement may be found in a variety of sources. For example, provisions for probationary periods have been based on personnel manuals, written employment contracts, city council resolutions, and government policy manuals.

The effect of having a probationary period varies and depends, in the first instance, on the agreement specifying a probationary period. Frequently, the agreement will specify that probationary employees may be discharged at will, whereas permanent employees may be discharged only for cause. For public employees, they may have no legally binding interest in their jobs until after the end of the probationary period.

TORT LIABILITY AND THE EMPLOYMENT
RELATIONSHIP

Although many aspects of modern employment law differ greatly from earlier common law rules, the tort consequences of the employment relationship still follow closely traditional common law doctrines. In particular, liability principles of employment law today are substantially based on the common law of master and servant. These rules remain extremely important and govern a wide range of tort actions, including the liability of an employer for the torts committed by an employee within the scope of employment.

Masters (Employers)

Generally, a master is a person who controls or has the right to control the details of the work of another person engaged in providing services for the master. Whether a particular person is the master of another becomes important when the other person commits a wrongful act. **As a general rule, a master is subject to liability for the wrongful acts of a servant when the servant commits the acts within the scope of employment**. A master may be liable for the conduct of a servant even if the servant's action is outside the scope of employment if the master intended the conduct, the master was negligent or reckless, the servant's conduct violated a nondelegable duty, or the agent committed the act with the aid of the agency relationship with the master. The term "employer" has displaced the term "master" in statutes and case law, and the terms are now used interchangeably.

In order to hold a master or employer liable for injury to a third party caused by a servant or an employee, the third party must first show that a master-servant or employer-employee relationship exists. Under one formulation, four factors are used to makes this determination: (1) the method of selection and engagement of the servant, (2) the basis of payment of compensation, (3) the power of dismissal, and (4) the power of control.[69] A number of courts use a 10-factor test to evaluate whether a master-servant relationship exists.[70] The most important

---

[69]Paxton v. Crabtree, 400 S.E.2d 245 (W. Va. 1990).
[70]*Restatement (Second) of Agency* §220(2) (1958).

element is the employer's right to control the physical details of the employee's work.

Servants (Employees)

A servant is a person who performs services for another and whose physical conduct while performing those services is subject to the control of the other. The term "servant" is not limited to persons who perform manual labor. Servants also need not even be paid for their services; they may be employed without compensation. The terms "servant" and "employee" are often used interchangeably. If a person performs the work of another, a presumption exists that the person is employed by the person whose work is being done.

Scope of Employment

Generally, an employer is liable for its employee's acts only if they are committed within the employee's scope of employment. The conduct of an employee is not within the scope of employment if the employee's actions are different in kind from those authorized, exceed the employee's authorized time or space limitation, or are not performed with a purpose to serve the employer. Another 10-factor test is used to determine whether conduct is within the scope of employment.[71]

An employer will not be liable for the acts of an employee engaged in a "frolic." In other words, if the employee's action is wholly motivated by his or her own interests with no underlying purpose to further the employer's business, then the employer will not be liable for the employee's wrongful negligent or intentional acts. An employee may temporarily depart from the scope of employment in time or space and reenter the scope of employment by resuming activity within the scope of employment. If an employee's deviation from the employer's business is slight and not unusual, a court may find that the employee continued to act within the scope of employment. If the employee's deviation is "marked and unusual," however, a court may find that the employee acted beyond the scope of employment.

---

[71]*Restatement (Second) of Agency* §229(2) (1958).

If an employee commits an intentional tort such as assault and battery, some courts require not only that the employee's acts be within the scope of employment, but also that the acts facilitate or promote the employer's business. Other courts use a foreseeability standard. Thus, no single test exists to determine what constitutes "scope of employment."

Generally, employees are not within the scope of employment while traveling to and from work. If the employer pays for employment-related travel, however, the employee is considered to be acting within the scope of employment. Also, if travel is part of employment, an employer will be liable for the employee's actions if the employment created the necessity for the travel. Accordingly, if an employee is on a purely personal errand while operating an automobile, the employer will not be liable for the employee's negligence. But, if an employee is engaged in a work-related errand, the employer will be liable for the employee's negligence.

Independent Contractors

Generally, an employer or master is not liable for wrongful acts committed by an independent contractor. The commonly accepted theory behind nonliability for the acts of an independent contractor is the fact that the employer has no right of control over the manner in which the contractor's work is done, and thus the work is regarded as the contractor's own enterprise.

An independent contractor is a person who, while pursuing an independent business, undertakes a specific job for another using his or her own means and methods without submitting to the control of the other except for the results of the work. An independent contractor may or may not be the agent of an employer.

Courts look at the hiring party's right to control the means or manner in which a worker performs a specific task. If the hiring party merely retains the right to require certain results, then the parties will be considered to have an independent contractor relationship. Thus, merely retaining the right to supervise or inspect the work of an independent contractor for compliance with the terms of a contract does not create a master-servant relationship.

Liability Arising from Social Events

An employee gets intoxicated at the company Christmas party and then gets involved in an automobile accident causing injury to a third party. Is the company liable to the injured party? This scenario and many variations of it have resulted in an increasing number of lawsuits. Although this is a serious concern of employers, the law varies so much among the states that it is impossible to express a general rule or even an accepted legal theory.

An employer's liability for the negligent act of its employee depends on the existence of a duty. Some courts hold that a duty is based on the employer's ability to control the employee,[72] other courts hold that there is simply no duty owed by the employer to third[73] parties or that the employee and not the employer was the proximate cause of the injury.[74] In many jurisdictions liability will depend on the nature of the event. If it was a business meeting or attendance was compulsory, liability is more likely to be found than where it was a purely social function with attendance optional.[75] Other courts limit employer responsibility to instances in which the employee was acting within the scope of employment at the time of the accident.[76] In light of this variation among the states as well as the magnitude of potential harm, it is important to be extremely careful with all company-sponsored events.

---

[72]*See, e.g.*, Gariup Constr. Co. v. Foster, 519 N.E.2d 1224 (Ind. 1988).

[73]*See, e.g.*, Overbaugh v. McCutcheon, 396 S.E.2d 153 (W. Va. 1990).

[74]*See, e.g.*, Rone v. H.R. Hospitality, Inc., 759 S.W.2d 548 (Ark. 1988).

[75]Chastain v. Litton Sys., 694 F.2d 975 (4th Cir. 1982); Divecchio v. Mead Corp., 361 S.E.2d 850 (Ga. App. 1987); Dickinson v. Edwards, 716 P.2d 814 (Wash. 1986).

[76]Mosko v. Raytheon Co., 622 N.E.2d 1066 (Mass. 1993); Joly v. Northway Motor Car Corp., 517 N.Y.S.2d 595 (App. Div. 1987); Sayles v. Piccadilly Cafeterias, 410 S.E.2d 632 (Va. 1991).

2

Employment Discrimination

INTRODUCTION

This chapter explores the federal statutory constraints on employment practices that disadvantage applicants and employees because of race, ethnicity, gender, religion, age, or disability. It also examines state statutory protections against discrimination and constitutionally based claims.

The centerpiece of employment discrimination law is Title VII of the Civil Rights Act of 1964 (Title VII), as amended by Congress on several occasions.[1] **Title VII prohibits employment discrimination on the basis of "race, color, religion, sex, or national origin" by employers, labor organizations, and employment agencies**. The term "sex" does not include sexual orientation. There is no federal protection against employment discrimination on the basis of sexual orientation, although some state and local laws prohibit discrimination on this ground. The Supreme Court has defined the term "national origin" as referring to "the country where a person was born, or, more broadly, the country from which his or her ancestors came."[2] Discrimination on the basis of religion refers not only to the adverse treatment of a worker because of religious affiliation, but also to the employer's

---

[1]42 U.S.C. §2000e *et seq.* (1993).
[2]Espinoza v. Farah Mfg. Co., 414 U.S. 86, 88, 6 FEP Cases 933 (1973).

failure to make reasonable accommodation to the religious beliefs of employees.

Several other sources of federally guaranteed rights against employment discrimination are examined at the end of this chapter. These include: constitutional claims of employment discrimination; claims derived from the Reconstruction Era Civil Rights Acts; actions for discrimination against individuals at least 40 years of age under the Age Discrimination in Employment Act (ADEA); and claims of discrimination based on disability under the Rehabilitation Act and the Americans with Disabilities Act (ADA). Finally, the chapter highlights state statutory prohibitions of discrimination.

COVERAGE AND EXEMPTIONS

Congress used the outer limits of its constitutional power when it enacted Title VII. Section 701(h) specifies that the Act covers any employer, labor organization, or employment agency that "affects commerce," which is not difficult to prove. The Supreme Court has interpreted broadly when activities "affect commerce" so that even local activities may have an effect on interstate commerce. In the context of Title VII, it is only the rare employer whose operations are almost completely confined within one state that will avoid coverage of the Act for failure to affect commerce.

The Act does not provide for individual liability. Only employers, labor organizations, and employment agencies can be liable. Although an individual person might be personally liable under state law for conduct concerning employment, the federal law does not impose such personal liability. The Title VII plaintiff must sue the employer either by naming the supervisory employees as agents or by naming the employer directly.

Limitations in Title VII Coverage

Congress imposed some limitations on the Act's coverage. One noteworthy limitation is that Title VII does not cover employers with fewer than 15 employees. Section 701(b) defines employer as "a person engaged in an industry affecting commerce who has fifteen or more employees for each working day in each of twenty or more calendar weeks in the current or preceding calendar year" or any agent of such person.

The legislative history indicates that Congress did not want to burden small businesses with federal requirements. The Act was amended in 1972 to reduce the threshold for coverage from 25 to the current number, 15 employees. Opponents of the reduction were concerned about the burden on small businesses, which are often family-run and which usually hire friends and relatives of the same ethnicity as the owner.

Employers Exempted from Title VII

There are very few employers who are exempt from Title VII. There is no Title VII exemption, for example, for charitable institutions. In contrast, there is an exemption for bona fide private membership clubs, other than labor organizations. Such clubs must (1) be exempt from taxation under the Internal Revenue Code, and (2) have a defined social or recreational purpose or promote a common literary, scientific, or political objective, and demand meaningful conditions of membership. The requirement of a defined purpose is not easily met. For example, a credit union does not have a sufficient purpose for exemption, nor does a retirement home restricted to members of a fraternal order.

Title VII expressly exempts "Indian tribes" so as not to interfere with their treaty-protected rights of self-government. This exemption includes corporations of a tribe designated to administer tribal assets.

Religious employers are not exempt from Title VII. Thus, they may not discriminate on the basis of race, color, national origin, or gender. The Act does make a specific exception, however, to allow religious employers to hire on the basis of religious belief and practice. The Supreme Court held in *Corporation of the Presiding Bishop of the Church of Jesus Christ of Latter-Day Saints v. Amos*[3] that this provision of the Act is constitutional, even though the exemption applies to the nonprofit secular activities of religious organizations.

Courts have interpreted the Act to exempt religious organizations from all interference with the employment relationship between a

---

[3]483 U.S. 327, 44 FEP Cases 20 (1987).

church and its minister. Therefore, the Act's prohibition against discrimination on the basis of race, gender, and national origin does not apply to this particular relationship. By reading this exemption into the Act, courts avoid the constitutional problem of state encroachment into religious freedom.

Title VII does protect employees of religious institutions if their duties do not go to the "heart" of the church's function. There is no encroachment into religious freedom to regulate the employment of sectarian employees, and Congress chose to prohibit religious institutions from discriminating on the basis of race, gender, and national origin—but not religion—of its nonministerial employees.

Defining "Employees"

Counting the 15 employees that are necessary for Title VII coverage is often not a simple matter. Section 701(b) requires that they be employed each working day for 20 or more calendar weeks in the current or previous year. It is noteworthy that the 20 weeks need not be consecutive, although the employees must work in each day during each of the 20 weeks counted. The 20 weeks with the minimum number of employees may be cumulated throughout the calendar year. Moreover, because the statute says that 20 weeks of 15 employees in the *previous* calendar year suffices for coverage, the employer is covered by Title VII for a year after meeting the minimum, even if the employer reduces the work force.

There is no statutory definition of "employee," so the courts have provided guidelines. Everyone who receives compensation from an employer is not necessarily an employee for purposes of counting the statutory minimum. Some individuals are management and therefore not employees. Corporate directors and managing partners of a partnership, for example, are not employees, even though the corporate legal entity pays them for their services.

Part-time workers do not count toward the minimum 15 employees necessary for coverage, but once the employer reaches the minimum for coverage, all employees are protected by the substantive provisions of the Act. It is not necessary to be a "counted" employee in order to have standing to complain of unlawful discrimination.

All employees of the employer's legal entity will be counted toward the minimum number, not just those in the particular department or branch where the discrimination took place. Furthermore, the plaintiff can amalgamate the number of employees of two or more distinct legal entities if they qualify as joint employers. The requirements are common ownership, unified control over both entities, an integrated economic relationship, and a common or centralized labor relations policy.

Defining the Employment Relationship

Each of the 15 workers necessary for application of the statute must have an "employment" relationship with the employer. Moreover, the relationship between an individual complainant and the employer must be one of "employment" for Title VII protections to apply to that individual, even if the employer otherwise has 15 employees.

This restriction to "employment" relationships applies regardless of whether the worker performs useful services. Thus, students are not employees, even when they assist in research or teaching at the direction of a professor, as long as the purpose of these compensated activities is "educational." An unpaid volunteer is also not an employee and is therefore not protected by the Act. The label "volunteer" is not controlling. Someone called a "paid volunteer" may qualify as an employee under the Act, but incidental remuneration is not sufficient to change the status of a volunteer to an employee.

The key in these cases is the economic reality of the relationship between the worker and the employer. Factors relevant to the economic reality test include the extent of the employer's right to control the means and manner of the worker's performance, the availability of leave time and retirement benefits, and the payment of Social Security taxes.

Independent contractors also are not covered by Title VII. Courts use the economic realities test to distinguish between an employee and an independent contractor. The primary factor is the extent of the employer's right to control the means and manner of the worker's performance. Other factors include: the owner of the worker's equipment, the duration of employment, the manner of terminating employment, the availability of leave, the accumulation of retirement benefits, the payment of Social Security taxes, and the intention of the parties.

The requirement of an employment relationship also excludes military personnel from coverage under the Act. Prisoners also are not employees unless the relationship meets the same economic realities test.

Corporate decisions that do not involve employment are not within the scope of Title VII. Examples of such decisions include the selection of corporate directors and eligibility to purchase stock. The Act is applicable, however, if stock is discriminatorily allocated as part of compensation. Moreover, an employer may not grant preferences to stockholder employees in terms of hiring, salary, job assignments, and promotion.

The limitation of Title VII's coverage to employer-employee relations further excludes entrepreneurial decisions such as the initial formation of a partnership or professional corporation. More difficult has been the question whether Title VII prohibits discrimination when established entities of this type break up and reorganize, excluding some partners.

Another question is whether the Act applies to the promotion of associates to partnership. The Supreme Court, in *Hishon v. King & Spalding*,[4] held that Title VII covered promotion to partnership in a law firm when that consideration was a term of employment of the associate. The case left unresolved whether Title VII covers partnership decisions in other contexts, but a subsequent comment by the Court strongly suggests that promotion to partnership is always covered by the Act. There has not been a direct holding to that effect, however.

Defining Protected Classes

Title VII proscribes "race" discrimination, which includes members of groups who trace their ancestry to Africa or Asia. The prohibition against "race" discrimination also encompasses indigenous Americans, including Native American Indians, Eskimos, Samoans, and Native Hawaiians.

The Supreme Court held in *McDonald v. Santa Fe Trail Transportation Co.*,[5] that the proscription applies not only to historically excluded "minorities" but to all racial groups. In that case the employer had discharged three Caucasian employees who were guilty of theft, but retained a black employee guilty of the same offense. The Court held that when such unequal treatment of similarly situated employees is premised upon race, it violates the Act.

---

[4] 467 U.S. 69, 34 FEP Cases 1406 (1984).
[5] 427 U.S. 273, 12 FEP Cases 1577 (1976).

The prohibition against race discrimination further includes discrimination because of the race of the applicant's or employee's spouse. An employer may not discriminate against an applicant or employee because that individual has an interracial marriage or otherwise associates with people of different racial backgrounds.

Congress did not provide much guidance on its intention with respect to the prohibition against discrimination on the basis of "sex." There is virtually no legislative history on the subject. This proscription became part of the Act only because a southern congressman who opposed the entirety of Title VII added "sex" as an amendment at the last minute in an effort to defeat the entire bill. Congress subsequently provided some clarification of the meaning of discrimination on the basis of "sex" when it amended Title VII with the Pregnancy Discrimination Act in 1978.[6] This Act defined discrimination on the basis of "sex" to include pregnancy, childbirth, and related medical conditions.

Title VII's prohibition against discrimination on the basis of "sex" does not include sexual orientation. The legislative history of Title VII does not support the extension of sex discrimination to include homosexuality or sexual disorders. More recently, Congress has expressly stated that sexual orientation is not a "disability" for purposes of the ADA.

The term "national origin" is broadly construed under Title VII. In the legislative history to Title VII Congress explained the term to mean the country from which one's forbearers came. The term appears to be synonymous with "ancestry," but a number of state statutes prohibiting discrimination in employment include "ancestry" as a term separate from "national origin."

The Title VII meaning of "national origin" includes the physical, cultural or linguistic characteristics of a national origin group. An allegation of discrimination on the basis of the plaintiff's Ukrainian roots, for example, is sufficient to establish membership in a protected class. The concept encompasses claims of discrimination against "hyphenated-American" groups such as Asian-Americans, Polish-Americans, and Italian-Americans. Discrimination on the basis of Spanish surname is discrimination on the basis of national origin. Further, it is not necessary for plaintiffs to allege a "nation" from which

---

[6]Pub. L. No. 95-555, 92 Stat. 2076 (1978).

"national origin" discrimination can arise; groups such as Cajuns and Gypsies are covered by the concept.

Title VII protects against discrimination on the basis of national origin, but not on the basis of citizenship. The Act thus affords no protection against an employer's decision to exclude lawful aliens because of their citizenship status. Citizenship discrimination is prohibited to a limited extent by the Immigration Reform and Control Act of 1986 (IRCA).[7]

Complainants cannot "bootstrap" coverage of an otherwise unprotected class on the basis that a protected class is adversely affected. For example, discrimination on the basis of sexual orientation is not covered by Title VII, even though the effect of this exclusion disproportionately disadvantages men. The fact that gender discrimination is covered by the Act, coupled with the adverse effect on men, does not overcome the fact that Congress did not intend to cover sexual orientation. Similarly, discrimination on the basis of citizenship is not covered by the Act, even when the effect is to disadvantage on the basis of national origin. For example, in *Fortino v. Quasar Co.*,[8] the court considered the effect of an American-Japanese treaty that permits foreign employers to engage managers of its own choosing. Quasar, now an American subsidiary of a Japanese company, fired American managers and replaced them with Japanese nationals. Although the effect of this process was to exclude on the basis of national origin, the plaintiffs could not use this effect to show a violation of Title VII. The court noted that "in the case of a homogeneous country like Japan, citizenship and national origin are highly correlated," but that "to use this correlation to infer national-origin discrimination from a treaty-sanctioned preference for Japanese citizens who happen also to be of Japanese national origin would nullify the treaty."

Congress recently amended Title VII to cover another category of workers that was not previously covered. The Supreme Court had held that Title VII does not apply to American citizens employed abroad by American companies. Congress responded by amending Title VII to cover such employees with the proviso that Title VII does not require American companies to engage in practices that would violate the laws of the host country.

---

[7] 8 U.S.C. §1324B (1993).
[8] 950 F.2d 389, 57 FEP Cases 712 (7th Cir. 1991).

State and Local Government Employers

The employment decisions of state and local governments are covered by Title VII if these employers otherwise meet the statutory minimum of 15 employees. These employers were excluded from coverage when the Act was originally passed in 1964, but Congress extended Title VII to state and local governments in the Equal Employment Opportunity Act of 1972.

Before the Civil Rights Act of 1991,[9] there was a Title VII exemption for employment decisions affecting three groups of officials appointed to assist elected officials: personal staff, immediate legal advisers, and policy-making assistants. Their exemption meant that they could be appointed or fired without the protection of the Act. Moreover, these employees did not count toward the statutory minimum number of 15 necessary for the Act's coverage. The Government Employees Rights Act of 1991, enacted as a part of the Civil Rights Act of 1991, extended the coverage of the Act to all except elected officials. Therefore, personal staff, legal advisers, and all assistants are now protected under Title VII. Under section 321 of the Act they can file complaints with the Equal Employment Opportunity Commission (EEOC) for agency review.

Federal Government

When Title VII was originally enacted it did not provide coverage for any public employers, including the federal government. The 1972 amendments to the Act extended the definition of employer to include state and local employers, but these amendments provided different coverage for federal employees. Title VII provides that its coverage of employers does not include the federal government or corporations wholly owned by the United States government. Although the federal government is not covered in the main body of Title VII, section 717 of the Act, as amended in 1972, provides substantive protection.

The primary difference between complaints against the federal employer and those against other employers is in the enforcement procedures. The employing federal agency has the primary

---

[9] 42 U.S.C. §1981, P.L. 102–166; 105 Stat. 1071 (1991).

responsibility for hearing complaints of discrimination against it. If the complainant is not satisfied with the resolution, suit may be brought in federal court.

The Civil Rights Act of 1991 extended the coverage of Title VII to previously excluded groups of federal employers: Congress, legislative agencies, and the President. First, the House of Representatives and legislative agencies are now covered by the remedies and procedures contained in the House Fair Employment Practices Resolution. The enforcement provisions of Title VII, however, do not apply, and there is no right to judicial review.

Senate employees are now protected by the Government Employee Rights Act of 1991, which was enacted as part of the Civil Rights Act of 1991. Although the same substantive provisions apply, the procedures and remedies are significantly curtailed. The Act creates an Office of Senate Fair Employment Practices with exclusive jurisdiction over claims in this category. The Office receives complaints, investigates, and holds hearings. The hearings board is authorized to order affirmative relief and award damages, not including punitive damages. Limited review is available in the Federal Circuit Court of Appeals.

Presidential appointees must file complaints with the EEOC or other entity as designated by Executive Order. The EEOC in such cases also investigates, holds hearings, and has the power to order affirmative relief and damages, not including punitive damages. Limited judicial review is available in the Federal Circuit Court of Appeals.

Title VII does not cover the relationship of the military to its uniformed military personnel. Issues involving the recruitment, enlistment, pay, discipline, and discharge of uniformed military personnel are thus beyond the scope of the Act. Civilian employees of the military are distinguishable and the military is not exempt from Title VII with respect to these employees.

Unions

Title VII imposes obligations on labor organizations. A "labor organization" is defined by its membership and purpose. The minimum number of members is 25. The purpose of the organization must be to deal in whole or in part with employers concerning grievances, labor disputes, wages, rates of pay, hours, or other terms or conditions of employment.

Section 703(c) of the Act forbids a labor organization from taking various actions on the basis of an individual's race, color, religion, sex, or national origin. These include: excluding or expelling from membership; limiting, segregating, or classifying its members or applicants for membership, and failing or refusing to refer for employment any member; and causing or attempting to cause an employer to discriminate. Section 703(d) prohibits discrimination on the same grounds in training programs, including apprenticeship and on-the-job training programs.

These provisions convey the twofold obligations of labor organizations, both internal and external. Internally, the union cannot discriminate in admissions, dues, facilities, allocation of union offices, and so forth. A union's internal obligation is violated when it segregates its membership according to race, national origin, or gender, even if there is no direct economic consequence resulting from the segregation.

Externally, the union cannot discriminate in its referrals and other relations with employers. The Supreme Court held in *Goodman v. Lukens Steel Co.*[10] that a union's external obligation included the obligation to process employees' grievances against the employer in a nondiscriminatory manner. The union, which failed to process grievances of race discrimination against the employer, could not defend on the ground that its actions were intended for strategic advantage on other issues that would benefit all employees.

Also noteworthy is the fact that employees may sue even if they are not union members. A union certified or lawfully recognized to represent all employees in a bargaining unit must meet its obligations to all employees represented by the union. A union further has a duty of fair representation imposed upon it by the labor relations statutes. The Supreme Court held in *Steele v. Louisville & Nashville Railroad*[11] that the union is obligated to represent all workers in the bargaining unit over which it exercises exclusive bargaining rights "without hostile discrimination, fairly, impartially, and in good faith."

The *Goodman* case left open the question whether a union is required to take affirmative steps to oppose an employer's discriminatory practices. The question is whether Title VII imposes an affirmative duty on the union to combat discrimination by an employer with which

---

[10]482 U.S. 656, 44 FEP Cases 1 (1987).
[11]323 U.S. 192, 9 FEP Cases 381 (1944).

the union has an exclusive bargaining relationship. The Supreme Court declined to address this broader obligation and affirmed the lower court's decision on the narrower ground of the union's obligation to process grievances in a nondiscriminatory manner.

The affirmative obligation of the union is clearer when an employer and union are engaged in a joint operation such as a training program. Section 703(d) of Title VII prohibits discrimination in training programs, including joint labor-management apprenticeship training programs. The failure of a union to monitor a joint apprenticeship committee or to police discrimination practiced by employers that employ journeymen referred to them as part of the apprenticeship training program is a violation of the Act.

When the union and the employer jointly violate the Act, they are both liable for the full amount of the plaintiff's recovery. An international union may be liable for the acts of a local. A union also may be liable under Title VII for discriminatory referrals by its agents. Finally, a union may be liable for a hostile environment in the union when its members engage in harassment. For example, a hostile environment can be created by pervasive racial epithets in the hiring hall.

Employment Agencies

Title VII also expressly covers discrimination on the basis of race, color, religion, sex, or national origin by employment agencies. Under section 703(b) agencies may not discriminate in job referrals in the same way that employers are prohibited from discriminating in hiring. Employers may not request discriminatory referrals, and agencies may not honor such requests.

Section 701(c) defines the term employment agency as "any person regularly undertaking with or without compensation to procure employees for an employer . . . and includes an agent of such a person." The number of employees at the agency and the volume of business of the agency are not controlling. Under this definition, coverage of employment agencies is based upon "regularly undertaking" the procurement of "employees" for "employers." Each of these terms has presented difficulties in interpretation. For example, an agency that operates a service to place nurses with out-patients who need private nursing in their homes is not covered by the Act as an "employment agency" because the employer to whom the employees are sent is not an "employer" covered by the Act. The size of the agency's business does not control; it is the size of the employer's business that controls. Once an agency is covered by any employer of sufficient size, however, then the agency is covered for all purposes. It cannot then make discriminatory referrals to anyone, even employers that are too small to be themselves in violation of the Act by requesting a discriminatory referral.

A newspaper is not an "employment agency" if it simply prints advertisements from employers in a "Help Wanted" section. An employment agency or employer covered by the Act cannot publish discriminatory advertisements, however. Section 704(b) provides that it is an unlawful employment practice for "an employer, labor organization, or employment agency to print or publish, or cause to be printed or published, any notice or advertisement relating to employment . . . indicating any preference, limitation, specification, or discrimination" on the basis of race, color, religion, sex, or national origin.

An educational institution, such as a college or a technical school, is an "employment agency" if it has a placement office. Its obligation under the Act is to refrain from discriminatory referrals. There is no affirmative obligation to monitor the practices of employers that recruit on campus, although many such institutions do so voluntarily.

It is clear that an agency has a duty to refrain from discriminatory referrals, but one problem is how the agency should distinguish between a legitimate request for limited referrals as opposed to an unlawful one. For example, an employer that wishes to interview only actresses for a woman's role in a play is legally permitted to do so under the defense of bona fide occupational qualification.[12] How can an agency distinguish between a lawful request for an employee defined by national origin or gender and an unlawful request that is discriminatory? The EEOC's Uniform Guidelines on Employee Selection Procedures (EEOC Guidelines)[13] say that the agency should receive such requests in written form for evaluation, and if they appear reasonable, the agency itself is protected.

---

[12]See below "Bona Fide Occupational Qualification" under the discussion of "Gender Stereotyping and Classification."
[13]29 C.F.R. §1607.4 (1992).

INTENTIONAL INDIVIDUAL DISCRIMINATION

The federal employment discrimination acts prohibit employers, labor organizations, and employment agencies from discriminating against individual employees or applicants on the basis of race, color, religion, national origin, gender, age (if 40 or over), or disability. Courts have interpreted the term "discrimination" broadly to include even conduct made in good faith. One type of prohibited conduct is "intentional" discrimination. This term is broadly construed and does not require malicious or overtly bigoted exclusion. It includes simply treating people differently on the basis of gender, for example, unless the employer has a defense.

Nature of "Intent"

The ordinary meaning of words like "discrimination" and "prejudice" does not determine liability under employment discrimination law. In one case the court declared that a jury was wrong to rely on the dictionary definitions of these words.[14] The plaintiff in that case alleged intentional discrimination and retaliation as a result of her complaints of racial discrimination. A handwritten note in the jury room revealed that the jury had improperly relied upon dictionary definitions, rather than legal definitions, of prejudice and discrimination.

The dictionary definition of prejudice used by the jury was "an opinion formed without taking time and care to judge fairly." The dictionary definition of discrimination was "to make or see a difference." Both of these definitions were improper because they focused upon a mental process rather than action. Further, the dictionary definition of "discriminate" was overly broad and did not accurately reflect the law because it focused upon difference in treatment rather than upon the *basis* of differential treatment. A claim of intentional employment discrimination under federal law requires that the plaintiff suffer from an adverse employment decision on the basis of a prohibited consideration.

---

[14]Mayhue v. St. Francis Hosp., Inc., 969 F.2d 919, 59 FEP Cases 405 (10th Cir. 1992).

The Supreme Court has explained that intent means doing something because of, not in spite of, a particular consequence. A state employer thus did not act illegally in granting a preference for veterans, even with knowledge that the effect of this preference was to advantage men applicants over women because more men are veterans.[15] If there is proof that the actions are motivated by prejudice, of course, then that conduct is intentionally discriminatory and is in violation of federal law if the prejudiced conduct bears some relation to employment opportunities. It is not sufficient to establish a violation of the Act, for example, for a supervisor to implicate minority employees in a criminal investigation unrelated to the workplace, even if the supervisor's suspicions are grounded in racial stereotyping. The Act relates only to opportunities for equal employment.

Violations of federal employment law require a connection between the adverse action and race, color, religion, sex, national origin, age 40 or over, or disability. Rejecting an applicant for being unclean, for example, is permissible as long as the employer's judgment is not clouded by stereotypes about certain groups. If the employer holds members of one race or gender to a higher standard of cleanliness, then there is a connection between adverse employment action and the protected categories. Otherwise, the law does not protect individuals who choose not to be clean.

A connection between the adverse employment action and the protected categories may be present even if it is not obvious. It is sufficient to show, for example, that the employer is motivated by racial considerations even if there is not literally racial animosity. Courts have found it unlawful for an employer to disadvantage an individual who has an interracial marriage, even if the employer is not prejudiced against either race but only against mixing races.

Similarly, favoritism on the basis of social relationships also may not be literally racial animosity, but can be connected with race sufficiently to violate federal employment law. In one case a supervisor promoted his "drinking buddy" whom he knew from social occasions.[16] The supervisor and his drinking buddy were both Caucasian; the plaintiff was an African-American who had not had the same

---

[15] Personnel Administrator v. Feeney, 442 U.S. 256, 19 FEP Cases 1377 (1979).
[16] Roberts v. Gadsden Mem. Hosp., 835 F.2d 793, 45 FEP Cases 1246 (11th Cir. 1988).

opportunities to participate in these social occasions. The plaintiff was more qualified for the promotion, but the supervisor "simply did not think of him" when making the decision. Although the promotion was literally based upon the social relationship rather than race, the promotion was "nothing more than a typical 'good ole boy' appointment" in violation of federal law.

Cases involving sexual favoritism present a similar issue because the employment disadvantage is based upon the sexual attractiveness of the other individual rather than gender itself. Sexual favoritism refers to a preference for an employee or applicant with whom the decision maker is romantically involved. In one such case the court found that the preference was sufficiently related to gender bias to be unlawful,[17] whereas another court found that the preference was based upon sexual attractiveness rather than gender discrimination.[18]

An employer's failure to follow federal requirements with respect to the posting of notices about federal employment discrimination law is not sufficient proof of "intentional discrimination" by itself. The purpose of these notices is to ensure that employees and applicants can know their rights. Failure to post such notices does not establish discrimination against a particular individual, although a willful failure to do so bears on the motive behind the discrimination against an individual.

Direct Evidence of Discriminatory Intent

Section 703(a) of Title VII makes it an unlawful employment practice for an employer covered by the Act to fail or refuse to hire or to discharge any individual on the basis of race, color, religion, sex, or national origin. The ADEA and the ADA have similar provisions for individuals who are at least 40 or who have disabilities. It is the plaintiff's responsibility to produce evidence to show a violation. One type of evidence is direct evidence, such as a statement of bigotry with reference to the plaintiff. For example, in a case challenging the denial of a promotion to a qualified candidate, the manager had said, "As long

---

[17]King v. Palmer, 778 F.2d 878, 39 FEP Cases 877 (D.C. Cir. 1985).
[18]De Cintio v. Westchester County Med. Ctr., 807 F.2d 304, 42 FEP Cases 921 (2d Cir. 1986).

as I'm the warehouse manager, no Jew will run the warehouse for me."[19] Such conduct is "direct evidence" of discrimination. Other types of evidence, examined later in this chapter, are "disparate treatment" and "disparate impact."

In one case the plaintiff alleged that the defendant college discriminated against her application as an administrator on the basis of gender.[20] The direct evidence included a conversation among college officials about the need to hire more minority and women administrators, but not for the higher positions. The plaintiff further alleged that her application for one of those higher administrative positions was rejected because the employer deliberately defined the job to require experience that women were unlikely to have. Specifically, the job description said that the position required a background of five years industrial experience. The plaintiff alleged that the decision maker for the position sought by plaintiff decided that the five years experience would have to be in "heavy industry" because few women would meet that narrowly defined qualification. The court held that such direct evidence would be sufficient to establish the plaintiff's case of intentional discrimination.

If the plaintiff establishes improper motivation with direct evidence, the defendant may present evidence that there were additional legitimate factors that affected the decision adverse to the plaintiff. If the defendant succeeds in proving that legitimate factors as well as illegal motivation affected the decision, the case becomes one of "mixed motive." By definition, a mixed motive case involves the simultaneous presence of legitimate and illegitimate factors motivating the decision process.

A case illustrating mixed motive is *Price Waterhouse v. Hopkins*.[21] In that case the plaintiff proved that the defendant had engaged in gender stereotyping when denying the plaintiff partnership status, but the employer proved that there were also legitimate reasons for the adverse decision. The plaintiff's proof of stereotyping included the advice she received that to improve her chances for partnership the next time she should "walk more femininely, talk more femininely, dress more

---

[19]Weiss v. Parker Hannifan Corp., 747 F. Supp. 1118, 57 FEP Cases 216 (D.N.J. 1990).

[20]Burns v. Gadsden State Community College, 908 F.2d 1512, 53 FEP Cases 1165 (11th Cir. 1990).

[21]490 U.S. 228, 49 FEP Cases 954 (1989).

femininely, wear make-up, have her hair styled, and wear jewelry." The employer's additional, legitimate reason was that the plaintiff had difficulty in relating to her co-workers.

Congress specifically addressed the issue of mixed motive cases in the Civil Rights Act of 1991. It amended Title VII to provide for the burdens of proof and the remedial consequences in a mixed motive case. Liability attaches when the plaintiff establishes that a decision was caused in part by illegal motives. Section 703(m) of the Act now provides that liability is established whenever "the complaining party demonstrates that race, color, religion, sex, or national origin was a motivating factor for any employment decision, even though other factors also motivated the practice."

Although the plaintiff can now prevail by showing partial illegal motivation in a mixed motive case, the remedies are limited. Congress further amended the Act in section 706(g) to preclude hiring or reinstatement orders when an employer can prove that it would have taken the same adverse decision even in the absence of the impermissible motivating factor. Although these remedies are limited, it is significant that plaintiffs in mixed motive cases can now recover attorney fees as prevailing plaintiffs. The practical effect is that plaintiffs with direct evidence of discrimination will more easily find attorneys to pursue their claims, because attorneys will be assured of recovering statutory fees from defendants once improper animus is established as a motivating factor. In choosing to take a case with direct evidence of discrimination, attorneys need not fear that the entire case will be lost if the employer can prove that there was also a legitimate reason for the action.

As with any discrimination claim, it is essential to the plaintiff's mixed motive claim that the direct evidence of discriminatory intent be connected to the adverse decision. It is not sufficient to demonstrate unrelated animus, such as a harassing environment, unless there is a connection between that unlawful animus and the employment decision. This principle applies even when the harassing environment itself may be actionable.

In one case, for example, a woman brought a claim of discriminatory discharge against her employer as well as a claim of hostile environment sexual harassment.[22] She had been the first woman

---

[22]Parton v. GTE North, Inc., 971 F.2d 150, 59 FEP Cases 707 (8th Cir. 1992).

assigned to the installation and repair department and the evidence revealed that the employer was responsible for a sexually harassing atmosphere in the warehouse out of which she worked. The evidence showed that sexually suggestive gestures and comments had been made and lewd cartoons were posted and distributed. Moreover, women in the warehouse were assigned to undesirable work when similarly situated men were not so assigned. The finding of a hostile work environment supported the award of nominal damages. The court did not sustain the plaintiff's claim of discriminatory discharge, however. The employer offered proof that she was discharged for poor performance, and the plaintiff did not show this reason to be pretextual. Her evidence of the hostile work environment was relevant to the claim, and separately actionable, but the court was not persuaded that the employer's reasons for her discharge were pretextual. She failed to establish a mixed motive claim because the court found the employer's motivation in her discharge to be only legitimate—not mixed.

Similarly, in another case the plaintiff failed to establish any causal connection between the alleged racial animus of his supervisor and his discharge by higher management after he broke a company rule.[23] In the absence of animus by the decision maker, miscellaneous proof of animus by even a supervisor is insufficient to establish a violation of federal law.

Disparate Treatment

Direct evidence of discriminatory animus is not always present in employment decisions challenged as intentionally discriminatory. **A plaintiff also may establish a case of intentional discrimination with circumstantial evidence**. The Supreme Court has held that a plaintiff in such a case has the burden of "showing actions taken by the employer from which one can infer, if such actions remain unexplained, that it is more likely than not that such actions were 'based on a discriminatory criterion illegal under the Act.'"[24]

The Supreme Court established in *McDonnell Douglas Corp. v. Green*[25] a three-part approach to cases with circumstantial evidence of

---

[23]Wilson v. Stroh Cos., 952 F.2d 942, 57 FEP Cases 1155 (6th Cir. 1991).
[24]Furnco Constr. Corp. v. Waters, 438 U.S. 567, 17 FEP Cases 1062 (1978).
[25]411 U.S. 792, 802, 5 FEP Cases 965 (1973).

discrimination. First, the plaintiff must establish differential treatment based on race, color, religion, sex, or national origin. If the plaintiff is successful, the defendant has the evidentiary burden of articulating a legitimate business purpose for the adverse decision. The defendant's articulation of a legitimate reason for the decision has the effect of dispelling the inference of improper motivation created by the plaintiff's proof. The third part of this approach permits the plaintiff to introduce evidence to show that the defendant's articulated reason is a pretext to hide the discriminatory animus.

The *McDonnell Douglas* case, in which the Court introduced this evidentiary scheme, was a hiring case. The Court detailed how the plaintiff can establish the first prong of the test for a claim of intentional exclusion in hiring in order to create the inference of improper motivation. To carry this initial burden of establishing a case of intentional discrimination, the plaintiff may show: "(i) that he belongs to a racial minority; (ii) that he applied and was qualified for a job for which the employer was seeking applicants; (iii) that, despite his qualifications, he was rejected; and (iv) that, after his rejection, the position remained open and the employer continued to seek applicants from persons of complainant's qualifications."

Courts have modified this original formulation to make it suitable for claims under Title VII other than race discrimination. Some courts have interpreted this requirement to mean simply that the plaintiff belongs to a minority group or protected class. Moreover, the Supreme Court held in *McDonald v. Santa Fe Trail Transportation Co.*[26] that federal employment law also protects majority group members, so that the first requirement of membership in a minority group cannot be taken literally.

When the plaintiff is a white male, some courts have modified the first prong of *McDonnell Douglas*. The rationale of the first prong has been said to reflect congressional efforts "to address this nation's history of discrimination against racial minorities, a legacy of racism so entrenched that we presume acts, otherwise unexplained, embody its effect."[27] In reverse discrimination cases, some courts have held that the plaintiff must make a special showing in order to enjoy the *McDonnell*

---

[26]427 U.S. 273, 12 FEP Cases 1577 (1976).
[27]Murray v. Thistledown Racing Club, Inc., 770 F.2d 63, 67, 38 FEP Cases 1065 (6th Cir. 1985).

Douglas presumption that discrimination is the most likely explanation for the adverse action unless the employer otherwise explains it. The Tenth Circuit Court of Appeals explained that a Title VII disparate treatment plaintiff who pursues a reverse discrimination claim under *McDonnell Douglas* "must, in lieu of showing that he belongs to a protected group, establish background circumstances that support an inference that the defendant is one of those unusual employers who discriminates against the majority."[28]

The requirement that the plaintiff "apply" for a position with the defendant is meaningful only in cases complaining of discrimination in initial hire or promotion. This requirement has been modified in the context of discharge.

The failure to make a formal application is not always fatal for a plaintiff, particularly in cases involving promotion or job assignment. The Supreme Court explained in *United States v. International Brotherhood of Teamsters*[29] that application for promotion to a racially exclusive division is not necessary when the plaintiff can demonstrate the futility of such application. An employer can create an atmosphere where it is understood that there is no prospect of some individuals holding certain jobs because of race, gender, national origin, religion, age 40 or older, or disability.

After the plaintiff creates the inference of discrimination from the four-part test, the burden then shifts to the employer to articulate some nondiscriminatory reason for the employee's rejection. In *McDonnell Douglas* the Court referred to this stage as the articulation of a "legitimate business purpose," but subsequent cases have made clear that the court should not be judging whether the reason is a rational business practice. Even irrational practices may be lawful. The sole reason for inquiring into the business purpose is to dispel the inference of intent. The onus on the employer is not great. Reasons sufficient to dispel the inference of discrimination include the greater communication skills of the individual selected and the probability that the selected individual would stay on the job longer.

---

[28]Notari v. Denver Water Dep't, 971 F.2d 585, 589, 59 FEP Cases 739, 742 (10th Cir. 1992). *See also* Livingston v. Roadway Express, Inc., 802 F.2d 1250, 41 FEP Cases 1713 (10th Cir. 1986).

[29]431 U.S. 324, 14 FEP Cases 1514 (1977).

The third prong of an individual case of disparate treatment arises after the employer has succeeded in dispelling the inference of discrimination. The plaintiff then has an opportunity to show that the employer's stated reason was pretextual. The Court in *McDonnell Douglas* noted that evidence relevant to a showing of pretext would include examples that similarly situated employees were treated differently. In the facts of that case, for example, the employer refused to rehire the black plaintiff after a layoff because during that time he had participated in an illegal demonstration against the employer. The Court said that this reason for refusing to hire an admittedly qualified worker was a nondiscriminatory one that rebuts the inference of intentional racial exclusion, but only if this criterion is applied alike to members of all races. For example, if other employees involved in acts against the employer of comparable seriousness to the plaintiff's act were nevertheless retained or rehired, then the employer's reason for refusing to rehire the plaintiff would be pretextual.

The Supreme Court noted in *McDonnell Douglas* that these four steps were not meant to be rigid and that lower courts should apply them flexibly. Since that time the courts have used this flexibility to adapt the steps to cases involving promotion, discharge, and constructive discharge. The ultimate question is whether the defendant intended to treat the plaintiff differently because of race, color, religion, sex, national origin, disability, or age. A race-blind rating system, for example, can defeat an inference that a plaintiff received disparate treatment on the basis of race, as long as the facts show that the raters were truly ignorant of racial information about the candidates.

DISCHARGE

A claim for discriminatory discharge proceeds in a manner generally like claims for discriminatory hiring or promotion. In a discharge case the plaintiff first must prove three basic elements: (1) membership in a class covered by the Act, (2) discharge despite qualification to perform the job, and (3) a person outside the class with equal or lesser qualifications was retained in, or hired for, the same or similar job.

Courts have differed in the application of these requirements. Some plaintiffs have had difficulty with the qualification requirement, for example, because some courts have required them to prove that they were performing at the level of the employer's legitimate expectations.

Other courts have applied a more lenient standard. Similarly, some courts have been flexible about the third requirement. Even when plaintiffs were not replaced by members outside their racial, ethnic, or gender group, some courts have said that other evidence of improper motivation will suffice.

Once the plaintiff establishes an initial case, the employer must articulate a legitimate nondiscriminatory reason for the discharge. The employer need not prove that the discharged employee's performance was inadequate; the employer need only dispel the inference of unlawful discrimination. The ultimate question is whether the employer was motivated to terminate the employee because of race, color, religion, sex, national origin, age, or disability.

It is the plaintiff's responsibility to convince the judge or jury that the employer was illegally motivated. Even if the employer's reason for the discharge is not a credible one, the plaintiff cannot win without establishing the illegality of the motive.

In a typical case the employee can establish the initial elements of the case and the employer rebuts with evidence of poor job performance. The plaintiff then must establish that the employer's reason is pretextual. Even direct evidence of animus or general evidence of disparate working conditions is not sufficient to establish that the termination itself was discriminatory.

In one case, for example, an Hispanic female plaintiff failed to prevail in her claim that the employer, the San Antonio Chamber of Commerce, discharged her in violation of Title VII.[30] She presented evidence that she was required to perform menial duties, such as preparing coffee, and that the president of the Chamber told her that she needed to work twice as hard as equivalent employees because she was young, Hispanic, and female. The district court judge believed that the employer discharged her because of her poor job performance, however, and not for discriminatory reasons.

Constructive Discharge

"Constructive discharge" refers to situations where an employer does not expressly fire an employee, but where the employer makes

---

[30]Valdez v. San Antonio Chamber of Commerce, 974 F.2d 592, 60 FEP Cases 93 (5th Cir. 1992).

conditions so difficult that the employee feels compelled to quit. Although the termination of employment appears voluntary, the employer's actions forcing the resignation make it a constructive discharge.

A constructive discharge occurs if working conditions are such that a reasonable person in the plaintiff's shoes would feel compelled to resign. As one court has explained, the employer has committed a constructive discharge "[w]hen an employee involuntarily resigns in order to escape intolerable and illegal employment requirements."[31] Constructive discharge claims often arise in the context of racial or sexual harassment.

The legal standards for a case of constructive discharge are like those of express discharge. The plaintiff must convince the judge or jury that the employer's motivation was illegal. Further, the employee's resignation must be caused by the employer's actions or inactions, rather than by personal reasons. The plaintiff need not prove that the employer intended to force the resignation, but the constructive discharge must be the reasonable and foreseeable result of the employer's conduct.

Retaliation for Opposing Discrimination

Section 704(a) of Title VII provides that it is an unlawful employment practice for an employer to discriminate against an individual "because he has opposed any practice made an unlawful employment practice by this title, or because he has made a charge, testified, assisted, or participated in any manner in an investigation, proceeding, or hearing under this title." This provision creates the cause of action for retaliation caused by opposition to discrimination or by participation in proceedings. "Opposition" refers to an individual's actions to protest an employer's unlawful employment practices, such as race discrimination. "Participation" refers to an individual's involvement in a proceeding concerning discrimination, such as filing a charge with the EEOC or testifying against the employer on behalf of another individual.

In a claim for retaliation the plaintiff must prove three elements: (1) that the plaintiff engaged in a protected activity, (2) that the plaintiff suffered an adverse employment decision, and (3) that the employer

---

[31]Henson v. Dundee, 682 F.2d 897, 29 FEP Cases 787 (11th Cir. 1982).

made the adverse decision because the plaintiff engaged in the protected activity.

This protection against retaliation applies even when the plaintiff is opposing discrimination directed against third parties. For example, an employer may not retaliate against a supervisor for hiring minority employees. Moreover, an employer may not retaliate against an employee or applicant because of the protected activities of a spouse, relative, or close friend.

When the plaintiff's claim for retaliation is based upon opposition to discrimination, the object of the protest need not be an actual violation of Title VII. In *Dimaranan v. Pomona Valley Hospital*,[32] for example, the plaintiff had refused to comply with the employer hospital's restriction on the speaking of Tagalog among its Filipino nurses. The court found that the "no Tagalog" rule itself did not have its genesis in discrimination, but that the plaintiff had been unlawfully retaliated against in her opposition to it.

Although the opposition to perceived discrimination need not in fact be a violation of the Act, there are further requirements for this legal action. The first is good faith; the plaintiff must have believed in good faith that discrimination had occurred. Second, the form of the opposition must be reasonable. A plaintiff's hostility alone does not destroy the reasonableness of conduct in opposition, but behavior that is deliberately disruptive of the work environment is not protected.

A retaliation claim based upon "participation" is different from one based upon "opposition" in one respect. In contrast to the requirements of good faith and reasonableness for an opposition claim, a claim based on retaliation for participation in proceedings may stand even if the plaintiff's conduct was malicious. This principle was established in *Pettway v. American Cast Iron Pipe Co.*,[33] where an employee knowingly made false statements in a request for reconsideration of his race discrimination case before the EEOC. The court chose the broad protective rule because a rule that protected only some statements would discourage employee speech. Therefore, the court held that even malicious materials contained in a complaint or communication with the EEOC entitled the employee to protection from retaliation. Title VII prohibits retaliatory discharge, demotion, or other adverse employment action.

---

[32]775 F. Supp. 338, 57 FEP Cases 315 (C.D. Cal. 1991).
[33]411 F.2d 998, 1 FEP Cases 752 (5th Cir. 1969).

Retaliation against federal employees is not expressly prohibited by the Act. The federal government is not a defined "employer" under section 704(a) and thus the provisions relating to retaliation do not directly apply. There are no parallel provisions under section 717(a), which prohibits discrimination by the federal government. Courts have implied such protection against retaliation, however.

The Act also does not literally prohibit retaliation against former employees with respect to employment records or references. The question is whether an employer violates Title VII by informing prospective employers of the fact that a former employee filed charges of discrimination or by giving an unjustifiedly negative reference in retaliation. Most courts have interpreted the Act to protect former employees from these types of retaliation as well, but not all courts have agreed.

RESTRICTIVE ADVERTISING AND CODING

Federal employment discrimination law protects from unlawful practices groups as well as individuals. Title VII prohibits employers from intentionally disadvantaging groups defined by race, color, religion, sex, or national origin. The Act made it unlawful, for example, to limit a job as a "man's job" or a "woman's job," or to post a Help Wanted sign in a store window with the specification that "No Irish need apply," such as was common in Boston at one time. Similarly, the ADEA prohibits employers from discriminating against workers age 40 or older by restricting jobs to "young" people.

Newspaper "Help Wanted" pages historically differentiated on the basis of gender and age. Virtually all newspapers had columns labeled "Help Wanted—Male" and "Help Wanted—Female," and it was routine to find advertisements requesting "young" applicants. Indeed, these advertising practices were so deeply ingrained in the culture that they persisted for many years after the federal guarantees of equal opportunity were enacted.

It is now well established that advertisements may not expressly describe desired applicants by gender or age. Nor may an advertisement use terms that suggest such preferences, such as "Gal Friday" or "recent graduate."

Because Title VII applies only to employers, labor organizations, and employment agencies, a newspaper is not liable simply for printing discriminatory advertisements for other employers. As an employer itself, of course, the newspaper cannot advertise discriminatorily for its own employees. For other employers, however, a newspaper does not become an "employment agency" subject to the Act by printing advertisements for other employers.

Efforts to restrict jobs with explicit but secretive preferences are as unlawful as the overt segregation in advertising. An interesting example of secretive job coding is alleged in *EEOC v. Recruit U.S.A.*[34] This case involved an appeal from an injunctive order requiring two employment agencies not to destroy records. The agencies operated referral agencies primarily for Japanese companies. The EEOC sought the preliminary injunction after receiving information from former employees that suggested invidious discrimination. The basis of the EEOC complaint was the alleged practice of these agencies to accommodate the racial, ethnic, gender, and age preferences of their clients. A former employee provided information that one agency had a secret coding system to keep track of the requests: "See Maria" meant that the client would prefer or accept Hispanics; "See Mary" meant Caucasians; "See Mariko" meant Japanese; "See Adam" restricted the job to males; "See Eve" restricted the job to females; "Suite 20-35" limited the job to ages 20-35; and "Floor 40" meant persons in their forties.

The prohibition against race coding should not be confused with the recordkeeping requirements of the EEOC's Uniform Guidelines. Employers, employment agencies, and labor organizations must make and keep records relevant to whether unlawful employment practices have been committed.

Lawful coding can be for the purpose of employment opportunity assessment or in preparation for litigation. The most common method of determining an individual's race, national origin, and gender is self-identification. Courts have sometimes accepted statistics based upon visual survey and name review even when self-identification records were available.

Because notations of race can be lawful in some circumstances but evidence of intentional discrimination in others, the purpose of the notations must be determined. In one case, for example, the trial judge found as a matter of fact that applications for certain positions were

---

[34]939 F.2d 746, 56 FEP Cases 721 (9th Cir. 1991).

racially coded by a circle in the lower lefthand corner of the first page.[35] A supervisor testified that the purpose of this coding was to keep records for purposes of assessing equal employment opportunity. The judge found this assertion discredited by the fact that when a black applicant filed a charge of discrimination against the company, someone in the company had whited out the racial coding on her application. If the notation had a lawful purpose, then it would be unnecessary to hide the notation in the face of litigation.

When employers surreptitiously make racial codes on applications, the secretive character can be evidence that the coding was invidious rather than lawful. An employer that relies heavily upon subjective evaluations of interviewers who make racial notations is especially vulnerable to a claim of intentional exclusion.

RACIAL SEGREGATION IN JOBS OR WORK CONDITIONS

Section 703(a)(2) of Title VII prohibits employers, labor organizations, and employment agencies covered by the Act "to limit, segregate, or classify" employees or applicants. Decisions since the Act's effective date in 1965 have identified many areas of such impermissible limitation, segregation, or classification.

Job segregation on the basis of race and gender was open and legal before 1965. It was generally understood by employers that Congress had targeted racial job segregation with the Civil Rights Act. The Act prohibits covert racial classifications as well as overt ones, but the plaintiff has problems of proof when such assignments are covert. The plaintiff class alleging disparate treatment in work conditions or assignments must show a deliberate pattern of racial disadvantage.

Statistics can help to establish such a pattern. In *International Brotherhood of Teamsters v. United States*[36] the Supreme Court considered the use of statistics to establish intentional exclusion. The employer had two truck driving classifications: city drivers and over-the-road drivers. The second category was considered more desirable and

---

[35]Calloway v. Westinghouse Elec. Corp., 642 F. Supp. 663, 41 FEP Cases 1715 (M.D. Ga. 1986).

[36]431 U.S. 324, 14 FEP Cases 1514 (1977).

the drivers were virtually all white. All the minority drivers were in the less desirable category. Impressed by the "inexorable zero" of minorities in the over-the-road job, the Court found that this fact, bolstered by anecdotal evidence, was sufficient to establish a pattern of intentional exclusion.

A manager's expression of stereotyped attitudes is also probative of intentional classification on the basis of race. In one case, a key manager responded to a question at trial concerning why blacks in the company were concentrated in the construction department: "I would presume that's the type of work that they like."[37] He discouraged inquiries from black workers about promotions and transfers, but facilitated the advancement of white workers about whom he did not have the same stereotyped attitude concerning their work preferences.

Conditions of employment other than job assignment can be impermissible classification. An employer cannot assign on the basis of race or national origin areas such as rest rooms or changing areas. The effect of such segregation is inherently demeaning and adversely affects the status of minority employees. The segregation of employees on the basis of gender for purposes of privacy in dressing and toilet, however, does not have the same demeaning effect.

It is important to distinguish between an invidious classification that is the employer's responsibility and self-imposed segregation of employees. An employer cannot condone employee segregation of work areas, such as firefighters who eat and sleep in groups defined by race. By contrast, an employer has no affirmative duty to eliminate self-segregation of employees at social events or eating places during nonworking hours.

The employer's lack of affirmative duty to monitor the self-imposed segregation of employees during nonwork hours is distinguishable from the employer's affirmative duty to control racially, ethnically, or sexually harassing behavior when the effect is to create a hostile working environment. Once on notice of such behavior on or off the worksite, the employer has a duty to take reasonable steps to stop co-worker harassment. Harassing behavior is conduct that goes beyond social segregation. An employer has an obligation to control conduct that affects the working environment sufficiently to make it a hostile

---

[37]Lams v. General Waterworks Corp., 766 F.2d 386, 38 FEP Cases 516 (8th Cir. 1985).

one. It does not matter if the conduct is occurring during nonworking hours if the effect is to create a hostile working environment.

The essence of the employer's obligation with respect to segregation of employees is to avoid conditions that adversely affect employment opportunities. Segregation for the purpose of disadvantaging or oppressing a group is unlawful. On the other hand, the *failure* to segregate on the basis of gender for toilet facilities or changing areas may have the effect of creating a harassing work environment. It is important for employers to focus on whether the segregation is demeaning or oppressive such that it adversely affects employment opportunities.

GENDER STEREOTYPING AND CLASSIFICATION

Employers may not operate on stereotyped assumptions in offering employment opportunities. As it is unlawful to make work assignments on the basis of racial stereotypes, an employer cannot assume that only one gender is capable of performing a job. An employer can limit jobs on the basis of gender only if gender is a "bona fide occupational qualification" (BFOQ). To establish this defense, which is explored later in this chapter, employers must demonstrate a factual foundation for the gender restriction; a stereotyped belief is not sufficient.

One early case that litigated gender stereotyping was *Diaz v. Pan American Airways, Inc.*[38] The defendant airline employed only women as flight attendants on the belief that men were not suited for the job. In an effort to establish stereotyped assumptions as a BFOQ, the airline introduced at trial expert testimony by a psychiatrist concerning the unique ability of women to calm passengers in the air. The expert explained that the cabin of a modern airplane is a "special and unique psychological environment"—a "sealed enclave"—in which women flight attendants are better able to calm passengers. The Court of Appeals for the Fifth Circuit rejected this basis for a BFOQ.

The Supreme Court addressed gender stereotyping in *City of Los Angeles Department of Water & Power v. Manhart*,[39] where the Court

---

[38]442 F.2d 385, 3 FEP Cases 337 (5th Cir)., *cert. denied*, 404 U.S. 950, 3 FEP Cases 1218 (1971).

[39]435 U.S. 702, 17 FEP Cases 395 (1978).

found unlawful the use of a gender-based rule for contributions to a pension plan. *Manhart* established that unsubstantiated beliefs cannot support employment decisions: "Myths and purely habitual assumptions about a woman's inability to perform certain kinds of work are no longer acceptable reasons for refusing to employ qualified individuals, or for paying them less." In this case the employment decision was based upon the "unquestionably true" fact that women as a group live longer than men as a group. In order to provide equal monthly pension benefits upon retirement, therefore, the employer withheld more from the paychecks of women than of men to fund these later benefits.

The Court said that the central issue is whether it is unlawfully discriminatory to operate on class characteristics rather than on individual characteristics. Even when the characteristics attributable to the class are true for the group as a whole, there are individual differences within the class. Although women as a group outlive men as a group, not every woman will outlive every man born at the same time. The Court found "unambiguous" the focus of the statute: "Even a true generalization about the class is an insufficient reason for disqualifying an individual to whom the generalization does not apply."

Other types of rules or practices that apply to only one gender are also unlawful. For example, a rule that prohibits the employment of women with preschool-age children is discriminatory when the rule does not apply equally to men. The Supreme Court held that such a rule violated Title VII in *Phillips v. Martin Marietta Corp.*[40] It did not matter that not all women have preschool-age children, nor did it matter that the rule did not have the effect of reducing employment opportunities for women in general because the job category in question was 70 to 75 percent women. Nonetheless, the rule affected employment opportunities for some individuals solely on the basis of gender without regard to the individual.

Rules that apply only to one gender are known as "sex-plus" rules. In *United Auto Workers v. Johnson Controls, Inc.*,[41] the Supreme Court found illegal a sex-plus rule that excluded women of childbearing capacity from jobs with potential exposure to lead. Similarly, an employer may not apply a no-marriage rule only to women and may not regulate the weight and appearance of only female employees.

---

[40]400 U.S. 542, 3 FEP Cases 40 (1971).
[41]499 U.S. 187, 55 FEP Cases 365 (1991).

It is important to note that in the sex-plus cases there is no violation of the Act unless there is a difference in treatment on the basis of gender. A rule applied equally to men and women, such as a rule against extramarital sexual relationships, is not a gender classification. The rule becomes unlawful when the employer applies it differentially, such as discharging females for transgressions while tolerating similar behavior from males. A rule also can violate the Act when there is greater chance that transgression of the rule will be observed for one group. For example, an employee's violation of a rule against unwed parenthood is more easily ascertained for women who conceive a child out of wedlock than for men who commit the same act.

Sex-plus rules are distinguishable from rules directed toward a category of workers who are all the same gender. It is not unlawful to apply rules to such workers unless the rules are directed at this job category precisely because of the gender of the workers. For example, a restriction on the weight of employees is permissible if applied in a similar fashion to men and women, even if gender-specific height and weight tables are used. It can be gender discrimination, however, to apply a stringent weight-maintenance requirement to a job category of all women solely because the employer values a svelte appearance more in women than in men.

Similarly, an employer violates Title VII by disadvantaging a single-sex category of workers because of their gender. The Supreme Court held in *County of Washington v. Gunther*[42] that an employer cannot pay less to female guards in county jails than the employer's own study indicated that they were worth, if the basis of that differential is gender based.

Pregnancy Discrimination

Another type of classification on the basis of gender is pregnancy discrimination. Congress amended Title VII with the Pregnancy Discrimination Act in 1978 to prohibit discrimination on the basis of pregnancy, childbirth, or related medical conditions. Section 701(k) of the Act provides that women affected by these conditions "shall be treated the same for all employment-related purposes" as other persons "not so affected but similar in their ability or inability to work."

---

[42]452 U.S. 161, 25 FEP Cases 1521 (1981).

Therefore, it is unlawful discrimination for an employer to require all pregnant women to quit or take leave at a certain point during pregnancy, unless such a rule is justified as a BFOQ.

The prohibition against pregnancy discrimination under section 701(k) also includes "receipt of benefits under fringe benefit programs." Employers need not provide such benefits at all, but any benefits provided cannot treat pregnancy, childbirth, and related conditions differently from other conditions.

The Pregnancy Discrimination Act further provides that employers are not required to pay for health insurance benefits for an abortion "except where the life of the mother would be endangered if the fetus were carried to term, or except where medical complications have arisen from an abortion." A proviso in the Act clarifies that although an employer need not provide abortion benefits, it is nonetheless permissible for an employer to provide such benefits. The EEOC interprets the Act to require an employer to grant sick leave for an abortion under the same terms that the employer grants sick leave for other medical conditions.[43] The EEOC interpretation of the Act also includes a prohibition on discharging an employee for having an abortion.

Prohibited gender classification of employees with respect to benefits is not limited to benefits for the employees themselves. The Supreme Court clarified this point in *Newport News Shipbuilding & Dry Dock Co. v. EEOC*,[44] which held that the Pregnancy Discrimination Act affects the ability of employers to fashion health benefits for dependents. The employer in that case provided for pregnancy benefits for employees but not for their spouses. The Court reasoned that this rule was discriminatory against men because only male employees could have spouses capable of becoming pregnant.

Bona Fide Occupational Qualification

The BFOQ defense under section 703(c) of Title VII and section 4(f)(1) of the ADEA allows for intentional classification of applicants or employees in the narrow circumstances where such classification is "reasonably necessary to the normal operation of that

---

[43]Questions & Answers on the Pregnancy Discrimination Act, 29 C.F.R. pt. 1604 (44 Fed. Reg. 23,804 (1979)).

[44]462 U.S. 669, 32 FEP Cases 1 (1983).

particular business or enterprise." **Title VII limits this defense to exclusion on the basis of gender, national origin, and religion; race is specifically excluded from this defense**.

The effect of the defense is that an employer can lawfully refuse to consider or hire certain individuals solely on the basis of their religion, gender, national origin, or age. The EEOC Guidelines interpret the defense narrowly, with a focus on its permissibility for authenticity. For example, a movie producer may restrict the screening for acting parts on the basis of gender; it is not necessary to consider actors for the role of a woman or actresses for the role of a man even if individual performers can credibly play opposite gender roles.

It is never permissible under the BFOQ defense to refuse to consider an individual on the basis of race. If a producer is casting a movie about historical characters, it is not permissible to refuse to consider individuals who are racially different than the historical people. Although it would be permissible to refuse to hire anyone whose appearance is too dissimilar to the historical figure, there can be no blanket refusal to consider all individuals on the basis of their racial identification. Thus, the producer of a movie about the life of Christopher Columbus cannot permissibly announce that the title role will be limited to individuals whose racial identification is Caucasian, although the producer can require that the person ultimately cast in the role bear a credible resemblance to the historical figure. The producer can refuse to consider any women for the title role, however, because of the BFOQ defense.

The Supreme Court has clarified the nature of this defense in three opinions. Two of these opinions concerned BFOQ for gender, and one involved the BFOQ defense under the ADEA. The Court has not indicated that the defense operates any differently under these two Acts.

In the most recent of these decisions, the Court held in *United Auto Workers v. Johnson Controls, Inc.*,[45] that the defense applies only to qualifications that affect an employee's ability to do the job. The employer in that case had adopted a gender-based fetal protection policy that excluded all fertile female employees from certain jobs because of a concern for the health of the fetus that a fertile woman might conceive. The employer manufactured batteries and workers were exposed to lead during the manufacturing process.

---

[45]499 U.S. 187, 55 FEP Cases 365 (1991).

The Court held that the total exclusion of all women of child-bearing capacity from jobs involving exposure to certain levels of lead violates the Act. The BFOQ defense did not apply because the rule did not relate to the ability of the employees to perform the job.

The Supreme Court had explained in an earlier case that the BFOQ defense is narrow. In *Dothard v. Rawlinson,*[46] the Court held that romantic paternalism is not sufficient to establish gender as a BFOQ for prison guards in a male penitentiary. Legitimate concerns for the safety of third parties is a legally sufficient basis for BFOQ, however. In the unique situation in that case, the male prisoners in the defendant-employer's penitentiary system were not segregated by type of offense. As a consequence, sex offenders were interspersed throughout the system and created a special threat to female guards. The Court said it was not permissible to deny women guard positions on the grounds that the employer was worried about their individual safety in any such possible attack, but it was permissible to deny such placement because of the threat such an attack would pose to third parties when the guard lost control.

In prison systems where the inmates are properly segregated on the basis of offense, the safety justification in *Dothard* does not apply to most of the guard positions. The question then becomes whether the employment of guards of the opposite gender threatens the privacy interest of the inmates. When it is possible to preserve privacy with simple measures, such as the availability of covering towels, gender is not a BFOQ in prisons.

As *Dothard* rejected romantic paternalism as a basis for its decision about women as prison guards, other cases have rejected the motivation to protect women from jobs that are dirty, dangerous, or strenuous.

Customer preference is not a sufficient reason for a BFOQ, except when privacy interests are involved. Even documented proof of customer preference, rather than mere assumptions, is not sufficient to create a BFOQ. In one early case, for example, an airline demonstrated through customer surveys that there was a preference for young female flight attendants among its passengers, who were primarily business-men. Such evidence was not sufficient for a BFOQ.[47]

---

[46]433 U.S. 321, 15 FEP Cases 10 (1977).

[47]Diaz v. Pan Am. World Airways, 442 F.2d 385, 3 FEP Cases 337 (5th Cir.), *cert. denied*, 404 U.S. 950, 3 FEP Cases 1218 (1971).

In another case, customer preference was insufficient for the defense, even though the strength of the preference threatened the ability of the employee to perform the job.[48] A woman was wrongfully denied a job as a sales representative who would need to conduct some overseas business out of her hotel room. The defendant argued that in Latin America she could not be effective as a sales representative because the cultural condition was such that men would be reluctant to do business with her. The court rejected the argument as a basis of a BFOQ. Similarly, an employer may not use a racial criterion when hiring a minority recruiter on the assumption that such an individual would be more credible with the target group. Such an assumption is a stereotype about the preferences of the target group. Similarly, an employer may not use racial or gender restrictions when hiring a social worker who would serve in part as a positive role model for young urban black males.

Other litigation on the BFOQ defense has concerned positions that require heavy lifting, arduous work, or providing physical security. In some cases, employers have argued that because men as a group are stronger, have more endurance, and are more physically threatening than women as a group, gender is a BFOQ for jobs requiring these traits. Under Title VII, however, even true stereotypes cannot be the basis of restricting employment opportunities.

The lower court cases that have considered the BFOQ defense in the context of physical stereotypes have generally rejected the defense because the individual who does not reflect the true stereotype is unfairly excluded. The employer cannot reject a woman applicant who is capable of performing the job requirements solely because many other members of her gender group cannot do so. One well-established legal test for a BFOQ is whether "all or substantially all" members of the excluded class would be unable to perform the essential job duties safely and efficiently. For example, if a job legitimately requires lifting heavy weights that most—but not "substantially all"—women cannot lift, the employer cannot limit the job to men; it is necessary to consider individual applications from women and to test their ability to perform the job.

The exception to the "all or substantially all" test for a BFOQ is when there is a risk to third parties and it is not practicable to test all

---

[48]Fernandez v. Wynn Oil Co., 653 F.2d 1273, 26 FEP Cases 815 (9th Cir. 1981).

individuals for this risk. The Supreme Court examined the safety principle in an age discrimination case concerning the BFOQ for airline personnel. In *Western Air Lines, Inc. v. Criswell*,[49] the Court provided a two-part approach. First, the employer must show that there are unacceptable risks to third parties if members of the protected class are employed. Second, the employer must show that it is impracticable to identify through individual evaluations those persons who cannot safely and efficiently perform those tasks. Although this case was brought under the ADEA, the principles are relevant to BFOQ litigation under Title VII.

The three Supreme Court cases concerning BFOQ make clear that the defense is most likely to be upheld when the issue is the safety of third parties for whom the employer has responsibility. In *Dothard*, the issue was the safety of those threatened by a prison riot. In *Criswell*, the safety of airline passengers was at issue. The employer in *Johnson Controls* presented the safety argument with respect to the potential health hazard to the potential fetuses that the women employees might carry. The safety argument in *Dothard* and *Criswell* related to the ability of the employees to do a job that has a safety component. In contrast, in *Johnson Controls*, the safety argument was unrelated to any direct aspect of the job. The Supreme Court thus made clear the essential focus of the defense; it applies only to qualifications that affect an employee's ability to do the job.

VOLUNTARY AFFIRMATIVE ACTION

Voluntary affirmative action refers to a choice by employers to take steps to ensure employment opportunities to groups historically excluded from various job categories. Such steps may include special efforts at recruiting, special training, and express consideration of race, national origin, and gender in decision making. These voluntary actions are distinguishable from court-ordered remedies against employers that have violated Title VII.

The Act makes no mention of preferential treatment except in two contexts. One is a provision in section 703(j) to clarify that the Act does not require preferential treatment even if the employer has a work force

---

[49]472 U.S. 400, 37 FEP Cases 1829 (1985).

that is not representative of the surrounding community. The other is a provision in section 703(i) that preferential treatment is permissible in the context of businesses near Indian reservations. Such businesses or enterprises may grant preferential treatment to any individual "because he is an Indian living on or near a reservation."

Federal contractors have affirmative action obligations under Executive Order 11246,[50] which is implemented by Department of Labor regulations. This Executive Order applies to all employers with construction contracts financed by the federal government and to employers with significant federal service or supply contracts. Their obligation is to remedy any underutilization of minorities and women, even though the individual employer may bear no responsibility for the relative underrepresentation of these groups in various job categories. The employer must adopt an affirmative action plan, which may include specific numerical goals and timetables.

The EEOC has promulgated guidelines with respect to the adoption of affirmative action plans for compliance with Executive Order 11246 or other purposes.[51] The guidelines permit plans if the employer's self-analysis indicates that one of the following three conditions exists: (1) the employer's practices have a potentially adverse effect on opportunities for women and minorities; (2) the effect of past discrimination has a continuing effect in the work force; or (3) the employer has a limited labor pool from which to select diverse candidates because of historical circumstances.

An employer that is not covered by Executive Order 11246 has no affirmative obligation to address any underutilization of groups in the work force except to the extent that the employer's own post-Act conduct is causing discriminatory exclusion. The Act specifically provides that employers are not under any affirmative obligation to achieve a work force representative of the population. Section 703(j) specifically provides that the Act does not require preferential treatment to any individual or to any group "on account of an imbalance which may exist with respect to the total number or percentage of persons . . . in comparison with the total number or percentages of persons of such race, color, religion, sex, or national origin . . . in the available work force in any community, State, section, or other area."

---

[50] 3 C.F.R. §1964 (1992).
[51] 29 C.F.R. §1608.1 (1992).

The Supreme Court considered the relationship of section 703(j) to the obligation of employers under Executive Order 11246 in *United Steelworkers of America v. Weber.*[52] This case concerned the legality of the admissions procedures for a special skills training program at a Kaiser aluminum plant. The plant was located in Gramercy, Louisiana, where the area population was approximately two-fifths black. The plant had a skills trade work force that was less than 2 percent black. As a federal contractor, Kaiser had affirmative action obligations that the Department of Labor enforced. Under federal pressure, the company and the Steelworkers Union agreed to a skills training program with a racial quota of equal numbers of black and white trainees. The plaintiff was a rejected white applicant who had qualifications equal to or greater than some of the accepted black trainees. He sued for reverse discrimination.

The Court in *Weber* first reconfirmed its prior holding that Title VII protects all groups from discrimination, not just the historically excluded groups that were the focus of the Act. The Court had held in *McDonald v. Santa Fe Trail Transportation Co.*[53] that an employer violated the Act by discharging white employees who had committed the same offense as a retained black employee. Unless the employer can explain the disparate treatment of the white employees with a nondiscriminatory reason, the employer's reverse discrimination was unlawful.

The *Weber* opinion explained that the *McDonald* principle did not compel a decision in favor of the plaintiff because the spirit of the Act is to provide opportunities for the historically excluded groups to advance in employment. The Act therefore permits voluntary efforts to remedy past patterns of exclusion. Although section 703(j) says that nothing in the Act "requires" affirmative action, the Court found that the section "permits" voluntary action. The plan in this case was voluntary despite the fact that the employer enacted it in response to the pressure of the Executive Order for federal contractors. The economic threat to the employer of losing federal contracts is not the kind of coercion that keeps the action from being "voluntary" under the Act.

The Supreme Court further explained the permissible reaches of voluntary affirmative action under Title VII in a subsequent opinion,

---

[52]443 U.S. 193, 20 FEP Cases 1 (1979).
[53]427 U.S. 273, 12 FEP Cases 1577 (1976).

Johnson v. Transportation Agency.[54] This case involved the use of an affirmative action plan to promote a woman named Diane Joyce to a position as a road dispatcher. No women had held this position in the defendant county previously. One of the components of the selection process was a highly subjective rating by a panel that interviewed the applicants. Joyce protested the objectivity of some of the members of her panel who had had poor interactions with her in the past. She complained that one panel member once had refused—until she filed a grievance—to issue her the same protective clothing that the men had, and that another had described her as a "rebel-rousing, skirt-wearing person." Her overall ratings from this panel were adequate for the promotion, but not as high as those of a man named Paul Johnson, who became the plaintiff in the suit. Rather than address the complaint by Joyce about the objectivity of her panel, the employer promoted Joyce instead of Johnson pursuant to its affirmative action plan.

The Supreme Court upheld the validity of this type of affirmative action. It was lawful for the employer to use gender as a factor in selection among qualified candidates. It was important in this case that the employer was acting under a valid affirmative action plan that met the criteria outlined in *Weber*.

Voluntary affirmative action is lawful under Title VII only if it is pursuant to a valid plan. In order for a plan to be valid it must remedy conspicuous racial imbalances in traditionally segregated job categories. It must not unduly trammel the rights of the majority. Moreover, it must be temporary; its purpose must be to eliminate a manifest racial imbalance rather than to maintain a racial balance. The fact that a plan does not have a stated termination date may be fatal to a plan that imposes quotas, as in *Weber*, but it is not fatal to a plan like the flexible one in *Johnson*. The *Johnson* plan did not set aside positions according to specific numbers, but simply took minority or gender status into account.

The cases in this area clarify the distinction between actionable reverse discrimination and lawful affirmative action. First, an employer cannot make an ad hoc decision preferring a member of an historically underrepresented group over another person similarly situated. A generalized desire to improve the opportunities for minorities or women is not sufficient. Next, even if there is an affirmative action plan in the

---

[54]480 U.S. 616, 43 FEP Cases 411 (1987).

company, its existence does not justify differential treatment on the basis of race. The fact that there is good cause to fire majority group employees, for example, does not justify preferential treatment to a minority group employee if the cause to discharge is equally strong.

The legality of affirmative action plans for public employers is less clear than for private employers. The *Johnson* case answered in part questions about the constitutionality of an affirmative action plan by a public employer because the defendant in that Title VII case was a public entity. *Johnson* made clear that a public employer can use gender as a factor in employment decisions, at least when qualification is rated subjectively. A plurality opinion by the Supreme Court in 1986 established that affirmative action plans by public employers are subject to exacting judicial scrutiny whenever racial or ethnic distinctions are involved. *Wygant v. Jackson Board of Education*[55] held unconstitutional a school board plan that required laying off white teachers who were more senior than minority teachers hired recently under this affirmative action plan. The divided Court found several infirmities. Several Justices noted problems with the plan, including: (1) its generalized desire to make the composition of the teachers represent the community rather than to redress underutilization of qualified teachers; (2) its permanent nature; and (3) its layoff policy that unduly trammeled the interests of the senior white teachers. The Constitution does not prohibit all affirmative action plans for public employers, but they are subject to "exacting judicial scrutiny" that can invalidate them.

INTENTIONAL EXCLUSION OF GROUPS

The plaintiff in a Title VII case alleging the intentional exclusion of a group protected by the Act must prove by a preponderance of the evidence that the employer has engaged in a regular pattern or practice of discrimination. A private plaintiff representing the group may bring the action if the court certifies the individual to be an appropriate representative of the class. Alternatively, the EEOC has authority to bring suit on behalf of a group.

There are two Supreme Court opinions involving pattern or practice cases, both decided in 1977. One is *International Brotherhood*

---

[55]476 U.S. 267, 40 FEP Cases 1321 (1986).

of *Teamsters v. United States*[56] and the other is *Hazelwood School District v. United States.*[57] Both were brought by the Department of Justice, which had the authority to bring pattern or practice suits before Congress transferred that authority to the EEOC.

Teamsters involved a challenge to the assignment of employees to truck driving categories because the line drivers were better paid than the city drivers. Nationwide the employer had 1,802 line drivers, all but 13 of whom were white. In the less desirable city driving jobs, there were 1,117 white employees and 167 minority employees. The government based its claim of intentional discrimination on these figures, plus anecdotal evidence of specific instances when black or Hispanic city drivers were discouraged from attempting to transfer to the better position.

Hazelwood involved a challenge to a school district's pattern of hires for school teaching. Less than 2 percent of the teachers in the entire school system were minority group members. The school district was in a suburb of St. Louis, whose school system employed many minority teachers. The Hazelwood School District had a practice of allowing the principals in the individual schools to hire the certified teachers of their choice. The plaintiff's claim was that the subjective hiring practices of the employer resulted in a virtually all white work force.

The Supreme Court explained the probative value of statistics in these cases. "Statistics showing the racial or ethnic imbalance are probative in a case such as this one," the Court noted, "only because such imbalance is often a telltale sign of purposeful discrimination." The purpose of statistical analysis is simply to probe such motivation and not to require employers to maintain a balanced work force.

The Court has refused to endorse any particular method of analyzing the effect of employer hiring practices. In *Watson v. Fort Worth Bank & Trust*,[58] the Court acknowledged the difficulty that its lack of specific guidance causes lower courts and litigators. There is no clear rule for when to use which method of analysis nor for when the extent of exclusion is legally significant. "At least at this stage of the law's development," the Court explained, "we believe that such a case-by-case approach properly reflects our recognition that statistics come in

---

[56]431 U.S. 324, 14 FEP Cases 1514 (1977).
[57]433 U.S. 299, 15 FEP Cases 1 (1977).
[58]487 U.S. 977, 47 FEP Cases 102 (1988).

infinite variety and . . . their usefulness depends on all of the surrounding facts and circumstances."

Population Comparisons

The Supreme Court provided the framework for population comparison analysis in *Teamsters* and *Hazelwood*. The premise of population comparison is that "absent explanation, it is ordinarily to be expected that nondiscriminatory hiring practices will in time result in a work force more or less representative of the racial and ethnic composition of the population in the community from which employees are hired." The Court further explained that evidence of "longlasting and gross disparity between the composition of a work force and that of the general population thus may be significant" to assess such intentional exclusion.

For this population comparison analysis the Court first distinguished between skilled and unskilled jobs. The facts of *Hazelwood* and *Teamsters* differ in that one case involved school teachers and the other concerned truck drivers. The Court observed that in *Teamsters* the comparison between the representation of minority group members among the over-the-road truck drivers and the percentage in the general population was "highly probative, because the job skill there involved—the ability to drive a truck—is one that many persons possess or can fairly readily acquire." By contrast, when jobs require special qualifications, "comparisons to the general population (rather than to the smaller group of individuals who possess the necessary qualifications) may have little probative value." In *Hazelwood*, the district court limited the comparison to the special skills group of school teachers.

In *Hazelwood*, the Supreme Court further clarified the population comparison approach and its relationship to applicant flow analysis. The defendant employer argued that applicant flow data would be better evidence of intentional exclusion than the comparative skilled population statistics, which have less probative value. Applicant flow statistics would show the actual percentage of white and minority applicants for teaching positions. The Court noted that there was no evidence of applicant flow statistics in the record, but agreed that such evidence "would, of course, be very relevant."

Statistical Disparities

The *Hazelwood* opinion further considered the degree of disparity between the population and the employer's work force necessary to show disproportionate exclusion. When the representation of the plaintiff class in the relevant population is a certain percentage, the employer's expected number of employees from the class is easily calculated. The issue then becomes how to assess the degree of the disparity between the expected and the actual number of employees from the class. The Court found it appropriate to calculate the "standard deviation" as a measure of predicted fluctuations from the expected value of a sample. The Court added that as a "general rule for such large samples, if the difference between the expected value and the observed number is greater than two or three standard deviations," then the hypothesis that employees are "hired without regard to race would be suspect."

The Court has since declined to provide further clarification. The plurality opinion in *Watson* noted that although the Court has "emphasized the useful role that statistical methods can have in Title VII cases," it has "not suggested that any particular number of 'standard deviations' can determine whether a plaintiff has made out a prima facie case in the complex area of employment discrimination."

An area of uncertainty in the litigation of group disparate treatment or pattern or practice claims is whether a claim can rest on statistics alone. In the usual case, plaintiffs present evidence of specific instances of discrimination because, as the Supreme Court explained in *Teamsters*, anecdotal evidence can bring "the cold numbers convincingly to life." Typically there are personal claims filed along with the group claim, and there are usually other witnesses testifying to incidents of discriminatory treatment. The uncertainty in the law is whether such evidence is necessary or whether specific incidents of discrimination simply bolster the statistics. Some cases have indicated that statistics alone can create a case of intentional group exclusion, but the issue remains an open one.

Group Claims of Disparate Impact

The disparate impact theory of discrimination is fundamentally different from the theory of intentional exclusion. **Motive is irrelevant in the disparate impact theory of discrimination.** This theory is premised upon unjustified exclusion caused by some hiring device that disproportionately disadvantages a group defined by race, color, religion, sex, national origin, age, or disability.

The Supreme Court first adopted the concept of disparate impact discrimination in its 1971 landmark decision in *Griggs v. Duke Power Co.*[59] The employer in that case required a high school diploma and a passing score on general aptitude tests for placement in any department except the lowest one. The unanimous opinion written by Chief Justice Burger said that Title VII proscribes conduct that is "fair in form but discriminatory in operation." When an employer uses procedures or testing mechanisms unrelated to measuring job capability, the absence of discriminatory intent does not redeem the conduct. The high school diploma requirement disproportionately excluded black applicants from the desirable jobs, and the aptitude tests were found also to impact applicants on the basis of race. **When such disparate impact occurs, it is incumbent upon the employer to demonstrate that such requirements are job related and governed by principles of business necessity**.

In 1977, the Court held in *Dothard v. Rawlinson*[60] that the disparate impact theory applies to gender discrimination. The plaintiff had been excluded from a position as a prison guard in Alabama penitentiaries because of a minimum height requirement for the job. The plaintiff's national statistics on the difference in height on the basis of gender were sufficient to shift the burden to the defendant to establish the business necessity of the requirement.

The Supreme Court held in *Watson v. Fort Worth Bank & Trust*[61] that the disparate impact theory can be applied to discretionary selection procedures like subjective evaluations and is not limited to objective standards like diploma requirements or height standards. The plaintiff was a black woman employee who had repeatedly failed in her quest for promotion. The employer defended each of the adverse decisions through subjective comparisons of the plaintiff to other candidates. The Court held that the plaintiff could establish a case if she could demonstrate that this subjective system had a disparate impact on black applicants. The burden would then shift to the defendant to justify the

---

[59]401 U.S. 424, 3 FEP Cases 175 (1971).
[60]433 U.S. 321, 15 FEP Cases 10 (1977).
[61]487 U.S. 977, 47 FEP Cases 102 (1988).

legitimacy of its subjective practices. Disparate impact discrimination is a separate theory of discrimination, distinct from disparate treatment discrimination. The confusing similarity in the names of these two theories of discrimination is unfortunate. The Supreme Court adopted these terms to make the distinction between *Griggs*-based impact claims and claims of intentional exclusion. The EEOC refers to "adverse impact" in the Uniform Guidelines, and *Griggs* itself referred to "disproportionate exclusion." These latter terms are thus used as synonymous with "disparate impact."

Plaintiffs can bring a theory of disparate impact under the modern federal employment discrimination statutes, but this theory is not sufficient to show a constitutional violation. The Supreme Court held in *Washington v. Davis*[62] that the disparate impact theory could not be used to challenge the Washington, D.C., police department's use of an aptitude test used to screen applicants for training. Although Title VII now covers governmental employees, at the time of this case the plaintiffs based their claim on the Constitution, and the Court held that there is no constitutional violation in the absence of motive. Similarly, the disparate impact theory cannot be used in a claim brought under section 1981 of the Reconstruction Era Civil Rights Acts.[63] The Supreme Court held in *General Building Contractors Association v. Pennsylvania*,[64] that discriminatory intent must be shown in such a claim.

Although it is not necessary to demonstrate the employer's motive in using any challenged selection device, the plaintiff's proof must be specific to establish the disproportionate impact of the device. It is not sufficient simply to assert that a selection criterion has an impact, nor is it sufficient to show that the employer's work force does not mirror the racial, ethnic, and gender composition of the surrounding population.

No "Bottom Line" Defense

It is not sufficient for an employer to defend a disparate impact case with evidence of a favorable "bottom line" of those hired, which

---

[62]426 U.S. 229, 12 FEP Cases 1415 (1976).
[63]42 U.S.C. §1981 (1993).
[64]458 U.S. 375, 29 FEP Cases 139 (1982).

matches the racial, gender, and ethnic characteristics of the applicants. In *Connecticut v. Teal*,[65] the Supreme Court held that an employer could not avoid the necessity of defending with business necessity the use of a test that has a disparate impact. The employer had a large pool of employees who were eligible for promotion to supervisor. The employees were given a test which disproportionately excluded black applicants. The employer then attempted to eliminate this effect by a second part of the selection process, which the Court characterized as an affirmative action program. The result was that the employer hired supervisors whose racial composition was very close to the composition of the applicants. The Court held that a favorable "bottom line" is not a defense when there is an identifiable selection device that disproportionately excludes on the basis of race. Unless the employer can demonstrate the business necessity of this device, individuals who would be otherwise qualified for the promotion are unfairly excluded. It is not sufficient that other members of the same racial group as the excluded individuals were advantaged by a subsequent selection device.

The Court thus held in *Teal* that if a test or other discrete pass/fail barrier has a disparate impact it must be individually validated even if there is no bottom line impact for the entire multicomponent selection process. The EEOC takes the opposite view in its Guidelines,[66] which the agency uses to guide its prosecutorial discretion. Although the EEOC takes a bottom line approach for its own purposes, the Guidelines are not binding on the courts and the Supreme Court refused to follow them in *Teal*.

Another technique that employers developed to eliminate the adverse effects of tests—and thus to avoid the necessity of demonstrating predictive validity—was to take the top scorers in each racial and gender group. Using this procedure, an employer would hire the top scoring man and top scoring woman, or the top scorers in groups defined by race or national origin, without regard to the possibly higher scores of other candidates in other groups. This practice, known as "race norming," is now prohibited by the Civil Rights Act of 1991. The Act amends section 703 of Title VII to provide that it is unlawful "to adjust the scores of, use different cutoff scores for, or otherwise alter the results of, employment related tests on the basis of race, color, religion, sex, or

---

[65]457 U.S. 440, 29 FEP Cases 1 (1982).
[66]29 C.F.R. §1607.4(C) (1992).

national origin." Employers thus may not impose an indirect quota system on test takers by taking the top scorers from each group without regard to the scores of other test takers.

Requirement Effect and Applicant Flow

One method by which the plaintiff may demonstrate the impact of a challenged selection device is to demonstrate the effect of the requirement on the relevant population. When a device has a demonstrable impact on the group from which the employer draws employees, the impact on that population establishes the plaintiff's case. Examples include state census figures for educational attainment by race to demonstrate the impact of a diploma requirement and statistics concerning the relative height of men and women to demonstrate the effect of a height requirement. The second method by which the plaintiff may demonstrate the disparate impact of a challenged selection device is applicant flow. This method is preferred by the EEOC in its Guidelines. Applicant flow analysis is the examination of the relative pass rates, or acceptance rates, of applicants on the basis of race, gender, and national origin. This method can be used to examine the effect of each separate requirement or to examine the effect of all the requirements taken together.

The Civil Rights Act of 1991 provides that the plaintiff must identify the particular practice that causes the impact, unless it is not possible to separate the employer's practices for individual analysis. Section 703(k)(1)(B)(i) of Title VII thus now provides that with respect to showing that particular requirements have a disparate impact, the plaintiff must demonstrate that each challenged practice causes a disparate impact, "except that if the complaining party can demonstrate to the court that the elements of a respondent's decisionmaking process are not capable of separation for analysis, the decision making process may be analyzed as one employment practice." If the plaintiff satisfies the court that the requirements are "not capable of separation," then presumably the plaintiff may demonstrate impact with the applicant flow throughout the entire process or perhaps by a general population comparison that would not otherwise be permitted.

One problem with applicant flow analysis is that potential applicants may be deterred from making a formal application because of the employer's reputation for discrimination or because the challenged requirement is known in advance such that potential applicants who do not satisfy the requirement do not pursue the position further. In *Dothard*, for example, the Supreme Court observed that plaintiffs need not always use comparative statistics concerning actual applicants. The Court reasoned that the application process might not reflect the actual potential applicant pool "since otherwise qualified people might be discouraged from applying because of a self-recognized inability to meet the very standards challenged as being discriminatory." A potential applicant would conclude that making an application would be futile if her height were below the announced standard.

Four-Fifths Guideline

The degree of disparity necessary to establish disparate impact is also unclear. When the Supreme Court cited the racial disparity in high school graduation rates in *Griggs* and the gender disparity in height in *Dothard*, it did not comment on the magnitude of disparity that was necessary to establish discrimination. The EEOC Guidelines have chosen a rule of thumb to assess the sufficiency of the disparity in the applicant flow data. The rule of thumb is called the "four-fifths rule" or "80 percent rule."

The "four-fifths rule" considers a selection device to have an adverse impact when it produces a pass rate for one group protected under the Act that is less than four-fifths, or 80 percent, of the pass rate of the group with the highest pass rate. For example, assume that there are 100 male applicants and 100 female applicants. The employer uses a timed test that requires applicants to sort cards alphabetically into bins. An applicant fails the test by taking longer than a proscribed cutoff time to sort the cards.

Assume first with this hypothetical employer that 60 of the 100 men pass the test and only 30 of the 100 women pass the test. The pass rate of the men is 60 percent and the rate for the women is 30 percent. The pass rate for the women is thus only half of the rate of the men. Under the "four-fifths rule" this difference is sufficient to show adverse impact because the comparative pass rate is only one-half and not at least four-fifths. If 50 of the women had passed, however, the female pass rate would have been 50 percent. To compare this pass rate with that of the men, divide the .50 rate by the .60 rate. The result is .83, which is greater than 80 percent (four-fifths).

To continue the example, assume now that the sorting test of this hypothetical employer results in 50 of the 100 women passing and fewer of the men passing. The pass rate for the women is one-half. Four-fifths of this rate is .40. Therefore, there will be adverse impact unless at least 40 of the men pass.

Some cases have followed the four-fifths rule of thumb to assess the sufficiency of the disparate impact, but others have not. In *Clady v. County of Los Angeles*,[67] for example, the court observed that the Uniform Guidelines are not binding and do not have the force of law. The four-fifths rule has been criticized by courts and commentators, the court noted, as an ill-conceived rule capable of producing anomalous results and trial courts need not adhere to it.

The Supreme Court subsequently confirmed that observation about the four-fifths rule and expressly refused to identify any single method by which the plaintiff's initial case for disparate impact can be established. In *Watson v. Fort Worth Bank & Trust*,[68] the Court refused to identify any single measure for assessing the sufficiency of the disparity in the success rate of the two groups being compared. The Court observed that although statistics can be very useful, it has never specified any guiding rule of thumb to determine whether a plaintiff has made out a statistical case of exclusion.

EMPLOYER'S BURDEN

Once a plaintiff class has established that a test has a disparate impact, the employer must then show that the exclusionary device is job related. The employer must demonstrate that any given requirement has a "manifest relationship" to the job.

Predictive Validity

Predictive validity is one important method by which an employer can establish that a test is job related and thus permissible to use under Title VII despite any unintended impact on the basis of race, gender,

---

[67]770 F.2d 1421, 38 FEP Cases 1575 (9th Cir. 1985), *cert. denied*, 475 U.S. 1109, 40 FEP Cases 792 (1986).

[68]487 U.S. 977, 47 FEP Cases 102 (1988).

national origin, religion, age, or disability. Predictive validity, also called criterion-related validity, means that a selection device is valid because empirical evidence establishes a close connection between the procedure and the job. Specifically, the evidence must show that there is a strong relationship between the results of the selection procedure and important elements of work behavior. In such a situation the selection device is predictive of performance because one's level of performance on the device predicts one's level of performance on the job.

The exact requirements for any method of validation are not fixed and inflexible. The key is whether the employer can establish a sufficiently strong relationship between the test and the job to show that the test predicts good job performance. The EEOC Guidelines provide the greatest source of guidance for assessing the sufficiency of a predictive validity study. These Guidelines require formal validation according to the standards of the American Psychological Association. In 1975, the Supreme Court held in *Albemarle Paper Co. v. Moody*,[69] that the Guidelines were entitled to great judicial deference on the subject of validation. The Guidelines have minimum technical standards with respect to:

- feasibility,
- analysis of the job,
- criterion measures,
- representativeness of the sample,
- statistical relationships,
- operational use of selection procedures,
- overstatement of validity findings, and
- fairness.

This last standard, "fairness," refers to a demonstration that a selection device is equally valid for minority group members as it is for majority group members. The cultural bias of a test, for example, could make it a valid predictor for one group but not for another. The original EEOC Guidelines required that employers study whether a test is

---

[69]422 U.S. 405, 10 FEP Cases 1181 (1975).

predictive for all groups, technically known as "differential validity." Subsequently, the Uniform Guidelines relaxed this requirement and urge examination of the fairness of the testing device to all groups.

Content Validity

Content validity is another form of test validation endorsed by the EEOC Guidelines. It refers to a demonstration that the test replicates the job, such as a typing test for a typist. The test must be representative of major portions of the job and the actual content of the job must require the tested abilities. Section 1607.14C(4) of the Guidelines requires for content validity that the employer, union, or labor organization "show that the behavior(s) demonstrated in the selection procedure are a representative sample of the behavior(s) of the job in question." The test need not measure all aspects of job performance in exact proportion to the job in order to be content valid, but the matters tested must be important aspects of the job. A firefighter exam, for example, may include the performance of specific tasks that a firefighter must undertake during the job itself: climbing ladders, removing ladders, carrying ladders, placing ladders, connecting and disconnecting hoses, turning on hydrants, dragging hoses, dragging and carrying tarpaulin. It does not matter that a firefighter does not perform these tasks constantly on the job; what is crucial is that they are essential tasks.

Determining what the exam measures is important to its content validity. A typing test for a typist may not measure speed, for example, if the job itself requires typing information on the lines of forms, such that accuracy rather than speed constitutes good job performance.

Because a firefighter's speed in performing physical tasks during a fire is crucial, an exam that measures abilities to perform essential tasks may measure the speed with which the tasks are successfully performed. The cutoff score must be logically and consistently applied, however. An employer cannot require a different minimum level of speed for the same job with each group of applicants.

A content valid test may be a paper and pencil test that asks questions about the tasks closely related to the job. In *Guardians Association v. Civil Service Commission,*[70] the employer used a written

---

[70]630 F.2d 79, 23 FEP Cases 909 (2d Cir. 1980), *cert. denied,* 452 U.S. 940, 25 FEP Cases 1683 (1981).

test for police officers. The test included an explanation of laws or circumstances under which arrests could be made. Then the test asked the applicant to apply the law to a certain fact situation. For example, it asked if a man making obscene gestures on the subway is committing (1) harassment, (2) jostling, (3) menacing, or (4) sexual misconduct. Because the ability to apply rules to factual situations was a skill that was a significant part of the job duties of a police officer, the test was content valid.

Construct Validity

A third type of validation is called construct validity, which refers to a showing that a test measures identifiable traits or characteristics important for successful job performance, such as leadership or aggressiveness. Such "constructs" may be measured by a testing device. Whereas content validity is appropriate for the measurement of a "skill" which comprises a significant portion of a job, construct validity is appropriate for the measurement of some personal trait or quality, called a "construct," desirable for the job.

Validation of a test that measures a construct requires proof that the construct itself is correlated statistically to the quality of job performance. In effect, employers need to validate such tests according to the standards demanded for criterion-related studies.

The greater difficulty in establishing construct validity compared with content validity makes the line between the two quite significant, but identification of the distinction can be difficult. "Intelligence" or "knowledge" are constructs because they are traits or characteristics, whereas the ability to read and effectively express oneself, and the knowledge of the subject matter that is the part of the job, could be considered a "skill" that is a part of the content of the job.

Business Necessity

Section 703(k)(1)(A) of Title VII provides that there is an unlawful employment practice based on disparate impact only if the plaintiff demonstrates that a person covered by the Act uses a particular employment practice that causes a disparate impact and the employer "fails to demonstrate that the challenged practice is job related for the position in question and consistent with business necessity."

When employers use criteria other than scored tests, the validation criteria do not easily apply. Common nontesting requirements include: education requirements, physical standards, criminal record inquiries, experience requirements, nepotism rules, and morality rules such as firing employees who conceive children out of wedlock. Although such requirements need not be strictly validated in order to be justified by business necessity, the employer must produce competent proof. A court will not assume, for example, the required relationship between a certain level of education and jobs that require general skills. Employers generally have not been successful in establishing the business necessity of an education requirement for semi-skilled jobs in production, transportation, maintenance, sales, and clerical positions. Courts have been more receptive to proof that education requirements are a business necessity for professional jobs.

There is general deference to public safety as an element of business necessity when the job clearly involves entrusting the public safety, such as airline pilots. In one case involving airline flight engineers, *Spurlock v. United Airlines,*[71] the court articulated a sliding scale, with a lesser showing of necessity required for jobs that require a high risk of harm to the public. Because piloting a commercial airliner clearly implicates public safety, the employer can require a college education, notwithstanding the absence of an empirical study correlating education and performance in the cockpit.

Physical requirements withstand scrutiny if they meet standards of content validity. For example, it is valid to require firefighter applicants to demonstrate an ability to do tasks specifically required for the job, such as carrying hoses. In contrast, courts will not assume that general physical requirements, such as height and weight requirements, are a business necessity without validation.

Employers must validate or defend with business necessity other kinds of nontesting requirements if they have a disparate impact. The disqualification of applicants with a criminal record, for example, may have a disparate impact. If the job does not specifically require trust and integrity more than most jobs, it is difficult for an employer to demonstrate the business necessity of such a requirement.

For some requirements of this type, courts have permitted employers to meet the requirement of "demonstrating" business necessity

---

[71]475 F.2d 216, 5 FEP Cases 17 (10th Cir. 1972).

without any effort to make an empirical demonstration. In *Chambers v. Omaha Girls Club, Inc.*,[72] for example, the employer operated a club for teenage girls in an inner city. The court found that the club's rule against single employees parenting children had a disparate impact on the basis of both race and gender, but that the employer successfully defended the rule with business necessity. The employer's evidence was not extensive; expert testimony confirmed the employer's assumption that an employee who had a child out of wedlock would defeat the employer's legitimate goal of providing positive role models.

Less Discriminatory Alternatives

Disparate impact cases have three phases. First, the plaintiff must establish that the employer uses a selection device that has a disparate impact on the basis of race, gender, national origin, religion, age, or disability. Next, the employer must demonstrate that the selection device is job related and consistent with business necessity. Finally, if the defendant succeeds with this defense, the plaintiff may demonstrate that the employer failed to use a different selection device that is equally effective but has a lesser disparate impact.

The Supreme Court introduced this third phase, proof of less discriminatory alternative, in its 1975 opinion in *Albemarle Paper Co. v. Moody*.[73] The Court explained that if an employer establishes the validity of a test, the plaintiff may show "that other tests or selection devices, without a similarly undesirable racial effect, would also serve the employer's legitimate interest in 'efficient and trustworthy workmanship.'" Such a showing, the Court explained further, would suggest "that the employer was using its tests merely as a 'pretext' for discrimination."

The Court further clarified this concept in *Watson v. Fort Worth Bank & Trust*.[74] On the subject of alternative selection devices with lesser disparate impact, the Court noted that relevant to the inquiry are factors such as the cost or other burdens of proposed alternative selection devices. The fundamental inquiry is determining whether they

---

[72]834 F.2d 697, 45 FEP Cases 698 (8th Cir. 1987).
[73]422 U.S. 405, 10 FEP Cases 1181 (1975).
[74]487 U.S. 977, 47 FEP Cases 102 (1988).

would be equally as effective as the challenged practice in serving the employer's legitimate business goals.

The Civil Rights Act of 1991 amended section 703 of Title VII to provide a statutory basis for the concept of less discriminatory alternatives. The Act now provides that a plaintiff can establish an unlawful employment practice by demonstrating the existence of such an alternative practice with a lesser disparate impact and the employer "refuses to adopt such alternative employment practice."

The exact meaning of this statutory requirement is unclear. The language "refuses to adopt" comes from a case[75] that Congress specifically rejected when it passed the Civil Rights Act of 1991, so the appearance of this language in this Act is confusing. Congress expressed an intent to affect this area of the law, but this amendment to Title VII fails to provide much guidance.

PROCEDURAL REQUIREMENTS

The procedural requirements under Title VII reflect the congressional goal that, if possible, parties should resolve employment discrimination disputes without trial. Plaintiffs must exhaust complicated state and federal administrative procedures before filing suit. During this time of administrative procedures, the state and federal agencies charged with investigating claims may attempt to conciliate or otherwise to resolve the dispute before litigation. If this process is not successful, the federal agency may sue in its own name or issue the complaining party a letter authorizing the party to sue on its own. Congress put these procedural impediments to litigation in Title VII in order to promote the conciliation of employment discrimination claims before litigation.

A second guiding principle in Title VII procedures is deference to state administrative agencies in states where there is a statutory scheme substantially similar to Title VII. Plaintiffs must first pursue their state administrative remedies and then pursue their federal administrative remedies. Under Title VII, a charge of discrimination against a nonfederal employer must be filed with the EEOC within a certain number of

---

[75]Wards Cove Packing Co. v. Antonio, 490 U.S. 642, 49 FEP Cases 1519 (1989).

days after the discriminatory act. Timely filing with the EEOC is a prerequisite to suit.

The complaining party has a limited number of days after the discriminatory act during which to file. The number of days is either 180 or 300, depending upon whether the complaining party lives in a state with a state agency charged with enforcing state law prohibiting race, gender, national origin, and religious discrimination.

Such state agencies, known as "deferral agencies" or "706 agencies," must have an opportunity to resolve employment discrimination claims before the federal agency. These agencies are designated at the discretion of the EEOC.[76]

Because of the policy of deference to an available state agency, the time limitation depends upon the presence of such an agency. A complaining party in a state without such an agency has 180 days in which to file with the EEOC, whereas a complaining party in a state with a deferral agency has 300 days.

The 300-day limitation is deceiving, however, in the sense that the complaining party must comply with the requirements of the state statute for filing the claim. Moreover, if the state agency terminates its jurisdiction, the complaining party must file the federal EEOC charge within 30 days. If the state agency has not terminated its jurisdiction, the complaining party may file with the EEOC within the 300-day period. The EEOC must grant exclusive jurisdiction to the state agency for 60 days. If the complaining party has not filed a complaint with the state agency, the EEOC will refer the complaint for the 60-day period and then reactivate the complaint for its own jurisdiction after that time. For purposes of counting the 300 days, however, the complaint is not "filed" with the EEOC until after the referral period. Therefore, as a practical matter, a complaining party filing with the EEOC needs to do so within 240 days of the discriminatory act.

---

[76]The following jurisdictions currently have one or more designated deferral agencies: Alaska, Arizona, California, Colorado, Connecticut, District of Columbia, Florida, Hawaii, Idaho, Illinois, Indiana, Iowa, Kansas, Kentucky, Maine, Maryland, Massachusetts, Michigan, Minnesota, Missouri, Montana, Nebraska, Nevada, New Hampshire, New Jersey, New Mexico, New York, North Carolina, Ohio, Oklahoma, Oregon, Pennsylvania, Puerto Rico, Rhode Island, South Carolina, South Dakota, Tennessee, Texas, Utah, Vermont, Virgin Islands, Virginia, Washington, West Virginia, Wisconsin, and Wyoming.

The state agency may waive its 60-day period if it has a "worksharing" agreement with the EEOC. A worksharing agreement is a contract between the federal and state agencies that establishes procedures for processing complaints. Part of that agreement may be a waiver of the 60-day period in some cases, such that the complaining party who files with the EEOC within the 300-day period but not with enough time for the 60-day deferral (i.e., after day 241) has still made a timely complaint.

The complaint (or charge) may be filed by the aggrieved individual or by someone acting on behalf of that person, such as a union or a civil rights organization. The EEOC also may file complaints. Upon receipt of the charge, the EEOC provides notice to the employer, union, or employment agency against whom the complaint is filed. The agency then has the power to investigate and determine if there is reasonable cause to believe that a violation of the Act has occurred. Upon such a filing, the Commission undertakes an investigation and makes an effort to conciliate. There is no time limit on this process, but after the statutory number of days have passed, the complaining party may demand a "right to sue" letter regardless of any agency action or inaction. After the EEOC issues a "right to sue" letter, a complaining party has 90 days in which to file a complaint in federal district court. The court is not bound by any findings made by the Commission.

The initial time for filing begins to run at the time of the discriminatory act. In hiring and promotion cases the discriminatory act is normally the date that the vacancy was filled on a discriminatory basis. It can be the date on which the employer made the decision adverse to the plaintiff if the facts give notice that the decision was discriminatory. In discharge cases the discriminatory act occurs on the day that notice is given.

The application of the time period to other kinds of continuing discrimination is more difficult. Discriminatory working conditions, such as assignment to a less desirable work facility, are clearly continuing violations until the practice changes. The creation of a hostile environment by racial or sexual harassment is a different kind of continuing working condition because the beginning and end of such working conditions are not as readily apparent. In sexual harassment cases alleging a hostile environment, for example, the time period runs from the last act that contributed to the claim. The continuing nature of the claim means that if a discrete act occurred within the time period for filing, the plaintiff can include earlier behavior as part of the proof of the harassing conditions. The fact that such earlier behavior falls outside the time period does not prevent its admissibility to show the pattern of behavior constituting the harassing environment.

Similarly, harassing behavior that occurred before the time period is admissible to probe the motivation behind a subsequent discharge. Such evidence can bear upon a dismissal that the complaining party challenges as discriminatory if the dismissal itself is within the statutory time limitation.

The time period for filing a complaint is not inflexibly fixed and a court may extend it in appropriate circumstances. Courts have extended the time period, for example, when the employer has misled the worker about the nature of its conduct. Such misconduct can occur when the employer presents a false reason for the discharge and thus prevents the complaining party from understanding the discriminatory nature of the conduct until further facts are discovered at a later time. In contrast, ignorance of the requirements of the law, or even bad advice from someone other than the employer, will not suffice to allow the complaining party a longer time period.

Both federal and state courts may hear Title VII claims. **Before the passage of the Civil Rights Act of 1991, Title VII cases were heard exclusively before a judge without a jury; the Act now authorizes jury trials for claims of intentional discrimination seeking compensatory and punitive damages**.

In general, the procedural philosophy of administrative agencies in the field of employment discrimination is to maximize chances for early resolution of the matter without diminishing the plaintiff's choices for state or federal trials. On the one hand, the statute requires the use of administrative procedures. On the other, the Supreme Court noted in *Alexander v. Gardner-Denver Co.*[77] that the legislative history of Title VII "manifests a congressional intent to allow an individual to pursue independently his rights under both Title VII and other applicable state and federal statutes." *Alexander* established the principle that an arbitration decision does not bind a court's subsequent consid-

---

[77]415 U.S. 36, 48, 7 FEP Cases 81 (1974).

eration of the same claim; the court hears the claim as if it had never been heard before.

The Court held further in *Gilmer v. Interstate/Johnson Lane Corp.*,[78] that an employee cannot avoid a contractual obligation to arbitrate simply by asserting that the dispute is a violation of federal discrimination law. Although there is a statutory scheme and administrative structure to process discrimination claims, the obligation to arbitrate remains. An arbitration obligation must be satisfied first and, if that process cannot resolve the dispute, then the regular procedures may be used.

REMEDIES FOR DISCRIMINATION

Judicial remedies for violations of Title VII can include any of the following:

- compensatory and punitive damages for intentional violations;

- reinstatement and back pay, seniority credit;

- affirmative action and other affirmative orders; and

- attorney fees and costs.

None of these remedies is awarded as a matter of right, although the Supreme Court has said that a court should ordinarily grant reinstatement to victims of discrimination, and that prevailing plaintiffs should ordinarily recover attorney fees.

As Congress originally enacted Title VII, the remedies provision was very limited. It did not provide for either compensatory or punitive damages, and limited the range of remedies. Moreover, Title VII actions were tried before a judge, without the right to a trial by jury.

Congress expanded the remedies available under Title VII in the Civil Rights Act of 1991. Part of that Act includes an amendment[79] providing for compensatory and punitive damages in a Title VII action "against a respondent who engaged in unlawful intentional discrimination (not an employment practice that is unlawful because of its

---

[78]500 U.S. 20, 55 FEP Cases 1116 (1991).
[79]42 U.S.C. §1981A (1993).

disparate impact). . . ." Recovery of punitive damages is allowed "if the complaining party demonstrates that the respondent engaged in a discriminatory practice or discriminatory practices with malice or with reckless indifference to the federally protected rights of an aggrieved individual." This provision is limited to respondents "other than a government, government agency or political subdivision." Plaintiffs never recover punitive damages as a matter of right; they are always discretionary with the judge or jury.

The 1991 Act provides for a right to trial by jury if the plaintiff seeks compensatory or punitive damages. When a plaintiff seeks both damages and affirmative relief from the judge, both the judge and jury can hear the case. Thus, for example, in a sexual harassment claim, the plaintiff may seek compensatory damages and reinstatement. The jury would hear the evidence, resolve any factual disputes, decide whether to award damages and, if so, determine the amount. The judge then may determine whether reinstatement is an appropriate remedy, but only in a manner consistent with the jury verdict.

Damages, Reinstatement, and Back Pay

"Compensatory damages" is a general term referring to monetary recovery for pecuniary and nonpecuniary losses. The 1991 Act enumerates types of compensatory damages that may be awarded. These are: future pecuniary losses (such as lost wages and out of pocket expenses), emotional pain, suffering, inconvenience, mental anguish, loss of enjoyment of life, and other nonpecuniary loss.

The 1991 Act places caps on the amount of compensatory and punitive damage recovery, depending on the size of the employer.

15-100 employees	up to $50,000
101-200 employees	up to $100,000
201-500 employees	up to $200,000
more than 500 employees	up to $300,000

Because of these caps, a prevailing Title VII plaintiff has less potential recovery than a prevailing plaintiff with a state tort claim arising from the same conduct or a prevailing plaintiff under section 1981 of the Reconstruction Era Civil Rights Act, where there are no caps.

Pecuniary losses in the form of back pay are not subject to the cap. The judge can award back pay representing compensation which the plaintiff would have received in the absence of unlawful discrimination. Such an award is determined by the judge rather than a jury.

"Front pay" is distinguishable from back pay. The term refers to monetary relief given in situations where a hiring or reinstatement order is not practical. Although affirmative orders to hire or reinstate employees are routinely granted upon a finding of liability under Title VII, in some cases such orders are impossible. Impossibility can occur if, for example, an order would require bumping innocent incumbent employees. For such situations, courts devised the award of "front pay" to compensate victims of discrimination with the pay that they would have received but for the discrimination. Front pay continues until the plaintiff receives the actual position, until the plaintiff receives substantially equivalent employment, or until the plaintiff fails to make diligent efforts to secure such employment. An area of uncertainty about damages under the 1991 Act is medical expenses. Victims of discrimination may have medical expenses and other out-of-pocket losses associated with the stress caused by the discrimination. Such losses were not compensable prior to the 1991 Act because medical expenses are considered compensatory damages. It remains unclear whether Congress intended to include medical expenses as compensable losses under the new Act and, if so, whether they are subject to the cap.

Retroactive seniority is another possible remedy for unlawful employment practices under Title VII. As with back pay, victims of discrimination ought ordinarily to receive retroactive seniority with a hiring or reinstatement order. The Supreme Court explained this principle in *Franks v. Bowman Transportation, Inc.*,[80] where the Justices noted that victims of discrimination should receive back pay and seniority relief unless there are reasons "which, if applied generally, would not frustrate the central statutory purposes of eradicating discrimination throughout the economy and making persons whole for injuries suffered through past discrimination."

Remedial seniority under *Franks* allows the victim of discrimination to receive seniority credit from the date of the discriminatory act. Although this approach affects the rights of innocent incumbent employees, the Court found more significant the interests of the victims of discrimination to receive complete relief.

---

[80]424 U.S. 747, 12 FEP Cases 549 (1976).

Attorney Fees

Federal employment discrimination law allows attorney fees for prevailing plaintiffs. The winner of a lawsuit in the United States ordinarily is not awarded attorney fees from the losing party, but Congress specifically provided an exception to this general rule. Title VII and other employment discrimination statutes provide for attorney fees to "prevailing parties." When it is the plaintiff who is the prevailing party, the award of fees is routinely granted. The theory is that the plaintiff is helping to eradicate discrimination in our society. When it is the defendant who is the prevailing party, the same rationale does not support the routine recovery of fees.

The Supreme Court in *Christiansburg Garment Co. v. EEOC*[81] considered how to interpret the statutory provision for fees to "prevailing parties" when the rationale for such recovery was much stronger for prevailing plaintiffs than for prevailing defendants. The Court rejected the defendant's argument that prevailing defendants should recover attorney fees on the same basis as prevailing plaintiffs. Nonetheless, the Court observed that "many defendants in Title VII claims are small- and moderate-size employers for whom the expense of defending even a frivolous claim may become a strong disincentive to the exercise of their legal rights." Therefore, the Court equally rejected the plaintiff's claim that defendants should recover attorney fees only when the plaintiff has litigated in bad faith. The Court therefore held that defendants can recover attorney fees in a Title VII case "upon a finding that the plaintiff's action was frivolous, unreasonable, or without foundation, even though not brought in subjective bad faith."

Christiansburg Garment also established the principle that attorney fees could be awarded to a prevailing defendant when the plaintiff is the government. The EEOC was the plaintiff in the case before the Court, and the agency argued that a higher standard should govern awards against a public entity. The Court disagreed; the standard for recovery of fees by prevailing defendants was already high enough to protect the public interest.

The ordinary procedure for the calculation of attorney fees is the calculation of the "lodestar." The lodestar is the amount representing the multiplication of the number of hours spent on the case times the

---

[81]434 U.S. 412, 16 FEP Cases 502 (1978).

attorney's hourly rate. In order to determine this amount, the trial court judge must first determine how many of the billable hours were reasonably spent on the portion or portions of the case on which the attorney prevailed. Next, the trial judge must determine a reasonable hourly rate for someone of the attorney's experience and the quality of the result in the case.

Enforcement of Consent Decrees

When the parties voluntarily settle a class-based employment discrimination claim, the settlement is reviewed and adopted by the trial court as a consent decree. Typically, the settlement includes an express statement that the defendant has not violated the law, but agrees voluntarily to take measures for the benefit of the class.

Problems have arisen when employees who are disadvantaged by a consent decree fail to protest in a timely manner. For example, when a consent decree provides for affirmative action in promotion on the basis of race or gender, there will be an adverse effect on some employees from the majority group. If the consent decree meets the relevant legal standards for an affirmative action plan, then this adverse effect is not legally significant. If the affirmative action plan is not properly constructed, however, the affected employees can intervene to protest. The question becomes whether they can protest the plan at any time.

Congress addressed this issue in the Civil Rights Act of 1991. The Act specifically precludes challenges to practices required by court orders or judgments entered in Title VII cases. Individuals cannot challenge decrees if they were fully apprised of their interest in the litigation and if they were given notice and an opportunity to intervene and participate at the time of such litigation, but chose not to do so.

A different kind of problem arises when the employer has engaged in separate agreements that conflict, as when a consent decree purports to override a prior collective bargaining agreement. The Supreme Court held in *W.R. Grace & Co. v. United Rubber Workers Local 759*[82] that if the union is not a party to the consent decree, it is not bound by it. An employee has an arbitrable grievance when the employer is ignoring the provisions of the collective bargaining agreement because of the

---

[82]461 U.S. 757, 31 FEP Cases 1409 (1983).

consent decree. The Court suggested, however, that the arbitrator is then free to decide in favor of either party, as long as the decision is based upon the agreement between the parties.

RELIGIOUS DISCRIMINATION

Discrimination for or against a person because of religion is a prohibited basis for providing employment opportunities. The plaintiff may establish a case of disparate treatment in the same manner as a case involving discrimination on the basis of race, gender, or national origin. Title VII also prohibits harassment on the basis of religion, with the same legal standards as for claims of sexual, racial, or national origin harassment.

The Act provides an exemption for religious institutions, but it is a narrow one. Section 702 provides that the Act does not apply to a "religious corporation" with respect to "employment of individuals of a particular religion to perform work connected with carrying on by such corporation of its activities." It is not a general exemption of religious corporations from the definition of "employers" covered by the Act. Rather, it is an exemption from the prohibition against religious discrimination by religious institutions. Thus, such employers may discriminate for or against individuals on the basis of religion, but they are still subject to the general proscriptions of the Act and may not discriminate on the basis of race, gender, or national origin.

The religious institution exemption applies to all employees in all the activities of the religious institution, not just in the religious ones. The original wording of section 702 qualified the exemption to "religious activities," but Congress removed this qualification in the 1972 amendments. Religious organizations now are free to discriminate on the basis of religion in all their activities, religious and secular.

The Supreme Court considered in part the constitutionality of section 702 in *Corporation of the Presiding Bishop of the Church of Jesus Christ of Latter-Day Saints v. Amos*.[83] The plaintiff in *Amos* was a former employee of a gymnasium run by the Latter-Day Saints Church, which is a religious institution under section 702. The employee lost his job because of his failure to remain a member in good standing in the church. The plaintiff argued that the exemption of a

---

[83]483 U.S. 327, 44 FEP Cases 20 (1987).

church's secular economic enterprises has the effect of "establishing" religion in violation of the First Amendment. The Supreme Court disagreed and upheld the constitutionality of section 702 as applied in this case. The Court explained that section 702 is a valid attempt by Congress to avoid the entanglement of courts in the fine distinction between religious and nonprofit secular activities. The Court left open the question of whether section 702 can constitutionally exempt profit-making secular enterprises.

Amos partially clarified the constitutionality of section 702, but other First Amendment issues surround the application of Title VII to religious institutions. The First Amendment protection of the free exercise of religion imposes constitutional limits on the literal application of Title VII to priests, ministers, and rabbis. Therefore, courts do not interfere with the ordination, pay, assignment, or removal of such core religious personnel. This constitutional constraint has presented courts with the necessity of distinguishing between religious personnel and personnel involved in secular activities. Religious personnel include not only priests, ministers, and rabbis, but also lay personnel who are directly involved in propagating religious doctrine. The question is whether the employment decision involves the religion's "spiritual function."

Courts have had difficulty distinguishing between religious personnel whose employment is protected by the First Amendment and individuals whose employment is covered by Title VII. One case found that a religious publishing house could not retaliate against a female editorial secretary who filed a complaint with the EEOC alleging gender discrimination in pay and job assignment.[84] The court found that Title VII applied to prohibit such retaliation even though the plaintiff broke a church rule when she filed secular charges against the church. The court did not find the intrusion into church doctrine under these circumstances to be sufficiently great to constitute a violation of the First Amendment.

In another case, Title VII applied to a claim of race discrimination in promotion at a liberal arts college.[85] A religious corporation financed

---

[84]EEOC v. Pacific Press Publishing Ass'n, 676 F.2d 1272, 28 FEP Cases 1596 (9th Cir. 1982).
[85]EEOC v. Mississippi College, 626 F.2d 477, 23 FEP Cases 1501 (5th Cir. 1980), *cert. denied*, 453 U.S. 912, 26 FEP Cases 64 (1981).

the college and appointed its managing board. The college emphasized Christianity in all courses, including secular ones, and imposed rules of conduct based upon Christian principles. The plaintiff taught one of those secular subjects. The court found that Title VII covered this teacher's employment because the faculty members who taught secular subjects were not "intermediaries between a church and its congregation." Further, they did not "attend to the religious needs of the faithful nor instruct students in the whole of religious doctrine."

Section 702 applies only to religious corporations, associations, educational institutions, and religious societies. It does not protect a secular employer who is religious. In *EEOC v. Townley Engineering & Manufacturing Co.*,[86] a manufacturer of mining equipment held mandatory devotional services for its employees. The company was a closely held corporation whose founders and principal owners made a covenant with God to operate the business as a Christian, faith-operated business. The court held that this secular employer could not discriminate on the basis of religion, which includes discrimination on the basis or absence of religion. The company could not inject religious practices into the workplace.

Religious Schools Exemption

Section 703(e)(2) of Title VII specifically exempts certain educational institutions from the prohibition on religious discrimination in hiring and employing individuals. The Act provides that it is not unlawful for a school, college, university, or other institution of learning to hire employees of a particular religion if such institution is "in whole or in part, owned, supported, controlled, or managed by a particular religious corporation, association, or society." This exemption further applies if "the curriculum of such school, college, university, or other educational institution or institution of learning is directed toward the propagation of a particular religion."

There is little case law on the meaning of this provision, probably because few religious schools are run by groups not already exempted as religions under section 702. One such case involved the Kamehameha

---

[86] 859 F.2d 610, 47 FEP Cases 1601 (9th Cir. 1988), *cert. denied*, 489 U.S. 1077, 49 FEP Cases 464 (1989).

School in Hawaii, founded by the estate of Bernice Pauahi Bishop.[87] Her will provided that teachers in the school "shall forever be persons of the Protestant religion." The plaintiff applied for a job and the school rejected her because she was not a Protestant. Among several grounds for decision, the district court held that the religious and moral curriculum of the school alone would be sufficient to exempt it under section 703(e)(2). The Ninth Circuit reversed and held that the school did not qualify for the religious exemption.

Religion as a Bona Fide Occupational Qualification

Section 703(e) of Title VII provides a BFOQ defense for religion as for gender and national origin. The provision allows the employment and classification of individuals on the basis of religion in "those certain instances" where religion is a "bona fide occupational qualification reasonably necessary to the normal operation of that particular business or enterprise."

There are only a few cases involving religion as a BFOQ, because it is a rare situation where an employer claiming a religion BFOQ would not already be a religious employer exempt under section 702 from the prohibition against religious discrimination. One case in which the BFOQ defense did appear was *Pime v. Loyola University of Chicago*.[88] In *Pime*, the defendant was a former Jesuit university seeking to maintain its religious identity even after it had evolved into a secular institution. At issue was the reservation of a certain number of positions for Jesuits in the philosophy department. The court found that "Jesuit presence" was important to the successful operation of the university. Although Jesuit training was not a superior qualification for any other reason, the court found that "having a Jesuit presence in the Philosophy faculty is 'reasonably necessary to the normal operation' of the enterprise, and that fixing the number at seven out of thirty-one is a reasonable determination."

The BFOQ for religion also applied to the job of transporting Moslem pilgrims into Mecca by helicopter. The employer limited the job to persons of that faith because only Moslems may enter the holy

[87]EEOC v. Kamehameha Schs., 990 F.2d 458, 61 FEP Cases 621 (9th Cir. 1993).
[88]803 F.2d 351, 42 FEP Cases 1 (7th Cir. 1986).

areas; others are subject to execution. The court upheld this religious BFOQ because of the threat of harm to third parties, not just to the non-Moslem pilot.[89]

Accommodating Religious Practices

Section 701(j) of Title VII defines the term "religion" as including "all aspects of religious observance and practice, as well as belief." This definition encompasses more than membership in traditional religious groups. The EEOC Guidelines on religious discrimination follow the Supreme Court's guidance under the First Amendment and define religious practices to include "moral or ethical beliefs as to what is right and wrong which are sincerely held with the strength of traditional religious views."[90] Under this interpretation, it is not necessary for a religious group to espouse the individual's beliefs, nor is it necessary for the religious group to which the individual professes to belong to accept all the particular beliefs held by the individual. A "religion" does not require a God or deity or even a written theology, but to be a "religion" the ideology must be more than a political, economic, or social philosophy.

The Act's further proscription on discrimination based on a religious "observance and practice" does not include definitions of these additional terms. Courts have tended to interpret this phrase broadly. Religious clothing or grooming standards required by a religion are protected practices. Moreover, an activity such as teaching a Bible class need not be required by the religion to qualify as a religious practice.

Although the Act covers church activities as "practices or observances," such activities must be religious. Purely secular activities, such as picnics or sporting events, are secular despite their church sponsorship and therefore they are not within the protection of the Act.

Congress clarified the employer's obligation in its 1972 amendments to Title VII. Section 701(j) now provides that the term religion includes all aspects of religious observance, practice, and belief "unless an employer demonstrates that he is unable to reasonably accommodate to an employee's or prospective employee's religious observance or

---

[89]Kerm v. Dynalectron Corp., 577 F. Supp. 1196, 33 FEP Cases 255 (N.D. Tex. 1983), *aff'd*, 746 F.2d 810, 36 FEP Cases 1716 (5th Cir. 1984).
[90]29 C.F.R. §1605.1 (1992).

practice without undue hardship on the conduct of the employer's business." The statute thus limits its protection of religious practices to those that can be reasonably accommodated.

The Supreme Court considered the relationship between "reasonable accommodation" and "undue hardship" in *Ansonia Board of Education v. Philbrook.*[91] The plaintiff was a high school teacher who converted to the Worldwide Church of God. The tenets of his new church required him to refrain from secular activities on numerous holy days. The union contract with the defendant school district provided teachers with three days off for religious purposes and other days off for personal convenience, not including religious observance. The plaintiff needed more than three days for holy days. The school board allowed him to take unauthorized days of leave without pay, but he was dissatisfied with this arrangement. He unsuccessfully sought permission either to use the personal convenience days for religious observance or to pay for the cost of the substitute (approximately $30 at the time) himself rather than lose the full amount of his own day's pay (approximately $130). After the rejection of these alternatives, he sued.

The Supreme Court held that it is not necessary for the employer to prove that each of the alternatives suggested by the employee would produce an undue hardship. It held that "an employer has met its obligation under §701(j) when it demonstrates that it has offered a reasonable accommodation to the employee."[92] Permitting an employee to take an unpaid leave for holy days beyond the number permitted in the collective bargaining agreement would be a reasonable accommodation. The Court explained that Congress was motivated by a desire to ensure individuals an opportunity to observe religious practices, "but it did not impose a duty on the employer to accommodate at all costs."[93]

The Court had earlier clarified the limited scope of the requirement of reasonableness in *Trans World Airlines, Inc. v. Hardison.*[94] This case involved a clerk in the supply department of the airline's 24-hour maintenance operation. The clerk gained sufficient seniority in one line of progression to be able to select shifts that avoided conflicts with religious observances. When the clerk successfully bid to change

---

[91]479 U.S. 60, 42 FEP Cases 359 (1986).
[92]479 U.S. at 69.
[93]*Id.* at 70.
[94]432 U.S. 63, 14 FEP Cases 1697 (1977).

building assignment in this operation, he fell to the bottom of the seniority list in accordance with the collective bargaining agreement. With less seniority, he lost the ability to avoid conflict with his Sabbath. The employee suggested several methods of accommodation that were rejected. Unlike the teacher in *Ansonia*, this employee was willing to take a cut in pay to have time off on the weekend for his religious observances, but the employer established that the work was essential on the weekend. To make this accommodation, the company would have to pay premium wages to someone not ordinarily assigned to that shift.

The Court found that the employer had taken reasonable steps by holding several meetings with the employee to attempt to find a solution to the problem. Further, the company allowed the plaintiff to observe special religious holidays and authorized the union steward to search for someone who would voluntarily swap shifts for regular Sabbath observances. The company also attempted to find the employee another position that did not pose the weekend conflict. These steps were sufficient. It was not necessary to pay premium wages to another employee to cover for the plaintiff, nor was it necessary to override the collective bargaining agreement and force an unwilling employee with no religious objection to work on the plaintiff's Sabbath.

RECONSTRUCTION ERA CIVIL RIGHTS ACTS

The purpose of the Reconstruction Era Civil Rights Acts was to grant civil rights to the newly freed slaves. One of these Acts of particular relevance to employment discrimination law is section 1981.[95] Congress originally passed this Act in 1866, following the abolition of involuntary servitude in the Thirteenth Amendment. This brief act provides to "all persons" the same right "to make and enforce contracts . . . as enjoyed by white citizens." Section 1981 was recodified in 1871, following the ratification of the Fourteenth Amendment, which provided citizenship for all persons born in the United States and prohibited states from making or enforcing any law that abridges privileges or immunities of citizens or denying them equal protection of the laws.[96]

---

[95] 42 U.S.C. § 1983 (1993).
[96] U.S. Const. Amend. XIV.

Section 1981 covers employment discrimination on the basis of race and ethnicity, but not religion or gender. The literal wording of the statute refers to the right of all persons to make contracts the same as "white citizens." The Supreme Court has interpreted this term to mean that the Act prohibits race discrimination as well as discrimination on the basis of ethnicity. Section 1981 reaches the relationship between an individual and an employer because it is a contractual one. In modern law it applies to both public and private employers and unions. Unlike Title VII, there is no statutory minimum number of employees for section 1981 coverage.

Because Title VII and section 1981 are separate and distinct, a plaintiff may take advantage of both avenues of redress if both apply. For claims of racial and ethnic discrimination, section 1981 provides plaintiffs procedural and remedial advantages compared with Title VII. First, the defendant employer need not have 15 employees. Section 1981 also differs from Title VII in that it does not specify a time limit for filing lawsuits. The court must apply the appropriate state time limit. This difference works to the advantage of a plaintiff who has a claim of discrimination on the basis of race or ethnicity and who has failed to make a timely complaint under Title VII. The absence of the Title VII requirements of using administrative procedures first also simplifies a claim under section 1981.

Another advantage of section 1981 is that plaintiffs may seek compensatory and punitive damages without statutory limitation. The Civil Rights Act of 1991 narrowed the difference between remedies for Title VII and for section 1981 by adding a new section, section 1981A, which provides for compensatory and punitive damages for intentional discrimination under Title VII. A difference remains, however, in that compensatory and punitive damages recoverable for Title VII violations are subject to caps that are determined by the defendant's number of employees, whereas these damages are recoverable under section 1981 without limitation. The practical effect is to permit greater recovery for claims of discrimination on the basis of race or national origin than for claims of gender or religious discrimination.

Unlike Title VII, a plaintiff bringing a claim under section 1981 must prove intentional discrimination. It is not sufficient to demonstrate discrimination on the basis of disparate impact; recovery under section 1981 requires proof of motivation.

Another Reconstruction Era Civil Rights Act is section 1983.[97] This Act prohibits any person acting under color of state law from depriving any person of life, liberty, or property, without due process of law; nor deny to "any person within its jurisdiction the equal protection of the laws." **Section 1983 does not govern private employers, only public ones.** Before Congress amended Title VII in 1972 to cover state and local governments, this section was the only statutory basis to challenge discrimination by such employers. Noteworthy employment discrimination cases brought under section 1983 have included claims against police departments, fire departments, and public schools.

Section 1983 remains useful for plaintiffs in employment cases against public employers for the recovery of damages without the statutory caps in the Civil Rights Act of 1991. There are also procedural advantages to section 1983 actions compared with Title VII. There is no time limit for filing claims contained in section 1983 and no requirement of using administrative procedures. The applicable time limit comes from the state, and the appropriate state statute is the one used for general personal injury cases. The federal courts as well as the state courts have jurisdiction over these claims.

A state is not a "person" subject to suit under section 1983 for the deprivation of a civil right under color of law. A plaintiff may sue a local government under section 1983 only for acts implementing an official policy, practice, or custom. Although the municipality may not be liable for the isolated acts of its employees, the policy or custom forming the basis of liability need not be an explicit rule or regulation. It is sufficient if there is an official action directed at the plaintiff, even if it is not part of a rule that is applicable to others.

AGE DISCRIMINATION IN EMPLOYMENT ACT

Congress enacted the Age Discrimination in Employment Act (ADEA)[98] in 1967 to prohibit discrimination against older workers. The basic substantive provisions of the Act are identical to Title VII, with the substitution of the word "age" as the prohibited basis

---

[97] 42 U.S.C. §1983 (1993).
[98] 29 U.S.C. §§621–34 (1993).

for discrimination in place of "race, color, religion, sex, or national origin."

The original impetus for the ADEA was a report from the Secretary of Labor which documented the problem of discrimination against older workers. Congress had directed the Secretary to prepare such a report when it decided not to include "age" as one of the prohibited bases of discrimination in the Civil Rights Act of 1964. When Congress enacted the ADEA in 1967, it was not acting to redress the omission of "age" in the 1964 Act. The ADEA is more narrow in its scope because the ADEA does not protect the young. Its protection extends only to individuals at least 40 years old.

Originally the Act prohibited discrimination against individuals between the ages of 40 and 65. Congress amended the Act in 1978 to extend the upper age limit to 70. Then, in 1986 Congress removed the upper cap altogether. In its current form, section 12(a) of the Act provides: "The prohibitions in this chapter shall be limited to individuals who are at least 40 years of age." Although some state statutes protect all adults from discrimination on the basis of age, the ADEA limits its protection to those at least 40 and does not recognize a cause of action for "reverse" age discrimination against the young.

The ADEA does not lend its protection to all individuals, even when they are at least 40. First, the ADEA does not apply to "bona fide executive or high policy-making positions" over the age of 65 if they have vested annual retirement benefits over $44,000. Next, individuals who are appointed by elected officials and who serve in a "policy making capacity" are not protected by the ADEA.

The coverage of the ADEA is similar to Title VII in that the ADEA regulates only the actions of "employers," "labor organizations," and "employment agencies." The definitions of these terms for ADEA coverage closely parallel those for Title VII. One difference is that the ADEA requires that the "person affecting commerce" have 20 or more employees rather than the requirement of 15 or more under Title VII.

The ADEA covers any labor organization if it maintains a hiring hall or has at least 25 members and is certified as a bargaining representative or seeks to be so recognized. Thus, a labor organization that does not otherwise meet the definition of employer because it hires only a few employees is nonetheless covered by the Act if it has the requisite number of members or is certified as a bargaining unit. The ADEA further governs the internal affairs of unions. Section 4(c)(1) of the ADEA makes it unlawful for a labor organization to "exclude or expel from its membership or otherwise discriminate against, any individual because of his age." That section further prohibits any classification or segregation that would tend to deprive employment opportunity on the basis of age. Finally, it prohibits a labor organization from causing or attempting to cause an employer from discriminating on the basis of age.

Some employers are exempt from the prohibitions of the ADEA regardless of their number of employees. Indian tribes are exempt employers, as they are under Title VII. The relationship of the military to its uniformed military personnel also is not covered by the ADEA.

Unlike Title VII, the ADEA does not exempt private clubs. A private membership club that qualifies for the Title VII exemption can discriminate on the basis of race, color, religion, sex, and national origin, but not age. Thus, a club could have enough employees to be an employer covered by the ADEA, but also be exempt from Title VII as a bona fide private membership club. The restriction of the ADEA on private membership clubs applies only to a club's employment practices and does not include its membership practices.

Public employers were not included in the ADEA as it was originally enacted, but the 1974 amendments expanded coverage to governmental employees. Congress approached this addition to the ADEA exactly as it had done for Title VII two years earlier. State and local governments, but not the federal government, were made subject to the ADEA by amending the definition of employer to include them.

Congress chose to treat the federal government differently, as it also had done under Title VII. Rather than include the federal government as an employer, Congress made separate provisions to protect federal employees from age discrimination. The ADEA provides that all personnel actions involving employees or applicants at least 40 years of age in executive agencies shall be made free from any discrimination based on age. Federal employees with an ADEA complaint are not burdened with the complicated requirements of using administrative agency procedures as they are under Title VII. The enforcement of their rights rests with the EEOC, but they have different waiting periods than other ADEA claimants.

Proving and Defending Age Discrimination

The substantive prohibition of section 4(a) of the ADEA is the same as section 703(a) of Title VII. It prohibits discrimination against an individual "because of such person's age." As previously noted, this protection extends only to individuals at least 40 years old. Because of the similar wording of these two provisions the substantive requirements for ADEA claims closely parallel those of Title VII. An individual may bring an individual claim of disparate treatment, or a plaintiff class can bring a claim of group disparate treatment or a claim of disparate impact.

For an individual claim of age discrimination, a plaintiff may introduce direct evidence of discrimination in the same manner as under Title VII. In one case, for example, the jury found that the employer violated the ADEA when it demoted an employee on the basis of age.[99] When the plaintiff complained about his small annual bonus after his division produced outstanding profits that year, he was told, "At your age, you shouldn't be rocking the boat." Shortly afterwards he was demoted. In another case, an employee in a cabaret survived summary judgment by alleging she was told that she could not be promoted from waitress to entertainer because she was "too old."[100]

The disparate treatment model of establishing discrimination under the ADEA parallels that of Title VII. The plaintiff can create an inference of unlawful disparate treatment in a hiring case by showing membership in the protected age category, qualification for a job, rejection despite that qualification, and that the job remained open or was filled by a younger person. In a discharge case the plaintiff must show membership in the protected category, satisfactory job performance, discharge, and replacement by a younger person. Some courts have defined the last requirement as "the employer did not treat age neutrally," or simply that "the employer sought a replacement."

Difficulty can arise in a discharge case with the requirement that the plaintiff demonstrate performance that meets the employer's reasonable expectation. Courts have phrased this requirement in various ways and applied it in a general way. If the plaintiff is challenging the

---

[99]Reyher v. Champion Int'l Corp., 975 F.2d 483, 61 FEP Cases 1675 (8th Cir. 1992).

[100]Lindsey v. Prive Corp., 987 F.2d 324, 61 FEP Cases 770 (5th Cir. 1993).

legitimacy of the expectation as a pretext for age discrimination, for example, the defendant cannot be insulated from liability by creating an unreasonable expectation. The plaintiff may attack the legitimacy of the expectation. The mere fact that the employer holds more experienced workers to a higher standard than less experienced workers, however, is not in itself age discrimination.

As with a Title VII disparate treatment claim, the defendant may dispel the inference of intentional discrimination by articulating a legitimate business reason for the adverse action. In a discharge case, the employer typically dispels the inference with evidence of the older employee's poor work performance. The burden then shifts back to the plaintiff to prove that the employer's proffered reason is pretextual.

When an employer articulates a "legitimate business purpose" to dispel the initial showing of a disparate treatment case, the purpose need not be "legitimate" in the sense of being a good business decision. As under Title VII, the purpose of this phase of the litigation is simply to dispel the inference of discrimination. Any nondiscriminatory reason for the adverse action suffices to meet this evidentiary burden. In *Lowe v. J.B. Hunt Transport*,[101] for example, a trucking company fired a 54-year-old manager for falsifying a petty cash report. The plaintiff could show that his job performance during his two years on the job was satisfactory, but the defendant could dispel the inference of intentional discrimination by articulating its specific, nondiscriminatory reason for the discharge. The court noted that his good job performance ratings were irrelevant when the reason for the discharge was not job performance.

A case of constructive discharge under the ADEA is governed by standards like those under Title VII. In *Wilson v. Monarch Paper Co.*,[102] for example, the employer reassigned a vice president with 30 years of experience to janitorial duties, sweeping the floors and cleaning up the employees' cafeteria. These demeaning conditions and additional age harassment caused the employee to suffer from a deep depression that eventually required hospitalization. The court held that the jury was justified in finding that the employer intentionally and systematically humiliated the plaintiff for the purpose of forcing his resignation.

---

[101]963 F.2d 173, 59 FEP Cases 74 (8th Cir. 1992).
[102]939 F.2d 1138, 56 FEP Cases 1005 (5th Cir. 1991).

Defenses to Intentional Age Discrimination

Employers may defend against a claim of intentional age discrimination not only by rebutting the plaintiff's evidence, but also by proving a specific defense. The ADEA provides for several defenses to intentional discrimination on the basis of age.

First, the ADEA protects actions that are based on the use of a bona fide seniority system. Although seniority is related to age in the sense that it is time-based, an employer nonetheless is permitted to observe the terms of a bona fide seniority system that is not intended to discriminate. This defense does not permit the involuntary retirement of workers because of age.

Voluntary early retirement incentive plans are permissible when they are consistent with the purposes of the statute, excepting two types of plans that are not subject to that standard: subsidized early retirement and Social Security "bridge" payments. Other plans must meet the standard of consistency with the purposes of the Act. It is not permissible, for example, to coerce employees to choose between early retirement with benefits and discharge without benefits. Another statutory defense under the ADEA is bona fide occupational qualification (BFOQ). Section 4(f)(1) provides that it is not unlawful to take any action otherwise prohibited under the Act "where age is a bona fide occupational qualification reasonably necessary to the normal operation of the particular business." Like this defense under Title VII, the defendant must prove a factual basis for the BFOQ and cannot rely upon stereotyped assumptions. Thus, it is not sufficient to say that a job is restricted to younger workers because it requires heavy work or long hours.

Although stereotyped assumptions are not sufficient for a BFOQ, the defense nonetheless does represent a congressional recognition that age may sometimes serve as a necessary basis for some employment decisions when it is not possible to use neutral qualifications instead. Like Title VII, the employer must show that all or substantially all individuals in the protected group would be unable to perform the job.

The Supreme Court considered the BFOQ defense under the ADEA in *Western Air Lines, Inc. v. Criswell*[103] and confirmed that the defense is governed by the same principles as Title VII. *Criswell* held

---

[103]472 U.S. 400, 37 FEP Cases 1829 (1985).

that an employer can establish age as a BFOQ by proving that some members of the age-defined group cannot perform the job safely and efficiently, and that they cannot be identified by means other than age. The case concerned a challenge to an airline's rule that flight engineers could not be over 60 because of the employer's concern for the safety of its passengers. The Court developed a two-part approach for cases involving safety as a BFOQ. First, the employer must establish that there is a potential for unacceptable risk to the employer or third parties that older employees are more likely to pose. Second, it is impractical to perform individual evaluations that could identify which of those older workers pose that risk. Rejecting the airline's argument that deference should be given to its rule, the Court held that mere convenience of the employer is not enough. There must be an objective justification.

Section 4(f)(1) also specifically provides that it is not an unlawful employment practice to take action "where the differentiation is based on reasonable factors other than age." Cost-cutting can be a legitimate, nondiscriminatory reason for discharging an older worker, but not if the employer's motivation is to replace the more highly paid older employee with a cheaper, younger person in the same position. The Seventh Circuit Court of Appeals held in *Metz v. Transit Mix, Inc.*,[104] that permitting such a defense to the ADEA would be to allow "industrial capital punishment" and to defeat the purpose of the Act.

The *Metz* type of cost-cutting is distinguishable from reductions that result from general company reorganization to trim the overall expense of the operation. When there is a general reduction in force, an individual plaintiff or class may claim intentional group discrimination on the basis of age if a disproportionate number of older employees is affected. As with other claims of group disparate treatment, statistics are relevant to probing the employer's motivation.

Disparate Impact Under the ADEA

Courts have generally held that disparate impact analysis is available for claims under the ADEA as it is under Title VII. In a disparate impact case it is not necessary to establish intentional conduct; liability

---

[104]828 F.2d 1202, 44 FEP Cases 1339 (7th Cir. 1987).

is premised upon the adverse effect of a particular employment practice that is not justified by business necessity.

One of the most noted circuit court cases permitting disparate impact analysis under the ADEA is *Geller v. Markham*.[105] In *Geller*, the defendant school board established a policy that in order to save money no newly hired teacher should have enough experience to be in the "sixth step" of the pay scale. The plaintiff was an experienced 55-year-old teacher who lost an employment opportunity to a less experienced 25 year old because of this policy. The Second Circuit Court of Appeals upheld the use of disparate impact analysis and permitted the plaintiff to establish an initial case with evidence that 92.6 percent of the teachers in the protected age group have enough experience to be in the sixth step. The school district attempted to show business necessity with its budgetary problems, but the court rejected this justification. The Supreme Court refused to review this case, over the objection of then-Justice Rehnquist (now Chief Justice). He dissented from denial of review because he questioned whether the disparate impact theory applies to age discrimination cases and also whether the cost-cutting defense should be allowed.

A separate but related issue is the effect of practices that have an impact on the basis of age only because the standards are necessarily correlated with age. The issue is whether such standards are permissible under the Act's exception in section 4(f)(1) for "reasonable factors other than age." For example, salary and age are positively correlated; it is generally true that older employees make a greater salary, although the correlation is not perfect because there are exceptions to the general trend. Nonetheless, discrimination on the basis of salary would have an impact on the basis of age for most employers. The EEOC has taken the position with respect to salary that differentiation based on the average cost of employing older workers is unlawful except for employee benefit plans qualifying for the statutory exception.[106]

This issue is unique to age discrimination and courts have not provided clear guidance. The Supreme Court's opinion in *Hazen Paper Co. v. Biggins*[107] had a fact situation that posed the issue with respect to

---

[105]635 F.2d 1027, 24 FEP Cases 920 (2d Cir. 1980), *cert. denied*, 451 U.S. 945, 25 FEP Cases 847 (1981).
[106]29 C.F.R. §1625.7(f) (1992).
[107]113 S. Ct. 1701, 61 FEP Cases 793 (1993).

a single employee, and thus the case was not brought as a disparate impact claim but as a disparate treatment claim. The employer fired the employee when he was within a few weeks of the vesting of his pension benefits upon 10 years of service. The Court observed that although years of service is correlated with age, it is an independent factor. Noting that a young employee may have worked for the same employer long enough for the pension to vest and that an older employee may be newly hired, the Court found age and years of service to be "analytically distinct." Therefore, it was incorrect to say that a decision based upon years of service is age-based and intentionally discriminatory under the disparate treatment theory.

An employer can defend a practice that causes an adverse impact on older workers by demonstrating its business necessity. Interpretation of the ADEA has followed Title VII in this regard, but an ambiguity exists after the Civil Rights Act of 1991 because the 1991 Act amends only Title VII in this regard, and does not address these issues under the ADEA.

Procedure and Remedies

Congress amended the ADEA in the Civil Rights Act of 1991 to provide for procedures like those under Title VII. A previously different scheme had caused unnecessary confusion.

Remedies under the ADEA include injunctions and damages. Injunctions may include reinstatement and other affirmative orders. Back pay and front pay may also be granted on the same principles as under Title VII. The ADEA does not permit damages for pain and suffering. Attorney fees are available as a remedy under the ADEA on the same basis that they are available under Title VII.

Unlike Title VII, the ADEA provides for double damages as "liquidated damages" in cases where the defendant commits a willful violation of the Act. In *Trans World Airlines v. Thurston*,[108] the Supreme Court defined willful conduct as occurring when the defendant "knew or showed reckless disregard" for whether the conduct was prohibited by the statute. This standard requires the plaintiff to prove more than simply that the defendant "should have known" that its conduct violated the Act or that the Act was "in the picture." Liquidated

---

[108]469 U.S. 111, 126, 36 FEP Cases 977 (1985).

damages are not permissible if the employer acted with an incorrect but good faith belief that the statute permitted the age-based distinction. Although the standard requires the plaintiff to make more than a showing that the employer was aware of the Act, it does not require the plaintiff to show that the employer's conduct was "outrageous."

DISABILITY DISCRIMINATION

In the past 20 years a variety of state and federal laws have been enacted to prohibit discrimination in employment on the basis of handicap and, more recently, disability. In 1973, Congress passed the Rehabilitation Act,[109] which prohibited discrimination on the basis of handicap but limited its coverage and remedies. During that decade most states enacted laws, or amended existing discrimination laws, to add disability to their list of protected categories. Then in 1990 Congress enacted the Americans with Disabilities Act (ADA),[110] which is the first comprehensive federal law to prohibit discrimination in employment on the basis of physical or mental disabilities.

Rehabilitation Act

The Rehabilitation Act was the groundbreaking legislation whose language was adopted in many state laws. It also served as the conceptual framework for the more comprehensive ADA.

Section 501, applicable to all federal departments, agencies, and other "executive instrumentalities," requires nondiscrimination, reasonable accommodation, and affirmative action for the "hiring, placement, and advancement" of individuals with disabilities. The term "individual with a disability" is defined as "any person who (A) has a physical or mental impairment which substantially limits one or more of such person's major life activities, (B) has a record of such an impairment, or (C) is regarded as having such an impairment." "Major life activities" means functions such as caring for oneself, performing manual tasks, walking, seeing, hearing, speaking, breathing, learning, and working.

---

[109]29 U.S.C. §§706, 791–94 (1993).
[110]42 U.S.C. §§12101–12213 (1992).

Section 503 provides that any contract in excess of $2,500 entered into with any federal department or agency shall contain a provision requiring that the contracting party take affirmative action to employ and promote qualified individuals with disabilities. Responsibility for enforcing section 503 is vested in the Office of Federal Contract Compliance Programs (OFCCP) in the Department of Labor. By regulation, the director of the OFCCP may seek to (1) withhold progress payments on the contract, (2) terminate the contract or, (3) bar the contractor from future contracts. The Labor Department also has awarded back pay to individuals who have been denied employment or advances in employment because of disability. Individuals who believe they have been discriminated against may only pursue their administrative remedies through the OFCCP; most courts have held that aggrieved individuals have no right to bring their own lawsuits in court.

Section 504 provides that no otherwise qualified individual with a disability shall, solely by reason of his or her disability, be (1) excluded from the participation in, (2) denied the benefits of, or (3) subjected to discrimination under, any program or activity receiving federal financial assistance. Unlike section 503, there is no monetary minimum amount of financial assistance required for coverage under section 504. By regulation, procedures for enforcement of section 504 by each federal agency must be the same as those used to implement Title VI of the Civil Rights Act of 1964, which prohibits racial discrimination in programs receiving federal financial assistance.[111] Also, unlike section 503, the courts have recognized that individuals may bring private lawsuits in court under section 504.

Americans with Disabilities Act

The ADA is a comprehensive federal law prohibiting discrimination on the basis of disability in employment, public services, public accommodations operated by private entities, and telecommunications. As of July 1994, Title I, dealing with employment discrimination, covers employers with 15 or more employees. From July 1992 to July 1994, the ADA only applied to employers with 25 or more employees. Besides most private sector employers, the ADA applies to state and

---

[111]45 C.F.R. §85.5 (1992).

local government employers and the United States Congress. Federal employees are not covered by the ADA, but they remain covered by comparable provisions of section 501 of the Rehabilitation Act.

As amended by the Civil Rights Act of 1991, remedies available under Title I of the ADA include reinstatement, back pay, compensatory damages, and punitive damages. Damages are only available for intentional violations and the total amount of damages available is limited by the size of the company with the same caps that apply under Title VII (see "Remedies for Discrimination," above). The responsibility for enforcement of Title I of the ADA rests with the EEOC.

Section 102(a) provides that entities covered by the ADA may not "discriminate against a qualified individual with a disability because of the disability of such individual in regard to job application procedures, the hiring, advancement, or discharge of employees, employee compensation, job training, and other terms, conditions, and privileges of employment." Congress intended this broad language to be consistent with section 504 of the Rehabilitation Act.

The definition of "disability" in section 3(2) of the ADA also is based on the Rehabilitation Act and its three-part definition of "disability" as a physical or mental impairment that substantially limits one or more of the major life activities of the individual, a record of such an impairment, or being regarded as having such an impairment. Section 101(8) of the ADA specifies that the term "'qualified individual with a disability' means an individual with a disability who, with or without reasonable accommodation, can perform the essential functions of the employment position that the individual holds or desires." The ADA expressly provides that homosexuality and bisexuality are not impairments and that various sexual and behavioral disorders are excluded from coverage under the Act.

The first prong of the three-prong definition of "disability" is a physical or mental impairment that substantially limits one or more of the major life activities of such individual. Although these terms are not further defined in the ADA, the legislative history clearly indicates that in adopting the same language as used in section 504 of the Rehabilitation Act, Congress intended that the regulations and case law under section 504 should be applied to the same terms when used in the ADA.[112]

---

[112]*See* 56 Fed. Reg. 35,726 app. at 35,746 (1991).

The EEOC used the section 504 regulations to define "physical or mental impairment" under the ADA. It includes any physiological disorder of various body systems, such as neurological, musculoskeletal, and sense organs, and therefore encompasses a wide range of medical conditions.[113] Only physical or mental impairments that *substantially* limit a major life activity are covered as disabilities under the ADA. The definition of impairment does not include physical characteristics such as eye color, hair color, handedness, or height, weight, or muscle tone that are within the "normal" range and are not the result of a physiological disorder. Personality traits and environmental, cultural, or economic factors also are not impairments.

To be a disability, the impairment must substantially limit a "major life activity," defined in the EEOC regulations as including, but not limited to, "caring for oneself, performing manual tasks, walking, seeing, hearing, speaking, breathing, learning, and working." These are "basic activities that the average person in the general population can perform with little or no difficulty."

According to the regulations, whether an individual is "substantially limited" depends on the nature and severity of the impairment, the duration or expected duration of the impairment, and the permanent or long-term impact of the impairment. Although determinations must be made on a case-by-case basis, it is clear that persons with minor, trivial impairments, such as a simple infected finger, are not impaired in a major life activity. Similarly, temporary impairments, such as "whiplash" or a broken leg, would not be considered substantially limiting. According to EEOC, broken limbs, sprained joints, concussions, appendicitis, influenza, and obesity are usually not disabilities. Federal and state cases decided before the ADA found a variety of minor "impairments" insufficiently severe to constitute disabilities or handicaps, including the following: acrophobia, chronic lateness, left handedness, mild to moderate varicose veins, minor osteoarthritis, muscular build, small stature, spider phobia, strabismus (cross-eye), and wearing eyeglasses.

The second prong of the definition of "disability" protects individuals with "a record of such impairment." Congress was aware that individuals with a history of cancer, heart disease, and other illnesses often face discrimination long after recovery from their illness.

---

[113]29 C.F.R. §1630.2(h) (1992).

According to EEOC's interpretive regulations, "[h]as a record of such impairment means has a history of, or has been misclassified as having, a mental or physical impairment that substantially limits one or more major life activities."[114]

The third prong of the definition of "disability," "being regarded as having such an impairment," is conceptually the most difficult. The EEOC has limited "being regarded as having a disability" to three situations: (1) individuals who have impairments that are not substantially limiting but are erroneously regarded as substantially limiting; (2) individuals who have impairments that are only substantially limiting because of the attitude of others; and (3) individuals who have no impairment at all but who are erroneously regarded as having a substantially limiting impairment.

The ADA has a special provision for infectious and communicable diseases. Pursuant to section 103(d), the Secretary of Health and Human Services was directed to publish a list of infectious and communicable diseases transmitted through handling food. An employer may refuse to assign an individual with one of the listed diseases to a job involving food handling. In 1991 the Public Health Service published a notice containing a list of six pathogens often transmitted by food contaminated by infected persons who handle food, such as hepatitis A.[115] HIV was not on the list.

The ADA also has special provisions for illegal drugs and alcohol. Section 104 excludes from the definition of "qualified individual with a disability," "any employee or applicant who is currently engaging in the illegal use of drugs, when the covered entity acts on the basis of such use." Individuals who are no longer using illegal drugs and who are in or who have completed a rehabilitation program and individuals who are erroneously regarded as engaging in illegal drug use are covered. It is not clear whether an individual who has a false positive drug test is covered under the ADA as someone erroneously regarded as engaging in illegal drug use. **The ADA gives employers wide discretion to combat the use of illegal drugs and alcohol in the workplace and neither requires nor prohibits drug testing**. Drug tests are expressly excluded from the definition of medical tests.

---

[114] 29 C.F.R. §1630.2(k) (1992).
[115] 56 Fed. Reg. 40,897 (1991).

An important issue regarding drug testing under the ADA concerns the timing of the tests. For employers subject to federal testing standards (as well as other employers using a good testing protocol), either before testing or after a positive test result, a medical review officer will interview the subject to inquire whether the individual is taking any medications that could have caused a false positive result. Under the ADA, however, it is illegal for an employer or any agent of the employer to inquire into the medications taken by an individual at the pre-employment stage. Therefore, good practice clearly suggests that any drug testing performed at the preassignment stage should be done at the preplacement stage—after a conditional offer of employment.

The ADA mandates major changes in the way some companies and physicians assess the health status of applicants and employees. Section 102(d)(2) prohibits preemployment medical examinations and questionnaires. An employer may not "conduct a medical examination or make inquiries of a job applicant as to whether such applicant is an individual with a disability or as to the nature or severity of such disability." The only permissible inquiries are about the ability of the applicant to perform job-related functions.

After a conditional offer of employment, an employer may require an "employment entrance examination" (preplacement examination) pursuant to section 102(d)(3). **To be lawful under the ADA all entering employees in the same job category must be subject to an examination, regardless of disability, and all medical information must be collected and maintained on separate forms and in separate medical files and treated as confidential**. The only exceptions to the confidentiality rules are that supervisors and managers may be informed about necessary work restrictions and accommodations, safety and first aid personnel may be informed if the disability might require emergency treatment, and government officials investigating compliance with the ADA may be provided with relevant information on request. Pursuant to section 102(d)(4), all medical examinations and inquiries of current employees must be "job-related and consistent with business necessity." Employers may offer medical examinations of a non-job-related nature, such as comprehensive medical examinations and wellness programs, but employee participation must be voluntary.

The ADA prohibits discrimination against a "*qualified* individual with a disability." Thus, it is essential to determine what it means to be "qualified." According to section 101(8), the term means "an individual with a disability who, with or without reasonable accommodation, can perform the essential functions of the employment position that such individual holds or desires."

In practice, determining whether an individual is medically qualified for a particular job is a two-step process. First, there must be an evaluation of the physical and mental demands of the job. Second, the applicant must undergo a job-related medical assessment. **Under the ADA, there must be an individualized determination of fitness**. In matching job demands with individual abilities, the individual need only be able to perform the "essential functions" of the job. Congress specifically intended that individuals with disabilities not be excluded because of their inability to perform functions that are "marginal" to the job. Whether a function is "essential" or "marginal" depends upon, among other things, the amount of time the employee spends on the activity and the effect on the business if the employee did not perform the function.

If an individual is unable to perform the essential functions of the job because of a disability, then the employer must determine whether reasonable accommodation would enable the individual to perform the essential functions. Under section 102(b)(5)(A), employers have a duty to make reasonable accommodations to the known physical or mental limitations of an otherwise qualified applicant or employee. Section 101(9) provides that reasonable accommodation may include the following:

- making facilities accessible;

- job restructuring, part-time or modified work schedules;

- reassignment to a vacant position;

- acquisition or modification of equipment or devices;

- appropriate adjustment or modification of examinations, training materials, or policies; and

- the provision of qualified readers or interpreters.

Reasonable accommodation is not required, however, if it results in "undue hardship" to the employer, defined in section 101(10) as "an action requiring significant difficulty or expense" in light of factors such as the nature and cost of the accommodation and the size and financial resources of the company.

One of the many reasons an individual with disabilities may be considered medically unqualified for a particular job is the employer's concern that the individual may pose a safety or health threat to the individual, co-workers, customers, or the public. Section 103(b) provides that "[t]he term 'qualification standards' may include a requirement that an individual shall not pose a direct threat to the health or safety of other individuals in the workplace." Although this language is narrow and does not include harm to the individual employee with a disability, the interpretive regulation of EEOC is broader. It defines "direct threat" to include the affected individual, requires these determinations to be made on the basis of reasonable medical judgment, and lists four factors to consider.[116] These factors are the duration of the risk, the nature and severity of the potential harm, the likelihood that the potential harm will occur, and the imminence of the potential harm. The legislative history and EEOC regulations make it clear that a "direct threat" claim of an employer is difficult to prove. Patronizing assumptions, generalized fears, and speculative or remote risks are insufficient.

Despite the congressional intent that the "direct threat" defense is to be construed narrowly, the courts in pre-ADA cases have given careful attention and some degree of deference to employer concerns about safety—especially public safety. Nevertheless, the safety defense must be substantiated by an individualized determination of fitness and objective, reliable evidence about the nature of the risk.

State Disabilities Laws

Nearly every state has its own civil rights law prohibiting discrimination in employment on the basis of disability or handicap. Section 501(b) of the ADA provides that the ADA does not preempt any state or local law "that provides greater or equal protection for the rights of individuals with disabilities than are afforded by this Act."

---

[116]29 C.F.R. §1630.2(r) (1992). *See* School Bd. of Nassau County v. Arline, 480 U.S. 273, 43 FEP Cases 81 (1987).

There are three main ways in which state laws are important to complement the protections of the ADA. First, the state law may apply to a wider class of employers.[117]

Second, the state law may apply to a wider range of impairments than the ADA, such as individuals who are obese or who have substance abuse problems.[118] Third, the state law may more closely regulate certain medical or hiring procedures in employment. For example, in 11 states (Alaska, California, Colorado, Kansas, Michigan, Minnesota, Missouri, Ohio, Pennsylvania, Rhode Island, and Utah) preplacement medical examinations must be limited to assessing job-related health conditions.

STATE FAIR EMPLOYMENT PRACTICE STATUTES

Most states, and many municipalities, have laws to promote fair employment, often as part of more comprehensive human rights legislation. State agencies to enforce these laws are present in most states as well. When these agencies qualify as deferral agencies for the federal EEOC, all complaints from those jurisdictions are deferred first to the state agency for resolution before there is any federal involvement. Complaints also may be filed directly with a state or municipal agency. These agencies are known variously as equal opportunity agencies, civil rights commissions, or human rights bureaus.

Unlike the federal law, state and local laws that prohibit employment discrimination are not restricted in their coverage to those persons who affect interstate commerce. Typically, state laws follow the federal law in their coverage of employers, labor organizations, and

---

[117]Twenty-five states and the District of Columbia have laws that apply to employers with fewer than 15 employees. They are: Alaska (1 or more), New Mexico (4 or more), California (5 or more), New York (4 or more), Connecticut (3 or more), North Dakota (1 or more), District of Columbia (1 or more), Ohio (4 or more), Hawaii (1 or more), Oregon (1 or more), Kansas (4 or more), Pennsylvania (4 or more), Kentucky (8 or more), Rhode Island (4 or more), Maine (1 or more), Tennessee (8 or more), Massachusetts (6 or more), Vermont (1 or more), Michigan (1 or more), Washington (8 or more), Missouri (6 or more), West Virginia (12 or more), Montana (1 or more), Wisconsin (1 or more), New Hampshire (1 or more), and Wyoming (2 or more).

[118]For a table listing the coverage of each state law, see Mark A. Rothstein, "Drug Testing in the Workplace: The Challenge to Employment Relations and Employment Law," 63 *Chi.-Kent L. Rev.* 683, 719–20 (1987).

employment agencies, but there are many differences between state and federal coverage and among the various states.

First, there are major differences among the statutes in the grounds on which employment discrimination is prohibited. The federal proscriptions include race, color, religion, sex, and national origin, as well as age and disability. Some states have fewer proscriptions and many have more. For example, several states do not prohibit discrimination on the basis of age, or limit that protection to public employees. In contrast, some of the states that prohibit age discrimination extend the prohibition against age discrimination to protect anyone over 18, rather than the federal approach of protecting only individuals at least 40. Many states also provide for an upper age limit, typically 70. The federal ADEA previously had this limitation, and the state statutes were generally modeled after the earlier version of the federal act. Some states subsequently amended their statutes to remove the upper age limit after the federal amendment, but others did not.

Many state statutes provide coverage that is virtually identical to the federal coverage. The significance of the overlap is that the state statute provides a state forum. Typically, there is an enforcing agency and state remedies that supplement the federal scheme. Two states have no comprehensive fair employment practice statute for private employers and no fair employment practice agencies. These are Alabama and Mississippi.

Beyond the identity of coverage between the federal law and most states, many of the state statutes are more expansive in their coverage than the federal law. These states thus permit a ground of complaint not otherwise covered by federal law, such as sexual orientation. Notably, the federal law does not include sexual orientation as a basis of proscribed employment discrimination, but several states have included this basis: California, Connecticut, Hawaii, Massachusetts, New Jersey, Vermont, Wisconsin, and the District of Columbia. The Massachusetts statute specifically excepts pedophilia from this category.

Discrimination on the basis of marital status, which is not prohibited by federal law, is covered by many states.[119] Alaska adds

---

[119]These jurisdictions include: Alaska, California, Connecticut, Delaware, Florida, Hawaii, Illinois, Maryland, Michigan, Minnesota, Montana, Nebraska, New Hampshire, New Jersey, New York, North Dakota, Oregon, Virginia, Washington, Wisconsin, the District of Columbia, and Puerto Rico.

"parenthood" with the proscription of discrimination on the basis of marital status. Pennsylvania broadly prohibits discrimination on the basis of "familial status."

Many states add "ancestry" in addition to "national origin" to the list of prohibited bases of employment discrimination.[120] Illinois adds "citizenship" to its list of proscribed dimensions of employment discrimination. The Vermont statute lists "place of birth." Puerto Rico includes "social position" as a prohibited basis of employment discrimination.

Some states make reference to military service in the list of protected individuals. Illinois prohibits discrimination on the basis of unfavorable discharge from the military. Georgia protects "wives whose husbands are on active duty in the Armed Forces." Wisconsin and New Jersey prohibit discrimination in general for "service in the armed forces."

Discrimination on the basis of arrest records is proscribed in Hawaii, Illinois, and Wisconsin. The Wisconsin act adds "conviction records" and the Hawaiian one refers generally to "court records." Oregon does not mention arrest or conviction records, but prohibits discrimination on the basis of a juvenile record that has been expunged.

Other proscriptions appear in various states. Michigan prohibits employment discrimination on the basis of "height and weight." The District of Columbia act covers more generally "personal appearance." Puerto Rico protects individuals from discrimination on the basis of "political beliefs." Oregon prohibits "bias because of legislative testimony" as well as "employment of another family member." Minnesota and North Dakota prohibit discrimination on the basis of acceptance of public assistance.

In addition to differences in the substantive coverage of the state statutes and federal law, there are differences in who is subject to the acts. First, the state fair employment practice statutes sometimes list exemptions or partial exclusions from coverage that differ from the federal law. Michigan and Oklahoma, for example, exclude from coverage the employment of individuals by their parents. Domestic servants are excluded by the statutes in Oklahoma and Ohio. Oklahoma

---

[120]California, Colorado, Hawaii, Illinois, Indiana, Kansas, Maine, Massachusetts, Missouri, New Jersey, New Mexico, Ohio, Pennsylvania, South Dakota, Washington, West Virginia, Wisconsin, Wyoming, and the Virgin Islands.

and Utah exempt religious associations that employ individuals of a particular religion to carry out their activities. Vermont makes a limited exception to the prohibition on sexual orientation for religious organizations that give preference to members of the same religion. Montana and New Hampshire exclude nonprofit private membership clubs.

Some states require a different minimum number of employees for coverage under separate, specialized acts than under their general discrimination act. California, for example, has a general statute that applies to employers with a minimum of five employees, but the prohibition against discrimination on the basis of mental disability applies only to employers with 15 or more. Similarly, Illinois' general statute applies to employers with a minimum of 15 employees, but complainants can bring claims of sexual harassment or handicap discrimination against employers with a minimum of only one employee.

The manner of proof in substantive claims brought under state employment discrimination law closely resembles the federal approach. Substantive differences sometimes develop, however, between federal and state employment discrimination laws. Remedial differences between Title VII and some state statutes have been important, especially before the expansion of federal remedies in the Civil Rights Act of 1991. It still remains true that many states provide criminal penalties or civil fines, unlike Title VII, for the violation of their employment discrimination laws. These sanctions are in addition to or in lieu of private remedies. Like Title VII, most states provide for attorney fees.

Most of the state statutes provide for affirmative orders like reinstatement, and many provide for some form of damages.[121] These provisions take various forms. One of the most expansive, for example, is the Michigan Civil Rights Act, known as the Elliott-Larsen Act, which provides simply for damages for an injury caused by an unlawful practice. Michigan state courts have interpreted this provision to permit prevailing plaintiffs to recover compensatory damages, including damages for humiliation, embarrassment, outrage, disappointment, and other forms of mental anguish.

---

[121]California, Idaho, Illinois, Iowa, Kansas, Kentucky, Louisiana, Michigan, Minnesota, Montana, Nevada, New Mexico, New York, Ohio, Oregon, Pennsylvania, South Dakota, Tennessee, Washington, and the District of Columbia.

Particularly before the enactment of the Civil Rights Act of 1991, the states that allowed damages under their statutes provided an attractive alternative forum for plaintiffs. Although federal law now permits limited compensatory and punitive damages under Title VII, the availability of damages under state law remains important because of the ceiling on the recovery of noneconomic damages under Title VII and because uncertainties remain about the application of the new federal provision for compensatory and punitive damages. It remains unclear under current Title VII law exactly when compensatory damages will be permitted for "intentional" conduct under the Civil Rights Act of 1991. Moreover, it remains unclear under the new federal law what elements of compensatory damages are permissible. For plaintiffs in a state like Michigan, therefore, the state act still has the advantage of permitting recovery for a broad range of noneconomic harm without any ceiling on such recovery.

Another area in which some states have recently enacted employment discrimination legislation concerns discrimination against smokers. Several states have statutes independent of other disability statutes that specifically prohibit employers from forbidding employees to use tobacco products outside the workplace or discriminating against them in compensation, terms, conditions, or privileges of employment because of such use. These state laws are discussed in chapter 1.

Although federal law dominates employment discrimination, state laws remain important. Many states provide alternative sources for redress and reconciliation as well as broader proscriptions or remedies. Despite the substantial overlap between the federal and state schemes, the states continue to play a significant role in resolving employment discrimination suits and in identifying other forms of discrimination that they find important to make unlawful.

3

Wages, Hours, and Benefits

INTRODUCTION

Perhaps more than any other area of employment law, the regulation of wages, hours, and benefits illustrates the conflict between improving and protecting conditions of employment, on the one hand, and preserving traditional employer prerogatives, on the other. Some aspects of compensation and benefit schemes are governed by a patchwork of federal and state laws with very detailed requirements, while others are not regulated at all. Some statutes require covered employers to provide specific benefits in specific ways, while others impose certain obligations once an employer voluntarily chooses to offer a benefit. In addition, unlike many other areas of employment law, to the extent that the provision of wages, hours, and benefits is regulated by law, that regulation is almost entirely statutory. Employees have few common law rights to require employers to provide specific wages or benefits.

The Fair Labor Standards Act (FLSA), first enacted in 1938, is the cornerstone of federal wage policy and exemplifies regulation through the imposition of detailed requirements. Although the FLSA has been amended a number of times since 1938, its basic scheme has remained essentially unchanged. It establishes a minimum wage for covered workers, but it does not limit hours they may be required to work. Rather, it attempts to discourage long work hours by requiring the payment of an overtime premium for all hours worked over 40 in a workweek. Over the years, the courts and the Department of Labor have developed extremely detailed rules governing various aspects of FLSA enforcement, such as the determination of compensable time and the scope of the exemptions from statutory coverage. The FLSA does not preempt state laws, and most states have wage-hour laws, although many are less protective than the FLSA. Most states also have laws protecting workers' rights to receive payment of their wages.

Since World War II employee benefits other than cash wages, such as pensions, health insurance, paid vacations, and leaves of absence, have become increasingly important aspects of compensation. Some benefits, such as unemployment compensation insurance coverage and Social Security taxes, are required by federal law, and many states require certain benefits, most commonly time off for jury duty, voting, or childcare. Until recently, however, Congress has resisted universal government-mandated benefits, and employers provide most benefits either unilaterally or as a result of collective bargaining with unions representing their workers. The Family and Medical Leave Act of 1993 (FMLA), which requires covered employers to grant leaves of absence for the birth or adoption of a child, or for the serious health condition of the employee or close family members, thus represents a significant departure from past practice.

The more common statutory approach to employee benefits has been not to require employers to provide a benefit, but to impose certain obligations once an employer chooses to offer one. Take, for instance, health care coverage. Except in Hawaii, no law currently requires employers to offer health care coverage to their workers. Once an employer provides this benefit, however, the Employee Retirement Income Security Act (ERISA) requires the provision of continuation coverage rights. If an employer provides health coverage through the purchase of insurance, every state requires some minimum level of coverage through its insurance laws, although the specific coverage requirements differ greatly from state to state. In addition, Title VII of the Civil Rights Act of 1964 (Title VII), as amended by the Pregnancy Discrimination Act of 1978, requires employers that offer health coverage to include coverage for pregnancy and childbirth.

ERISA has been one of the most significant developments in the law regulating employee benefits. Although primarily concerned with pensions, it also covers a vast array of nonpension benefits. It imposes certain procedural obligations on employers that provide covered benefits, including reporting and disclosure requirements and the requirement of internal claims and appeal mechanisms, and it creates a federal cause of action for challenges to benefits denials. Its most important and controversial aspect, however, is its broad preemption provision, which has displaced large bodies of state law dealing with the enforcement of benefit promises.

FAIR LABOR STANDARDS ACT

Overview

The Fair Labor Standards Act (FLSA)[1] contains four major requirements: a minimum wage, an overtime standard, restrictions on child labor, and equal pay. These requirements apply to all covered employees who are not specifically exempt. There are three ways in which employees can be covered by the FLSA: individual employee coverage, enterprise coverage, and coverage of public employees. The first two types of coverage are based on broad interstate commerce tests that most employers probably meet. Enterprise coverage, however, also contains a $500,000 business volume test, so many employees of small businesses may not be covered by the Act.

The FLSA is administered and enforced by the Secretary of Labor and the Administrator of the Wage-Hour Division of the Department of Labor. The Wage-Hour Division conducts inspections of workplaces and the records employers are required to keep. Failure to keep required records is a violation of the FLSA, even if the employer has not committed any wage violations.

The FLSA is enforced primarily through civil suits by the Secretary of Labor or by individual employees. Unlike the employment discrimination statutes, the FLSA does not require employees to file charges with the government before bringing suit. FLSA plaintiffs must simply file suit within the Act's two- or three-year statute of limitations. Remedies for FLSA violations include unpaid minimum wages and overtime pay and an equal amount as liquidated damages, plus attorney fees. The Secretary of Labor can sue for injunctive relief, including a ban

---

[1]29 U.S.C. §§201–19 (1993).

on interstate shipment of goods produced in violation of the Act. The Secretary can also impose a civil penalty of up to $10,000 for each violation of the child labor provisions and up to $1,000 per violation for repeated or willful violations of the minimum wage and overtime provisions. Finally, the FLSA authorizes a criminal sanction of a fine of not more than $10,000 or imprisonment for not more than six months, or both, for willful violations.

Coverage

The FLSA applies to all covered employees unless the Act specifically exempts them from one or more of its provisions. Two of three types of coverage, individual employee and enterprise coverage, are discussed below. Coverage of public employees will be discussed separately later in this chapter.

Individual Employee Coverage

Individual employee coverage is based on an employee's job duties, not on the nature of the employer's business. It includes employees who are "engaged in commerce" or in the "production of goods for commerce." This commerce requirement is very broad. Employees are engaged in commerce if their work involves the movement of goods, people, or communications across state lines. Employees are engaged in the production of goods for commerce if they manufacture, produce, handle, or work on goods that cross state lines. For example, employees in communications industries, employees who load, unload, or handle goods received directly from outside the state, and employees who regularly use telephones and the mail are all included in individual employee coverage.

Enterprise Coverage

Individual employee coverage focuses on each worker's duties, and therefore some employees of a company can be covered by this test, while others are not. Enterprise coverage, on the other hand, focuses on the nature of the employer's business. **If a business meets the tests for enterprise coverage, all of its employees are automatically covered, regardless of their individual duties**. To be covered as an enterprise, a firm (or firms) must meet three requirements. It must satisfy the statutory definition of "enterprise," it must have two or more employees engaged in commerce or the production of goods for commerce, and most businesses must satisfy a dollar-volume test.

The FLSA defines "enterprise" as "related activities performed (either through unified operations or common control) by any person or persons for a common business purpose." Under this broad definition, physically separate locations or legally distinct firms can be treated as a single enterprise, so that all of their employees are covered by the FLSA. The definition's requirement of a common business purpose can be established by a profit motive or commercial activity, even if conducted by a nonprofit organization. Currently, the dollar volume test is $500,000 in annual gross sales or business. Companies that meet the first two elements but do not do enough business to meet the dollar-volume test are not covered as enterprises, and their employees will be covered by the FLSA, if at all, only under individual employee coverage.

Hospitals, nursing homes, or other similar residential institutions, schools, colleges, universities, various types of urban and interurban mass transit, and public agencies receive special treatment under the statute. They are deemed to satisfy the common business purpose requirement of the definition of enterprise, and they do not have to satisfy the dollar-volume test. As a result, virtually all of these institutions are covered as enterprises.

Independent Contractors

Inclusion of individual workers under any form of coverage depends on the existence of an employer-employee relationship. Although the FLSA contains a very broad definition of "employee," not everyone who works is an employee. The most common dispute over employee status involves the distinction between employee and independent contractor. If an individual hired to perform work for a firm is a true independent contractor, no employment relationship and therefore no FLSA coverage exist.

The basic test is economic reality: Are individuals economically dependent on the business for which they labor? In interpreting the economic realities test, courts have applied a number of factors. They include:

- the degree of control exercised by the employer,

- the extent of the relative investments in equipment and material,

- the worker's opportunity for profit and loss through managerial skill,

- the skill and initiative required by the work,

- the permanence of the relationship, and

- the extent to which the service rendered is an integral part of the employer's business.

Agreements between the parties about the nature of their relationship are not controlling. Instead, courts examine all the circumstances of each situation. For instance, a firm's lack of actual day-to-day control over an individual's work does not prevent a finding of employee status if the nature of the job, such as private-duty nursing, precludes direct supervision. Additionally, workers do not have to be completely dependent on a business for their basic source of income. Otherwise, workers in seasonal businesses, part-time workers, and workers with more than one job might never be covered. Rather, the question in such situations is whether workers depend on the business for their continued employment during the period the business operates.

Courts disregard sham arrangements set up to provide the appearance of an independent contractor relationship. For example, an employer might arrange to have an employee perform after-hours work, either at the employer's place of business or at the employee's home. Except under highly unusual circumstances, the worker remains an employee, even if the after-hours work is different from the work he or she performs during normal business hours.

Wages

The FLSA requires employers to pay at least the minimum hourly wage, which is currently $4.25, to all covered employees who are not specifically exempt. The unit of measurement for determining compliance with the minimum wage requirement is the workweek. Each workweek is considered separately; a workweek in which an employee receives less than the minimum wage cannot be averaged with one in which he or she receives more than the statutory minimum.

Although the FLSA states the minimum wage as an hourly rate, it does not require employers to pay by the hour. Other compensation systems, such as piece rates and weekly, monthly, or yearly salaries, are perfectly legal, as long as the employee's total straight-time compensation for a workweek divided by the total number of hours worked equals at least the minimum wage. The result of this computation will also be the "regular rate of pay," which determines the amount of any overtime compensation required by the FLSA.

Deductions From Wages

With two exceptions, employees must receive the minimum wage in cash or negotiable instrument, free and clear. Employers may credit against the minimum wage the reasonable value of board, lodging, or other facilities customarily furnished to their employees. Reasonable cost may not exceed the employer's actual cost, and the employer is responsible for maintaining and preserving records documenting its costs. Under Department of Labor regulations, the facilities must be of a kind normally furnished by the employer, such as meals provided by a restaurant, and they must be furnished primarily for the benefit of the employees; the employees must be told that the value of the facilities is being deducted from their wages; acceptance of the facilities must be voluntary.[2] The Eleventh Circuit Court of Appeals has, however, rejected the regulation's voluntariness requirement and allowed a restaurant to take a credit for meals provided to employees even though the employees did not have the choice of receiving the cash instead.[3]

Items that do not meet these requirements, such as tools of the trade, set-offs for breakage, and uniforms, may not be credited against payment of the minimum wage. The FLSA does not prohibit employers from requiring employees to wear uniforms, but an employer may not require employees to pay for the uniforms or even for the cost of cleaning them, if those payments reduce the employee's hourly rate below the minimum wage in the week in which the uniforms are bought or cleaned. Similarly, employers may not deduct from an employee's pay losses for breakage, cash register shortages, or suspected theft if the

---

[2]29 C.F.R. pt. 531 (1992).
[3]Davis Bros. v. Donovan, 700 F.2d 1368, 26 WH Cases 29 (11th Cir. 1983); Morrison, Inc. v. Donovan, 700 F.2d 1374, 26 WH Cases 33 (11th Cir. 1983).

deduction will have the effect of reducing the employee's hourly wage for that week below the statutory minimum. Deductions for theft that would result in less than the statutory minimum may be made only following an adjudication of guilt against the employee in a criminal proceeding.

Employers may deduct from the employee's pay the employee's share of Social Security and any other federal, state, and local taxes, but not any tax the employer is required to bear. Deductions for amounts ordered paid to a third party under garnishment, wage attachment, or bankruptcy proceedings are lawful, as are deductions as a result of the employee's voluntary assignment to a third party. Typical assignments include union dues, charitable contributions, and insurance premiums.

It is important to keep in mind that FLSA restrictions on deductions from an employee's pay apply only when the effect of the deduction is to reduce the employee's hourly rate of pay below the required minimum wage for the workweek in which the deduction is made. Otherwise, the FLSA does not limit the items or amounts of deductions. State law, however, often does regulate deductions for all employees, including employees who are exempt from the federal minimum wage requirement and employees who are so highly paid that compliance with the FLSA requirement is not in jeopardy. State wage payment laws will be discussed in further detail later in this chapter.

Tip Credit

The second statutory exception to the requirement that the minimum wage be paid free and clear is for tipped employees. The employer may take a tip credit of up to 50 percent of the minimum wage for employees who customarily receive over $30 a month in tips. The current minimum wage for these employees, therefore, is effectively $2.12 1/2 per hour. The tip credit can not exceed the value of the tips received, so tipped employees must actually receive at least $2.12 1/2 in tips for each hour worked.

Overtime Requirement

The FLSA does not restrict the number of hours employers may require employees to work. It simply requires that employees who are not specifically exempt from the overtime provision be paid at least one-and-a-half times their regular rate of pay for all hours they work over 40 in a workweek. As with the minimum wage requirement, the basic unit of measurement for computation of overtime is the workweek. For instance, if an employee works 30 hours in one week and 50 the next, the employer may not average the two weeks to avoid payment of overtime; the employee is entitled to 10 hours of overtime for the second week.

Although employees may be paid on an hourly, salary, piece rate, commission, or some other basis, each employee has a "regular rate of pay," which must be computed in order to determine the amount of overtime pay required. The regular rate is an hourly rate. It is often more than the minimum wage, but it can never be less.

Calculation of the amount of overtime due to a worker paid on an hourly basis is simple. The regular rate is the employee's hourly rate. In addition to the straight-time hourly earnings, the employee must receive one-half the hourly rate for every hour over 40. For example, an employee with an hourly rate of $8.00 who works 44 hours in a workweek is entitled to $368 (44 hours at $8.00, plus four hours at $4.00).

Computing overtime due salaried employees can be more complex. A salaried employee's regular rate of pay is the amount of the salary divided by the number of hours of work for which the salary is intended to compensate. Therefore, a worker whose weekly salary of $500 is intended to compensate for a workweek of 40 hours has a regular rate of $12.50 and must be paid, in addition to the salary of $500, one-and-one-half times that rate, or $18.75, for each hour over 40. If the salary is intended to cover only a 35-hour workweek, the employee's regular rate is $14.29. The employee would be entitled to receive the salary plus $14.29 per hour for hours 36 to 40, and $21.44 ($14.29 × 1½) for all hours in excess of 40.

Compensable Time

The FLSA requires that employees be paid at least the minimum wage for the first 40 hours they work in a workweek and one-and-a-half times their regular rate of pay for all additional hours worked. Therefore, a key to compliance with the Act's minimum wage and overtime requirements is determining the number of "hours worked." In a series of decisions in 1944, the United States Supreme Court set forth a test that is still used as the basis for determining compensable time today. Employees must be paid not only for all time spent in "physical or mental exertion (whether burdensome or not) controlled or required by the employer and pursued necessarily and primarily for the benefit of the employer or his business," but also for idle time or time spent in incidental activities.[4]

Under this test, time actually spent in production and related activities is clearly compensable. This includes not only the normal work day, but also any other time employees are required or permitted to perform work. Work not required or requested by the employer counts as hours worked if the employer actually knew about it or should have known about it. For instance, if an employee arrives early and does things like starting machines or answering the phone, that time is compensable if the employer knew or should have known of the employee's actions. The same is true if an employee stays late to finish a project or takes work home and completes it there. Employers who wish to avoid liability for these hours should prohibit unauthorized work beyond the normal working day and establish a system to police compliance with the rule.

Waiting Time

The critical question in most waiting time cases is whether employees can make effective use of the time for their own purposes. If they cannot, the time is considered primarily for the employer's benefit and compensable. Time spent waiting for work during the work day because of machinery breakdowns, delivery delays, a shortage of customers, or other similar reasons is normally compensable. Even if employees are permitted to leave the employer's property, courts generally find the waiting time compensable if it is too short for employees to use the time for their own benefit. On the other hand, if

---

[4]Tennessee Coal, Iron & R.R. v. Muscoda Local 123, 321 U.S. 590 (1944); Armour & Co. v. Wantock, 323 U.S. 126 (1944); Skidmore v. Swift & Co., 323 U.S. 134 (1944).

employees are completely relieved of duty during the waiting time and the periods are long enough to permit them to pursue their own activities, the time is not compensable.

On-Call Time

A similar analysis applies to employees who are "on call" and must be available to return to work on short notice. Obviously, these employees are not completely free to do whatever they want when they are off duty but on call. Depending on the employer's requirements, they may not be able to leave their homes, travel out of town, or even be alone with their children without having a babysitter on call too. Constraints on an employee's freedom, however, do not by themselves make on-call time compensable. If employees must remain on or so near the employer's property that they cannot engage in personal activities, the on-call time is compensable. If employees are permitted to go home while on call, courts rarely find the on-call time compensable, regardless of the restrictions on the employees' movements.

In *Bright v. Houston Northwest Medical Center Survivor, Inc.*,[5] for instance, a hospital biomedical equipment repair technician had to wear a beeper, arrive at the hospital within 20 minutes after being called, and not be intoxicated or so impaired that he could not work on the equipment. The court held that the on-call time was not compensable, even though the employee was on call during all of his off-duty hours and had had no relief from this status for almost an entire year. On-call hours will be compensable only where callbacks are so frequent that employees cannot effectively use their off-duty time or where the employer's on-call system is so distracting or burdensome that personal activities are inhibited. For instance, in *Renfro v. City of Emporia*,[6] firefighters were subject to constraints almost identical to those in *Bright* and a number of other cases, but with one critical difference. The firefighters were called back to work for at least an hour on an average

---

[5] 934 F.2d 671, 30 WH Cases 609 (5th Cir. 1991) (en banc), *cert. denied*, 112 S. Ct. 882, 30 WH Cases 1176 (1992).

[6] 948 F.2d 1529, 30 WH Cases 1017 (10th Cir. 1991), *cert. dismissed*, 112 S. Ct. 1310 (1992).

of three to five times during a 24-hour on-call period. The frequency of the callbacks was so burdensome that the entire on-call time became compensable.

Sleep Time

Sleep time is compensable under certain circumstances. Employees who are on duty for less than 24 hours are considered to be working even if they are allowed to sleep during part of that time. Employees who are on duty for 24 hours or more may agree with their employer to exclude from compensable time bona fide meal periods and bona fide sleeping periods of no more than eight hours. The employer must furnish adequate sleeping facilities, and employees must normally have an uninterrupted sleep period. Any actual interruptions for calls to duty are compensable, and if employees do not get at least five hours' sleep during a sleep period, the entire time is compensable. Employees who reside on their employers' property permanently or for extended periods of time are probably not working the entire time they are there. The Department of Labor will recognize any "reasonable agreement" between the parties concerning exclusion of sleep time.

Travel Time

Travel from home to work and back is normally not compensable time. If, however, employees are required to report to one location, such as the employer's dispatching office, to receive assignments or instructions, and then travel to a job site, the time spent traveling from the office to the job site is compensable. If travel is part of an employee's principal job activities, travel time is compensable. Overnight travel is compensable if it occurs during regular working hours, but not otherwise, unless the employee is required to perform work while traveling.

Rest and Meal Periods

Rest and meal periods are governed by straightforward rules. Break periods of 20 minutes or less are compensable. Meal periods of at least 30 minutes are not compensable if employees are completely relieved of duty. If employees remain on call during the meal period or are required to remain at their work station while eating, they must be paid for the time.

Miscellaneous

Finally, many other miscellaneous activities may be compensable if the employer requires them or if they primarily benefit the employer. These include attendance at lectures, meetings, and training programs, adjusting grievances during the regular workday (unless otherwise agreed in a collective bargaining agreement), and waiting for and receiving medical attention on the employer's property or at the employer's direction during normal working hours.

White-Collar Exemptions

The FLSA contains a complex scheme of exemptions, under which covered employees may be fully or partially exempt from the Act's minimum wage requirement, its overtime requirement, or its restrictions on child labor. Most exemptions are measured on a workweek basis. Usually, if an employee performs both exempt and nonexempt work during a workweek, the exemption is lost for the entire week, although some exemptions permit the performance of a specified amount of nonexempt work, as long as all the other requirements of the exemption are met. In addition, in some circumstances the regulations allow the combination, or tacking, of exempt work during a workweek in which part of an employee's work satisfies one exemption, and part of it another. Courts interpret exemptions narrowly, and the employer must prove that an employee satisfies an exemption.

Although almost all of the FLSA exemptions apply to specific industries, the most significant, the "white-collar exemptions," are based on job duties and cut across all sectors of the economy.[7] The white-collar exemptions are for those employed "in a bona fide executive, administrative, or professional capacity." They relieve the employer from both the minimum wage and the overtime requirements. Of all the exemptions, these contain the greatest potential for error, with possibly devastating results. White-collar employees are often highly paid and therefore have high hourly rates of pay, and they may routinely work more than 40 hours a week. A mistake in classifying them as exempt can result in large awards for unpaid overtime.

---

[7] 29 C.F.R. pt. 541 (1992).

Salary Basis Test

To satisfy any of the white-collar exemptions, employees must be paid on a salary basis. This means that for each week during which employees perform any work, they must receive a predetermined amount of money that constitutes all or part of their compensation. The salary may not be subject to reduction because of the quality or quantity of work performed, or because of absences of less than one day. If an employer docks the pay of an otherwise exempt employee because of an absence of less than a day, the exemption is lost and the employee is entitled to overtime. Some courts have applied this rule even when the employee avoided a pay reduction by using accumulated paid leave, if the employer otherwise would have docked the pay. The Family and Medical Leave Act of 1993, discussed later in this chapter, creates an exception to this rule for the unpaid leaves it requires.

Hourly rates of pay, no matter how high, are antithetical to the concept of a salary, and employees who are paid on an hourly basis do not qualify for the white-collar exemptions. In 1990, however, Congress passed a law directing the Secretary of Labor to allow skilled workers in the computer industry to qualify as exempt white-collar employees if their hourly rate of pay is at least six-and-one-half times the applicable minimum wage.[8] Accordingly, the Department of Labor issued a regulation under which employees who perform "[w]ork that requires theoretical and practical application of highly-specialized knowledge in computer systems analysis, programming, and software engineering, and who [are] employed and engaged in these activities as a computer systems analyst, computer programmer, software engineer, or other similarly skilled worker in the computer software field" are exempt as professional employees if they either meet the salary test for other professional employees, discussed below, or are compensated on an hourly basis at a rate in excess of six-and-one-half times the minimum wage (currently $27.625).[9]

Executive Employees

In addition to the salary basis test, each exempt executive, administrative, or professional employee must also satisfy a duties test, either

---

[8]Pub. L. No. 101-583 (1990).
[9]57 Fed. Reg. 46,742 (1992).

the "short test" or the "long test," depending on the amount of the employee's salary. Under the long test, workers are exempt as executive employees if they receive a salary of at least $155 per week and meet five other requirements:

- their primary duty must be management of an enterprise or one of its subdivisions or departments;

- they must customarily and regularly direct the work of two or more employees;

- they must have the authority to hire or fire or to make meaningful recommendations about these decisions;

- they must customarily and regularly exercise discretion; and

- they must not spend more than 20 percent of their time (40 percent for retail or service establishments) performing nonexempt work.

The percentage limitations on nonexempt work do not apply to an employee who is in sole charge of an independent establishment or a physically separate branch, or who owns at least a 20 percent interest in the enterprise. Under the short test, employees are exempt executives if they receive a salary of at least $250 per week and meet the first two long-test criteria.

Administrative Employees

Employees who qualify for the administrative exemption generally perform office work. They include executive and administrative assistants; specialists in technical areas, such as credit managers, purchasing agents, and labor relations directors; and individuals who work on special assignments with only general supervision and who are often away from the employer's place of business, such as field representatives and account executives. The long test for administrative employees requires a weekly salary of at least $155 and satisfaction of the following tests:

- the employee's primary duty must be either (a) office or nonmanual work directly related to management policies or the general operations of the company, or (b) administration of a school system or educational institution in work directly related to academic instruction or training;

- the employee must customarily and regularly exercise discretion and independent judgment;

- the employee must either (a) regularly and directly assist a proprietor or bona fide executive or administrative employee, or (b) work under only general supervision along specialized or technical lines, or (c) execute special assignments and tasks under only general supervision; and

- the employee must not spend more than 20 percent of his or her time (40 percent for retail or service establishments) performing nonexempt work.

Under the short test, employees who receive salaries of at least $250 per week qualify for the exemption if they satisfy the primary duty test (first requirement of the long test) doing work that requires the exercise of discretion and independent judgment.

Professional Employees

The exemption for professional employees includes the traditional professions of law, medicine, and theology, as well as work requiring advanced instruction in a field of science or learning and work that is original and creative in character. Under the long test, employees are exempt as professionals if their salary is at least $170 per week and

- their primary duty consists of either (a) work requiring advanced knowledge acquired by a prolonged course of scientific or specialized study, (b) original and creative work depending on imagination, talent, or invention, (c) teaching, or (d) computer programming or other highly skilled computer work;

- they consistently exercise discretion and judgment;

- their work is predominately intellectual, varied, and incapable of being standardized by time; and

- they do not spend more than 20 percent of their time in work not essential and necessarily incident to the work described above.

The short test is satisfied if employees receive a salary of at least $250 per week, they satisfy either (a) or (c) of the primary duty criteria, and their work requires the consistent exercise of discretion and judgment, or of invention, imagination, or talent in a recognized field of artistic endeavor. The salary requirement does not apply at all to attorneys, physicians, and teachers, or to highly skilled computer workers who are paid on an hourly basis at a rate exceeding six-and-one-half times the minimum wage.

An interesting phenomenon in recent years has been lawsuits in which individuals who work in fields that many people probably consider professions argue that they are not exempt professionals and are therefore entitled to be paid overtime. In *Dalheim v. KDFW-TV*,[10] the Fifth Circuit Court of Appeals found that television news producers were not exempt as professional employees because they worked within a well-defined framework of management policies and any discretion they exercised was governed by skill and experience, not by originality and creativity. Similarly, most of the work done by the station's general assignment reporters depended on skill, diligence, and intelligence, not originality or creativity. In *Sherwood v. Washington Post*,[11] the D.C. Circuit Court of Appeals ordered a trial on the question whether the work performed by newspaper reporters and editors was predominately original or creative, or whether the paper had to pay them overtime.

"Outside Salesmen"

A fourth white-collar exemption exists for any "employee employed . . . in the capacity of outside salesman." There is no salary test for this exemption. Employees qualify if (1) they are employed for the purpose of and are customarily and regularly engaged away from their employer's place of business in either (a) making sales or (b) obtaining orders or contracts for services or for the use of facilities for which the customer will pay, and (2) their hours of work in other activities "do not exceed 20 percent of the hours worked in the workweek by nonexempt employees of the employer."

Outside salespeople must perform their work away from the employer's place of business; inside salespeople do not come within

---

[10]918 F.2d 1220, 30 WH Cases 113 (5th Cir. 1990).
[11]871 F.2d 1144, 29 WH Cases 399 (D.C. Cir. 1989).

the exemption. The sale of services as well as goods qualifies for the exemption, but the performance of services does not. For instance, route drivers whose primary responsibility is delivery of their employer's products to retail outlets, with little or no direct sales activity, do not come within the exemption.

Other Exemptions

Exemptions From Minimum Wage and Overtime Requirements

Aside from the white-collar exemptions, the FLSA contains other exemptions from both the minimum wage and overtime requirements. These include:

- employees employed in agriculture under certain circumstances,
- employees employed by seasonal amusement and recreational businesses,
- certain employees in fishing and other fishing-related and aquatic businesses,
- "seamen" on foreign vessels,
- domestic employees employed on a casual basis to provide babysitting services and those employed to provide companionship services to aged and infirm individuals,
- employees of small newspapers, and
- certain switchboard operators.

Exemptions From Minimum Wage Only

Certificates issued by the Department of Labor can permit the employment of apprentices, learners, messengers, workers with disabilities, and students at special rates below the minimum wage. In 1989, amendments to the FLSA permitted employers to pay a subminimum training wage to teenage employees, under certain limited circumstances.[12] By its terms, this provision expired on April 1, 1993. Experience revealed that few employers used the training wage, and it is unlikely that it will be reenacted.

---

[12]Fair Labor Standards Amendments of 1989, §6, Pub. L. No. 101-157, 103 Stat. 938 (1989).

Exemptions From Overtime Only

The FLSA also contains exemptions from its overtime requirements only. The major provisions affect the transportation industry. Employees covered by the Motor Carriers Act, employees of employers engaged in the operation of a common carrier by rail, employees of air carriers subject to the Railway Labor Act, and "seamen" on U.S. vessels are all exempt from FLSA overtime requirements. In addition, a number of employees in agriculture and related industries are exempt from the overtime requirements, as are other specialized workers, including certain television and radio broadcasters, live-in domestic workers, and houseparents for institutionalized orphans. Special overtime rules for public sector firefighters and law enforcement officers are discussed later in this chapter.

Child Labor

The FLSA and Department of Labor regulations contain detailed restrictions on the employment of minors.[13] In nonagricultural employment, the minimum age for most jobs is 16. For 17 hazardous occupations, including such jobs as coal mining, logging, driving motor vehicles, and operating power woodworking machines, the minimum age is 18.

Fourteen- and 15-year-olds may work in certain specified jobs in office and sales work, retail, food service, and gasoline service establishments, as long as the working conditions do not interfere with their education, health, or well-being. There are limits on the number of hours these minors may work, both per day and per week. Their employment must be outside of school hours and between the hours of 7:00 a.m. and 7:00 p.m., except from June 1 to Labor Day, when the evening limit is 9:00 p.m. Additionally, during the school year, 14- and 15-year-olds may work no more than three hours per day and 18 hours per week. During vacation periods, they may work no more than eight hours per day and 40 hours per week.

Exemptions

As with its other requirements, the FLSA provides some exemptions from the child labor prohibitions. They cover agriculture, actors

---

[13] 29 C.F.R. pt. 570 (1992).

and performers, newspaper delivery, evergreen wreath making, and employment by a parent or guardian.

The most significant and controversial exemption is that for agriculture. Minors 14 and older may work in any agricultural occupation outside of school hours unless the Secretary of Labor has declared that occupation hazardous. Twelve- and 13-year-olds may work in agriculture outside of school hours on the same farm where their parent is employed or on another farm with parental consent. Children under 12 may be employed by their parent on the parent's farm.

Public Employees

Since 1985 the FLSA has applied to employees of state and local governments. Generally, the rules governing private sector employees apply in the public sector as well, but Congress has added a few provisions to deal with the unique fiscal problems and historical practices of public employers. These include the use of compensatory time off instead of cash payments for overtime, the status of volunteers, and special overtime rules for public safety employees.[14]

Compensatory Time Off

Public employers may make compensatory time off, or "comp time," available to employees instead of paying for overtime in cash. Comp time must be awarded at a rate of at least one-and-one-half hours off for each hour of overtime worked. There are limits on the amount of comp time employees may accumulate before they must either receive time off or be paid in cash for any additional overtime. For employees engaged in public safety, emergency response, and seasonal activities, the limit is 480 hours of comp time, which is the equivalent of 320 hours of overtime. For all other employees, the cap is 240 hours of comp time, or 160 hours of overtime. An employee's request to use comp time must be honored within a reasonable period unless the time off would unduly disrupt the agency's operations. The statute does not, however, condition the use of comp time on employee requests. Absent an agreement to the contrary, a public employer may unilaterally require its employees to use accumulated comp time when it chooses. When employees

---

[14]29 C.F.R. pt. 553 (1992).

leave a job, they must be paid for any unused comp time at their final regular rate, or at their average regular rate for the last three years, whichever is greater.

Public employers may provide comp time instead of paying for overtime only if there is an agreement between the employer and the employee. The statute describes three kinds of agreements. The first kind is available only in states that permit public sector collective bargaining.[15] In those states, a public agency whose employees have organized may address the issue of comp time in a collective bargaining agreement or other similar agreement with the employees' representative. The other two kinds may be used if the employees are not unionized or if the state prohibits public sector bargaining. In either of these situations, the employer must reach an agreement with each individual employee hired after April 15, 1986, before the employee performs any work. For employees hired before April 15, 1986, the regular practice in effect on that date constitutes an agreement that satisfies the statute.

Volunteers

The FLSA's definition of "employee" contains a provision making it clear that individuals performing volunteer services for state and local governments are not covered by the Act, even if they receive expenses or a nominal payment for their work. For instance, a volunteer school crossing guard is not an employee merely because he or she receives a uniform allowance or travel expenses. To prevent abuse and undue pressure, however, public employees may not volunteer to perform the same kind of services for which they are employed for the same public agency that employs them.

Overtime Exemptions

The FLSA contains three different kinds of overtime exemptions for firefighters and law enforcement personnel. First, there is a complete exemption from the overtime requirements for public employees engaged in fire protection or law enforcement activities for workweeks in which the public employer has fewer than five employees employed in these activities.

---

[15]Moreau v. Klevenhagen, 113 S. Ct. 1905, 1 WH Cases 2d 569 (1993).

Second, public employers too large for the complete exemption may structure their employment practices to come within a partial exemption. For fire protection employees with work periods of 28 consecutive days, overtime must be paid for all hours worked over 212 in a work period; if the work period is less than 28 but more than six consecutive days, no overtime compensation is required until the ratio of the number of hours worked to the number of days in the work period exceeds that of 212 hours to 28 days. For instance, if a city established a work period of 14 consecutive days for firefighters, overtime would be required for all hours in excess of 106 (106/14 = 212/28). For employees engaged in law enforcement activities, the rules are the same, but the number of hours that triggers overtime is 171 for a work period of 28 consecutive days. Thus, a city with a work period of 14 consecutive days would owe overtime to its police officers after 86 hours (86/14 = 171/28). Employees with a work period less than seven consecutive days do not qualify for this partial exemption, and they must receive overtime for all hours over 40 in a workweek.

The third exemption allows public employers to exclude from the computation of hours worked special detail work performed for a separate and independent employer by the public employer's fire protection or law enforcement employees, as long as this work is at the employee's option. This exemption also permits public employees, at their option, to engage in occasional or sporadic part-time employment for the same employer but in a different capacity, without having the hours worked on the occasional job count toward calculation of overtime in the regular job. Employees may also trade shifts with other employees, and those hours will be excluded from calculation of overtime.

Ambulance and rescue service employees may be treated as fire protection or law enforcement personnel for purposes of these exemptions if they "form an integral part" of the public employer's fire protection or law enforcement activities or if their services are "substantially related" to those activities. To satisfy the substantially related test, the ambulance and rescue employees must have received training in the rescue of fire, crime, and accident victims, and they must be regularly dispatched to fires, crime scenes, riots, natural disasters, and accidents. Performance of nonexempt work by fire protection or law enforcement personnel will not defeat the exemptions as long as the nonexempt work does not exceed 20 percent of the total hours worked by an employee during the applicable work period.

Salary Basis Test

Although Congress has recognized many special needs of public sector employers, most of the FLSA applies in the same manner to all covered employers, whether public or private. As discussed elsewhere in this chapter, the exemption for executive, administrative, and professional employees requires, among other things, that employees be paid on a salary basis. Under Department of Labor regulations, employees are not paid on a salary basis if their pay is subject to reduction for absences of less than one day. In *Abshire v. County of Kern*,[16] the public employer required salaried employees to use accrued sick leave or vacation time to compensate for absences of less than one day. The Ninth Circuit Court of Appeals held that these employees were not paid on a salary basis, because their pay was subject to reduction, even though it may not actually have been reduced. Concern that decisions like *Abshire* could result in enormous unexpected liability for public sector employers and that they conflict with common governmental payroll systems prohibiting payment for time not spent working led the Department of Labor to revise its salary basis regulations. Under the revision the exemption is preserved for otherwise exempt public sector executive, administrative, and professional employees who work under a system that requires the use of paid leave for absences of less than one day or reduces their salaries if paid leave is not used.[17]

Retaliation

Like most other remedial labor legislation, the FLSA prohibits discrimination against employees because they have filed complaints or instituted or testified in proceedings under the Act. Although employees must take some overt action to gain the protection of the antiretaliation provision, filing a complaint with the Department of Labor is not necessary. Discussing a problem with a Department investigator, refusing to release back pay claims or return back pay awards, and protesting violations to the employer all have been found protected. The

---

[16] 908 F.2d 483, 29 WH Cases 1417 (9th Cir. 1990), *cert. denied*, 498 U.S. 1068, 30 WH Cases 208 (1991).

[17] 57 Fed. Reg. 37,666 (1992) (final rule, effective September 18, 1992, adding 29 C.F.R. §541.5d).

prohibition also applies to employers who attempt to blacklist or otherwise retaliate against former employees. The employee does not have to be correct in asserting a FLSA violation; a good faith belief that the employer is violating the Act is enough. The Third Circuit Court of Appeals has held that the FLSA protects an employee from retaliation even where the employer erroneously believed the employee had filed a complaint.[18]

Administration and Enforcement

The FLSA is administered and enforced by the Secretary of Labor and the Administrator of the Wage-Hour Division of the Department of Labor, to whom the Secretary has delegated most statutory responsibilities. The Secretary and the Administrator issue regulations interpreting the Act, and the Administrator issues interpretive bulletins and opinion letters.

Inspections

The FLSA authorizes the Wage-Hour Division to enter and inspect workplaces and the records employers are required to keep. If the employer denies entry, the Administrator may issue a subpoena for records. Employers must permit entry for service of the subpoena, even if the investigator does not have a warrant.[19] Because there are not enough Wage-Hour investigators to visit all of the nation's workplaces, inspections generally occur as a result of an employee complaint, as a reinspection of an establishment previously found in violation, or as part of a plan targeting industries with high levels of violations. The Division does not tell the employer the reason for the inspection, however. Because the Act does not require an administrative complaint as a prerequisite to governmental inspection or to suit by either the government or the employee, the names of any complainants are not relevant to any subsequent action.

Recordkeeping Requirements

Employers subject to the Act must make, keep, and preserve records of the individuals they employ and their wages, hours, and other

---

[18]Brock v. Richardson, 812 F.2d 121, 27 WH Cases 1689 (3d Cir. 1986).
[19]Donovan v. Lone Steer, Inc., 464 U.S. 408, 26 WH Cases 933 (1984).

conditions of employment. Depending on their type, records must be preserved for two or three years.[20] Payroll records, collective bargaining agreements or other employment contracts or agreements on which the employer relies to establish various exemptions, and records of the total dollar volume of sales or business and goods purchased or received must all be kept for three years. Among the records that need be preserved only two years are time or earning cards or sheets; wage rate tables; order, shipping, and billing records; and documentation of the basis for additions to or deductions from individual employees' wages.

Although failure to comply with the recordkeeping requirements is a violation of the FLSA independent of any other violations, the most significant impact of an employer's failure to keep required records is its effect on the proof in a suit seeking unpaid minimum wages or overtime. If the employer has not maintained records from which an employee's hours of work and wages can be determined, the employee merely has to produce evidence to show the "amount and extent of that work as a matter of just and reasonable inference."[21] If the employee does so, the burden shifts to the employer to rebut the inference, a difficult task if it has not kept adequate records.

Enforcement Actions

The FLSA authorizes five enforcement actions: three by the Secretary of Labor, one by private plaintiffs, and one by the Department of Justice. First, the Secretary may sue on behalf of affected employees to recover unpaid minimum wages and overtime compensation and an equal amount in liquidated damages.

Second, the Secretary may seek injunctive relief to restrain any violation of the Act, including minimum wage, overtime, retaliation, and child labor violations. The injunction may also prohibit the interstate shipment of goods produced in violation of the FLSA. This "hot goods" ban applies to "any person" who ships goods produced in violation of the Act's minimum wage, overtime, and child labor requirements.

Third, the Secretary may impose civil penalties of up to $10,000 for each violation of the child labor provisions and up to $1,000 per

---

[20] 29 C.F.R. pt. 516 (1992).
[21] Anderson v. Mt. Clemens Pottery Co., 328 U.S. 680 (1946).

violation for repeated or willful violations of the minimum wage and overtime provisions. The Secretary determines the amount of the proposed civil penalty administratively, and employers objecting to the penalty may request a hearing before an Administrative Law Judge. Ultimately, the Secretary may sue to collect the penalty.

Fourth, employees may sue for unpaid minimum wages and overtime compensation and an equal amount as liquidated damages, and to enforce the Act's antiretaliation provision. Employees lose their individual right to sue if the Secretary of Labor files an action on their behalf.

The fifth action authorized by the FLSA is a criminal prosecution for willful violations. The Department of Justice prosecutes these actions, and maximum penalties are a fine of not more than $10,000 or imprisonment for not more than six months, or both. Prison sentences may not be imposed for a first conviction.

Defenses

The Portal-to-Portal Act of 1947[22] established two good faith defenses for employers found in violation of the FLSA. The first provides a defense to liability if the employer proves that it acted in good faith in conformity with and reliance on a written opinion of the Wage-Hour Administrator, even if the opinion is later rescinded or invalidated. This defense is very difficult to meet, and employers rarely satisfy it. The opinion must be in writing, and it must come from the Wage-Hour Administrator. Oral statements from any official or written opinions from lower-level officials within the Wage-Hour Division do not satisfy the statute. To be "in conformity with" a written opinion, the employer's situation must be identical to the facts described in the opinion. If some elements are missing or different, or if the opinion does not take a clear position on the issue, the employer may not take advantage of this defense, regardless of its state of mind.

The second defense authorizes the court, in its discretion, to reduce or eliminate an award of liquidated damages if the employer proves that it acted in good faith and had reasonable grounds for believing that it was not violating the FLSA. This defense, however, applies only to the liquidated damages portion of plaintiff's recovery. There can be no

---

[22]29 U.S.C. §§251–62 (1993).

reduction of liability for unpaid minimum wages and overtime compensation. Because a written opinion from the Wage-Hour Administrator is not required for this defense, courts can consider such factors as reliance on advice of counsel or personnel experts. The employer must satisfy both the subjective and objective prongs of the defense, however. If the law in an area is clear, the employer will not be able to prove it reasonably believed it was acting lawfully.

Waivers, Releases, and Settlements

The FLSA severely restricts the ability of employees to waive, release, or settle their claims for unpaid wages. No settlement will be binding on the employee unless it is supervised by the Secretary of Labor or part of the resolution of a lawsuit. Unsupervised private agreements between an employer and its employees are not valid, and employees or the Department of Labor remain free to sue the employer for any remaining unpaid wages and for liquidated damages.

RESTRICTIONS ON GARNISHMENT

The Consumer Credit Protection Act of 1968[23] restricts creditors' ability to garnish workers' earnings and employers' rights to fire workers whose wages have been garnished. As a general matter, creditors may not garnish more than 25 percent of a worker's disposable earnings in any week. "Disposable earnings" means the earnings left after deduction of any amounts withheld by law. Exceptions to the general 25 percent limit exist for support orders, orders of bankruptcy courts, and debts due for federal or state taxes. Support orders may garnish as much as 50 percent of a worker's disposable earnings, and as much as 60 percent if the employee subject to the support order is not also supporting a spouse or dependent child apart from the spouse or child involved in the support order. These percentage limitations increase to 55 and 65, respectively, if the worker is more than 12 weeks behind in support payments.

The second prong of the Act restricts discharges. **Employers may not fire any employee because his or her earnings "have been**

---

[23]15 U.S.C. §§1671–77 (1993).

subject to garnishment for any one indebtedness." The phrase "subject to garnishment" means that the earnings must actually be withheld from the employee's pay. Therefore, mere service on the employer of a second garnishment order does not constitute garnishment for a second debt, and firing the employee would violate the Act. In one case, an employer was served with a second garnishment but did not withhold any money because the maximum amount allowed by law was already being withheld for a first garnishment. It fired the employee for having a second garnishment, but the court held that the employee had not been "subject to garnishment" for a second debt, and therefore the employer had violated the Act.[24] Willful violation of the restriction on discharge is punishable by a fine of $1,000 or imprisonment for one year, or both.

The Act does not preempt state laws prohibiting garnishments or imposing greater restrictions on garnishments than federal law, or laws providing greater rights against discharge because of garnishments.

STATE WAGE AND HOUR REGULATION

Almost every state has a wage-hour law setting at least a minimum wage. Most also contain an overtime requirement and restrictions on child labor. While some states have lower minimum wages and higher overtime thresholds than federal law, others provide more protection for workers than does the FLSA. **The FLSA does not preempt state laws that impose higher standards than federal law**. Therefore, if the state minimum wage is higher than the federal minimum, if state law imposes a daily overtime requirement, if it covers workers who are exempt under the FLSA, or if it imposes more severe restrictions on child labor than does the FLSA, state law controls.

A more significant source of wage-related rights is found in state wage payment or wage collection statutes. These laws regulate the specifics of wage payment in ways not touched by federal law. Although statutes vary from state to state, they share some common elements. They contain a definition of "wages" and require that employers pay wages in legal tender. They generally require payment of wages on a regular periodic basis, either monthly, semi-monthly, or

---

[24]Brennan v. Kroger Co., 513 F.2d 961 (7th Cir. 1975).

weekly. Many states require employers to notify workers of the dates on which they will be paid and the place where they will receive their paychecks.

State wage payment laws commonly limit deductions and withholding from employees' pay. Most states prohibit deductions unless required or permitted by law or with the written consent of the employee. Some states prohibit deductions for damage to the employer's property, shortages, robberies, or debts, while others, such as Iowa, permit deductions for such items if the losses result from the worker's gross negligence, willful misconduct, or dishonesty.

Most state wage payment laws also regulate the payment of wages upon termination of employment. In some states, the employer must pay all accrued wages on the last day of employment, while in others the payment may be made on the next regularly scheduled payday. Some states draw a distinction between voluntary and involuntary separation from employment and require immediate payment only in cases of involuntary separation. If there is a dispute about the amount of wages owed to an employee, some states require the employer to pay the amount it concedes to be due. On the death of an employee, some states permit the employer to pay a specified portion of the wages due the deceased worker to his or her surviving family members before transferring the rest to the estate.

Enforcement of wage payment laws is generally entrusted to an administrative agency, with an appeal of the agency's decision to the state trial courts. Aside from unpaid wages, penalties often include liquidated damages, and criminal sanctions may be available, especially for willful violations. Generally, employees may not waive their rights under state wage payment statutes.

A dispute under a state wage payment law may involve the question whether the employer actually owes certain amounts to the employee. Resolution of the issue may require looking to the same kind of evidence that is often used to support claims of discharge in breach of an implied contract.[25] Thus, for instance, whether a worker who quit or was fired before his or her employment anniversary date is entitled to vacation pay for the year depends, in most states, on the terms of the employer's vacation policy, which might normally be found in an employee handbook or other similar document.

---

[25]See chapter 8.

A caveat to this discussion of rights under state wage payment or collection laws is that ERISA, discussed later in this chapter, preempts these laws as they relate to the payment of fringe benefits under an ERISA-covered plan. For instance, because severance pay plans are covered by ERISA, state wage payment laws may not regulate the circumstances under which employees receive severance pay. The employee's recourse is suit under ERISA, not a complaint under the state wage payment law. Claims to vacation pay, however, are normally not preempted by ERISA, because ERISA does not cover unfunded, single-employer vacation pay plans.

EQUAL PAY ACT

Overview

The Equal Pay Act of 1963 (EPA), the first modern employment discrimination statute, was enacted as an amendment to the FLSA.[26] Coverage under the EPA is identical to that of the FLSA, based on individual employee coverage, enterprise coverage, or federal, state, and local government coverage. The EPA is enforced in the same manner as the FLSA, except that the enforcement agency is the Equal Employment Opportunity Commission (EEOC).

The EPA requires that men and women doing "equal work" in the same "establishment" receive equal pay, unless the employer can justify a pay differential by a seniority, merit, or piecework system, or by "any other factor other than sex." The statute describes equal work as work that requires equal skill, effort, and responsibility and is performed under similar working conditions. Although enacted to correct wage discrimination against women, the EPA also protects men who receive lower pay than women who perform the same work. The EPA prohibits only one form of gender-based wage discrimination—unequal pay for equal work. Unequal pay for unequal (but comparable) work is not illegal under the EPA, even where intentional discrimination caused the inequality in work assignments. Remedies, if any, for this problem lie under Title VII.

---

[26]29 U.S.C. §206(d) (1993).

Elements of a Violation

Employees wishing to sue under the EPA must prove the elements of a violation. These elements are that (1) within the same establishment the employer paid (2) unequal pay (3) to men and women (on the basis of sex) who (4) performed equal work. The plaintiff has the burden of proof on each of these elements.

Establishment

The term "establishment" generally means a physically separate place of business. Thus, wages paid to employees who work in separate facilities operated by the same employer may not always be compared for EPA purposes. Circumstances such as centralized hiring, frequent interchange of employees, and identical duties among locations may result in the treatment of two or more distinct physical parts of a business as a single establishment. For instance, in *Brennan v. Goose Creek Consolidated School District*,[27] the Fifth Circuit Court of Appeals found that where a centralized administration controlled all personnel decisions and each school building had essentially the same working conditions, all of the schools in a school district constituted a single establishment under the EPA.

Unequal Pay

The second element of an EPA case is unequal pay. The EPA prohibits an employer from paying "wages to employees . . . at a rate less than the rate at which he pays wages to employees of the opposite sex. . . ." The statute commands equal *rates of pay*, not necessarily an equal bottom line. In *Bence v. Detroit Health Corp.*,[28] the managers of the men's division of a chain of health spas received a higher percentage commission on their membership sales than did the managers of the women's division. Although the total remuneration for both groups was equal because more women than men bought memberships,

---

[27]519 F.2d 53, 11 FEP Cases 313 (5th Cir. 1975).
[28]712 F.2d 1024, 32 FEP Cases 434 (6th Cir. 1983), *cert. denied*, 465 U.S. 1025, 33 FEP Cases 1884 (1984).

the court found the employer in violation of the equal pay requirement. The rate of pay was the unequal commission rate, not the equal bottom line.

On the Basis of Sex

To prove pay discrimination on the basis of gender, a female plaintiff need only find one man doing equal work at a higher rate of pay. If some men also receive the same pay as the plaintiff, the employer may be able to establish an affirmative defense by attributing the pay differential to some factor other than gender. Plaintiffs may also compare their pay to that of a predecessor or successor in the same position, if no intervening changes in job content or other circumstances destroy the equality of the job held by different employees. In one case, the female plaintiff received the same pay as her immediate male predecessor, but less than several men who preceded him. The court allowed her to compare her pay to that of her nonimmediate predecessors.[29]

Equal Work

The equal work standard is the battleground in many EPA cases. In performing an equal work analysis, actual job content, not job title or description, controls. Similarly, courts look to the requirements of the job itself, not the skills and qualifications of the individual holding the job. Factors such as experience and training may justify a pay differential between two employees performing equal work, but they enter the case as defenses, not as part of the plaintiff's case.

"Equal" means "substantially equal," not "identical." The substantially equal test prevents employers from avoiding EPA liability by assigning one inconsequential task to male workers only. Nevertheless, for work to be equal, the two jobs must look alike; the courts have construed the EPA's equal work requirement as applying only to jobs within the same job family. To satisfy the substantial equality test, jobs must share a common core of tasks; a significant portion of the two jobs must be identical.

---

[29]Clymore v. Far-Mar-Co., Inc., 709 F.2d 499, 42 FEP Cases 439 (8th Cir. 1983).

Rarely are two sets of jobs identical; one or both jobs may have additional duties that the other does not. Once a court determines the existence of a common core of tasks, it must then evaluate the differences between the jobs and decide whether those differences make the jobs unequal. The statute's three criteria, skill, effort, and responsibility, generally come into play at this point, although the courts often do not treat them separately or with much meaningful analysis.

Skill includes factors such as experience, training, education, and ability. Very few cases have dealt specifically with the skill criterion. Effort is physical or mental exertion. Most of the cases dealing with the significance of additional duties involve the equal effort requirement. Responsibility is the accountability the job requires. For instance, supervisory responsibilities can render jobs unequal.

A test developed in *Hodgson v. Brookhaven General Hospital*,[30] an extra effort case, states principles courts often use in assessing the significance of extra duties to the equal work determination. Generally, extra duties assigned to the higher paid workers will not destroy the substantial equality of two jobs unless the extra duties actually require extra effort (or skill or responsibility), take a significant amount of the time of all of the higher paid workers, and have an economic value to the employer commensurate with the pay difference. Extra duties that do not require extra effort, skill, or responsibility are treated as inconsequential, and the jobs retain their substantial equality. If not all members of the higher-paid group perform the extra duties, the obvious conclusion is that the basis for the pay differential is something else, like the gender of those holding the higher-paid jobs. Moreover, if a lower-paid woman can point to just one higher-paid man whose work is substantially equal to hers and who does not perform the extra duties, she has established this element of her case. That other men receive the same higher pay but actually do the extra tasks is irrelevant.

The fourth requirement for equal work, similar working conditions, is the only one the United States Supreme Court has specifically addressed. In *Corning Glass Works v. Brennan*,[31] the Court held that Congress intended the phrase "similar working conditions" to be defined according to commonly used principles of job evaluation. Under those principles, "working conditions" means "surroundings"

---

[30] 436 F.2d 719, 9 FEP Cases 599 (5th Cir. 1970).
[31] 417 U.S. 188, 9 FEP Cases 919 (1974).

and "hazards," not, as Corning argued, time of day. Thus, a finding of dissimilar working conditions requires jobs with exposure to a greater level of risk or a more unpleasant environment than those to which they are compared.

Defenses

Once the plaintiff in an EPA case has proved the elements of a violation, the defendant can win only by justifying the pay differential under one of the EPA's four exceptions:

- a seniority system,

- a merit system,

- a system that measures earnings by quantity or quality of production, or

- a differential based on any factor other than sex.

Seniority, Merit, and Incentive Systems

The first three defenses share the requirement that the employer have a system. A formal written document may not be necessary, but an employer must regularly use an organized and structured procedure with identified criteria to determine wage differences. Employees should be aware of the system, and, of course, the system must not be based on sex.

Of the three, only the merit system defense has generated much litigation. "Merit" is a vague term, and a scheme of merit evaluations can disguise the very kinds of gender discrimination the EPA was intended to eliminate. **Ratings under a merit system must be based on predetermined criteria applied systematically, not on highly subjective, standardless factors applied haphazardly.** After-the-fact testimony about an employee's merit is not a merit system. An employer should be able to explain how it used its merit system to arrive at each worker's rating and how that rating caused any pay discrepancies among employees doing equal work. A system that merely classifies jobs without providing a basis of evaluation, advancement, or reward does not qualify as a merit system.

Any Factor Other Than Sex

Most of the case law on the EPA affirmative defenses involves the fourth, catch-all defense, "any other factor other than sex." Overt gender considerations of any sort obviously preclude its use, as does blatant reliance on gender-biased market forces. Beyond these bright lines, theoretically almost any justification could be advanced under the fourth affirmative defense. In practice, however, most of the case law centers on a handful of reasons. These include various factors related to the labor market, the economic value of the work performed, head-of-household classifications, training programs, red-circling, temporary or part-time work, and shift differentials.

One of the most difficult questions is the role of market forces in setting wages. Employers may not pay men more than women simply because men have greater bargaining power in the market, but that rule is not always easy to apply in individual cases. For instance, in settings where salary bargaining takes place on an individual basis and the employer has a random pay structure, one man may receive a higher salary because he in fact has more experience or greater skills, and not because of any gender bias in the market. In *Horner v. Mary Institute*,[32] a school hired a male teacher at a higher salary than a female teacher after the man refused to accept the amount offered to (and accepted by) the woman. The Eighth Circuit Court of Appeals said that the school had merely "consider[ed] the market value of the skills of a particular individual," and therefore, the pay difference was based on a factor other than sex.

A related issue is an employer's use of an employee's prior salary in setting initial wages. This practice allows the current employer to take advantage of gender biases in the market and thus perpetuates the underpayment of women. In *Kouba v. Allstate Insurance Co.*,[33] Allstate based an employee's initial salary on several elements, including his or her prior salary. The court recognized that this practice could result in the incorporation of prior discriminatory practices into Allstate's wage structure. It said Allstate could win by showing that its use of prior salaries served as a sales incentive or as a predictor of ability. Similarly,

---

[32]613 F.2d 706, 21 FEP Cases 1069 (8th Cir. 1980).
[33]691 F.2d 873, 30 FEP Cases 57 (9th Cir. 1982).

Price v. Lockheed Space Operations Co.[34] held that basing an employee's pay on prior salary is not a factor other than sex unless the employer can prove business reasons for the practice.

Another category of "factor other than sex" cases that tends to disadvantage women is the payment of benefits only to a "head-of-household." If the employer defines the head of household as the man, the factor is explicitly gender-based and unlawful. If the head of household is defined in neutral terms as an employee who earns more than his or her spouse, men continue to be the primary beneficiaries because of the market forces that undervalue work done by women. Moreover, unlike prior salary, a head-of-household rule is not even arguably job related. Nevertheless, all of the courts of appeals to consider this practice have upheld it as a factor other than sex.

Curing Violations

The EPA contains a "no wage reduction" proviso, which states: "An employer who is paying a wage rate differential in violation of this subsection shall not, in order to comply with this subsection, reduce the wage rate of any employee." Employers can come into compliance with the EPA only by raising the wages of the lower-paid employees immediately, not by reducing the wages of the higher-paid employees or by opening opportunities in the higher-paid jobs that may previously have been unavailable to the lower-paid workers.

The United States Supreme Court's landmark EPA case, *Corning Glass Works v. Brennan,*[35] illustrates the operation of this requirement. For 40 years Corning had operated segregated shifts, with men working at night being paid more than women doing the same jobs during the day. In 1966, the company allowed women to bid for night shift jobs, and within two years half of the night shift jobs were filled by women. In 1969, Corning signed a collective bargaining agreement establishing a uniform wage rate for all new workers on both shifts. The collective bargaining agreement, however, provided for a higher rate for incumbent night shift workers that effectively preserved the 40-year differential between day and night shift workers. By this time both shifts were fully integrated, so that the incumbent night shift consisted of both

---

[34] 856 F.2d 1503, 47 FEP Cases 1851 (11th Cir. 1988).
[35] 417 U.S. 188, 9 FEP Cases 919 (1974).

men and women, as did the lower-paid incumbent day shift. The Court held that the 1966 integration of the night shift was not enough; Corning could cure its violation only by equalizing the wages of the female day shift workers. The wage provision in the 1969 collective bargaining agreement suffered from the same flaw, for the rates it preserved violated the EPA. To cure the violation, the incumbent day shift workers had to receive the same higher rate as the night shift workers.

Comparable Worth

The EPA applies to gender-based wage discrimination only where men and women perform substantially equal work. Title VII of the Civil Rights Act of 1964, enacted the year after the EPA, prohibits gender discrimination in all aspects of employment, including compensation, without an equal work requirement. In *County of Washington v. Gunther*,[36] the United States Supreme Court held that the female plaintiffs could win their Title VII wage discrimination suit if they could prove that their employer intentionally depressed their wages because they were women even if they could not point to any higher-paid men doing equal work.

Gunther thus permitted employees to try to assert claims of comparable worth under Title VII. The premise of this theory is that widespread occupational segregation has caused some jobs to be filled predominantly by women, while other, entirely different jobs are held predominantly by men. The theory asserts that, precisely because women hold them, predominately female jobs receive lower wages than male-dominated jobs of equal value, or comparable worth, to the employer.[37] Comparable worth claims have involved such disparate jobs as nurse and tree trimmer, and secretary and carpet layer. The EPA does not reach this kind of discrimination, because admittedly the two sets of jobs do not satisfy that Act's equal work requirement. The vehicle for asserting claims of comparable worth is Title VII. *Gunther* did not, however, specify the kinds of evidence that could be used to prove sex-based wage discrimination in cases where the work done by men and women was not equal, nor did it endorse a comparable worth

---

[36]452 U.S. 161, 25 FEP Cases 1521 (1981).
[37]Paul Weiler, "The Wages of Sex: The Uses and Limits of Comparable Worth," 99 Harv. L. Rev. 1728 (1986).

theory that would require a comparison of the intrinsic worth of jobs or consideration of statistical evidence quantifying the role of sex discrimination in wage rates.

While *Gunther* permitted the assertion of comparable worth claims, the lower courts have shown great reluctance to find that a wage scheme violates Title VII absent strong "smoking gun" evidence of intentional sex discrimination. When virtually the only evidence of discriminatory intent is a job evaluation or wage survey revealing an undervaluation of predominantly female jobs, courts have not found a violation of Title VII. In *American Federation of State, County & Municipal Employees (AFSCME) v. Washington*,[38] the state commissioned a job evaluation study that disclosed serious disparities between wages paid to predominantly female jobs and those paid to predominantly male jobs with similar rankings in the study. When the state did not correct the situation immediately, the plaintiffs sued, claiming that a failure to correct the known undervaluation of women's jobs supplied the necessary discriminatory intent. The Ninth Circuit Court of Appeals disagreed. The state's practice of setting wages for various jobs based on market rates, rather than on their rating in the job evaluation study, was not enough to prove intentional discrimination. The court said that mere knowledge of a wage disparity is not enough; the plaintiffs must prove that the employer chose the policy because of its discriminatory effect.

AFSCME was a major blow to the comparable worth movement. With its "because of" standard, *AFSCME* created a burden of proof that will be almost impossible for Title VII wage discrimination plaintiffs to meet. Courts cite *AFSCME* for the proposition that an employer's mere reliance on prevailing wages in the labor market is a defense to a Title VII wage discrimination claim.

EMPLOYEE RETIREMENT INCOME SECURITY ACT

Overview

Aside from basic wages or salaries, employers often provide part of an employee's compensation in the form of fringe benefits, such as paid vacations, severance pay, medical coverage, or disability pay-

---

[38]770 F.2d 1401, 38 FEP Cases 1353 (9th Cir. 1985).

ments. In 1974, Congress transformed the law governing most fringe benefits by enacting the Employee Retirement Income Security Act (ERISA).[39] Although much of the legislative history dealt with abuses in the administration and investment of private pension plans, ERISA also covers a wide variety of other common employment fringe benefits. **ERISA does not require employers to provide pensions or any other benefit, nor does it mandate any specific level of benefits if employers choose to offer plans.** Rather, it protects the interests of participants in employee benefit plans and their beneficiaries in enforcing any benefit promise the employer does make by establishing certain minimum standards for all covered plans.

Title I of ERISA deals with the protection of employee rights. It is administered and enforced by the Department of Labor.[40] ERISA covers any employee benefit plan established or maintained by an employer, a union, or both. Exempted are governmental plans; tax-exempt church plans; plans maintained solely to comply with workers' compensation, unemployment compensation, or disability insurance laws; plans maintained outside the United States primarily for nonresident aliens; and excess benefit plans.

Under ERISA the universe of benefit plans is divided into two types, pension benefit plans (or just "pension plans") and welfare benefit plans (or "welfare plans"). Both are subject to statutory structural requirements, reporting and disclosure obligations, fiduciary standards of care, broad preemption of state law, federal court enforcement by the government and private plaintiffs, and civil and criminal remedies for violations. While pension plans are subject to participation, vesting, and funding requirements,[41] ERISA has almost no substantive requirements for welfare plans. ERISA displaces much of the preexisting state law governing welfare benefits, but it does not impose any significant content regulation of its own.

Coverage of Welfare Plans

A welfare benefit plan under ERISA is (1) "any plan, fund or program" (2) established by (3) an employer, an employee organization,

---

[39]29 U.S.C. §§1001-1461 (1993).
[40]29 C.F.R. pts. 2509–70 (1992).
[41]See chapter 10.

or both, (4) for the purpose of providing certain listed benefits, through the purchase of insurance or otherwise, (5) to participants and their beneficiaries. A plan must cover participants because of their status as employees. In *Nationwide Mutual Insurance Co. v. Darden*,[42] the Supreme Court held that ERISA's definition of the term "employee" incorporates traditional principles of law for distinguishing employees from independent contractors.

ERISA's statutory definition of welfare plans lists many common employment fringe benefits:

- medical, surgical, or hospital care or benefits;
- benefits in the event of sickness, accident, disability, death, or unemployment;
- vacation benefits;
- apprenticeship or training programs;
- day care centers;
- scholarship funds;
- prepaid legal services; and
- any benefit allowed by section 302(c) of the Labor Management Relations Act (LMRA) other than pensions.

Section 302(c) of the LMRA authorizes collectively bargained trust funds, jointly administered by employers and unions, that provide certain fringe benefits to employees. It largely duplicates the benefits listed in the ERISA definition, except for the addition of holiday and severance benefits and financial assistance for employee housing.[43]

The Department of Labor has exempted from ERISA coverage certain payroll practices and one-time payments by employers to employees. They include overtime, shift, holiday, or weekend premiums; wage payments out of an employer's general assets, rather than from a trust fund, for absences because of illness, vacations, holidays, active military duty, jury duty, training periods, or sabbatical or other educational leave; and holiday gifts such as turkeys or hams. In *Massachusetts v. Morash*,[44] the United States Supreme Court agreed

---

[42]112 S. Ct. 1344, 14 EB Cases 2625 (1992).
[43]29 U.S.C. §302(c) (1993).
[44]490 U.S. 107, 29 WH Cases 369 (1989).

with the Department of Labor that an employer's practice of paying discharged employees a lump sum for unused vacation time out of its general assets is not a welfare plan under ERISA.

Although the statute imposes various structural requirements on ERISA plans, compliance with these requirements is not necessary for coverage. Courts have found that very casual practices, including oral promises or a few sentences in an employee handbook, are covered plans, even when the employer was not aware it was maintaining an ERISA plan.

Requirements

ERISA requires all benefit plans to be in writing. Failure to comply with this requirement does not, however, affect coverage. If a plan meets the statutory definition, which does not contain a written document requirement, ERISA applies. If the employer has not prepared a written document, it probably has not complied with other statutory obligations, such as the reporting and disclosure requirements, but these are independent violations with their own penalties, and they do not affect the question of coverage.

Summary Plan Descriptions

ERISA also requires the plan administrator to issue a summary plan description (SPD), providing a plain English version of the plan to participants and beneficiaries. The SPD must be in writing, written in a manner calculated to be understood by the average plan participant, and sufficiently accurate and comprehensive to apprise participants and beneficiaries of their rights and obligations under the plan. The statute and accompanying regulations set forth a detailed list of the information the SPD must contain. The plan administrator must furnish an SPD to each participant or beneficiary within 90 days after that person becomes a participant or starts receiving benefits, and updated SPDs must be provided periodically. In addition, the administrator must furnish a copy of the latest updated SPD upon written request of a participant or beneficiary.

Although the formal plan document can sometimes serve as the SPD as well, normally the SPD is a separate document, printed in booklet or brochure form, like an employee handbook. The SPD may be the only written explanation employees receive about their benefits. Although the SPD must be an accurate summary of the plan, subtleties in eligibility and coverage may become lost in the translation from the formal plan document to the SPD. When the SPD entitles an employee to benefits, but the formal plan document does not, courts generally enforce the SPD if the participant or beneficiary reasonably relied on it, even if the SPD contains a statement that the plan document will control in case of conflict.

Other Reporting and Disclosure Requirements

ERISA imposes extensive reporting and disclosure requirements on all covered plans. The plan administrator must file an annual report and other information with the Department of Labor. The plan administrator must periodically furnish certain documents and information directly to participants and beneficiaries. These include summary annual reports, summary plan descriptions, summaries of material modifications, and for pension plans, statements of total accrued benefits and vested pension benefits. Information must also be provided upon the written request of participants and beneficiaries, or upon the occurrence of a COBRA qualifying event (as described below in "COBRA Amendments").

Claims Procedures

Every ERISA plan must establish and maintain a claims and appeal procedure. The plan must give participants or beneficiaries whose claims for benefits have been denied written notice of the specific reasons for the denial and provide them a reasonable opportunity for a full and fair review of that decision.

Every plan is thus required to establish a "reasonable claims procedure," as defined in Department of Labor regulations. **The summary plan description must describe the procedures for presenting claims for benefits and the remedies available under the plan if a claim is denied.**

The plan must give a claimant notice of denial of the claim for benefits within a reasonable period of time, no more than 90 days, after filing of the claim. If the plan does not give notice within that time, the claim is considered denied, and the claimant may proceed to the review stage of the claims procedure. A notice denying a claim for benefits must be written in plain language, and it must provide specific reasons for the denial. It must refer to the specific plan provisions on which denial is based, it must give a detailed description of any additional material or information the claimant needs to complete the claim, and it must provide information on the steps necessary to appeal the denial.

Each ERISA plan must also establish a procedure for the appeal of a denial of benefits. The appeals procedure must allow claimants to make a written request for review, to review pertinent documents, and to submit issues and comments in writing. The plan may establish a time limit for appeals of at least 60 days after the claimant receives written notice of the claim denial. The review decision must normally be made within 60 days after receipt of the request for review or the appeal is treated as denied. The decision on review must be in writing and include specific reasons for the decision, with specific references to the plan documents. Generally, a participant or beneficiary may not sue under ERISA to challenge a denial of benefits unless he or she has first used the plan's claims procedures.

COBRA Amendments

While ERISA contains detailed substantive regulation of pension benefit plans, as originally enacted it did not regulate any of the terms of welfare benefit plans. The one departure from this norm came in the Consolidated Omnibus Budget Reconciliation Act of 1985 (COBRA),[45] which requires sponsors of group health plans to offer participants and beneficiaries the chance to elect continuation coverage under the plan when a "qualifying event" that would otherwise cause a loss of coverage occurs. COBRA applies to group health plans maintained by all employers except churches, federal government entities, state and local government entities that do not receive funds under the Public Health Service Act, and employers that "normally employed fewer than 20 employees on a typical business day during the preceding calendar year."

---

[45]Pub. L. No. 99-272, 100 Stat. 82, as amended, Pub. L. No. 99-509, 100 Stat. 2076 (1986); Pub. L. No. 99-514, 100 Stat. 2085 (1986); Pub. L. No. 101-239, 103 Stat. 2106 (1989).

Qualified Beneficiary

ERISA requires the plan to offer continuation coverage to "each qualified beneficiary" who suffers a "qualifying event." A qualified beneficiary is an employee who was covered by the plan on the day before the qualifying event, as well as the covered employee's spouse or dependent children who were covered on the day before the qualifying event. Retired employees, their spouses (or surviving spouses), and their dependent children can also be qualified beneficiaries in certain circumstances.

Qualifying Event

An event is a qualifying event only if it would result in loss of coverage under the plan but for the right to elect continuation coverage. There are different qualifying events for employees and for their spouses and dependents. For employees, there are two qualifying events, a termination of employment for any reason other than discharge for "gross misconduct," or a reduction of hours. The statute does not define the kind of termination for "gross misconduct" that will cause the loss of COBRA rights. The few courts to consider the question have adopted the gross misconduct standard used under state unemployment insurance laws, which requires proof of willful, wanton, intentional, or substantial disregard of the employer's interests.

For spouses and dependents, the qualifying events are the same as for employees, plus the death of the covered employee, divorce or legal separation from the employee, the employee's becoming entitled to Medicare benefits, and a dependent child's ceasing to be a dependent under the terms of the plan. Additionally, for retired employees, a bankruptcy reorganization proceeding that results in a "substantial elimination of coverage" within one year of its commencement is a qualifying event.

Commencement and Length of Continuation Coverage

As a general matter, the period of continuation coverage begins on the date of the qualifying event, not the date on which coverage would otherwise have been lost. For instance, if an employee is fired in the middle of a month, but the employer has paid for coverage under the health care plan through the end of the month, the COBRA period (assuming the employee elects continuation coverage) runs from the date of discharge. Under a 1989 amendment to COBRA, a plan may choose to follow this general rule, or it may choose to defer the beginning of the COBRA period until the loss of coverage actually occurs.

The length of required continuation coverage depends on the qualifying event. If the qualifying event is termination of employment or reduction in hours, the COBRA period is normally 18 months. If, however, the qualified beneficiary is determined to have been disabled under Title II or XVI of the Social Security Act at the time of the loss of employment or reduction of hours, the COBRA period is extended to 29 months. If another qualifying event, like a divorce or separation, occurs during the original 18- or 29-month period, the COBRA period is extended to 36 months, but only for individuals who were qualified beneficiaries when the first qualifying event took place and who remained covered at the time of the second event.

If the qualifying event is the death of the employee, divorce or separation, loss of dependent child status, or eligibility for Medicare, the COBRA period is 36 months. Any time an employee becomes eligible for Medicare, regardless of whether there is a qualifying event, COBRA coverage must be provided for the spouse and dependent children for at least 36 months following the date of eligibility. For retirees whose qualifying event is the employer's bankruptcy, COBRA coverage must be offered for the life of the retiree. If the retiree dies and leaves a surviving spouse or dependent children, COBRA coverage for them extends an additional 36 months beyond the date of the retiree's death.

COBRA coverage can end before the expiration of any of these periods if the employer stops providing any group health plan to any employee, if the beneficiary fails to pay the premium, or if the beneficiary becomes entitled to Medicare. Coverage under another group health plan terminates COBRA coverage only if the second plan does not exclude or limit any preexisting condition of the beneficiary. If the employee or dependents were covered under a preexisting plan before the date of the qualifying event, they are considered covered under this test. For instance, an employee who is covered under both his employer's plan and as a spouse under his wife's employer's plan is not eligible for COBRA under his employer's plan.

Type of Coverage and Premium

Coverage offered under COBRA must be identical to the coverage available to the beneficiary immediately before the qualifying event. If coverage provided similarly situated active employees is changed, the COBRA beneficiary must be given the same rights with respect to the new coverage as active employees who have not had a qualifying event.

The plan may charge a COBRA beneficiary a premium for continuation coverage of no more than 102 percent of the plan's cost for a similarly situated beneficiary; a disabled beneficiary who is entitled to 29 months of coverage may be charged 150 percent of the applicable premium after the first 18 months of COBRA coverage. The plan may not require payment of any premium until 45 days after the date on which the beneficiary makes the initial election for continuation coverage.

Notice Requirements and Election Rights

COBRA contains two separate notice requirements. Upon the commencement of coverage under a health care plan to which COBRA applies, the plan administrator must provide each participant and his or her spouse a notice of continuation coverage rights. Coverage can commence because an employee is hired by the plan sponsor, or because the plan becomes subject to COBRA by, for instance, meeting the 20-employee requirement.

The second notice requirement is triggered by a qualifying event. The employer must notify the plan administrator within 30 days after a covered employee's death, termination of employment, reduction of hours, or Medicare eligibility, or the commencement of bankruptcy proceedings. If the employer continues to pay for coverage after the qualifying event, it may delay this notice until the date coverage is lost, but then the COBRA period does not begin to run until the loss of coverage. The qualified beneficiary has the duty to notify the plan administrator within 60 days after a divorce, legal separation, or a child's loss of dependency status. The plan administrator then has 14 days to notify each qualified beneficiary of the right to elect continuation coverage.

A qualified beneficiary must elect coverage within 60 days after the date coverage terminates under the plan because of the qualifying event or the date he or she receives notice of COBRA election rights from the plan administrator, whichever is later. An election made any time during the 60-day period relates back to the date coverage was lost because of the qualifying event. The Eleventh Circuit Court of Appeals has held that if the plan administrator knows that the qualified beneficiary is incompetent at the time of the qualifying event, the COBRA notification is effective only if it is mailed to a person capable of making, and willing to make, an informed decision about the election of continuation coverage on behalf of the beneficiary.[46]

Remedies

Failure to comply with COBRA requirements can be remedied through suit under ERISA, and relief can include all the benefits that would have been paid if no violation had occurred. In addition, failure to provide the required notices can subject plan administrators to a $100 per day penalty. In addition to the ERISA penalties, the Internal Revenue Code imposes severe tax consequences on nongovernmental employers that fail to comply with the COBRA requirements.

Interference With Benefit Accrual

Like most other remedial labor legislation, ERISA contains an antiretaliation provision that safeguards workers' statutory rights by protecting the underlying employment relationship on which those rights are based. It is unlawful "for any person to discharge, fine, suspend, expel, discipline, or discriminate against a participant or beneficiary for exercising any right to which he is entitled under the provisions of an employee benefit plan, [or] this title, . . . or for the purpose of interfering with the attainment of any right to which such participant may become entitled under the plan, [or] this title. . . ."

This provision contains two separate protections. The first, patterned on the antiretaliation provisions of other labor laws, is straightforward; it prohibits any adverse employment action in retaliation for the exercise of a right to seek benefits. For instance, an employer violates the Act if it fires an employee because the employee filed a claim for benefits under an ERISA plan or sued under ERISA to recover denied benefits.

---

[46]Meadows v. Cagle's, Inc., 954 F.2d 686, 14 EB Cases 2513 (11th Cir. 1992).

The second form of antiretaliation protection is unique to ERISA. Congressional committees heard stories of employees who were fired after many years of faithful service, just before they were to become eligible for a pension or other employment benefit. Congress sought to deter this kind of employer misconduct both by imposing relatively short vesting requirements for pension plans[47] and by prohibiting employers from discriminating against employees in order to prevent them from attaining rights under ERISA plans. Thus, an employer that fires an employee in order to block that employee's vesting in the employer's pension plan violates the Act. Although Congress was concerned with protecting employees' ability to obtain vested pension rights, the courts have given this provision a much broader reading. Discrimination intended to interfere with the attainment of *any* rights under an ERISA plan is prohibited. Employees who are already fully vested in the employer's pension plan are protected from discharge or other adverse actions aimed at preventing them from accruing additional pension rights. Participation in ERISA welfare plans is also protected, even though welfare plans rarely provide for vested rights.

Another unique aspect of ERISA's antiretaliation provision is that it provides rights to both "participants" and "beneficiaries." Participants are employees or former employees who are or may become eligible for benefits, and beneficiaries are those "designated by a participant" to receive benefits, normally an employee's spouse and children. **Thus, employers are prohibited from firing an employee to prevent medical claims on behalf of the employee's dependent child**. Although one group of nonemployees, beneficiaries, is protected by this section, another significant group, job applicants, is not. Applicants do not satisfy the statutory definition of participant, which is pegged to employee status. Therefore, applicants who are refused employment because they or their dependents may make large claims against the employer's health care plan do not have a claim under ERISA. Those applicants may, however, have rights under the Americans with Disabilities Act (ADA).[48]

A major problem under ERISA's antiretaliation provision, as with other discrimination statutes, is proof of the necessary employer intent. In one sense, every discharge interferes with the employee's ability to

---

[47]See chapter 10.
[48]See chapter 2's discussion of "Disability Discrimination."

accrue and receive benefits offered by the employer, because fired employees normally lose all nonvested benefits. The courts have not allowed this provision to become a general wrongful discharge statute, however. Plaintiffs must prove more than the fact that their discharge prevented them from receiving future benefits; they must prove that the employer acted with specific intent to interfere with their ERISA rights. The loss of benefits must have been a motivating factor for the employer's actions, not merely a consequence of them. The mere fact that the employer's actions resulted in a savings is not enough, standing alone, to prove the necessary intent. Absent evidence that the employer was concerned only with benefit costs, as opposed to general payroll costs, plaintiffs have to find other strong circumstantial evidence, such as the timing of the discharge.

Folz v. Marriott Corp.[49] illustrates the use of circumstantial evidence to prove a violation. The general manager of a hotel was fired shortly after he told his supervisor he had multiple sclerosis. The employer claimed the discharge was for poor performance, but the court found that reason pretextual. Among other things, the plaintiff had a history of good performance during his 18 years with the company, he had never received poor evaluations until his illness, the employer failed to follow its normal procedure of probation rather than discharge, and the employer had a strong financial incentive to fire him, because its medical and disability plans were self-funded. On the other hand, the court found no violation in *Phelps v. Field Real Estate Co.*,[50] in which a sales manager with AIDS was fired. The court noted that the plaintiff was not fired until 14 months after he initially disclosed his illness, his sales division had not been meeting the company's expectations, and there was no evidence that management officials ever calculated the potential benefit costs of plaintiff's illness.

Instead of firing an employee to avoid paying benefit claims, an employer might decide simply to eliminate the particular benefit. ERISA does not require employers to provide benefits, nor does it regulate the level of benefits that employers do offer. While ERISA regulates some kinds of pension plan terminations, employers can freely terminate or modify welfare plan benefits unless they have promised not to do so.

---

[49]594 F. Supp. 1007, 5 EB Cases 2244 (W.D. Mo. 1984).
[50]991 F.2d 645 (10th Cir. 1993).

The much-discussed case of *McGann v. H & H Music Co.*[51] involved not a plan termination, but a modification affecting only the plaintiff. After learning that McGann had been diagnosed as having AIDS, his employer modified its health care plan by becoming self-insured and placing a $5,000 cap on lifetime benefits for AIDS. It retained the preexisting $1 million lifetime cap for all other medical conditions. The company conceded that its action was prompted by knowledge of McGann's illness and a desire to avoid the high medical costs associated with AIDS. McGann's claim that this change violated ERISA's antiretaliation section was rejected by the Fifth Circuit Court of Appeals. The court reasoned that the employer had never promised not to change the terms of its health care plan, and therefore it had an absolute right to do so. Because McGann did not have a right to the continued availability of the $1 million cap, he was not deprived of any right to which he was entitled under the employer's plan. The court noted that although McGann was the company's first employee with AIDS, the $5,000 limit on AIDS coverage applied to all employees.

McGann also illustrates a major advantage to employers of having a self-funded health care plan. Commercial health insurance is subject to regulation by each state. In many states, changes without notice to policyholders and the exclusion, differentiation, or elimination of coverage for particular medical conditions are unlawful. Indeed, following *McGann*, Texas amended its insurance laws to prohibit the cancellation of an accident or sickness policy during its term because the insured has been diagnosed with HIV infection or AIDS. Even if the amendment had predated his illness, however, it would not have benefited Mr. McGann. As discussed more fully later in this chapter, ERISA permits the operation of state insurance laws, but it neither allows states to regulate the content of self-funded ERISA plans nor imposes its own substantive requirements for those plans.

Civil Enforcement of Benefit Rights

The civil enforcement provision of ERISA authorizes a number of legal actions, four of which may be used for benefit claims litigation. First, participants or beneficiaries may bring lawsuits to recover ben-

---

[51]946 F.2d 401, 14 EB Cases 1729 (5th Cir. 1991), *cert. denied sub nom.* Greenberg v. H & H Music Co., 113 S. Ct. 482, 16 EB Cases 1432 (1992).

efits due them under the plan, to enforce their rights under the plan, or to clarify their rights to future benefits under the plan. Second, participants, beneficiaries, or fiduciaries may sue to prevent any act that violates ERISA or the terms of the plan, or to obtain "other appropriate equitable relief" to redress statutory or plan violations or to enforce provisions of the statute or the plan. Third, a participant, beneficiary, fiduciary, or the Secretary of Labor may seek relief for breach of ERISA's fiduciary obligations. Fourth, a plan participant or beneficiary may sue the plan administrator for failure to comply with a request for information that ERISA requires the administrator to furnish. The remedy for this violation is a civil penalty of up to $100 per day.

Judicial Review of Fiduciary Decisions

Questions of coverage under welfare benefit plans, especially health care plans, arise constantly. Some involve interpreting the terms of the benefit plan and applying them to undisputed facts, while others may require decisions about the underlying facts. For example, is a particular medical procedure an "experimental" treatment excluded from coverage under a health care plan? Are services rendered to a patient at an extended care facility medical treatment or merely "rehabilitative" or "custodial" in nature? When a company sells a plant or a division, are employees who continue in the buyer's employment without missing a day of work entitled to benefits under the seller's severance pay plan? These questions, plus many more, eventually find their way to court as ERISA suits. Those courts must then determine the standard of review to apply to the plan fiduciary's decision.

In *Firestone Tire & Rubber Co. v. Bruch*,[52] the United States Supreme Court said that courts should review benefits decisions under a de novo standard, "unless the benefit plan gives the administrator or fiduciary discretionary authority to determine eligibility for benefits or to construe the terms of the plan." De novo review means that the reviewing court is free to make its own decision, without regard to the decision of the administrator. If the plan does give the administrator discretion, the standard of review is arbitrary and capricious. Under this standard, a court will uphold a decision denying benefits if the decision

---

[52] 489 U.S. 101, 10 EB Cases 1873 (1989).

is based on a reasonable interpretation of the plan's terms and the evidence before the fiduciary at the time of the decision. Procedural violations, such as failure to file required documents with the Department of Labor, failure to provide summary plan descriptions to participants and beneficiaries, or failure to comply with requests for information, normally do not affect the application of the arbitrary and capricious standard of review.

Therefore, the threshold question in any suit challenging a benefits denial is whether the plan language gives the administrator or fiduciary the kind of discretionary authority that will cause a court to use an arbitrary and capricious, rather than a de novo, standard of review. Clauses granting administrators the power "to interpret," "to construe," "to determine eligibility," "to determine coverage," "to determine all questions arising in connection with the administration, interpretation, and application of the Plan" have been held to confer *Firestone's* discretionary authority. On the other hand, language that fails clearly and expressly to delegate some form of discretion in decision making does not invoke deferential review. While one court has commented that "magic words (such as 'the committee has discretion to . . .') are unnecessary," presumably a body of judicially approved clauses is fast developing, and plan sponsors and administrators who want to be certain of obtaining deferential review of their benefits decisions will amend their plans to include that language.

Preemption

ERISA contains an extremely broad preemption provision. It bars state regulation of benefit plans even as to matters on which ERISA is silent. For that reason, ERISA preemption has had its most dramatic effect on welfare plans. Although state laws relating to pensions are also preempted, ERISA contains substantive federal standards for pension plans. ERISA does not, however, regulate the content of welfare plans. Federal preemption thus displaces a vast body of state law dealing with fringe benefits. **If the state law requires an ERISA-covered benefit plan to offer a particular benefit, ERISA preemption prevents the enforcement of that law and leaves a void in its place**. If the state law provides a means for enforcing benefit rights, ERISA preempts it, and the claimant must bring an action under ERISA instead.

ERISA preempts "any and all State laws insofar as they may now or hereafter relate to any employee benefit plan" covered by the Act. Exceptions include state laws that regulate insurance, banking, or securities; generally applicable criminal laws; parts of Hawaii's Prepaid Health Care Act; qualified domestic relations orders that are exempted from ERISA's anti-alienation provision;[53] and state laws prohibiting health care plans from requiring beneficiaries to use Medicaid before they may receive plan benefits.

Covered Plan

ERISA's preemption provision applies only to employee benefit plans covered by the statute. States may apply their own laws to plans that are exempt from ERISA coverage, such as government plans and church plans. In *Massachusetts v. Morash*,[54] the United States Supreme Court approved Department of Labor regulations exempting from ERISA coverage certain "payroll practices," including the payment of vacation pay out of an employer's general assets. Under the regulations, the employer's practice of paying terminated employees for their unused vacation time was not a covered plan, and therefore Massachusetts could apply its wage payment law to require payment in full on the date of the discharge.

"Relate to"

ERISA preempts state laws that "relate to" an ERISA-covered plan. The Supreme Court has said that these words should be construed expansively, and that a law "relates to" an employee benefit plan "if it has a connection with or reference to such a plan."[55] Both direct and indirect state actions that relate to covered plans are preempted. State laws that relate to ERISA plans are preempted even if they do not conflict with ERISA's requirements, even if they are consistent with ERISA's underlying purposes, and even if they deal with matters that ERISA does not address. For example, ERISA does not mandate that plans provide any particular level of welfare benefits, yet state laws

---

[53]See in chapter 10, "Alienation or Assignment of Benefits."
[54]490 U.S. 107, 29 WH Cases 369 (1989).
[55]Shaw v. Delta Air Lines, Inc., 463 U.S. 85, 32 FEP Cases 121 (1983).

requiring welfare plans to provide certain benefits are preempted. Similarly, an employee who claims he or she was fired to prevent vesting in the employer's pension plan may not bring a wrongful discharge suit under state law. That state claim is preempted, and the employee must sue under ERISA for violation of its anti-alienation provision.[56]

The Insurance Saving Clause and the Deemer Clause

Although the scope of ERISA's preemption provision is very broad, its "saving clause" returns significant power to the states by exempting from the scope of the preemption provision "any state law that regulates insurance . . ." and permitting states to continue their traditional role as primary regulators of the insurance industry. At the same time, Congress wanted to prevent the states from subjecting ERISA plans to their general insurance laws by claiming the plans were insurers under state law. The "deemer clause" qualifies the saving clause by providing that no employee benefit plan shall be deemed to be an insurance company "for purposes of any law of any state purporting to regulate insurance companies, [or] insurance contracts. . . ." The combination of these confusing clauses means that any entity engaged in the business of insurance, except an ERISA plan, is subject to state insurance regulation.

In *Metropolitan Life Insurance Co. v. Massachusetts*,[57] the United States Supreme Court held that the saving clause applies both to traditional insurance laws, such as those that regulate the manner in which insurance may be sold, and to laws that deal with the content of insurance contracts. States may regulate the content of insurance policies by, for instance, requiring certain benefits to be included in any health care policy sold in the state, but they may not impose the same requirements on self-funded ERISA plans.

The combination of these clauses results in different treatment of insured and uninsured plans. **Employers that are able to self-insure can avoid the increasing number of state laws mandating minimum health care benefits**. This distinction has enormous significance for health policy. Our current system of health care relies heavily on

---

[56]Ingersoll-Rand Co. v. McClendon, 498 U.S. 133 (1990).
[57]471 U.S. 724, 119 LRRM 2569 (1985).

benefits provided through employment. Any state attempts at improving the delivery of health care services or controlling health care costs through regulation of employer-provided health care plans will never be fully effective because of ERISA preemption. States can regulate insured plans through their insurance laws, but they cannot reach self-insured plans. *Standard Oil Co. v. Agsalud*[58] struck down the Hawaii Prepaid Health Care Act, which required all workers in the state to be covered by a comprehensive health care plan, on exactly these grounds. After years of effort, Hawaii's congressional delegation obtained passage of an amendment to ERISA's preemption provision exempting portions of the Hawaii law. Hawaii remains the only state whose health care law is exempted, although only partially, from ERISA preemption. Any further state efforts at reform in this area would require a waiver from ERISA.

LEAVES OF ABSENCE

Federal Law

Maternity, Paternity, and Family Leave

The Family and Medical Leave Act of 1993 (FMLA)[59] for the first time requires as a matter of federal law that employers provide leaves of absence for childbirth, for the care of sick children or other family members, or for an employee's own illness. The FMLA covers employers with 50 or more employees and state and local government agencies. These employers must permit eligible workers to take up to 12 weeks of unpaid leave in any 12-month period for the birth, adoption, or placement for foster care of a child, to care for a child, spouse, or parent with a serious health condition, or for the worker's own serious health condition that makes him or her unable to perform the job. To be eligible for FMLA leave, a worker must have been employed by the employer for at least 12 months and have at least 1,250 hours of service in the 12-month period preceding the leave. In addition, the employer must

---

[58]442 F. Supp. 695 (N.D. Cal. 1977), *aff'd*, 633 F.2d 760, 2 EB Cases 1559 (9th Cir. 1980), *aff'd*, 454 U.S. 801, 2 EB Cases 2044 (1981).
[59]29 U.S.C. §§2601–54 (1993).

have at least 50 employees within a 75-mile radius of the employee's worksite. Thus, an employee who works at a small far-flung branch of a major employer might not qualify for FMLA leave.

A "serious health condition" is an illness, injury, impairment, or physical or mental condition that involves inpatient care or continuing treatment by a health care provider. Department of Labor regulations specifically include prenatal care as a serious health condition, but they exclude routine physical examinations.[60] An employer may require medical certification, including a second or third opinion at its expense, of the need for a leave to care for a sick relative or for the employee's own illness. The employer may request recertification at reasonable intervals (not more than once every 30 days). As discussed in chapter 2, the Americans with Disabilities Act generally prohibits employers from asking about employees' or applicants' medical conditions or from requiring physical examinations of employees unless the examinations are job related and consistent with business necessity. The medical certification provisions of the FMLA create one situation in which employers may acquire information about an employee's health condition. Courts may well interpret these provisions narrowly to harmonize them with the ADA, so employers should be careful not to ask for information the FMLA does not specifically authorize.

When leave for childbirth, adoption, or placement for foster care is foreseeable, the employee must give at least 30 days' notice of his or her intention to take a leave. When medical leave is foreseeable because of a planned treatment, the employee must make a reasonable effort to schedule the treatment in a manner that will not unduly disrupt the employer's operations, and give 30 days' notice. If the employee cannot give 30 days' notice, he or she must give notice as soon as possible. Leave for birth, adoption, or placement for foster care must be completed within one year of the event. If a husband and wife work for the same employer, the employer may limit their aggregate number of weeks of leave for birth, adoption, placement for foster care, or care of a sick parent to 12 in a 12-month period. Employees taking leave to care for a sick family member or because of their own serious health condition may take their leave intermittently or on a reduced leave schedule when medically necessary. When an employee requests intermittent or reduced schedule leave, the employer may temporarily

---

[60]29 C.F.R. pt. 825 (1992).

transfer him or her to a different job that can better accommodate the recurring periods of leave, as long as the employee is qualified for the job and the new job has equivalent pay and benefits.

The FMLA does not require paid leave, although an employee may elect, or the employer may require, the substitution of accrued paid leave for any part of the 12-week leave provided by the Act. The Act specifically states that providing unpaid FMLA leave to a salaried employee who would otherwise come within one of the FLSA's white-collar exemptions, discussed earlier in this chapter, will not cause the loss of the FLSA exemption.

During the leave the employer must continue to provide health care benefits at the same level and under the same conditions as if the employee were actively at work. If the employee fails to return from leave for a reason other than the continuation, recurrence, or onset of a serious health condition that would entitle the employee to FMLA leave, or for some other reason beyond the employee's control, the employer may "recover" any premium it paid to maintain the employee's coverage during the leave. The FMLA does not specify how this "recovery" is to be made. If the employer deducts the premiums from any amounts due to the employee, it may violate the restrictions on deductions contained in most state wage payment laws, discussed earlier in this chapter. Unless the courts find that the recovery of premiums provision of the FMLA preempts state law, an employer may be limited to suing an employee who does not voluntarily repay the premiums.

When the employee returns from leave, the employer must restore him or her to the same or an equivalent position, with no loss of employment benefits accrued before the date the leave began. There is an exception to the requirement of reinstatement for "key employees." The employer may deny reinstatement (but not the granting of leave in the first place) to a salaried employee who is among the highest paid 10 percent of the employees within 75 miles of the facility where the employee works, if the denial is "necessary to prevent substantial and grievous economic injury" to its operations, if the employer notifies the employee of its determination, and if the employee does not return to work after receiving this notice.

The enforcement mechanisms of the FMLA are similar to those under the FLSA. The FMLA may be enforced through suit in either federal or state court by employees individually or on behalf of themselves and other similarly situated employees, or by the Secretary of Labor. An employee's right to bring suit terminates if the Secretary brings a legal action on his or her behalf. The statute of limitations is two years, or three years for willful violations. The Department of Labor may receive and investigate employee complaints, but, as under the FLSA, there is no administrative prerequisite to suit.

Remedies for violations of the Act include lost wages and benefits plus interest, or, if the employee has not lost any wages or benefits, any actual monetary losses the employee sustained as a direct result of the violation, up to the equivalent of 12 weeks' pay, plus interest. In addition, plaintiffs may recover an amount equal to the monetary recovery as liquidated damages, subject to reduction by the court if the employer proves it acted in good faith and with reasonable grounds for believing it was not in violation of the Act. The court must award a victorious plaintiff reasonable attorney fees, reasonable expert witness fees, and costs.

Employers with fewer than 50 employees are not covered by the FMLA and therefore are not required by that Act to grant any leaves. The provision of leaves of absence is also regulated less directly by Title VII. If an employer not covered by the FMLA does choose to offer leaves, or if covered employers offer leaves under more generous conditions than required by the FMLA, they must do so on a nondiscriminatory basis.

The Pregnancy Discrimination Act (PDA), an amendment to Title VII,[61] requires that employers treat workers disabled by pregnancy, childbirth, or related medical conditions the same for all employment-related purposes as employees disabled by other conditions. Therefore, if an employer provides leaves of absence for employees who cannot work because of illness or injury, it must provide leaves on the same basis and with the same conditions for the period of a female employee's pregnancy-related disability. An employer may not, for instance, limit the length of a leave for pregnancy-related disabilities if it does not place the same limit on other kinds of medical leaves. In addition, a failure to provide any leave at all for pregnancy-related disabilities, or the provision of seriously inadequate leave, may, upon

---

[61]42 U.S.C. §2000e(k) (1993).

a proper statistical showing, constitute unlawful pregnancy discrimination under Title VII's disparate impact theory.[62]

Employers may, if they wish, treat workers with pregnancy-related disabilities more favorably than they treat workers with other conditions. In *California Federal Savings & Loan Association v. Guerra*,[63] the United States Supreme Court held that the PDA did not preempt a California statute requiring employers to provide up to four months' unpaid leave to workers disabled by pregnancy and childbirth. One of the Court's rationales was that "Congress intended the PDA to be a floor beneath which pregnancy disability benefits may not drop—not a ceiling above which they may not rise." The Court carefully noted that the California statute was limited to the period of actual disability and therefore did not reflect stereotypes about the general abilities of pregnant workers. Under *Cal Fed*, then, employers may provide a leave of absence for the period of disability caused by pregnancy and childbirth, even if the FMLA does not require them to offer any other form of disability leave.

It is important to distinguish between a leave granted because of the disability caused by pregnancy and childbirth and a leave granted for other reasons. If a "maternity leave" extends beyond the time when the female worker is actually disabled by pregnancy and childbirth, it becomes to that extent a childcare, or personal, leave. *Cal Fed* does not apply to nondisability personal leaves of absence for reasons such as childcare, and such leaves must be equally available to men and women. An employer would violate Title VII if, for example, it allowed female employees, but not male employees, to take a one-year leave of absence to care for a newborn child, without regard to the length of time the woman was actually disabled.

Leaves for Military Service

The Veterans' Reemployment Rights Act (VRRA),[64] also known as the Vietnam Era Veterans' Readjustment Assistance Act, gives

---

[62]Abraham v. Graphic Arts Int'l Union, 660 F.2d 811, 26 FEP Cases 818 (D.C. Cir. 1981). See chapter 2 for a discussion of the disparate impact theory under Title VII.

[63]479 U.S. 272, 42 FEP Cases 1073 (1987).

[64]38 U.S.C. §§4301–07 (1993). The current Act is essentially a reenactment of legislation in effect since the Selective Training and Service Act of 1940.

individuals who have completed their military service with an honorable discharge the right to reemployment with their former employer upon certain conditions. The Act protects both individuals who have enlisted or been inducted into full time active duty, and members of the Reserves and the National Guard, whose service is generally for shorter periods of time. It applies to public sector as well as private sector employers.

Returning veterans must apply for reemployment with their preservice employer within 90 days after discharge from the military. Reservists and members of the National Guard who are ordered to active duty for training for a period of not less than 12 weeks and reservists who are ordered to active duty for not more than 90 days must apply for reemployment within 31 days after release from active duty. Although a written application is not required, the returning veteran must give adequate notice to the preservice employer of his or her veteran status and desire for reemployment.

The preservice employer must restore a returning veteran to his or her previous job or to a similar position, unless the veteran is no longer qualified to perform the job duties. The veteran must be reemployed without loss of seniority and treated as if there had been no absence for military service. Therefore, the returning veteran is entitled to any general pay raises or automatic promotions granted in his or her absence, but not to increases or promotions made on the basis of merit, experience, or similar factors. Similarly, returning veterans are entitled to pension credit for the time they spent on military leave. A returning inductee or enlistee may not be fired without cause for one year following reemployment; a reservist or National Guard member called to active duty training or a reservist called to active duty receives a six-month protection from discharge without cause.

The statute places some limits on the duration of these reemployment rights. While there is no limit on the duration of the service of inductees, those who enlist in the Armed Forces and those who go on active duty as a result of an order or call to duty retain their right to reemployment with their preservice employers as long as their tours do not exceed a maximum of five years.

Special rules apply to members of the Reserves and the National Guard for periods of active or inactive duty that do not fall within any of the other categories. This includes, for instance, weekend drills, summer training sessions, or even longer periods of active duty.

Employers must grant the reservist or National Guard member a leave of absence for these periods upon request, and they may not fire or otherwise deny any "incident or advantage of employment" to those individuals because of their military obligations. This prohibition provides the reservist with rights similar to the for-cause protection accorded other returning veterans. In *Monroe v. Standard Oil Co.*[65] the United States Supreme Court read this protection narrowly and refused to impose a reasonable accommodation requirement that would have forced employers to provide special scheduling privileges to reservists.

LEAVES OF ABSENCE

State Law

Maternity, Paternity, and Family Leave

Approximately half the states have legislation requiring covered employers to provide family or medical leaves in certain circumstances. In addition, a number of states have leave laws that apply only to state employees.[66] These are often part of general personnel or civil service statutes governing the state and its subdivisions, and they will not be discussed in this chapter.

The most comprehensive of the state laws applicable to the private as well as the public sector require covered employers to grant employees of either sex unpaid leave for the birth or adoption of a child or for the serious illness of an immediate family member. Eight states and the District of Columbia currently have such family leave laws;[67] in addition, Hawaii's family leave law became effective on July 1, 1994. Of these, six also require leaves for the employee's own medical condition.[68] Minnesota's law permits leave only for birth or adoption,

---

[65]452 U.S. 549, 107 LRRM 2633 (1981).

[66]Alaska, Arizona, Colorado, Delaware, Florida, Georgia, Illinois, Iowa, Kansas, Kentucky, Maryland, Montana, Nebraska, North Carolina, North Dakota, Oklahoma, South Carolina, Utah, and West Virginia.

[67]California, Connecticut, District of Columbia, Maine, New Jersey, Oregon, Rhode Island, Vermont, and Wisconsin.

[68]Connecticut, District of Columbia, Maine, Rhode Island, Vermont, and Wisconsin.

but it also requires employers to permit workers to use their sick leave to care for an ill or injured child. Washington permits leave for birth, adoption, or to care for a terminally ill child.

The length of the required leave varies from four weeks in one calendar year to four months in a 24-month period.[69] A few states impose restrictions, similar to those found in the FMLA, on the aggregate amount of leave a husband and wife working for the same employer may take.[70] Oregon requires parents to share parental leave even if they work for different employers.

All of these family leave statutes require that employees have worked for the employer for a specified period of time before being eligible for family leave.[71] Employees are generally required to give advance notice of the need for a leave whenever possible, and many statutes permit the employer to require medical certification of the illness.[72] Hawaii's law permits employers to require certification of a birth or adoption, but it does not mention any certification of serious health conditions. In some states, employers may deny family leave to certain highly compensated employees, generally on the conditions that the employer show its need to deny the leave and give the employee notice of the decision.[73] In California, an employer may deny leave to

---

[69]California (4 months in a 24-month period); Connecticut (16 weeks in a 24-month period); District of Columbia (16 weeks in a 24-month period); Hawaii (4 weeks in a calendar year); Maine (10 weeks in 2 years); Minnesota (6 weeks); New Jersey (12 weeks in 24-month period); Oregon (12 weeks in 24 months); Rhode Island (13 weeks in 24 months); Vermont (12 weeks in 12 months); Washington (12 weeks in 24 months); Wisconsin (2 to 8 weeks in 12 months, depending on the reasons).

[70]Connecticut, District of Columbia, and Washington.

[71]California (1 year of continuous service and eligible for at least one employer-provided benefit); Connecticut (12 months and 1,000 hours); District of Columbia (1 year and 1,000 hours); Hawaii (6 consecutive months); Maine (12 consecutive months); Minnesota (12 months and an average number of hours equal to one-half the full-time equivalent position in the employee's job classification); New Jersey (12 months and 1,000 hours); Oregon (for family medical leave, 180 days and an average of 25 hours per week; for parental leave, 90 days); Rhode Island (average of 30 hours per week for 12 consecutive months); Vermont (1 year for an average of 30 hours per week); Washington (52 weeks of continuous employment for at least 35 hours per week); Wisconsin (52 consecutive weeks and 1,000 hours).

[72]California, Connecticut, District of Columbia, Maine, New Jersey, Oregon, Vermont, Washington, and Wisconsin.

[73]California (undue hardship, or if employee is among the 5 highest paid employees or in the top 10%); District of Columbia (5 highest paid employees or

care for a sick child if the other parent is unemployed and able to care for the child.

Although they do not have parental leave laws, Colorado and New York require that employers give adoptive parents the same leave privileges they provide to biological parents. Finally, seven states that do not have family and medical leave laws require employers to provide disability leaves to pregnant workers.[74]

At the conclusion of any of the leaves described in this section, the employer must normally reinstate the worker to his or her former job or a substantially equivalent position, with no loss of accumulated seniority or benefits. The FMLA requires employers to continue health coverage while workers are on leave. State laws imposing the same requirement, however, may well be preempted by ERISA.[75]

The federal FMLA, which covers employers with 50 or more employees, does not preempt state and local laws providing more generous leave rights. For instance, a state's leave law may apply to smaller employers that are not covered by the FMLA. The FMLA permits those laws to continue to operate, and eligible employees may take leave under state law, even though they have no rights under the FMLA. A more difficult problem occurs when an employer is covered by both the FMLA and a state leave law. The Department of Labor states that if leave qualifies under both the FMLA and state law, the leave used counts against the employee's entitlement under both laws. For instance, if the state law provides for 16 weeks of leave in a two-year period, the employee would be entitled to take 16 weeks one year under the state law and 12 weeks the next under the FMLA.

---

among the highest paid 10%, depending on employer's size); New Jersey (highest paid 5% or among the 7 highest paid employees); Vermont (reinstatement may be denied if the employee performed unique services and hiring a replacement was necessary to prevent substantial and grievous economic injury); Washington (highest paid 10%).

[74]Iowa (up to 8 weeks); Kansas (reasonable period of time); Louisiana (up to 4 months); Massachusetts (8 weeks); Montana (reasonable leave of absence); New Hampshire (for the period of temporary physical disability); Tennessee (4 months).

[75]New Jersey Business & Indus. Ass'n v. State of New Jersey, 592 A.2d 660, 13 EB Cases 2012 (N.J. Super. Ct. 1991).

Leaves for Military Service

Several states have enacted laws to broaden protection for employees returning from active military service. For example, California and Maryland provide certain public employees returning from active military service with reemployment rights.

JURY SERVICE LAWS

Federal Law

Under the Jury System Improvements Act,[76] an employee is protected from discharge, intimidation, and coercion by an employer because of the employee's service on a jury in federal court. Thus, an employer violates the Act if it intimidates the employee, even if it does not fire him or her. The courts consider any hostile comments by the employer about an employee's jury service as evidence of coercion. In addition, hostile comments may indicate the employer's true reasons for firing an employee.

The Act also prohibits an employer from changing an employee's working conditions while the employee serves as a juror. Thus, a company may not reassign an employee to a new position or change an employee's work schedule during jury service without an explanation unrelated to jury service. Further, an employer may not suggest that it will fire an employee if the employee serves as a federal juror in the future, nor may an employer withhold wages while an employee serves on a federal jury.

Remedies for a violation of the Act include lost wages and benefits, injunctive or other appropriate relief, including reinstatement, and reasonable attorney fees. Additionally, the employer is subject to a civil penalty up to $1,000. Although employees may sue under the Act after they have been fired, a judge may hear an action independently if a juror is being harassed or coerced while serving on a jury in the judge's court.

State Laws

Currently every state except Montana has a statutory provision protecting an employee from discharge because of serving on a jury

---

[76]28 U.S.C. §1875 (1993).

panel in state or federal court. Protection under state law, however, is usually not as broad as protection under the Jury System Improvements Act. For example, New Jersey's statute applies only to public and mass transit employees. A number of states prohibit an employer from threatening or coercing an employee because of jury service, but many states merely focus on protection against wrongful discharge. In some states, an employee must give reasonable notice to the employer of impending jury service in order to receive statutory protection.

In most states employees may bring a civil action for violation of the state statute. Remedies include lost wages, reinstatement, and reasonable attorney fees, and, in some states, punitive damages. Many states provide for criminal sanctions, ranging from fines to imprisonment in addition to or instead of providing for a civil cause of action.

Some statutes specifically provide that the employer is not required to compensate the employee for time on jury duty; a few states require the employer to compensate the employee; others have determined that an employer is simply not legally bound to pay an employee during an absence for jury duty.

Most state statutes do not address whether statutory protection applies to both potential and actual jurors or only to those individuals actually selected as jurors. At least one state, Texas, recognizes statutory protection for a potential juror appearing for the limited reason of claiming an exemption from jury duty.

VOTING TIME OFF LAWS

Most states permit an employee statutorily protected time off from work to vote.[77] Generally, an employee is allowed time off to vote varying from one to four hours unless the employee has the same amount of time to vote outside of working hours while the polls are open. Minnesota allows an unspecified amount of time off during the morning of election day. Ohio allows a "reasonable time" off to vote.

As a general rule, an employer may not deny an employee compensation for the time that an employee is away from work to vote.

---

[77]Alaska, Arizona, Arkansas, California, Colorado, Georgia, Hawaii, Illinois, Iowa, Kansas, Kentucky, Maryland, Massachusetts, Minnesota, Missouri, Nebraska, Nevada, New Mexico, New York, Ohio, Oklahoma, South Dakota, Tennessee, Texas, Utah, Washington, West Virginia, Wisconsin, and Wyoming.

Nevertheless, the courts in a few states have struck down pay-while-voting regulations as unconstitutional.[78] Further, if an employee takes the time off but does not vote, a number of states allow the employer to dock the employee's pay for that time or to discipline him or her. Many states allow an employer to designate what hours may be taken off for voting and to request notice before an employee takes time off to vote.

Although most states do not indicate what penalty exists for violation of the voting time off laws, some statutes provide that an employer will be guilty of a misdemeanor for violations.

---

[78]Heimgaertner v. Benjamin Elec. Mfg. Co., 128 N.E.2d 691 (Ill. 1955); Illinois Central R.R. v. Commonwealth, 204 S.W.2d 973 (Ky. 1947), *cert. denied*, 334 U.S. 843 (1948).

4

Conditions of Employment

INTRODUCTION

Traditionally, employers have had wide discretion to establish all of the conditions of employment. It was the employer's property and the employer's business and therefore the employer decided the means of operation and employee conduct in the workplace. As discussed in chapter 1, it is precisely this point that differentiates an employee from an independent contractor. Simply stated, the employer retains the right of control over employees.

The principle of the master (later the employer) having total control of the servants' (later employees') activities in the workplace and beyond was not inconsistent with eighteenth and nineteenth century American values, in which the law sanctioned indentured servitude, slavery, and limitations on women's employment. Today, even a much lesser degree of control over individuals by employers conflicts with a society that places great value on individual autonomy, privacy, freedom of expression, and freedom of association. Thus, although employers still have unchallenged authority to determine the essential aspects of the business operation, unreasonable intrusions into the personal lives of employees or other similar practices by employers are less likely to be countenanced by either employees or the institutions with the authority to regulate employment—the courts and legislatures.

As in other areas of employment law, many of the first successful actions challenging employer practices have involved public sector employees. Using the governmental action of public employment, employees have sought to invoke constitutional protections, such as freedom of expression, freedom of association, and freedom from unreasonable searches and seizures. In the private sector, civil rights statutes and common law principles have been relied upon by employees, with varying degrees of success. The expectations of employees also have been influenced by collective bargaining agreements, which have set industry standards regarding conditions of employment.

For private sector employees, where the law regarding conditions of employment is least developed, it is important to distinguish between at-will employees and employees who may be discharged only for just cause. With regard to at-will employees, in the absence of outrageous employer conduct or violation of a statute, employees are still likely to have relatively few legal rights. With regard to employees who may be discharged only for just cause, for many conditions of employment related to on-the-job (e.g., grooming, dress) or off-work (e.g., associations, political activities) activities, employers are likely to have a difficult time establishing just cause for discharge.

This chapter considers a range of conditions subject to regulation by employers. It is an area of employment law that is likely to see tremendous growth for at least three reasons. First, as the nature of what people do on the job continues to change, it will raise new questions regarding the legitimate rights of employers and employees. For example, computer monitoring and other surveillance measures raise a conflict between privacy and productivity. Second, as the identity and relationships of the workers change, new issues arise. Sexual harassment as a social matter has arisen because greater work force participation by women has resulted in new working relationships as well as a new societal ethos. Third, the range of employee interests deemed worth protecting, through legislative action or litigation, is likely to continue to expand. The privacy of employment records, the right to dress or be groomed as one wishes, and the right to be free of employer interference with off-work activities are examples of employee interests seriously asserted only recently.

GROOMING

Employers sometimes establish grooming standards for their employees that regulate hair length, hair style, facial hair, or hair coverings.

The policies are most often imposed for two reasons: health and sanitation and the "image" of the company for employees in public contact positions. Grooming policies have been challenged on constitutional grounds, under Title VII of the Civil Rights Act of 1964 (Title VII),[1] and under various state statutes similar to Title VII.

Constitutional Law

Constitutional challenges to grooming policies are usually based on either the First Amendment right to personal expression or the Fourteenth Amendment right to equal protection and due process. In the leading case of *Kelley v. Johnson*,[2] a police officer challenged a county regulation limiting the length of male police officers' hair. The Supreme Court held that the regulation did not violate due process of law under the Fourteenth Amendment. Justice Rehnquist's majority opinion noted that law enforcement officers are subject to many regulations not applicable to the public at large, such as those requiring them to wear a police uniform, prohibiting them from smoking in public, and requiring them to salute the flag while in uniform. Viewed in this context, the Court considered the hair-length regulation a reasonable restriction.

Based on *Kelley*, the First Circuit Court of Appeals also upheld a ban on mustaches and goatees as well as beards for police officers.[3] The court held that ease of recognition and promotion of esprit de corps were sufficient reasons to uphold the rule. According to the court, "*Kelley's* grip on the instant case is unrelenting."

Kelley's grip on cases involving other types of public safety officers is also significant. For example, the Supreme Court has held that hair-length regulations for firefighters were rationally related to safety because the rules ensure proper functioning of gas masks and promote discipline within the department.[4] The Eighth Circuit Court of Appeals also has held that a county policy prohibiting emergency medical technicians from wearing mustaches or beards did not violate due process.[5] The policy was justified by the need for esprit de corps, a

---

[1] 42 U.S.C. §2000e (1993).
[2] 425 U.S. 238 (1976).
[3] Weaver v. Henderson, 984 F.2d 11, 8 IER Cases 431 (1st Cir. 1993).
[4] Quinn v. Muscare, 425 U.S. 560 (1976).
[5] Hottinger v. Pope County, 971 F.2d 127 (8th Cir. 1992).

professional image, and possible interference with the performance of their job.

Grooming policies also have been challenged as unconstitutional religious discrimination. One police officer asserted that a police department regulation required him to break his religious vow not to cut his hair or shave his beard and therefore infringed upon his First Amendment freedom of religion.[6] The court held that the plaintiff's First Amendment rights were not violated and that the police department owed him no duty to accommodate his religious beliefs. The public health and safety interest promoted by the regulation outweighed the plaintiff's interest in wearing his hair and beard as his religious beliefs dictated.

Several rationales have been applied in the dismissal of constitutional gender discrimination claims by lower courts. The cases often have involved regulations requiring only men to have short hair. One court stated that the right to wear one's hair in a certain way is not a right found within the periphery of any specific constitutional right. Another said that the right to personal expression is subject to abridgment in the interest of health and safety.

Title VII

While Title VII does not specifically address grooming policies, courts have regularly accepted that the policies fall within "terms and conditions of employment," about which discrimination is forbidden by Title VII. The grooming policies most often attacked under Title VII are those setting different hair-length standards for males and females. While a majority of courts hold that the application of different grooming standards to the sexes is not gender discrimination under Title VII, a minority of courts and the Equal Employment Opportunity Commission (EEOC) have declared such policies to be the type of discrimination Title VII is intended to prevent.

Title VII also has been used to challenge regulations related to hair coverings worn in the workplace. A regulation allowing long-haired women who work with exposed food to wear hair nets, but requiring men in the same position to wear hats, was found to be discrimination

---

[6]Marshall v. District of Columbia, 392 F. Supp. 1012 (D.D.C. 1975), *remanded*, 559 F.2d 726 (D.C. Cir. 1977).

on the basis of gender. The court held that grooming regulations must be rationally related to a legitimate goal and may not be based on stereotypes.

The vast majority of courts, however, have found that enforcing different grooming policies for males and females does not necessarily constitute gender discrimination under Title VII. For example, in one case, different hair length standards applied to the male and female employees of a food store chain were found to have no significant effect upon the employment opportunities afforded one sex in favor of the other. Grooming standards also have been held to be nondiscriminatory when applied to diverse employees, including employees who service and repair bank equipment, bus drivers, copy layout artists, artist-craftpersons for an amusement park operator, and railroad procedures analysts. These decisions have been explained in different ways. One rationale is that it is an employer's right to impose standards necessary to the success of its business. Another theory is that discrimination is only illegal when based on immutable or protected characteristics, such as unchangeable gender characteristics, being married, or having children. Because hair length is easily changeable, it does not qualify as an immutable characteristic.

Most race discrimination claims related to grooming policies involve no-beard rules. Pseudofolliculitis barbae is a skin disorder resulting from hairs in the beard area of the face and neck when the individual is clean shaven. Because the condition is found in 25 percent of black males but far less than 1 percent of white males, black men have asserted that no-beard rules constitute disparate impact race discrimination. Some cases have upheld no-beard rules because health and sanitation, cleanliness, hygiene, and public image involved in certain businesses outweighed the disparate impact resulting from the grooming policy. Other cases, however, have found that no-beard rules constitute disparate impact race discrimination for which employers have the burden of proving job relatedness or business necessity.

No-beard rules also have been alleged to constitute religious discrimination under Title VII. Whether the plaintiff wins or loses generally turns on the overall conduct of the employer and the type of business in which the employer is engaged. **Employer grooming rules are more likely to be upheld if they are applied consistently and based on substantial concerns, such as safety**. For instance, a company was required to accommodate a Jewish computer programmer's religious beliefs requiring him to have a beard when it was shown that the company accommodated members of other religions.[7] On the other hand, accommodation may not be possible because of the nature of the business. This rationale was applied to a plaintiff who was the manager of a family restaurant and to an employee who had potential exposure to toxic gases and who was unable to wear a respirator because of a beard.

State Fair Employment Laws

Plaintiffs also have brought race, sex, religion, and national origin discrimination claims under state law. For example, a prospective busboy sued successfully under New York state law when a restaurant hired females with long hair, but refused to hire him.[8] On the other hand, some courts have been extremely deferential to employers by stating that a "hiring policy that distinguishes on some other ground [than a fundamental right], such as grooming codes or length of hair, is related more closely to the employer's choice of how to run his business than to equality of opportunity."[9]

In Illinois, a prospective mailroom employee claimed discrimination on the basis of race, religion, and national origin.[10] The plaintiff, a Jamaican-born black man, was a member of the Ethiopian Orthodox Church, one of two fundamental branches of the Rastafarian religion. He was rejected because he wore his hair in dreadlocks. His employment discrimination action was dismissed because there was no evidence that the employer knew or should have known the plaintiff's hairstyle was mandated by religion or national origin, and because no pretext was shown for hiring another employee. The result may be questioned, however, as protecting employers who choose not to learn about practices of minority groups.

Discrimination based on physical appearance also has been alleged to be unlawful disability discrimination. For example, in one case, a

---

[7]EEOC v. Electronic Data Sys., 31 FEP Cases 588 (W.D. Wash. 1983).

[8]Doyle v. Buffalo Sidewalk Cafe, Inc., 333 N.Y.S.2d 534, 4 FEP Cases 1140 (Sup. Ct. 1972).

[9]Pik-Kwik Stores, Inc. v. Commission on Human Rights & Opportunities, 365 A.2d 1210, 26 FEP Cases 848 (Conn. 1976).

[10]Gayle v. Human Rights Comm'n, 578 N.E.2d 144 (Ill. App.), *appeal denied*, 584 N.E.2d 129 (Ill. 1991).

chambermaid at a "four-star" ski resort was discharged because she was toothless and she did not wear her dentures to work because they were too painful to wear.[11] The Vermont Supreme Court held that the plaintiff had a physical impairment under Vermont law. The case was remanded on the issue of whether her contact with hotel guests rendered her unfit to perform the job.

The District of Columbia is the only jurisdiction with a statute specifically prohibiting discrimination based on personal appearance, including grooming practices. Personal appearance is defined in the statute as "the outward appearance of any person, irrespective of sex, with regard to bodily condition or characteristics, manner or style of dress, and manner or style of personal grooming, including, but not limited to, hair style and beards." In a case brought under this law, the employer was held to have violated the statute for discharging a receptionist for, among other things, having disheveled hair and wearing low-cut and tight blouses.[12] This case demonstrates the difficulty in regulating such a variable subject as personal appearance.

DRESS

Employers often regulate the appearance of their employees by establishing dress codes, including regulation of uniforms, eyeglasses, head coverings, earrings, and certain types of religious garb. As with grooming rules, dress codes have been challenged under the Constitution, as discrimination based on gender, race, and religion under Title VII, and under state law.

Constitutional Law

The leading constitutional dress code case involved the military, but is nevertheless instructive. In *Goldman v. Weinberger*,[13] the plaintiff, an Orthodox Jew and an ordained rabbi, was a captain at a military hospital. The Air Force refused to grant him an exemption to its dress

---

[11]Hodgdon v. Mt. Mansfield Co., 624 A.2d 1122, 2 AD Cases 499 (Vt. 1992).

[12]Atlantic Richfield Co. v. District of Columbia Comm'n on Human Rights, 515 A.2d 1095, 41 FEP Cases 1489 (D.C. App. 1986).

[13]475 U.S. 503, 40 FEP Cases 543 (1986).

code to allow him to wear a yarmulke while on duty. In holding that the Air Force did not violate the plaintiff's First Amendment right of free exercise of religion, the Supreme Court stated that because the military is a specialized society separate from that of civilians, the review of constitutional challenges to military regulations is "far more deferential" than that for regulations applied to civilians. The Air Force argued that the wearing of a yarmulke would open the door to dress code challenges by members of all religions, compelling them to allow all exceptions, including the turbans of Sikhs and dreadlocks worn by those of the Rastafarian faith. Alternatively, the Air Force argued that refusing exemptions for the religious garb of other faiths would create the appearance of religious favoritism. The Court found that the dress code served a legitimate purpose by encouraging "the subordination of personal preferences and identities in favor of the overall group mission." Courts reviewing dress codes for civilian employees of the government are likely to be less deferential to the government.

Title VII

Title VII also has been used in religion and gender discrimination dress code cases. Dress codes challenged as discriminatory on the basis of gender have involved requiring uniforms for women only, uniforms which subject the wearer to sexual harassment, and even prohibitions on the wearing of eyeglasses. Personal appearance standards sometimes have been used to deny or terminate employment, as well as to deny promotions.

Where uniforms are prescribed, employers may not discriminate between male and female employees in the nature of the uniform, even though the uniforms need not be identical. In *Carroll v. Talman Federal Savings & Loan Association*,[14] a bank required all female tellers to wear uniform attire, while male tellers could wear business suits. The women were expected to pay for the cleaning and maintenance of their uniforms and income tax on the value of the uniforms was deducted from their earnings. In ruling that the uniform rule discriminated on the basis of gender, the Seventh Circuit Court of

---

[14]604 F.2d 1028, 20 FEP Cases 764 (7th Cir. 1979), *cert. denied*, 445 U.S. 929 (1980).

Appeals said that it was irrelevant that some female employees liked the uniforms. The uniform rule constituted disparate treatment and was demeaning to women because customers generally assume that uniformed employees have less authority than those in normal business attire. In another case, female sales clerks were required to wear smocks, while male sales clerks could wear customary business attire consisting of slacks, a shirt, and a necktie.[15] The court held that this was disparate treatment discrimination and also ruled that discriminatory intent is not necessary for gender discrimination based on uniforms.

Uniforms which subject women to sexual harassment also constitute discrimination on the basis of gender. In *EEOC v. Sage Realty Corp.*,[16] the plaintiff was a lobby attendant in a building managed by the defendant. The plaintiff was issued a "bicentennial uniform," designed to resemble the American flag and worn as a poncho, with only dancer pants and sheer stockings underneath. Because the plaintiff was tall, the standard-size uniform was very short and revealing. While wearing the uniform, she was subjected to repeated sexual harassment, including sexual propositions and lewd comments and gestures from visitors to the building. When she resorted to wearing her old uniform, she was given a "lay-off" letter stating that she had lost her job because of a lack of work. The court held that the employer violated Title VII by requiring the plaintiff to wear a uniform the employer knew was revealing and sexually provocative and could reasonably have been expected to subject her to sexual harassment when worn on the job. Cocktail and restaurant waitresses also have alleged gender discrimination when they were required to wear uniforms that subjected them to verbal and physical sexual harassment from customers, as well as to physical discomfort and colds. In one case, cocktail waitresses were instructed to "project an air of sexual availability through the use of provocative outfits."[17] Unless sexiness is part of the "essence of the business," such as a topless bar, requiring female employees to wear sexually alluring outfits may constitute gender discrimination.

In some instances, dress codes may be closely related to single-sex employment policies. For example, in *Wilson v. Southwest Airlines*

---

[15]O'Donnell v. Burlington Coat Factory Warehouse, Inc., 656 F. Supp. 263, 43 FEP Cases 150 (S.D. Ohio 1987).

[16]507 F. Supp. 599, 24 FEP Cases 1521 (S.D.N.Y. 1981).

[17]EEOC v. Newtown Inn Assoc., 647 F. Supp. 957, 958, 42 FEP Cases 480 (E.D. Va. 1986).

Co.,[18] the airline employed only attractive young women for the positions of ticket agent and flight attendant and required them to wear high boots and hot pants. In defending an action alleging gender discrimination against men, the airline asserted that the dress code and hiring restrictions were essential because the airline was attempting to project an image of "feminine spirit, fun and sex appeal." The court rejected the claim and concluded that female sexual allure was not essential to the airline's primary function of transporting passengers.

A regulation requiring female airline employees to wear contact lenses and not eyeglasses also was found to be discrimination on the basis of gender. The court based its decision on the fact that the contact lens requirement imposed a substantially greater cost on female employees and was not reasonably related to performance of the job.

Dress code regulations requiring different attire of male and female employees, but which are not demeaning or costly to the female employees, are sometimes upheld. In one such case, the court upheld an employer's dress code which prohibited women from wearing pants in the executive office portion of the defendant's offices.[19]

General personal appearance standards are often upheld. In *Craft v. Metromedia*,[20] a television news station relied partially on market surveys in terminating the employment of a female news anchor. When told that she was fired because she was not feminine enough in her clothing and makeup, the plaintiff sued on the basis of gender discrimination, alleging that the station did not apply similar standards to male news anchors. The court held that while there was some emphasis on the feminine stereotype of "softness" and bows and ruffles, and on the fashionableness of female news anchors, the real reason for termination was a nondiscriminatory concern for appearance, colors, textures, lighting, and conservatism.

General personal appearance standards have been used to deny promotions to women. In *Price Waterhouse v. Hopkins*,[21] however, the Supreme Court held that the comments of partners in an accounting firm

---

[18]517 F. Supp. 292, 26 FEP Cases 989 (N.D. Tex. 1981).

[19]Lanigan v. Bartlett & Co. Grain, 466 F. Supp. 1388, 19 FEP Cases 1039 (W.D. Mo. 1979).

[20]766 F.2d 1205, 38 FEP Cases 404 (8th Cir. 1985), *cert. denied*, 475 U.S. 1058 (1986).

[21]490 U.S. 228, 49 FEP Cases 954 (1989).

concerning a female candidate's manner and grooming were sufficient to show that her rejection for partnership was based on gender discrimination. The decision was based on evidence that the man who explained to the plaintiff the decision to place her partnership candidacy on hold advised her to "walk more femininely, talk more femininely, dress more femininely, wear make-up, have her hair styled, and wear jewelry."

It is not clear to what extent *Price Waterhouse* will be applied in cases involving grooming and dress codes. If viewed more broadly as a case of gender stereotyping, *Price Waterhouse* will have little direct impact. If viewed in a more fact-specific manner, however, *Price Waterhouse* could result in closer judicial scrutiny of employment decisions based on considerations of grooming and dress.

Men who challenge dress code restrictions tend to lose when the regulations are based on traditional cultural norms. For example, a male grocery store employee unsuccessfully challenged a tie requirement on the basis that the female dress code had been modified to allow women to wear pants. In another case, a male loan counselor claimed gender discrimination when the dress code prohibited men from wearing earrings, while permitting women to wear them.[22] In ruling for the defendant, the court stated that the "imposition of grooming standards designed to project, in the employer's view, a conservative banking image is within the employer's discretion."

Religious discrimination claims also have been based on employer dress codes. Whether the policy is found to be discriminatory usually turns on the nature of the job in question. In one of these cases, the defendant was a private corporation providing auxiliary services to nonpublic school students under a contract with the school district.[23] The plaintiff, a Muslim woman, alleged religious discrimination when she applied but was not hired for a position as a third-grade counselor for Catholic elementary schools because she wore a head covering. In ruling for the plaintiff, the court said that although the plaintiff's head covering was worn for a religious purpose, it did not clearly indicate to others that she belonged to any certain religion, and therefore the refusal to hire her could not have been religious discrimination.

---

[22]Capaldo v. Pan Am. Fed. Credit Union, 43 Empl. Prac. Dec. ¶ 37,016 (E.D.N.Y. 1987).

[23]EEOC v. READS, Inc., 759 F. Supp. 1150, 58 FEP Cases 49 (E.D. Pa. 1991).

In *United States v. Board of Education*,[24] the plaintiff, a Muslim school teacher, was not permitted to wear religious head coverings and other attire. The school district took the action because a Pennsylvania "garb statute" expressly prohibits public school teachers from teaching in any religious garb. In a lawsuit brought by the federal government, representing the teacher, the plaintiff argued that the Pennsylvania law was unconstitutional and preempted by Title VII. The Third Circuit Court of Appeals upheld the law, and said the law served the compelling state interest of preserving religious neutrality.

State Fair Employment Laws

State law gender discrimination claims have paralleled those under Title VII. Thus, for example, gender discrimination lawsuits are likely to be successful if the dress codes are based on stereotypes or encourage sexual harassment. In a Michigan case, a hospital's dress code required female technologists to wear a white or pastel-colored uniform and males in the same position to wear a white laboratory coat over regular street clothing.[25] This rule was found to constitute gender discrimination because the hospital conceded that the regulation was adopted because the administration believed patients expect females to look like nurses and males to look like doctors. In summary, there is little direct regulation of employer policies prescribing dress codes for employees. An employer may require an employee to wear a uniform or similar attire, but policies that have the purpose or effect of unreasonably discriminating against employees on the basis of gender, religion, or other proscribed factors will violate Title VII.

SEXUAL HARASSMENT

Title VII prohibits discrimination against any individual with respect to "compensation, terms, conditions, or privileges of employment" because of the individual's sex. Sexual harassment has been recognized as a form of discrimination based on sex. The EEOC has defined sexual harassment in the following way:

---

[24]911 F.2d 882, 53 FEP Cases 1077 (3d Cir. 1990).
[25]Michigan Dep't of Civil Rights v. Edward A. Sparrow Hosp. Ass'n, 377 N.W.2d 755, 43 FEP Cases 1062 (Mich. 1985).

Unwelcome sexual advances, requests for sexual favors, and other verbal or physical conduct is of a sexual nature . . . when (1) submission to such conduct is made either explicitly or implicitly a term or condition of an individual's employment, (2) submission to or rejection of such conduct by an individual is used as the basis for employment decision affecting such individual, or (3) such conduct has the purpose or effect of unreasonably interfering with an individual's work or performance creating an intimidating, hostile, or offensive working environment.[26]

Quid Pro Quo

Two forms of sexual harassment have been recognized, quid pro quo and hostile environment. Quid pro quo harassment involves unwelcome sexual advances, requests for sexual favors, or other verbal or physical conduct of a sexual nature in which acquiescence to the sexual conduct is made a condition of employment. Thus, quid pro quo sexual harassment would exist when a supervisor conditions tangible job benefits, such as a promotion or continued employment, on the employee's submission to the supervisor's sexual advances. Quid pro quo harassment may only involve persons in a position of authority over the employee.

Under a quid pro quo theory, the employee must show that he or she suffered or was threatened with an economic injury. Consequently, if a supervisor never relates submission to the sexual advances to the employee's employment prospects, and the employee is not fired, then the employee suffers no economic injury and there is no quid pro quo sexual harassment. On the other hand, if an employee is terminated because he or she refuses to submit to a supervisor's sexual advances, then quid pro quo sexual harassment would be established. A single act of sexual harassment may be sufficient to sustain a lawsuit based on quid pro quo harassment.

A quid pro quo sexual harassment case requires proof that (1) the employee belongs to a protected group; (2) the employee was subjected to unwelcome sexual harassment; (3) the harassment was based on sex; and (4) the employee's reaction affected a tangible aspect of the employee's compensation, terms, conditions, or privileges of employment.

---

[26]29 C.F.R. §1604.11(a) (1993).

An employer has a duty to investigate complaints based on sexual harassment. If the employer fails, then the employer will be considered to have condoned the conduct.

Hostile Environment

Hostile environment sexual harassment is much more common than quid pro quo sexual harassment. It occurs when an employer creates or allows others to create a pattern of conduct relating to sex that establishes an unpleasant, intolerable, or hostile environment. Hostile environment harassment involves misconduct that has the effect or purpose of unreasonably interfering with an employee's work performance or creating an intimidating, hostile, or offensive working environment. In a hostile environment situation, the misconduct must be sufficiently severe or pervasive to alter the employee's conditions of employment and create a hostile working environment. Hostile environment sexual harassment involves subjecting employees, usually females, to sexual advances, suggestions, jokes, or pornography without threatening the loss of tangible job benefits. Hostile environment harassment may involve supervisors, co-workers, or third parties. Employers may be held liable for the misconduct of supervisors, co-employees, and third parties.

The United States Supreme Court recognized the viability of a sexual harassment claim based on a hostile environment in *Meritor Savings Bank v. Vinson*.[27] In *Vinson*, the Court determined that Title VII did not limit its protection to "economic" or "tangible" discrimination. Nevertheless, hostile environment discrimination must be "sufficiently severe or pervasive to alter the conditions of the victim's employment and create an abusive working environment." The Court determined that the key inquiry regarding sex-related conduct is not whether the victim's conduct is voluntary, but whether the sexual advances are unwelcome.

The EEOC defines hostile environment harassment as "conduct [which] has the purpose or effect of unreasonably interfering with an individual's work performance or creating an intimidating, hostile, or offensive working environment."[28] Conduct that has been considered sufficiently severe or pervasive includes name calling, pornography,

---

[27]477 U.S. 57, 40 FEP Cases 1822 (1986).
[28]29 C.F.R. §1604.11(a) (3) (1993).

keeping sexual objects on desks, anonymous phone calls, bizarre love-letters from a co-worker, and displaying sexually oriented posters.

In *Weiss v. Coca-Cola Bottling Co.,*[29] the plaintiff alleged that her supervisor asked her for dates, called her a "dumb blond," put his hand on her shoulder several times, placed "I love you" signs in her work area, and attempted to kiss her in a bar. The Seventh Circuit Court of Appeals held that these "relatively isolated" incidents were insufficient to establish sexual harassment.

The elements of a successful claim for hostile environment harassment are as follows: "(1) the employee was a member of a protected class; (2) the employee was subjected to unwelcome sexual harassment; (3) the harassment was based on sex; (4) the harassment affected a term, condition, or privilege of employment; and (5) the employer knew or should have known of the harassment and failed to take proper remedial action."[30]

Generally, a single incident will not support a hostile environment sexual harassment legal action, but it may be sufficient if it is severe enough. To determine whether conduct is so severe or pervasive that it creates a hostile environment, some courts use a "reasonable person" standard. Other courts, however, have adopted a "reasonable victim" or "reasonable woman" standard. Under the "reasonable person" standard, the court will determine whether the complained-of conduct would interfere with a reasonable person's work performance and seriously affect the individual's psychological well-being in the same or similar circumstances. Under the "reasonable victim" or "reasonable woman" standard, courts view the harassment from the perspective of the female victim, rather than that of a hypothetical gender-neutral person, who arguably reflects a male perspective. Thus, if the plaintiff is a female, then the standard is that of a reasonable woman; in the unusual case where the plaintiff is a male, then the standard is that of a reasonable man.

In *Harris v. Forklift Systems,*[31] the Supreme Court held that a plaintiff need not suffer psychological harm to establish a claim of hostile environment sexual harassment.

---

[29]990 F.2d 333, 61 FEP Cases 773 (7th Cir. 1993).

[30]Henson v. Dundee, 682 F.2d 897, 903–04, 29 FEP Cases 787 (11th Cir. 1982). *See also* B. Lindemann & D.D. Kadue, *Sexual Harassment in Employment Law* 169 (Washington, D.C.: BNA Books, 1992).

[31]114 S. Ct. 367, 63 FEP Cases 225 (1993).

The effect on the employee's psychological well-being is, of course, relevant to determining whether the plaintiff actually found the environment abusive. But while psychological harm, like any other relevant factor, may be taken into account, no single factor is required.[32]

To hold an employer liable for harassment based on hostile environment, the employer must have known of the conduct or could have discovered it with the exercise of reasonable diligence. An employer's response to alleged harassment "must be reasonably calculated to prevent further harassment under the particular facts and circumstances of the case at the time that the allegations are made."[33] The test is not whether the harassment ultimately succeeded, but whether the employer's actions were reasonable. Thus, in instances in which an employer knows of harassment and takes prompt remedial action, courts may not find the employer liable.

OTHER HARASSMENT

Although gender-based harassment is the most common form of harassment in the workplace, it is not the only form of harassment recognized by the courts. Harassment based on race, national origin, religion, age, and disability also are actionable, while harassment based on sexual orientation will not succeed unless there is an express law prohibiting this form of discrimination. The legal actions have been brought pursuant to federal and state statutes, principally Title VII, as well as common law.

Harassment for reasons other than sex is invariably of the hostile environment type. The essence of the action is that an employer, supervisor, or fellow employees create or permit the existence of an intimidating, offensive work environment. The courts have long held that the "practice of creating a working environment heavily charged with ethnic or racial discrimination" is prohibited by Title VII.[34]

---

[32]114 S. Ct. at 371.

[33]Brooms v. Regal Tube Co., 881 F.2d 412, 50 FEP Cases 1499 (7th Cir. 1989).

[34]Rogers v. EEOC, 454 F.2d 234, 237–38, 4 FEP Cases 92 (5th Cir. 1971), *cert. denied*, 406 U.S. 957, 4 FEP Cases 265 (1972).

Race

A variety of conduct has been alleged to constitute racial harassment. Even though some general conclusions may be drawn from the cases, there is some variability in the standards applied by the courts and an even wider disparity in the results. For example, in *Daniels v. Essex Group, Inc.*,[35] a black plaintiff was subjected to racial harassment, which included race-oriented graffiti, racial slurs, and a doll hung in effigy. In upholding a finding of unlawful discrimination, the Seventh Circuit Court of Appeals considered the nature of the alleged harassment; the background and experience of the plaintiff, her co-workers, and supervisors; the totality of the physical environment of the plaintiff's work area; the level of obscenity in the workplace before and after the plaintiff began working there; and the reasonable expectations of the plaintiff.

A contrary result was reached by the Sixth Circuit in *Davis v. Monsanto Chemical Co.*,[36] a case with facts similar to *Daniels*. In *Davis*, a black plaintiff was subjected to racial slurs, racial graffiti, restrictions on lunchroom use, and spitting on time cards. In finding no Title VII violation, the court emphasized that the racial epithets were directed only once at the plaintiff, that the company acted quickly to correct the situation, and that other assertions of the plaintiff were contradicted by the evidence.

Many cases are based on the use of racist language or disparate treatment. In *Johnson v. Bunny Bread Co.*,[37] black employees complained that their supervisors and co-workers often referred to them as "niggers." The Eighth Circuit Court of Appeals, in an unenlightened opinion, conceded that a Title VII action is available for a "steady barrage of opprobrious racial comment," but it held that there was no violation because the remarks were merely a part of casual conversation, accidental, or sporadic. Virtually all of the other cases of repeated, racially abusive language go the other way. According to one court, while Title VII was not intended to be a "clean language" act, an employer may not hide racist comments behind a "thicket of race neutral insults and profanities."[38]

---

[35]937 F.2d 1264, 56 FEP Cases 833 (7th Cir. 1991).

[36]858 F.2d 345, 47 FEP Cases 1825 (6th Cir. 1988), *cert. denied*, 490 U.S. 1110 (1989).

[37]646 F.2d 1250, 25 FEP Cases 1326 (8th Cir. 1981).

[38]Rodgers v. Western-Southern Life Ins. Co., 792 F. Supp. 628, 635, 58 FEP Cases 1364 (E.D. Wis. 1992).

Racial harassment actions also have been brought under state civil rights laws. In addition, common law actions for intentional infliction of emotional distress may be brought for intentional racial disparagement conducted in a rude, insolent, or violent manner for the purpose of causing emotional and physical distress.

National Origin

Cases alleging workplace harassment based on national origin have applied principles common to other forms of harassment. For example, it is not necessary for the plaintiff to prove a tangible economic harm in order to prevail in a claim for national origin-based harassment. The plaintiff is also more likely to prevail if the harassing conduct has occurred with some frequency or there is evidence that ethnic slurs were encouraged, permitted, or condoned by supervisory personnel.

Courts will look at the entire workplace atmosphere to determine whether the complained-of conduct created a hostile environment. For example, in *Valdez v. Mercy Hospital*,[39] a supervisor who was known for telling ethnic jokes, circulated among the employees a handwritten "Mexican Sex Manual" and a "Polish Sex Manual." The Eighth Circuit Court of Appeals held the conduct was not sufficiently severe or pervasive to be actionable under Title VII, especially in light of the ongoing personality conflict between the plaintiff and his supervisor.

Religion

There are some unique elements of religious harassment claims. First, all aspects of religious observance, practice, and belief are protected under Title VII. Second, harassment based on religious ancestry is also protected. For example, a Title VII violation was found where an employee was subjected to a course of religious harassment because his paternal grandmother was Jewish, even though the plaintiff was never a member of the Jewish faith.[40] Third, religious harassment may be established by an employer's failure to make reasonable

---

[39] 961 F.2d 1401, 58 FEP Cases 1137 (8th Cir. 1992).

[40] Compston v. Borden, Inc., 424 F. Supp. 157, 17 FEP Cases 310 (S.D. Ohio 1976).

accommodation to an individual's religious beliefs, such as by failing to remedy unintentional conduct that created an offensive or hostile environment.

The most frequent source of religious harassment claims is the use of demeaning and offensive religious slurs. **Liability is most likely to be found where the conduct is highly offensive, on a continual basis, or engaged in by supervisors**. On the other hand, conduct considered by the courts to be less extreme, such as a supervisor's referring to the plaintiff as a "Jewish-American princess" and asking her who she slept with to get her job, has been held not to be actionable.[41]

Once an employer has been put on notice about workplace harassment, it must do more than merely show that it has an official policy against such conduct. This is especially true when the unlawful activities are engaged in by supervisors or managers. Where harassment is shown, courts are more likely to find that the defendant's after-the-fact assertions of plaintiff's work deficiencies are pretextual.

Age

Claims of harassment based on age are most frequently based on the Age Discrimination in Employment Act (ADEA).[42] The elements of the cause of action under the ADEA are comparable to those under Title VII. According to one court, the plaintiff must prove that (1) he or she was a member of the protected class (age 40 or over); (2) he or she was subject to unwelcome harassment; (3) the harassment was prompted solely because of age; (4) the harassment affected a term, condition, or privilege of employment; (5) respondeat superior liability existed; (6) the employer provided no reasonable avenue for complaint; and (7) the employer knew of the harassment but did nothing about it.[43]

A wide range of conduct may give rise to an action for age-based harassment. For example, it has been held to be unlawful age harassment to taunt an employee by calling him "old man" and "grandpa," to repeatedly urge that an employee retire, and, among other things, to tell

---

[41]Meek v. Michigan Bell Tel. Co., 483 N.W.2d 407, 59 FEP Cases 177 (Mich. App. 1991) (action based on state law).

[42]29 U.S.C. §621–34 (1993).

[43]Spence v. Maryland Casualty Co., 803 F. Supp. 649, 62 FEP Cases 131 (W.D.N.Y. 1992).

a senior employee that he need not make a contribution to the office "flower fund" because he would not be around to work that much longer and sending him out in the rain to do another employee's work. On the other hand, where the harassment was not directly based on the employee's age, it was not continuous, pervasive, and concerted, and where the employee failed to complain about the conduct to supervisors, no age-based harassment was found.

Disability

Harassment based on an individual's disability violates section 102(a) of the Americans with Disabilities Act (ADA).[44] Although there have not been any harassment cases decided yet under the ADA, several already have been filed. Extreme cases of harassment also have been alleged to constitute intentional infliction of emotional distress, although the courts have been very reluctant to permit recovery in such cases.

A variety of conduct has been alleged to be the source of disabilities-based harassment under pre-ADA laws. These cases have included excessive scrutiny and criticism of an employee who had returned to work after recovery from severe depression and anxiety, constant mimicking of an employee who stuttered, verbally harassing an employee about his mental condition, deliberately transferring an employee to a job she was unable to perform, and harassing an arachnophobic employee by putting rubber spiders on her desk. Because the results have varied widely, it is hard to predict the outcome of future cases.

Sexual Orientation

Claims of harassment based on sexual orientation have become increasingly common, but the courts are unlikely to recognize the existence of the claim in the absence of a state statute prohibiting discrimination on the basis of sexual orientation. For example, in one case the court held that neither Title VII nor state discrimination law afforded relief to an employee who was subject to

---

[44]42 U.S.C. §§12101–12213 (1992).

continuous derogatory comments, such as "faggot," as well as physical assaults.[45]

In *Zaks v. American Broadcasting Corp.*,[46] however, an action for intentional infliction of emotional distress was permitted where an employer and co-employees allegedly harassed, vandalized, assaulted, stabbed, and stuffed into a closet an unconscious employee because of his homosexual orientation. Obviously, this is an atypical case.

SEARCHES

Employers sometimes believe it is necessary to search employees, the personal property of employees, and employer property under the control of employees to locate money, merchandise, contraband, or other things. **The lawfulness of a workplace search depends, primarily, on whether constitutional principles apply and the reasonableness of the search**.

Public Employers

Workplace searches by government employers are controlled by the Fourth Amendment of the U.S. Constitution, which prohibits unreasonable searches and seizures. Hallways, offices, desks, closets, and file cabinets are considered to be part of the workplace. Fourth Amendment rights do not depend on who owns either the place searched or its contents, "but upon whether the area was one in which there was a reasonable expectation of freedom from governmental intrusion."[47] For a search to violate the Fourth Amendment, the employee whose work space is searched must have a subjective expectation of privacy that would be considered reasonable by society.

In the leading case of *O'Connor v. Ortega*,[48] the Supreme Court found a reasonable expectation of privacy in the desk and file cabinets of a physician whose hospital-employer accused him of work-related improprieties. The physician had exclusive use of the office, desk, and

---

[45]Carreno v. Local Union No. 226, IBEW, 54 FEP Cases 81 (D. Kan. 1990).
[46]626 F. Supp. 695, 121 LRRM 2624 (C.D. Cal. 1985).
[47]Mancusi v. De Forte, 392 U.S. 364, 368, 68 LRRM 2449 (1968).
[48]480 U.S. 709, 1 IER Cases 1617 (1987).

file cabinets, occupied his office for 17 years, kept personal materials there, and kept work-related files outside the office. In addition, the hospital had no regulation or policy discouraging employees from storing personal papers and effects in their desks or file cabinets.

While employees do not waive their Fourth Amendment rights merely because they work for the government, "the operational realities of the workplace . . . may make some employees' expectations of privacy unreasonable when an intrusion is by a supervisor rather than a law enforcement official."[49] Thus, employee awareness of the practice of regularly conducted searches, possession of locker keys or combinations by the employer, and workplace regulations that authorize searches are sufficient to negate an employee's reasonable expectation of privacy. Abandonment of the object of the search or a waiver signed by the employee also may negate any privacy right in the subject of the search.

The *O'Connor* case also introduced a second factor into Fourth Amendment search analysis—whether the government employer's search of the area was reasonable under the circumstances. This requires a balancing of the governmental interest in the efficient and proper operation of the workplace with the employee's privacy interests. Thus, for example, the government would have a more compelling interest in searching the lockers of employees of the United States Mint than it would in a search involving clerical workers at another agency.

A heightened standard has been applied in Fourth Amendment challenges to strip searches. Correctional facility officers and other government employees with public safety duties have been found to have a diminished reasonable expectation of privacy. In *McDonell v. Hunter*,[50] the Eighth Circuit Court of Appeals held that to determine if an individual's expectation of privacy is reasonable there must be both an objective and a subjective expectation, and the expectation must be one which society will accept as reasonable. The court adopted a reasonable suspicion standard for strip searches of correctional officers based on the legitimate government interest in maintaining security. A "reasonable suspicion" must be based on specific objective facts and rational inferences that the employee is in possession of contraband hidden on his or her person.

---

[49]O'Connor v. Ortega, 480 U.S. 709, 717, 1 IER Cases 1617 (1987).
[50]809 F.2d 1302, 1 IER Cases 1297 (8th Cir. 1987).

Another type of search addressed in *McDonell*, vehicle searches, was found to be much less intrusive than the search of one's person. An individual's expectation of privacy in his or her vehicle is less than in other property and the expectation of privacy as to packages or containers within a vehicle is less than that which would exist if the packages were in the employer's offices. Therefore, privately owned vehicles of correctional facility employees may be searched without cause if parked where they are accessible to inmates and if the search is done uniformly or by systematic random selection of employees whose vehicles are to be searched.

Private Employers

Searches by private employers pose different legal issues than challenges brought under the Fourth Amendment, although privacy standards for public employees may provide a reasonable basis for the privacy expectations of private sector employees. Searches by private employers are usually challenged under state tort law, such as invasion of privacy or intentional or negligent infliction of emotional distress. For example, in one case[51] an invasion of privacy claim was brought where an employer searched an employee's locked file cabinet, desk, and personal papers. The court found for the defendants because the plaintiff failed to allege a lack of authority for the search. Similarly, the search of an employee's briefcase and random vehicle searches with prior notice of the policy were found not to meet the level of outrageousness necessary for a claim of intentional infliction of emotional distress.

In other cases, however, courts have held that employer searches constituted an invasion of privacy. For example, in one case,[52] the court held that mere suspicion that another employee had stolen watches or that unidentified employees may have stolen price-marking guns was found insufficient to justify the employer's search of the employee's locked locker and her personal possessions without her consent. In another case,[53] the search of an employee's motel room was held to be an invasion of privacy.

---

[51]Hoth v. American States Ins. Co., 735 F. Supp. 290 (N.D. Ill. 1990).
[52]K-Mart Corp. v. Trotti, 677 S.W.2d 632 (Tex. App. 1984).
[53]Sowards v. Norbar, Inc., 605 N.E.2d 468 (Ohio 1992).

Searches of one's person may raise other issues. For example, in one case,[54] a liquor distiller began having security guards conduct pat-down searches of employees as they left the plant to prevent the theft of tools and small bottles of liquor ("miniatures"). When some of the 500 male workers and their wives objected to a woman guard conducting the pat-down searches, she was transferred and replaced with a male guard. According to the court, her transfer did not violate Title VII.

Strip searches are one of the most intrusive types of searches. In *Bodewig v. K-Mart, Inc.*,[55] an Oregon court held that the plaintiff could recover under the tort of outrageous conduct where a store manager, after concluding that the plaintiff, a part-time checker, did not take a customer's money, nevertheless forced her to submit to a strip search to appease the customer, who was permitted to witness the search. The court found that the manager's conduct was unacceptable by society's standards and showed complete disregard for any subsequent effect on the plaintiff.

Although there are still relatively few private sector search cases, it is an area of law that is likely to expand. The numerous challenges to employer-mandated drug testing (discussed in chapter 1) have, to some extent, established a legal framework for asserting these claims. Moreover, as society increasingly values the right of individuals to be free from intrusive searches of their person and property, then unreasonable searches of even private sector employees will be held to be actionable.

SURVEILLANCE

An emerging issue in employment law involves the surveillance of employees in the workplace by their employers. Workplace surveillance takes various forms, such as using one-way mirrors, surveillance cameras, listening devices, monitoring of phone conversations, monitoring of electronic mail, and computer monitoring. Although there is, as yet, relatively little statutory or case law, it is an area where increased legislation and litigation is certain, especially because new computer technologies enable wide scale monitoring of workers.

---

[54]Sutton v. National Distillers Prods. Co., 445 F. Supp. 1319, 27 FEP Cases 323 (S.D. Ohio 1978), *aff'd*, 628 F.2d 936 (16th Cir. 1980).
[55]635 P.2d 657 (Or. App. 1981).

Federal Law

Most of the current litigation has focused on the monitoring of employee telephone conversations by private or public employers. This is an area specifically covered by federal statute. Title III of the Omnibus Crime Control and Safe Streets Act of 1968 (Omnibus Act)[56] protects both wire and oral communication from interception by employers. The statute has two exceptions, which allow monitoring: (1) if it is performed in the ordinary course of business, either in any business or by a telephone service provider, or by a law enforcement officer; and (2) if one party consents or is the interceptor. The law requires that the plaintiff have a reasonable expectation of privacy, defined by the courts as a subjectively held expectation that society would be prepared to regard as reasonable under the circumstances.

Under the statute, "any person whose wire, oral, or electronic communication is intercepted, disclosed, or intentionally used in violation of" the law may recover in a legal action. Appropriate relief includes injunctions, damages, attorney fees, and litigation costs. If the conduct is for an illegal purpose or for purposes of direct or indirect commercial advantage, damages are the greater of the sum of actual damages suffered by the plaintiff and any profits made by the violator or the statutory damages of between $100 a day for each violation or $10,000.

In *Simmons v. Southwestern Bell Telephone Co.*,[57] the plaintiff operated a phone company "testdesk" from which personal phone calls were not permitted. The company provided an unmonitored phone line for personal use, warned the employee repeatedly about use of the testdesk for personal calls, and the employee knew that the testdesk lines were monitored. These facts led the court to conclude that the plaintiff had no reasonable expectation of privacy with regard to the testdesk lines and therefore there was no violation of the statute.

Under the Omnibus Act, a telephone extension used without authorization or consent to surreptitiously record a private conversation is not used in the "ordinary course of business." Both "sporadic illegal eavesdropping" and indiscriminate wiretapping of private telephone conversations have been held to violate the statute. On the other hand,

---

[56]18 U.S.C. §§2510–21 (1992).
[57]452 F. Supp. 392 (W.D. Okla. 1978), *aff'd*, 611 F.2d 342 (10th Cir. 1979).

monitoring of employee phone calls dealing with the general public has been held to fall within the "extension telephone exception" where the employees had advance knowledge of the monitoring and because there was a legitimate business purpose for the practice.

In *Deal v. Spears*,[58] the owners of a small liquor store, in attempting to discover whether an employee played a role in a recent burglary, secretly recorded and listened to more than 22 hours of employee phone calls. Many of the calls were sexually provocative and involved an extramarital affair. When the recording was finally used to justify the discharge of an employee for selling a keg of beer to a friend at cost, the two employees whose calls were taped sued the store owners. The Eighth Circuit Court of Appeals affirmed an award for the plaintiffs and rejected the owner's claim that the recordings were made in the "ordinary course of business."

Prior consent is another exception that may make employer monitoring of personal phone calls permissible. The knowledge of monitoring capability alone, however, does not constitute implied consent. Also, the consent must extend to the specific nature of the call. For example, where an employee did not consent to general monitoring but only to the monitoring of sales calls, the asserted consent was ineffective.[59] The court concluded that consent can be limited and that the presence of a general monitoring policy does not submit the employee to unlimited surveillance.

The Omnibus Act contains a very specific exception for an investigative or law enforcement officer in the ordinary course of duties. Thus, there was no violation of the Act for a police department to monitor the calls of a police officer who was using a regularly recorded police telephone line to place a personal call to his lover.[60] The court stated that Congress did not intend the Act to apply to routine recording of emergency and investigative calls as an integral part of a police telephone system. Similar reasoning was used in a case involving the monitoring of a two-way radio system for communication between school bus drivers and their dispatchers. The court said that a person broadcasting by radio did not have a reasonable expectation of privacy under the Act because anyone with a radio could monitor the

---

[58]980 F.2d 1153, 8 IER Cases 105 (8th Cir. 1992).
[59]Epps v. St. Mary's Hosp. of Athens, Inc., 802 F.2d 412 (11th Cir. 1986).
[60]Jandak v. Village of Brookfield, 520 F. Supp. 815 (N.D. Ill. 1981).

communications.[61] In a case involving the surreptitious cassette recording of an argument between the plaintiff and his foreman, the court held
that there was no reasonable expectation of privacy under the Act
because the argument took place in a small shop with no walls and other
workers could enter and leave the area freely.[62]

State Law

Nearly 40 states protect privacy rights in personal communications
by statute, many of which are based on the federal statute. Some states
protect privacy rights in the state constitution, usually by creating a
general right to privacy. A few states specifically protect the privacy of
communications. For example, Connecticut law prohibits "electronic
surveillance, including video surveillance, of any area designed for the
health and comfort of employees or for safeguarding of their possessions, including rest rooms, locker rooms, and lounges."

Some states require the consent of all parties to a conversation
before it may be recorded; others require consent by only one of the
parties. California prohibits monitoring without a beeptone or verbal
announcement.

Electronic surveillance in the workplace also may constitute
common law invasion of privacy. For example, an employer was liable
for invasion of privacy where a supervisor concealed an electronic
listening device in the ceiling of an employee's office and monitored her
private conversations for four years.[63]

INTERROGATION

An employee suspected of stealing or other serious misconduct
frequently will be brought in for questioning by a manager, supervisor,
or security guard as part of an internal investigation. **Employers have
a privilege to conduct investigations, and there is no common law
right for an employee to refuse to participate in an interrogation or**

---

[61]Goodall's Charter Bus Serv., Inc. v. San Diego Unified Sch. Dist., 178 Cal.
Rptr. 21 (Cal. App. 1981).

[62]Kemp v. Block, 607 F. Supp. 1262 (D. Nev. 1985).

[63]Slack v. Kanawha County Housing Auth., 423 S.E.2d 547 (W. Va. 1992).

to insist upon having one's attorney present. Although union employees have the right to have a representative present at a disciplinary interview, the right has not been extended to nonunion employees.

If an interrogation is conducted in an unreasonable manner, the employee may have a legal action in tort. The most frequently asserted claims are false imprisonment, intentional infliction of emotional distress, invasion of privacy, and defamation.

False Imprisonment

False imprisonment is usually the most serious tort arising from an interrogation. It occurs when the employer or its representative intentionally confines the employee within a fixed area. For example, in one case, while accusing the plaintiff of stealing, the defendant repeatedly put his hands on the plaintiff's shoulders to restrain her when she rose in an attempt to leave the room.[64] Threats made during the course of the interrogation and excessively long interrogations are also factors accounting for liability.

If the interrogation is conducted in a generally reasonable manner, then there will be no liability. For example, the employers have prevailed in false imprisonment cases where the plaintiff showed no apprehension or fear, where the employee was questioned during business hours in familiar surroundings, and where the employer was acting in good faith.

Frequently, the employer's representative will tell the employee being interrogated that if he or she leaves the room then the employee will be fired. If the employee remains to keep his or her job or to "clear" his or her name, has the employee been "confined" by the employer sufficiently to establish false imprisonment? The courts are in agreement that this "compulsion" is inadequate to establish false imprisonment. Even a threat to call the police if the employee does not remain has been insufficient to establish false imprisonment.

Another issue is whether a "shopkeeper's privilege" statute, which shields merchants from liability for detaining and interrogating individuals suspected of shoplifting, applies to the detention of employees. At least one court has held that it did not apply, and even if it did, it did

---

[64]Skillern & Sons v. Stewart, 379 S.W.2d 687 (Tex. 1964).

not protect the defendant's conduct consisting of shouting at the employee in a four-hour interrogation and forcing her to admit to a crime she did not commit.[65]

Intentional Infliction of Emotional Distress

Unreasonable employer interrogation also has been alleged to constitute intentional infliction of emotional distress. The employee must prove that the employer intentionally or recklessly engaged in conduct "so outrageous in character and extreme in degree as to go beyond all bounds of decency."[66] The employer-employee relationship establishes a clear duty not to engage in such behavior. The more difficult question is determining what type of employer conduct is sufficiently outrageous to establish liability. For example, liability was found where the defendant intended to frighten the plaintiff by raising his voice, pounded his fist on the table, and threatened to have her arrested, but there was no liability where the defendant threatened to obtain a search warrant to check the plaintiff's house.

Factors considered by the courts in similar cases include the length of the interrogation, whether the employee was paid for the time spent in the interview, whether the employer's conduct during the interrogation was reasonable, and whether the employer had a good faith belief in the employee's guilt. Often, the plaintiff must meet a stringent burden of proof to show that the defendant's actions were so "terrifying or insulting as naturally to humiliate, embarrass, or frighten the plaintiff."[67] If the employer acts in good faith, or if the plaintiff failed to request that the interview be terminated, or the plaintiff was rude to the interviewer as well, then the claim has failed.

Regardless of the severity of the conduct required to establish liability, unfortunately, a few employers have exceeded it. Thus, in one case, while interrogating a female manager, one of the employer's representatives left his pants unzipped, laughed at the employee and accused her of lying, did not permit her to smoke or eat, accused her of having a lesbian affair with a co-worker, and did not permit her to leave

---

[65]DeAngelis v. Jamesway Dep't Store, 501 A.2d 561 (N.J. Super. 1985).
[66]National Loss Control Serv. Corp. v. Dotti, 467 N.E.2d 937, 942 (Ill. App. 1984).
[67]Sossenko v. Michelin Tire Corp., 324 S.E.2d 593 (Ga. App. 1984).

until she signed a statement.[68] In another case, store security officers questioned a female sales representative in a small, windowless room for over three hours, during which time she was led to believe that she was not free to leave.[69]

In deciding whether the defendant's conduct is sufficiently outrageous the courts consider whether it would be considered extreme and outrageous by the plaintiff of ordinary sensitivities— unless the defendant knew that the plaintiff was a person of special sensitivities. For example, in one case, the employer knew that the employee was emotionally frail. Nevertheless, the employee was interrogated most of the day at 30-minute intervals without a lunch break, he was cursed at, accused of stealing, threatened with arrest, and denied access to and use of his prescription tranquilizer.[70]

The plaintiff must establish that the defendant's conduct caused the plaintiff to suffer severe emotional distress. In one case,[71] the plaintiff failed to prove emotional distress where her physical symptoms were associated with a preexisting medical condition and she failed to see her physician immediately after the incident.

Defamation

False accusations made by a representative of the employer to the employee are generally not actionable because the statements are not made to a third party and because the communication may be privileged. Occasionally, however, the interrogation is conducted in such an unreasonable manner that a legal action for defamation may lie. For example, in one case, the employer's security guards interrogated the employee in a glass-enclosed guardhouse at the plant gate through which numerous employees passed as they entered or left the large plant. Even though none of the passers-by could hear what was being said, the court held that an action for slander could be brought because

---

[68]Mansfield v. American Tel. & Tel. Corp., 747 F. Supp. 1329, 5 IER Cases 1383 (W.D. Ark. 1990).

[69]Smithson v. Nordstrom, Inc., 664 P.2d 1119, 118 LRRM 3019 (Or. App. 1983).

[70]*See* Tandy Corp. v. Bone, 678 S.W.2d 312 (Ark. 1984).

[71]Bridges v. Winn-Dixie Atlanta, Inc., 335 S.E.2d 445 (Ga. App. 1985).

of the clear nonverbal implication that the employee had engaged in some serious wrongdoing.[72]

EMPLOYMENT RECORDS

Employment records consist of both personnel files and employee medical records. Statutory and case law involving employment records have centered around three factual situations. First, an employee may seek access to his or her own records. This is usually pursuant to a state statute. Second, some third parties may seek access to an employee's records. Examples of third parties include journalists, unions, co-employees, attorneys, and citizen groups. Third, the employee may claim that improper information is contained in his or her employment records or that the contents of the records have been wrongfully disseminated. Legal actions for negligent maintenance of employment records, defamation, and invasion of privacy have been brought based on this third category.

Legislation has been enacted to regulate various aspects of employment records. Fourteen states[73] have laws giving public and private sector employees access to their own personnel files. Two states (Connecticut, Minnesota) allow access only to private employees and seven states (North Carolina, North Dakota, South Dakota, Tennessee, Utah, Virignia, and the District of Columbia) allow access only to public employees. These laws usually grant an employee "reasonable" access to his or her own records, but employers may be able to limit the frequency of access to the records. Private sector employees in nine states[74] can request that inaccurate information be expunged from their personnel file, and if there is a dispute about the accuracy of the information employees may write an explanatory letter which is then included in the file and sent out any time the disputed information is requested. A Minnesota law requires an employer to provide a copy of

---

[72]General Motors Corp. v. Piskor, 381 A.2d 16 (Md. 1977).

[73]Alaska, California, Delaware, Iowa, Maine, Massachusetts, Michigan, Nevada, New Hampshire, Oregon, Pennsylvania, Rhode Island, Washington, and Wisconsin.

[74]Connecticut, Delaware, Massachusetts, Michigan, Minnesota, Nevada, New Hampshire, Washington, and Wisconsin.

a personnel record to an employee after the employee reviews his or her record and files a written request.

The rights of third parties to access the personnel files of federal employees is regulated by the Freedom of Information Act[75] and the Privacy Act.[76] Twenty states have some type of public records statute using language similar to that of the Privacy Act, and regulate access to the files of state or other public employees. Some states regulate access to employee files of specific public or private employees, including police officers, firefighters, and teachers. Public records statutes usually limit access to personnel files of public employees if that access would constitute an "unwarranted invasion of personal privacy," and require balancing the public's right to government information with the employee's right of privacy.

Laws enacted in five states (Iowa, Maine, Ohio, Oklahoma, and Wisconsin) give employees a right of access to some or all of their medical records within the possession of their employer. Certain medical information, however, may be withheld if, in the opinion of the employer's physician, it would be injurious to the health of the employee. In addition, under many workers' compensation laws, employees have a right of access to any physician report prepared for workers' compensation purposes. Perhaps the most sweeping right of access for employees to their medical records is contained in a regulation issued pursuant to the Occupational Safety and Health Act, discussed in chapter 5.

Access to one's own file is generally limited by the type of information contained in the file. In *Board of Trustees v. Superior Court*,[77] a physician sought access to his own personnel, tenure, and promotion files. The court balanced the physician's right of access to private information about himself with the rights of the individuals whose confidential letters of reference were in the requested files. A California statute allowed an employee access to his own personnel file, excluding letters of reference. The court found no compelling state purpose to maintain the confidentiality of the information contained in the letters, but required that the letters be disclosed with identifying

---

[75] 5 U.S.C. §552(a) (1992).
[76] 5 U.S.C. §552(b) (1992).
[77] 174 Cal. Rptr. 160 (Cal. App. 1981).

information deleted to maintain the rights of privacy of those who had furnished the information.

In *Ollie v. Highland School District No. 203*,[78] a discharged school library aide sought access to information contained in co-workers' personnel files to support her claim that she had been subject to harsher treatment. Under the state's public disclosure act, public records were exempt from disclosure if they were "personal information, maintained for employees, [and] disclosure . . . would violate the employee's right to privacy." The court held that information contained in personnel evaluations and personnel records was privileged, but information about public, on duty job performances could be disclosed if the employees' names and identifying information were removed to protect their privacy.

This method of deleting information to maintain privacy was discussed in *Department of the Air Force v. Rose*,[79] in which the United States Supreme Court interpreted the section of the Privacy Act dealing with personnel files. The Supreme Court stated that courts would have to examine any records to which access was requested and require disclosure of information to which the exemption would not apply.

FREEDOM OF EXPRESSION

Employers have long been interested in regulating what employees say, where they say it, and to whom they say it. Where there is a legitimate basis for the employers' concerns, such as trade secret disclosures, the law has sanctioned employer regulation of employee expression. Where the employers' interests are less direct, however, the law has sometimes granted a remedy to employees whose freedom of expression has been limited. As with many of the conditions of employment explored in this chapter, the most important consideration in analyzing the rights of employees is whether the employment at issue is public or private.

---

[78]749 P.2d 757, 3 IER Cases 167 (Wash. App.), *review denied*, 110 Wash. 2d 1040 (1988).

[79]425 U.S. 352, 1 Media L. Rep. 2509 (1976).

Public Employment

Public employee freedom of expression is protected by the First Amendment. In *Pickering v. Board of Education*,[80] the Supreme Court established a three-part test to determine whether the discharge of a public employee was made on the basis of protected speech. First, the employee must be speaking on a matter of public concern. Second, the court must balance the interests of the employee, as a citizen, in commenting on matters of public concern against the governmental employer's interest in running an efficient operation. Third, the employee's protected conduct must be a motivating factor in the governmental employer's decision to discharge.

The first issue, whether the speech addresses a matter of public concern, is evaluated according to the "content, form, and context of the statement."[81] The manner, time, and place of the statement is very important. The burden is on the employee to show that the speech deserves First Amendment protection. Although the Supreme Court has not defined "public concern," statements addressing matters of public concern tend to fall within certain categories. These include speech related to broad social or policy issues or allegations of discrimination, inefficiency, or improprieties by a government office. These types of statements have been held to be matters of public concern. On the other hand, mundane employment grievances relating primarily to the individual employee have been held not to be matters of public concern. Some examples include individual job evaluations, complaints about individual working conditions, and employer grooming requirements.

Because these general distinctions are not always easy to apply to the wide range of cases, the Supreme Court has said that the context of the statement is important. If a statement is made in the course of an ongoing debate about public issues, such as in testimony before the legislature or in comments to the news media, then the speech is more likely to be considered to involve a matter of public concern.

If employee speech is found to involve a matter of public concern, then the employee's interest in speaking on matters of public concern is balanced against the governmental employer's interest in promoting

---

[80]391 U.S. 563, 1 IER Cases 8 (1968).
[81]Connick v. Myers, 461 U.S. 138, 1 IER Cases 178 (1983).

workplace efficiency. The Supreme Court in *Pickering* and in *Connick v. Myers*[82] suggested the following factors to consider:

- maintenance of discipline by immediate superiors;

- preservation of harmony among co-workers;

- maintenance of personal loyalty and confidence when necessary to the proper functioning of a close working relationship;

- maintenance of the employee's proper performance of daily duties;

- public impact of the statement;

- impact of the statement on the operation of the government entity;

- the existence or nonexistence of an issue of legitimate public concern;

- whether the speaker was in a position in which the need for confidentiality was so great as to justify dismissal for even completely accurate public statements;

- whether narrowly drawn grievance procedures required submission of complaints about the operation of the agency to superiors for action prior to taking complaints to the public;

- whether a statement that was knowingly or recklessly false would still be protected by the First Amendment.

Not surprisingly, application of these myriad factors has proven to be difficult. For example, *Rankin v. McPherson*[83] involved a 19-year-old probationary clerical employee with the title of "deputy constable," who worked in a room where there was no public access, in the Harris County, Texas, constable's office. On March 30, 1981, upon hearing a radio report that there had been an attempt to assassinate President Reagan, the plaintiff told a co-worker, who was her boyfriend, "If they go for him again, I hope they get him." After another employee overheard the remark, she was summoned into the constable's office and fired.

---

[82]461 U.S. 138, 1 IER Cases 178 (1983).
[83]483 U.S. 378, 2 IER Cases 257 (1987).

The Supreme Court, five-to-four, held that the employee's First Amendment rights outweighed the employer's interests. The majority relied on the fact that the employee served no confidential, policy making, or public contact role; the employee was not a peace officer, did not wear a uniform, and was not authorized to make arrests or carry a weapon; and the statement was made in a private conversation in an area where the public did not have access. The dissent challenged whether a distinction should be drawn between non-policy-making and policy-making employees. It further argued that the need to maintain esprit de corps and public image of a law enforcement agency outweighed the employee's First Amendment freedom of expression. Because of the closeness of the case and the changes in Court composition, it is hard to predict how a comparably close case would be decided today.

Although there was little question in *Rankin* that the discharge was based on the speech in question, the third part of the *Pickering* test requires that the court determine that the protected activity was a motivating factor in the action of the public employer. In *Mount Healthy City School District Board of Education v. Doyle*,[84] the Supreme Court enunciated a test which "protects against the invasion of constitutional rights without commanding undesirable consequences not necessary to the assurance of those rights." The test formulated by the Court places the initial burden of proving causation on the employee, who must show that the conduct was a "motivating" or "substantial" factor in the termination of employment. Once the employee has carried that burden, the employer must show by a preponderance of the evidence that the employee would have been discharged even if the protected conduct had not occurred. The policy behind this test is to keep an employee who would not otherwise have been retained from being put in a better position merely because the employee also engaged in constitutionally protected conduct.[85]

Private Employment

Because direct federal constitutional protection is limited to instances of governmental action, private sector employees have fewer rights to express their opinions than public employees. Potentially, the

---

[84]429 U.S. 274, 1 IER Cases 76 (1977).
[85]429 U.S. at 286.

most likely basis for a sweeping expansion of the right to freedom of expression for private sector employees would be through an expansion of the public policy exception to the at-will rule. In a leading but still singular case, *Novosel v. Nationwide Insurance Co.*,[86] a district claims manager for an insurance company was discharged for refusing to lobby the Pennsylvania legislature in opposition to a "no fault" insurance bill under consideration. The Third Circuit Court of Appeals concluded that concern for the rights of political expression and association is sufficient to state a public policy under Pennsylvania law. The case was remanded for application of balancing considerations based on *Pickering* and later cases.

In evaluating freedom of expression claims in the private sector, the courts often differentiate between internal and external speech. Statements made by employees within the workplace are generally afforded less protection by the courts. Thus, for example, discharges have been upheld where employees complained about internal accounting practices, inadequate service to customers, and defective products. By contrast, external speech is much more likely to be protected under either whistleblowing laws or common law. This includes statements to government agencies, the news media, and in public forums.

Otherwise protected employee speech may lose its protection if it is made in an unreasonable time, place, or manner. For example, discharges have been upheld where an employee stood in front of the employer's customer's place of business and expressed his dissatisfaction with the customer's product and service[87] and where a hospital employee discussed incidents of abuses and improper conduct by hospital employees with her taxi driver, her neighbor, and the newspaper, but later denied discussing the incidents.[88]

FREEDOM OF ASSOCIATION

The First Amendment protects public sector employees from interference with their right of association outside the workplace. While the freedom of association was once held to apply only to the advancing

---

[86]721 F.2d 894, 1 IER Cases 286 (3d Cir. 1983).
[87]Prysak v. R.L. Polk Co., 483 N.W.2d 629 (Mich. App. 1992).
[88]Rozier v. St. Mary's Hosp., 411 N.E.2d 50 (Ill. App. 1980).

of political beliefs, the concept now includes the right to meet with others regardless of whether the association is to advance common beliefs.

Public Employees

In *Shelton v. Tucker*,[89] the Supreme Court declared unconstitutional an Arkansas statute which conditioned the employment of every teacher in a state-supported school or college on annually filing an affidavit listing, without limitation, every organization to which the teacher belonged or regularly contributed money over the previous five years. While conceding that fitness for teaching depends on many factors, including conduct outside the classroom, the Court stated that to compel a teacher to list every organization with which he or she associates is a clear violation of the freedom of association.

The use of questionnaires by government employers also has been a source of litigation. In *American Federation of Government Employees v. Schlesinger*,[90] employees of the Department of Energy challenged a mandatory questionnaire that required them to divulge employment and financial interests, creditors, and interests in real property of the employee, spouse, and dependents. The court stated that while some intrusion upon an employee's privacy will be tolerated when it is relevant to the purpose or function of the governmental agency, this sort of broad-sweeping invasion should not be allowed.

In another questionnaire case, an employee who worked as an administrator in a city alternative sentencing program was terminated for her failure to complete a questionnaire that asked about arrests and convictions of the employee or immediate family members, previous sexual relations with a member of the same sex, the details of previous marriages, divorces, and annulments, and all outstanding debts or adverse judgments.[91] The Fourth Circuit Court of Appeals upheld the dismissal on the ground that the information was either public information or not constitutionally protected. The court further held that the employer had a legitimate interest in the information and that it took adequate steps to prevent further disclosure.

---

[89]364 U.S. 479 (1960).
[90]443 F. Supp. 431 (D.D.C. 1978).
[91]Walls v. Petersburg, 895 F.2d 188, 52 FEP Cases 39 (4th Cir. 1990).

The choice of marriage partner also may implicate the freedom of association. For example, the Sixth Circuit Court of Appeals held that a school board employee made out a case of a constitutional violation by alleging that her discharge was the result of her marriage to a person with whom the superintendent had a disagreement.[92] The employee had a legitimate interest in not being denied employment for exercising her First Amendment right to freedom of association.

Private Employees

Some types of associations may be protected by civil rights statutes. For example, under Title VII it is unlawful for an employer to discriminate against an applicant or employee because the individual is married to or associates with members of another racial, religious, or ethnic group. To be protected under Title VII, however, a religious association must be bona fide. For example, a court rejected the argument that discharging an employee because he belonged to the Ku Klux Klan was religious discrimination under Title VII.[93] The court ruled that the Klan is a political and social organization and is not a religion for purposes of Title VII.

In addition to Title VII, section 102(b)(4) of the ADA expressly includes within the definition of unlawful discrimination "excluding or otherwise denying equal jobs or benefits to a qualified individual because of the known disability of an individual with whom the qualified individual is known to have a relationship or association." The purpose of the provision was to prohibit discrimination against family members and friends of people with AIDS, but it has broader applicability, including prohibiting discrimination against individuals who have a spouse or child with a chronic illness.

The right of association has not yet been afforded much recognition in common law actions by at-will employees. For example, a Maryland statute made it a criminal offense "for any person, group, or organization to engage in any act or conduct for the sole purpose of coercing or intimidating another person to contribute or donate any goods, materials, services, or moneys to any social, economic, or political association

---

[92]Adkins v. Board of Educ., 982 F.2d 952, 61 FEP Cases 252 (6th Cir. 1993).
[93]Slater v. King Soopers, 809 F. Supp. 809, 60 FEP Cases 963 (D. Colo. 1992).

or organization." An employee who was terminated for refusing to make a contribution to the United Way brought a wrongful discharge action in which she alleged that her employer was in violation of the Maryland statute on contributions and therefore that her discharge violated public policy. The Maryland Court of Appeals upheld the discharge on the ground that the United Way was not a social or economic organization and therefore the discharge did not violate the statute or public policy.[94]

POLITICAL ACTIVITY

Public Employees

Employee political activity is subject to constitutional protection and statutory regulation. Most of the leading cases involve public sector employees, especially those who have been dismissed because of political patronage. In *Elrod v. Burns*,[95] the Supreme Court reiterated the constitutional rule that a public employee may not be excluded from employment on the basis of political affiliation unless the affiliation is with a subversive organization. The Court found that the state interest in political patronage (preservation of the two-party political system) did not outweigh the freedoms of belief and association upon which the system infringed. Individuals in policy-making positions, however, may be dismissed based on political affiliation because the use of these positions to sabotage the policies of the opposing party would defeat the purpose of representative government.

Based on *Elrod*, it is important to determine whether an employee occupies a policy-making position. A policy maker is an employee whose responsibilities are "not well defined or are of broad scope," or one who "acts as an adviser or formulates plans for the implementation of broad goals." Confidentiality is an indicator of a policy-making position only when the employee obtains access to information of partisan political importance, not information relating only to the needs of individual clients. The Fifth Circuit Court of Appeals, in finding that a school superintendent occupied a policy-making position, listed the following relevant factors to be considered: a general statement of

---

[94]Ball v. United Parcel Serv., 602 A.2d 1176, 7 IER Cases 394 (Md. 1992).
[95]427 U.S. 347, 1 IER Cases 60 (1976).

responsibilities; a position demanding more than ministerial competence; discretion in performing duties which is not severely limited by statute, regulation, or policy determinations made by supervisors; and an employee whose decisions create or implement policy.[96] The broad criteria used in defining "policy making" means that cases must be decided on an ad hoc basis.

In *Branti v. Finkel*,[97] the Supreme Court further held that political affiliation may be the basis of a retention decision if the affiliation is relevant to the effective discharge of the duties of the office. The Court rejected inquiries based on policy making or confidentiality requirements before holding that the proper question is whether the hiring authority can demonstrate that party affiliation is an appropriate requirement for the effective performance of the public office involved. If an individual's private political beliefs would interfere with the discharge of his or her public duties, the interest in maintaining governmental effectiveness and efficiency will outweigh the interest in protecting those beliefs.

In *Rutan v. Republican Party*,[98] the Supreme Court forbid patronage-based decisions in promotion, transfer, recall, and hiring. The majority asserted that the burdens on free speech and association imposed by patronage hiring are similar to those involved in patronage promotions, transfers, and recalls. While government employees have no entitlement to promotions, transfers, and recalls, the government may not withhold these benefits on a basis that violates employees' First Amendment rights.

An employee need not prove that the employer attempted to change his or her political allegiance through coercion, only that the sole reason for the discharge or other adverse action was affiliation with a certain political party. A plaintiff must show that the discharge grew out of constitutionally protected activities; thereafter, the defendant has the burden of proving that another reason existed for the adverse action.

Refusal to hire on the basis of the political *beliefs* of a potential employee is unlawful, but the employee must prove that the political beliefs were a substantial or motivating factor in the decision not to hire. In one case, a Marxist political science professor was unable to prove

---

[96]Kinsey v. Salado Ind. Sch. Dist., 950 F.2d 988 (5th Cir. 1992).

[97]445 U.S. 507, 1 IER Cases 91 (1980).

[98]497 U.S. 62, 5 IER Cases 673 (1990).

that his Marxist beliefs were a substantial or motivating factor in the decision to deny his appointment.[99] The Supreme Court, however, has held that a requirement that public employees execute affidavits disclosing or denying membership in the Communist Party was a reasonable requirement of fitness for employment and not a violation of due process.[100]

Loyalty oaths long have been used to restrict public employees' political activities. In early cases, the Supreme Court held that the denial of public employment on the basis of subversive association could not be justified when the employee was innocent of the group's illegal and subversive goals. In the leading case, *Elfbrandt v. Russell*,[101] the Supreme Court found that mere knowledge of illegal aims of the "subversive organization" with which one is associated is insufficient to terminate an individual's employment. The Court also has struck down state statutes requiring one to forgo any involvement with the Communist Party,[102] as well as statutes that required respect for the flag and the forswearing of membership in subversive organizations.[103]

Employment may not be conditioned on an oath that one has not or will not engage in protected speech activities such as the following: criticizing institutions of government, discussing political doctrine that approves the overthrow of certain forms of government, and supporting candidates for political office. Loyalty oaths are upheld even when they paraphrase constitutional oaths, as long as such oaths are addressed to future action and promise constitutional support in broad terms. In contrast, an oath requiring a state employee to swear that he is not a "subversive person" was held to be unconstitutionally vague and broad, in violation of the First and Fourteenth Amendments.

The Hatch Act[104] is the federal statute that limits the rights of federal employees to engage in partisan political activities. The purpose of the Hatch Act is to ensure political neutrality of federal and state bureaucracies. The statute was meant to prevent the bureaucracy from becoming a unified political power, to prevent the party in power from

---

[99]Ollman v. Toll, 518 F. Supp. 1196 (D. Md. 1981), *aff'd*, 704 F.2d 139 (4th Cir. 1983).

[100]Garner v. Board of Pub. Works, 341 U.S. 716 (1951).

[101]384 U.S. 11 (1966).

[102]Cramp v. Board of Pub. Instruc., 368 U.S. 278 (1961).

[103]Baggett v. Bullitt, 377 U.S. 360 (1964).

[104]5 U.S.C. §§1501–08 (1992).

using government workers improperly, to prevent competition between the party and the department heads, and to prevent employee demoralization based on politics, not merit. All 50 states have passed statutes modeled on the Hatch Act, which limit the political activities of state employees.

The Hatch Act prohibitions apply to nearly all employees of the executive branch of the federal government, with the exception of certain employees appointed by or paid by the executive department, and persons employed as the head or assistant head of an executive department. Nonpartisan political activities, such as voter registration, are exempted from the scope of the Act. Violators of the Act may receive penalties from 30 days' unpaid suspension to removal from office.

While the First Amendment nearly always protects nonpartisan activity, partisan activity is regulated more closely. In *United States Civil Service Commission v. National Association of Letter Carriers*,[105] the Supreme Court listed various partisan political activities that may be regulated by public employers. Among the activities of public employees that may be regulated are the following:

- holding a party office;
- working at the polls;
- acting as party paymaster for other party workers;
- organizing a political party or club;
- actively participating in fund-raising activities for a partisan candidate or political party;
- becoming a partisan candidate for, or campaigning for, an elective public office;
- actively managing the campaign of a partisan candidate for public office; and
- serving as a delegate, alternate, or proxy to a political party convention.

The outward expression of political affiliation also is constitutionally protected, subject to restriction only when necessary to protect a

---

[105]413 U.S. 548 (1973).

legitimate government interest. When a ban on wearing political buttons was challenged by Veteran's Administration employees, the court found that a balancing test would be required because wearing political buttons is not prohibited by the Hatch Act.[106] Factors to be considered include the type of expression, the nature of the agency seeking the ban, and the context in which the expression is made. The court found that restrictions on this type of activity must be based on efficient performance of duties or prevention of conflicts of interest, and that the ban must be restricted to a particular class of employees.

Private Employees

Private sector employees also have alleged that restrictions on their political activity are unlawful. Many states have laws protecting specific political activities of private sector employees, such as joining political parties and running for office. Broader assertions of political rights in the absence of express statutory language have been less successful.

OTHER OFF-WORK BEHAVIOR

Some employers have long been interested in the off-duty activities of their employees, such as personal associations or behavior which could disrupt the job performance of the employee or fellow workers, favor business competitors, or reflect negatively on the image of the enterprise. Off-duty sexual relationships and illegal activity are the most frequently cited "unacceptable behavior." An employee's right to challenge employer disciplinary action depends on whether the employer is public or private, the nature of the unacceptable activity, and the respective interests of the employer and employee.

Public Employees

Public employees may invoke constitutional protections unavailable to private sector employees. When discipline or dismissal results

---

[106]American Fed'n of Gov't Employees v. Pierce, 586 F. Supp. 1559 (D.D.C. 1984).

from lack of adherence to general standards, variously defined as "immoral acts," "conduct unbecoming" or "lack of good moral character," a public sector employee may challenge the action on equal protection, due process, or "void for vagueness" grounds. The results have varied. For example, dismissals have been upheld where a married employee left his wife and moved in with his pregnant girlfriend; where male police officers consorted with women with criminal records, with the wife of an alleged mobster, and with women of "loose morals"; and where the employee practiced "plural marriage." On the other hand, dismissals have been held to violate the right to privacy of an employee who refused to answer questions about her sex life, an employee who had a relationship with a co-worker, an employee who cohabited with his girlfriend, and an employee who refused to terminate an affair.

Police officers and teachers appear to be held to a higher standard of conduct (and afforded fewer privacy protections) than are other public employees because of their function as "role models" and their potential influence on the public and students. In addition, the quasi-military structure of most police units, with their need for discipline, has also been used by the courts to justify lessened privacy rights for employees. Generally, the courts have required only a rational relationship between a regulation and the government's intended objective in order to uphold the regulation as constitutional.

Federal employees have greater protection against dismissal based on their off-work activities than do other public sector employees because of the federal statutory requirement that the "efficiency of the service" be impaired. The issue has been framed as whether the misconduct has a sufficient relationship to the agency's operations so that disciplinary action would promote the efficiency of the service. It is the agency's burden to show by a preponderance of the evidence that a nexus exists, and the employee may successfully rebut by showing the absence of any adverse impact.

A sufficient relationship may be shown to exist because the egregious nature of the conduct presumes a nexus, because the conduct is so at odds with the employee's job duties that a nexus is created, or because the notoriety accompanying the misconduct has discredited the agency or affected the performance of other employees. When the conduct is unrelated to job duties and there is no notorious publicity, a nexus generally is not found. Being charged with a crime does not automatically establish a nexus, although conviction may.

The discharges of state and local employees have been upheld where an employee was engaged in egregious sexual misconduct, where an off-duty employee engaged in anti-Semitic verbal abuse in public, where an employee assaulted a fellow off-duty employee, and where an employee engaged in disorderly conduct. The Kentucky Supreme Court even upheld the discharge of an at-will public employee, a secretary with the Louisville Housing Authority, who filed a negligence action after her infant son was injured in an apartment owned and managed by her employer.[107] Successful challenges, however, have been brought against the refusal to hire unwed mothers, the discharge of a middle-aged, divorced school teacher who had a male guest stay overnight, the discharge of a state college director of residence halls for women who had a child out of wedlock, and the discharge of a teacher for a single, noncriminal homosexual episode with a fellow teacher.

Private Employees

Private sector employees have fewer protections against employer discipline for off-duty behavior. Thus, the courts have upheld the discharge of employees for dating or marrying co-workers. The courts also have given deference to the rights of religious organizations to oversee the morals of their employees.

Off-duty conduct rarely falls into the category of behavior protected by the public policy exception to the at-will rule, but employees may be protected if they are working pursuant to an express or implied contract. In *Rulon-Miller v. International Business Machines Corp.*,[108] an employee was discharged for dating an employee of a competitor. Because there was a written company policy acknowledging the privacy rights of employees with regard to their off-the-job behavior, the court held that the employee had stated a cognizable claim for wrongful discharge. In the absence of such policies, however, the courts will not require a nexus between off-the-job conduct and on-the-job performance, leaving employers largely free to impose whatever standards of conduct or discipline they choose.

---

[107]Boykins v. Housing Auth., 842 S.W.2d 527, 8 IER Cases 1 (Ky. 1992).
[108]208 Cal. Rptr. 524, 1 IER Cases 405 (Cal. App. 1984).

Some employer attempts to regulate off-work behavior or lifestyle may implicate Title VII. In *Chambers v. Omaha Girls Club, Inc.*,[109] a black, single woman was employed by the Club as an arts and crafts instructor. When she later informed her supervisor that she was pregnant, she was discharged pursuant to the Club's written "role model" rule. The plaintiff brought a Title VII action in which she alleged that the "role model" rule amounted to race and gender discrimination, but the court upheld the rule.

Some states have enacted laws forbidding employers from coercing employees to deal with or refrain from patronizing particular stores. These laws date back to the days of "company stores." Additional state legislation to limit employers from inquiring into off-work activities of employees or from discharging employees because of off-work activities is likely. For example, several states have enacted laws prohibiting employers from refusing to hire or discharging employees because they smoke cigarettes off work. Some of the laws enacted for this purpose are written more broadly to prohibit discrimination because of the use of a "lawful product," or even because of "lawful activity off the premises of the employer during nonworking hours." It remains to be seen how broadly these laws will be construed.

INVASION OF PRIVACY

Employees have become increasingly sensitive about employer intrusions on their privacy and they have brought a wide range of lawsuits seeking redress. Public employees have raised federal constitutional claims. State constitutions and state statutes have been invoked by private sector employees. The most frequently asserted privacy claims, however, have been for common law invasion of privacy.

Invasion of privacy encompasses a wide range of factual situations of alleged wrongdoing. The tort of invasion of privacy, often the legal basis of the case, actually consists of four separate types of cases: public disclosure of private facts, intrusion upon seclusion, false light, and appropriation of name or likeness. Each of these claims has been asserted in the employment context.

---

[109]834 F.2d 697, 45 FEP Cases 698 (8th Cir. 1987).

Public Disclosure of Private Facts

Public disclosure of private facts is the tort most often asserted by employees in invasion of privacy actions. The elements necessary to establish a claim for invasion of privacy based on public disclosure of private facts are: "Publication or publicity absent any waiver or privilege of private matters in which the public has no legitimate concern so as to bring shame or humiliation to a person of ordinary sensibilities."[110] "Publicity" occurs when a matter is made public by communicating to the public at large, or to so many persons that the matter must be regarded as substantially certain to become one of public knowledge. Oral communications as well as written communications may qualify as "publication." Where no publicity is proven, no cause of action exists.

The majority rule is that private information must be made widely public, with disclosure made to people outside the workplace who have no need to know the information. A balancing of interests usually occurs in these cases, where the court weighs the degree of exposure, the sensitivity of the private facts disclosed, and the need for legitimate business communication. For example, the publication requirement was not satisfied where a treating psychologist's letter to the employee's division supervisor was reviewed only by supervisors and others with a legitimate and direct interest in the plaintiff's employment.[111] Similarly, a former employer's mailing a letter to the plaintiff's ex-wife requesting verification that the ex-wife would exercise no claim to plaintiff's retirement benefits, was held to be a private and not a public communication.[112]

Discussion of a plaintiff's private matters with fellow employees does not reach the requisite level of publicity to state a claim for public disclosure of private facts. For instance, the disclosing to a few co-workers the fact that the plaintiff-employee was undergoing psychiatric treatment did not reach the requisite level of "publicity."[113] Also, when an employer responded to customer inquiries regarding the reason for the discharge of a sales representative, the court held that there was no

---

[110]*Restatement (Second) of Torts* §652D (1977).
[111]Childs v. Williams, 825 S.W.2d 4, 7 IER Cases 255 (Mo. App. 1992).
[112]Lodge v. Shell Oil Co., 747 F.2d 16, 5 EB Cases 2225 (1st Cir. 1984).
[113]Eddy v. Brown, 715 P.2d 74 (Okla. 1986).

invasion of privacy because the customers asked and only a few were told the information.[114]

The opposite result, finding an invasion of privacy, was reached in *Levias v. United Airlines*.[115] An airline's medical examiner was supplied with the plaintiff flight attendant's medical information by her gynecologist. The medical supervisor then disclosed most of the information to the plaintiff's male flight supervisor, who had no compelling reason to know it, as well as to the plaintiff's husband. In addition, the supervisor repeatedly contacted the plaintiff to reveal the details of her medical condition and also raised the issue with the plaintiff in the presence of her appearance supervisor.

The employer-defendant in an invasion of privacy action may claim that a waiver or privilege precludes the invasion of privacy action. Written or oral releases authorizing a physician to reveal information acquired in the course of the employee's examination or treatment may operate as a waiver of any potential invasion of privacy claims by the employee. Where a psychologist revealed information about a patient's neuroses and psychoses to the patient's employer in the course of recommending that she be transferred to a less stressful position, the court found that the plaintiff had waived her right to keep the information confidential.[116]

Some communications may be absolutely privileged. For example, the employer of an employee who worked with potentially dangerous chemicals and was believed by a mental health professional to be lethally dangerous to himself and those around him was found to have an absolute and a qualified privilege to confer with others in order to determine whether the employee should continue working.[117] The employer was found to have an absolute privilege because of the statutory requirement that employers make the workplace safe.

Matters which are already public knowledge as the result of a public incident, and which are the subject of disciplinary action by a public body, are not sufficiently private to provide an invasion of privacy cause of action. In one case, three public school teachers who

---

[114]*See* Lemnah v. American Breeders Serv., Inc., 482 A.2d 700 (Vt. 1984).

[115]500 N.E.2d 370 (Ohio App. 1985).

[116]Childs v. Williams, 825 S.W.2d 4, 7 IER Cases 255 (Mo. App. 1992).

[117]Davis v. Monsanto Co., 627 F. Supp. 418, 7 EB Cases 1048 (S.D. W. Va. 1986).

became drunk at an end-of-the-year teachers' retirement party and later crashed their car into a cement abutment failed to prove any actionable publicity by the school district, which publicized the disciplinary action taken in regard to the plaintiffs.[118]

Another limitation on the cause of action for invasion of privacy is that the private matter disclosed publicly must be outrageous or highly offensive to a reasonable person. In order to constitute outrageous conduct, the defendant's conduct must inflict actual mental suffering on the plaintiff.

While the employment relationship may work against the employee by creating a waiver or privilege, the relationship may also provide a basis for a claim of invasion of privacy. For example, one court found an employee's physical, mental, and emotional distress resulting from her employer's disclosure of the facts surrounding her mastectomy to co-employees to be a question for the jury.[119]

Intrusion Upon Seclusion

The tort of intrusion upon seclusion has been defined in the following manner: "One who intentionally intrudes, physically or otherwise, upon the solitude or seclusion of another or his private affairs or concerns, is subject to liability to the other for invasion of his privacy, if the intrusion would be highly offensive to a reasonable person."[120] The legitimacy of the reason for inquiring into the employee's private concerns is an important factor in determining liability.

In *Mares v. Conagra Poultry Co.,*[121] the plaintiff's employment was terminated following her failure to fill out a form dealing with prescription drug usage in connection with a routine drug test. The court, while recognizing that the absence of public disclosure does not preclude a legal action for intrusion upon seclusion, nevertheless held that the legitimate business interests cited by the employer (protecting employees from false positives and maintaining the integrity of its drug testing) were enough to support the employer's request for information.

---

[118]Trout v. Umatilla County Sch. Dist., 712 P.2d 814, *review denied*, 716 P.2d 758 (Or. 1986).

[119]Miller v. Motorola, Inc., 560 N.E.2d 900, 5 IER Cases 885 (Ill. App. 1990).

[120]*Restatement (Second) of Torts*, §652B (1977).

[121]971 F.2d 492, 7 IER Cases 997 (10th Cir. 1992).

Although most jurisdictions hold that no physical intrusion is necessary, several jurisdictions require a physical intrusion to maintain an action. For example, the Georgia Court of Appeals found that a physical intrusion, like that of a trespass, is necessary for the tort of intrusion upon seclusion.[122] Also, if no intrusion actually takes place because of the employee's refusal to participate in the questioning or activity, no cause of action for invasion of privacy will exist.

Courts generally agree that an employer has a legitimate business interest in determining the mental and physical condition of an employee to the extent that it relates to employment. That interest, however, must be balanced against the nature and extent of intrusion in determining if an invasion of privacy has occurred. Where an employee was discharged after her supervisors questioned her clinical psychologist, with whom she met at her own expense regarding her mental state, the court found an actionable invasion of her privacy.[123] The plaintiff had not consented to the release of the information by her private psychologist, and the court found that her employer had no legitimate business interest in trying to garner information without the plaintiff's consent.

On the other hand, some courts have refused to find an invasion of privacy even where the employer engaged in or authorized highly questionable conduct. In one case, investigators conducting an undercover investigation of the plaintiff's husband's workers' compensation claim represented themselves to be employed by a marketing company and used that story to gain access to the plaintiff's home.[124] They gathered information about the activities of her husband, as well as later asking the plaintiff to test various consumer products and inviting her to participate in a shopping spree, which was later canceled. The court found no invasion of privacy because the purpose and scope of the investigation was limited to gathering information concerning the workers' compensation claim, the investigators never entered the plaintiff's home without her permission, the investigation took place for a relatively short period of time, and the credibility of the plaintiff's husband was called into question by competent evidence.

---

[122]Kobeck v. Nabisco, Inc., 305 S.E.2d 183, 185, 1 IER Cases 200 (Ga. App. 1983).

[123]Leggett v. First Interstate Bank, 739 P.2d 1083 (Or. App. 1987).

[124]Turner v. General Adjustment Bureau, Inc., 832 P.2d 62 (Utah App. 1992).

Courts have construed an "offensive intrusion" to require either an unreasonable manner of intrusion or intrusion for an unwarranted purpose. In one case, two of the plaintiff's supervisors, allegedly concerned about his health, hired a locksmith to open his trailer home, where they observed the plaintiff sleeping and possibly intoxicated.[125] After this incident, during which the two supervisors took notes on the number of liquor bottles present in the plaintiff's trailer, the plaintiff was told he could not return to his place of work in a supervisory capacity, and as a result, he signed a termination agreement. The court found that there was no error in the jury finding that an unreasonable intrusion occurred.

A manager's intrusive interrogation and coercive behavior were found to be so offensive as to support a jury award of damages for the invasion of the plaintiff's privacy.[126] The manager repeatedly called the plaintiff into his office, closed and locked the door, questioned her about her sex life, propositioned her, and threatened to fire her if she did not have sex with him. The plaintiff refused to answer any of the questions and spurned the advances. Significantly, the court held that there was an intrusion, even though the manager was rebuked. If the behavior is sufficiently offensive, actual receipt of the private information is not necessary.

False Light

The tort of false light publicity has been defined in the following manner:

> One who gives publicity to a matter concerning another that places the other before the public in a false light is subject to liability to the other for invasion of privacy, if: (a) the false light in which the other was placed would be highly offensive to a reasonable person, and (b) the actor had knowledge of or acted in reckless disregard as to the falsity of the publicized matter and the false light in which the other would be placed.[127]

---

[125]Love v. Southern Bell Tel. & Tel. Co., 263 So.2d 460 (La. App.), *cert. denied*, 266 So.2d 429 (La. 1972).

[126]Phillips v. Smalley Maintenance Servs., Inc., 711 F.2d 1524, 32 FEP Cases 975 (11th Cir. 1983).

[127]*Restatement (Second) of Torts* §652E (1977).

The injury in a false light claim is mental distress resulting from the publicity.

False light requires that the published matter be untrue. Therefore, if the published matter is expressed as an opinion and not as a matter of fact, no cause of action exists. Facts must actually be made public in a false light invasion of privacy claim. One court found sufficient publication to uphold a jury verdict for the plaintiff where a supervisor falsely stated to a subordinate in front of other employees that the subordinate's wife was sexually promiscuous.[128] When an employee's former supervisor made comments following the plaintiff's resignation indicating that he was terminated for embezzlement or similar activities, the court found that a jury question existed as to whether any information placing the plaintiff in a false light was communicated to "so many persons that the matter must be regarded as substantially certain to become one of public knowledge."[129]

The "publication" at the root of an invasion of privacy claim may consist of acts rather than words. In one case, a trader for a securities firm fell out of favor with management for voicing his objection to the firm's participation in what he believed were unlawful trading practices.[130] The firm, deciding to terminate his employment, made a surprise visit to his office in front of the other traders, refused to allow him to speak to his staff, remained with him while he packed his personal belongings, interrogated his fellow employees about entries in his travel and entertainment expense reports, and then escorted him out of the building. The court agreed with the trader's claim that the series of acts taken by management had the cumulative effect of creating a false impression among his co-workers that he had engaged in serious misconduct or a substantial breach of ethics before his discharge.

Appropriation of Another's Name or Likeness

One form of the tort of invasion of privacy which occasionally arises in the employment context is appropriation of name or likeness.

---

[128]Keehr v. Consolidated Freightway, Inc., 825 F.2d 133, 2 IER Cases 565 (7th Cir. 1987).

[129]Krochalis v. Insurance Co. of N. Am., 629 F. Supp. 1360 (E.D. Pa. 1985).

[130]Zechman v. Merrill Lynch, 742 F. Supp. 1359, 29 WH Cases 1456 (N.D. Ill. 1990).

The case law in this area generally involves whether the employer used the employee's name, picture, or other likeness for commercial use without the employee's consent.

A common example is a case in which a Boeing Airplane employee was in a photograph used by the company in magazine advertisements.[131] The employee made no complaint at the time the photograph was taken, nor did he complain when the photograph was posted around the plant on company bulletin boards. The focus of the photograph was on the airplane pictured, with the employee serving mainly as a prop, with no identification of him made by name or otherwise. The court, determining that the employee's real complaint was that he had not been compensated for the use of his photograph, not the fact that the photograph was published, found that there was no invasion of the employee's privacy.

Similarly, a former laboratory director claimed that his name continued to appear on various forms and documents by the company after his employment with the company was terminated.[132] The court found that the plaintiff had originally consented to the use of his name, but that a question of fact existed as to whether the company had ceased use of the plaintiff's name within a reasonable time after his dismissal.

[131]Johnson v. Boeing Airplane Co., 262 P.2d 808 (Kan. 1953).
[132]Alonso v. Parfet, 325 S.E.2d 152 (Ga. 1985).

5

Occupational Safety and Health Act

INTRODUCTION

The Occupational Safety and Health Act of 1970 (OSH Act or Act)[1] is the primary federal law regulating workplace safety and health. It covers private sector employment in every state, the District of Columbia, Puerto Rico, and all U.S. territories. Among other requirements, each employer must comply with occupational safety and health standards set by the Secretary of Labor. Each employer also must keep its workplace free from "recognized hazards that are causing or likely to cause death or serious physical harm to its employees."

The job of enforcing the Act rests with the Occupational Safety and Health Administration (OSHA) of the United States Department of Labor. OSHA compliance officers (COs) may inspect any workplace covered by the Act. The CO must present his or her credentials to the owner, operator, or agent in charge before proceeding with the inspection. The employer and an employee representative have a right to accompany the inspector. A closing conference is held after the

---

[1] 29 U.S.C. §§651–78 (1993). For a further discussion, see M.A. Rothstein, *Occupational Safety and Health Law* (St. Paul, Minn.: West Publishing Co., 3d ed. 1990).

inspection, during which the CO and the employer's representative discuss safety and health conditions and possible violations.

After the CO files a report of the inspection with the OSHA area director, the Department of Labor decides whether to issue a citation against the employer, computes any penalties to be assessed under the Act, and sets the date for correction of each alleged violation. If a citation is issued, it is mailed to the employer as soon as possible after the inspection, but in no event can it be issued more than six months after the alleged violation occurred. Citations must be in writing and must describe with particularity the violations alleged, including the relevant OSHA standards and regulations.

The Act, as amended in 1990, provides for a wide range of penalties based on the degree of violation, i.e., de minimis; nonserious or serious; whether it is a repeated or willful violation; and whether the violation is for failure to abate (correct) a previously cited violation. (Penalties are discussed later in this chapter).

The good faith of the employer, the gravity of the violation, the employer's past history of compliance, and the size of the employer are all considered in penalty assessment. There are also criminal sanctions under the Act, including fines and imprisonment, for willful violations that have caused the death of one or more employees.

Under the Act, an employer, an employee, or an authorized employee representative (union) has 15 working days in which to object to the citation by filing a notice of contest. If no contest is filed, the citation becomes final and may not be challenged later. The Secretary must immediately forward any notice of contest received by OSHA to the Occupational Safety and Health Review Commission (Commission or OSHRC), an independent administrative agency. The Commission will then hold a hearing presided over by an administrative law judge (ALJ). After the hearing, the ALJ will issue a decision, affirming, modifying, or vacating the citation, penalty, or time given to correct the violation (abatement date). The ALJ's decision may then be reviewed by the Commission. Appeals from Commission decisions may then be filed in the United States courts of appeals.

JURISDICTION

The OSH Act applies to all private sector employers in the United States. This has been estimated to include at least six million workplaces and 90 million employees. Unlike the National Labor Relations Act and Title VII of the Civil Rights Act of 1964, coverage under the OSH Act is not based on a minimum volume of business or number of employees.

State and Local Governments

The Act does not apply to state and local governments. This exemption, however, has been narrowly construed. Consequently, private employers with a contractual or other relationship with a state or political subdivision have been unsuccessful in avoiding coverage by asserting that their working conditions are governmental. For example, an architecture and construction management firm that was supervising the construction of a building at a state university was held to be an employer covered under the Act because the company dealt with the state "at arm's length." Similarly, the Commission held that joint supervisory control over a private employer's workers by a municipal sewer department did not relieve the private employer of its duty to comply with the Act. In general, some of the significant factors in determining whether an employer is exempt under the Act as a state or political subdivision are whether it makes a profit, whether it pays taxes, whether it pays the salary of the employees, and whether it is administered by a public official.[2]

Federal Government

Section 19(a) of the Act requires the head of each federal agency to establish, develop, and maintain a comprehensive occupational safety and health program. This express congressional mandate of federal government compliance has been implemented by presidential executive orders. The main problem with federal government programs is the lack of an enforcement mechanism comparable to the private sector.

Interstate Commerce Requirement

Section 3(5) of the Act defines an employer as "a person engaged in a business affecting commerce who has employees." Proof that an

---

[2]See the Secretary's regulations at 29 C.F.R. §1975.5 (1992).

employer is in a business affecting commerce is necessary to give the Secretary jurisdiction under the Act. It is quite easy for the Secretary to prove that an employer is engaged in a business affecting commerce. For example, it has been held that an employer was engaged in a business affecting commerce because it hired employees from a union hall, used the telephone and mails, and purchased supplies from out of state. Similarly, an employer's use of goods manufactured out of state, which moved in interstate commerce, was sufficient to establish jurisdiction under the Act.

Preemption by Another Agency

Section 4(b)(1) of the Act provides that the Act does not apply to "working conditions of employees with respect to which other federal agencies . . . exercise statutory authority to prescribe or enforce standards or regulations affecting occupational safety and health." Congress intended to avoid the duplication of enforcement by OSHA and other federal agencies that regulate employee safety and health. The most recent Commission decisions suggest a three-part test to determine whether OSHA is precluded from exercising jurisdiction by virtue of section 4(b)(1). The OSH Act will not apply if the following requirements are met.

First, the employer must be covered by another federal act directed exclusively at employee safety and health or directed at public safety and health and employees directly receive the protection the act is intended to provide. An example is the Federal Mine Safety and Health Act.

Second, the other federal agency must have exercised its statutory authority by prescribing and enforcing safety and health standards. Nevertheless, the other federal agency's regulations need not be similar or equally stringent to OSHA's. In addition, according to the Commission, "[a]ny oversight of another agency's enforcement activities is beyond the scope of a permissible inquiry under section 4(b)(1)."[3]

Third, the other federal agency must have acted in such a manner as to exempt the working conditions from OSHA jurisdiction. In general, industrywide exemptions have not been granted and the facts of each case have been reviewed independently.

---

[3]Pennsuco Cement & Aggregates, Inc., 8 OSH Cases 1378 (1980).

STATE PLANS AND STATE REGULATION

Section 18 of the Act permits states to assert jurisdiction over job safety and health matters by submitting a plan for OSHA approval. The Act sets the minimum acceptable safety standards in order to maintain some semblance of uniformity. Nevertheless, the standards merely serve as starting points for state programs; the Act does not require that state plans be identical to federal OSHA. The standards prescribed for employers may even be more stringent under a state plan.

The Act leaves the choice of submitting a plan to the individual state. If a state does not submit a state plan, it is precluded from enforcing state laws, regulations, or standards relating to "issues" covered by the Act. This preclusion, however, does not extend to a state's enforcement of a law or standard directed to an issue upon which there is no OSHA standard. Boilers and elevators are two issues over which OSHA has not promulgated standards and, therefore, over which state enforcement is not preempted.

States without approved plans also retain jurisdiction in three other areas. First, states may enforce standards, such as state and local fire regulations, designed to protect the general population. Second, states retain jurisdiction over consultation, training, and safety information activities. Third, states may enforce standards to protect state and local government employees who are not covered by federal OSHA.[4]

As of 1994, there were 23 jurisdictions with approved state plans for private and public sector employees and two state plans covering only state and local government employees.[5]

The District of Columbia, Maine, New Hampshire, New Jersey, Rhode Island, West Virginia, and Wisconsin have laws protecting public employees, but they are not OSHA-approved state plans. Because federal grants of 90 percent for planning and development are no longer available, it is unlikely that any new state plans will be submitted for approval.

---

[4]The Secretary has promulgated regulations for state plans that cover only state and local employees. 29 C.F.R. pt. 1956.

[5]States with approved plans are: Alaska, Arizona, California, Hawaii, Indiana, Iowa, Kentucky, Maryland, Michigan, Minnesota, Nevada, New Mexico, North Carolina, Oregon, Puerto Rico, South Carolina, Tennessee, Utah, Vermont, Virgin Islands, Virginia, Washington, and Wyoming. States having plans covering only public employees are Connecticut and New York. Descriptions of each state plan appear at 29 C.F.R. pt. 1952.

In *Gade v. National Solid Wastes Management Ass'n,*[6] the Supreme Court considered whether two Illinois laws, which required state licensing of hazardous waste workers, were preempted by the OSH Act. The dual purposes of the state laws were to protect both employees and the general public. A detailed OSHA standard also addressed training requirements for hazardous waste workers. The Supreme Court, five to four, held that the Illinois law was preempted by the federal law. According to Justice O'Connor, the OSH Act "precludes any state regulation of an occupational safety and health issue with respect to which a federal standard has been established, unless a state plan has been submitted and approved pursuant to section 18(b)."

State Criminal Laws

Since the mid-1980s there has been a substantial increase in the number of state criminal prosecutions brought as a result of fatalities or injuries in the workplace. The charges have included reckless endangerment, manslaughter, and even murder. One reason for this increased local activity is a perception of lax federal enforcement efforts in occupational safety and health.

In many of these cases the defendants have argued that state criminal laws may not be applied where the prosecution is based on working conditions regulated by OSHA. The state courts generally have not been receptive to these arguments. In fact, decisions in Illinois, Michigan, New York, Texas, and Wisconsin, and an advisory opinion by the United States Department of Justice, all have concluded that state criminal prosecutions may be based on conduct in the workplace.

DEVELOPMENT OF OSHA STANDARDS

Although the language of the OSH Act is quite general, Congress envisioned that employers would have clearly expressed duties to take specific measures to provide safe and healthful workplaces. Thus, Congress delegated to the Secretary of Labor the responsibility for developing specific OSHA standards.

---

[6]112 S.Ct. 2374, 15 OSH Cases 1673 (1992).

Section 6 of the Act describes three different types of standards: existing standards (interim standards) adopted under section 6(a) of the Act; new standards (permanent standards) added pursuant to section 6(b) of the Act; and emergency temporary standards adopted under section 6(c) of the Act. Although the Secretary of Labor is authorized to develop and enforce the standards, technical assistance in developing standards is provided by another agency. Section 22 of the Act created the National Institute for Occupational Safety and Health (NIOSH), headed by a director appointed by the Secretary of Health and Human Services (HHS) for a term of six years. Within HHS, NIOSH is a part of the Centers for Disease Control and Prevention.

NIOSH has no authority to set or enforce standards, but it is responsible for conducting research and making recommendations to the Department of Labor. In addition to recommending new standards, NIOSH is also responsible for updating and revising all prior standards. NIOSH has authority to conduct inspections and question employers and employees for research purposes.[7] Many of these inspections are "health hazard evaluations" initiated by an employee's filing of an inspection request with NIOSH.

Existing Standards

Under section 6(a) of the Act, the Secretary of Labor was required to adopt as occupational safety and health standards all "national consensus standards," unless the Secretary determined that a particular standard would not result in improved safety and health for employees. National consensus standards are privately written standards produced by a body of diverse professionals, such as the American National Standards Institute (ANSI). The purpose of section 6(a) was to permit OSHA enforcement activities without a time lag for development of standards.

In attempting to give binding effect to these private standards, the Secretary in some instances changed the wording of a standard from "should" to "shall." In *Usery v. Kennecott Copper Corp.*,[8] however, the Tenth Circuit affirmed the Commission's holding that the Secretary was not authorized by section 6(a) of the Act to make such changes.

---

[7]NIOSH workplace investigation procedures appear at 42 C.F.R. pt. 85 (1992).
[8]577 F.2d 1113, 6 OSH Cases 1197 (10th Cir. 1977).

Furthermore, the court in *Marshall v. Pittsburgh Des Moines Steel Co.*[9] held that the Secretary's subsequent "interpretation" of an ANSI standard could not change the effect of an already adopted standard from optional to mandatory.

Section 6(a) of the Act also permitted the Secretary of Labor to adopt "established federal standards." These are federal safety and health standards previously adopted under another, pre-OSHA federal statute, such as the Walsh-Healey Act, which prescribed the working conditions for employees of federal contractors. As with the national consensus standards, the adoption of established federal standards pursuant to section 6(a) has raised a number of legal issues. Of particular importance are OSHA's changes in language and changes in scope from the original standard.

New Standards

Section 6(b) of the Act provides that when OSHA adds a new standard, or modifies or revokes an existing OSHA standard, it must comply with specific procedures.[10] The Secretary of Labor is required to publish a notice in the Federal Register and must allow 30 days after publication for interested parties to submit written data or comments. In practice, the process for adopting new OSHA standards, especially new health standards, often takes years.

In *Industrial Union Department, AFL-CIO v. American Petroleum Institute (The Benzene Case)*,[11] the Supreme Court addressed several important issues in ruling on the validity of OSHA's benzene standard. In a sharply divided opinion, the Supreme Court held that "[Section 3(8)] requires the Secretary, before issuing any standard, to determine that it is reasonably necessary and appropriate to remedy a significant risk of material health impairment." In proving that a standard is reasonably necessary, the Secretary must first show that there exists a significant risk at current exposure levels. Then, the Secretary must prove that the new standard will lead to appreciable benefits.

---

[9]584 F.2d 638, 6 OSH Cases 1929 (3d Cir. 1978).
[10]The Secretary's rulemaking procedures appear at 29 C.F.R. pt. 1911 (1992).
[11]448 U.S. 607, 8 OSH Cases 1586 (1980).

In *American Textile Manufacturers Institute, Inc. v. Donovan (The Cotton Dust Case)*,[12] the Supreme Court addressed the issue of whether the Act requires the Secretary to determine that the costs of a new standard bear a reasonable relationship to its benefits. The Court rejected the argument that the Act requires the use of cost-benefit analysis. The statute requires only that standards be both technologically and economically "feasible," which the Court defined as capable of being achieved.

Revising and updating existing health standards also have been difficult for the Secretary. *AFL-CIO v. OSHA*[13] involved a challenge to OSHA's attempt to revise at one time its standards for 428 toxic substances. The Eleventh Circuit Court of Appeals held that the Act does not preclude "generic" rulemaking, but the court held that each new permissible exposure limit (PEL) must be supported by substantial evidence. The court held that OSHA failed to prove the "significant risk" posed by each substance to be regulated or that the new standards eliminate or substantially lessen the risk.

Emergency Temporary Standards

Section 6(c)(1) of the Act provides that if the Secretary determines that employees are "exposed to grave danger from exposure to substances or agents determined to be toxic or physically harmful or from new hazards," an emergency temporary standard (ETS) may be issued. These standards are effective immediately upon publication in the Federal Register. An ETS may remain in effect for only six months; thereafter the Secretary must issue a permanent standard under section 6(b) of the Act. An emergency temporary standard must be based on the existence of a grave danger and the need for a standard to protect workers from the danger. The first element, therefore, is proving that there is a grave danger. The Act does not require an absolute certainty of the deleterious effect of a substance, but there must be evidence showing "more than some possibility" of a grave danger.

The second element of an ETS is the need to protect workers from the danger. In *Asbestos Information Association/North America v.*

---

[12]452 U.S. 490, 9 OSH Cases 1913 (1981).
[13]965 F.2d 962, 15 OSH Cases 1729 (11th Cir. 1992).

OSHA,[14] the Fifth Circuit Court of Appeals held that the ETS for asbestos was invalid. The court said that OSHA had failed to prove the need to adopt an ETS for asbestos under section 6(c) rather than modifying the existing standard pursuant to section 6(b).

Judicial Review

The validity of OSHA standards may be reviewed by the courts in two ways. First, within 60 days of the issuance of a standard, any party (typically a trade association or union) may file a "petition for review" (an appeal). These petitions may be filed in the United States court of appeals for the circuit in which the party resides or has its principal place of business.

Second, a postenforcement challenge to the validity of a standard may be brought. After being issued a citation by the Secretary and challenging the citation before the Commission, an employer may file a petition seeking review of the Commission's decision. These petitions also must be filed within 60 days in a United States court of appeals for the circuit in which the violation is alleged to have occurred, for the circuit in which the employer has its principal office, or in the District of Columbia Circuit. Waiting until after being issued a citation to challenge the validity of a new standard, however, has some risk attached, because some courts hold that the validity of a standard may only be challenged at the time the standard is issued.

COMPLIANCE WITH STANDARDS

OSHA standards are grouped under four industry categories: General Industry, Construction, Maritime and Longshoring, and Agricultural. An employer must be cited under an applicable standard appropriate to the employer's business, and the burden is on the Secretary of Labor to prove that the standard applies.

General Industry

General industry standards apply to all employers, subject to two exceptions. First, the general industry standard may be specifically

---

[14]727 F.2d 415, 11 OSH Cases 1817 (5th Cir. 1984).

limited to a certain type of business. For example, subpart R of the general industry standards contains "special" standards for bakery equipment, laundry machinery, sawmills, and the like. Nevertheless, employers covered by these "special industry" general industry standards still must comply with all other general industry standards unless the specific condition is actually covered by a "special industry" standard.

Second, the specific working conditions may be subject to a standard contained in the construction, maritime and longshoring, or agricultural standards. General industry standards will apply, however, if there is no specific construction, maritime and long-shoring, or agricultural standard covering the hazardous condition. For example, "even in areas properly citable under specific maritime standards, the Secretary may hold an employer to the general industry standards in those situations where no specific standard is applicable."[15]

Construction

The construction standards apply to employers with employees "engaged in construction work," defined as "work for construction, alteration, and/or repair, including painting and decorating."[16] Several cases have involved whether the employer's operations came within this definition. For example, in *Brock v. Cardinal Industries, Inc.*,[17] the employer was manufacturing modular housing units in a factory. It was cited under the general industry standards for failing to have guardrails on two platforms. The ALJ affirmed the violations, but the Commission reversed. The Commission majority concluded that the general industry standards did not apply because the employer was engaged in construction. The Sixth Circuit Court of Appeals reversed the Commission. According to the court, in determining whether the work performed is "construction," it is not the nature of the work in the abstract, but the nexus of the work to a particular construction site.

---

[15]Dravo Corp. v. OSHRC, 613 F.2d 1227, 1234, 7 OSH Cases 2089 (3d Cir. 1980).

[16]29 C.F.R. §1910.12(b) (1992).

[17]828 F.2d 373, 13 OSH Cases 1377 (6th Cir. 1987).

Maritime and Longshoring

The terms "ship repairing," "ship building," "shipbreaking," and "longshoring" are defined in the OSHA standards. Ship repair means "any repair of a vessel, including, but not restricted to, alterations, conversions, installations, cleaning, painting, and maintenance work." Shipbuilding means "the construction of a vessel, including the installation of machinery and equipment." Shipbreaking means "any breaking down of a vessel's structure for the purpose of scrapping the vessel, including the removal of gear, equipment, or any component part of a vessel." Longshoring operation means "the loading, unloading, moving, or handling of, cargo, ship's stores, gear, etc., into, in, on, or out of any vessel."

Agricultural

There are two types of OSHA agricultural standards. First, certain general industry standards have been made applicable to agricultural operations. Second, certain standards have been issued that apply only to agricultural operations.

Other Ways to Categorize Standards

Besides the four broad industry categories, OSHA standards may also be broken down, unofficially, in other ways. For example, standards are often referred to as being "horizontal" or "vertical." Horizontal standards are broadly worded standards covering many employers in various industries. Vertical standards are detailed, specific standards applied to a smaller number of employers—usually in a particular industry. Standards also may be divided into "specification" standards and "performance" standards. Specification standards detail the precise equipment, materials, and work processes required to eliminate hazards. Performance standards indicate the degree of safety and health protection to be achieved, but are more flexible and leave the method of achieving the protection to the employer. Finally, standards may be "general" or "specific." General standards, such as those dealing with housekeeping or personal protective equipment, apply to a variety of workplace settings. Specific standards, such as a requirement that a precise type of machine be guarded in a precise manner, apply only to prescribed situations.

As a general rule, when two or more standards apply to a particular working condition, a vertical standard will take precedence over a horizontal standard and a specific standard will take precedence over a general standard.

Employee Training and Education

Many OSHA standards require employers to provide specific safety training for employees. The failure to provide adequate safety training may constitute a violation of a specific training standard. For example, the Second Circuit Court of Appeals held that a standard requiring an employer to designate a competent person to inspect machinery and equipment meant that the employer was required to select a specific employee and to notify the employee of the existence and nature of his or her safety inspection duties.[18]

Along with the duty to comply with specific safety training standards, employers have an overall duty to train employees adequately for their jobs. Employers must take reasonable precautionary steps to protect employees from hazards. "And precautionary steps, of course, include the employer's providing an adequate safety and training program."[19] The reasonableness of training depends upon the obviousness of the hazard, the experience of the employee, the likelihood that an accident will occur, and the degree of harm likely to result from an accident.

It is important to remember that the degree of safety training required of a particular employee performing a specific job will vary considerably. Some of the factors considered in determining the amount of safety training required are the following: (1) the employee's experience, expertise, and other qualifications; (2) the nature of the employee's job function; and (3) the nature of the hazards to which the employee may be exposed in the normal course of work.

---

[18]Brennan v. OSHRC (Gerosa, Inc.), 491 F.2d 1340, 1 OSH Cases 1523 (2d Cir. 1974).

[19]Brennan v. Butler Lime & Cement Co., 520 F.2d 1011, 1017, 3 OSH Cases 1461 (7th Cir. 1975).

Supervision

Employers are required to provide adequate supervision of employees, although the degree of supervision required depends on several factors. In general, less supervision is required where employees are well trained, competent, experienced, and have good safety records; where the work involved is not overly hazardous; or where constant supervision is impractical. The Fifth Circuit Court of Appeals held that the owner of a company with an excellent safety program was not required to remain on the job and direct the employees himself.[20] The court stated that this would be unreasonable and infeasible. Similarly, the Commission has held that an employer was not required to supervise constantly its employees who were working at another employer's worksite and were under the direction of the other employer.[21]

Safety Equipment

Many OSHA standards require compliance by adopting prescribed safety procedures or by modifying machinery to include safety devices. Employers also have a duty to supply their employees with tools and equipment in safe condition. The Commission has held, however, that this duty is not absolute, and that employers will not be liable for latent defects in machinery or tools manufactured or repaired by another company. Nevertheless, employers must exercise reasonable diligence in providing safe tools, including periodically examining and testing equipment. It is not necessary for the Secretary to observe defective tools or machinery in use to establish a violation where other evidence indicates that defective tools or machinery were in use at the time of the alleged violation or were available for use.

Employers may also be required to provide, and to insist on the use of "personal protective equipment." Examples of personal protective equipment are safety shoes, safety belts, goggles, and hard hats. OSHA does not certify, approve, or endorse brands of safety equipment and

---

[20]Horne Plumbing & Heating Co. v. OSHRC, 528 F.2d 564, 569–70, 3 OSH Cases 2060 (5th Cir. 1976).

[21]Ira Holliday Logging Co., 1 OSH Cases 1200 (1973), *petition for review dismissed*, No. 73-2170 (9th Cir. 1973).

manufacturers may not represent that their products are recommended by OSHA.

The Fifth Circuit Court of Appeals reviewed a standard requiring the use of personal protective equipment "wherever it is necessary by reason of hazards of process or environment." The court applied a "reasonable man" test and held, contrary to the employer's contention, that the standard was not impermissibly vague.[22] Other cases have held that the need for using safety shoes was not dependent on any evidence of prior accidents.

Many safety standards simply read that the employer must "provide" safety equipment. Thus, it has been important to determine whether "provide" means that the employer must simply "make available" the equipment to employees or whether "provide" means that the employer must also "require the use of" the equipment. In *Usery v. Kennecott Copper Corp.*,[23] the Tenth Circuit Court of Appeals reversed the Commission and held that "provide" does *not* mean "require the use of." According to the court, this result was mandated by the plain meaning of the word. The Commission has followed *Kennecott.*

The question also has been raised whether the word "provide" means that the employer must pay for personal protective equipment. The Third Circuit Court of Appeals has held that the word "provide" in a personal protective equipment standard did not mean that the employer was required to bear the cost for safety shoes worn by employees.[24] Although the question of cost should be resolved during collective bargaining, the court held that the employer still must require the use of protective footwear.

Health Hazards

An area in which employers have a heightened duty is in protecting employees from exposure to health hazards such as asbestos, vinyl chloride, and lead. Because of the dangers associated with these substances, preventive duties are extensive and explicit.

---

[22]Ryder Truck Lines, Inc. v. Brennan, 497 F.2d 230, 2 OSH Cases 1075 (5th CIr. 1974).

[23]577 F.2d 1113, 6 OSH Cases 1197 (10th Cir. 1977).

[24]Budd Co. v. OSHRC, 513 F.2d 201, 2 OSH Cases 1698 (3d Cir. 1975).

The first responsibility of the employer is to conduct periodic atmospheric tests to determine the presence and concentration of hazardous substances. The standards differ on the frequency of the testing, but even stringent requirements have been upheld. For example, the Second Circuit Court of Appeals held that an employer must monitor *every* operation in which vinyl chloride was released, regardless of the employer's prediction that only negligible concentrations of the gas were released.[25] The Commission, however, has held that the asbestos standard does not require environmental monitoring or medical examinations where employees are not regularly exposed during the course of their work, even though their sporadic exposures sometimes exceeded the standard.[26]

In detecting health hazards, an employer is only required to exercise reasonable diligence. A citation was vacated where the employer had retained an independent testing laboratory to conduct atmospheric tests, even though those tests failed to discover excess levels of asbestos fibers.[27]

An employer may also be required to provide periodic medical examinations for each employee. The D.C. Circuit Court of Appeals affirmed the Commission's holding that this requirement exists where employees are exposed to *any* concentration of asbestos fibers, even if below the permissible limit.[28] In addition, employers are required to keep detailed records of all medical examinations and atmospheric tests.

OSHA's health standards require that medical examinations be provided "without cost" or "at no cost" to the employee. The Commission has held that a provision in the inorganic arsenic standard providing that medical examinations be provided without cost required the employer to compensate employees for time spent taking the examination (outside normal working hours) and for extra transportation expenses.[29]

---

[25]Marshall v. Western Elec., Inc., 565 F.2d 240, 5 OSH Cases 2054 (2d Cir. 1977).

[26]Duquesne Light Co., 11 OSHC 2033 (1984), *petition for review dismissed*, No. 84-3538 (3d Cir. 1984).

[27]Dunlop v. Rockwell Int'l, 540 F.2d 1283, 4 OSH Cases 1606 (6th Cir. 1976).

[28]GAF Corp. v. OSHRC, 561 F.2d 913, 5 OSH Cases 1555 (D.C. Cir. 1977).

[29]Phelps Dodge Corp., 11 OSH Cases 1441 (1983), *aff'd*, 725 F.2d 1237, 11 OSH Cases 1769 (9th Cir. 1984).

Variances

Pursuant to section 6(d) of the Act, an employer may petition the Secretary for a "permanent" variance when its safety practices are not in strict compliance with a standard, but still achieve the same result. A "temporary" variance may be sought under section 6(b)(6)(A) of the Act when an employer cannot meet the requirements of a standard within the time specified for compliance. The filing of a variance does not prevent an employer from being found in violation of the Act during the pendency of the variance application.

ELEMENTS OF A VIOLATION

To establish that an employer has violated section 5(a)(2) of the Act by failing to comply with a standard, the Secretary of Labor must prove that (1) the cited standard applies, (2) there was a failure to comply with the cited standard, (3) an employee had access to the violative condition, and (4) the employer knew or could have known of the condition with the exercise of reasonable diligence. The Secretary also has the burden of proving the reasonableness of the proposed time for correcting the violations, the "abatement date."

Exposure

A violation of section 5(a)(2) requires that there must be at least some possibility that an employee could come into contact with the hazard. This is referred to as "exposure." In *Gilles & Cotting, Inc.*,[30] the Commission announced that its exposure rule was based on the concept of access. Access was said to be present whenever employees in the course of their work, their personal comfort activities while on the job, or their normal means of ingress and egress to their workplaces have been, are, or will be in a "zone of danger" where they could be exposed to the hazard. Subsequent Commission decisions have modified *Gilles & Cotting* to permit the Secretary to prove exposure by showing that employees may reasonably be expected to come into danger considering

---

[30] 3 OSH Cases 2002 (1976).

the nature of the work, the work activities required, and the routes of arrival and departure.

Access to the zone of danger is relatively easy to prove. The Secretary need not prove the identity of exposed employees. It is not necessary that machinery be observed in operation where other evidence indicates that it was in use at the time of the alleged violation or was available for use. On the other hand, it has been held that access may not be based on the exposure of the employer's representative during the OSHA inspection or on the exposure of an employee conducting a safety inspection.

Knowledge

The Secretary also must prove an element of "knowledge" on the part of the employer. In this context, "knowledge" refers to an awareness of the existence of the conditions allegedly in noncompliance with OSHA standards. It is not necessary to prove that the employer knew the requirements of the standard.

For OSH Act purposes, "knowledge" includes both what the employer and its officials actually know about workplace conditions and what they could have discovered with the exercise of reasonable diligence. This latter situation is referred to as "constructive knowledge." Constructive knowledge has been found where the employer failed to inspect its workplace to discover readily apparent hazards, where there were inadequate safety instructions, where safety rules were not enforced, where there were prior instances of employee noncompliance, where an employee had been injured previously by the same hazard, and where the employer had received at least three written complaints from employees before the OSHA inspection. Even under the constructive knowledge principle an employer need only do what is reasonable to discover hazards. Thus, the Secretary failed to prove employer knowledge where the employer had retained a consulting firm to conduct atmospheric tests and the consultant failed to discover that employees were exposed to excess levels of airborne contaminants.

Feasibility

OSHA standards generally specify the means for compliance but do not contain specific language relating to the feasibility of compliance. Thus, the question has been raised whether the Secretary has the burden of proving that compliance with a standard is feasible or whether feasibility is presumed and the burden of proving a lack of feasibility is on the employer.

Commission decisions have held that the Secretary does not have the burden of proving feasibility for most violations of standards under section 5(a)(2). A small number of standards, however, particularly health standards, actually use the word "feasible" in the standard and condition an employer's obligation to comply on the existence of "feasible methods." The Commission has held that, when a violation of one of these standards is alleged, the Secretary has the burden of proving technological feasibility. Thus, the Secretary must prove that *some* controls are feasible and that the compliance measures are feasible at the cited employer's workplace.

Because the Secretary is presumed to have considered economic factors before issuing a standard, the Secretary will not normally have the burden of proving the economic feasibility of compliance in a contest before the Commission. But, where the word "feasible" is used in a standard, the Secretary also must prove economic feasibility.

DEFENSES

Employers charged with failing to comply with an OSHA standard may avoid liability under the Act if they can prove one of several defenses that have been recognized by the Commission and courts. These defenses are based on the Act and are unrelated to "common law" defenses that might be raised in a civil negligence action.

Vagueness of Standard

Some standards containing general language have been attacked because they are allegedly too vague to give employers an adequate explanation of what conduct is required. Although vagueness challenges have been common, they have not met with much success at either the Commission or Court of Appeals level.

Ryder Truck Lines, Inc. v. Brennan[31] was the first judicial decision to consider the vagueness issue. The Fifth Circuit Court of Appeals, in

---

[31] 497 F.2d 230, 2 OSH Cases 1075 (5th Cir. 1974).

affirming the validity of a general personal protective equipment standard, held that "[s]o long as the mandate affords a reasonable warning of the proscribed conduct in light of common understanding and practices, it will pass constitutional muster."

Whether a standard provides fair notice to an employer cannot be determined solely from the words of the standard, but the facts of each case must be considered. Nevertheless, some general principles can be discerned from the cases decided on the basis of vagueness. First, flexibility in wording, or even imprecise or inartful drafting, does not necessarily mean that a standard is impermissibly vague. Second, a standard is not vague simply because its application requires the exercise of judgment. Third, a vague standard "may be cured by authoritative judicial or administrative interpretations which clarify obscurities or resolve ambiguities."[32] Fourth, where the standard's terms are "unequivocal," the Commission will not even apply a reasonable person test in rejecting a vagueness challenge.

Unpreventable Employee Misconduct

Unpreventable employee misconduct is the most important defense. It also has been referred to as "isolated occurrence," "isolated incident," "isolated misconduct," and "employee misconduct." Regardless of the name, the basic premise of this defense is that it would be unfair and would not promote employee safety and health to penalize an employer for conditions that were unpreventable and not likely to recur.

In *Jensen Construction Co.*,[33] the Commission listed the four elements of the defense: (1) the employer has established work rules designed to prevent the violation; (2) it has adequately communicated these rules to its employees; (3) it has taken steps to discover violations; and (4) it has effectively enforced the rules when violations have been discovered. The defense focuses on the employer's overall safety program rather than on the events surrounding the specific incident of violative conduct.

---

[32]Diebold, Inc. v. Marshall, 585 F.2d 1327, 1338, 6 OSH Cases 2002 (6th Cir. 1978).

[33]7 OSH Cases 1477 (1979).

Greater Hazard

In some instances employers have been able to prove that compliance with a standard would actually create a greater hazard than noncompliance. The Commission will vacate a citation under the greater hazard defense if the employer can prove (1) the hazards of compliance are greater than the hazards of noncompliance, (2) alternative means of protecting employees are unavailable, and (3) a variance application would be inappropriate. This three-part test has received widespread judicial approval.

The essence of the greater hazard defense is that the hazards of compliance with a standard are greater than the hazards of noncompliance. The evidence of a greater hazard, however, must be clear. The "mere verbalized fears" of employees and an employer's unsupported opinion have been held to be inadequate. Similarly, it is not enough that compliance with the standard will cause momentary lapses of protection or inconvenience to employees.

GENERAL DUTY CLAUSE

The general duty clause, section 5 (a)(1), was included in the Act to cover serious hazards to which no specific standard applies. Because section 5(a)(1) was designed to augment rather than supplant standards, citation by the Secretary under section 5(a)(1) is improper where a specific standard is appropriate.

To prove a violation of section 5(a)(1) the Secretary must establish that the employer failed to render its workplace free of a hazard, which was "recognized" by the employer or its industry, and which was causing or likely to cause death or serious physical harm. In addition, the Secretary must demonstrate the feasibility and likely utility of specific corrective measures. Nevertheless, as with section 5(a)(2) violations of standards, section 5(a)(1) does not require the actual occurrence of an accident, nor does the occurrence of an accident, by itself, prove the existence of a violation.

Decisions of the Commission and courts of appeals have held that citation under section 5(a)(1) of the Act is only proper if no specific standard applies. "The standards presumably give the employer superior notice of the alleged violation and should be used instead of the general duty clause whenever possible."[34]

Elements of a Violation

Section 5(a)(1) of the Act specifically requires that "each employer shall furnish to each of *his employees* employment and a place of employment" (emphasis added) free from recognized hazards. Thus, unlike section 5(a)(2) of the Act, which mandates compliance with standards without qualification, section 5(a)(1) limits the employer's duty to protecting its own employees from recognized hazards.

The most distinctive and significant element of section 5(a)(1) violations is that they are limited to "recognized hazards." The "recognition" requirement serves to ensure that cited employers at least have constructive knowledge of the existence of specific hazardous conditions. In this way, Congress sought to eliminate the unfairness of assessing penalties based on such a sweeping and broadly worded provision.

A hazard is considered recognized if it is common knowledge in the employer's industry *or* if the employer has knowledge of the hazardous condition. Thus, recognition may be established either objectively or subjectively. In *National Realty & Construction Co. v. OSHRC,*[35] the D.C. Circuit Court of Appeals held that whether a hazard is recognized by an industry is determined by the "common knowledge of safety experts who are familiar with the circumstances of the industry or the activity in question." The Commission has followed *National Realty* and also has held that the expert testimony of an OSHA compliance officer about industry practice may be used to show that a hazard was recognized.

The second way in which a hazard may be recognized is if the employer has actual knowledge of the hazard. In *Brennan v. OSHRC (Vy Lactos Laboratories, Inc.),*[36] the Eighth Circuit Court of Appeals held that an employer's personal knowledge of the existence of a hazard

---

[34]Usery v. Marquette Cement Mfg. Co., 568 F.2d 902, 905 n. 5, 5 OSH Cases 1793 (2d Cir. 1977).

[35]489 F.2d 1257, 1 OSH Cases 1422 (D.C. Cir. 1973).

[36]494 F.2d 460, 1 OSH Cases 1623 (8th Cir. 1974).

was sufficient to make the hazard "recognized." This view has been followed by the Commission.

Burden of Proof

The Secretary's burden of proving a violation of the general duty clause is greater than the burden of proving a violation of a standard. In *National Realty* the D.C. Circuit Court of Appeals held that the Secretary must prove (1) that the employer failed to render its workplace free of a hazard which was (2) recognized, and (3) causing or likely to cause death or serious physical harm, and (4) the Secretary must specify the particular steps the cited employer should have taken to avoid citation and demonstrate the feasibility and likely utility of those measures. This formulation of the burden of proof has been adopted by the Commission, the other courts of appeals, and the Secretary.

Defenses

Employers have a wide range of defenses available against alleged section 5(a)(1) violations. For example, the employer can show that a specific standard applied, that the hazard was not "recognized," that there was insufficient employee exposure, that the employer had no knowledge of the violation, or that the Secretary failed to indicate what method of compliance was feasible.

Employers also may raise many of the same defenses that can be raised in a section 5(a)(2) case. The Secretary's heightened burden of proof under section 5(a)(1) of the Act, however, has the effect of allocating to the Secretary the burden of proving some of these matters. For example, the Ninth Circuit Court of Appeals has held that the Secretary must prove that the proposed method of abatement will not result in a greater hazard.[37]

RECORDKEEPING

All covered employers are subject to the Act's recordkeeping and reporting requirements unless specifically exempted. Even federal

---

[37]Donovan v. Royal Logging Co., 645 F.2d 822, 830, 9 OSH Cases 1755 (9th Cir. 1981).

agencies and state and local government employers in state plan states are required to keep records. An important exemption is provided for small employers. According to the Secretary's regulation, an employer with no more than 10 employees at any time during the prior calendar year need not comply with any recordkeeping requirement except the obligation to report fatalities or multiple hospitalization accidents and the obligation to participate in Bureau of Labor Statistics (BLS) statistical surveys. Other exemptions, such as for certain retail firms and services, farmers, and employers of domestic servants, are set out in the Secretary's regulations.[38]

The recordkeeping system consists of three forms for the recording of occupational injuries and illnesses: a log, a supplementary record, and a summary. Employers must request each of these forms from OSHA. The records must be kept on a calendar-year basis (January 1 to December 31). The completed forms should *not* be sent to OSHA, but must remain at the establishment and be available for inspection and copying by the BLS, the Department of Labor, HHS, or states with authority to inspect and compile records. The records must be maintained at the establishment for five years following the end of the year to which they refer.

OSHA regulations require records to be kept at each "establishment," defined as a single physical location where business is conducted or where services or industrial operations are performed.[39] Employers without a fixed establishment, such as construction, installation, and repair and service operations, may maintain records in an established central place.

OSHA classification rules describe the recordkeeping duties created by each occupational injury or illness. The injury or illness must be entered into the log as either a fatality, lost workday case, or nonfatal case without lost workday. All fatalities, defined as occupational injuries or illnesses resulting in death, must be reported to the nearest OSHA office within 8 hours. Lost workdays are the number of days after, but not including, the day of an injury or illness during which an employee could not perform all or any part of the normal work shift duties due to the injury or illness. To be recordable, nonfatal cases without lost workdays must result in transfer to another job, termination

---

[38]29 C.F.R. §1904.16 (1992).
[39]29 C.F.R. §1904.12(g)(1) (1992).

of employment, medical treatment, loss of consciousness, or work or motion restriction. If an employee's condition changes, the initial entry in the log may be lined out and a new entry added.

Each employer is also required to display in each establishment an official poster explaining the protections of employees under the Act. In states with approved state plans, only a state poster need be used. All posters are supplied by OSHA or the applicable state agency responsible for administering an approved state plan.

Employee Access to Exposure and Medical Records

The primary purpose of OSHA's access to exposure and medical records regulation is "to enable workers to play a meaningful role in their own health management."[40] The regulation applies to all covered general industry, maritime, and construction employers. It is, however, limited to employers having employees exposed to toxic substances or harmful physical agents. Unlike other OSHA recordkeeping requirements, the access regulation does *not* require that certain documents be prepared, but only that existing records be maintained and made available to employees and other parties designated in the regulation.

Any current or former employee or an employee being assigned or transferred to work where there will be exposure to toxic substances or harmful physical agents has a right of access to four kinds of exposure records: (1) environmental monitoring records, (2) biological monitoring results, (3) material safety data sheets, and (4) any other record disclosing the identity of a toxic substance or harmful physical agent. Any worker who has a right of access to exposure records may designate a representative to exercise his or her access rights. Recognized or certified collective bargaining agents (labor unions) are automatically considered "designated representatives" and have a right of access to employee exposure records without individual employee consent. OSHA also has a right of access to exposure records.

Access to employee medical records is more restricted. Employees have a right of access to their entire medical files regardless of how the information was generated or is maintained. Excluded from the definition of "employee medical record" are certain physical specimens,

---

[40]45 Fed. Reg. 35,212 (1980), codified at 29 C.F.R. §1910.20 (1992).

certain records concerning health insurance claims, and certain records concerning voluntary employee medical assistance programs. A limited discretion is also given physicians to deny access where there is a specific diagnosis of a terminal illness or psychiatric condition. Collective bargaining agents must obtain specific written consent before gaining access to employee medical records. OSHA has a right of access to employee medical records, but those records in a personally identifiable form are subject to detailed procedures and protections. The Commission has held that OSHA has a right of access to employee medical records as part of its enforcement process and in a Commission hearing.

With a few exceptions, employers must preserve exposure records for at least 30 years and must preserve medical records for the duration of employment plus 30 years. With the exception of X rays, employers may keep the records in any form, such as microfilm, microfiche, or computer. Upon receipt of a request, access must be provided in a reasonable time, place, and manner within 15 days. In responding to an initial request, an employer may provide a copy without cost, provide copying facilities at no cost, or may loan the record for a reasonable time. Administrative costs may be charged for subsequent copying requests.

Although identities of substances, exposure levels, and health status data may not be withheld, the employer may delete trade secret data that discloses manufacturing processes or discloses the percentage of a chemical substance in a mixture, as long as the employee or designated representative is notified of the deletion. Access to other trade secrets may be conditioned upon a written agreement not to misuse this information.

Hazard Communication/"Right to Know"

OSHA's original Hazard Communication Standard covered an estimated 14 million employees in 300,000 manufacturing establishments. Among other things, it required chemical manufacturers and importers to assess the hazards of chemicals they produce or import, and all employers engaged in manufacturing to provide information to their employees concerning hazardous chemicals by means of hazard communication programs including labels, material safety data sheets, training, and access to written records. One of the purposes of the standard was to preempt state "right to know" laws. The standard originally applied only to chemical manufacturers and importers (Standard Industrial Classification (SIC) Codes 20-39) and applied only to 600 substances and excluded hazardous wastes, foods, drugs, and pesticides. In 1987 OSHA published an amendment to the Hazard Communication Standard that expanded coverage beyond the manufacturing sector to cover all workers.

In the 1980s about half the states enacted "right to know" laws. Most of these laws were passed before the adoption of OSHA's Hazard Communication Standard. Although the coverage and requirements of the laws vary widely, it now appears that state laws limited to the workplace as well as "dual purpose" laws that apply to the workplace as well as other areas are preempted by the OSHA Hazard Communication Standard. According to the Supreme Court in *Gade v. National Solid Wastes Management Ass'n*,[41] a state law that addresses public safety as well as occupational safety concerns will be preempted, regardless of whether it serves any other objective, so long as it "directly, substantially, and specifically regulates occupational safety and health."

EMPLOYEE RIGHTS AND DUTIES

Employees have numerous rights conferred upon them by the OSH Act, the Secretary's regulations, and the Commission's rules of procedure. The most important of these rights is contained in section 11(c) of the Act, which protects employees from employer discrimination.[42]

It is unlawful for an employer to discharge or in any manner discriminate against any employee because the employee has filed a complaint or instituted any proceeding under or related to the OSH Act. It is also unlawful to discriminate against an employee because he or she has testified or is about to testify in any proceeding or because of the exercise by the employee of any right afforded under the Act.

The Secretary's regulations contain two important interpretations of section 11(c). First, the term "employee" is considered to include job

---

[41] 112 S.Ct. 2374, 15 OSH Cases 1673 (1992).

[42] The Secretary's regulations implementing this section appear at 29 C.F.R. pt. 1977 (1992).

applicants and former employees who were employed at the time of the alleged discrimination. Second, the employee's engaging in protected activity (such as filing a complaint with OSHA) need not be the *sole* consideration behind the employer's action. Section 11(c) is violated if protected activity was a substantial reason for the employer's action or if the discrimination would not have taken place "but for" the employee's engaging in protected activity.

An employer's discharging or otherwise sanctioning an employee will be upheld if the employer can prove that its action is not a retaliation, but is based on another valid reason. Thus, unsatisfactory work performance, disruption of the business, insubordination and destruction of the employer's property, lack of cooperation with management, and other "good cause" have been held to be valid reasons for discharge. Similarly, to be protected under section 11(c) employee activity must be in good faith.

Under section 11(c)(2) employees must file a complaint with the Secretary within 30 days after the occurrence of the alleged discrimination. A discrimination complaint may be filed by the employee or by any representative of the employee who is authorized to do so. The complaint may be filed with the OSHA area director for the region in which the employee resides or was employed. No particular form of complaint is required.

After the filing of a complaint, the Secretary customarily will conduct an investigation to determine the validity of the allegation. Section 11(c)(3) requires the Secretary to notify the complainant within 90 days of receipt of the complaint of OSHA's determination. If the complaint is found to be meritorious and if attempts at reaching a settlement between the employer and employee are unsuccessful, the Secretary may file a lawsuit in United States district court on behalf of the complainant. There is no right for individuals to sue under section 11(c), and therefore individuals may not bring lawsuits on their own, regardless of whether complaints were initially filed with the Secretary.

Section 5(b) provides that "[e]ach employee shall comply with occupational safety and health standards and all rules, regulations and orders issued pursuant to this Act which are applicable to his own actions and conduct." This language, however, is not enforceable. Neither the Secretary nor the Commission or courts have any power to fine or otherwise sanction disobedient employees.

Final responsibility for compliance with OSHA's requirements rests with the employer. Employers are not relieved of their obligations under the Act because of employee reluctance to comply. Therefore, employers must take every measure possible to ensure employee compliance, including the sanctioning of recalcitrant employees. According to the Secretary's regulations, disciplinary measures taken by employers solely in response to employee refusals to comply with appropriate safety rules and regulations are not considered discrimination in violation of section 11(c).

INSPECTION PRIORITIES

OSHA inspections may be divided into four categories, which have been assigned the following priority by the Secretary of Labor: (1) imminent dangers, (2) fatality and catastrophe investigations, (3) investigations of complaints and referrals, and (4) programmed inspections.

Imminent Dangers

Section 13(a) defines an "imminent danger" as a danger "which could reasonably be expected to cause death or serious physical harm immediately or before the imminence of such danger can be eliminated through the enforcement procedures otherwise provided by this Act." For imminent danger purposes the Secretary has identified two types of "serious physical harm." First is where there is permanent, prolonged, or temporary impairment, in which part of the body is made functionally useless or is substantially reduced in efficiency on or off the job. This would include fractures, serious cuts and burns, and concussions. Second are illnesses that could shorten life or significantly reduce physical or mental efficiency by inhibiting the normal function of a part of the body. This would include cancer and serious hearing or vision impairments. For a health hazard to constitute an imminent danger there must be a reasonable expectation that "irreversible harm" will result.

An imminent danger inspection may result from the filing of an employee complaint or from some other source. Any allegation of imminent danger is given OSHA's highest priority, regardless of weekends, holidays, leave, or other considerations. Except in extraordinary circumstances an inspection will be conducted not later than the next working day of the employer.

Fatality and Catastrophe Investigations

Fatality and catastrophe investigations are second in OSHA priority. The purpose of these inspections is to determine if noncompliance with OSHA standards has caused the injuries, and thereby to prevent future accidents. Most fatality and accident investigations result from the employers' reporting requirement. A fatality or catastrophe investigation will be conducted if an accident has (1) caused one or more deaths or (2) resulted in the hospitalization of five or more employees for more than 24 hours.

Complaints and Referrals

According to OSHA procedures an inspection will be conducted in response to a formal (written) complaint unless the complainant does not establish reasonable grounds to believe that a violation threatening physical harm or an imminent danger exists. OSHA will respond to formal complaints alleging an imminent danger within 24 hours, serious hazards within five working days, and other conditions within 30 working days.

If a nonformal complaint is received, OSHA will usually respond by sending a letter to the employer describing the alleged hazard and requesting abatement within a certain time. The complainant will also be notified and requested to inform OSHA if no corrective action is taken by the specified time. An inspection will be conducted if the employer fails to respond to OSHA's letter or if the complainant indicates that no abatement measures have been taken. Inspections also will be conducted for all imminent danger situations and where there is employee exposure to toxic substances.

If a complaint is filed against an employer in an industry with a high accident rate, the scope of the inspection generally will be the entire facility. If the complaint involves a low rate industry, only the conditions identified in the complaint will be inspected. Complaints by former employees alleging unsafe conditions and that they were discharged in violation of section 11(c) of the Act are treated as nonformal complaints.

Programmed Inspections

According to OSHA regulations, programmed inspections for general industry will be conducted only in "high hazard" establishments, those with lost workday injury rates at or above the national lost workday injury rate for manufacturing. Whether an establishment is considered "high hazard" is based on the nature of the enterprise. For example, scheduling for general industry safety inspections is based on statewide industry ranking reports rating four-digit Standard Industrial Classifications (SICs). General industry health inspection scheduling uses statewide four-digit SICs with high potential for employee exposure to dangerous substances. Due to the mobility of the construction industry, the transitory nature of construction work sites, and the fact that construction work sites frequently involve more than one construction employer, inspections are conducted from a list of construction work sites rather than construction employers.

Administrative exemptions from programmed inspections have been increasing and presently there are four exemptions in effect. First, establishments with 10 or fewer employees are not subject to programmed inspections. Second, an employer will be deleted from OSHA's schedule for programmed safety inspections if a substantially complete safety inspection has been conducted within the current or previous fiscal year, regardless of whether violations were cited. Third, an employer will be exempt from a programmed health inspection if one was conducted within the current year or the previous three fiscal years and no serious violations were cited. Fourth, inspections must be in accord with the latest congressional funding limitations.

INSPECTION WARRANTS

In *Marshall v. Barlow's, Inc.*,[43] the Supreme Court held that unless the employer consents, OSHA inspections can only be conducted

---

[43]436 U.S. 307, 6 OSH Cases 1571 (1978).

pursuant to a search warrant. The Court stated that section 8(a) of the Act provides adequate statutory authority for the issuance of warrants. Furthermore, the Court held that it is permissible for the Secretary to obtain a search warrant without giving the employer prior notice, thereby permitting the Secretary to conduct unannounced inspections.

Three exceptions to the warrant requirement apply to OSHA. The first exception is for emergencies. According to this traditional approach, exigent circumstances eliminate the warrant requirement because the urgent need for an immediate search outweighs the right to privacy. The emergency exception, however, can only be invoked in the most extreme instances. For OSHA inspections, the emergency exception would appear to be limited to imminent dangers and other exigencies *and* where it is impossible to obtain consent.

Most administrative inspections are conducted on the basis of consent. In fact, the Supreme Court in *Barlow's* suggested that "the great majority of businessmen can be expected in normal course to consent to inspection without warrant. . . ." Valid consent operates as a waiver of the right against unreasonable search and seizure contained in the Fourth Amendment of the U.S. Constitution. For OSHA inspections, the courts have adopted a standard of consent that is less stringent than that required for criminal searches. Consent to an OSHA inspection need not be express, and the failure to object to a known search constitutes consent. Thus, consent has been found where a company foreman accompanied the compliance officer (CO) on a walkaround without protest.

The failure of the inspector to warn the company managers of their right to insist on a warrant does not render the consent unknowing or involuntary. The COs have been instructed, however, that they may not mislead, coerce, or threaten the employer and if the employer asks questions about the *Barlow's* decision, the CO must answer in a "straightforward" manner. Consent to an OSHA inspection may be given by any competent management official. Inspections have been upheld where the consent was given by a plant manager, a foreman, and a superintendent. In addition, a general contractor may consent to the inspection of a common worksite where a subcontractor is working.

A warrant is not required where the premises are open to the public. An important factor is whether an individual or business has a "reasonable expectation of privacy," even if the inspection is in an area open to the public. In *Marshall v. Western Waterproofing Co.*,[44] COs attempted to inspect scaffolding on the 11th floor of a building from which an employee had fallen the previous day. Despite being unable to contact a company official, the COs began the inspection after learning that the scaffolding would be dismantled the next day. Accompanied by the building manager, the COs examined the fifth floor mezzanine, onto which the employee fell. They also viewed the scaffold from a window of the 11th floor office of an attorney, who had consented to the presence of the COs. The Eighth Circuit Court of Appeals rejected the employer's claim that the search was illegal. The court pointed out that the COs were given consent to enter the mezzanine and office by the building manager and attorney. In addition, the scaffold was exposed to public view while suspended on the building and was also readily observable by the tenants in the building.

Similar results have been reached in other cases. The Fifth Circuit Court of Appeals upheld the warrantless inspection of a caved-in trench along a public street.[45] In another case, an agent of the employer directed the CO to wait in the parking lot until the company president or supervisor would arrive and give him permission to conduct an inspection.[46] The Commission held that the CO's observations of violative conditions, which he made from the parking lot, were lawful.

Warrant Procedure

United States magistrate judges have the authority to issue OSHA warrants, and the Secretary and the Secretary's agents (including Labor Department attorneys) have authority to obtain warrants. It is also clear that employers have no right to advance notice of a warrant application, no right to be present or to have counsel present at the warrant hearing, and no right to receive copies of the materials submitted to the magistrate. OSHA has the authority to seek a warrant before attempting to make an inspection. Nevertheless, except under special

---

[44]560 F.2d 947, 5 OSH Cases 1732 (8th Cir. 1977).

[45]Accu-Namics, Inc. v. OSHRC, 515 F.2d 828, 3 OSH Cases 1299 (5th Cir. 1975), *cert. denied*, 425 U.S. 903, 4 OSH Cases 1090 (1976).

[46]Ackerman Enter., Inc., 10 OSH Cases 1709 (1982).

circumstances, the Secretary will not seek a warrant until after an employer refuses to permit an inspection.

Probable Cause

The Supreme Court in *Barlow's* addressed the issue of probable cause as follows: "For purposes of an administrative search such as this, probable cause justifying the issuance of a warrant may be based not only on specific evidence of an existing violation but also on a showing that "reasonable legislative or administrative standards for conducting an . . . inspection are satisfied with respect to a particular [establishment]."[47]

OSHA's first priority is the inspection of imminent dangers. There would appear to be little problem in establishing probable cause where a valid imminent danger exists. Indeed, for some imminent dangers a warrant may not even be necessary under the emergency exception.

OSHA's second priority is for the investigation of fatalities and catastrophes. In *Donovan v. Federal Clearing Die Casting Co.*,[48] OSHA sought an inspection warrant based on (1) the fact that the employer had been cited for violations four years earlier, and (2) the submission of two newspaper articles reporting that an employee of Federal had both hands amputated in a recent accident. The Seventh Circuit Court of Appeals held that there was no probable cause because there was inadequate "specific evidence" of a violation.

OSHA's third type of unprogrammed inspection is based on the filing of a complaint. Although the filing of an employee or union complaint will usually establish probable cause, the magistrate must be presented with some additional information. The Seventh Circuit Court of Appeals has held that the mere allegation that a complaint has been filed is not sufficient to establish probable cause.[49] There must be an indication that inspections based on employee complaints are a part of an overall administrative program and that the specific complaint sets forth adequate facts to justify an inspection.

---

[47]436 U.S. at 320.

[48]655 F.2d 793, 9 OSH Cases 2072 (7th Cir. 1981).

[49]*See In re* Midwest Instruments Co., 900 F.2d 1150, 14 OSH Cases 1569 (7th Cir. 1990).

If possible, a signed employee complaint with supporting statements should be presented to the judge or magistrate with the warrant application. Nevertheless, probable cause may be based on an anonymous or informal employee complaint.

Scope of Inspection

The permissible scope of an OSHA inspection warrant is an important but, as yet, unresolved issue. Some courts hold that under most circumstances when an OSHA inspection is based on an employee complaint, the inspection must be limited to the work area of the complaining employee. Other courts hold that when an inspection is based on an employee complaint the CO may inspect the entire workplace—a "wall-to-wall" inspection. In *In re Inspection of Workplace (Carondelet Coke Corp.)*,[50] the Eighth Circuit Court of Appeals adopted a middle approach, which requires the Secretary to make "some showing" of why a broad warrant is appropriate in the particular case. In *Carondelet* the court held that the Secretary satisfied this burden by showing that the employer was in a high hazard industry, had a lost work day injury rate nearly four times the national average for manufacturers, and was due to have a programmed wall-to-wall inspection when the complaint was filed.

INSPECTION TOUR

Section 8(a)(1) of the Act conditions the Secretary's authority to inspect on the presentation of proper credentials. This provision protects against forcible entry and snooping as well as guarding against unauthorized individuals representing themselves as COs. Section 8(a)(1) provides that credentials must be presented to the "owner, operator, or agent in charge." As with the general consent provisions, this includes all management personnel in a position of authority. For example, the Commission upheld the validity of an inspection where the CO made a reasonable attempt but was unable to locate the owner and then presented his credentials to the employee authorized to handle matters in the owner's absence.

---

[50]741 F.2d 172, 11 OSH Cases 2153 (8th Cir. 1984).

An employer's argument that there was a failure to present credentials will probably not succeed unless there has been prejudice to the employer. "Prejudice" refers to an employer's ability to present an effective defense on the merits. The Fifth Circuit Court of Appeals, in *Accu-Namics, Inc. v. OSHRC*,[51] held that technical violations of section 8(a) of the Act "cannot operate to exclude evidence obtained in that inspection when there is no showing that the employer was prejudiced in any way."

After the presentation of credentials, the CO will conduct an opening conference with a representative of the employer and a representative of the employees, at which time the procedures for conducting the inspection will be discussed. If the inspection is a result of an employee complaint, the complaint will be shown to the employer, although the employee's name will be withheld if the employee has so requested.

The opening conference is brief and should not exceed one hour. During this time the employer is told what safety records the CO wants to inspect, told what the inspection tour will encompass, and given copies of applicable laws, standards, and regulations. At the opening conference the employer should indicate what trade secrets will be encountered during the inspection and the employer may request confidentiality. The employer also should indicate to the CO any special conditions related to the inspection, such as the need for the CO to wear personal protective equipment or the need to have valid immunization papers or a security clearance.

Section 8(e) of the Act provides that an employer and employee representative "shall be given" an opportunity to accompany the inspection tour "for the purpose of aiding such inspection." Despite some early confusion, it is now clear that any defense based on the failure to afford "walkaround" rights must focus on whether there was substantial compliance by the Secretary and whether there was prejudice to the employer.

During the course of an inspection the CO is authorized to record all pertinent information, including the making of diagrams and the taking of environmental samples and photographs. An important, related issue is whether, during an inspection, the company may refuse

---

[51]515 F.2d 828, 3 OSH Cases 1299 (5th Cir. 1975), *cert. denied*, 425 U.S. 903, 4 OSH Cases 1090 (1976).

to permit the CO to attach sampling devices to employees to measure the level of noise or airborne contaminants. OSHA has adopted a regulation providing that personal sampling devices attached to workers may be used by COs as an aid to workplace inspections. Decisions of the First and Fifth Circuits have upheld the validity of OSHA's regulation on the use of personal sampling. The employer has the burden of demonstrating the existence of special or exceptional circumstances that would make the use of personal sampling uniquely burdensome at its workplace.

The closing conference takes place after the inspection tour, and its purpose is to review the findings of the inspection with the employer and employee representative. It also affords the employer an opportunity to confer with the CO before a citation is issued. At this time the CO will inform the employer of any apparent violations and the employer may indicate what steps will be taken to abate the hazards.

During the closing conference the CO also will inform the employer about other matters related to enforcement, including variances, abatement dates, notices of proposed penalties, and how to file a notice of contest. The CO also should indicate if there will be a referral or follow-up inspection.

CITATIONS

Section 9(a) of the Act provides that a citation must "describe with particularity the nature of the violation, including reference to the provision of the Act, standard, rule, regulation, or order alleged to have been violated." In other words, a citation must contain two elements, a description of the alleged violation and a reference to the standard allegedly violated.

The requirement that citations be reasonably specific is designed to apprise the employer of the alleged violation so that corrective action may be taken and so that the employer may be able to decide whether and how to proceed with a contest. It must be remembered, however, that section 9(a) does not require that a citation state the legal elements of an OSHA violation or that an employer be informed with particularity how to abate a hazardous condition. A citation will be dismissed only if it fails to contain a description of the alleged violation or a reference to the standard allegedly violated.

Time for Issuance

Until the issuance of a citation an employer is under no legal duty to correct a hazardous condition. To promote the expeditious correction of violations, section 9(a) of the Act provides that citations must be issued with "reasonable promptness." This requirement also serves to ensure that the employer receives prompt notice of the Secretary's allegations so that it may begin preparing its defense while the evidence is still fresh.

In *Coughlan Construction Co.*,[52] the Commission held that regardless of the delay in issuing a citation, a citation will not be dismissed for lack of "reasonable promptness" unless the employer was prejudiced by the delay. Under this rule, unless the delay impairs an employer's ability to prepare and present a defense, the citation will be deemed to have been issued in accordance with section 9(a).

Amendments and Settlements

The Secretary's regulations provide that OSHA may unilaterally amend a citation before the employer files a notice of contest or before the expiration of the 15 working day contest period. For amended items only, a new 15 working day contest period begins to run upon receipt of the amended citation. The Secretary's regulations also provide that when a citation is amended both the original citation and the amended version should be posted.

OSHA area directors are authorized to enter into settlement agreements with employers before the filing of a notice of contest. In some instances a settlement results after an informal conference with the employer. Settlements finalized after the filing of a notice of contest must be approved by the Secretary's regional solicitor. In *Marshall v. Sun Petroleum Products Co.*,[53] the Third Circuit Court of Appeals held that if no notice of contest has been filed the Commission has no jurisdiction to review a settlement.

---

[52] 3 OSH Cases 1636 (1975).
[53] 622 F.2d 1176, 1185, 8 OSH Cases 1422 (3d Cir.), *cert. denied*, 449 U.S. 1061, 9 OSH Cases 1134 (1980).

Service of Citations

The Act does not specifically provide for a method of service for citations. Section 10(a) of the Act, however, authorizes service of notices of proposed penalties by certified mail and, as a practical matter, the two usually have been sent together by certified mail.

An issue that arises occasionally is what official at the workplace is authorized to receive service of a citation. In *B.J. Hughes, Inc.*,[54] the Commission held that service upon the district superintendent at a local job site was valid. According to the Commission, service is proper if it "is reasonably calculated to provide an employer with knowledge of the citation and notification of proposed penalty and an opportunity to determine whether to contest or abate." Therefore, it is proper to serve an employee who will know to whom in the corporate hierarchy to forward the documents. Even if an employee without authority signs the certified mailing receipt, the date of the receipt starts the notice of contest period. An employer's internal mail routing policies are not within the Secretary's control.

Where two companies are closely related, service on one company may be considered adequate service on the other company. Similarly, service on one member of a joint venture constitutes service on the entire joint venture.

Section 9(b) of the Act requires that the cited employer post a copy of the citation at or near each place of a violation referred to in the citation. The posting requirement is for the benefit of employees. Therefore, the employer must post the citation at a place where it may be readily observed by all affected employees. Where employees are engaged in physically dispersed activities, the citation may be posted at the location to which employees report each day. If the employees do not report to a single location, the citation may be posted at the location from which the employees carry out their activities.

Employers are permitted to post, along with the citation, a notice informing employees that the citation is being contested and the basis of the contest. A substitute or edited version of the citation, however, may not be posted. The employer also must take steps to ensure that the citation is not altered, defaced, or covered by other material. According

---

[54] 7 OSH Cases 1471 (1979).

to the Secretary's regulations, the citation must be posted immediately upon receipt and must remain posted until the violation is abated or for three working days, whichever is longer. The failure to keep the citation posted will result in a penalty.

Section 17(i) of the Act provides that a civil penalty of up to $7,000 for each violation "shall be assessed" for failure to comply with the Act's posting requirements. The Commission has held that this language makes it mandatory that a penalty be assessed for each violation. Nevertheless, the employer's size, its good faith, its prior history of violations, and the gravity of the original violation will be considered in the penalty assessment for a failure to post.

The assessment of monetary penalties is the only sanction that may be imposed against employers for failing to comply with the Act's posting requirements. The Commission has held that an ALJ has no authority to dismiss an employer's notice of contest as a sanction for failing to post the citation.

EMPLOYER CONTESTS

Under section 10(a) of the Act an employer has 15 working days from the date of receipt of the notice of proposed penalty (or no penalty) in which to file a notice of contest. Weekends and federal holidays are excluded, as is the day on which the employer received the notice of proposed penalty. The notice of contest must be in writing and should be mailed to the area director who issued the citation and proposed penalty. The postmark date on the notice of contest is controlling. Although the date of receipt of the notice of proposed penalty, rather than the citation, is determinative, OSHA uses a single form for both the citation and notice of proposed penalty. The short notice of contest period, which begins to run upon receipt of the form, is designed to promote the prompt abatement of hazards while preserving the employer's right to adequate time to consider a response.

An employer may contest any part or all of the citation, the proposed penalty, the abatement dates, or all of these elements. In no event, however, may the employer take more than 15 working days to file its notice of contest. Under section 10(a) an uncontested citation is "deemed a final order of the Commission and not subject to review by any court or agency."

There is no prescribed form for a notice of contest. Technically, the communication need only be a notice of "intent to contest." To avoid problems, however, a notice of contest should be signed and dated, list what items are being contested, and indicate whether the notice of contest is of the citation, penalty, abatement date, or all three. It is not necessary to indicate the grounds on which the contest is based.

Notices of contest should be mailed promptly to the area director who issued the citation. Employers also should be certain to serve copies of the notice of contest on all proper parties. All authorized employee representatives, such as labor unions, may be served personally or by regular first class mail. The employer must notify unrepresented employees by posting, at the same place the citation is posted, a copy of the notice of contest and a notice informing the employees of their right to elect party status in the proceedings. The employer also must make all documents in the matter available for inspection and copying at reasonable times. This same information also should be sent to the union. Proof of service consists of a written statement setting forth the date and manner of service, which is filed with the notice of contest. The employer is supposed to complete a postcard form, advising the Commission about notification of employees and their representatives, but the Commission will not impose the sanction of dismissing the notice of contest for failure to provide proof of posting.

Although section 10(a) merely requires that an employer "notify" the Secretary of an intent to contest, the Secretary's regulations have interpreted this as requiring that the notification be in writing. The Commission also has held that a notice of contest must be in writing.

Under section 10(a) the failure to file a notice of contest results in the citation and proposed penalty becoming a final order of the Commission, "not subject to review by any court or agency." This provision has been strictly construed by the Commission.

EMPLOYEE CONTESTS

Under section 10(c) of the Act "any employee or representative of employees" may file a notice of contest to challenge the reasonableness of the abatement date in a citation. Any "affected employee," including supervisors and officers, or the employees' collective bargaining agent, may file a notice of contest. Like employer contests, employee contests must be sent to the area director who issued the citation and must be postmarked within 15 working days of the employer's posting of the citation. The area director must then forward the notice of contest to the Commission within seven days.

Employee contests under section 10(c) are limited to challenging "that the period of time fixed in the citation for the abatement of the violation is unreasonable. . . ." Commission and judicial decisions have narrowly construed this provision, with the result of greatly decreasing the effectiveness of employee contests. In *United Auto Workers, Local 588 (Ford Motor Co.) v. OSHRC*,[55] the Seventh Circuit Court of Appeals affirmed the Commission's holding that employees may only contest the reasonableness of the date for abatement and may not challenge the adequacy of an abatement plan agreed to by the Secretary.

The Commission has held that in employee contests the burden of proof rests with the Secretary to show that the proposed abatement date is reasonable. Employers also may elect party status after the filing of an employee notice of contest. Thus, employees and employers may present their own evidence at the hearing.

Even without filing their own notice of contest, employees may elect party status and participate at the employer's hearing. This election can be made up to 10 days before the hearing, and by permission of the Commission, for good cause within 10 days of the hearing.

DEGREES OF VIOLATIONS

The Act provides for a wide range of violations, from de minimis notices to criminal violations.

De Minimis

Section 9(a) of the Act provides for "the issuance of a notice in lieu of a citation with respect to de minimis violations which have no direct or immediate relationship to safety and health." When the Secretary issues a de minimis notice, the employer does not have to post the notice, there is no abatement requirement, and there are no penalties.

---

[55]557 F.2d 607, 5 OSH Cases 1525 (7th Cir. 1977).

Because it is not a citation there can be no notice of contest filed. De minimis notices are only issued when there is no direct and immediate relationship between the noncomplying conditions and employee safety and health. Thus, de minimis notices have been issued for trifling items like a minor breach of a toilet partitioning standard and a failure to provide a receptacle for disposable cups.

The Commission has the authority to amend a citation to a de minimis notice. It has used this authority as a way of removing the abatement requirement where noncompliance with a standard creates no real hazard to employees. The Commission has held that a de minimis violation may be found only when, at worst, only extremely minor injuries are possible from the hazard, such as when there was only a "technical noncompliance" with a standard and when the employer complied with an updated version of a consensus standard not adopted by the Secretary.

Nonserious

The Act does not specifically define a nonserious violation. Because there are express definitions for both de minimis and serious violations, however, a nonserious violation is between the two. "Accordingly, a non-serious violation is one in which there is a direct and immediate relationship between the violative condition and occupational safety and health but not of such relationship that a resultant injury or illness is death or serious physical harm."[56]

Section 17(c) of the Act provides that "[a]ny employer who has received a citation for a violation . . . and such violation is specifically determined not to be of a serious nature, may be assessed a civil penalty of up to $7,000 for each such violation." The quoted language would seem to require that the Secretary make a specific determination that a violation is nonserious. In practice, however, the opposite is true. Violations are, in effect, "presumed" to be nonserious unless the Secretary proves the elements of a serious violation.

The most important difference between a serious and nonserious violation is that under section 17(k) of the Act a serious violation requires a "substantial probability that death or serious physical harm

---

[56]Crescent Wharf & Warehouse Co., 1 OSH Cases 1219 (1973).

could result. . . ." This language has been interpreted as referring to the severity of an injury if an accident occurs, rather than the likelihood of an accident.

Unlike serious violations, the Secretary is not required to assess a penalty for a nonserious violation. Although the maximum possible penalties for serious and nonserious violations are the same, $7,000 for each violation, as a practical matter, nonserious violations usually carry much lower penalties.

Serious

The finding of a serious violation under section 17(k) of the Act requires "a substantial probability that death or serious physical harm could result." Decisions of the Commission and courts have consistently held that it is not necessary for the Secretary to prove that there is a substantial probability that an accident will occur. It is only necessary to prove that an accident is possible and that death or serious physical harm could result. The likelihood of an accident is an important factor in determining the gravity of the violation. Thus, it is quite possible for a serious violation to be of low gravity and a nonserious violation to be of high gravity. Even where there has been a fatality in the workplace, the cited OSHA violation is not necessarily serious. The Secretary must prove a connection between the cited violation and the fatality or that the violative condition could lead to death or serious physical harm.

In *Anaconda Aluminum Co.*,[57] the Commission held that if a standard is intended to protect against a life-threatening disease, then a violation of the standard is deemed to be serious. The Secretary need not prove that the levels of exposure at the cited employer's workplace would lead to a serious disease.

The Secretary's regulations also provide that two or more nonserious violations may be grouped to form a serious violation if the combination of the nonserious violations results in a substantial probability that death or serious physical harm could result. The Commission has specifically approved this procedure.

Section 17(b) of the Act provides that an employer that receives a citation for a serious violation *shall* be assessed a penalty of up to

---

[57]9 OSH Cases 1460 (1981).

$7,000. The Commission has construed this section as requiring that a penalty be assessed for each serious violation.

Repeated

Section 17(a) of the Act provides that "any employer who willfully or repeatedly violates the requirements of section 5 of this Act, any standard, rule, or order promulgated pursuant to section 6 of this Act, or regulations prescribed pursuant to this Act, may be assessed a civil penalty of not more than $70,000 for each violation."

In *Potlatch Corp.*,[58] the Commission set forth the elements of a repeated violation. The Commission held that "[a] violation is repeated under section 17(a) of the Act if, at the time of the alleged repeated violation, there was a Commission final order against the same employer for a substantially similar violation." Based on *Potlatch*, to establish a repeated violation the Secretary must prove the following: (1) the same employer (2) was cited at least once before (3) and a final order was issued (4) for a substantially similar violation.

Citations for repeated violations may be issued for serious and nonserious violations—and conceivably even willful violations. While penalties of up to $70,000 for each violation are possible, the penalty assessment factors of section 17(j) of the Act must be considered. Also, because section 17(a) of the Act provides that penalties up to $70,000 *may* be assessed, it is possible that a repeated nonserious violation could carry no penalty.

Willful

The Act does not define a willful violation. Section 17(a) of the Act simply provides that an employer "who willfully . . . violates [the Act] . . . may be assessed a civil penalty of not more than $70,000 for each violation, with a minimum of $5,000 for each violation." Although there is no requirement that willful violations be serious, many willful citations are issued where there is death, serious injury, or the potential for serious injury. Willful violations may be alleged under both section 5(a)(1) and section 5(a)(2) of the Act.

---

[58] 7 OSH Cases 1061 (1979).

The Commission has held that to prove a willful violation the Secretary must prove that the employer has committed a violation of the Act and the violation was committed voluntarily with intentional disregard or demonstrated plain indifference to the Act. In *John W. Eshelman & Sons*,[59] the Commission held that the Secretary need not prove that the employer knew it was violating a specific standard or the Act in general. Nevertheless, proof of employer knowledge of the Act or a specific standard is one of the most effective ways of proving that the employer's conduct was marked by "careless disregard of" or "plain indifference to" employee safety and health. Employer knowledge of a standard and a subsequent violation of that standard, however, do not *necessarily* establish a willful violation.

Willful violations require that the employer have a particular state of mind. The Commission has held that "'wilful' means intentional, knowing, or voluntary as distinguished from accidental conduct and may be characterized as conduct marked by careless disregard."[60] In *Intercounty Construction Co. v. OSHRC*,[61] the Fourth Circuit Court of Appeals agreed with the Commission and defined "willful" as action being taken knowledgeably by one subject to the statutory provisions in disregard of the action's legality. No showing of malicious intent is necessary. A conscious, intentional, deliberate, voluntary decision is properly described as willful, "regardless of venial motive." The court pointed out that "[t]o require bad intent would place a severe restriction on the statutory authority of OSHA to apply the stronger sanctions in enforcing the law, a result we do not feel was intended by Congress." This interpretation has been widely followed.

As mentioned earlier, penalties of up to $70,000 may be assessed for each willful violation, with a $5,000 minimum for each violation. The Commission, in applying the section 17(j) penalty assessment factors, has held that the consideration of an employer's good faith is not inconsistent with the finding of a willful violation.

---

[59]9 OSH Cases 1396 (1981).

[60]C.N. Flagg & Co., 2 OSH Cases 1195 (1974), *aff'd*, 538 F.2d 308, 3 OSH Cases 2029 (2d Cir. 1976).

[61]522 F.2d 777, 3 OSH Cases 1337 (4th Cir. 1975), *cert. denied*, 423 U.S. 1072, 3 OSH Cases 1879 (1976).

Failure to Abate

The most severe civil penalties in the Act are provided for employers failing to correct (abate) violations for which they were previously cited. Section 17(d) of the Act provides that "any employer who fails to correct a violation . . . may be assessed a civil penalty of not more than $7,000 for each day during which such failure or violation continues." Separate citations are not issued to employers that fail to abate violations. Instead, the Secretary will issue a notice of failure to correct and a notice of proposed additional penalties. A notice of failure to correct may be issued at any time after the abatement date. If the proposed abatement date occurs before the end of the 15 working day period in which the employer may contest the original citation, a notice of failure to correct may be issued as soon as the abatement date has passed. An employer has 15 working days to contest additional penalties for failure to abate, but the notification of additional penalties need not be posted.

In assessing penalties for failure to abate, the Commission considers the penalty assessment factors of section 17(j) of the Act. One important consideration is the amount of the original penalty. Other significant factors are whether the employer has taken any steps toward abatement, the gravity of the violation, and overall good faith.

Imminent Danger

Section 13(a) of the Act defines "imminent danger" as a condition "which could be reasonably expected to cause death or serious physical harm immediately or before the imminence of such danger can be eliminated through the enforcement procedures otherwise provided by this Act." If an OSHA compliance officer finds an imminent danger, the CO will ask the employer to remove endangered employees and to abate the hazard voluntarily. Most employers have abated voluntarily, thereby eliminating the need for other action. If, however, the employer refuses to abate voluntarily, the CO notifies the regional director who, through the regional solicitor, seeks a court order from the nearest United States district court pursuant to section 13(b) of the Act, which orders the immediate abatement of the hazard.

Criminal Sanctions

Section 17(e) of the Act provides that "any employer who willfully violates [the] Act, and that violation caused death to any employee" may be punished, upon conviction, by a fine up to $10,000 or six months imprisonment, or both, For second offenses, the punishment may be a fine up to $20,000 or one year imprisonment, or both. Criminal cases under the Act are brought by the United States Department of Justice and are prosecuted by the local United States attorney. The cases are tried in United States district court.

The Act contains other criminal sanctions. Section 17(f) prohibits any person from giving advance notice of an inspection. Section 17(g) makes it a crime for any person to make false statements or file false reports. Section 17(h) makes it a crime to interfere with an OSHA compliance officer by using force. These provisions have been used in only a few cases.

PENALTIES

The Act provides for a wide range of penalties. As amended in 1990, the penalty ranges for each of the violations are as follows:

De minimis notice	$0
Nonserious	$0-$7,000
Serious	$1-$7,000
Repeated	$0-$70,000
Willful	$5,000-$70,000
Failure to abate notice	$0-$7,000 per day

Section 17(j) of the Act provides that "the Commission shall have authority to assess all civil penalties provided in this section. . . ." In *Brennan v. OSHRC (Interstate Glass Co.)*,[62] the Eighth Circuit Court of Appeals held that "the Commission shall be the final arbiter of penalties if the Secretary's proposals are contested and that, in such a case, the Secretary's proposals merely become advisory." The Commission has enthusiastically endorsed the principle that in contested cases it assesses a penalty independently.

---

[62]487 F.2d 438, 1 OSH Cases 1372 (8th Cir. 1973).

The Commission has held that in assessing penalties under the Act it is not bound to follow the Secretary's penalty computation formula. In applying the statutory penalty assessment factors of gravity, size, good faith, and compliance history, the Commission further declared that it need not accord these factors equal weight. Despite a long-standing rejection of the Secretary's formula, the Commission has never formalized a calculation method of its own. Cases are still decided on a case-by-case basis.

The Commission has held that an administrative law judge (ALJ) may not routinely affirm the proposed penalty of the Secretary, but the ALJ must make an independent determination based on the section 17(j) factors and the particular facts of each case. This same principle applies to all types of violations. For example, the Commission has held that a blanket $100 per day penalty for failure to abate used by the Secretary was invalid. Penalties for failure to abate must bear a reasonable relationship to the penalties assessed for the violations in the first instance.

Although the Commission has staunchly defended its right to be the final arbiter in penalty assessments, in practice, the Secretary's proposals are often given considerable deference. If the ALJ's assessment, often identical to the Secretary's proposal, is not substantially unreasonable, it is usually upheld. The main reason for this unannounced policy is that penalty assessment is subjective and it is difficult and time consuming for the commissioners to agree on an appropriate penalty.

Assessment Factors

The gravity of the violation is the starting point and most important factor in penalty assessment. "Gravity, unlike good faith, compliance history and size is relevant only to the [specific] violation being considered in a case and therefore is usually of greater significance. The other factors are concerned with the employer generally and are considered as modifying factors."[63] Consequently, it is possible for the gravity to be so high that even with full consideration for good faith, size, and compliance history the penalty assessed will be the maximum amount. The Commission has held that gravity is composed of (1) the number

---

[63]Natkin & Co., 1 OSH Cases 1204 (1973).

of employees exposed to the hazard, (2) the duration of exposure, (3) whether any precautions have been taken against injury, and (4) the degree of probability that an accident would occur.

The Commission has indicated that good faith should be determined by a review of the employer's safety and health program, its commitment to job safety and health, and its cooperation with persons and organizations (like OSHA). Good faith can be shown by the employer's conduct before or after the time of the alleged violation. Nevertheless, the Commission has declined to give the term a specific definition. "The phrase good faith is not capable of precise definition but must be ascertained from the facts in each case."[64] A review of Commission decisions in this area reveals four main categories of conduct that the Commission has found to evidence good faith. They are the employer's (1) overall safety program, (2) attempts at compliance, (3) cooperation with the OSHA compliance officer, and (4) prompt abatement of violations.

Section 17(j) of the Act requires that the size of the business be considered in penalty assessment. "Adjustment of the penalty for the employer's size is primarily an attempt to avoid destructive penalties" that could cripple a small business.[65] The First Circuit Court of Appeals has held that it was not unreasonable to differentiate in penalty assessment based on the size of the employer.[66] The Commission has refrained from narrowly defining what it considers to be a "small business." Instead, it evaluates the facts of each case individually, considering both the gross dollar volume of the business and the total number of employees, including those at other worksites. The Commission also is not restricted to the amount of relief it can grant a small employer, but it attempts to assess a penalty that is fair. Many of the reductions for employer size also are based, in part, on the employer's financial condition.

The final penalty assessment factor specifically mentioned in section 17(j) of the Act is the employer's history of compliance. Frequently, this factor is related to the employer's good faith. A history of few or no prior violations will usually result in a lower penalty than

---

[64]Marino Dev. Corp., 2 OSH Cases 1260 (1974).
[65]Colonial Craft Reprods., 1 OSH Cases 1063 (1972).
[66]Desarrollos Metropolitanos, Inc. v. OSHRC, 551 F.2d 874, 5 OSH Cases 1135 (1st Cir. 1977).

where the employer has a history of several violations. An employer need not have a perfect safety record to have a good history of compliance with the Act. This is especially true where the employer is a large company with many employees.

Collection

Section 17(l) of the Act provides that all civil penalties owed under the Act are payable to the Secretary of Labor for deposit in the United States Treasury. For uncontested citations, the penalty is due at the end of the notice of contest period. For contested cases, the penalty is due upon the issuance of a final order of the Commission. According to the Secretary's regulations, the area director will send a collection letter to any employer that fails to pay an uncontested penalty within 15 working days of receipt of a citation. Any form of payment other than cash will be accepted.

PREHEARING PROCEDURE

The Occupational Safety and Health Review Commission has the responsibility of adjudicating contested cases under the Act. It is an indpendent body comprised of three members appointed by the President. One of the members is designated as Chairman and is responsible for the administrative operations of the Commission. Members serve staggered six-year terms.

The main office of the Commission is in Washington, D.C. Each commissioner has a legal staff and support personnel. All Commission hearings and records are open to the public. The Commission has issued regulations indicating its methods of compliance with the Freedom of Information Act[67] and the Privacy Act,[68] and also has published Standards of Ethics and Conduct for its employees.[69]

The Chairman of the Commission has responsibility for appointing ALJs who have life tenure. A number of ALJs work out of each one

---

[67]5 U.S.C. §552 (1993); 29 C.F.R. pt. 2201 (1992).
[68]5 U.S.C. §552a (1993); 29 C.F.R. pt. 2400 (1992).
[69]29 C.F.R. pt. 2202 (1992).

of the Commission's regional offices from which they are assigned cases, so that hearings may be held in a community as close as possible to the location of the alleged violation. The Commission has its own rules of procedure which govern its proceedings.[70]

Complaint

No later than 20 days after forwarding a notice of contest to the Commission, the Secretary of Labor must file a complaint. In the complaint the Secretary must set forth the following: all violations and proposed penalties being contested; the basis for jurisdiction; the time, location, place, and circumstances of each alleged violation; the considerations upon which all abatement periods and proposed penalties are based; and, if the complaint seeks to amend the citation or proposed penalty, the reasons for the amendment and the change sought.

Answer

The employer must file an answer within 20 days after service of the complaint. The answer must contain a short and plain statement denying those allegations in the complaint which the employer intends to contest. When an employer fails to file an answer, the Commission will issue an order to show cause why the notice of contest should not be dismissed. This allows employers a second chance to file an answer. If the employer fails to respond to repeated notices or to an order to show cause, or fails to prove excusable neglect, the notice of contest may be dismissed.

Settlements

The Commission encourages settlements at any stage of the proceedings. Settlement agreements do not need to include any particular language as long as the terms are expressed clearly, unresolved issues are noted, and any employee parties' objections to the reasonableness of abatement times are indicated.

---

[70]The rules are codified at 29 C.F.R. pt. 2200 (1992).

HEARING PROCEDURE

The Commission's policy is to conduct a hearing in or near the community where an alleged violation occurred. In *Bethlehem Steel Corp.*,[71] the Commission reversed an ALJ's notice of hearing, which set the hearing 50 miles from the employer's plant, and ordered that the hearing be held in a smaller city only six miles from the employer's plant. According to the Commission, a hearing should be held as close as possible to the site of an alleged violation.

All parties must receive at least 30 days notice of the time, place (city), and nature of a hearing. If there has been a prior postponement or if there are exigent circumstances, at least 10 days notice is required. A motion to postpone must be filed at least seven days in advance of a hearing unless there is good cause for a late filing.

The failure of a party to appear at a hearing may result in a decision against that party. The Commission or the ALJ, however, may excuse the failure to appear and reschedule the hearing if good cause is shown. In the absence of extraordinary circumstances, requests for reinstatement must be made within five days after the scheduled hearing date.

Representation

Any party may appear at the hearing in person or through a representative. A representative need not be a lawyer.

Burden of Proof

In all proceedings initiated by the filing of a notice of contest, the burden of proof rests with the Secretary. This includes all employer contests and employee challenges to the reasonableness of the abatement date. The Commission has held that the civil "preponderance of the evidence" test applies in Commission proceedings. In other words, the Secretary must prove that it is more probable than not that a violation existed in order to prevail at the hearing.

---

[71] 6 OSH Cases 1912 (1978).

Fees

Occasionally the Secretary will issue an OSHA citation and prosecute the matter through a hearing before the Commission even though the case against the employer is extremely weak. Although the employer prevails at the hearing, it may have cost hundreds or thousands of dollars for the employer to vindicate its position. The Equal Access to Justice Act[72] may permit the awarding of attorney fees to a private party in an OSHA (or other administrative) proceeding in these circumstances.

Under this law, if the ALJ or Commission finds that OSHA failed to prove that its action was "substantially justified," attorney fees, expert witness fees, and other costs may be awarded against the United States. In OSHA cases, fees may be awarded only against the Secretary. There can be no recovery against the Commission because its role is limited to adjudication. The test of whether the Secretary's action is substantially justified is essentially one of reasonableness. Where the Secretary can show that a case had a reasonable basis both in law and fact (even if ultimately unsuccessful), no attorney fees will be awarded.

The Commission's regulations implementing the Equal Access to Justice Act provide (1) to be eligible there is a ceiling on net worth of $2 million for individuals and $7 million for partnerships, corporations, and other entities; (2) units of a local government (erroneously cited) are eligible for fee awards; (3) "substantially justified" is defined to include the underlying governmental action or failure to act that the proceeding is based on, as well as the government's position in litigation; and (4) the Secretary may seek additional proceedings to show that a position was substantially justified, especially where the action was dismissed before any record was developed.[73]

POSTHEARING PROCEDURE

A copy of an ALJ's decision is mailed to every party, and the parties then have 20 days in which to file exceptions. During this period the ALJ is free to reconsider the decision and correct clerical errors and

---

[72]5 U.S.C. §504 (1993).
[73]29 C.F.R. pt. 2204 (1992).

errors arising through oversight or inadvertence. The ALJ must transmit the decision and all other accompanying documents to the Commission no later than the 21st day following the date of mailing to the parties.

Once an ALJ's decision is received and docketed by the Commission, the ALJ has no jurisdiction to amend the decision. The ALJ's report becomes a final order of the Commission unless it is directed for review by the Commission within 30 days of docketing. The Executive Secretary of the Commission will notify all parties that an ALJ's decision has been docketed by the Commission.

Commission Review

Review by the Commission is not a matter of right, but rests within the sound discretion of the Commission. There are two distinct, but related, ways in which an ALJ's decision may be directed for review by the Commission. First, the Commission may grant a petition for discretionary review (PDR) filed by any aggrieved party. This is essentially a request for the Commission to grant an appeal. Second, a Commission member may direct review of the ALJ's decision on his or her own initiative even without the filing of such a petition.

Although a direction for review gives the Commission jurisdiction to review the entire case, ordinarily the issues will be limited to those stated in the formal direction for review issued by the Commission or in a later order. In its direction for review the Commission may raise new issues to which the parties will be asked to respond.

The Commission ordinarily will not review issues on which an ALJ did not have an opportunity to rule. In exercising discretion to consider issues raised for the first time on review, the Commission "may consider such factors as whether there was good cause for not raising the issue before the Judge, the degree to which the issue is factual, the degree to which proceedings will be disrupted or delayed by raising the issue on review, whether the ability of an adverse party to press a claim or defense would be impaired, and whether considering the new issue would avoid injustice or ensure that judgment will be rendered in accordance with the law and facts."[74]

---

[74]29 C.F.R. § 2200.93(c) (1992).

When the Commission directs review of an ALJ's decision, the entire decision is on review. The failure to direct a particular citation item for review does not make the ALJ's disposition of that item a final order of the Commission. Therefore, there is no abatement requirement for any contested item until the Commission issues a final order.

Judicial Review

Section 11(a) of the Act provides that "any person adversely affected or aggrieved by a final order of the Commission" may seek review by filing a petition for review in any United States Court of Appeals for the circuit in which the alleged violation occurred, where the employer has its principal office, or in the Court of Appeals for the District of Columbia Circuit. Under section 11(b) of the Act, the Secretary may seek review only in the circuit in which the alleged violation occurred or where the employer has its principal office.

Petitions for review must be filed with the clerk of the court within 60 days following the issuance of the Commission's final order. The 60-day period may not be extended. For an unreviewed ALJ's decision, the 60-day period begins to run on the day the ALJ's decision becomes a final order of the Commission, *not* 30 days after the Commission's notice to the employer that its PDR was denied. The date of filing with a court is the date the petition arrives at the office of the clerk of the court.

6

Workers' Compensation

INTRODUCTION

Every year, millions of workers sustain employment-related injuries or contract work-related diseases. Some result from single accidents, while others, such as carpal tunnel syndrome, are caused by repeated traumas or the performance of repetitive job tasks. Many workers contract diseases, such as asbestosis, silicosis, cancer, pneumoconiosis, and lead poisoning, that are related to their work environments. Job stress may contribute to cardiovascular disease or mental illness. Many employment-related health conditions require medical treatment. A number cause short-term job interruptions, while a few generate prolonged periods of unemployment or result in death.

As the United States was transformed from an agricultural to an industrial society, the number of employment-related injuries and diseases increased sharply. Employees who sustained economic losses were forced to seek redress through common law tort actions. They had to prove that their injuries had been caused by the negligent acts of individuals who were acting as agents of their employer. If they were unsuccessful in this regard, they were denied relief.

Even when injured workers were able to establish negligence attributable to their employer, there was still a good chance they would be unable to obtain favorable judgments. If the employer could demonstrate that the employee's own negligence contributed to his or her condition, the worker's "contributory negligence" would usually preclude monetary relief. Many courts also adopted the "fellow servant" doctrine to narrow employer liability for the negligent acts of workers. Under this approach, employers were not held liable for injuries caused to employees by the negligent actions of their fellow workers. The third concept that shielded employers against liability for employee injuries was the "assumption of risk" doctrine. Courts applying this rule held that employees assumed the risks associated with their employment and were thus unable to sue their employer for industrial accidents caused by work-related circumstances.

By the late 1800s, courts began to recognize the harsh results generated by application of the contributory negligence, fellow servant, and assumption of risk doctrines, and several exceptions were developed to limit application of those rules. As a result, an increasing number of tort actions culminated in verdicts favorable to injured workers. Although employers were dissatisfied with these developments, many injured employees continued to be denied relief due to the contributory negligence, fellow servant, and assumption of risk concepts. They were also unable to obtain compensation for accidental injuries that were not caused by negligence that was attributable to their employer. State legislatures began to consider the need for legislative reform.

In 1884, Germany adopted a comprehensive compensation approach that provided benefits to all workers affected by sickness or accidental disability. This was the first major legislation that did not require claimants to demonstrate some fault attributable to their employer. England extended the "liability without fault" concept to its workers through the Workmen's Compensation Act of 1897, and other European countries quickly adopted similar statutes.

In the early 1900s, state legislatures began to adopt compensation laws that provided injured workers with medical and disability benefits. The adversely affected individuals no longer had to demonstrate fault attributable to their employer. They were merely required to show that their injuries arose out of and during the course of their employment. Furthermore, the traditional contributory negligence, fellow servant, and assumption of risk defenses were abolished. Even workers who sustained injuries as a result of their own carelessness were entitled to workers' compensation. All 50 states and the District of Columbia now have workers' compensation laws.

The statutory acceptance of the liability without fault concept was of significant benefit to injured workers. The new laws, however, also provided employers with several important benefits. While injured employees were guaranteed medical coverage and specified amounts for lost earnings, the liability imposed on business firms was limited. Punitive damages could normally not be awarded, and disability benefit awards could not exceed statutorily prescribed maximums. Employers were also provided with expansive tort immunity. The new workers' compensation enactments generally prevented injured workers from obtaining tort judgments against their employer for compensable injuries, even when those injuries were caused by negligent actions attributable to their employer.

COVERAGE

Most workers' compensation laws cover all private and most public employers. Idaho excludes nonprofit businesses, and Arkansas, Mississippi, and North Dakota exclude both charitable and religious employers. In states that do not expressly exclude charitable and religious enterprises, courts generally find those organizations covered by workers' compensation statutes. These decisions are based on the assumption that social welfare laws are intended to provide expansive coverage.

The vast majority of workers' compensation statutes apply to all employers with one or more full-time employees and to many firms that have one or more regular part-time workers. Nonetheless, seven states[1] require a minimum of three employees, two states[2] require at least four workers, and three states[3] require five or more employees. Some small firms in states that require three, four, or five regular employees for coverage may employ more than the minimum number during most of the year and fewer than that figure during the remainder of the year. To avoid the uncertainty that would result if such employers were only covered during the periods they employ a sufficient number of workers,

---

[1]Alabama, Arkansas, Florida, Georgia, Virginia, New Mexico, and North Carolina.
[2]Rhode Island and South Carolina.
[3]Mississippi, Missouri, and Tennessee.

courts generally extend full-year coverage to companies that regularly employ the minimum number of persons during significant portions of the year.

A separate federal law extends workers' compensation protection to maritime employees under the Longshore and Harbor Workers' Compensation Act (LHWCA).[4] Coverage is provided to individuals who are injured while working on piers, wharfs, terminals, buildings, or vessels loading, unloading, building, or repairing ships associated with navigable waters. Injured maritime workers may seek benefits under both the LHWCA and the applicable state workers' compensation law, with the administrative agency making the more recent award deducting amounts previously granted under the other enactment.

All workers' compensation statutes cover some or all government employers. Forty states[5] extend mandatory protection to all public personnel. Six states[6] cover public employees, but exclude government officials. Texas extends coverage to county workers and to state highway and college personnel, and it authorizes municipalities to elect coverage for their employees. The Delaware and Tennessee statutes permit voluntary coverage of government workers. Federal civilian employees enjoy statutory protection under the Federal Employees Compensation Act (FECA).[7]

Statutory Employers

Business firms frequently hire independent contractors to perform tasks that would otherwise be performed by regular company personnel. Although the independent contractor employees are directly employed by their contractor, they may function like employees of the principal party. Such contractor employees may work for small contractors that are not required to provide workers' compensation coverage or that fail

---

[4]*See* 33 U.S.C. §§901–50 (1993).

[5]Alabama, Alaska, Arizona, Arkansas, California, Colorado, Connecticut, Georgia, Hawaii, Idaho, Illinois, Indiana, Iowa, Kansas, Kentucky, Maine, Maryland, Massachusetts, Michigan, Minnesota, Mississippi, Missouri, Montana, Nebraska, Nevada, New Hampshire, New Jersey, New York, North Carolina, North Dakota, Ohio, Oklahoma, Oregon, Pennsylvania, Rhode Island, Utah, Washington, West Virginia, Wisconsin, and Wyoming.

[6]Florida, Louisiana, South Carolina, South Dakota, Vermont, and Virginia.

[7]5 U.S.C. §§8101–93 (1993).

to do so. The workers' compensation laws in the vast majority of states[8] contain special provisions pertaining to so-called statutory employers. These apply to principal parties that are not technically the employers of contractor employees but use those individuals as their own workers.

If the work being performed by contractor employees would ordinarily be accomplished by employees of the principal party, considering the past practices of this firm and of comparable companies, the principal party generally will be held secondarily liable for the workers' compensation of those contractor personnel. The principal firm is thus held responsible for injured contractor employees when their actual employers lack adequate workers' compensation coverage. When the principal is held liable, it may usually seek reimbursement from the primarily responsible contractors. Principal firms may protect themselves against such liability by requiring their contractors to provide sufficient insurance to cover the workers' compensation of their employees.

Statutory employer cases often involve the use of contractor personnel to perform maintenance, construction, and delivery work. Courts resolving statutory employer questions usually consider:

- the past and present practices of the principal firm and of similar companies;

- whether the activities are customarily conducted by the principal's own employees;

- whether the activities relate to the regular operations of the principal firm;

- whether the job functions are being performed on the principal firm's premises or at another location;

- whether the principal possesses the right to exercise meaningful control over the manner in which the contractor employees perform their work;

---

[8]Alaska, Arizona, Arkansas, Colorado, Connecticut, Florida, Georgia, Hawaii, Idaho, Illinois, Indiana, Kansas, Kentucky, Louisiana, Maryland, Massachusetts, Michigan, Minnesota, Mississippi, Missouri, Montana, Nebraska, Nevada, New Hampshire, New Jersey, New Mexico, New York, North Carolina, North Dakota, Ohio, Oklahoma, Oregon, Pennsylvania, South Carolina, South Dakota, Tennessee, Texas, Utah, Virginia, Vermont, Washington, Wisconsin, and Wyoming.

- whether the job tasks are regularly or irregularly carried out; and

- the specialized or nonspecialized nature of the work.

If the work being performed by contractor employees is not part of the regular business of the principal party and the principal exercises minimal control over their job functions, the principal would probably not be held responsible for contractor employees' compensation coverage. If, however, the contractor personnel are carrying out regular maintenance or delivery work and the principal has the right to control their actual work, the principal would most likely be considered their statutory employer. If a statutory employer relationship is found and the statutory employer is liable for the workers' compensation of injured individuals, that party will enjoy immunity against tort liability relating to those injuries.

Exempt Employees

The fact that an employer is subject to workers' compensation coverage does not mean that all of its employees are entitled to statutory protection. Certain groups of workers are specifically excluded from coverage in many states. Twenty-six states[9] exempt persons who perform domestic services. The other 24 states[10] provide limited coverage for such workers, typically requiring a minimum number of hours worked per week or a minimal amount of earnings per calendar quarter for inclusion. Individuals who perform domestic work on a part-time or sporadic basis are rarely entitled to mandatory protection, but most state laws permit employers to provide excluded domestic employees with voluntary coverage.

Most workers' compensation statutes provide coverage for agricultural workers. Some restrict coverage by requiring a minimum amount of annual earnings, while others limit protection to persons who

---

[9]Alabama, Arizona, Arkansas, Florida, Georgia, Idaho, Indiana, Louisiana, Maine, Mississippi, Montana, Nebraska, Nevada, New Mexico, North Carolina, North Dakota, Oregon, Pennsylvania, Rhode Island, Tennessee, Texas, Virginia, Vermont, West Virginia, Wisconsin, and Wyoming.

[10]Alaska, California, Colorado, Connecticut, Delaware, Hawaii, Illinois, Iowa, Kansas, Kentucky, Maryland, Massachusetts, Michigan, Minnesota, Missouri, New Hampshire, New Jersey, New York, Ohio, Oklahoma, South Carolina, South Dakota, Utah, and Washington.

operate power equipment or work in hazardous jobs. The laws in 11 states[11] expressly exclude agricultural employees. When deciding coverage questions, courts in these states generally consider the actual job functions being performed by the workers involved, rather than focusing on the nature of the employer's business. While individuals directly involved with the cultivation of crops or the raising of livestock are clearly "agricultural" employees, courts often reach conflicting decisions with respect to persons who process crops or livestock. People who perform tasks associated with the initial processing of farm products (e.g., gathering the crops or transporting them to canneries) are more likely to be found "agricultural" workers than persons who are more directly involved with the final production process. Most state laws allow farmers to grant voluntary coverage to excluded agricultural workers.

A majority of workers' compensation laws exclude "casual" employees who perform work on an irregular or sporadic basis. Although four states[12] exempt all casual workers, 27 states[13] limit the casual employee exception to persons who perform job functions that are outside the normal trade or business of their employer. In these 27 jurisdictions, casual workers who perform tasks related to the regular business of their employer are entitled to workers' compensation protection. Eight other states[14] do not exempt "casual" employees, but do exclude all persons who perform work that is not within the normal trade or business of their employer. Individuals who engage in maintenance or repair work are usually considered within the normal business of their employer, because such work is essential to the basic operation of any business. Construction workers who engage in remodeling projects are likely to be found within the regular trade or business of their employer, while persons who work on the construction of new buildings are generally found outside the normal trade or business of an employer that is not engaged in the construction business.

---

[11]Arkansas, Georgia, Idaho, Indiana, Kentucky, Mississippi, Nebraska, Nevada, New Mexico, Tennessee, and Texas.

[12]Idaho, Maryland, New Jersey, and Tennessee.

[13]Alabama, Arizona, Arkansas, California, Colorado, Connecticut, Delaware, Florida, Indiana, Iowa, Minnesota, Montana, Nebraska, Nevada, New Mexico, North Carolina, North Dakota, Ohio, Oregon, Pennsylvania, Rhode Island, South Carolina, Utah, Vermont, Virginia, Washington, and Wyoming.

[14]Georgia, Illinois, Louisiana, Maine, Massachusetts, South Dakota, Texas, and Wisconsin.

Employment Relationship

Workers' compensation coverage is normally limited to employees who have been retained under express or implied contracts of hire to perform services for other parties. This requirement concerns the belief that employers should not be held responsible for work-related injuries in the absence of mutual employment relationships. Nonetheless, where such relationships are established, statutory coverage is likely to be provided, even when the employees are spouses or minor children of the employer or are undocumented aliens who have been unlawfully employed. So long as they are employed on a regular, rather than a casual, basis, spouses, minor children, and undocumented aliens are normally granted workers' compensation coverage.

A number of coverage cases have concerned prisoners who perform services for correctional institutions or for other government agencies or outside parties. Prisoners who receive modest compensation for their prison services are usually denied workers' compensation protection either by express statutory exclusion or by judicial decision. The judicial determinations are generally based on the premise that convicts are required to work and cannot be considered to have entered into voluntary employment arrangements. On the other hand, when prisoners are farmed out to work for other government agencies or for private employers, courts are more likely to find covered employment relationships.

It is normally acknowledged that employment relationships involve some form of remuneration. As a result, judicial decisions have uniformly concluded that individuals who perform gratuitous services without any expectation of compensation are not entitled to workers' compensation protection. Even volunteers who are provided with free meals by charitable organizations are generally denied coverage, due to the absence of any real remuneration. On the other hand, individuals do not have to receive cash for their services to obtain statutory protection. If they are given meaningful in-kind payments consisting of room and board or training, they will probably be found covered employees.

Independent Contractors

Even when individuals enter into contractual relationships with employers providing for the performance of remunerated services, they do not necessarily create covered "employment" relationships. Courts distinguish between employees, who are entitled to statutory protection, and independent contractors, who are not. Because it is clear that most state legislatures contemplated common law master-servant concepts when they adopted statutory provisions covering employees and exempting independent contractors, courts frequently consider various factors to determine whether covered employment relationships exist.

Court decisions regularly emphasize the so-called right-to-control test to resolve questions regarding the existence or nonexistence of employment relationships. When the evidence indicates that the principal party possesses the authority to exercise meaningful control over the individual's actual job performance, a covered employment relationship is usually found. In situations in which the principal party merely specifies the final product but lacks the right to control the person's job performance, an exempt independent contractor relationship is normally determined.

Close cases often involve individuals with attenuated work arrangements, such as truck drivers, taxi drivers, and commission salespeople. When the principal party retains the right to exercise meaningful control over the actual job performance of these persons, courts tend to find covered employment relationships. On the other hand, when truck or taxi drivers may work for different firms and determine when and how they will conduct their own business, exempt independent contractor relationships are likely to result. Similar considerations are used to distinguish between covered and uncovered commission salespeople.

When the right-to-control factor does not clearly support a covered employment or an uncovered independent contractor relationship, courts usually evaluate other factors. The criteria suggesting a covered employment relationship include:

- the worker is not engaged in a distinct occupation or business;
- the work is usually performed in this area under the direction of an employer;
- the work does not require the services of a highly skilled individual;
- the principal supplies the tools and the place of work;
- the employment is for an extended period of time and involves regular hours;

- the worker is to be paid by the hour, week, or month, and has not assumed the risk of loss if the work does not generate profits;

- the work being performed is part of the regular business of the principal party;

- the parties thought they were creating an employer-employee relationship; and

- the principal party is engaged in a recognized business.

Most courts do not apply these factors on a strictly numerical basis. The results in particular cases involve weighing the applicable criteria and applying a significant degree of judicial discretion. Because workers' compensation laws are designed to provide social insurance for injured employees, courts tend to resolve close cases in favor of coverage. They thus examine the nature of the work involved and endeavor to find employment relationships whenever the circumstances suggest that the injured individuals are in need of statutory protection.

Professional and Executive Personnel

Professional and executive personnel occasionally raise interesting coverage problems because of the substantial discretion they exercise over their own job performance. Professionals who work regularly for a specific firm and are subject to a meaningful degree of management control in their job tasks are clearly entitled to statutory protection. Even professionals who enjoy expansive work discretion are likely to be considered covered employees if they work continuously for the same party. Nevertheless, professionals who enter into service contracts with various firms and retain primary control over their own work activities are normally found ineligible for statutory protection.

Most corporate executives, including those who formulate and effectuate basic managerial policies, are provided with statutory coverage. Even officers with substantial or total stock ownership continue to enjoy workers' compensation protection when they perform managerial functions. On some occasions, however, executives who exercise pervasive shareholder authority may be considered so identified with the corporation itself that they will be denied statutory coverage. This is especially likely when they are acting in an entrepreneurial, rather than an executive, manner.

Similar issues arise when equity partners in business firms sustain work-related injuries. Most courts treat equity partners as exempt employers, rather than covered employees. Very few states have extended mandatory protection to equity partners. Laws in eight states[15] permit business firms to cover their equity partners on a voluntary basis.

Borrowed Servants

Employees who work for one company are sometimes required to perform services for a second firm. Many judicial decisions have struggled with the so-called borrowed servant doctrine to determine when the borrowing company should be considered the employer of the loaned individuals for workers' compensation purposes. Courts generally recognize that no employment relationship can exist without evidence of an express or implied contract of hire. If it is clear that the loaned employee and the borrowing firm have not entered into an explicit or implicit work arrangement, no covered employment relationship between those two parties is likely to be found. On the other hand, when there is any indication of a consensual agreement between the loaned worker and the borrowing company, courts usually find the requisite contract of hire. Such an arrangement will often be implied from the fact that the loaned individual willingly complied with work directions issued by the borrowing party.

Once an express or implied contract of hire is found, courts look for other indicia of employment. If the borrowing firm is empowered to exercise control over the manner of the loaned individual's work and the tasks being performed by that person are primarily for the benefit of the borrowing company, that entity is likely to be held responsible for that person's workers' compensation coverage. When both the lending company and the borrowing firm may simultaneously control the worker's performance, a "joint employer" relationship is usually found, with both parties being held jointly responsible for that person's workers' compensation protection. On the other hand, when the loaned employee engages in separate activities during discrete time periods for the lending party and the borrowing concern, a "dual employment" relationship is normally determined, with each firm being held

---

[15]Florida, Nebraska, New Mexico, Oregon, Tennessee, Utah, Vermont, and Virginia.

exclusively responsible for the occupational injuries sustained by the affected worker while that person is performing duties for that particular firm.

ARISING DURING THE COURSE OF EMPLOYMENT

Workers' compensation laws do not protect individuals against all accidental injuries. They only cover employment-related occurrences. Claimants seeking compensation must demonstrate that their conditions arose *during the course of* their employment. If their injuries have no connection with their employment, they are not compensable. If, however, their injuries arose in the employment environment while they were performing work tasks, they would clearly be covered.

The most frequently litigated cases involve occurrences that have a tenuous connection to the employment of the injured workers. They may be injured while commuting to or from work, eating, changing their clothes, cleaning up, resting, or performing other acts of a personal nature. Their accident may occur while they are participating in employer-related recreation or social activities, or while they are engaged in horseplay or misconduct. In all of these situations, compensation administrators must decide whether there is a sufficient connection to employment to warrant statutory protection.

Traveling to and From Work

Employees regularly travel to and from their places of work, to and from different jobs during their shift, and to and from meal and rest areas. Accidents may occur while they are driving, riding, or walking. Individuals who are injured at home while preparing to leave for work or who are injured while commuting to and from work on public roads or sidewalks are normally denied workers' compensation coverage due to the absence of any direct connection to their employment. On the other hand, commuters who are accidentally injured *after* they have entered their employer's premises, including company parking lots, on the way to work or *before* they have left their employer's premises at the end of the work day are likely to be accorded statutory protection. The fact that the injury occurred on company premises is considered sufficient to supply the required employment connection.

Courts have generally applied the same "going-and-coming" rule with respect to employees injured while traveling to and from external eating establishments during meal or rest breaks. People injured while driving, riding, or walking on company premises are entitled to compensation because of the immediate connection to their employer. Individuals who are injured while away from company premises, however, are almost always denied statutory coverage.

When employers own several, noncontiguous premises, employees may have to travel from one location to another on public roads or sidewalks. Courts recognize that it would be illogical to regard worker trips on public thoroughfares connecting company facilities as beyond the scope of their employment. As a result, employees who are injured on public roadways while traveling between employer facilities are generally found eligible for workers' compensation. The fact that they are traveling between firm premises for the direct benefit of their employer causes their trip to be considered during the course of their employment. Many courts have extended this concept to injuries sustained by employees injured while walking on public sidewalks or streets between a company parking lot and the main facility. Coverage is especially likely if employees are expected to park in the noncontiguous company lot.

Although employees injured on public thoroughfares while traveling to and from work are generally denied workers' compensation coverage, courts occasionally extend statutory protection to injuries caused by special hazards located adjacent to company premises. They treat such special dangers as employment-related, due to their proximity to firm property. Typical cases involve employees struck by vehicles while they are traveling to or from work in extremely congested areas near their work premises.

Special Errands and Travel on Company Vehicles

Employees are sometimes required to make special trips to their place of employment to perform specific tasks. For example, an individual may be required to return to work each evening to turn off particular machines. If this person were injured during the trip to or from work in connection with this assignment, a number of courts would provide compensation. They would find the travel of this employee sufficiently work-related, because the special trip would be a fundamental aspect of that person's employment. Coverage would be particularly likely if the individual were compensated for the travel time or reimbursed for travel expenses.

The "special errand" rule is usually applied to people with specified work hours who are required to make special trips back to work during their off-duty hours to perform limited tasks. The special trip does not have to occur on a regular basis to result in statutory protection. For example, if an employee were injured while returning to work for the purpose of unlocking the door to admit a repair person, benefits would probably be awarded. On the other hand, if the person were returning to employer premises to perform more extensive job functions, courts would be unlikely to apply the "special errand" rule.

Statutory coverage would also be likely with respect to employees injured while commuting to and from work in personal vehicles their employer requires them to use to travel from job to job during the work day. Most courts would find that they are driving their vehicles to and from work for the direct benefit of their employer. As a result, their commute would be regarded as part of their employment.

Another exception to the traditional going-and-coming doctrine has been adopted by most courts for employee travel on company conveyances. When workers sustain injuries while traveling to and from work in employer-supplied vehicles, they are normally found eligible for workers' compensation. Accidents that occur during commutes in company vehicles are regarded as having arisen during the course of the riders' employment, even when the workers are charged a fee for the company-provided transportation. On the other hand, if the employer was in the transportation business and allowed its employees to ride its buses or trains to and from work, a number of courts would deny injured riders statutory coverage. They would find that the company conveyances were primarily for the benefit of the riding public, not commuting employees.

Dual Purpose Doctrine

Workers occasionally take trips that serve both business and personal interests. For example, an individual going on vacation to a particular location may be asked to conduct company business on the way. Or a person traveling to a city on firm business may decide to take several vacation days in conjunction with that trip. When a "dual purpose" trip combines business and personal aspects, it is generally considered personal and uncovered if the travel would have been carried out despite the presence or absence of the business objective and would have been canceled without the existence of the personal consideration. On the other hand, the trip would constitute covered business travel if it would have had to be carried out by some employee even in the absence of the personal motivation. The critical question is not whether the trip would have been made by the injured worker, but whether it would have had to be undertaken by some employee. The mere fact that the employer asked the individual to carry out the business objective after it learned of the planned personal trip would not preclude coverage, so long as the business aspect is of sufficient importance that some employee would have been asked to make the trip.

Personal Comfort Doctrine

During the normal work day, employees frequently perform acts of a personal nature. They eat, drink, relieve themselves, wash up, change clothes, and rest. If their actions are found to advance employer interests or are an inherent aspect of the employment relationship, they take place on firm property, and they do not involve substantial departures from their customary employment endeavors, workers' compensation coverage is likely to be provided. For example, if employees on paid or unpaid rest or meal breaks sustain injuries while on company premises, their injuries would normally be considered compensable. The fact they are still on firm property and are ministering to personal needs that must be satisfied during their work day would lead most courts to conclude that their injuries arose during the course of their employment.

Statutory coverage would similarly be available to employees who stop briefly during the work day to get a drink, smoke a cigarette, or use the bathroom. It would also protect people injured while they are cleaning up or changing clothes at the beginning or conclusion of the work day. Many courts are even willing to extend coverage to workers who take short swims on firm property to obtain relief from summer heat. On the other hand, when employees leave company premises to satisfy personal needs, they are usually considered to have temporarily abandoned the course of their employment and to have lost their right to workers' compensation coverage. A lack of coverage is also likely with respect to employees who are merely hanging around before or after their shift and who sustain injuries that have no meaningful connection to their employment.

Unique coverage issues are raised by employees who reside in company-provided housing. While they may have fixed hours of work, they remain on employer premises during many of their off-duty hours. Because statutory protection is extended to nonresidential personnel who are injured on company property while eating, resting, changing clothes, cleaning up, and engaging in other personal activities incident to their employment, courts generally provide similar protection for fixed-hour residential employees while they are carrying out such tasks on firm premises. Nonetheless, when fixed-hour residential workers engage in wholly personal tasks in their rooms that have no meaningful connection to their employment, coverage is normally denied. Coverage for such purely personal endeavors is only available in most instances for residential personnel who are continuously on call and are required to be available at all hours.

Recreational and Social Activities

Many companies permit, encourage, or require employee participation in various recreational or social activities. These undertakings may occur during the regular work day or before or after work. If individuals are injured while participating in such endeavors, they would probably be granted workers' compensation if they could establish that their injuries (1) arose on company property as an incident of their employment, (2) originated during activities expressly or implicitly required by their employer, or (3) occurred while they were participating in recreational or social programs of significant benefit to their firm.

Numerous cases involve company parties. If these social events take place on firm property, coverage is generally available. Statutory protection for parties conducted away from company premises is also likely when workers are encouraged by managers to attend or if their employer hopes to enhance business opportunities through their attendance. Nonetheless, workers who sustain injuries while driving home from company parties are usually denied coverage under the traditional going-and-coming rule that excludes travel to and from work.

When workers are injured while participating in employer-mandated sporting events, they are almost always entitled to workers' compensation because they are satisfying company obligations. They would have more difficulty if they sustained their injuries during voluntary events. The laws in several states[16] expressly deny coverage to employees who voluntarily participate in activities that are not directly sponsored by their employer. Individuals who sustain injuries while participating in athletic events in these states must establish that they were either required or strongly encouraged to participate if they wish to obtain benefits.

Courts in states that do not have specific statutory provisions pertaining to this area usually consider various factors when deciding whether to extend statutory protection to employees injured while participating in voluntary recreational events. Coverage is likely if (1) the games occur on firm premises, (2) the company expressly promotes the activities or supplies the equipment, the uniforms, or the prizes, or (3) the firm derives commercial benefits through its sponsorship of team sports.

Traveling Employees

Some individuals regularly travel away from their employer's premises as part of their job. While they are on the road, they perform various tasks that relate directly to their work, and they engage in activities of a wholly personal nature. Injuries sustained by these persons while they are performing actual job functions are clearly compensable, and courts are increasingly extending coverage to injuries that arise during their personal endeavors. When traveling employees stay at hotels and motels, most courts apply the same rules as are applied to residential employees who live in company housing. Injuries sustained while they are obtaining meals on the road are usually covered as if they were eating in employer cafeterias. Application of the "special errand" rule also extends statutory protection to them while they are driving or walking from their hotel to eating establishments in the same way it would with respect to regular personnel traveling from one part of their employer's premises to another.

---

[16]California, Colorado, Illinois, Massachusetts, Nevada, New Jersey, New York, and Oregon.

Traveling employees injured by conditions indigenous to their out-of-town residences, such as hotel fires or personal assaults by intruders, are often given statutory protection. This is especially true when they are injured while on call. Most courts even extend coverage to injuries that arise while they are bathing or dressing, on the ground they are expected by their employer to maintain appropriate appearances. A growing number of decisions have also covered injuries occurring during recreational activities, based on the premise that while they are on the road, they may reasonably be expected to engage in some recreational endeavors to maintain their physical and mental health.

Horseplay and Employee Misconduct

It is not unusual for employees to engage in horseplay or prohibited misconduct at work. Innocent persons injured by the pranks or misconduct of fellow employees are generally eligible for benefits because their employment exposed them to the relevant behavior. On the other hand, persons who injure themselves while engaged in deliberate misconduct are usually denied benefits because of specific statutory provisions excluding such behavior or court decisions recognizing that such conduct is not reasonably related to the employment environment. When horseplay participants are injured, their right to coverage is less certain.

Courts have traditionally applied the "aggressor" defense that enables employers to defeat compensation claims filed by employees injured by horseplay carried out by themselves. This approach is based on the notion that individuals who engage in deliberate horseplay temporarily abandon their employment and thus forfeit their right to statutory protection. Nevertheless, some courts occasionally use different theories to award compensation to workers injured by their own horseplay. A number of courts have adopted a rule that allows individuals who are injured while engaged in horseplay that has become an accepted incident of their employment to obtain compensation. Only persons who participate in atypical pranks are denied compensation.

A second approach merely asks whether it would be reasonable to conclude that the injury caused by the claimant's horseplay arose out of the employment setting. So long as the relevant behavior does not involve a substantial departure from the claimant's regular employment, courts applying this rule tend to award compensation. When more than a minimal departure from expected conduct is involved, statutory protection is likely to be denied.

A few courts have effectively abolished the historic distinction between mere bystanders and active participants. These judges view injuries caused by shop mischief as an expected byproduct of crowded and stressful employment environments. As a result, they extend coverage to individuals who are injured by their own horseplay, so long as the relevant conduct does not involve a truly substantial departure from "acceptable" shop behavior.

Activities Beyond Regular Duties

It is not unusual for employees to engage in acts beyond their normal duties. They may assist fellow workers, customers, or members of the general public, and they may undertake actions that are designed to enhance their own employment skills. Modern courts usually recognize that actions taken to assist other employees with their job functions or to help customers have a sufficient employment connection to warrant statutory protection. These courts realize that a contrary rule would discourage actions that clearly benefit employers. Many courts use similar reasoning to extend coverage to acts intended to assist members of the general public. They believe that such worker conduct is likely to enhance company good will. Nonetheless, other courts continue to deny coverage to individuals who engage in such personal endeavors that lack a direct relationship to their employment. A loss of eligibility is particularly likely when employees assist fellow workers with the performance of wholly personal tasks.

When employees are injured carrying out private tasks they are directed to perform for the personal benefit of supervisors or their employer, statutory protection is normally available. Despite the personal nature of these actions, the workers are merely following supervisory instructions. Workers' compensation coverage is similarly likely when individuals attempt to enhance their overall skills by learning to operate or practicing on machines they do not usually operate, or by enrolling in training programs. Coverage may even be granted to employees who use other machines for personal benefit, if they can demonstrate that their employer has customarily allowed workers to work on such jobs.

People who become bored with their own work may decide to exchange jobs with fellow workers. If they do so with the express or implied permission of their employer, statutory protection will normally be provided. On the other hand, when they do so without the consent or knowledge of their employer, courts frequently find a lack of coverage. If company rules specifically prohibit job trading, coverage will almost always be denied.

Individuals who sustain injuries while attending conventions or seminars related to their occupations are generally entitled to statutory protection if they can demonstrate that their employer directed or encouraged them to attend. If, however, there is no evidence of employer encouragement and the workers decided on their own to attend, coverage would most likely be denied, even though their employer indirectly benefited from their efforts.

Many business firms permit their employees to engage in community service activities on company property. Workers may participate in Red Cross blood drives or charitable fund raising campaigns. Although these efforts take place on employer premises, their overwhelming personal nature causes most courts to conclude that the participants are acting outside the scope of their employment.

During their employment, individuals sometimes encounter emergency situations involving fellow workers, firm customers, or members of the general public. When claimants can demonstrate that employer interests were threatened by the emergency, statutory protection is usually provided. As a result, efforts to protect firm premises or equipment or to assist other workers endangered by employment-related conditions are generally found covered. If firm customers or members of the general public have been threatened by employer-related factors, employee efforts to protect those people and to limit employer liability will usually be given statutory protection. On the other hand, when employees assist customers or citizens who have been endangered by circumstances having no relationship to the employer, coverage is normally denied. Only a few courts extend protection to these good Samaritan actions, and they do so by reasoning that the actors' employment placed them in the situations that induced them to act.

Prehire and Post-Termination Injuries

Individuals applying for employment may sustain injuries while on the premises of prospective employers, and people who accept new positions may injure themselves on firm property before they actually begin their employment. **Because courts generally require evidence of an employment relationship before they extend workers' compensation protection to injured claimants, people who sustain injuries while they are attempting to obtain work and before they are formally hired are normally denied coverage.** This lack of coverage is even likely with respect to applicants injured during preemployment physical ability tests. Nonetheless, once it is clear that specific persons have actually been employed, they are generally entitled to statutory protection. If they are injured on company premises while walking or riding to their assigned place of work or while leaving the personnel office, they would probably be granted compensation. Even if the new workers were hired on a temporary basis until they complete probationary periods, they would be given the same protection as regular employees.

Persons who voluntarily quit or who are discharged may suffer harm while they are preparing to remove themselves or their belongings from employer premises. Courts recognize that these individuals must be given a reasonable opportunity to pick up their personal belongings and their final check, and to leave firm premises. If they sustain injuries while engaged in these activities within a reasonable period of time after the conclusion of their employment, coverage would generally be available. Even terminated workers who return several days later to retrieve their final checks or their personal tools are likely to be entitled to protection, so long as the time between their last day and the date of their injury is not inordinate. Benefits tend to be denied to these individuals only when there is an extended hiatus between their final day of work and the date they return to retrieve their belongings or their check.

ARISING OUT OF EMPLOYMENT

Almost all state workers' compensation laws require claimants to demonstrate not only that they sustained injuries *during the course of* their employment, but also that their conditions *arose out of* their employment.[17] **Courts have generally recognized that the "course of employment" prerequisite concerns the time, place, and circumstances surrounding the incident in question, while the "arising out of" component pertains to the underlying cause of the resulting injuries.**

Various risk concepts have been formulated by courts in an effort to distinguish between compensable and noncompensable injuries. When the operative circumstances contributing to worker harm are directly related to the worker's employment, it is clear that the "arising out of" requirement is satisfied. A typical case would involve an employee injured by a malfunctioning machine. On the other hand, other industrial accident cases concern situations that are more equivocal. Individuals may suffer unexplainable accidents where the underlying cause is not discernible, or they may be adversely affected by acts of nature.

People sometimes sustain injuries that are only related to their employment because the operative circumstances occurred at their place of work. For example, they may be struck by stray bullets fired from outside the workplace or they may be assaulted by other workers or strangers. They may experience inexplicable dizzy spells, suffer heart attacks, or develop nervous disorders that are more indigenous to their personal circumstances than to their employment environments. They may become ill because of contaminated food or drink they brought to work. Clearly compensable injuries may become infected or be exacerbated by careless medical treatment.

Compensation administrators and courts have developed various risk theories to determine when claimants who have suffered injuries under equivocal circumstances should be granted or denied coverage. It is important to note that there has been a clear tendency over the past half century to expand statutory protection. The decisions resolving close cases in favor of coverage have usually been based on the belief that employers are in a better position to spread the risk of marginal conditions than are individual employees.

---

[17]The Utah statute requires proof that the harm either resulted during the course of claimant employment *or* arose out of it. The laws in North Dakota, Pennsylvania, Texas, Washington, and Wisconsin, and the Federal Employees Compensation Act, have omitted the "arising out of" requirement. *See* Larson, A. *Larson's Workmen's Compensation Law* §6.10. (New York: Matthew Bender, 1992).

Traditional Risk Concepts

Some of the early workers' compensation decisions found it difficult to accept the "liability without fault" concept included in the new statutes. They often used the "peculiar risk" approach, which required claimants to demonstrate that their employment conditions significantly enhanced the likelihood they would suffer the type of harm involved. If members of the general public were exposed to similar hazards, compensation was usually denied the injured workers.

Increased Risk Doctrine

Courts soon realized that the "peculiar risk" doctrine placed an unreasonably high burden on claimants, and they replaced that approach with the less onerous "increased risk" rule that continues to be the predominant American standard. Under this approach, employees no longer have to prove that their injuries were caused by risks peculiar to their employment. They need only demonstrate that their employment environment increased the likelihood of harm similar to that they sustained.

Courts applying the "increased risk" doctrine have developed a special "street risk" rule for workers required by their employment to travel on public thoroughfares. Application of this doctrine is discussed below.

Actual Risk Doctrine

A number of courts have further expanded statutory protection through adoption of the "actual risk" doctrine. These decisions no longer require claimants to show that they work in settings that expose them to a greater probability of injury. They need only establish that the type of harm suffered may reasonably be considered a risk associated with their employment, even if members of the general public are exposed to similar danger.

Positional Risk Doctrine

Some courts have extended the "actual risk" approach through acceptance of the "positional risk" rule. Under this progressive formulation, injuries are considered to have arisen out of employments if claimants can demonstrate that their adverse consequences would not have occurred *but for* the fact that their employment duties placed them in the positions in which they were injured. This broad concept enables employees to obtain benefits for occurrences having no direct relationship to their employment beyond the fact that they sustained their injuries while at work.

States applying the "positional risk" rule tend to award benefits to claimants who can establish that their employment required them to be in areas that contained the hazards that caused their injuries. The results are similar to those reached in "street risk" cases for traveling employees, but they extend coverage to dangers encountered throughout the employment relationship.

"Employment Risks," "Neutral Risks," and "Personal Risks"

Courts attempting to distinguish between compensable and noncompensable injuries have recognized three distinct types of risks. The first group covers "employment risks" that are directly related to the work environment. Typical examples include machine malfunctions and production processes that do not develop properly. Injuries caused by such "employment risks" are uniformly regarded as having arisen out of claimant employment.

The second category includes "neutral risks" that are neither employment related nor personal to the individuals involved. These entail acts of nature that affect employees while they are at work, as well as conditions caused by external human factors, including accidental injuries that have no apparent cause, such as an inexplicable fall. Various theories are used to decide whether claimants injured by "neutral risks" should be granted compensation.

"Personal risks" involve circumstances related to particular individuals. This risk concept includes persons with heart or vascular conditions who suffer heart attacks or strokes while at work, and people with other medical disorders that coincidentally manifest themselves in the employment setting. It also covers people who become ill because of contaminated food or drink they bring to work. Courts frequently deny benefits to individuals who have been injured by purely personal risks.

Acts of Nature

Although most courts award workers' compensation to employees who are injured by acts of nature, they do so through application of various legal theories. Some courts cover acts of nature through application of either the "actual risk" or the "positional risk" doctrine. These decisions provide protection for injuries that may reasonably be characterized as actual risks of employment or that affect employees because of the location where they are working when the critical circumstances arise. Classic cases involve people injured by hurricanes, tornadoes, and earthquakes. Because these acts of nature tend to affect everyone in their path, it is difficult for claimants injured by these storms at work to demonstrate that their employment increased the risk of harm. Nonetheless, in states applying the "actual risk" approach, they may obtain benefits if they can show that the type of harm sustained was an actual risk associated with their employment. In "positional risk" states, they need only establish that their jobs placed them in positions that exposed them to the harm caused, even though members of the general public were similarly exposed. Some courts may also extend statutory protection to individuals injured by acts of nature while they are traveling on public thoroughfares during the course of their employment through application of the "street risk" doctrine.

Even when employment did not increase the risk of injury, many "increased risk" states still provide protection for people hurt by acts of nature if they were injured by physical contact with part of their employer's premises. Claimants are thus entitled to compensation for harm caused by glass from broken windows, flying brick or lumber, collapsed roofs, or fallen walls. The fact that they came into contact with employer property is sufficient to establish a connection to their employment.

Stray Bullets and Unexplained Accidents

Courts in states such as California, Louisiana, Massachusetts, and New Jersey have used the "positional risk" doctrine to cover employees struck at work by stray bullets or other objects emanating from persons outside the employment setting. Other decisions have awarded benefits to individuals injured while at work by unexplained accidents or inexplicable falls. Courts that still apply the conventional "increased risk" rule would not extend coverage to these people, unless they could demonstrate that their particular employment situations exposed them to a greater likelihood of such injuries than members of the general public.

A growing number of courts have decided to extend statutory protection to employees who suffer unexplained falls during the course of their employment. Although these decisions often refuse to adopt formally the "positional risk" doctrine, they use reasoning that is analogous to that employed in "positional risk" states. Nonetheless, they tend to make a critical distinction between unexplained falls and idiopathic falls. Unexplained falls normally involve neutral risks indigenous to the work environment, and many courts extend protection to these events. Idiopathic falls concern incidents attributable to physical or mental conditions, such as epilepsy or vertigo, that are personal to the affected employees. Due to the personal nature of idiopathic falls, courts tend to deny coverage to these incidents, unless the claimants can demonstrate some reasonable connection to their employment. They may accomplish this objective by showing that their injury was exacerbated by a table or chair they struck during their fall.

Unexplained Deaths

The unexplained-idiopathic distinction also arises with respect to deaths that occur at work. When employees die during the course of their employment on firm property due to unexplained circumstances, most courts assume that the fatal conditions arose out of the deceased workers' employment. They regard these situations as neutral risk cases and effectively apply "positional risk" concepts. Only when it is clear that the deaths were caused by personal conditions that were not exacerbated by employment-related factors is compensation likely to be denied.

Street Risks

Some employees, such as truck drivers, taxi drivers, and traveling salespeople, regularly drive, walk, or ride on public roads and conveyances in connection with their employment. Other individuals are occasionally required to journey from place to place during their employment. While workers are engaged in these excursions, they may be injured in vehicular accidents or sidewalk falls. When courts applied the "increased risk" doctrine to these cases, only the relatively few individuals who could establish that their regular employment-related travel exposed them to a greater risk of harm than members of the general public were granted benefits. Because judges did not believe that this approach was fair to other workers who were injured while traveling on public thoroughfares, they developed the "street risk" doctrine.

Under the generally followed "street risk" rule, injuries that are sustained by employees while they are walking, driving, or riding on public sidewalks or roads during the course of their employment are granted statutory protection. Their adverse consequences are regarded as arising out of their employment, even when the claimants are unable to show that their work-related travel exposed them to greater risks of harm than members of the general public. As a result, persons asked to cross the street to make bank deposits, to mail letters, or to carry out other employment errands are given statutory protection when they suffer accidental injuries during their travels.

A number of courts have expanded the "street risk" doctrine to include other risks that are not always associated with travel. For example, they have recognized that people who are walking or driving may be assaulted by thieves, struck by falling debris, or stabbed by deranged persons. Under the expanded "street risk" approach taken by these courts, claimants injured by such occurrences during the course of their employment are entitled to compensation. Other courts, however, continue to confine "street risk" coverage to accidents that are more traditionally associated with public travel.

Personal and Imported Risks

Employees are often injured, not by employment risks associated with their work or by neutral risks indigenous to their employment environments, but by personal risks unique to themselves. Typical cases involve idiopathic falls that result from nonoccupational heart attacks, epileptic seizures, vertigo, and other similar conditions. When it is clear that these incidents have been entirely caused by medical conditions personal to the claimants, compensation is almost always denied because the resulting harm has not "arisen out of" employment. Benefits tend to be awarded only in cases in which claimants can demonstrate that the work environment meaningfully contributed to the ultimate harm they sustained. For example, individuals hurt when they fall off ladders or scaffolds or when they fall onto company machinery or equipment would be likely to obtain compensation because of the connection between the employment setting and their injuries.

Victims of other idiopathic conditions that flare up in work environments may similarly obtain benefits if they can establish that employment-related stress, excitement, exertion, or pollution aggravated their preexisting infirmities. For example, individuals whose preexisting back weaknesses or heart conditions are aggravated by job-related stress or exertion are usually granted compensation. Statutory coverage is also likely with respect to persons whose pulmonary conditions, such as asthma, emphysema, or lung cancer, are exacerbated by the inhalation of particles found in their work environments. A number of decisions have also extended protection to nervous disorders that are affected by job stress. Even though the work-related factors might not cause such problems in people without preexisting personal weaknesses, courts emphasize that workers' compensation laws require employers to take their employees as they find them.

Because many personal risk cases involve preexisting weaknesses or predispositions that have allegedly been aggravated by job-related factors, medical testimony is often determinative. **To obtain benefits, claimants must establish a causal connection between their employment setting and the relevant harm**. Some of the most controverted cases concern medical conditions that do not have universally accepted causes. Classic cases involve cancers that victims claim were exacerbated by work-related factors. In the absence of credible medical testimony suggesting a reasonable connection between the employment environment and the cancerous conditions, coverage is not likely to be provided.

Some employees are injured at work by personal risks brought by themselves into the employment environment. They may become ill after they consume contaminated food or drink brought from home, or they may burn themselves while lighting a match or a cigarette. Unless these claimants can demonstrate that their job functions or the employment setting contributed to their harm, compensation is usually denied. Even though statutory protection would normally be provided under the personal comfort doctrine for illness caused by contaminated food purchased at the company cafeteria or eaten at near-by restaurants when their employment obligations effectively require them to patronize those establishments, courts tend to view food and drink brought from home as wholly personal risks that have no reasonable connection to the employment setting.

Because cigarette smoking continues to be tolerated during work breaks by most employers, accidents caused by matches, lighters, or cigarettes on firm premises are generally found covered. These activities are considered personal ministrations that constitute incidental aspects of the employment relationship. The resulting injuries are thus regarded by most courts as "arising out of" claimant employment. On the other hand, when employees are, for example, injured in company parking lots while handling weapons they brought to work for subsequent hunting, the absence of any meaningful connection to their jobs usually results in benefit denials.

Personal Assaults

Individuals are occasionally injured during the course of their employment by assaults committed on them by fellow employees or members of the general public. Claimants who can demonstrate that their particular job duties exposed them to a greater likelihood of attack than ordinary citizens may usually obtain benefits under the conventional "increased risk" theory. Statutory protection is thus likely with respect to public safety personnel, plant guards, cashiers, couriers who transport valuable merchandise, bartenders, bus and taxi drivers, and other workers whose job functions expose them to an increased risk of physical responses from other parties. Compensation is generally available to regular employees assaulted by angry supervisors and persons struck by fellow employees during arguments regarding their job responsibilities. Courts are only likely to deny statutory protection in those cases in which the disputants had adequate time to cool down between their employment-related disputes and their physical altercations. Under such circumstances, judges often view the subsequent assaults as personal, rather than job-related.

When claimants are unable to establish that their job functions, work environments, or shift schedules exposed them to a greater probability of assault than members of the general public, the majority of courts that continue to apply the "increased risk" doctrine are unlikely to provide them with statutory coverage. They may only obtain compensation if they are assaulted on a public thoroughfare during the course of their employment and can thus rely upon the more expansive "street risk" theory. Some courts have extended protection to assault victims through application of the "positional risk" concept. These decisions simply regard assaults by fellow workers or strangers as compensable risks associated with one's employment. In jurisdictions applying the "positional risk" rule, claimants are only required to show that they were assaulted during the course of their employment.

Early workers' compensation decisions frequently used the "aggressor" defense to deny benefits to employees injured during altercations they instigated. More recent decisions have rejected the "aggressor" approach, and have sustained compensation awards to claimants who precipitated physical confrontations with other people. A number of state laws now contain specific provisions that disqualify claimants whose injuries have been caused by their intentional efforts to hurt others. Nonetheless, courts in these states do not deny compensation to all persons injured in confrontations they initiated. They limit these exclusions to individuals who precipitate altercations through deliberate and premeditated aggression of a serious nature. Mere profanity and even minimal shoving are often found insufficient to warrant disqualification.

Direct and Proximate Consequences of Compensable Injuries

When employees sustain injuries that arise out of and during the course of their employment, they are clearly entitled to workers' compensation. Statutory protection is available not only for their immediate conditions, but also for the direct and natural consequences of their original injuries. For example, individuals who sustain employment-related conditions must frequently obtain medical treatment and courts recognize that imperfect treatment is a reasonably foreseeable consequence. As a result, it is universally acknowledged that the results of careless treatment constitute compensable conditions. **Claimants whose conditions are aggravated by unsanitary instruments, antibiotics, pain killers, surgical complications, or other medical errors would be eligible for benefits covering their total injuries.** Statutory protection is even available for entirely new conditions, such as impotence, heart and vascular problems, and neurosis, that are found to be direct and natural consequences of claimants' treatment.

Claimants seeking compensation for injuries aggravated by careless medical treatment are not obliged to demonstrate negligent conduct. So long as they can show that their worsened conditions are the direct and proximate consequence of their employment-related incidents, they are entitled to full statutory coverage. Furthermore, the fact that health care professionals acted negligently or even recklessly does not normally sever the causal link to their original injuries. While this issue would be relevant if the claimants were to bring lawsuits against the negligent actors, it would have no relevance with respect to their right to receive workers' compensation benefits for their overall conditions.

Treatment for compensable injuries may sometimes exacerbate preexisting conditions. Courts generally find aggravation of preexisting conditions subject to statutory coverage as foreseeable consequences of the work-related situations. Typical preexisting conditions aggravated by job-connected incidents include heart disease, phlebitis, varicose veins, back problems, cancer, and mental disorders. When courts find that these preexisting circumstances would not have become serious so quickly had it not been for the impact of the job-related events, the resulting conditions are considered the direct and proximate consequences of the original injuries. Statutory protection is similarly provided for preexisting conditions that deteriorate because of a lack of treatment caused by employment-related injuries. For example, if a job-related infection precluded treatment of an existing cancerous condition, the exacerbation of the cancer would be covered.

Individuals injured in employment-related accidents often have to travel to and from hospitals or medical offices for treatment. Because their travel is a direct and natural consequence of their compensable injuries, if they were to sustain further injuries as a result of travel-related accidents, most courts would extend coverage to these additional medical problems.

Compensable conditions are occasionally worsened by the conduct of claimants themselves. They may negligently treat their own wounds or obtain the assistance of quacks. They may alternatively refuse to submit to treatment recommended by physicians. Because careless treatment by claimants is considered a foreseeable consequence of employment-related accidents, statutory coverage would generally include the results of that negligent treatment. Courts would only be likely to deny coverage for worsened conditions where it is clear that the claimant's conduct was wholly unreasonable. Because judges view resort to unqualified charlatan healers as completely irrational acts, they similarly refuse to extend statutory coverage to the aggravated results of such "treatment."

When claimant conditions are worsened by their refusal to submit to recommended medical procedures, courts generally evaluate the reasonableness of the conduct. Courts balance the likely success of the proposed courses of action against the risk of harm involved. **When the probability of medical success is high and the risk to claimants is minimal, the unreasonable refusal of the claimants to submit to treatment will normally prevent compensation for the exacerbation of their original conditions**. On the other hand, when the risk to claimants is real, their failure to submit will rarely cause a loss of protection for any aggravation they may suffer.

Some of the most contested cases involve individuals with back difficulties who refuse to undergo myelograms or decline surgery. A majority of courts continue to find the risks and discomfort associated with these procedures sufficient to excuse the unwillingness of persons to submit to them. Nevertheless, when claimants decline minor surgery that would correct work-related conditions with minimal discomfort, they are likely to forfeit their right to continued benefits. This is true in most states whether their refusal is based on a subjective fear of surgery or on religious convictions that forbid resort to medical treatment.

Various workers' compensation statutes provide that claimants must obtain treatment from employer or compensation commission approved physicians. Injured workers occasionally ignore this requirement and have their injuries exacerbated by the careless treatment of unapproved health care specialists. It is generally recognized that the employer is not liable for the cost of the medical treatment obtained from unapproved physicians, unless the claimants can demonstrate that relevant circumstances caused them to seek the assistance of the specialists they chose. Nonetheless, most courts still provide coverage for injuries aggravated by the treatment of unapproved physicians.

Employees with work-related injuries may sustain subsequent injuries outside the employment setting that are at least partially attributable to their previously weakened conditions. If the later events had no employment connection, they would not be compensable.

Nevertheless, when claimants can demonstrate a reasonable causal relationship between their previous compensable injuries and their subsequent conditions, they normally receive statutory coverage for their most recent difficulties. Typical cases involve people who sustain nonoccupational falls as a result of previous job-related injuries that weakened their legs, ankles, knees, or feet.

Even when the previous occupational injuries do not directly cause the subsequent nonoccupational accidents, compensation may still be available for the resulting conditions. Claimants only have to establish a reasonable connection between the prior employment-related events and the subsequent incidents to be eligible for total coverage. They may do this by showing that the earlier accidents weakened limbs and made them more susceptible to the types of fractures experienced in the later incidents. Similar logic is frequently used to provide statutory protection for heart attacks, leg injuries, and back problems that may reasonably be attributed to preexisting weaknesses caused by previous work-related accidents.

CAUSATION

The fact that physical or mental conditions arise *during* the course of people's employment does not necessarily result in statutory coverage. Claimants must also demonstrate that their conditions arose out of their employment. This "arising out of" requirement includes a causation component. Claimants must usually establish a causal connection between their injuries and their job situations.

In addition, workers' compensation laws in all but nine states[18] expressly or implicitly require proof that employee injuries were caused by "accidental" events. In states with this prerequisite, claimants must normally demonstrate that the circumstances causing their conditions were of an unexpected nature. As a result, if their injury was caused by their own intentional actions, they are usually found ineligible for benefits. Many courts also require proof that the relevant incident occurred within a relatively definite time frame. This concept is

---

[18]California, Colorado, Iowa, Maine, Massachusetts, Minnesota, Pennsylvania, Rhode Island, and South Dakota. *See* Larson, A. *Larson's Workmen's Compensation Law* §§37–38 (New York: Matthew Bender, 1992).

especially important with respect to conditions that develop gradually, rather than instantaneously, such as repetitive trauma disorders or occupational diseases.

"Exertion" cases that are most likely to result in benefit awards concern job activities that cause immediate "breakage"—i.e., sudden structural changes in the body. Classic cases involve work-related efforts that precipitate relatively instantaneous hernias, ruptured discs, hemorrhages, or strokes. That these injuries have arisen in a comparatively immediate manner would be sufficient to establish their "accidental" nature. In most states, the fact that the operative circumstances merely involved usual work exertion would not preclude benefit awards.

Heart Conditions

Employees regularly seek compensation for heart attacks, heart disease, and related conditions they claim were caused or aggravated by employment exertion. Employers often contest these cases, contending that the claimants suffered from preexisting heart conditions that had no relationship to their employment. Courts need to determine the degree of work exertion that must be shown to make these conditions compensable, and they must decide whether the existence of preexisting nonoccupational heart weaknesses should affect the right of claimants to obtain compensation.

A majority of states have adopted the "usual exertion" approach under which claimants who sustain heart injuries while engaged in normal work exertion are entitled to statutory coverage.[19] They are merely obliged to show that their conditions arose out of and during their employment. The fact they had preexisting heart conditions would not preclude coverage for work-related complications, because employers take their employees as they find them. Courts applying the usual exertion doctrine would probably even sustain benefit awards for heart problems that did not manifest themselves until the evening or the day following the job exertion that ultimately precipitated those attacks.

---

[19]Alabama, Arizona, Arkansas, Delaware, Georgia, Idaho, Illinois, Kentucky, Maine, Michigan, Minnesota, Mississippi, Missouri, Montana, Nebraska, New Hampshire, New Jersey, New Mexico, New York, Ohio, Oklahoma, Oregon, Pennsylvania, Tennessee, Texas, Utah, and West Virginia.

A sizable minority of states continue to believe that coverage should not be extended to heart problems that only have attenuated connections to employment settings.[20] Courts in these states only award compensation to claimants who can demonstrate that their injuries were caused by unusual, rather than ordinary, job exertion. Claimants must show that the critical events involved exertion beyond the normal demands of their employment. Due to the somewhat subjective nature of the "unusual exertion" approach, it is often difficult to predict how courts will resolve particular cases.

Back Injuries

Most states extend workers' compensation coverage to all back injuries that arise out of and during the course of employment, even when the conditions are caused by usual job efforts.[21] This is true whether a claimant's normal work exertion is greater than or similar to that associated with ordinary life. Statutory protection is even likely to be afforded to individuals who aggravate preexisting back conditions while performing normal job tasks, if they can show that their employment efforts meaningfully contributed to their back problems.

Some states refuse to extend coverage to workers who sustain back injuries during usual employment exertion.[22] They require evidence of unusual work exertion as a prerequisite to benefit awards. People who develop back problems as a result of normal job exertion are usually unable to obtain compensation in these states. Judicial decisions occasionally distinguish between claimants who had preexisting back weaknesses and those who did not. They permit coverage for back injuries caused by usual employment exertion, when there is no evidence of preexisting back difficulties. When there is a record of prior back problems, however, these courts only cover exacerbations generated by unusual job exertion.

---

[20]Colorado, Florida, Indiana, Kansas, Louisiana, Maryland, North Carolina, North Dakota, South Carolina, Virginia, Washington, and Wyoming.

[21]Arkansas, Colorado, Connecticut, Delaware, Florida, Idaho, Indiana, Kansas, Kentucky, Louisiana, Massachusetts, Michigan, Missouri, Montana, Nebraska, New Jersey, New York, Ohio, Oklahoma, Texas, Utah, Vermont, and Washington.

[22]Maryland, North Carolina, Pennsylvania, and Virginia.

Exposure to Extreme Temperatures and to Diseases

It is uniformly recognized that people who sustain employment-related heatstroke or frostbite are entitled to statutory coverage. Their conditions are considered sufficiently sudden and unexpected to be considered "accidental" events. Decisions relating to conditions resulting from extreme heat or cold do not consider whether exposure to high or low temperatures was a usual or unusual aspect of claimant employment. They merely consider whether the adversely affected employees were subject to temperature extremes that were greater than those associated with ordinary life. If they were, statutory protection will be provided.

Individuals are often exposed to diseases during the course of their employment. The diseases may include pneumonia, pleurisy, influenza, tuberculosis, common colds, and other similar maladies. Employee exposure may be due to their proximity to sick co-workers, customers, or members of the general public, or it may result from unhealthful conditions in their work environments. If individuals who become infected can demonstrate that their illnesses were caused by their particular employment, they would probably be covered by occupational disease provisions. In the absence of occupational disease coverage, however, they would have to demonstrate that they sustained "accidental" injuries that arose out of and during the course of their employment.

When individuals develop diseases or infections from relatively sudden and unexpected exposure to germs at work, they are generally found eligible for benefits. Courts consider such conditions to constitute "accidental" injuries that arose out of and during the course of claimant employment. As a result, diseases transmitted at specific moments through cuts or abrasions, pimples on the skin, insect bites, or similar events are usually considered "accidental" injuries. On the other hand, when workers develop diseases or infections due to prolonged exposure to germs, it is more difficult to obtain coverage. The absence of a relatively sudden triggering event may induce some courts to find a lack of any "accidental" occurrence. Most courts, however, find the unexpected nature of claimant contraction and the specific time at which the condition manifested itself sufficient to satisfy the "accidental" prerequisite.

When claimants contract diseases or infections from routine exposure to germs to which members of the general public are exposed, it is frequently difficult for them to establish the requisite employment connection. Many courts refuse to award benefits to persons who contract nonoccupational diseases from routine exposure to others in the work environment. Some find a lack of causation, because the claimants have not been exposed to greater risks of illness than ordinary citizens, while others find no "accidental" events, on the ground that normal exposure to the diseases of life can hardly be thought of as sudden or unexpected. Although some of the cases extending statutory protection to such diseases involve normal exposure to germs affecting members of the general public, most concern exposure to illnesses that transcend the risks associated with ordinary life. These decisions find the diseased conditions compensable, since claimants' exposure is viewed as an increased risk associated with their employment. Even though members of the general public may be exposed to similar illnesses, they are not obliged to remain for prolonged periods in work environments that contain infectious germs.

Some of the most contested claims concern illnesses that develop slowly over weeks or months of exposure to germs. Courts evaluating claimant benefit eligibility in these "repeated trauma" cases are often concerned that the absence of any immediate triggering event suggests the lack of "accidental" injuries. Nevertheless, most courts extend statutory protection to conditions that develop over prolonged periods. They usually use one of three theories to satisfy the "accidental" prerequisite: (1) a few simply eliminate the time element, and find the unexpected nature of the illness sufficient to satisfy the "accidental" requirement; (2) some find the time factor satisfied if the physical condition manifests itself at an identifiable time, despite the number of weeks or months it may have taken for the injury to become apparent; (3) other courts rely on the "repeated trauma" doctrine, under which they treat each distinct, job-related exposure as a separate "accident" for coverage purposes. A few states continue to deny "accidental" injury coverage to illnesses that develop over prolonged periods, and courts in states that are willing to extend protection to many prolonged exposure cases deny compensation in close cases. These tend to involve claimants who are unable to show clear employment-related causal connections or who sustain conditions that do not manifest themselves at identifiable times.

Employment Stress Affecting Physical Conditions

Individuals exposed to continuous employment stress may develop physical conditions. They may suffer heart attacks, strokes, hypertension, thrombosis, or similar maladies. When such health problems are caused by sudden and unexpected shocks, they are generally considered compensable "accidental" injuries. When, however, the physical manifestations of job stress develop over prolonged periods, it is more difficult for claimants to establish job-related causal connections.

If workers can demonstrate meaningful connection with employment, statutory coverage will usually be provided. Typical cases resulting in coverage involve individuals who are affected by heavy work loads, clear job-related tension, serious employment problems, and similar concerns. Favorable awards are most likely when claimants can show that they were exposed to unusual levels of job tension or anxiety.

Courts are most likely to find a lack of statutory protection in cases in which the employment-related stress is not significantly different from the stress associated with ordinary life. Some courts denying benefits in these cases find that the claimants were unable to establish sufficient causal connections to their work. Others decide that the adversely affected individuals failed to demonstrate that they sustained "accidental" injuries.

Employment Traumas Affecting Emotional Conditions

Many employees exposed to physical or mental traumas at work sustain emotional, rather than physical, conditions. Courts must regularly determine whether their resulting depression, neuroses, or other psychological disorders constitute compensable injuries. **When the underlying emotional difficulties are generated by physical traumas, statutory protection is usually provided. On the other hand, when the causative factors are entirely psychological, statutory coverage is less certain.**

Courts are generally willing to award benefits to employees who suffer physical traumas that generate emotional difficulties. So long as the causative events occur in a relatively sudden and unexpected manner, the resulting conditions are considered "accidental" injuries. Typical cases involve individuals who are struck in the head or back and develop emotional disabilities. The fact these claimants had preexisting neurotic tendencies does not usually affect their right to compensation. Courts apply the usual rule that employers take their employees as they find them. The individuals seeking benefits need only demonstrate that employment-related physical traumas meaningfully contributed to their disabling conditions.

Some workers develop emotional difficulties that result from psychological, rather than physical, traumas. Statutory coverage is most likely for mental conditions that arise from particular psychological traumas. The sudden and unexpected nature of the triggering events is sufficient to satisfy the "accidental" injury requirement imposed by most states. For example, workers may be emotionally affected by explosions or sudden injuries to fellow employees. The fact that other nonemployment stress may have also affected the psychological state of the claimants does not preclude statutory coverage, so long as the job-related incidents meaningfully contributed to the final result. Nonetheless, some courts continue to deny coverage to individuals who develop mental problems as a result of single-incident physical traumas. Courts denying compensation in these cases generally base their decisions on the absence of any physical ramifications. They are simply hesitant to award benefits for wholly psychological difficulties.

Many claimants' emotional problems arise slowly as a result of prolonged employment-related stress, anxiety, or frustration. Even though the individuals affected by these circumstances are unable to identify specific events precipitating their disabling mental conditions, a majority of contemporary courts find these persons eligible for compensation. *Carter v. General Motors Corp.*[23] is a classic case. A worker on an automotive assembly line was unable to keep up with the machine-driven pace. When he worked on one hub assembly at a time, he fell behind. When he worked on two at a time, in a desperate attempt to keep up, he often put the assemblies back on the line in the wrong

---

[23]106 N.W.2d 105 (Mich. 1960).

order. He was regularly chastised by his supervisor and eventually suffered an emotional collapse. Because the court found that his mental problems were directly related to the stress associated with his work, he was awarded benefits. Other courts have followed this approach. These decisions either ignore the "accidental" injury requirement or find the sudden and unexpected manifestations of the disabling conditions sufficient to satisfy this prerequisite.

On rare occasions, employees who have been severely affected by physical or emotional traumas commit suicide. Even though states normally exclude conditions that are intentionally self-inflicted, they cover suicides that may reasonably be attributed to employment-related circumstances beyond claimant control. While early decisions required evidence of uncontrollable impulses or unconscious deliriums as prerequisites to coverage, contemporary courts find suicides compensable whenever job-related traumas generate mental derangements that cause a loss of self-control and result in self-inflicted death.

A psychological condition that generates more controversy than suicide is called "compensation neurosis." It involves injured workers who assert that anxiety over their industrial accidents or the outcomes of their compensation cases has exacerbated their situations by producing a disabling neurosis that may only be cured through the award of additional compensation. If it appears that the claimants are malingerers who simply do not wish to return to work, their requests for further benefits are generally denied. On the other hand, if psychiatrists or psychologists convince compensation administrators that persons who have sustained job-related injuries continue to be disabled due to compensation neurosis, a majority of states permit a continuation of benefits. A number of states, however, remain skeptical of this condition and refuse to permit continued benefit payments.

OCCUPATIONAL DISEASES

The original workers' compensation laws were designed to substitute no-fault coverage for common law tort remedies. Because occupational diseases were not conditions subject to tort liability, state legislatures did not address those particular problems in their initial statutes. Although a few early court decisions interpreted general "injury" provisions to encompass some job-related diseases, most "non-accidental" illnesses were not regarded as compensable conditions.

Legislators quickly recognized that employees could be as economically devastated by diseases contracted in work environments as they were by job-related "accidental" injuries. In 1920, New York became the first state to add specific occupational disease coverage to its compensation law, and other states rapidly followed suit. Many enactments currently provide general coverage—i.e., they extend protection to all employment-related diseases. Some laws, however, provide more limited coverage. They list scheduled conditions that are protected, but many now contain catch-all clauses that extend statutory protection to other nonspecified occupational diseases. Several states[24] have adopted entirely separate occupational disease laws. Courts in these states occasionally encounter difficulties when they attempt to determine whether particular conditions are compensable under the "accidental" injury law, the occupational disease enactment, or both.

Occupational disease coverage is quite different from "accidental" injury protection. Occupational disease provisions do not require evidence of sudden and unexpected triggering events as prerequisites to benefit awards. If a diseased condition arises in an unexpected manner from a relatively definitive exposure to particular germs, it is normally treated, not as an occupational disease, but as an "accidental" injury. Most occupational diseases develop slowly over prolonged periods and are not entirely unexpected occurrences. While occupational diseases may be unanticipated from the perspective of the specific individuals who contract them, they are hardly unexpected events from the perspective of people who are familiar with the hazards associated with the occupations or industries involved. It is the fact that certain diseases are an inherent risk of particular occupations or industries that renders them compensable illnesses.

Courts deciding whether specific medical conditions constitute compensable occupational diseases must initially review the relevant statutory language. Most workers' compensation laws expressly define the term "occupational disease" in a way that differentiates between covered conditions and uncovered diseases that are associated with ordinary life. Some include elaborate definitions, while others contain

---

[24]Idaho, Illinois, Indiana, and Pennsylvania.

more general language. When the applicable law fails to provide specific guidance, courts use similar language to distinguish between covered and uncovered conditions. "An ailment does not become an occupational disease simply because it is contracted on the employer's premises. It must be one which is commonly regarded as natural to, inhering in, an incident and concomitant of, the work in question."[25]

Whether the relevant statutory language is specific, general, or nondefinitive, courts considering occupational disease claims tend to evaluate the cases in a similar manner. They initially review the medical evidence to determine if there appears to be a causal connection between the claimant's illness and the job. If no causal link can be established, compensation is generally denied. They also attempt to ascertain whether the claimants are suffering from diseases of ordinary life to which members of the general public are equally exposed. Individuals seeking benefits for such conditions must demonstrate that their employment exposed them to an unusually high risk of those diseases.

Compensable cases involving common diseases typically concern persons exposed to specific germs, chemicals, dusts, or similar substances found in their respective work environments in harmful quantities. For example, health care workers often work in close proximity to contagious patients. If it appears that they have contracted tuberculosis, hepatitis, or other diseases from those patients, they will normally be found eligible for benefits. Their repeated exposure to contagious patients is sufficient to distinguish their conditions from diseases associated with ordinary life. Statutory coverage is also likely for people who contract asbestosis, asthma, bronchitis, emphysema, pneumoconiosis, pulmonary fibrosis, or other respiratory diseases because of their excessive exposure in work settings to the substances that cause those conditions.

The most difficult problem for claimants who contract diseases of ordinary life is the need to show that their job settings meaningfully contributed to their maladies. Common ailments are frequently found compensable if the germs, fumes, or other substances causing those disorders are present in the workplace at unusually elevated levels. The establishment of this causal link is especially hard for individuals who have previously experienced similar, nonoccupational conditions or have exacerbated their medical problems through smoking. Coverage is

---

[25]Harman v. Republic Aviation Corp., 82 N.E.2d 785, 786 (N.Y. 1948).

also likely to be denied in states with laws that appear to exclude all diseases of ordinary life no matter how much the employment environment may have contributed to those disorders.

Similar rules are applied to other common conditions that may have been significantly affected by the claimant's job functions. Employees who lift heavy objects or engage in repeated twisting may develop back problems. People who must sit for long periods may injure their tail bones, while workers whose jobs require extensive walking or standing may develop varicose veins. If these individuals could establish a reasonable connection between their back difficulties or their varicose veins and their job functions, statutory protection would usually be provided.

Persons who repeatedly move their arms and hands during their work are more likely than other people to develop carpal tunnel syndrome, bursitis, or similar disorders. Most courts are thus willing to award compensation to workers who are affected by these conditions. Nonetheless, some courts continue to deny coverage for these maladies, because they do not consider the employment-related connection sufficient to warrant statutory protection.

Judges are occasionally presented with medical conditions that are not clearly included or excluded under applicable "occupational disease" provisions. When workers' compensation laws generally define "occupational disease" to cover disorders peculiar to specific occupations or industries, it is relatively easy for sympathetic courts to expand the scope of protection in appropriate cases. Even though back strains, herniated discs, foot problems, bursitis, arthritis, and similar disorders may not technically constitute "diseases" under the statute, most courts include these medical problems within general "occupational disease" provisions. They assume legislators intended to provide statutory protection for all medical conditions that are reasonably related to employment, and they interpret the term "disease" accordingly.

Even though most workers' compensation laws provide general "occupational disease" coverage, a number also list specific conditions that are associated with particular occupations or industries. The most frequently listed maladies include anthrax, asbestosis, dermatitis, pneumoconiosis, radiation-related illnesses, silicosis, and various types of chemical poisonings. Workers who develop these conditions are presumptively entitled to benefits. Employers attempting to defeat compensation claims must usually prove that the relevant disorders did not arise out of and during the course of claimant employment.

A number of courts have recently been asked to determine whether stress-related nervous conditions that develop over prolonged periods should be considered covered under "occupational disease" provisions. *James v. State Accident Insurance Fund*[26] provides a classic example. The claimant, who had previously suffered from anxiety, became an Information Referral Counselor. She experienced significant personality and professional conflicts with her supervisor. He criticized her work and gave her conflicting job assignments that required her to be in two locations simultaneously. She became increasingly nervous and took many tranquilizers. After finally concluding that her nervous condition prevented further employment, she filed for workers' compensation. The Oregon Supreme Court ruled that emotional disorders caused by unusual job-related stress transcending that experienced by ordinary people could constitute compensable "occupational diseases." Although some other courts have sustained benefit awards for such stress-related conditions, other courts have refused to do so. Courts refusing to cover these conditions do not consider it proper to include nervous disorders that are affected by repeated, work-related psychological traumas within either "accidental injury" or "occupational disease" provisions.

Allergies and Preexisting Conditions

Most states recognize that employees with allergies should not be denied statutory protection for allergic reactions generated by exposure to substances in their work environments. So long as claimants can show that their medical problems were significantly affected by employment-related factors, coverage is likely to be available. Furthermore, the fact that a particular allergy affects few individuals does not diminish the right of the affected persons to compensation for job-related flare-ups.

The vast majority of courts follow the same rule with respect to workers whose preexisting weaknesses are exacerbated by employment factors. Although a few courts deny "occupational disease" protection

---

[26]624 P.2d 565 (Or. 1981).

to these claimants due to their personal susceptibility to the particular maladies, most find the propensities of individual workers irrelevant to their right to coverage. The critical factor in most states is causation. So long as claimants can show a meaningful causal connection between their employment and their conditions, benefits are likely to be awarded.

Diseases Caused by Both Occupational and Nonoccupational Factors

Individuals occasionally seek benefits for conditions that have been jointly caused by employment and nonemployment factors. Typical cases involve workers with pulmonary difficulties that appear to have been caused by their inhalation of fumes or substances in the work environment and by their own smoking. Most courts recognize that even people who smoke are entitled to statutory protection for lung conditions that have been significantly affected by employment-related factors. As a result, when claimants can establish that they worked in employment settings that exposed them to unusual levels of carcinogenic substances, their resulting lung cancer will normally be covered. Smokers who can prove that excessive shop fumes meaningfully contributed to their emphysema, bronchitis, or other pulmonary diseases are normally accorded similar protection.

When the causal link between employment and a claimant's lung problems is not clear, coverage may be denied. These cases tend to involve heavy smokers who work in environments that contain airborne substances that could have contributed to their pulmonary disorders. Courts refusing to extend protection to these claimants usually find an absence of any significant connection to their employment settings and attribute the claimants' lung difficulties to their own smoking.

Several states[27] have sought to accommodate the dual-causation cases through specific statutory provisions that apportion coverage between the occupational and nonoccupational causative factors. When claimants in these states seek compensation for disorders affected by employment and nonemployment factors, courts try to determine the degree of disability attributable to the occupational and nonoccupational elements. Benefit awards are then based on the proportion of the total disability pertaining to the occupational component.

---

[27]*E.g.,* Alabama, Arkansas, and Georgia.

The vast majority of state legislatures have refused to adopt special apportionment provisions, and courts in these states have declined to establish such an approach in their decisions. They continue to believe that employers take their workers as they find them. So long as employment-related factors meaningfully contribute to diseases contracted by employees, full compensation is awarded, despite the fact that nonemployment elements may have also contributed to the final result.

Timing Issues Relating to Causation, Statutes of Limitation, and Benefit Levels

Some state legislatures were initially worried that occupational disease coverage would be so broad that it would jeopardize the financial viability of workers' compensation systems. To prevent fiscal difficulties, several states adopted special provisions designed to limit occupational disease protection. Some require minimal periods of exposure to employment-related substances as a prerequisite to benefit eligibility. Others deny statutory coverage to disorders that do not become apparent within specified periods following the most recent exposure of claimants to the work-related hazards.

Statutes in 12 states[28] require minimal periods of exposure to certain substances as a condition of occupational disease coverage. These provisions most frequently apply to asbestosis, silicosis, and pneumoconiosis. They state that benefits may not be awarded to persons affected by the listed conditions unless claimants can show that they were exposed to the airborne triggering agents for minimal periods of time—typically ranging from two to five years.

Laws in eight states[29] impose somewhat different time restrictions. They limit benefit awards to claimants who can establish that they were exposed to the harmful work-related inhalants for minimal periods of time within their states. They most often require a minimum of two to five years of exposure within their jurisdictions.

Statute of limitation provisions in 10 states[30] impose other time restrictions that affect occupational diseases. While statutes of

---

[28]Arizona, Georgia, Idaho, Iowa, Kansas, Maine, Nevada, New Mexico, North Carolina, South Carolina, South Dakota, and Virginia.

[29]Idaho, Iowa, Montana, Nevada, Ohio, Pennsylvania, South Dakota, and Utah.

[30]Georgia, Idaho, Illinois, Indiana, Maine, Montana, Oregon, Vermont, Virginia, and Wyoming.

limitation in most workers' compensation laws do not begin to run until claimants either become aware or should reasonably be aware of their employment-related conditions, the statutes in these states start to run when the affected individuals were last exposed to the underlying causative agents. These special provisions generally impose one to five year time limits.

The final time-related issue concerns the date to be used to calculate the benefit levels available to persons who contract occupational diseases that do not manifest themselves until several years after claimant exposure to work-setting hazards. Should benefit levels be determined as of the date of last exposure to the harmful substances or the date the disabling conditions become apparent? In most states, benefit levels are calculated as of the date occupational diseases manifest themselves. Nonetheless, a number of states continue to use the date of last exposure as the critical moment for benefit determination purposes.[31] This difference may profoundly affect claimants whose wages at the time their conditions became apparent are substantially higher than when they were last exposed to the work-related causative factors.

Special Police and Firefighter Provisions

The workers' compensation laws in over half the states[32] contain special provisions pertaining to active police officers and firefighters. These "heart and lung" statutes typically establish presumptions in favor of statutory coverage for heart conditions and respiratory diseases sustained by individuals employed in these occupations. While they usually apply to all covered police officers and firefighters, the laws in several states limit application to claimants who were found free of heart disease or respiratory problems during their prior medical examinations.

---

[31]*See, e.g.*, E.I. Du Pont de Nemours & Co. v. Green, 411 A.2d 953 (Del. Super. 1980); Hawkins v. Johns-Manville, 418 So.2d 725 (La. App. 1982).

[32]Alabama, California, Connecticut, Florida, Georgia, Hawaii, Illinois, Louisiana, Maine, Maryland, Massachusetts, Michigan, Minnesota, Missouri, Nebraska, Nevada, New Hampshire, New Jersey, New York, North Dakota, Ohio, Oklahoma, Oregon, Pennsylvania, South Carolina, Tennessee, Texas, Vermont, Virginia, and Wisconsin.

The degree to which an employment connection is presumed for heart and lung conditions developed by police and fire personnel varies from state to state. Courts in several states interpret these provisions as merely creating rebuttable presumptions in favor of compensability. In some cases, government employers need only raise honest questions regarding the occupational nature of claimant conditions to rebut the statutory presumption of coverage. In other states, however, employers are required to present more substantial evidence indicating that the police or firefighter duties did not meaningfully contribute to their disorders.

Courts in some states treat these provisions as establishing almost irrebuttable presumptions in favor of compensability. Judges assume that police and fire personnel covered by these enactments are entitled to benefit awards for all heart and lung disorders. Government employers can only defeat worker claims by unequivocally establishing that their conditions were caused entirely by nonoccupational factors. In these states, employers rarely overcome the statutory presumption favoring coverage.

Black Lung Provisions

The repeated inhalation of coal dust by coal miners frequently results in black lung disease (pneumoconiosis). In 1969, Congress sought to enhance the protection available to affected miners through the enactment of the Coal Mine Health and Safety Act.[33] Title IV of that statute created a compensation program for coal miners who became "totally disabled" due to black lung disease. It also provided death benefits for surviving dependents of miners who either died from pneumoconiosis or were totally disabled from that condition when they died from some other cause. The federal government initially accepted financial responsibility for the coal miner benefit program, hoping that states would ultimately enact their own black lung laws. By the late 1970s, the annual cost of that federal program exceeded $1 billion.

In late 1977, Congress enacted the Black Lung Benefits Reform Act[34] and the Black Lung Benefits Revenue Act.[35] These laws created

[33]Pub. Law No. 91-173, 83 Stat. 742 (1969).
[34]Pub. Law No. 95-239, 92 Stat. 95 (1978).
[35]Pub. Law No. 95-227, 92 Stat. 11 (1978).

the Black Lung Disability Trust Fund financed by a per-ton tax imposed on coal operators. They also liberalized the statutory presumptions favoring coverage for miners who contracted pneumoconiosis. In 1981, Congress sought to protect the financial viability of the black lung program through enactment of the Black Lung Benefits Revenue Act and the Black Lung Benefits Amendments.[36] These amendments terminated the right of surviving dependents to obtain benefits for miners who died from other causes while totally disabled by pneumoconiosis. Survivor benefits were thereafter limited to miners who died from black lung disease. The 1981 amendments also eliminated several presumptions that favored coverage for individuals who had worked in mines for minimal periods of time, even when they died from pulmonary disorders other than pneumoconiosis.

Claimants seeking benefits under the Federal Black Lung Act must demonstrate that (1) they are "miners" within the meaning of the statute and (2) they are "totally disabled" because of pneumoconiosis. The term "miners" now includes people who work or have worked in underground or surface mines. Claimants must then present medical testimony verifying their pneumoconiosis and suggesting a causal connection with their mining employment.

There is an irrebuttable presumption in favor of total disability coverage for individuals suffering from "complicated" pneumoconiosis—a condition involving lung opacities exceeding one centimeter in diameter. Claimants without such extreme lung incapacities may take advantage of a rebuttable presumption of benefit entitlement if they can establish "simple" pneumoconiosis plus a minimum of 10 years employment in coal mines. When neither of these presumptions is applicable, claimants are required to demonstrate independently that they suffer from pneumoconiosis that was caused by their work in coal mines. They must also establish that their condition has rendered them totally disabled. Many of the contested cases involve claimants whose own smoking may have significantly contributed to their pulmonary disorders.

Claimants who establish their benefit eligibility are entitled to comprehensive medical coverage and disability payments. Their surviving spouses are also entitled to benefits. Department of Labor administrators have to identify the coal operators responsible for

---

[36]Pub. Law No. 97-119, 95 Stat. 1635 (1981).

claimant benefits. Under the "most recent one-year rule," the operator with which the claimant had the most recent period of employment of at least one year is normally held to be the responsible operator. Coal operators are expected to satisfy their compensation obligations through insurance policies or self-insurance plans.

COMPENSATION

Claimants who have been affected by accidental employment-related injuries or occupational diseases are eligible for broad medical coverage and, if they suffer job impairments, disability payments. They may have partial or total disabilities, and their conditions may be temporary or permanent. In some cases, they may be granted scheduled benefits for specific physical impairments, such as the loss of a leg, hand, or eye.

Medical Benefits

Claimants who sustain occupational injuries and diseases are entitled to medical and hospital coverage. Their right to medical benefits is independent of their right to disability benefits. They are thus eligible for medical protection even when their condition has no impact on their ability to work.

Under most workers' compensation laws, employers are required to provide injured employees with initial medical and hospital services. Many statutes thereafter permit claimants to select their own physicians. Some states require claimants to select from a panel of doctors compiled by the state agency or their employer, while others permit their employer to designate the physicians who must be used.

Injured workers must usually notify their employer of job-related medical problems and give their employer the chance to authorize the necessary medical assistance. Individuals who inexcusably fail to notify their employer and obtain their own medical help are likely to be held personally liable for the expenses they incur. The primary exception to this rule concerns emergency situations in which injured workers may obtain needed medical care without prior employer authorization.

The employer is responsible for the claimant's reasonably necessary medical treatment, including the services of physicians, nurses, and rehabilitation specialists. When appropriate, the services of psychiatrists and psychologists are covered. The cost of cosmetic treatment is included for individuals who have suffered disfigurements. Although most state laws cover chiropractic treatment, some laws limit benefits to medical doctors.

Transportation costs incurred in connection with appropriate medical treatment or rehabilitation also are covered. Injured workers who must purchase hearing aids, glasses, appliances, special beds, or similar items are usually entitled to reimbursement. Claimants experiencing substantial pain may now obtain covered treatment in most states that is merely designed to alleviate their discomfort.

Some claimants who require nursing assistance may ask family members to help them. Although early decisions often refused to approve payments for the services of family members, most contemporary decisions permit coverage for such assistance. They recognize that the employer is responsible for such care, and they do not believe that individuals providing bona fide nursing services should be denied compensation simply because they are related to the claimants.

Unscheduled Disability Benefits

Disability benefits are designed to offset earnings lost by individuals who sustain work-related injuries. These payments are normally limited to claimants who can demonstrate reduced earning capacity. All state laws contain brief waiting periods—ranging from three to seven days—that must elapse before injured workers become eligible for disability benefits. If the disabling condition continues for more than a specified period, the disability payments are made retroactive to the date of injury. This time period varies from five days to four weeks.

Workers' compensation systems divide disabilities into four basic categories:

- temporary partial
- temporary total
- permanent partial
- permanent total

Most injured workers experience temporary total or temporary partial disabilities. As soon as their conditions improve and they are able to resume work, their right to benefits ends. Once the healing process runs its course and their conditions stabilize, claimants may continue to have reduced capabilities. At this point, their right to temporary benefits ends and they must apply for permanent partial or total disability payments. If they have suffered specific losses, they may be entitled to scheduled benefits. In most cases, however, they must request unscheduled disability payments.

Courts use different tests to determine whether claimants have unscheduled permanent disabilities. The traditional "wage loss" and "earning capacity" tests used by most courts focus on the claimant's earning potential. These courts estimate the future earnings impairment caused by the occupational injuries involved. They consider the claimant's age, education, training, and work experience when attempting to calculate the loss of earning potential associated with their conditions.

Courts also review the present earnings of claimants who are seeking permanent disability benefits, because they believe that post-injury earnings are a good indication of a claimant's earning capacity. Nevertheless, if claimants can demonstrate that their current postinjury earnings do not truly reflect their future earning capacities, they may be awarded benefits despite the fact they are now earning as much as they earned before their injuries.

Most courts define disability in terms of the ability of claimants to perform work commensurate with their training and job experience. If they have obtained postinjury employment suitable to their particular backgrounds that pays them as much as their previous jobs, they will normally be presumed to have suffered no loss in earning capacity, even though they may be engaged in different lines of work. On the other hand, some claimants may be forced to accept employment that is not commensurate with their backgrounds because their employment-related conditions prevent them from performing tasks suitable to people with their training and experience. These persons are likely to be granted permanent partial disability payments, even though they may currently be earning wages equal to their preinjury salaries.

When occupational diseases are involved, courts in North Carolina, Maryland, Minnesota, New Mexico, and New York apply an occupation-specific test to determine benefit eligibility. If claimants are no longer able to engage in their prior occupations, they are granted permanent disability benefits. The fact that these individuals may currently earn as much as before while working in other lines of work is not considered controlling. Most states, however, refuse to apply the occupation-specific standard. So long as they conclude that the claimant's earning capacity is as high as it previously was, they refuse to award permanent benefits, even if the injured persons have to work in other suitable occupations.

Claimants seeking total disability payments are not required to show that their occupational conditions have deprived them of absolutely all earning capacity. Under the generally accepted "odd-lot" doctrine, courts recognize that even persons who may be able to earn occasional wages or to perform limited kinds of work may be entitled to total disability awards. The critical question is whether the evidence indicates that the claimants, as a result of their conditions, are really incapable of obtaining and holding steady employment. Once they establish their inability to work regularly in any recognized branch of the labor market, they are usually found eligible for total disability payments, even though they may sometimes be able to locate gainful employment. Many of these cases involve individuals with limited education who have previously performed physical labor and whose job-related injuries have severely affected their physical capabilities.

Scheduled Disability Benefits

The workers' compensation laws in every state, except Alaska, Florida, Kentucky, Maine, Minnesota, Montana, Nevada, and Texas, contain special scheduled benefit provisions. These sections usually cover specific physical impairments, such as the loss of one or both eyes, ears, arms, legs, hands, or feet, or one or more fingers or toes. They also include combined losses, such as one arm and one leg, several fingers and one hand, or a foot and a leg. They provide disability payments for a certain number of weeks for each particular loss without regard to the actual wage loss associated with the listed condition. These benefits are based on the conclusive presumption that people who sustain such occupational losses suffer diminished earning capacities over their remaining lives.

It is relatively easy to determine claimant eligibility for scheduled benefits when an entire arm or leg has been amputated or vision in one eye has been completely lost. It is more difficult, however, when amputation does not involve the whole arm or leg or minimal vision is retained in the affected eye. Courts usually hold that the loss of a significant portion of a finger, toe, arm, or leg will be treated as a loss of the entire limb for scheduled benefit purposes. When injuries or the pain generated by those conditions causes the substantial loss of *use* of particular limbs, courts tend to permit scheduled benefit awards. Nonetheless, when loss-of-use cases involve less substantial impairments, courts are likely to require claimants to seek unscheduled disability payments. The controlling issue in these cases is normally whether the affected limb is no longer of any real use to the injured worker.

Courts do not always agree whether loss-of-use determinations should consider the relevant members in the abstract or as they currently function with the assistance of eye glasses, hearing aids, or artificial limbs. A majority believe that scheduled benefits should be based on the uncorrected sight or hearing possessed by the affected workers. Most courts similarly award full scheduled benefits to employees who lose particular limbs, despite their subsequent replacement with prosthetic devices.

Some industrial accidents do not diminish the ability of the affected employees to perform their jobs, but they do result in serious physical disfigurements. These maladies may well affect future claimant earnings. To compensate claimants with these conditions, the vast majority of states now permit scheduled-type benefit awards for occupational disfigurements. They typically provide a certain percentage of weekly earnings for a specified number of weeks. When occupational accidents cause the loss of particular members *and* accompanying disfigurement, some courts permit scheduled awards for both the lost members and the disfigurement. Other courts, however, refuse to allow payments pertaining to both the lost members and the disfigurement.

When certain injuries cause the loss of particular members, they also affect the use of larger limbs. For example, claimants who lose two or three fingers or toes may effectively lose the use of the affected hands or feet. Courts in a number of states limit benefits to the exact scheduled losses sustained. Nonetheless, courts in other jurisdictions recognize that for some people, the loss of two or three fingers or toes is the equivalent of a lost hand or foot. They thus permit benefit awards covering the entire hand or foot.

If employees sustain scheduled and unscheduled injuries in work-related accidents, they may usually obtain benefit awards covering both their scheduled and unscheduled conditions. On the other hand, if they merely sustain scheduled losses, may they be granted unscheduled benefits? A majority of state laws permit temporary unscheduled benefit payments while such persons are recuperating, followed by their full scheduled benefits. Some other enactments allow temporary benefits when the convalescence period for the scheduled injuries is protracted. The laws in a few states require the deduction of previously awarded temporary benefits from scheduled payments covering the same injuries.

When claimants awarded scheduled benefits exhaust their benefits, they may continue to be partially or totally disabled. If they then request unscheduled benefits based on their current conditions, the courts in many states will deny their requests. They consider the scheduled benefits the exclusive workers' compensation remedy for scheduled losses. On the other hand, a growing number of courts have indicated a willingness to reassess claimant circumstances once scheduled benefits have been exhausted. If claimants demonstrate continued disabilities, they permit unscheduled benefit awards.

Second Injury Problems

Second injury questions usually involve scheduled injuries. They result from the fact that the combined impact of successive injuries may be far greater that the mere sum of the parts. For example, workers who have previously lost the use of one arm, leg, or eye in occupational or nonoccupational incidents will be more devastated by current industrial accidents that result in the loss of their other arm, leg, or eye than would individuals with no preexisting disabilities who sustain the identical present losses. Because courts generally recognize that employers take their employees as they hire them, courts tend to hold employers responsible for the total disabilities resulting from the combined impact of successive injuries. The companies employing the workers when they lost their second arm, leg, or eye would thus be held responsible for scheduled benefits pertaining to the loss of *both* arms, legs, or eyes, rather than for the mere loss of one such member. While this approach fairly compensates employees who suffer successive injuries, it imposes liability on employers that transcends the degree of loss arising from the most recent accident involving their workers. It also discourages the employment of individuals with preexisting disabilities.

A number of state legislatures have sought to limit employer liability for successive injury cases through the enactment of apportionment provisions.[37] These generally provide that firms are not liable for the additional consequences created by preexisting conditions. When the ultimate disability results from successive occupational events, the adversely affected employees are reasonably protected, with each of the respective employers being held responsible for the degree of disability that arose out of and during a claimant's employment with them.

Apportionment statutes have a harsh impact on employees whose present industrial accidents exacerbate preexisting, nonoccupational disabilities. If their employer is only held liable for the proportion of their combined disability attributable to the recent industrial accident, they are denied compensation for their overall disabilities. State laws have sought to accommodate the competing interests of employees with successive injuries and their employers through the creation of second injury funds. **Although second injury provisions hold employers responsible only for the degree of disabilities attributable to the injuries arising out of the claimant's employment with them, they guarantee individuals who sustain successive injuries full compensation for their combined disabilities**. Second injury funds are normally financed through state appropriations or employer assessments.

Two-thirds of second injury fund programs are limited to successive injury situations that result in permanent total disabilities.[38] The statutes in 18 states,[39] however, impose no such restrictions. Fund provisions in half of the state laws specifically cover scheduled injuries, but do not apply to unscheduled disabilities.[40] Statutes that do not contain this limitation are usually found applicable to successive injury

---

[37]Arkansas, California, Florida, Kentucky, Maine, Maryland, Michigan, Minnesota, Mississippi, New York, North Carolina, North Dakota, Oklahoma, Oregon, South Carolina, Texas, Washington, and West Virginia.

[38]See Larson, A. *Larson's Workmen's Compensation Law* §59.31. (New York: Matthew Bender, 1992).

[39]Alaska, California, Connecticut, Florida, Iowa, Kansas, Kentucky, Maryland, Minnesota, Missouri, Nebraska, New Mexico, New York, North Dakota, Oklahoma, Oregon, Utah, and Wisconsin.

[40]Alabama, Arkansas, Colorado, Georgia, Idaho, Illinois, Indiana, Iowa, Kansas, Louisiana, Maine, Massachusetts, Michigan, Mississippi, Nevada, New Hampshire, North Carolina, Ohio, Pennsylvania, South Carolina, South Dakota, Tennessee, Texas, Virginia, West Virginia, and Wyoming.

cases concerning preexisting unscheduled disabilities and to cases involving occupational diseases.

Claimants seeking second injury fund benefits must be able to demonstrate that the most recent incident combined with some preexisting condition to increase their overall degree of disability. In some states, they would obtain full compensation for their combined disabilities from their most recent employers, who would then seek reimbursement from the second injury fund for the portion of benefits attributable to the aggravation of the preexisting disabilities. In other states, the responsible employers would merely be obliged to compensate the claimants for their most recent losses. The affected workers would then have to request compensation for the remaining part of their combined disabilities from the second injury fund. A number of statutes set maximum weekly benefit amounts that may be awarded to disabled people or limit the number of weeks benefits may be received, to avoid disability awards that exceed the amount available for total disability cases.

Calculating the Wage Basis

State compensation laws typically provide disabled workers with from one-half to two-thirds of their "average weekly wage." The weekly benefit amounts for partially disabled claimants are usually the same as the amounts for totally disabled persons, but the affected persons receive their benefit payments for proportionately fewer weeks.

Statutes generally provide that the three, six, or 12 month period preceding claimant disability will be used to calculate the relevant weekly wage rate. If claimants were employed on a relatively full-time basis during this period, compensation administrators use their actual earnings to compute their average weekly wage rate. If they were not employed during substantially all of the specified period, their weekly wage rate is determined by reference to employees of the same class who worked throughout the relevant time frame. The weekly wage rate includes tips, commissions, regular bonuses, and customary overtime earnings, but it usually excludes employer contributions to fringe benefit plans.

When claimants were voluntarily employed on a part-time basis prior to the development of their occupational conditions, some courts require the weekly wage rate to be calculated in a manner that reflects the part-time nature of claimant employment. Other courts, however, believe that the wage rate should be computed by reference to similar employees who have been working on a full-time basis. These courts think that this approach best reflects the loss of future earning capacity caused to claimants by their current injuries. Nonetheless, when claimants who wished to work on a full-time basis were required shortly before their industrial accidents to accept part-time hours due to circumstances beyond their control, courts generally use the earnings of full-time personnel to calculate the weekly wage rates of the claimants.[41]

If claimants were employed by two different firms when they developed their occupational conditions, a number of states use combined claimant earnings to compute their weekly wage rate if the two employments were "related" or "similar." Other states use the combined earnings in their calculations even when the separate employments were not related or similar. A few states refuse to combine the earnings from different jobs even when they were related or similar.

Death Benefits

Certain surviving dependents of workers who die as a result of occupational injuries or diseases are entitled to prescribed death benefits. Surviving spouses and dependent children usually receive specified percentages of the deceased employees' weekly earnings—most frequently one-third, one-half, or two-thirds for surviving spouses and two-thirds or three-fourths for surviving spouses with dependent children. These benefits are usually provided for a set number of weeks, ranging from 300 to 700 for surviving spouses and continuing for dependent children until they reach 18. Many statutes terminate death benefits for surviving spouses when they remarry. Burial expenses are also provided, ranging from $2,000 to $3,000 in most states.

If the disabled workers established their right to benefits while they were alive, most states do not require their surviving dependents to relitigate these issues. If the disabled employees did not demonstrate their right to benefits while alive, their dependents must do so after they

---

[41]*See, e.g.,* State ex rel., Branham v. Industrial Comm'n, 443 N.E.2d 1019 (Ohio App. 1981); Traders & General Ins. Co. v. Nored, 341 S.W.2d 492 (Tex. Civ. App. 1960).

die. In many states, spouses and minor children who resided with deceased workers when they died are conclusively presumed to be eligible for death benefits. Because the rights of surviving dependents are usually considered independent of the rights of the workers themselves, most states do not deduct disability payments given to injured or diseased workers before they died from the death benefits payable to their survivors. Survivors who were totally dependent on the deceased workers are entitled to full benefits, while partially dependent survivors, who only received part of their financial support from the deceased workers, are generally given proportionately reduced benefits.

Compensation administrators often must decide how to divide death benefits among multiple surviving dependents. In most states, totally dependent survivors—usually spouses and minor children living with the deceased—have first priority. If there are several totally dependent survivors, they normally share the benefits specified for total dependents. Partial dependents share the remaining sums, if any. Most laws list the relatives eligible for death benefits. They generally include spouses, minor children, and parents. Some cover siblings, grandparents, and other more distant relatives. People who do not fall within the list of covered dependents are not entitled to death benefits, despite their actual dependence on the deceased.

CLAIMS ADMINISTRATION AND RESOLUTION

Administrative and Judicial Enforcement

Most workers' compensation laws are enforced by administrative agencies. Louisiana is the only state that relies entirely on judicial enforcement. While Alabama, New Mexico, Tennessee, and Wyoming require some judicial involvement, they also use administrative agencies to handle many aspects of the enforcement process.

Because it is recognized that claimants are not likely to be knowledgeable regarding technical legal procedures, administrative agencies apply informal procedural rules. For example, informal benefit applications, such as letters sent to compensation administrators generally describing the relevant circumstances, are usually found sufficient. Claims must normally identify the claimant, indicate that a compensable condition has developed, and suggest that benefit payments are desired.

The failure of claimants to describe the pertinent circumstances in detail or the inclusion of erroneous dates will rarely defeat their claims.

Duty to Notify Employer of Injuries

Injured employees are usually required to notify their employers promptly of their job-related conditions. When latent injuries are involved, notice must be provided as soon as the claimants become aware of their conditions. The failure of claimants to give their employers notice of their conditions may be excused if the employers were not prejudiced by their omission. For example, a claimant's employer may have learned of the situation from a supervisor or the firm's health care professional. On the other hand, if employers are actually prejudiced by the failure of claimants to provide them with timely notice, the affected workers may lose their right to obtain benefits. The critical question in these cases is whether the employers could have provided more effective medical treatment if they had known of claimant's condition or could have ascertained and preserved the relevant facts for a workers' compensation hearing.

If deceased workers fail to give their employers proper notice of their conditions while they are alive, the right of their surviving dependents to death benefits may be forfeited if their employers were prejudiced by the lack of notice. This result is quite likely when the notice provision specifically applies to death benefit claims. On the other hand, when statutory provisions requiring claimants to provide notice do not expressly cover death benefits, courts tend to permit awards to surviving dependents despite the failure of the deceased workers to provide that notice while they were alive.

Statute of Limitations Periods

Individuals who develop job-related conditions must file claims with state agencies within specified time periods—usually one or two years—following their industrial accidents or the manifestation of their occupational diseases. Nonetheless, when their injuries initially seem insignificant, states generally refuse to begin the running of these limitation periods until they become aware or should reasonably have become aware of their disabling conditions. Typical cases involve minor eye injuries that develop into cataracts or seemingly inconsequential lesions that become cancerous.

Most state laws contain separate statute-of-limitation provisions for death benefits. Because the right of a surviving dependent does not accrue until the worker dies, the limitation period for a dependent does not begin to run until the death of the injured employee. Even when no specific provisions regulate this area, courts usually hold that the limitation period for a surviving dependent commences at the time of the worker's death. The fact that a deceased employee failed to file a claim in a timely manner while alive does not normally affect the right of a surviving dependent to obtain death benefits.

Informal Hearing Procedures

Compensation proceedings are usually conducted in an informal manner, and compliance with technical rules of evidence are not required. **Although the *exclusion* of competent evidence may result in a judicial reversal of the agency's compensation determination, the *admission* of incompetent evidence rarely results in judicial reversals**. So long as some competent evidence supports the agency decision, it is likely to be sustained.

Most controverted cases include medical evidence. The fact that the claimant's medical evidence does not establish a definite connection between employment and injury or disease is not determinative. The record need only be sufficient to enable administrators to reasonably find that the relevant conditions are job-related. The claimant's testimony and the testimony of other lay witnesses will often be enough to support a benefit award.

Agency and Court Review

Initial compensation determinations are generally made by administrative examiners. Their factual findings and legal conclusions are usually subject to thorough administrative review by agency directors or compensation review boards. Parties dissatisfied with final administrative decisions may seek judicial review. Many state enactments expressly state that agency fact findings are conclusive, so long as they are supported by substantial evidence. Similar judicial deference is usually given to agency fact findings in states that do not have statutory provisions requiring such deference. As a result, judges do not ask whether they would have reached the same factual conclusions if they had been the deciding officials. They simply ask whether there is substantial evidence in the record supporting the agency findings. Only when records contain no rational evidence supporting challenged factual determinations are reviewing courts likely to reverse those findings.

When courts are asked to review administrative interpretations of statutory provisions and other legal issues, they engage in more intensive scrutiny. They examine the statutory language and the relevant legislative history to ascertain the intent of the legislators who adopted the pertinent sections. While reviewing judges are not bound by agency interpretations, they generally give substantial deference to the decisions of the administrative agencies that were created to interpret and apply the workers' compensation laws. Nonetheless, when reviewing courts conclude that administrative agencies have clearly misinterpreted or misapplied statutory provisions, they do not hesitate to reverse those decisions.

Voluntary Settlement Agreements

The vast majority of workers' compensation claims are resolved without agency adjudication through negotiated settlement agreements. Employers or their insurance carriers expressly or implicitly acknowledge that the claimants' conditions arose out of and during their employment, and they voluntarily provide medical coverage and, where appropriate, disability benefits. Some state laws contain provisions that prohibit settlement agreements that include waivers of claimant statutory rights. Courts in these states usually refuse to allow individuals to settle claims for less than the statutorily prescribed benefit amounts. Many courts in states that do not have such explicit provisions similarly refuse to allow settlements that provide claimants with benefits below those prescribed by statute. Other courts, however, do accept settlements that compromise claimant rights, so long as they are reached in good faith.

Compensation laws in numerous states permit lump-sum settlements. In states that do not allow the compromise of worker claims, lump-sum settlements must approximate the present value of the prescribed weekly benefit amounts to which claimants would otherwise be entitled. In states that accept compromise settlements, lump-sum agreements may provide for reduced benefit payments. Some states only permit lump-sum settlements when claimants can demonstrate that lump-sum payments are in their best interest.

Reopening Prior Awards

In recognition of the fact that a claimant's condition may improve or deteriorate over time, the compensation laws in all 50 states permit awards to be reopened in appropriate situations. Most of these provisions impose various time limits on the right to reopen prior awards. Some only permit reopening within a set number of years after the initial injuries or benefit awards, or following the last benefit payment, while others allow reopening even after the last benefit payment has been made.

Requests to reopen benefit awards must be based on changed circumstance. Claimants seeking benefit increases must usually show that their conditions have either worsened or been aggravated by other developments. Employers or insurance carriers seeking reduced or terminated benefits must establish that claimant conditions have significantly improved. Although most states even allow previously negotiated settlement agreements to be reopened because of changed medical circumstances, some statutes expressly preclude reopening of settlement agreements.

Attorney and Expert Witness Fees

Although employers and their insurance carriers must generally assume responsibility for the cost of lawyers and expert witnesses they employ, statutes in 35 states[42] authorize the awarding of extra benefits

---

[42]Alaska, Arkansas, California, Connecticut, Delaware, Florida, Georgia, Hawaii, Idaho, Illinois, Indiana, Kentucky, Louisiana, Maine, Maryland, Massachusetts, Minnesota, Montana, Nebraska, Nevada, New Hampshire, New Jersey, New Mexico, North Carolina, North Dakota, Oregon, Pennsylvania, Rhode Island, South Carolina, South Dakota, Texas, Vermont, Virginia, Washington, and Wyoming. *See* Larson, A. *Larson's Workmen's Compensation Law* App. B., Table 18. (New York: Matthew Bender, 1992).

to prevailing claimants to cover the cost of their attorneys and a few permit extra benefits to reimburse prevailing claimants for their expert witnesses. Attorney fee add-ons most often range from 10 to 30 percent of disability benefit awards. In the absence of these special provisions, however, injured workers are normally obliged to bear their own litigation costs. Attorneys in these states generally charge prevailing clients a percentage of their benefit awards. Most statutes contain provisions that either require agency approval of lawyer fees or limit contingent fees to 20, 25, or 30 percent of compensation awards.

When employers or their insurance carriers contest benefit awards, months or years may elapse before prevailing claimants receive their benefits. A number of laws permit interest to be awarded on unpaid benefit amounts. Some enactments even authorize the imposition of special penalties in cases involving unreasonable nonpayment.

WORKERS' COMPENSATION EXCLUSIVITY AND EXCEPTIONS

The enactment of workers' compensation laws involved a critical tradeoff. In exchange for the liability-without-fault protection given to employees whose conditions arose out of and during the course of their employment, their employers were granted expansive tort immunity with respect to statutorily covered injuries and diseases. **As a result, individuals who sustain job-related conditions are usually unable to bring personal injury lawsuits in court against their employers for injuries that were caused by negligence attributable to those companies**. Furthermore, the fact that the adversely affected workers failed to file compensation claims is not controlling. Nor is the fact that they suffered no *compensable* harm. So long as their conditions arose out of and during the course of their employment, their situations will generally be subject to tort immunity.

When employees are injured or killed in employment-related accidents, their dependents also may be affected. Spouses or children may be left without financial support or companionship. These persons may decide to sue the responsible employers. Suits by such dependents are usually barred by the statutory immunity granted to employers.

Individuals injured in employment-related incidents often attempt to sue fellow workers or other parties. Many workers' compensation statutes grant co-workers and supervisors the same tort immunity that is given to their employers. As a result, injured persons are unable to seek tort damages from fellow employees or supervisors whose negligence may have contributed to their injuries. In nine states,[43] however, statutory immunity is limited to employers. In these states, people injured by the negligence of co-workers or supervisors may seek tort damages from those persons. Statutory immunity includes the employers of "borrowed servants" who are injured while they are on loan to those firms. Where co-workers and supervisors of injured individuals are given similar immunity, the fellow employees of the "borrowing" companies enjoy the same protection.

Despite the tort immunity that is generally granted to the employers of injured workers, adversely affected employees occasionally attempt to obtain tort damages from those firms. Some courts have allowed tort actions against employers under the "dual capacity" doctrine, which permits employees to sue their employer if they are injured by their employer while it was acting in a wholly separate capacity. For example, persons employed by a physician may be injured in the course of their employment and then receive negligent treatment from that doctor. Courts that follow the "dual capacity" doctrine would most likely permit the injured employees to sue the physician for negligent treatment, on the ground the treatment occurred when the physician was acting as a health care specialist rather than their employer. A majority of states have refused to adopt the "dual capacity" exception.

Workers' compensation laws provide the exclusive remedy vis-à-vis employers with respect to "accidental" injuries sustained by their employees. Nonetheless, if workers are injured as a result of intentional assaults committed by employer officials, the resulting harm is not considered "accidental," and statutory immunity is no longer available to the responsible employer. Some state laws allow employees injured by intentional employer assaults to seek either workers' compensation benefits or tort damages. A few provide extra workers' compensation benefits for individuals injured by intentional employer torts. This exception is usually limited to truly intentional torts. If the employer officials are merely acting with gross negligence or even

---

[43]Alabama, Arkansas, Maryland, Minnesota, Missouri, New Hampshire, Rhode Island, South Dakota, and Vermont.

recklessness, most courts refuse to permit tort actions against that company.

Intentional misconduct may similarly affect the immunity available to co-workers. Statutory provisions in 12 states[44] and court decisions in seven other states[45] deny statutory immunity to workers whose intentional misbehavior causes injury to fellow employees. In these states, employees injured by the deliberate misconduct of co-workers may bring lawsuits against those persons.

A number of states refuse to extend statutory immunity to employers that fraudulently conceal from employees work-related conditions detected by company physicians in the course of medical examinations. While tort immunity would prevent any suit based on the initial injury, courts in these states would allow employees to sue for the additional harm caused by the fact that their employer's concealment caused them to delay treatment for the undisclosed conditions.

THIRD PARTY TORT ACTIONS

Employees who sustain job-related injuries occasionally attempt to sue other parties whose negligence contributed to their conditions. Although statutory immunity is not a bar to these actions—so long as they are not against their employer or co-workers—the injured workers must prove that negligence by the third-party defendants caused them harm. Typical cases are brought against negligent drivers, manufacturers of defective products used by injured employees, negligent persons employed by other companies, careless health care providers, and other similar parties. When negligent actions by such third parties have adversely affected individuals employed by other companies, the injured persons may normally sue the responsible third parties for damages.

Cases of greater interest to employers concern job applicants or employees who have medical conditions that are not properly diagnosed during employer-mandated medical examinations. Courts traditionally

---

[44]Arizona, California, Connecticut, Florida, Louisiana, Mississippi, Montana, Nebraska, New Hampshire, New Jersey, Pennsylvania, and Texas.

[45]New York, North Carolina, Ohio, Oklahoma, Tennessee, Utah, and Washington.

refused to permit such adversely affected individuals to sue the examining physicians, due to the absence of physician-patient relationships and the lack of any duty of care owed by the doctors to the workers being examined at company expense. A growing number of decisions, however, have permitted employees to sue physicians whose negligent failure to diagnose injuries or diseases has exacerbated those conditions.

RETALIATION AGAINST EMPLOYEES WHO FILE CLAIMS

Many state laws contain specific provisions making it unlawful for employers to discriminate against individuals because of their filing of workers' compensation claims. Some statutory provisions permit individuals who are the victims of retaliatory discharges to seek reinstatement and back pay through workers' compensation agencies, while other enactments authorize judicial actions to obtain the same relief.

Courts in most states that do not have statutorily prescribed antiretaliation provisions have granted workers' compensation claimants similar protection through the public policy exception to the traditional employment-at-will doctrine. Courts in these states recognize that access to compensation benefits is an important public policy that cannot be thwarted by discriminatory employer action. As a result, employees who are fired in retaliation for filing of workers' compensation claims may sue their employer in tort for damages. Because these public policy actions do not involve the enforcement of rights set forth in the applicable workers' compensation law, the culpable employers enjoy no statutory immunity against such actions.

7

Noncompetition Agreements and Related Matters

INTRODUCTION

A variety of legal issues can arise when an employee leaves employment voluntarily. Unlike wrongful discharge cases, discussed in chapter 8, in which lawsuits are invariably brought by discharged employees, when employees quit their jobs any lawsuits are likely to be brought by employers. This chapter discusses the legal bases for these legal actions. There are two main areas of discussion. First, many employees agree that if they leave their current employer they will not work for a competitor or start a competing business of their own. The enforceability of these noncompetition agreements varies widely based on the jurisdiction and the facts of the case. Second, intellectual property issues of trade secrets, copyrights, and patents can arise when an employee seeks to use valuable information acquired during the course of employment. These issues are discussed at the end of the chapter.

INVOLUNTARY SERVITUDE

Congress enacted the Thirteenth Amendment to the Constitution after the Civil War in order to incorporate the prohibition against slavery into the Constitution. The amendment prohibits "involuntary servitude, except as a punishment for crime whereof the party shall have been duly convicted." The Supreme Court has interpreted this amendment to apply to labor contracts and refused to restrict it to slavery or to African-Americans.[1] This interpretation extends the prohibition against involuntary work to protect individuals from both private and public entities, except the armed services.

This guarantee against involuntary servitude protects individuals from court orders mandating certain work and thus gives employees a right to refuse to perform further services for an employer. Even when an employee has a contract promising to perform, a court cannot grant specific performance by ordering personal services.

The constitutional right not to perform personal services is limited, however. Although it protects individuals from being forced to work, it does not otherwise protect them from the legal consequences of breaching an employment contract. They are still subject to lawsuits for damages resulting from the refusal to perform promised work. Moreover, it does not protect them against court orders requiring individuals to keep contractual promises not to perform similar work for other employers. Because some employees can be restrained from working for competitors, the practical effect often is to keep them from quitting the employer who has a contract with them. The economic coercion that keeps such employees from quitting is not "involuntary servitude" within the meaning of the Constitution.

EMPLOYEE BREACH OF CONTRACT

When an employee refuses further performance in violation of a contract to work under specific terms, the employer often suffers consequent losses. In the usual case, it is necessary to find and train a replacement employee on short notice. If the employee was not justified in the breach, the employer can sue for such losses under a theory of breach of contract.

As a practical matter, employers rarely recover substantial damages in actions against former employees for breach of contract.

---

[1]Bailey v. Alabama, 219 U.S. 219 (1911).

First, courts and juries have generally been unsympathetic to employers in such cases. Even when employers win, monetary judgments against former employees are usually difficult to collect. Moreover, the monetary loss is typically too small to justify the cost of litigation. For these reasons, employers rarely initiate such actions; the cases for breach of employee contract typically arise in response to an employee's suit to collect wages withheld for past work.

An employer is obligated to "mitigate" damages caused by the employee's breach. The obligation to mitigate means that a plaintiff cannot recover for avoidable losses that occur after the defendant's wrong. In the context of employee breach, the obligation to mitigate means that the employer must make every effort to avoid losses that can be prevented. One common step is to secure a substitute employee as soon as possible.

Damages are usually limited to the costs of replacing the employee. If the employer is able to replace the employee quickly with someone else at the same salary or lower, there may not be any damages at all. Some employment contracts contain clauses providing for reimbursement of costs to train a new employee in the event of breach. Such costs may be recoverable with or without such a clause, but some courts have been unreceptive to such claims.

Employees can defend actions for breach of contract by establishing a legally sufficient justification for their actions. An employee need not honor the terms of a contract for personal services when the work is illegal, for example.

Impossibility of performance caused by the employee's illness is also generally recognized as an excuse from personal service obligations. A noteworthy Wisconsin Supreme Court opinion[2] considered this excuse and created a distinction between unforeseeable illness and illness caused by the employee's hypertension on the job. The case concerned a teacher who quit mid-year because of an illness caused in part by her resentment and agitation on the job. The court reasoned that self-induced illness is not an excuse, so the teacher was liable for the higher cost of her replacement. To date, this distinction has not been adopted by other jurisdictions.

---

[2]Handicapped Children's Educ. Bd. v. Lukaszewski, 332 N.W.2d 774 (Wis. 1983).

NONCOMPETITION AGREEMENTS AND
PUBLIC POLICY

Employment contracts often contain noncompetition clauses in which the employee agrees not to work for competitors after leaving the employer. These promises, which are called "covenants not to compete" or "noncompetition agreements," have been the subject of extensive litigation. **Courts enforce noncompetition agreements only when their terms are narrowly tailored to meet the employer's legitimate interest in keeping confidential information away from competitors without unduly interfering with the worker's ability to earn a living**.

Several states have statutes directly governing covenants not to compete: Alaska, California, Colorado, Florida, Hawaii, Louisiana, Michigan, Montana, Nevada, North Carolina, North Dakota, Ohio, South Dakota, Tennessee, Texas, West Virginia, and Wisconsin. Most of these statutes declare covenants not to compete to be void as against public policy, but provide exceptions. In addition, Massachusetts and Minnesota have provisions in their state constitutions that emphasize the right to work or the right to choose one's occupation or labor freely.

Even in the absence of statutory curtailment, courts have found that public policy dictates restrictions on noncompetition agreements. The public has an economic interest in free and open competition between product and service providers. That competition is affected by covenants not to compete, which are drafted for the exclusive benefit of one employer. They discourage new competition in providing goods and services because former employees are a likely source of new entrants into the market.

Enforcement of such agreements against competition also prevents individuals from maximizing their labor for society. There is a public interest in allowing free mobility of labor, in human satisfaction, and in maximizing the productivity of skilled individuals. There is a further social interest in allowing individuals who have invested in their own skills to put those skills to use and to earn a livelihood by their use. **A court enforces a promise not to compete only after the judge has determined that the circumstance does not work an unjustified hardship on the former employee and that the restrictions on time, geography, and scope of business are appropriate**.

Another reason that noncompetition contracts are generally not favored in modern law is that they are typically very one-sided agreements that are executed completely under the employer's terms. Some jurisdictions consider whether the employee agreed to the terms at the time of hiring, rather than at any point after the employee is on the job. If the covenant is presented to the employee at the outset, the employee at least has adequate notice before committing to that employment relationship. In one Arizona case,[3] the judge denied enforcement in part because the individual did not know that signing a noncompetition covenant was a condition of employment until he had resigned his other job and appeared for the first day for work.

The same rationale applies when an employee is promoted or trained for a different job. The covenant should be signed before the employee receives the promotion or training to avoid the impression that the covenant is an afterthought by the employer to recapture an unplanned advantage in the form of control over the employee. The key is whether the employer appears to be taking advantage of the employee's vulnerable situation. For example, a Kansas court held that continued employment of an employee after execution of a covenant was sufficient where the evidence showed he was given promotions, increased responsibilities, and greater importance in the company operation after signing the covenant.[4]

Employees rarely receive additional compensation during employment for agreeing to the covenant. Similarly, it is rare for an employer to provide separate compensation to a former employee during the time that the restriction applies. A factor in favor of the enforceability of a noncompetition agreement is the presence of some separate monetary incentive to sign the contract or some continuing payment during the period that the covenant is in force.

A former employee's covenant not to compete is distinguishable from two special situations that also involve promises not to compete. One is a noncompetition agreement incorporated in the sale of a business and its goodwill. Courts are more likely to enforce a promise

---

[3]American Credit Bureau, Inc. v. Carter, 462 P.2d 838 (Ariz. App. 1969).
[4]Puritan-Bennett Corp. v. Richter, 657 P.2d 589 (Kan. App. 1983), *modified*, 679 P.2d 206 (Kan. 1984).

not to compete when it is part of an arm's-length sale of a business than when it restricts a former employee for the benefit of the former employer. In the sale of a business, the parties are generally engaged in a one-time commercial relationship, rather than a continuing relationship in which there may be an inequality of power. The buyer's interest in the goodwill of the ongoing business is protected by a covenant preventing the seller from starting a rival new business immediately after selling the old one.

The second special situation involves covenants not to compete in partnership arrangements. Such agreements are not one-sided like the typical covenant in the employment relationship. Whereas the noncompetition agreement in the employment context is entirely for the benefit of the employer, such agreements in the partnership context are mutually beneficial because it is similarly binding on all partners. For example, Partner A cannot compete with the partnership in the specified area for the specified term, but Partner A gets the reciprocal benefit that Partner B is similarly bound. Thus, the burdens and benefits of enforcement fall evenly upon both parties.

In both of these special cases involving covenants not to compete, courts apply rules that are similar to the rules applied to former employees' covenants. Their enforceability depends upon the time, geography, and scope of the business. Nonetheless, these special cases are not very useful in resolving issues of covenants not to compete in the employment context because different policy issues affect the legal resolution of these otherwise similar situations.

ENFORCEABILITY OF NONCOMPETITION AGREEMENTS

There are four elements that determine the enforceability of a covenant not to compete against a former employee. First, the employer must have a substantial and legitimate interest to be protected. Second, the restriction on the employee must be relevant, reasonable, and no broader than necessary to protect that right. Third, there must not be any undue hardship on the employee. Fourth, there must not be any harm to the public as a result of enforcing the covenant not to compete.

Legitimate Interests in Noncompetition

An employer's need to protect its business interests is well recognized in two common circumstances. The first is where the employer has contributed extensively to the employee's training and productivity and the employee leaves before the employer has been able to realize a reasonable return on that investment. For example, this interest is recognized in a Colorado statute as an exception to a general prohibition on noncompetition agreements. The statute permits the recovery of training expenses for persons employed less than two years.

The second well-recognized employer interest arises when the employee has acted in bad faith by selling secrets to a competitor, sabotaging the firm's business position, or otherwise engaging in an unfair business practice. In *Texas Road Boring Co. v. Parker*,[5] for example, an employee left the employer after less than a year as a manager and established his own competing business. He hired some of the company's employees and began soliciting the company's clients. The court found a significant invasion of the employer's legitimate interests and enforced the noncompetition covenant.

In contrast, the mere fact that the employer has invested in training an employee is not in itself enough to support enforcement of a covenant not to compete. Many courts have held that the knowledge, skill, expertise, and information acquired by an employee during employment become part of the employee's person. The distinction is between specialized training amounting to a trade secret and general skills acquired during employment. Such specialized skills legitimately belong to an employer whereas generalized training does not. A North Carolina court held, for example, that an employee's skill in removing asbestos was a general skill that belonged to him; such knowledge therefore did not constitute a protectable interest for the employer.[6]

The legitimacy of the employer's interest requires that the employer be able to benefit from enforcing the noncompetition agreement in some way other than indirectly coercing the employee to continue to work for the employer. For example, a covenant cannot operate in an area where the employer no longer engages in the activity the covenant

---

[5]194 So. 2d 885 (Miss. 1967).
[6]Masterclean of N.C., Inc. v. Guy, 345 S.E.2d 692 (N.C. App. 1986).

was designed to protect. Similarly, an employer cannot prevent a former employee from soliciting customers of a firm with whom the employee had no significant contact during the time of employment.

Standard of Reasonableness

After the threshold question of the employer's legitimate interest, the issue becomes the reasonableness of the restriction on competition. In most states, there are no firm guidelines to delineate when limits are reasonable. A few state statutes specify standards of duration that are presumptively reasonable or presumptively unreasonable, but in most states the courts consider the reasonableness of the restriction. Factors determining its reasonableness include the scope of the work considered competing, the geographical limits, and the duration of the restraint. Because courts weigh the circumstances as a whole, no one factor controls.

The flexibility of the reasonableness standard allows judges to balance the stringency of one factor against the leniency of another. For example, a court may allow a longer period of competitive restraint in a relatively small geographic area. In any case, however, the restraint should be no greater than is necessary to protect the employer's legitimate business interests. Courts consider the time period, the geographic area, and the scope of activity that the employer seeks to restrict. Hence, an agreement preventing a former newspaper employee from competitive publishing within a 50 mile radius may be reasonable,[7] whereas a similar covenant imposed upon an automobile roof installer may not be.[8]

The reasonableness of a restriction depends upon the employer's individual circumstances. In one case a court concluded that certain two-year and one-year time restrictions in a covenant were reasonable in light of the firm's testimony that it takes one to three years to establish a major account.[9] Several courts have taken the view that the duration should be no longer than is necessary for a replacement employee to learn the business. Other courts hold that the duration should be no longer than is necessary to obliterate the identification

---

[7]*See* Tyler v. Eufaula Tribune Publishing Co., 500 So. 2d 1005 (Ala. 1986).
[8]*See* DeVoe v. Cheatham, 413 So. 2d 1141 (Ala. 1982).
[9]McRand, Inc. v. Van Beelen, 486 N.E.2d 1306 (Ill. App. 1985).

between the firm and the former employee in the minds of the firm's customers.

As many firms have begun to compete in an increasingly statewide, national, or international marketplace, reasonable geographical restrictions become more difficult to identify. Courts rarely enforce extensive geographic limitations except in cases where traveling sales representatives seek to serve that same region or route with a basically fungible product.

Increasingly, customer restrictions are used to complement or substitute for geographic restrictions. Employers can protect their legitimate interests in noncompetition by restricting the former employee from contacting its customers. **Courts apply the same standards of reasonableness to customer restrictions, and broad restrictions barring the former employee from contacting any of the employer's customers are rarely enforced.** A restriction is overbroad and therefore unreasonable if the former employee had not personally served those customers and had never represented the firm's goodwill to those customers.

A restraint on contact with former customers is reasonable if the former employee gained special knowledge and familiarity with the customers' requirements while working for the employer. The reasonableness of a restraint can depend on many factors, including the complexity of the products being sold, the frequency of calls made by the sales representative, and the length of time customers have been associated with the employer. Finally, the time, expense, and difficulty of developing the clientele can be important factors when the court determines the reasonableness of restraining a former employee from contact with the employer's customers.

A court may always consider the hardship that its decrees may have on litigants in a particular case. Therefore, it is appropriate to consider the potential hardship on a former employee when an employer seeks to enforce a noncompetition agreement. Relevant to the inquiry are factors such as the educational level of the individual, family support obligations, and the probability of finding other employment. In one case,[10] for example, the court considered that the individual was 50 years old, married, and had significant financial obligations.

---

[10]Sheffield v. Stoudenmire, 553 So. 2d 125 (Ala. 1989).

A few courts have focused on whether the enforcement of the covenant would require the employee to move from the area in order to engage in the same type of work. In one case,[11] a Texas court found a noncompetition agreement oppressive because it prevented the individual from using his acquired skills to support himself in the place he lived.

Cause of Termination

Anticompetitive covenants are most appropriate when the employee quits and unfairly competes with the former employer by taking customers or by leaving immediately after receiving specialized training. In contrast, it often seems unfair to prevent the employee from engaging in other similar employment when the employer terminates the employee.

Courts have not been consistent in developing rules concerning whether to enforce noncompetition agreements in the situation where the employer terminates the employee. Some courts have held that the employer loses the benefit of the covenant upon the termination and therefore refuse to enjoin the employee from competing employment. Others find this factor irrelevant and do not consider it. Still others find the circumstance of the termination to be simply one factor among all the factors to weigh in deciding whether to enforce the noncompetition agreement.

Some courts have focused upon whether the termination was for good cause. The Arkansas Supreme Court expressed concern that any other rule might result in anticompetitive behavior contravening public policy. The court explained that if an employer "obtained an agreement of this nature from an employee, and then, without reasonable cause, fired him, the agreement would not be binding." The reason is that "an employer cannot use this type of contract as a subterfuge to rid himself of a possible future competitor."[12]

Other jurisdictions distinguish between termination without just cause and termination in bad faith. Termination without just cause does not affect the decision whether to enforce the covenant in these states, but bad faith bars the employer from the benefits of the agreement. An

---

[11]*See* Hill v. Mobile Auto Trim, 725 S.W.2d 168 (Tex. 1987).
[12]Bailey v. King, 398 S.W.2d 906, 908 (Ark. 1966).

NONCOMPETITION AGREEMENTS 411

employer cannot, for example, threaten termination to prevent an employee from exercising rights under a stock option plan.

ANTISOLICITATION AGREEMENTS

Antisolicitation agreements are a form of covenant not to compete that prohibit people who sell goods or services on behalf of an employer from soliciting former customers or clients after leaving the employer. A former employee's ability to attract the customers can threaten the former employer's business. **Most courts have held that an employer has a legitimate interest in enforcing an antisolicitation agreement when the former employee may be able to divert all or part of the business.** The assessment of this risk includes consideration of the extent to which the customer is likely to identify the product or service being sold with the employee rather than the employer. The nature, extent, and locale of the employee's contacts with customers are relevant considerations.

The nature of the employee's contact with customers includes consideration of the quality of the employee-customer contacts, ranging from door-to-door sales of basic consumer goods to the work of an account executive at an advertising agency specifically assigned to assess a client's needs. The risk to an employer arises in situations where the employee works closely with the client or customer over a long period of time.

Also relevant is the extent to which the employee's services are a significant part of the total transaction. In situations where there are substantial services performed by the salesperson, there is a greater identification likely in the customer's mind. For example, in one case,[13] a court held that a salesperson in the seismographing and core bit drilling branches of the petroleum industry was engaged in highly specialized, individually cultivated sales, where an unprotected employee-customer relationship could seriously threaten the employer. Similarly, one court has found that salespeople of water treatment products were in an industry where the personal relationships between the salesperson and the customer and the service record developed by the salesperson were of paramount importance.[14]

---

[13]Spinks v. Riebold, 310 S.W.2d 668 (Tex. App. 1958).
[14]Olin Water Servs. v. Midland Research Labs., 596 F. Supp. 412, 415 (E.D. Ark. 1984), *appeal dismissed as moot and remanded*, 774 F.2d 303 (8th Cir. 1985).

To evaluate the extent of the customer contact courts consider how often and how regularly the salesperson contacts the firm's customers. Continuous or constant contact between the salesperson and the client contributes to a protectable employer interest. In contrast, a restraint would not be justifiable when repeat sales are less common, as with residential real estate or major household appliances.

Finally, the site of the employee-customer contact is relevant to the court's decision whether to enforce an antisolicitation agreement. A court is less likely to grant the restraint in situations where the customer interacts with the salesperson on the premises of the employer's business because customers are less likely to direct their loyalty primarily to the employee.

Employers have been more successful in obtaining restraints on former employees when they have taken lists of customers and or lists of expiration dates for service contracts with them upon leaving employment. Conversely, the failure to take any lists is evidence of the salesperson's independence from the firm's resources during subsequent competition with the firm. In an Alabama case,[15] for example, the court refused to enforce a covenant against an insurance agent because he had not taken any lists with him on termination.

TRADE SECRETS

An employee is not privileged to take trade secrets from an employer, with or without an enforceable noncompetition or antisolicitation agreement. Trade secrets are distinguishable from the employee's general skill and expertise. For example, if a salesperson took a customer list that the firm had assembled, it may be protected as a trade secret. Even if the former employee had not signed an antisolicitation agreement, the employer may be able to restrain the former employee from use of a trade secret.

The law concerning trade secrets is related to the principles of trademark and patent law, but the protection of trade secrets is more comprehensive. **Unlike patents, a trade secret need not be novel; rather, the essence of a trade secret is its relative secrecy.** Additionally, unlike patent law, trade secret law draws less from the principles

---

[15]Sheffield v. Stoudenmire, 553 So. 2d 125 (Ala. 1989).

of property and more from the principles governing confidential relationships.

The types of information employers have sought to claim as trade secrets fall into two groups. One group is customer lists, organizational practices, and those items akin to goodwill. The other is formulas, designs, and other more technical information more closely related to patentable items.

Any individual can be liable for the disclosure or use of a trade secret in the absence of a privilege to do so. Such liability can occur if (1) the individual discovered the secret by improper means, (2) the disclosure or use constitutes a breach of confidence, or (3) the secret came from a third person under improper circumstances.

It is not possible to provide an exact definition of trade secret. Courts consider several factors, including the extent to which the information is known inside and outside the particular business, the cost of developing the information, the ease or difficulty with which the information could be properly acquired or duplicated by others, and measures taken by the employer to guard the secrecy of the information.

The Uniform Trade Secret Act[16] has been adopted in 35 states.[17] Under section 3426.1(d), a trade secret is any information, including a formula, pattern, compilation, program, device, method, technique, or process that:

> (1) Derives independent economic value, actual or potential, from not being generally known to the public or to other persons who can obtain economic value from its disclosure or use; and

> (2) Is the subject of efforts that are reasonable under the circumstances to maintain its secrecy.

Under this definition, information need only be valuable by virtue of its relative secrecy and be reasonably protected in order to qualify as a trade secret.

Secrecy is a key element, but the secrecy need not be absolute. The efforts expended to protect the secrecy are more important than the

---

[16]Uniform Trade Secrets Act tit. 18, §1905 (1988).
[17]Alaska, Arizona, Arkansas, California, Colorado, Connecticut, Delaware, Florida, Hawaii, Idaho, Illinois, Indiana, Idaho, Kansas, Kentucky, Louisiana, Maine, Maryland, Minnesota, Mississippi, Montana, Nebraska, Nevada, New Hampshire, New Mexico, North Dakota, Oklahoma, Oregon, Rhode Island, South Dakota, Utah, Virginia, Washington, West Virginia, and Wisconsin.

relative success of those efforts. One need not go to "heroic" lengths to guard secrecy in order to achieve trade secret status.

The Minnesota Supreme Court has discussed the effort necessary to maintain secrecy in *Electro-Craft Corp. v. Controlled Motion, Inc.*[18] The court noted that some effort to guard secrecy was required in order to prevent employers from holding their employees in "mental bondage." A mere intention to maintain secrecy is therefore insufficient to confer trade secret status.

The necessary amount of effort to maintain secrecy varies with the circumstances. The court in *Electro-Craft* drew a distinction between "obvious" trade secrets such as formulas and "non-intuitive" secrets, such as motor dimensions. An "obvious" trade secret requires little effort at protection, whereas a "non-intuitive" one requires substantially more effort at protection. The idea is that efforts at guarding secrecy should be at least enough to place employees on notice that they cannot take the information with them.

The definitions and guiding factors are helpful, but the cases applying them offer little in the way of consistency. For example, in *American Paper & Packaging Products v. Kirgan*,[19] the court held that a list of customers who operate manufacturing concerns and who need shipping supplies was not a trade secret because it was "known or readily ascertainable" to other persons in the shipping business. The court further noted that "the compilation process [was] neither sophisticated nor difficult nor particularly time consuming."

Other cases have looked to the efforts made by the owner to protect the secrecy of the list. In *Allied Supply Co. v. Brown*[20] the Alabama Supreme Court refused to extend trade secret protection to a customer list. Although the court recognized that such a list could be a trade secret, the employer must have made reasonable efforts to protect the secrecy of the information. The employer in *Allied* had permitted multiple copies of the list to be made, permitted employees to take the lists home, and had failed to mark the copies "confidential" or the like. The court regarded this behavior as an insufficient effort under the circumstances to guard the secrecy of the list, and therefore it was not a trade secret.

---

[18]332 N.W.2d 890 (Minn. 1983).
[19]228 Cal. Rptr. 713 (Ct. App. 1986).
[20]585 So. 2d 33 (Ala. 1991).

In *Dionne v. Southeast Foam Converting & Packaging, Inc.*,[21] a family business turned into a family feud when one of the brothers who helped develop the company's principal product left the firm to start a competing business. The court emphasized that secrecy, not novelty, is the essence of a trade secret, and although the defendant-brother helped develop the product, the closely knit, confidential nature of a family business left no doubt that the product was to be a trade secret. By contrast, another court found that a collection of computer programs, each of which was in the public domain (and therefore hardly secret), was nevertheless a trade secret because of the novel way in which they had been linked.[22]

An additional consideration stems from the inherent conflict between the principles of trade secret law and those manifested in antitrust law. Trade secret law is premised on the idea that, as a matter of sound public policy, innovation and technological development should be encouraged. Thus, trade secret law was developed for the purpose of protecting rights in trade secrets and to foster innovation. On the other hand, antitrust law serves to encourage competition rather than to preserve a marketplace advantage.

These policies conflict sharply in situations where an individual seeks to compete with a former employer. Although the former employer is entitled to have its trade secrets protected, the law is reluctant to deprive an individual of the means of a livelihood. Consequently, court orders prohibiting the use of former employers' trade secrets have been narrowly drawn to avoid depriving individuals of the opportunity to earn a living.

COPYRIGHTS

Employee-designers and their employer-commissioner counterparts often become involved in disputes over who has the right to copyright a work produced by the former for the use of the latter. These disputes fall within the purview of the federal Copyright Act,[23] which preempts all state laws covering the same or equivalent rights.

---

[21]397 S.E.2d 110, 17 USPQ2d 1565 (Va. 1990).
[22]Computer Assocs. Int'l, Inc. v. Bryan, 784 F. Supp. 982 (E.D.N.Y. 1992).
[23]17 U.S.C. §§101–914 (1988).

Ordinarily, the right to copyright belongs to the author or authors of the work. The Copyright Act, however, creates an important exception in the employer/employee context for "works made for hire." **Section 201(b) vests the right to copyright such works in the employer or commissioner, unless the parties expressly agree otherwise.**

Section 101 of the Act defines "work made for hire" as:

> (1) a work prepared by an employee within the scope of his or her employment; or

> (2) a work specially ordered or commissioned for use as a contribution to a collective work, as a part of a motion picture or other audiovisual work, as a translation, as a supplementary work, as a compilation, as an instructional text, as a test, as answer material for a test, or as an atlas, if the parties expressly agree in a written instrument signed by them that the work shall be considered a work made for hire.

Because the exception in section 201(b) changes the right to ownership of a copyright, whether a work qualifies as a work made for hire is of crucial importance. The situation described in section 101(2) is fairly clear-cut—the work must be part of a collective piece and subject to an express written agreement covering the work's status. The more important (and difficult) provision is section 101(1). By its terms, a work's status depends on how one characterizes the relationship between the author and the commissioner. A work made for hire under this provision must stem from an employment relationship.

Prior to 1988, the lower federal courts were split as to what test to use in characterizing the relationship between the parties as it pertained to section 101(1). Some courts held that, for purposes of copyright law, employees were those individuals receiving formal salaries. Others looked to the degree of supervision and control exercised over the work. Yet a third approach was to look to general principles of agency law.

In 1988, the Supreme Court resolved this conflict in *Community for Creative Non-Violence v. Reid*.[24] CCNV commissioned Reid to create a sculpture based on a modern nativity motif devised by CCNV. Although Reid accepted some suggestions from CCNV personnel regarding pose and general setting, Reid retained control over the actual creation of the work. There were no discussions of the possibility of copyrighting the

---

[24] 490 U.S. 730 (1989).

work, and both parties filed competing copyright claims following its completion. Thus, at trial the issue was whether the sculpture was a "work made for hire." The Court concluded that the appropriate test was the third one, basing the characterization on the "general common law of agency."

A "servant" is defined as "a person employed to perform services in the affairs of another and who with respect to the physical conduct in the performance of the services is subject to the other's control or right to control."[25] Among the factors a court is to consider are:

- the extent of control which, by the agreement, the master may exercise over the details of the work;

- whether or not the one employed is engaged in a distinct occupation or business;

- the kind of occupation, with reference to whether, in the locality, the work is usually done under the direction of the employer or by a specialist without supervision;

- the skill required in the occupation;

- whether the employer or the workman supplies the instrumentalities, tools, and the place of work for the person doing the work;

- the length of time for which the person is employed;

- the method of payment, whether by the time or by the job;

- whether or not the work is a part of the regular business of the employer;

- whether or not the parties believe they are creating the relation of master and servant;

- whether the principal is or is not in business.[26]

Although the *Reid* Court referred to most of these considerations, it should be noted that the list is not exclusive. Moreover, no one factor alone is determinative.

Applying these principles, for example, a court held that a photographer commissioned by a trade magazine to photograph jewelry was an

---

[25]*Restatement (Second) of Agency* §220(1) (1958).
[26]*Id.* §220(2).

independent contractor, so his photographs were not "works for hire."[27] In applying the *Reid* factors, the court noted that the photographer used his own equipment, paid his own taxes, supplied his own studio, did not receive employee benefits, worked in a distinct occupation, and was paid by the job. These factors militated in favor of his status as an independent contractor. On the other hand, the publisher supplied the jewelry, props, models, sketches intended to describe the exact composition of the photographs, and, at some sessions, an art director to "supervise" the mood. The court said that these factors were not determinative because the publisher controlled only the details of the subject matter and the composition of the images, and the control did not extend to most aspects of the photographic work including choice of light, sources, filters, lenses, camera, film, perspective, aperture setting, shutter speed, and processing techniques.

PATENTS

A variety of employer-employee conflicts have arisen in the context of intellectual property falling within the scope of patent law. Certainly, an employee who invents something has an interest in the rights that attach to that invention. Likewise, an employer that furnishes the time, equipment, expertise, and other assistance also has an interest in those rights.

Ordinarily, when an employee creates a new invention, the rights to the patent, which are tantamount to actual ownership of the invention itself, reside in the employee. **The mere existence of an employment relationship does not automatically entitle the employer to assignment of the patents to inventions created by its employees.** Thus, when the employment relationship is said to be "general"—when the employee has been hired for purposes other than to invent—the patent properly belongs to the employee. Two important exceptions exist to this general rule.

One exception vests the patent in the employer when the employee was hired for the specific purpose of creating the invention or solving the particular problem. It is a "true" exception, because application of the rule results in the employee being completely divested of ownership of the invention.

---

[27]Marco v. Accent Publishing Co., 969 F.2d 1547 (3d Cir. 1992).

This rule applies to situations other than "general" employment. In *Wommack v. Durham Pecan Co.*,[28] the company hired Wommack to work as a janitor in its pecan-processing plant. While there, Wommack observed the difficulty the line workers experienced in removing worms from the nuts and the resulting inefficiency of the process. He then devised a method to treat the nuts so that the worms are easily identified under black light. Because Wommack was hired as a janitor, his employment was general, and the resulting patent belonged to him, not the company. Had the company hired Wommack as an engineer to solve its efficiency problem, his employment would have been specific, and the company would have been entitled to the patent.

Wommack nevertheless lost because he was subject to the other exception, the "shop-right" doctrine. The shop-right doctrine is based on the presumption that, when an employee creates an invention at work, the employer has contributed to the invention through materials, equipment, and the like. Under the shop-right doctrine, the employer gains an equitable, nonexclusive right to use the invention. The doctrine is not a true exception to the original rule, because the employee is not divested of ownership of the invention. It is, however, an exception *to the patent itself*, because the employer retains a right to use the invention, royalty-free. Thus, Wommack could keep the patent, but the company was entitled to use the process under the shop-right doctrine.

Unlike copyright, the shop-right rule does not turn on the existence of a true employment relationship. The New Jersey Supreme Court considered this principle in *Ingersoll-Rand Co. v. Ciavatta*.[29] The *Ciavatta* case pertained to a "holdover" agreement on inventions developed after the employee left employment. Under the agreement, the employee promised to assign his rights in inventions created during a specified period following termination, if the invention was conceived as a result of or was attributable to work done during employment. The court held that the validity of the agreement turned on its reasonableness. It held that a holdover clause is unreasonable if it: (1) extends beyond any apparent protection that the employer reasonably requires, (2) prevents the inventor from seeking other employment, or (3) adversely impacts the public.

---

[28]715 F.2d 962 (5th Cir. 1983).
[29]542 A.2d 879 (N.J. 1988).

The court recognized that the rules governing holdover agreements are closely related to the rules governing trade secrets. Both involve the conflict between the interest in protecting the employer's innovation and the employee's right to earn a living after termination. It is from this conflict that the reasonableness requirement is derived. The idea is to balance the protection against unfair employment restrictions with the equitable concern that an employee will take ideas so related to prior work that in good conscience they should belong to the former employer.

8

Wrongful Discharge

INTRODUCTION

In a treatise published in 1877, Horace G. Wood stated that an employee who did not have an employment contract for a fixed term could be fired at any time for good cause, bad cause, or no cause at all.[1] American courts quickly adopted this "employment at will" concept and applied it to all workers who were not guaranteed continued employment in individual employment contracts.

The courts consistently followed the employment at will approach well into the second half of the twentieth century, although three developments undoubtedly influenced the later course of employment law. First, the legal recognition of unions in the National Labor Relations Act of 1935 meant that employees could bargain collectively for job security. As a result of collectively bargained agreements, a substantial percentage of the private sector work force became subject to discharge only for "just cause," with arbitration to resolve grievances. Second, the emergence of civil service protection for state and local government employees increased even further the number of workers who could not be fired arbitrarily. Third, major civil rights legislation enacted in the 1960s gave further support to the notion that unchallenged

---

[1]*See* Wood, H.G. *A Treatise on the Law of Master and Servant* (1877).

employer prerogative in hiring and firing decisions had to give way to other social interests.

The first major nonstatutory crack in the employment at will rule came in 1959. An at-will employee who was fired after he refused to commit perjury on his employer's orders sued the employer. The California Court of Appeal held that the right to fire an at-will employee could be restricted by statute or public policy.[2] During the last two decades, a series of state court decisions challenged unfair discharges with a variety of legal theories. Gradually three major "exceptions" to the at-will doctrine emerged. They are (1) breach of an express or implied promise, including representations made in employee handbooks; (2) breach of the implied covenant of good faith and fair dealing; and (3) wrongful discharge in violation of public policy.

Courts do not always agree upon the exact scope or nature of the three major employment at will exceptions established in judicial decisions. Suits based on express or implied contract obligations are generally regarded as contract actions, as are legal actions based on implied covenants of good faith and fair dealing. Claims based on public policy, however, are more likely to be viewed as tort actions. While parties adversely affected by contract breaches are normally limited to actual damages that are designed to compensate them for their lost bargain, people asserting tort claims may often obtain more expansive monetary relief based on the desire of courts to vindicate the social policies involved. As a result, tort claimants may even obtain punitive damage awards that are intended to punish the policy violators and to deter others who might contemplate such socially inappropriate behavior.

The Fifth and Fourteenth Amendments to the U.S. Constitution prohibit, among other things, government action that deprives persons of property rights without due process. In *Cleveland Board of Education v. Loudermill*,[3] the Supreme Court acknowledged that many federal, state, and local government employees have a property right to continued employment. As a result, government employers may not dismiss employees who have reasonable expectations of ongoing employment without affording them due process.

---

[2]Petermann v. Teamsters Local 396, 344 P.2d 25, 1 IER Cases 5 (Cal. App. 1959).

[3]470 U.S. 532 (1985).

WRITTEN CONTRACTS

Most employees do not have individual employment contracts; they are hired on an at-will basis and enjoy no employment tenure. Some company executives and a few highly skilled professionals, however, are able to obtain written contracts governing their employment relationships. These contracts usually specify a minimum term of employment and indicate that the covered individuals may not be terminated before the end of that period except for cause. Individuals who have written contracts may bring breach of contract lawsuits if their employment is ended prematurely.

The first issue that must be addressed in these cases concerns the actual existence of an enforceable contract. The dissatisfied employees must demonstrate that they and their employer entered into written agreements specifying their employment terms. The next issue is whether any terms of the contract have been breached. Individuals employed under a contract for a definite term may not be fired before the expiration of the term except for cause, unless the contract specifically states a different rule. Therefore, employees must establish that their contracts provide them with employment for a definite term of months or years. This is critical, because written contracts that fail to specify any duration will normally be regarded as terminable at will by either party.

Courts are not in agreement concerning the impact of written statements in employment contracts or confirmation letters indicating that the employees are to receive monthly or annual salaries. Some decisions treat such language as creating employment security for a minimum of one month or one year. Other decisions, however, refuse to do so. They require additional evidence suggesting that the contracting parties intended the stated compensation to create more than employment at will relationships. **Individuals who wish to obtain term agreements with for-cause protection should carefully specify the term of employment involved. On the other hand, employers who wish to avoid unintended term relationships should include language expressly preserving the right of either party to terminate the relationship at any time for any reason.**

People who sue to enforce written employment contracts occasionally claim that their written terms were affected by oral promises of employment for a minimum period of time or a promise of reappointment if they performed their work satisfactorily. If the written documents appear to represent the entire understanding of the parties, courts generally will not consider oral representations made before or after execution of the written agreements. In the absence of fraudulent misrepresentations that were deliberately designed to induce persons to think they were actually entering into term arrangements, courts almost always look exclusively to the written documents themselves. If the documents do not suggest a mutual intent to create more than at-will relationships, courts usually find no continuing employment rights.

Companies sometimes ask new employees to sign form employment contracts. These may contain ambiguous terms that might suggest both term appointments and at-will arrangements. **Firms that use form agreements must recognize that courts tend to construe these contracts against the parties that drafted them**. As a result, if these documents suggest employment for a minimal period of time, courts may decide to enforce those term provisions despite the presence of contrary provisions indicating at-will relationships.

Some written contracts contain provisions indicating that they continue in force until either party gives the other advance notice of an intention to terminate the relationship. If no notice is provided, courts generally find ongoing arrangements that may not be terminated. On the other hand, once proper notice is given, the relationship becomes for a definite term ending at the conclusion of the notice period. During the notice period the employer must have cause to fire the employee.

REPRESENTATIONS IN EMPLOYMENT MANUALS

As small shops began to expand into larger corporations, business firms created centralized personnel departments to monitor employment-related issues. These departments developed employment manuals or handbooks to inform all workers of basic company policies. Group meetings were used to review applicable personnel rules. The vast majority of contemporary companies have written employment manuals that are amplified by oral discussions conducted by personnel representatives.

Some employment manuals merely contain general statements regarding firm personnel policies. Others, however, include specific language describing detailed evaluation policies, disciplinary practices, and internal appeal procedures. Some include statements indicating that workers with satisfactory performance may expect continued employment so long as favorable economic conditions exist.

Prior to the 1980s, courts were generally unwilling to permit employees to bring breach of contract lawsuits based on statements set forth in employment manuals. The courts did not believe that the affected employees had given the company anything of value ("consideration") in exchange for the firm's promises articulated in these handbooks. The mere fact that these individuals performed their regular job functions was not considered sufficient to convert personnel manual representations into legally enforceable obligations. Courts also thought it would be unfair to impose binding duties regarding continued employment on employers while workers were free to resign at any time for any reason. Judges thus continued to apply the traditional employment at will doctrine despite contrary language set forth in employment manuals.

During the 1980s, many courts began to recognize that promises made in written employment handbooks could generate express or implied contractual obligations that could be legally enforced. Most contemporary courts are now willing to enforce clear employment representations contained in employment manuals. Some courts, however, still find such statements unenforceable absent some additional benefit given by the affected workers to their employer in exchange for those handbook protections.

Courts that are willing to enforce representations made in employment manuals normally use either of two legal theories to render those statements binding on employers. Some find that personnel handbook statements may be viewed as unilateral offers that are accepted by continued employee performance. Once workers remain with their employer after issuance of the handbook, they have provided consideration, and the policies embodied in those pronouncements become legally binding.

Judicial decisions also use the reliance theory to render handbook representations enforceable. When employers make statements that are reasonably designed to encourage employees to remain with the firm and that actually induce them to do so, the employees' reliance on those policies converts the employer promises into binding obligations. These individuals have effectively foregone other potential employment opportunities to retain the protections afforded them in the personnel handbooks.

Communication to Employees

An employer policy cannot be considered an offer unless it is communicated to employees. Obviously, an employee handbook or personnel manual that the employer distributes to all employees has been adequately communicated, whereas a policy that is never distributed or otherwise made known to employees has not. Most courts will not permit rank-and-file workers to base breach of contract claims on the terms of policies circulated only to supervisors and not otherwise made known to them.

Although communication of the handbook is necessary for a valid offer, many courts do not require that an employee have actually made a reasoned decision to continue to work in reliance on the promises in the handbook. It is enough that the employee merely continues to work after the handbook is issued. These courts express concern that requiring actual reliance would result in protection only for those employees who actually read the handbook, and not for the others.

Language Needed to Create an Enforceable Contract

When employees bring breach of contract lawsuits claiming that their unwarranted terminations contravened promises of continued employment contained in employment handbooks, courts must determine whether they had any reasonable expectation of ongoing employment. They review the handbook language to ascertain whether it appears to indicate that workers would be retained for as long as their performance was acceptable. Oral representations explaining the import of the relevant handbook provisions will also be considered. When ambiguous language is involved, courts tend to construe it against the employers that drafted the handbook provisions in question.

Reasonable expectations of continued employment are often raised by handbook terms that indicate that workers may only be terminated for "just cause." Most courts hold that such language prohibits discharges that are not based on valid reasons. Expectations of employment security may also be created by detailed provisions that list specific grounds for discharge, because the implication is that persons who do not violate these specific proscriptions will be retained by the firm. A number of court decisions have held unlawful discharge decisions that were not based on the listed factors. On the other hand, if the handbook describes the stated grounds for termination as illustrative, rather than exhaustive, courts may sustain firings based on other similarly offensive behavior.

Sometimes descriptions of the standards of behavior and performance expected of employees is found to be the equivalent of a for-cause standard. In one case,[4] the employee handbook stated that all actions affecting employees "shall be based solely on merit, ability (performance) and justice," and "an employee who provides unsatisfactory service or who is guilty of substantial violation of regulations shall be subject to dismissal without prior notice." The court found that this language described a for-cause standard and limited the employer's ability to fire at will.

Some employment manuals set forth progressive disciplinary steps to be followed when workers engage in misconduct. They may begin with oral or written warnings, progress to suspensions, and conclude with discharge. If courts find that employees were induced to believe that these procedures would be followed prior to termination, they may find that discharges failing to comport with the stated progressive steps are a breach of contract. **If companies with progressive discipline programs wish to retain the unfettered right to fire individuals for particular conduct without the need for prior discipline, they should say so expressly in their handbook provisions**.

Revision and Revocation of Handbook Promises

Firms with handbook language promising limits on the right to fire at will may decide to revise or revoke those sections. Although employers must comply with unrevoked promises of job security contained in a handbook, they are free unilaterally to change those promises at any time, as long as they do so properly. The same theory that permits employees to rely on handbook promises—continued employment after the handbook is issued—permits employers to revoke them. Once employees have received the revisions or amendments and continue to work for the company, the new terms become the employment contract between the parties. **Amendments must be carefully**

---

[4]Cummings v. South Portland Housing Auth., 985 F.2d 1 (1st Cir. 1993).

**drafted and communicated to all employees, and all contrary
language should be simultaneously eliminated.**

Employers must be precise in the language they use to revise or
revoke handbook promises. In one case,[5] the original handbook contained a progressive discipline system and representations of "maximum job security." A few years later the employer issued a revised
handbook with a disclaimer stating that the handbook was "not intended
to create, nor should be construed to constitute, a contract of employment between the Company and any one or all of its personnel." The
court said that this language did not adequately explain how it affected
the original representations of job security and therefore did not
effectively create at-will status.

It is important to note that employers may not unilaterally modify
or revoke rights that employees have already earned, such as vacation
pay. Courts do not, however, place job security in the category of earned
or accrued rights. As long as the employer does not manipulate the
timing of a handbook amendment in order to retaliate against a particular employee, employers are free to eliminate promises of job security.

Disclaimers

Some employers attempt to avoid handbook problems by including disclaimers indicating that nothing in the manuals should be read as
creating any right to continued employment and expressly reserving the
right to terminate employees at any time for any reason. Even when
specific disclaimers are included, however, firms may encounter difficulties if other handbook provisions or oral representations contain
contrary language suggesting the creation of more permanent relationships. When other handbook sections or verbal statements cause employees reasonably to think their positions are secure so long as their
performance is acceptable, courts may enforce those promises despite
the presence of disclaimer clauses. Judges usually review the entire
handbook to determine the overall impression given to employees.

If disclaimer provisions are prominently displayed, courts are
more likely to respect those sections than if they are not so conspicuous.
A few firms attempt to deal with this issue by providing new workers

---

[5]Preston v. Claridge Hotel & Casino, Ltd., 555 A.2d 12, 4 IER Cases 493 (N.J.
Super. 1989).

with written disclaimers that explicitly preserve the employment at will concept. Many of these companies require new personnel to sign forms acknowledging that they have received and understand these disclaimer provisions.

Employees who wish to challenge the propriety of their terminations may use different techniques to avoid the impact of disclaimer clauses. They may emphasize specific handbook provisions indicating that satisfactory workers will enjoy continued employment security. They may cite oral assurances suggesting similar protection. They may rely on progressive disciplinary procedures that have not been satisfied or on detailed provisions listing the exclusive acts for which individuals may be summarily discharged.

Companies with employment manuals should carefully review their handbooks to be certain they are not promising employees greater job security than is actually intended. **Disclaimers preserving at-will relationships should be prominently and unambiguously stated.** Managers should be certain that employer agents do not provide new workers with oral representations counteracting the disclaimer language. They should also emphasize the establishment of at-will arrangements at the time new personnel are hired, not weeks or months thereafter.

Firms with handbook provisions giving employees unlimited employment tenure may decide to modify those sections. They must carefully draft the modified terms and transmit those terms to all employees, and all contrary language should be simultaneously eliminated. Once companies explicitly notify workers that they will henceforth be considered at-will personnel, those businesses should be able to rely on the amended terms with respect to future employment decisions.

ORAL CONTRACTS

Under traditional employment at will decisions, courts rarely found oral statements regarding continued employment sufficient to rebut the legal presumption that the relationship could be terminated by either party at any time for any reason. As courts have recognized the legal enforceability of promises contained in written contracts and in employee handbooks, however, some have evidenced a willingness to reconsider the status of oral representations concerning job security.

Few wrongful discharge cases are based exclusively on oral statements. Most concern claims based on express or implied promises set forth in written handbooks. Employees often enhance their handbook claims with oral statements that purportedly explained the rights given them in handbook provisions. Judges frequently permit the introduction of such evidence to determine whether the employees were induced to believe they would not be terminated except for just cause.

Courts have recently acknowledged that oral promises of continued employment may themselves be legally enforceable, so long as the affected workers can demonstrate the existence of clear and definite terms. The employees must prove that they reached a mutual understanding with their employer. The oral contract must normally specify the duration of the intended relationship and the applicable salary. It must also be clear that the worker has accepted those terms and agreed to perform specified job functions in return for the employer's promises.

Oral representations made during prehire interviews and at the time job offers are being made and accepted are usually relied on to establish verbal contracts of employment. Courts must decide whether employer agents have told new employees they would only be discharged for cause or could expect continued employment if their performance was satisfactory. Similar issues might arise with respect to statements made to induce current employees to reject offers from other companies and remain with their present firm.

Some courts do not find mere employee promises to perform their jobs sufficient "consideration" to support the enforceability of oral company representations concerning ongoing employment. A growing number of courts, however, do consider satisfactory performance adequate to sustain such company statements. In these states, the affected workers must merely demonstrate the existence of the alleged oral promises.

Statute of Frauds

Almost all states have enacted laws modeled on the English Statute of Frauds of 1677. Statute of frauds provisions generally require agreements that are not to be performed within one year to be embodied in written documents if they are to be enforceable. As a result, oral contracts that have a duration exceeding one year are normally unenforceable. Most courts that have considered the legal enforceability of oral employment contracts have refused to permit employers to use Statutes of Frauds to defeat otherwise valid worker claims.

Some judges accomplish this result by finding Statutes of Frauds inapplicable to employment agreements that *could be* completely performed in less than one year. Because workers might resign, retire, or be discharged during the first year of their employment, these courts decline to find that their contracts are for more than one year in length. Other courts accomplish the same result by distinguishing between agreements for definite and indefinite terms. While contracts for definite terms exceeding one year must be in writing to be enforced, accords for indefinite terms do not have to be. These decisions at least implicitly recognize that employment contracts for indefinite terms could be completed within one year if the parties ended their relationships within 12 months.

A few courts use the doctrine of reliance to prevent employers from using Statute of Frauds arguments to defeat otherwise valid employee contract claims. This doctrine applies when workers rely to their detriment on promises made by their employer. Typical cases involve workers who have rejected outside job offers in response to promises from their current employer for continued employment security if they remain with that firm.

CONTRACTS IMPLIED FROM CONDUCT

In some situations in which workers and their employer do not have formal employment contracts, courts may imply contractual obligations from the overall conduct of the parties themselves. These implied-in-fact contracts may arise from oral representations made by employer agents, statements contained in employee handbooks, or specific circumstances of the employer-employee relationship that suggest restrictions on traditional employment at will arrangements. This theory can be used by employees who may reasonably believe they have been promised job security, but who cannot point to any explicit words to that effect. Even when employees can point to express oral promises or handbook provisions, their claims may well be bolstered by proof of other employer conduct consistent with these representations.

For instance, in *Morriss v. Coleman Cos.*,[6] male and female co-workers who were not married to each other were fired after their supervisor learned they had taken an overnight trip together. They sued for breach of an implied contract of discharge for cause only and based their claim on the employer's personnel manual, the employer's established method of dealing with employees, and other verbal and nonverbal conduct indicating tht the employer would treat its employees fairly. The Kansas Supreme Court held that the employees had raised legitimate issues concerning the existence of a contract, implied from the course of conduct between the company and its employees, not to fire employees without just cause.

Similarly, in *Kestenbaum v. Pennzoil Co.*,[7] the New Mexico Supreme Court held that oral statements made by an employer may be sufficient to create an implied just cause contract. The employee had a variety of evidence to establish that his employment contract was for an indefinite period of time and allowed dismissal only for a good reason. First, Kestenbaum showed that during his initial employment negotiations, his supervisor said that the employment would be long-term and permanent as long as he did his job. Second, company officials testified that the company fired permanent employees only for "a good reason, a just cause." Third, both the insurance benefits manual and the employee handbook contained provisions describing conversion privileges after termination of employment, but neither manual mentioned termination without cause.

Courts are usually unwilling to enforce oral limitations on employer action unless the verbal representations regarding employment security are definitive. General statements about good employer-employee relations are unlikely to create judicially enforceable obligations, but specific statements concerning the right to continuing employment if work performance is acceptable or indicating that individuals can only be discharged for "good cause" may generate implied contractual duties.

Employees attempting to rely on implied-in-fact contractual duties to preserve their jobs must demonstrate that they received clear expressions of continuing employment security. They may prove that

---

[6]738 P.2d 841, 2 IER Cases 844 (Kan. 1987).

[7]766 P.2d 280, 4 IER Cases 67 (N.M. 1988), *cert. denied*, 490 U.S. 1109, 4 IER Cases 672 (1989).

company agents orally promised them that they would not lose their jobs if their performance was satisfactory or that they would only be discharged for cause. They might alternatively cite written employee manual representations of a similar nature. Because U.S. courts continue to assume the existence of at-will relationships in the absence of specific indications to the contrary, workers must usually present definitive representations before courts are likely to impose implied restrictions on the traditional right of their employer to terminate their employment at any time. Mere statements to new employees that the company expects a long and mutually rewarding relationship would probably be insufficient.

The fact that individuals have maintained satisfactory employment relationships with the same company for a number of years may assist them in establishing implied-in-fact contracts. Judges usually assume that such long-term workers have received written or oral statements indicating that their performance has been satisfactory. They may also have been given some assurances of continuing employment during their periodic evaluations. When long, established relationships are involved, courts have a greater tendency to find implied promises of continuing job security from less definitive statements that might not be sufficient to protect the rights of short-term personnel. It is thus important for company agents to be careful when reviewing employee performance to avoid the use of phrases that might induce those workers to think they are being promised unintended employment protection.

Pugh v. See's Candies, Inc.[8] provides a classic example. An employee who was discharged after 32 years of employment brought a wrongful termination suit. The court emphasized the factors from which the jury could have found the existence of an implied promise that it would not treat its personnel unfairly: (1) the long period of satisfactory employment, (2) the commendations and promotions given to the worker, (3) the lack of any meaningful criticism of his performance, (4) the general assurances he was given, and (5) the employer's acknowledged practice of treating employees fairly. Although one or two years would probably be insufficient to support an implied contract claim to continuing employment, satisfactory performance over 10, 15, or 20 years would cause a number of courts to find implied contractual

---

[8]171 Cal. Rptr. 917 (Ct. App. 1981).

obligations from oral statements or employee manual provisions suggesting that workers would not be unfairly discharged. In most states, longevity of service alone, without additional employer communications about its significance, is not enough to establish an implied promise of job security. As a practical matter, however, it is unlikely that an employee who has performed acceptably for a long period of time has not received some communication, written or oral, of the employer's continued satisfaction that looks like a settled pattern of continued employment.

IMPLIED COVENANT OF GOOD FAITH AND FAIR DEALING

A small minority of jurisdictions (about one-fifth of the states, including California) recognize that the law reads into every employment contract an implied obligation on the parties to engage in good faith and fair dealing. Although the theory of an implied covenant of good faith and fair dealing is widely recognized as a principle of contract law, most courts have refused to apply the concept to employment contracts on the grounds that the doctrine is amorphous, too broad, and destructive of employer prerogatives.

The courts that have adopted this theory generally have used it to prevent employers from depriving employees of benefits the employees have earned. Consequently, most of the courts have held that the remedy for breach of the implied covenant is based on contract rather than tort.[9] Because there are no compensatory and punitive damages available, the awards are much smaller than in tort cases. This, in turn, makes lawyers less anxious to take such cases.

It is important to emphasize that even where the implied covenant theory is recognized, this does not impose a requirement that the employer must have good cause to terminate an at-will relationship.[10] Indeed, the improper motive or bad faith of the employer is the key element of this type of lawsuit. For example, in *Merrill v. Crothall-American, Inc.*,[11] the employer, which provided facilities management

---

[9]Foley v. Interactive Data Corp., 765 P.2d 373 (Cal. 1988).
[10]Carbone v. Atlantic Richfield Co., 528 A.2d 1137 (Conn. 1987).
[11]606 A.2d 96 (Del. 1992).

services for institutions such as schools and hospitals, had a contractual obligation to supply a Director of Plant Operations for a health care facility by October 14, 1986. On that date it offered the job to Mr. Merrill, even though he expressed concern about his qualifications. A few months later, Merrill was fired. In his lawsuit, Merrill alleged that the employer hired him because it needed a "warm body" to fill the position and never intended to employ him on a long-term basis. In fact, he contended that the employer was interviewing the person who replaced him only two days after he (Merrill) began work. He asserted that the employer induced him to take the job under the belief that the job, while at-will, would be of indefinite duration, all the while concealing its intention to employ him only temporarily. The Delaware Supreme Court held that Merrill had alleged a valid claim under the implied covenant of good faith and fair dealing. Here, it was the deceptive inducement that constituted the breach, and the firing was only the logical extension of that wrong.

CONSTRUCTIVE DISCHARGE

Ordinarily, an employee who quits his or her job does not have a claim for breach of contract or retaliatory discharge, because quitting is a voluntary act. If, however, the conditions that cause the employee to quit constitute a "constructive discharge," courts will treat the employee as if he or she had been fired. Most constructive discharge cases fall into one of two basic fact patterns. First, the employer can cause a constructive discharge by breaching the employee's contract of employment in some way other than firing the employee. Second, the employer can make working conditions so intolerable that the employee feels compelled to quit. It is important to remember that a constructive discharge is not a legal claim in and of itself. Proof that an employee who quit was really constructively discharged merely demonstrates that the employee was fired. The employee must still prove that the underlying circumstances that led him or her to quit were somehow wrongful.

Employer Breach of Contract

Most cases of constructive discharge caused by the employer's breach of contract involve employees who have express contracts of employment. If an employee was hired for a particular position, a major change in duties, a significant reduction of rank and responsibility, or a reassignment to another position will normally entitle the employee to quit and sue for damages. Another reason for a finding of a constructive discharge is the employer's refusal to pay agreed-upon wages.

Intolerable Working Conditions

A constructive discharge can also take place if the employee quits because of intolerable working conditions. Many cases involving this branch of the constructive discharge doctrine arise under the employment discrimination laws, where the intolerable conditions are the result of racial, ethnic, or sexual harassment.[12] The theory can apply equally to claims of retaliatory discharge or discharge in breach of contract, however.

Most courts require that the employer must have created or maintained working conditions so intolerable that any reasonable employee would have felt compelled to quit rather than endure them. A few courts also require the employee to prove that the employer created the intolerable conditions with the specific intent of forcing the employee to quit.

Relatively minor abuse of an employee is not enough to prove a constructive discharge. Unfavorable evaluations, criticisms of poor performance, transfers, and demotions, without more, do not justify an employee's resignation. Rather, the adverse conditions must be ongoing, repetitive, pervasive, and severe. In many cases, the intolerable working conditions that permit a finding of constructive discharge may also support a claim for intentional infliction of emotional distress.

As with the first branch of constructive discharge doctrine, an employee cannot prevail merely by proving the intolerable nature of the working conditions. The working conditions must be related to the facts supporting a claim of retaliatory discharge or breach of contract. For instance, the employee in *Kestell v. Heritage Health Care Corp.*[13] could be fired only for good cause. The court found that he was justified in quitting after the employer abruptly removed him from his office,

---

[12]See chapter 2.
[13]858 P.2d 3, 8 IER Cases 1233 (Mont. 1993).

isolated him in a remote area of its facility, and deprived him of any meaningful activity. The court said, however, that the employer's actions may have been justified by good cause; if they were, the employee would lose his claim, because a constructive discharge for good cause was not actionable.

JUST CAUSE

Issues of "just cause," or "good cause," or simply "cause" arise when an employee claims breach of the terms of an employment contract stating that discharge will be only for just cause. Just cause is based on contract, either express or implied. This includes written contracts, oral agreements, and employee handbooks or manuals. In some instances, the agreement will merely provide that the employee will not be fired except for just cause. In other instances, the agreement will define particular grounds for discharge, such as theft, absenteeism, and insubordination. As discussed earlier in this chapter in the section on employment handbooks, depending on the specific language used, courts may permit other, undefined reasons to constitute just cause.

Just cause may be divided into two categories: (1) business or economic reasons unrelated to the employee, and (2) employee miscon- duct or inadequate performance. The first category, economic reasons, is the easiest. If the employment agreement is for an indefinite term, a bona fide reduction in force or a plant closing or reorganization will establish just cause. On the other hand, a cessation of business due to poor economic conditions may not establish just cause for a discharge if the contract was for a definite term.

The second category, employee-based reasons for just cause, includes inadequate performance, as well as offenses against the em- ployer or its business, such as resume fraud, sexual harassment, fighting, drinking, assaulting a customer, and insubordination.

Not all employee misconduct will meet the standard for just cause, however. In general, the misconduct must be *substantial*. Thus, a minor neglect of duty, an excusable absence, a minor misrepresentation, rudeness, and even filing a defamation action against the employer have been held not to establish just cause. Moreover, in some situations, misconduct, such as the failure to follow unreasonable orders, may be justified. Courts are reluctant to find just cause based on employee activity off the job, unless there is a direct, adverse effect on the employer's business.

When the employer contends it fired an employee for reasons attributable to the employee, an issue closely related to whether the conduct amounts to just cause is whether the employee must actually have committed the acts for which he or she was fired. Some courts say that it is enough if the employer based the decision to fire on facts it reasonably believed to be true, while others require that the employee actually be guilty of the conduct.

Instead of providing for discharge only for just cause, some employment contracts permit discharge if an employee's performance is not "acceptable" or "satisfactory" to the employer. Courts generally agree that this "satisfaction" standard is inherently subjective and permits discharges as long as the employer is actually and in good faith dissatisfied with the employee. Employees fired under a satisfaction contract may win a breach of contract action only by showing that the employer was not in fact dissatisfied with them, or that the employer fired them for reasons other than dissatisfaction.

PUBLIC POLICY EXCEPTION

In General

The public policy exception to the employment at will doctrine provides that employers may not fire workers for reasons that violate public policy. The public policy exception does not give at-will employees the right to be fired only for cause; it simply protects employees from being fired for a reason that is against public policy. Public policy cases are sometimes called retaliatory discharge cases, because the employee may claim he or she was fired in retaliation for acting pursuant to public policy. Every state except Alabama, Florida, Georgia, Louisiana, New York, and Rhode Island recognizes some form of the public policy exception. The breadth of the exception varies from state to state, however, depending on what the courts of each state consider to be an important enough public policy to protect from retaliatory discharge. Courts generally find public policy in the state constitution, statutes, regulations, court decisions, or occasionally, in ethical codes.

Although the public policy exception is particularly important for private sector at-will employees, who have no contractual rights to job security, the protection of the exception extends to almost all types of employment relationships. Courts have recognized public policy protections as extending to public sector employees and to employees covered by collective bargaining agreements. The reason for this broad coverage is that the public policy exception derives from the overriding public significance of the policies themselves, and courts will not permit the protection to be bargained away.

While the courts of each state must decide whether and how to apply the public policy exception, most cases involving the exception can be grouped into four broad categories. These categories are:

- refusing to perform unlawful acts,
- reporting illegal activity (whistleblowing),
- exercising rights under state law, and
- performing a civic duty.

Some cases may fall into more than one category, and some may not fit neatly into any of them, but these four groups are a helpful way to think about state law on wrongful discharge. It is important to keep in mind that not every state recognizes every possible category of the public policy exception.

Refusing to Perform Unlawful Acts

Virtually all states that recognize the public policy exception apply it to the situation in which an employee is fired for disobeying an order to violate the law. In fact, this is the only exception recognized by Texas and the District of Columbia. The clearest example of this "illegal act" category occurs when an employee is fired for refusing to do something that would subject him or her to personal criminal liability. For instance, in one of the earliest public policy cases, *Petermann v. Teamsters Local 396*,[14] the employer fired an at-will employee when he disobeyed an order to commit perjury at a legislative hearing. The court reasoned

---

[14]344 P.2d 25, 1 IER Cases 5 (Cal. App. 1959).

that the employer's conduct violated the state's public policy of encouraging truthful testimony and therefore was an abuse of the employer's rights. The facts in *Petermann*, coercing an employee to commit the crime of perjury, for which he could have been imprisoned, are so compelling that the outcome is hard to question.

The rationale for the "illegal act" exception is to prevent an employer from placing an employee in the position of keeping a job only by performing the illegal act. The more clearly the public's interest is implicated, the more likely the courts are to permit the employee to recover. For example, in *Martin Marietta Corp. v. Lorenz*,[15] the employee was the principal investigator on several NASA projects, and one of his duties was to report quality control deficiencies. His employer fired him when he refused an order to misrepresent deficiencies to the government and to report false contract prices. Because carrying out the order would have violated specific provisions of a law prohibiting false statements to the United States, his discharge for refusal to obey his employer's order violated public policy.

The importance of finding a criminal law on which to base a retaliatory discharge action is illustrated by another famous case, *Wagenseller v. Scottsdale Memorial Hospital*.[16] Wagenseller was a staff nurse who went on a camping trip with her supervisor and other hospital workers. During the trip, she refused to participate in a skit parodying the song "Moon River," which concluded with members of the group "mooning" the audience. She claimed that afterwards her relationship with her supervisor deteriorated. Less than three months later she was fired. The Arizona Supreme Court held that she could bring a retaliatory discharge case based on her refusal to commit an act that might have violated the state law prohibiting indecent exposure.

Not all illegal act cases involve violations of criminal laws, however. Some laws and regulations provide only for civil penalties. Some punish only the employer that ordered the violation, not the employee who carried out the order. Some behavior might result in a civil suit brought by a private individual, but would not cause any governmental action against the employer or the employee. As the activity involved gets further away from the criminal law, courts may become more reluctant to find a discharge in breach of public policy.

---

[15]823 P.2d 100, 7 IER Cases 77 (Colo. 1992).
[16]710 P.2d 1025, 1 IER 526 (Ariz. 1985).

Despite this reluctance, courts have permitted suit in many situations in which the employee was not faced with personal criminal liability. For instance, courts have allowed wrongful discharge actions for employees' refusals to participate in the employer's theft scheme; to take part in predatory price setting in violation of antitrust laws; to alter data in pollution control reports submitted to a state agency; to pump a ship's contaminated bilges into open water in violation of federal law; to fix an advertised raffle; to drive an overloaded truck in violation of state maximum weight limits; and to falsify tax and customs documents.

Reporting Illegal Activity

The second major category of public policy exceptions to the employment at will rule involves employees who are fired because they have reported illegal or harmful activity. Three-quarters of the states have statutes protecting employee "whistleblowers" in some situations. These statutes are discussed later in this chapter. Even where no statute applies, however, many courts permit employees to bring retaliatory discharge actions under the public policy exception.

In these public policy whistleblower cases, courts often make a distinction between employees who report wrongdoing to an outside agency and those who report it within the company. **Courts are more likely to protect whistleblowing employees who report illegal activity to outside public bodies charged with policing the specific type of activity involved**. Employees tend to fare less well when they are fired for reporting information on wrongdoing to their superiors internally.

Reports to Outside Agencies

Most courts that recognize the public policy exception permit an employee who was fired for making a good faith report of wrongdoing to outside agencies to sue for discharge in violation of public policy. Usually, the employee has reported wrongdoing by his or her employer, although courts have applied the whistleblower exception to reports of misbehavior by fellow employees. For example, in *Palmateer v. International Harvester Co.*,[17] an employee was fired for supplying

---

[17]421 N.E.2d 876, 115 LRRM 4165 (Ill. 1981).

information to law enforcement officials about a co-worker's possible criminal behavior. The employee had also agreed to gather additional evidence implicating the co-worker and to testify at any criminal trial. The court emphasized that for public policy purposes, the nature of the crime was irrelevant. "[P]ublic policy . . . favors citizen crime fighters."

Similarly, in *Garibaldi v. Lucky Food Stores, Inc.*,[18] an employee claimed he was fired for reporting a shipment of adulterated milk to health authorities after his supervisors ordered him to deliver it. The court found that whistleblowing to protect the health and safety of the citizens of the state was exactly the type of conduct that the public policy exception to the employment at will rule was designed to protect.

The employer cannot avoid liability by firing the employee in anticipation that he or she might report wrongdoing to an outside agency. For example, an Oregon court held that a nursing home violated public policy when it fired a nurse who threatened to report abuse of patients to the state health department.[19] It was immaterial to the court that she was fired before she had actually filed a complaint.

Protests or Complaints Made Within the Company

While one might think employees would receive better treatment from the courts when they allow employers the opportunity to cure potential problems by taking steps internally instead of filing a report with an outside agency, employees actually tend to fare less well when they are fired for "internal whistleblowing."

The states that recognize the public policy exception for whistleblowing are divided about whether to protect an employee who reports alleged wrongdoing internally within the company. When courts deny protection, it is usually because they believe internal reporting does not implicate a strong public interest in the way that a report to a governmental official does. Rather, internal complaints about a corporate decision may merely reflect a difference of opinion between the employee and those with decision-making authority. Courts that reason in this manner require the employee to go outside the company

---

[18]726 F.2d 1367, 1 IER Cases 354 (9th Cir. 1984), *cert. denied*, 471 U.S. 1099, 1 IER Cases 848 (1985).

[19]McQuary v. Bel Air Convalescent Home, Inc., 684 P.2d 21, 120 LRRM 3129 (Or. App. 1984).

to report violations to some public authority before they can gain the protection of the public policy exception.

One of the best known internal whistleblowing cases is *Foley v. Interactive Data Corp.*[20] In *Foley*, the employee was fired after reporting to his superiors that his new supervisor was under investigation by the FBI for embezzlement from a former employer. The superiors told Foley to forget what he had heard and not to discuss rumors. (These "rumors" were later borne out when the supervisor in question pleaded guilty to a felony count of embezzlement.) A relatively short time later, Foley, who had previously had high performance ratings, was fired. In his lawsuit, Foley argued that his discharge violated public policy because, under California law, an employee "is required to disclose to his employer all information relevant to [his employment]." The California Supreme Court held that the duty of an employee to disclose information to his employer serves only the private interest of the employer. Even if the employee serves that private interest, the employer can still fire him without violating public policy. Courts in Illinois, Ohio, Pennsylvania, Massachusetts, and New Jersey have reached similar results.

Reports About Company Policy

A few states have protected whistleblowers who complain about company policy rather than violations of the law. For example, the New Hampshire Supreme Court held that the public policy exception applied to the discharge of an employee because he refused to lie to the company president on behalf of a co-worker.[21] Protection of these whistleblowers remains the exception, however. Courts are understandably reluctant to protect every employee who claims that his or her discharge was the result of a complaint about company policy. Courts worry that the employee's complaint may rest on questionable information or may simply reflect a difference of opinion about the wisdom of company policy. In such circumstances, courts would impermissibly inject themselves into corporate decision making by protecting the discharged employee who disputed company policy. In Kansas, for instance,

---

[20]765 P.2d 373, 3 IER Cases 1729 (Cal. 1988).
[21]Cilley v. New Hampshire Ball Bearings, Inc., 514 A.2d 818, 1 IER Cases 521 (N.H. 1986).

employees must show that they were fired for reporting "activities in violation of rules, regulations, or the law relating to public health, safety, and the general welfare."[22] Although this definition is broad, it excludes employee complaints about personnel issues, budgetary priorities, or other kinds of internal disagreements.

A Massachusetts case illustrates the tension over protecting whistleblowers whose complaints fall in the gray area between allegations of illegalities and disagreements with employer policy. In *Wright v. Shriners Hospital for Crippled Children*,[23] a nurse was fired in reprisal for critical remarks she made to a survey team inspecting the hospital. The court majority was unwilling to find that her firing violated the public policy represented by Massachusetts laws requiring reports of patient abuse, because the nurse had not complained about abuse, neglect, or mistreatment of patients. Rather, she reported her concerns about a lack of consistent procedures and standards for patient care, and a breakdown in communications between the nursing staff and the physicians. The court said this report was about "an internal matter, and internal matters . . . could not be the basis of a public policy exception to the at-will rule." The dissenting justices disagreed, arguing that the public interest in good patient care must protect employees who report detriments to patient care.

Protests or Complaints Made to Third Parties

Sometimes employees disclose their knowledge of their employer's wrongdoing directly to a client or customer. In *Knight v. American Guard & Alert, Inc.*,[24] a security guard claimed he was fired for reporting to his employer's client that co-workers were drinking and using drugs while on duty. The employee testified that he tried to report the drinking and drug abuse to his supervisors, but he gave up because he "wasn't getting anywhere." The Alaska Supreme Court said that his case should go to trial, and he should be given a chance to prove that he was fired in retaliation for informing the client.

Courts have generally not protected whistleblowers in the private sector who take their grievances directly to the press. The First

---

[22]Palmer v. Brown, 752 P.2d 685, 3 IER Cases 177 (Kan. 1988).
[23]589 N.E.2d 1241, 7 IER Cases 553 (Mass. 1992).
[24]714 P.2d 788 (Alaska 1986).

Amendment protection enjoyed by public employees to speak out on matters of "public concern," however, includes the right to talk to the press.

Nonetheless, the law in this area is still developing, and some courts may well extend protection to internal whistleblowers whose information is accurate and whose decision to complain is based on an unwillingness to allow some company policy to take advantage of clients, customers, or the general public.

Exercising Rights Under State Law

The third category of public policy exceptions encompasses employees who are fired because they have exercised a right afforded them by state law. Courts generally require that this right relate to employment; that is, courts require that employees enjoy the right because of their status as employees, and not because of some other status they may have, such as citizen, taxpayer, or parent. A rare example of an exception to this rule is a Virginia case in which two employees who also owned stock in the employer-corporation were fired because they refused to vote their stock as the company wanted. The court found a public policy in the state securities and corporation laws, which contemplate freedom from coercion in exercising shareholders' rights.[25]

The most widely found subset of cases in this category involves employees who were fired because they filed or pursued workers' compensation claims. In many states the workers' compensation laws expressly permit employees to sue if they are fired in retaliation for filing claims. Employees in these states do not need to rely on the public policy exception, because there is a statutory cause of action to protect them. In other states the workers' compensation statutes prohibit retaliatory discharge but do not expressly permit employees to sue. In virtually all of these states, courts allow suit under the public policy exception.

In some states, courts have extended the public policy exception to protect employees who are fired because the employer believes they intend to file workers' compensation claims in the future. Kansas protects a noninjured spouse from retaliation because the other spouse has filed a workers' compensation claim.

---

[25]Bowman v. State Bank, 331 S.E.2d 797, 1 IER Cases 437 (Va. 1985).

It is important to note that in many (but not all) states, employers may fire an employee for absenteeism, including absenteeism caused by recuperation from a work-related injury or illness, as long as the employer applies a uniform and neutral absenteeism rule. States that do not follow this rule and instead prohibit the application of an absenteeism rule to workers with compensable injuries include Maine and California. Moreover, under the Family and Medical Leave Act,[26] discussed in chapter 3, employees of employers with 50 or more employees have a right to 12 weeks of unpaid leave to recover from an injury or illness, and they may not be fired for absenteeism during that time. A number of states have similar medical leave laws. These laws are also discussed in chapter 3.

Other state laws may also provide work-related rights that are protected by the public policy exception. They include occupational safety and health laws, wage-hour laws, and polygraph statutes. Most of these laws expressly permit employees to sue for retaliation, but sometimes courts permit suit under the public policy exception.

In *D'Angelo v. Gardner,*[27] an employee who had an unclosed surgical wound was fired when he refused to perform work that required contact with cyanide. The Nevada Supreme Court used the state Occupational Safety and Health Act as its source of public policy and held that firing an employee for refusing to work in unreasonably dangerous conditions violates that policy. A discharge in this situation might also violate the federal Occupational Safety and Health Act, as discussed in chapter 5.

In *Wilcox v. Niagara of Wisconsin Paper Co.,*[28] Wilcox, the company's director of computer operations, was fired after he failed to come to work on a weekend. The year before, Wilcox had undergone heart bypass surgery. During the week he was fired, he had worked 61 hours, including 35 hours on Thursday and Friday alone. He went home at 9:30 p.m. on Friday after suffering angina pains and was hospitalized later that evening. He was released from the hospital on Saturday with instructions to take it easy. The court held that the employee was entitled to a trial on whether a Wisconsin statute prohibiting employment that is "dangerous or prejudicial to the person's

---

[26]29 U.S.C. §§2611–53 (1993).
[27]819 P.2d 206, 6 IER Cases 1545 (Nev. 1991).
[28]965 F.2d 355, 7 IER Cases 812 (7th Cir. 1992).

life, health, safety or welfare" established a public policy violated by the employer.

In *Amos v. Oakdale Knitting Co.*,[29] the North Carolina Supreme Court held that the employer violated public policy by firing employees because they refused to work for less than the state minimum wage.

As discussed in chapter 1, some states have statutes that prohibit or restrict employers from requiring employees to take a polygraph test. Even when the statute does not expressly give workers a right to sue for violations of the statute, courts often protect them under the public policy exception.

Performing a Civic Duty

Under the fourth category, some courts have found that employees are entitled to public policy protection when they are fired for performing a civic duty. There are very few civic duties in American society, however. This category may be limited to serving on a jury, obeying a subpoena, and testifying in a legal proceeding. As discussed in chapter 3, every state except Montana has a statute prohibiting the discharge of an employee because of jury service. In some states, the statute expressly permits fired employees to sue; in the others, the courts may allow fired employees to bring an action under the public policy exception.

Courts also have protected employees for obeying a subpoena and for testifying in court. Testifying at nonjudicial grievance hearings has not always been accorded the same type of public policy recognition, however. In *Miller v. Sevamp, Inc.*,[30] an employee claimed she was fired in retaliation for appearing as a witness at a fellow employee's grievance hearing. The Virginia Supreme Court acknowledged that the right to testify was protected by the employer's personnel manual, but it said that violation of the manual would affect only private rights, not public policy. In a similar setting, however, the California Supreme Court held that an employee who testified at an administrative investigation about another employee's claim of sexual harassment was protected against retaliatory discharge. The court viewed sexual harassment, the topic of the investigation, as sufficiently a matter of public policy to protect.[31]

---

[29]416 S.E.2d 166, 7 IER Cases 714 (N.C. 1992).
[30]362 S.E.2d 915, 2 IER Cases 1202 (Va. 1987).
[31]Gantt v. Sentry Ins., 824 P.2d 680, 7 IER Cases 289 (Cal. 1992).

WHISTLEBLOWER AND ANTIRETALIATION LAWS

Many states and the federal government have laws affording protection against retaliation for employees who complain about illegal or improper practices by their employers. These are commonly called "whistleblower" laws, although many state statutes do not expressly use this term. In addition, most state and federal laws governing the employment relationship specifically prohibit retaliation against workers who assert rights under them.

State Laws

Thirty-seven states have whistleblower protection laws. Of these, 20 states[32] protect only public sector employees, while 17 states[33] protect both public and private sector employees. In addition, Montana's Wrongful Discharge from Employment Act prohibits public and private sector employers from discharging workers in retaliation for reporting violations of public policy.

The scope of protection under these laws varies from state to state. Some state laws require employees to report their concerns internally first and to give employers a reasonable time to correct alleged improprieties. For example, Ohio requires that the employee first orally notify the employer of a violation and then submit a written report to the employer describing in detail the alleged violation. If the employer fails to remedy the violation within 24 hours, the employee may then file a complaint with the appropriate government agency. Eleven other states[34] have employer notification requirements, although Colorado requires only a good faith attempt at notification and in Florida, internal reporting is unnecessary if it would be futile and there is an imminent danger to public health and safety. On the other hand, four

---

[32]Alaska, Arizona, Colorado, Delaware, Iowa, Kansas, Kentucky, Maryland, Mississippi, Missouri, Nevada, Oklahoma, Pennsylvania, South Carolina, Tennessee, Texas, Utah, Washington, West Virginia, and Wisconsin.

[33]California, Connecticut, Florida, Hawaii, Illinois, Indiana, Louisiana, Maine, Michigan, Minnesota, New Hampshire, New Jersey, New York, North Carolina, Ohio, Oregon, and Rhode Island.

[34]California, Colorado, Florida, Maine, Michigan, Montana, Nevada, New Hampshire, New Jersey, New York, and Wisconsin.

states[35] specifically forbid any requirement that the employee report the alleged violation to the employer.

In states specifying a statutory reporting scheme, it is essential that employees follow statutory procedures. The failure to do so may result in a loss of statutory protection. For instance, in one case involving Ohio's whistleblower law, the employee complained orally to several company officials, including the company's president, that minor employees were consuming alcohol on company premises, but she did not follow up with a written report as required by the statute. (There was some evidence that she had drafted a memorandum to the president, but she was fired before she gave it to him.) The court held that her failure to comply with the statutory requirements prevented her suit.[36]

Statutorily protected activity varies significantly among the states and between public and private employees. In general, whistleblowing statutes covering public employees protect them from retaliation for reporting violations of laws or regulations, mismanagement, gross waste of money, abuse of authority, neglect of duty, or endangerment of public health and safety. For instance, in one Texas case, the court held that reports of improper expenditures of public funds, extortion of money and favors by city employees, and misbehavior by public officials involved matters of public interest protected by the state whistleblower statute.[37]

In contrast, statutes covering private sector employees are often more limited in their scope. As a general matter, these workers are protected from retaliation for disclosing or threatening to disclose violations of laws, rules, or regulations to any appropriate government agency. Statutes in five states (Florida, Minnesota, New Hampshire, North Carolina, and Utah) protect employees who have objected to or refused to participate in a violation of a law, rule, or regulation. Some state statutes, however, are much narrower. The Louisiana whistleblower law covers only violations of environmental laws, rules, and regulations. New York also has a very strict law that protects an employee who discloses or threatens to disclose a violation that "creates and presents a substantial and specific danger to the public health and safety." New York courts have held that refusal to participate in fiscal im-

---

[35]Kansas, Kentucky, Missouri, and Oregon.
[36]Bear v. Geetronics, Inc., 614 N.E.2d 803, 8 IER Cases 1128 (Ohio App. 1992).
[37]City of Houston v. Leach, 819 S.W.2d 185 (Tex. App. 1991).

proprieties, reporting fraudulent billing, and reporting the neglect of a mental patient are all unprotected under this law.

Whistleblower laws generally do not protect private sector employees who reporting of alleged violations of company policy, waste, or mismanagement. For example, an employee who reported alleged breaches of his employer's contract with the U.S. Navy was not protected by Maine's Whistleblowers' Protection Act. That Act requires that the employee have reasonable cause to believe the employer is violating a law, and the employee was claiming only a breach of contract.[38] Similarly, except in Wisconsin, state laws do not protect reports of unethical conduct.

Generally, employee complaints covered by a whistleblower statute will be protected if they are made in good faith and with reasonable belief that they are true, even if the factual assertions are later found to be incorrect. Three states (Indiana, North Carolina, and Ohio) require that employees take steps to verify the accuracy of any allegations. California requires a sworn statement as to the truth or believed truth of the matters reported.

Most state laws are silent about whether an employee's own wrongdoing will negate the protection of the law. Four states (Alaska, Florida, Missouri, and Oregon) specifically remove the statutory protection from an employee who has participated in the unlawful activity he or she has reported. In Louisiana, an employee is protected only if the employer requested the employee's involvement in the challenged activity.

In addition to state whistleblower protection, most state labor laws contain provisions protecting employees who file complaints, assist investigations, testify in proceedings, or otherwise assert their rights under the particular law. In contrast with the whistleblower laws, these provisions apply only to the assertion of rights under the specific law of which they are a part. For example, state fair employment practice laws, which are discussed in chapter 2, commonly prohibit retaliation against employees who file complaints alleging discrimination. State occupational safety and health laws generally prohibit retaliation against employees who file complaints or assert their rights to a safe workplace. Most state workers' compensation laws prohibit retaliation because workers have filed claims for compensation. Not all of these provisions

---

[38]Bard v. Bath Iron Works Corp., 590 A.2d 152 (Me. 1991).

specifically authorize employees to sue for retaliation, but states that recognize the public policy exception to the employment at will rule often use these provisions as the basis for a wrongful discharge suit.

Federal Laws

Two federal statutes, the Civil Service Reform Act[39] and the Whistleblower Protection Act,[40] protect federal employees from retaliation based on whistleblowing.

In addition, most federal statutes regulating occupational safety and health, public health, and the environment contain provisions protecting both public and private employees against retaliation for reporting violations, making claims, or otherwise asserting rights under these laws. These provisions are found in such statutes as the Asbestos Hazard Emergency Response Act,[41] Asbestos School Hazard Detection and Control Act,[42] Clean Air Act,[43] Clean Water Act,[44] Comprehensive Environmental Response, Compensation and Liability Act,[45] Department of Defense Authorization Act,[46] Energy Reorganization Act,[47] Federal Mine Safety and Health Act,[48] Hazardous Substances Releases Liability Compensation Act,[49] Migrant and Seasonal Agricultural Worker Protection Act,[50] Occupational Safety and Health Act,[51] Public Health Service Act,[52] Railroad Safety Act,[53] Safe Containers for International Cargo Act,[54] Safe Drinking Water Act,[55] Solid Waste Disposal Act,[56]

---

[39] 5 U.S.C. §2301(b)(9) (1993).
[40] *Id.*
[41] 15 U.S.C. §2651(a) (1993).
[42] 20 U.S.C. §3608 (1992).
[43] 42 U.S.C. §7622 (1992).
[44] 33 U.S.C. §507 (1992).
[45] 42 U.S.C. §9610(a) (1993).
[46] 10 U.S.C. §2409(a) (1993).
[47] 42 U.S.C. §5851(a) (1993).
[48] 30 U.S.C. §815 (1993).
[49] 42 U.S.C. §9610(a) (1993).
[50] 29 U.S.C. §1855(a) (1993). For a further discussion, see chapter 6.
[51] 29 U.S.C. §660(c) (1993). For a further discussion, see chapter 5.
[52] 42 U.S.C. §300a-7 (1993).
[53] 45 U.S.C. §441(a) (1993).
[54] 46 U.S.C. App. §1506(a) (1992).
[55] 42 U.S.C. §300j-9(i) (1993).
[56] 42 U.S.C. §6971(a) (1993).

Surface Mining Control and Reclamation Act,[57] Surface Transportation Assistance Act,[58] and Toxic Substances Control Act.[59] These antiretaliation provisions seek to protect the public interest by encouraging the reporting of suspected violations.

It is often difficult to distinguish antiretaliation provisions that protect the public or co-workers from provisions that protect only the individual interest of the complaining employee. Antiretaliation provisions in occupational safety and health laws are perhaps the best example of a single provision attempting to protect employees in general as well as the particular employee who filed a complaint or otherwise asserted a right under the law. Many federal employment statutes seek to protect employees who exercise their statutory rights under those laws. These include the Age Discrimination in Employment Act,[60] Americans with Disabilities Act,[61] Employee Polygraph Protection Act,[62] Employee Retirement Income Security Act,[63] Fair Labor Standards Act,[64] Family and Medical Leave Act,[65] Immigration Reform and Control Act,[66] and Title VII of the Civil Rights Act of 1964.[67]

Each of these statutes has its own definition of protected activity.

RELEASES AND WAIVERS

Many employers ask workers whose employment has been terminated to sign a release or waiver promising not to sue the employer in exchange for the employer's payment of various benefits. Although there are restrictions on an employee's ability to waive rights under some employment statutes, including the Fair Labor Standards Act and the Age Discrimination in Employment Act,[68] generally courts uphold

---

[57]30 U.S.C. §1293(a) (1993).
[58]49 U.S.C. App. §2305(a) (1993).
[59]15 U.S.C. §2622(a) (1993).
[60]29 U.S.C. §623(d). See also chapter 2.
[61]42 U.S.C. §12203. See also chapter 2.
[62]29 U.S.C. §2002(4). See also chapter 1.
[63]29 U.S.C. §1140. See also chapter 3.
[64]29 U.S.C. §215(a) (3). See also chapter 3.
[65]29 U.S.C. §2615. See also chapter 3.
[66]8 U.S.C. §1324b(5). See also chapter 1.
[67]42 U.S.C. §2000e-3(a). See also chapter 2.
[68]See chapers 3 and 10.

releases and waivers of other employment rights as long as the releases are knowing and voluntary.

An employer's misrepresentation, fraud, or duress may invalidate termination agreements, but employees who wish to avoid the effects of a release must normally repay any benefits they received under the release. For instance, in a Michigan case the employee signed a release when he resigned from his job. One year later he brought a wrongful discharge action, and a year after that he tried to return the benefits he received when he signed the release. The court held this was an unreasonable delay, and the release prevented him from suing for wrongful discharge.[69] This view was also taken by another court when an employee accepted a check for severance pay and told others that he had resigned, and the former employer gave the former employee favorable references.[70] The court held that the employee had accepted the benefits of his release of claims against the former employer, acted in accordance with it, and ratified the release, thereby waiving any claim of duress he may otherwise have had.

REMEDIES

The remedies available in a wrongful discharge claim depend upon the legal theory of liability under which the plaintiff prevails. If the recovery is based upon a statute, then the remedies specified in the statute govern the recovery. If there is no statute, then the remedies are governed by either contract law or tort law. The California Supreme Court explained the difference between contract and tort in wrongful discharge cases: "Contract actions are created to enforce the intentions of the parties to the agreement, but tort law is primarily designed to vindicate "social policy."[71] **As a general rule, tort damages are greater than contract damages**.

Traditional contract remedies are usually applied where the discharge is found to violate promises made by an employer. Such promises (1) may be express representations made at the time of hiring,

---

[69]Davis v. Bronson Methodist Hosp., 406 N.W.2d 201, 2 IER Cases 376 (Mich. App. 1986).

[70]Anselmo v. Manufacturers Life Ins. Co., 771 F.2d 417, 120 LRRM 2384 (8th Cir. 1985).

[71]Foley v. Interactive Data Corp., 765 P.2d 373 (Cal. 1988).

(2) may be implied from an employee handbook, or (3) may come from other employer actions or promises.

Tort remedies are awarded if the employee demonstrates that the discharge was wrongful because it violated public policy, or because the discharge was abusive, malicious, or retaliatory. Most courts that permit employees to sue on the theory that the employer breached the implied covenant of good faith and fair dealing allow only contract damages.

Lost Wages

Lost wages are an available remedy both in cases for breach of contract and for wrongful discharge tort actions. The term "lost wages" refers both to wages that would have been earned between the time of the termination and the trial as well as to the period of time after the trial when the plaintiff is not reinstated and is unlikely to secure other employment. Wages lost before the time of trial are called "back pay," whereas anticipated wage loss after the trial is known as "front pay." Both types of wage loss are permissible only until such time as the plaintiff can find comparable employment.

As a general matter, in either an action for breach of contract or for tort, courts adhere to the principle that prevailing employees should be placed in the same economic position they would have enjoyed if they had not been wrongly fired. Generally, back pay damages are measured by the amount the employee would have received from the employer from the date of the discharge until the date of the trial, less any income the employee actually earned or could have earned if he or she had exercised reasonable diligence in searching for similar employment.

In addition to compensation lost in the past, plaintiffs often seek future damages, or front pay, for some period of time beyond the date of the trial. The duty to mitigate means that, if the courts permit awards of front pay, they can go only to those plaintiffs who have not been able to find other comparable employment after their discharge. In many future damages cases, however, the employee has another job that pays less than the former employment and argues that the defendant should have to compensate him or her for the lifetime earnings differential.

Juries have some latitude to consider the uncertainties of the future, but verdicts cannot be speculative. Front pay is permissible only when there is some basis for the award. The basis cannot be pure conjecture, but there need not be absolute certainty. The evidence must afford a reasonable basis for estimating the loss.

In *Worrell v. Multipress, Inc.*,[72] the Ohio Supreme Court identified four factors to consider in determining front pay damages in breach of employment contract cases:

- the age of the employee and his or her reasonable prospects of obtaining comparable employment elsewhere,

- salary and other tangible benefits such as bonuses and vacation pay,

- expenses associated with finding new employment, and

- the replacement value of fringe benefits for a reasonable time until new employment is obtained.

In *Beales v. Hillhaven*,[73] the Nevada Supreme Court upheld a jury verdict of $208,476 in front pay based upon an economist's expert testimony that a permanent employee, age 62 at the time of trial, would sustain front pay damages of $49,152 if she retired at age 65 and front pay damages of $315,791 if she retired at age 70. In *Stark v. Circle K Corp.*,[74] the Montana Supreme Court upheld a jury verdict of 28 years of front pay damages also based upon the expert testimony of an economist.

Reliance Damages

Even if the court does not permit an award of front pay, plaintiffs can sometimes recover their reliance damages. For instance, in *Pearson v. Simmonds Precision Products, Inc.*,[75] the plaintiff was hired as a senior test engineer on a design project for the B-2 bomber. During his preemployment interviews, he expressed concern about job security, given the unpredictable nature of defense contracting. The employer replied that much of its business was in nondefense areas, and that, even if the B-2 project failed, there would be work for him. The plaintiff accepted the job, moved to Vermont, and took out a loan to buy a house;

---

[72]543 N.E.2d 1277 (Ohio 1989).
[73]825 P.2d 212, 1 IER Cases 260 (Nev. 1992).
[74]751 P.2d 162, 3 IER Cases 53 (Mont. 1988).
[75]624 A.2d 1134, 8 IER 535 (Vt. 1993).

within a few months, cutbacks in the B-2 project led to his discharge. Although he had signed a contract clearly indicating his at-will status, he prevailed against the employer on the theories of negligent failure to disclose and negligent misrepresentation. The employer knew at the time it was negotiating with him that the project was facing serious cutbacks and that there was a good chance his job would be eliminated. Therefore the court held the employer had a duty to disclose that information to him. The employee was permitted to recover the damages he incurred in relying on the employer's misrepresentations.

Emotional Distress

Damages for emotional distress generally depend on whether the action is in contract or tort. In general, emotional distress damages are not recoverable in an action for breach of contract. In *Silva v. Albuquerque Assembly & Distribution Freeport Warehouse Corp.*,[76] for example, a discharged employee sought distress damages for the employer's failure to provide health insurance coverage as required by the employment contract. The New Mexico Supreme Court held that emotional distress damages are not available in a breach of an employment contract action unless the parties agreed at the formation of the contract that such damages would be recoverable.

In most types of tort cases prevailing plaintiffs can recover damages for emotional distress. Courts that recognize the public policy exception to the employment at will doctrine generally allow such damages. Damages for emotional distress are available if the distress is caused by intentional, outrageous, or reckless conduct.

Punitive Damages

The purpose of punitive damages in tort cases is to punish and deter the defendant and others from acting in a similar manner under similar circumstances. Furthermore, punitive damages express society's disapproval of a defendant's conduct. Their function is to create a strong incentive to conform to clearly defined legal duties.

Generally, punitive damages are not recoverable for a breach of contract regardless of the character of the breach. **Most jurisdictions**

---

[76]738 P.2d 513, 2 IER Cases 446 (N.M. 1987).

do not allow recovery of punitive damages unless there is tortious behavior in addition to the breach of contract. In *D'Angelo v. Gardner*,[77] for example, the Nevada Supreme Court found that punitive damages were properly awarded to an employee in his breach of employment contract and tortious discharge action. There was evidence to support the conclusion that the charge of "insubordination" leveled by the employer against him was a contrivance and a fraud, and there was evidence to support a finding of malicious intent and oppressiveness on part of the employer.

States have various formulations for the degree of culpability that must be established to justify an award of punitive damages. Some states hold that punitive damages are recoverable only upon a showing that the employer acted in bad faith. A deliberate breach by an employer does not necessarily constitute a culpable mental state sufficient for punitive damages. An intent by the employer to injure the employee or actions in heedless disregard for the employee's rights can constitute bad faith.

Many states use the standard that punitive damages may be recovered only when the defendant's conduct is "wanton, willful or malicious." Such conduct may be found in situations where the employer spreads malicious or false statements concerning the employee before or after discharge, where the employer harasses the employee in an effort to force the employee to resign, or where the employer seriously undermines the employee's chances of obtaining other employment. In *K Mart v. Ponsock*,[78] the Nevada Supreme Court held that discharging an employee in order to defeat that employee's retirement entitlement was malicious and oppressive, and thus justified a punitive damage award in the employee's favor.

Some courts have refused to award punitive damages where the employer could not have reasonably known that its actions would result in liability because the law changed. In *Springer v. Weeks & Leo Co.*,[79] for example, an employee who was wrongfully discharged for exercising her right to file a workers' compensation claim sought punitive damages against her employer. The Iowa Supreme Court denied the employee's claim for punitive damages because the employer's conduct

---

[77]819 P.2d 206, 6 IER Cases 1545 (Nev. 1991).
[78]732 P.2d 1364, 2 IER Cases 56 (Nev. 1987).
[79]475 N.W.2d 630, 7 IER Cases 1573 (Iowa 1991).

occurred before the court recognized a tort action for retaliatory discharge.

Mitigation of Damages

An employee seeking damages in a wrongful discharge case has a duty to mitigate those damages by reasonably seeking and obtaining other, comparable employment. Damages are reduced by the amount of any wages that are actually earned after termination and by amounts that could have been earned with reasonable diligence.

Courts describe the employee's duty to mitigate as requiring due diligence or reasonable care, effort, or expenditure by the employee. **Generally, an employer can demonstrate that an employee failed to mitigate damages by showing that the employee refused to accept the same or a substantially similar position with similar compensation.** A position is not considered substantially similar if it is (1) another line of work, (2) an inferior position or a demotion, or (3) a position that may be considered offensive or degrading. An employee is not required to relocate to find employment or to conduct a nationwide job search. Further, a wrongfully discharged employee is entitled to recover reasonable expenses incurred while seeking alternative employment.

The best way for an employer to show a failure to mitigate is to demonstrate that the employee rejected an offer of the identical job from which he or she was fired—that is, to show that it offered to reinstate the employee. To operate in this fashion, the offer of reinstatement must be bona fide and made in good faith. It must not be conditioned on dismissal or compromise of the employee's claim, nor may it require a demotion, lower pay, or less responsibility. Even if the offer is to reinstate the employee to his or her old job with identical salary and benefits, the employee may still refuse it if reasonable grounds exist for the refusal, as where further association between the parties would be offensive or degrading.

Reinstatement

Although courts routinely order hiring or reinstatement in statutory cases, such as under Title VII of the Civil Rights Act of 1964, **it is rare for courts to make hiring orders in wrongful discharge cases**. One reason articulated by some states is the lack of "mutuality of remedies" between the employer and the employee; employers cannot get orders requiring employees to perform, so employees should not get orders to require employers to receive their work .

In any legal context, courts award reinstatement only in circumstances where the parties would be capable of a productive relationship after the litigation. When the plaintiff would be working in a close, personal employment relationship with the defendant, reinstatement is inappropriate. Animosity from the trial is not a sufficient basis to deny the reinstatement remedy, however, when the circumstances of the workplace are more impersonal. As a practical matter, few employees seek reinstatement in wrongful discharge actions. By the time of litigation, few plaintiffs want to return to their former jobs.

CONSTITUTIONAL ISSUES IN PUBLIC EMPLOYMENT

The Fourteenth Amendment to the United States Constitution provides that no state shall "deprive any person of life, liberty, or property without due process of law."[80] A public employee with a legally recognized interest in continued employment has a "property right" that the state cannot deprive without due process. A public employee also has a protected "liberty interest" in his or her good name, reputation, honor, and integrity.

Property Rights

A public employee has a property right in a job if he or she has a continuing right to employment. This is determined by state law. A property interest in employment can be created by a statute, an ordinance, or an express or implied contract that creates a term of office or establishes specific reasons for which a public employee may be fired. Thus, if state law provides that public employees or permanent or classified civil servants are entitled to remain in their positions as long as they provide efficient service and good behavior, those employees have a property right in their positions. For instance, a tenured faculty member at a public school, college, or university has a constitutionally

---

[80]U.S. Const. amend. XIV.

protected property right because tenure is a promise of continued employment. On the other hand, if an employee's status is provisional, probationary, or untenured, he or she does not have a property right to employment.

Due Process Rights

Once it is established that a public employee has a protected property right in employment, the state cannot deprive the employee of that property without due process.[81] Although state law defines an employee's property interests, federal law determines what procedural due process requirements must be met. **At a minimum, due process requires that an employee have notice and an opportunity to be heard before termination.** A terminated employee also must have an opportunity to be heard after discharge. The level of due process protection differs between pretermination and post-termination hearings. At the pretermination stage, an employee is entitled to "some opportunity to be heard," but at the post-termination stage, an employee has a right to a full hearing.

A public employee is entitled to oral or written notice of the charges against him or her, although states may require that the notice be in writing. The notice must describe the nature of the charges against the employee and the general substance of the evidence against the employee. For example, a letter stating that the reason for an employee's discharge was a pattern of sexual harassment and including specific instances of the conduct was sufficient notice, even though the letter did not include the names of the women allegedly harassed.[82] The notice should include a statement that the employee will be fired on a particular date and that the employee must respond to the charges or be fired. The notice must also include a statement of the employee's right to an appeal.

An employee must have an opportunity to be heard, either in writing or orally, at a pretermination hearing. The pretermination hearing need not be elaborate, especially if a more detailed post-termination procedure exists. The hearing also need not be a full evidentiary hearing. An employee is not entitled to a stenographic

---

[81]Cleveland Bd. of Educ. v. Loudermill, 470 U.S. 532, 1 IER Cases 424 (1985).
[82]Roberts v. Greiner, 386 S.E.2d 504 (W. Va. 1989).

recording or a tape recording of a pretermination hearing. When an elaborate post-termination proceeding is available, a pretermination hearing does not have to "definitively resolve the propriety of the discharge." Rather, "[i]t should be an initial check against mistaken decisions." Thus, a pretermination hearing should merely resolve "whether there are reasonable grounds to believe that the charges against the employee are true and support the proposed action."

The decision maker at a pretermination hearing does not have to be an impartial outsider or an impartial insider. The party proposing that the employee be terminated may also preside over the hearing. Moreover, the same party may order an investigation into the employee's conduct, issue a notice of proposed discharge, and sign the final discharge letter without violating an employee's due process rights at the pretermination stage.[83]

State law may allow an employee to be represented by counsel at a pretermination hearing, but representation by counsel is not included in federal due process protection. If an employee fails to secure a legal representative, there is no due process violation.

Liberty Interests

A public employee has a protected liberty interest in his or her "good name, reputation, honor, or integrity."[84] An injury to an employee's reputation alone, however, is not a deprivation of a liberty interest. A deprivation of a liberty interest occurs if a public employer fires or refuses to rehire an employee and at the same time makes charges against that person that are so stigmatizing that his or her freedom to pursue other employment is foreclosed.[85] Examples of such charges would be accusations of dishonesty or immorality.

To be actionable under the Fourteenth Amendment, the charges made against the employee must be false, they must be made public, and the employee must have been denied a meaningful opportunity to clear his or her name. The employee must show either that the stigmatizing allegations were actually made public or that a likelihood of future

---

[83]Hanley v. General Servs. Admin., 829 F.2d 23, 2 IER Cases 892 (Fed. Cir. 1987).

[84]Bishop v. Wood, 426 U.S. 341 (1976).

[85]Seigert v. Gilley, 500 U.S. 226, 6 IER Cases 705 (1991).

disclosure exists. Unpublicized accusations or criticisms do not harm an employee's good name, reputation, honor, or integrity.

Assertions surrounding a dismissal are considered unpublicized if they are communicated only in a judicial proceeding occurring after the employee's discharge. Privileged communications to a state unemployment office have been held not to be publicized. The inferences that may be drawn from dismissal alone are not sufficient to implicate a liberty interest. Also, the presence of derogatory information in confidential files is not sufficient to infringe upon an employee's liberty interests.

An employee whose liberty interests are violated has a right to notice and a hearing to clear his or her name. This hearing is merely to clear the employee's name and reputation, and it does not affect employment status.

EMPLOYMENT FRAUD

An employer may be held liable for fraudulently inducing an applicant to accept a job or an incumbent employee to turn down an offer from another employer and continue in the current job by misrepresenting facts about the employment. It is immaterial whether the employment is at will or for cause. An employer is not shielded from liability for fraudulent concealment merely because it has a right to terminate the employment relationship at any time. The employee sues not for wrongful discharge, but for fraud in the inducement, and promises that will not support a claim for breach of contract may well support a claim for fraud.

To prevail on a claim of fraud, an employee must generally prove (1) a misrepresentation of a material fact, (2) made knowingly, (3) with the intent to mislead, (4) reasonable reliance by the misled party, and (5) resulting damage to the misled party. Thus, if an employer conceals or misrepresents its financial position in order to induce the employee to enter a position under a false impression of the position's stability, the employer will be liable for fraudulent inducement. Actionable misrepresentations can include the employer's omission of facts when it has stated other facts it knows will create a false impression unless it also discloses the omitted facts, as well as the failure to correct a material representation once it learns it is false.

In *Stewart v. Jackson & Nash*,[86] an attorney alleged that she resigned her position with her prior law firm and joined the defendant law firm because she was told that the new firm had secured a large environmental law client and that she would head the firm's new environmental law section. After two years, the new firm still had not formed an environmental law section and she realized that there never was an environmental law client. She resigned from the firm and brought an action for fraudulent inducement. The Second Circuit Court of Appeals held that the alleged misrepresentations of fact could establish the basis of liability as could her allegation that the firm never intended to fulfill its promise to make the attorney the head of the environmental law section.

In *Shebar v. Sanyo Business Systems Corp.*,[87] another fraud case, Shebar, who worked for Sanyo, used an executive search firm to secure a job offer from Sony. When he submitted his resignation to his superiors at Sanyo, they told him they would not permit him to resign and assured him he would have a job at Sanyo for life. Based on this conversation, Shebar rescinded his acceptance of the Sony offer. When Shebar told his contact at the search firm what he had done, the contact expressed surprise at Sanyo's behavior, claiming he knew Sanyo was trying to find a replacement for the employee. Shebar immediately confronted his superiors, who denied the whole thing and claimed that the search firm was just trying to get him to take the Sony job so that it could get its placement fee. Four months later, Sanyo fired Shebar. The court held that Shebar could sue Sanyo for fraud on the theory that at the time the Sanyo executives were denying any efforts to replace him, they in fact intended to fire him shortly.

To make out a claim for fraud, the employee must show he or she reasonably relied on the employer's misrepresentations. In one Alabama case, the employee signed an at-will disclaimer in the employment application for a job at a jewelry store that was about to open. She admitted she had read and understood the disclaimer. In response to her questions, the hiring representative then told her she would have permanent employment and would not be laid off immediately after the

---

[86]976 F.2d 86, 7 IER Cases 1322 (2d Cir. 1992).
[87]526 A.2d 1144, 3 IER Cases 1380 (N.J. Super. 1987), *aff'd*, 544 A.2d 377, 3 IER Cases 1385 (N.J. 1988).

store's grand opening. She quit her current job, took the job with the employer, and was fired a week later. The court held that she could not reasonably have relied on the employer's misrepresentations in light of the clear disclaimer she had just signed.[88]

ABUSIVE DISCHARGE

In its heyday, the employment at will doctrine not only permitted employers to fire an employee for any reason, but it permitted employers to fire employees in any manner. Today, just as certain reasons for discharge are unlawful, such as those that violate public policy, so too are discharges effected in an abusive manner—regardless of the merits of the decision to discharge the individual. These cases are often referred to as abusive discharge cases, although some courts use "abusive" discharge as synonymous with "wrongful" discharge. For clarity, as used here, abusive discharge is a description of the circumstances surrounding a discharge. Accordingly, abusive discharge cases include intentional torts (assault, battery, false imprisonment), intentional infliction of emotional distress, defamation, invasion of privacy, and other theories.

The legal theories underlying each of these causes of action are discussed at greater length in other sections of the book. This section will focus on five stages in which abusive discharge actions may arise: (1) the employer's method of investigating alleged employee misconduct, (2) the employer's method of disciplining individual employees short of discharge, (3) the employer's method of deciding which employee to discharge for a particular offense, (4) the employer's method of informing the individual of the discharge, and (5) the employer's conduct after the employee's termination. As in other areas of employment law, the nascent state of the law has resulted in wide variability among jurisdictions.

Investigations

Overzealous surveillance, interviews, and interrogation are a frequent source of litigation. For example, interrogating an employee for

---

[88]Shelby v. Zayre Corp., 474 So.2d 1069, 120 LRRM 2224 (Ala. 1985).

three hours without a break and then summarily firing him, and threatening an employee for hours while using loud, obscene language and gestures have been held to constitute intentional infliction of emotional distress. Coercive interrogation lawsuits may be more likely to be successful when the employer knows that the employee is in poor health.

Unreasonable interrogation also may give rise to an action for false imprisonment. For example, detaining an employee to secure a confession has been held to be illegal. On the other hand, if the employee is free to leave, even if leaving would result in discharge, the employee cannot prevail in an action for false imprisonment.

Other unlawful conduct has included intentionally placing company-endorsed checks in an employee's possession to make it appear that she was stealing from the company and conspiring with a security firm so that an employee would fail a polygraph examination.

Outrageous Treatment

An employer's overall pattern of dealing with an employee may be so outrageous that it constitutes intentional infliction of emotional distress. As discussed earlier in this chapter, employees who quit rather than endure the treatment may also have a claim for wrongful discharge on the theory that their quitting was a constructive discharge. For example, in *Wilson v. Monarch Paper Co.*,[89] the plaintiff was a 60-year-old vice-president of a corporation. When a new president took over, the plaintiff was given three options: (1) he could take a sales job at half his former pay; (2) he could be terminated with three months' severance pay; or (3) he could accept a job as warehouse supervisor with the same pay but a reduction in benefits. He chose the third option, but the warehouse position turned out to be a janitorial job, in which he had the responsibility for sweeping the floors and cleaning the employee cafeteria. He quit after four months because of a severe case of clinical depression and respiratory problems caused by dust. The Fifth Circuit Court of Appeals affirmed an award of $3.4 million for age discrimination and intentional infliction of emotional distress.

Racial, ethnic, and sexual harassment on the job can violate Title VII of the Civil Rights Act of 1964, which is discussed in

---

[89] 939 F.2d 1138, 6 IER Cases 1344 (5th Cir. 1991).

chapter 2, and courts may find the same conduct to be tortious under state law as well. In *Ford v. Revlon, Inc.*[90] the plaintiff complained repeatedly about sexual harassment by her supervisor, yet the company did not respond, even though it had a policy against sexual harassment that required investigation of complaints. This failure to investigate supported a claim for intentional infliction of emotional distress.

Discharge Decision

The courts will sometimes tolerate the discharge of at-will employees for highly objectionable reasons so long as the method of discharge is not sufficiently extreme. In *Madani v. Kendall Ford, Inc.*,[91] an automobile salesperson was fired when he refused his supervisor's order to pull down his pants and expose himself in full view of fellow employees and customers. The Oregon Supreme Court, in a questionable ruling, held that the manner of discharge was not sufficiently outrageous to constitute intentional infliction of emotional distress.

In instances of suspected employee wrongdoing, there may be more than one employee under suspicion. Deciding which employee is responsible and taking action against the employee may constitute abusive discharge. In *Agis v. Howard Johnson Co.*,[92] the manager of a restaurant notified all of the waitresses that someone was stealing from the cash register and that, until the person or persons were discovered, he would begin firing all of the waitresses in alphabetical order. The plaintiff, Debra Agis, was the first to be fired and she sued for intentional infliction of emotional distress. The court held that the plaintiff had alleged facts sufficient to establish extreme and outrageous conduct.

Method of Discharge

A wide range of employer actions at the time of discharge have given rise to abusive discharge claims. In general, the courts have been reluctant to permit the former employee to recover unless the employer has engaged in truly outrageous conduct. For example, escorting an employee off the premises has been held not to constitute intentional

---

[90]734 P.2d 580, 1 IER Cases 1571 (Ariz. 1987).
[91]818 P.2d 930 (Or. 1991).
[92]355 N.E.2d 315 (Mass. 1976).

infliction of emotional distress, but stabbing an employee during a discharge-related argument was held to be an assault and battery. A supervisor's yelling at an employee on the sales floor that he did not trust the employee did not constitute extreme and outrageous conduct, but the use of abusive racial epithets in the course of discharge did.

In one case,[93] the Oregon Court of Appeals held that employees failed to state a claim for intentional infliction of emotional distress where the employer, in discharging them, directed them to hold hands, demanded that they surrender their keys, accused them of being liars and saboteurs, and ordered them off the premises without an opportunity to collect their personal items.

Postdischarge Acts

The most common basis for liability after a discharge is through defamatory communications to third parties, such as prospective employers. Nevertheless, other actions are possible. For example, in *Diamond Shamrock Refining & Marketing Co. v. Mendez*,[94] the plaintiff worked for 10 years as one of four chief operators at a refinery. At the end of one night shift he was ordered to clean up some debris, including some loose nails, which had been left by carpenters working in the area. He threw the nails in a small box and placed the box in his lunch bag, which he inadvertently took home. He was later fired for theft, and word of his discharge for stealing was widely disseminated around the plant. The lower court held that the excessive publication of the incident placed the plaintiff in a false light, which was actionable as an invasion of privacy. The Texas Supreme Court, however, held that the plaintiff could not recover without proof that the employer acted with actual malice.

In *Taiwo v. Vu*,[95] the plaintiff was a certified school teacher who was hired by the defendant to bring a day care center into compliance with state law. The plaintiff soon resigned when the defendant would not agree to follow state laws. When the plaintiff tried to get her last paycheck, the defendant assaulted, battered, and falsely imprisoned her;

---

[93]Watte v. Maeyen, 828 P.2d 479 (Or. App.), *review denied,* 836 P.2d 1345 (Or. 1992).
[94]844 S.W.2d 198 (Tex. 1992).
[95]822 P.2d 1024 (Kan. 1991).

she filed false police reports against the plaintiff and her husband; and she induced another employee to lie to the police about the plaintiff. The Supreme Court of Kansas held that the defendant's post-termination conduct was so extreme and outrageous as to permit the plaintiff to recover for intentional infliction of emotional distress.

9

Bankruptcy, Plant Closings, and Unemployment

INTRODUCTION

Each year, millions of employees are adversely affected by economic difficulties experienced by business firms that result in compensation reductions, layoffs, or permanent job losses. These experiences may create substantial financial and psychological problems for the affected individuals. This chapter will explore the ability of companies with financial difficulties to obtain relief through bankruptcy procedures, and the rights of employees affected by employer bankruptcies. It will then cover state and federal laws that encourage or require companies to provide advance notice of plant closings or mass layoffs. The chapter will finally review the federally mandated unemployment compensation insurance system.

BANKRUPTCY

Companies experiencing financial problems frequently attempt to reduce operating expenses by decreasing labor costs through wage and fringe benefit reductions. With respect to the 85 percent of workers who are not covered by collective bargaining agreements and have no individual employment contracts, firms are generally free to modify worker wages and fringe benefits without discussing the changes with the affected personnel. These companies are not even required to file bankruptcy petitions before they implement such changes. Nonetheless, employers that wish to reduce the labor costs of personnel covered by collective contracts must either obtain the consent of the representative labor unions or obtain bankruptcy court approval.

Modifying and Rejecting Bargaining Agreement Provisions

Chapter 11 of the Bankruptcy Code[1] sets forth the detailed procedures that must be satisfied by corporate debtors that wish to avoid liquidation through reorganization of financially troubled enterprises. Section 1113 specifies the prerequisites that must be satisfied before an economically depressed firm may reject or modify the terms of a collective bargaining agreement. The company must make a proposal to the union based on the most complete and reliable information then available, which provides for those modifications that are required to permit the successful reorganization of the debtor. The proposal must treat the creditors and affected employees "fairly and equitably."

The firm must supply the union with all relevant information and confer with the union in a good faith effort to reach mutually satisfactory modifications. Management officials need not engage in the detailed bargaining that would otherwise be required under the National Labor Relations Act with respect to other changes they wish to make in existing terms of employment. They must, however, give union representatives the opportunity to discuss the suggested changes and to consider less drastic alternatives that might equally satisfy company financial concerns. If the union rejects the suggested changes "without good cause" and the company convinces the bankruptcy court that "the balance of the equities clearly favors rejection" of the existing contract terms, the employer will be authorized to implement the proposed modifications.

An employer seeking to modify the terms contained in an existing collective bargaining agreement must suggest only those changes that are necessary to achieve a successful reorganization. If the bankruptcy

---

[1]11 U.S.C. §§1101–74 (1993).

court finds that the proposed terms go beyond what is realistically necessary, it will refuse to approve the requested changes. The petitioning employer must also treat all of the affected parties "fairly and equitably" by ensuring that the economic hardships do not disadvantage the unionized employees to a disproportionate degree compared to other creditors.

Priority for Unpaid Wages and Benefits

When a company seeks bankruptcy protection, it usually has outstanding wage and fringe benefit obligations. If it attempts a financial reorganization, it will incur additional wage and benefit liabilities during the reorganization period. Although employees are not secured creditors who may have recourse to particular company assets, they are granted certain wage and fringe benefit priorities under section 507 of the Bankruptcy Code.[2]

Section 507 carefully distinguishes between wage and benefit obligations incurred before versus after the filing of a petition in bankruptcy. After outstanding company liabilities are satisfied pertaining to administrative expenses and parties furnishing goods, services, or credit during the period between filing the bankruptcy petition and the appointment of a bankruptcy trustee, the remaining company assets are used to reimburse employees for wages, commissions, and vacation pay, severance benefits, and sick leave earned within 90 days prior to the filing of the bankruptcy petition. Vacation pay, severance pay, and sick leave are generally treated as if they accrue continuously as work is performed, with priority preference for these items being limited to the portion that accrued during the 90 day prepetition period. The next priority is for claims for unpaid employer contributions to employee benefit plans, such as pension, health insurance, and life insurance, that pertain to services performed by employees within 180 days prior to the filing of the petition. Compensation and fringe benefits earned too early to be entitled to priority status are treated as unsecured claims that are entitled to no priority.

Wages and fringe benefits earned by employees after a bankruptcy petition has been filed and during the reorganization period are accorded

---

[2]11 U.S.C. §507 (1993).

first priority treatment as "administrative expenses." Courts accord similar priority to vacation pay, severance pay, and employer contributions to insurance and pension programs to the extent those obligations accrue during the reorganization period.

PLANT CLOSINGS AND MASS LAYOFFS
UNDER STATE LAW

Eleven states have laws regulating plant closings and mass layoffs.[3] Some impose affirmative obligations on employers, while others merely encourage voluntary behavior. When businesses fail to satisfy mandatory obligations, fines or severance payments may be imposed. Connecticut law requires firms with 100 or more employees to pay for continued health benefits for up to 120 days for employees displaced by plant closings or substantial job relocations to other states.[4] Hawaii law obliges companies with 50 or more employees to provide affected employees and the State Director of Labor Relations with 45 days advance notice of plant closures and substantial job relocations to other states.[5] Employers are also required to pay displaced workers eligible for unemployment compensation the difference between their prelayoff wages and their unemployment benefits during the four weeks following their dislocation.

Maine law obliges companies with 100 or more employees that terminate operations or relocate all or substantially all operations to a new location more than 100 miles from the original location to grant one week's severance pay for each year of employment to affected personnel who have at least three years of service, unless the closure or relocation is caused by a physical calamity.[6] The Director of the State Bureau of Labor must be given 60 days advance written notice of proposed plant closures and relocations, and affected employees must be given 60 days notice of job relocations to other states.

---

[3]*See generally* J.F. Fitzpatrick, *WARN Act and State Plant-Closing Handbook* (Washington, D.C.: BNA Books, 1993), ch. 3.
[4]Conn. Stat. Ann. §§31-51o(a)–(c) (1993).
[5]Haw. Rev. Stat. §394B-1 through -8 (1993).
[6]Me. Rev. Stat. Ann. tit. 26, §625-B(1)–(7) (1992).

Maryland law covers companies with at least 50 employees that have been in business for over one year.[7] It suggests that such firms voluntarily provide at least 90 days advance notice to employees who would be affected by job relocations or layoffs that would reduce operations by 25 percent or 15 employees, whichever is greater, over any three-month period.

Massachusetts encourages companies with 50 or more employees to voluntarily provide affected employees and the State Director of the Division of Employment Security with advance notice of proposed plant closings that will result in the dislocation of over 90 percent of workers.[8] Firms with 12 or more employees are required to provide the Director with advance notice of planned facility relocations within Massachusetts.

Michigan encourages employee-owned businesses with 25 or more workers to provide affected personnel and the State Department of Labor with advance notice of plant closings and production relocations.[9] Minnesota directs the Commissioner of Jobs and Services to encourage firms contemplating plant closures, operational relocations, or substantial layoffs to give advance notice to representative unions, affected employees, and the local government unit involved.[10]

Oregon requires employers covered by the Federal Worker Adjustment and Retraining Notification Act to provide advance notice of plant closures and mass layoffs to the Economic Development Department and directs that Department to inform affected employers of state assistance programs that are available to communities, companies, and workers affected by such closures and layoffs.[11]

South Carolina only regulates companies that oblige their own employees to provide advance notice before they quit. These firms are required to post written notices regarding proposed plant closures not less than two weeks in advance or the same length of time required of workers before they resign.[12]

---

[7]Md. Code Ann. art. 83A, §§3-301 through -304 (1993).
[8]Mass. Laws Ann. ch. 149, §179B, ch. 151 A, §71A-G (1982).
[9]Mich. Comp. Laws §450.736 (1992).
[10]Minn. Stat. §268.976 (1989).
[11]Or. Rev. Stat. §285.453 through .463 (1993).
[12]S.C. Code §41-1-40 (1986).

Tennessee obliges companies with 50 to 99 full-time employees to provide advance notice to affected workers and the State Department of Labor of contemplated plant closures, facility relocations more than 50 miles from the existing site, or reductions that will displace 50 or more employees within a three-month period.[13]

Wisconsin requires companies with at least 50 employees to provide affected workers, the Department of Industry, Labor, and Human Resources, and the highest official of the local municipality with 60 days advance notice of any proposed plant closure that will displace 25 or more personnel or any mass layoff affecting 25 employees or 25 percent of the company's work force, whichever is greater.[14] Advance notice is not required if the business is relocated to another area within a reasonable commuting distance from the closed facility and the firm offers to retain the affected workers at the new location or the reductions are due to unforeseeable business exigencies or a natural or human-generated disaster beyond the control of the company.

WORKER ADJUSTMENT AND RETRAINING NOTIFICATION ACT

In 1988, Congress enacted the Worker Adjustment and Retraining Notification Act (WARN).[15] WARN covers companies that employ 100 full-time workers or 100 or more full- and part-time employees who work a combined total of at least 4,000 hours per week, not counting overtime. Section 2101(a) requires covered firms to provide 60 days advance notice of planned "plant closings" or "mass layoffs" to affected employees or their representative unions, if any, and to interested state and local government units.

A "plant closing" involves the permanent or temporary shutdown of a single site of employment resulting in an employment loss during any 30-day period for 50 or more employees, not counting "part-time employees" who average fewer than 20 hours per week. A "mass layoff"

---

[13]Tenn. Code §§50-1-601 through 604 (1991).

[14]Wis. Stat. Ann. §109.07 (1993).

[15]29 U.S.C. §§2101-09 (1993). *See* J.F. Fitzpatrick, *WARN Act and State Plant-Closing Handbook* (Washington, D.C.: BNA Books, 1993); Bureau of National Affairs, Inc., *Plant Closings: The Complete Resource Guide* (Washington, D.C.: Bureau of National Affairs, Inc., 1988).

entails single site employment losses within a 30-day period of at least one-third of the full-time employees and at least 50 full-time personnel, or the displacement of at least 500 full-time workers. "Employment losses" include layoffs that exceed six months in duration and work reductions of more than 50 percent of normal hours during any six-month period. Under section 2101(b)(1), a company selling its business is responsible for advance notice of plant closures or mass layoffs until the effective date of the sale, with the purchaser being responsible for WARN notices due after that date.

The WARN notice requirements do not apply to plant closings or mass layoffs caused by natural disasters, or to consolidations or production relocations if the company offers displaced workers jobs at the new location and it is within a reasonable commuting distance from the previous facility. The WARN notice obligations are similarly inapplicable to employment losses caused by strikes or lockouts, even when employers exercise their right to hire permanent replacements for striking employees.

In certain circumstances, employers may be permitted to provide less than 60 days advance notice of plant closings or mass layoffs. For example, a firm may be actively seeking new capital or new business that would enable it to avoid or postpone the need for any shutdown and it might believe that giving notice might jeopardize the likelihood of obtaining the needed capital or business. In such a situation, the company would not have to provide advance notice until it became clear that it would be unable to obtain the new financing or business. A business may also order a plant closing or mass layoff before the conclusion of the 60-day notice period, when the closing or layoff is caused by business circumstances that were not reasonably foreseeable at the time the usual notice would have had to be given.

Employers do not have to give advance notice of substantial layoffs that are not expected to exceed six months in duration. Once it becomes clear, however, that a seemingly short-term layoff will extend beyond six months, the firm must immediately notify the affected personnel of the likely continued employment loss. If the company fails to provide the requisite notice, it will expose itself to WARN liability.

Adversely affected employees, including personnel who suffer work hour reductions of more than 50 percent during each month of a six-month period, who are not given timely advance notice of plant closings or mass layoffs may sue their offending employer in federal district court. These workers are entitled to back pay for each of the 60 days the employer failed to give them the required notice, and they may receive an award of reasonable attorney fees. The firm's liability is reduced by any wages actually paid to the affected workers covering the period of the violation and by any voluntary payments given to the employees that are not required by any legal obligation. If the company failed to provide timely advance notice to the appropriate local government unit, it would also be liable to a civil fine of up to $500 per day for each day of the violation. Nonetheless, if the company could demonstrate that its failure to give the requisite notice was caused by a reasonable belief that its omission was not a violation of WARN, the court may reduce the amount of statutory liability involved.

UNEMPLOYMENT COMPENSATION

The unemployment of millions of workers during the Great Depression induced Congress to recognize the need for a national unemployment compensation program. To accomplish this objective, Titles III and IX of the Social Security Act of 1935 imposed a federal payroll tax of 3 percent on all covered employers. A credit of up to 90 percent, or 2.7 percent, was provided for amounts paid by employers into qualified state unemployment compensation funds. This offset feature functioned as expected, as every state and the District of Columbia quickly established unemployment compensation programs. To reward firms that rarely laid off employees, the federal law allowed companies that did not pay the full 2.7 percent tax into a state unemployment fund to retain the 2.7 percent federal offset when they were assessed state unemployment tax rates of less than 2.7 percent based on their beneficial experience ratings with respect to layoffs over the prior three or four years.

The federal unemployment tax provisions that were originally contained in Title IX of the Social Security Act were subsequently incorporated in the Federal Unemployment Tax Act (FUTA).[16] The FUTA currently imposes a 6.2 percent payroll tax on the first $7,000 paid annually by covered employers to each employee. Of this amount, 6 percent constitutes the basic tax rate, with employers receiving a

---

[16]26 U.S.C. §§3301-11 (1993).

90 percent, or 5.4 percent, offset for amounts paid to state unemployment funds. The extra 0.2 percent represents a surtax that partially finances extended unemployment benefits that are available during recessionary periods. The other 0.6 percent federal tax is used to finance administration of the overall federal/state unemployment compensation system.

Covered Employers and Employees

All states are required to cover employers that paid wages of $1,500 or more during any calendar quarter during the current or preceding calendar year or that employed at least one worker on at least one day of each of 20 weeks during the current or preceding calendar year. Firms that paid cash wages of at least $20,000 for agricultural labor during any calendar quarter during the current or preceding calendar year or that employed at least 10 agricultural workers on at least one day of each of 20 weeks during that period are also covered. Employers that paid cash wages of $1,000 or more during any calendar quarter during the current or preceding calendar year for domestic service in a private home, college club, or college fraternity or sorority are similarly included, as are nonprofit organizations that employed four or more employees for one day during each of 20 different weeks during the current or preceding calendar year, and state and local governments. The term "wages" for coverage purposes does not include remuneration in excess of $7,000 paid to individual workers during a calendar year or fringe benefit contributions. Although 33 states[17] have adopted these federal coverage standards, 17[18] have established more expansive definitions.

The FUTA does not require state coverage of self-employed individuals or persons who work for personal relatives. Nor must states include temporary, nonresident aliens or individuals employed by

---

[17]Alabama, Arizona, Connecticut, Delaware, Florida, Georgia, Idaho, Illinois, Indiana, Iowa, Kansas, Kentucky, Louisiana, Maine, Michigan, Minnesota, Mississippi, Missouri, Nebraska, New Hampshire, New Mexico, North Carolina, North Dakota, Ohio, Oklahoma, South Carolina, South Dakota, Tennessee, Texas, Vermont, Virginia, West Virginia, and Wisconsin.

[18]Alaska, Arkansas, California, Colorado, Hawaii, Maryland, Massachusetts, Montana, Nevada, New Jersey, New York, Oregon, Pennsylvania, Rhode Island, Utah, Washington, and Wyoming.

foreign governments. People who work for churches or religious organizations also may be excluded. Even though states may voluntarily extend coverage to these groups, most have not done so.

The FUTA and state unemployment compensation statutes only cover parties with employer-employee relationships. The federal enactment and the laws of 14 states[19] expressly include those persons who have employment relationships within the meaning of the common law doctrines governing these issues. The most significant factor used by the courts tends to be the degree of control the principal party can exercise over the work being performed by the agent involved. When the principal can exercise meaningful control of the worker's actual job performance, a covered employment relationship is normally found, while uncovered independent contractor relationships are generally found when the principal lacks such control.

When the right-to-control factor does not clearly support covered employment or uncovered independent contractor status, courts applying the common law rules tend to evaluate the other *Restatement* factors.[20] Criteria supporting a covered employment relationship include:

- the worker is not employed in a distinct occupation or business;

- the work is usually performed in the geographical area under the direction of an employer;

- the work does not require the services of a highly skilled individual;

- the principal supplies the tools and place of work;

- the employment is for a considerable period of time and involves regular hours;

- the individual is to work exclusively for one party;

- the worker is to be paid by the hour, week, or month, and has not assumed the risk of loss if the work does not generate profits;

- the work being performed is part of the regular business of the principal;

---

[19]Alaska, Arizona, California, Florida, Iowa, Kentucky, Michigan, Minnesota, Mississippi, New York, North Carolina, Oklahoma, South Carolina, and Texas.
[20]*Restatement of Agency* §220 (1992).

- the parties believed that they were creating an employer-employee relationship; and

- the principal party is engaged in a business activity.

Courts do not apply these factors on a strictly numerical basis. They usually weigh all of the criteria to determine whether a covered employment relationship should be found, and they usually resolve close cases in favor of coverage. Most states have adopted language providing unemployment compensation coverage that is more inclusive than that determined by application of the traditional common law doctrines.

Eligible for Unemployment Benefits

The mere fact that individuals are out of work does not automatically entitle them to unemployment benefits. They must first demonstrate that they have earned a sufficient amount of wages during the "base period" to establish their benefit eligibility.[21] Most states also require claimants to show that they have been employed for a minimum amount of time during the base period. These eligibility rules are intended to limit unemployment benefits to those persons who have a continuing attachment to the covered labor force.

In 44 states and the District of Columbia, the base period includes the first four calendar quarters of the five calendar quarters immediately preceding the filing of the claim for unemployment compensation.[22] Every state and the District of Columbia restricts benefit eligibility to those persons who had specified minimum earnings during the base period. Most statutory minimums fall between $1,000 and $2,500. Every state, except California, Colorado, Delaware, Massachusetts, and Washington, also requires claimants to have been employed during at least two of the calendar quarters during the base period.

Able to Work

Unemployment benefits are intended to provide financial assistance to people who are out of work and who want to obtain gainful

---

[21]*See* U.S. Department of Labor, *Comparison of State Unemployment Insurance Laws* (updated semiannually), at 3-23 through 3-24, Table 300 (1993).

[22]The other six states, California, Massachusetts, Michigan, Nebraska, New Hampshire, and New York, use slightly different 52-week base periods.

employment. As a result, all 50 states and the District of Columbia limit unemployment compensation eligibility to claimants who are "able to work." Claimants who have disabilities precluding their employment must apply for workers' compensation if their conditions arose during and out of their employment, or nonoccupational disability benefits if they did not. Nevertheless, the mere fact that benefit applicants have physical or mental problems does not automatically cause a loss of benefit eligibility. So long as they are able to perform work suitable for individuals with their training and experience, they will retain their eligibility. Even when they cannot presently pursue their regular occupation, they will be entitled to benefits if they are still able to engage in other gainful employment. Some states do not consider short-term illness or disability to constitute disqualifying conditions, but others do during the period those conditions preclude gainful employment.

Available for Work

The unemployment regulations in all 50 states and the District of Columbia also require claimants to demonstrate that they are "available for work"—i.e., ready and willing to work. They must generally register at the appropriate public employment office, and most states require some additional indication that they are attempting to locate employment suitable to their skills and experience. Two-thirds of states expect claimants to establish that they are actively seeking work as part of the "available for work" prerequisite. This requirement normally obliges applicants to make reasonably diligent efforts each week to locate suitable employment. If they usually obtain their work through union hiring halls, they must register with those entities. In other cases, they must file applications with area firms that might need workers with their skills and experience.

Claimants who temporarily withdraw from the labor force do not necessarily forfeit their benefit eligibility. For example, individuals who take short vacations or who enroll in training courses will continue to be eligible for unemployment compensation, so long as they continue to look for employment and would be willing to accept suitable jobs they may locate. It is only when claimants truly withdraw from the active labor force that they lose their benefit eligibility. Doubts tend to be resolved in favor of continued eligibility.

Claimants who relocate to other geographical areas while they are unemployed may encounter eligibility problems. This issue often concerns workers who move to other regions to get married, to follow transferred spouses, or to find less expensive housing. People who move to regions with as much employment potential as the areas they left are normally still considered "available for work," even when they move to different states.

Difficulties may arise when benefit applicants relocate to areas that have fewer job opportunities. If there are almost no jobs suitable to individuals possessing the skills and experience of the claimants, they may lose their eligibility. Nonetheless, so long as there is a reasonable market in the new location for the services the claimants are willing and able to perform, courts tend to find them "available for work."

Similar eligibility issues are raised by benefit applicants who place restrictions on the types of employment they are willing to accept. Individuals who do not handle stress well might refuse to consider employment opportunities that would involve unusual pressure. If they do not impose extreme limitations on the kinds of work they will accept and they continue to seek less stressful work that might be available, they will usually be found eligible for benefits. On the other hand, if they place undue restrictions on the types of work they will accept, they will most likely forfeit their entitlement to benefits.

Family obligations or personal considerations may occasionally cause some claimants to indicate that they are unwilling to work the night shift or the day shift, or to accept jobs requiring weekend work. For example, single parents may only be willing to consider day work that would not necessitate the performance of weekend tasks. If courts find that such limitations significantly reduce their availability for suitable work, the persons will be found ineligible for benefits. On the other hand, claimants who refuse to accept employment that would require Saturday or Sunday work due to religious convictions may not be deprived of benefit eligibility due to their limited availability, because such action would violate their First Amendment right to freedom of religion.[23]

A few benefit applicants may impose other employment restrictions that raise availability issues. These limitations may concern the

---

[23]*See* Frazee v. Illinois Dep't of Employment Sec., 489 U.S. 829 (1989); Sherbert v. Verner, 374 U.S. 398 (1963).

physical environment, the location of work, the duration of employment, dress or grooming requirements, or wage levels. The critical question in these cases involves the degree to which such claimants have decreased their likelihood of obtaining suitable employment. If the restrictions imposed by claimants meaningfully diminish their job prospects, they will normally be found ineligible for unemployment benefits. On the other hand, if their limitations are not unreasonably expansive and it appears that they have not unduly restricted their employment opportunities, they will continue to be entitled to unemployment compensation.

Individuals who are temporarily laid off from their regular positions may inform prospective employers that they plan to return to their former jobs as soon as their former jobs become available. Such representations may cause many firms to hire other applicants who would be more likely to remain with them for extended periods. Courts frequently find that benefit applicants who effectively limit their interim job searches to companies that would be willing to hire short-term personnel have rendered themselves unavailable for work.

Unemployment claimants are not normally required to seek employment that would involve compensation substantially below that generally paid to persons with their skills and experience. As a result, they are not rendered ineligible for benefits by their unwillingness to look for work that would entail significantly reduced pay. Nonetheless, as the duration of their unemployment increases, claimants may be expected to "lower their sights" and indicate a willingness to accept employment that might involve skill levels or compensation below that normally associated with persons with their particular backgrounds. If they fail to consider job opportunities that are not wholly unsuitable to people possessing their skills and experience, they may well forfeit their right to continued unemployment compensation.

Disqualification

Discharge for Employment-Related Misconduct

The unemployment laws in all 50 states and the District of Columbia expressly disqualify claimants who have been recently discharged because of employment-related misconduct. In Alaska, Arkansas, Colorado, Florida, New Jersey, and West Virginia, the disqualification period is for a specified number of weeks, while in Alabama, Maryland, Missouri, Nebraska, South Carolina, and Vermont, it is for a variable number of weeks depending on the severity of the misconduct involved. In the remaining 38 states and the District of Columbia, the disqualification applies throughout the resulting period of unemployment. People disqualified in these states can only regain benefit eligibility through post-termination employment with covered employers for specified minimum periods of time.

Twenty-two state laws have additional disqualification provisions covering individuals terminated because of "gross misconduct." These provisions cover discharges based on admitted or convicted criminal theft connected with employment (Florida, Illinois, Indiana, Nevada, New York, Oregon, Utah, and Washington); employment-related felony or misdemeanor convictions (Maine and Utah); employment-related dishonest or criminal acts (Alabama); gross or aggravated misconduct at work (Missouri and South Carolina); willful or flagrant work-related misconduct (Maryland and Nebraska); or other similar acts of egregious misbehavior.

Courts have acknowledged that the general "misconduct" disqualification is intended to affect workers who have engaged in acts of wanton or willful misbehavior—deliberate violations of company rules or gross departures from accepted standards of conduct. As a result, mere inadvertence or inattention is normally not sufficient to disqualify benefit claimants.

Employers frequently challenge claimant eligibility for unemployment compensation when they discharge employees based upon their discovery of false statements made on initial job applications. These misrepresentations may concern applicant qualifications, criminal records, medical information, or other relevant factors. When job applicants have deliberately distorted information that is material to their ability to perform the requisite work, they may lose their right to benefits if their misrepresentations are discovered and lead to their termination.

On the other hand, if they successfully performed their jobs for several years before the misstatements were discovered, courts may refuse to disqualify the discharged individuals based on the theory that their application falsifications must not have been truly material.

Job applicants do not always provide complete answers to health questions. They may erroneously think that inquiries regarding back difficulties, chest pains, or other ailments are designed to elicit information regarding their current status. If they have previously suffered from such conditions but have not experienced any recent attacks, they may decide not to mention these circumstances. When courts conclude that health omissions were due to errors of judgment rather than to deliberate deceit, they usually refuse to disqualify the affected benefit claimants. It is only when it is clear that job applicants willfully misrepresented relevant medical information that they are likely to be disqualified on that basis.

Job applicants who fail to disclose criminal records are not automatically rendered ineligible for unemployment benefits when they are terminated as a result of their omissions. If their convictions did not involve violent acts or serious dishonesty and they were applying for positions that did not entail exposure to valuable property, their intentional failure to provide the requested information may not cause them to become disqualified for unemployment benefits. On the other hand, if the omitted criminal information concerned violent conduct or behavior evidencing a serious lack of integrity and the applicants were seeking employment that involved positions of trust, their omissions would most likely result in disqualification.

Employees who are discharged because of insubordination do not necessarily forfeit their unemployment benefit eligibility. Claimants who can establish that they refused to obey supervisory directives because of mitigating circumstances, such as confusion regarding the orders being given or concern about health and safety risks associated with the assigned tasks, are likely to be found eligible for unemployment compensation. Nonetheless, employees who willfully and inexcusably refuse to follow proper supervisory orders are likely to be found guilty of disqualifying misconduct.

The conduct of employees toward other workers or third persons may render them ineligible for unemployment benefits. While the use of profanity that would be considered mere "shop talk" would be unlikely to result in disqualification, the use of excessive or abusive profanity would usually cause a loss of eligibility. Disqualification is especially likely when vulgar remarks are directed toward customers or members of the public.

Employees who are fired because of their threats of physical violence against other workers or outside persons are almost always considered ineligible for benefits. Workers who resort to physical assaults are usually found disqualified. Only when claimants can demonstrate that their physical violence was used in an effort to defend themselves against the unprovoked aggression of others or was isolated and of a truly insignificant nature would they be likely to avoid benefit disqualification.

One of the most difficult questions raised under misconduct disqualification provisions concerns the eligibility of persons fired because of inefficient or negligent work performance. While it is recognized that occasional performance lapses should not be considered "misconduct," isolated acts of gross negligence or repeated acts of mere negligence may well cause a loss of benefit eligibility.

> [T]he intended meaning of the term 'misconduct' . . . is limited to conduct evincing such wilful or wanton disregard of an employer's interests as is found in deliberate violations or disregard of standards of behavior which the employer has the right to expect of his employee, or in carelessness or negligence of such degree or recurrence as to manifest equal culpability, wrongful intent or evil design, or to show an intentional and substantial disregard of the employer's interests or of the employee's duties and obligations to his employer.[24]

Infrequent errors due to mere inattention are usually not considered disqualifying. Nonetheless, if numerous mistakes are made, misconduct is often found, especially when the inattentive acts have caused significant harm. Furthermore, even single acts of gross negligence or reckless behavior that evidence a clear disregard for employer interests may be found disqualifying, particularly when substantial employer interests are threatened.

Companies often discharge employees because of absenteeism or tardiness. When continued absenteeism or repeated tardiness is found to constitute "misconduct," the affected workers are rendered ineligible for unemployment benefits. Courts usually base their determinations on several factors: (1) the frequency of absence or lateness; (2) whether the absent individuals have notified their employer of expected nonattendance; (3) whether the employer has cautioned employees with attendance problems of the negative consequences that are likely to result from continued absences; and (4) the reasons for the claimants' unavailability.

---

[24]Fitzgerald v. Globe-Union, Inc., 151 N.W.2d 136 (Wis. 1967).

When specific employees establish patterns of repeated absence or tardiness and are discharged because of that conduct, they are often found to have engaged in disqualifying misconduct. This result is especially likely when they have failed to provide valid reasons for their recurrent absences. It is also probable if they have received specific warnings regarding their unacceptable attendance. Even though courts are more lenient with employees whose repeated absences have been caused by personal illness, if these individuals have failed to notify their employer of expected absences and have not provided acceptable medical explanations, they may forfeit their entitlement to unemployment compensation.

In rare situations, even a single absence may be found disqualifying. For example, if supervisors specifically deny employee requests for time away from work for personal reasons and the workers deliberately ignore supervisory warnings of dire consequences if they fail to report to work, the offending individuals may lose their benefit eligibility. Similar disqualification may result when employees who are critical to the production process are absent and fail to notify their employer of their anticipated absence.

Employees who are terminated because of employment-related drug or alcohol abuse are often found guilty of disqualifying misconduct. This may occur when they report for work in an unfit condition or use illegal drugs or alcohol on employer premises. Disqualification is similarly likely with respect to employees who possess illicit drugs on company premises. Even individuals who violate company rules prohibiting off-duty drinking or drug use may forfeit their benefit eligibility, if the employer can demonstrate that the rule is reasonably related to valid employment interests. On the other hand, when such prohibitions have no demonstrable connection to bona fide firm interests, persons fired for violating those rules would probably not be found disqualified.

Unemployment benefit applicants who have been discharged because of work-related drinking or drug use occasionally argue that they are alcoholics or drug addicts whose compulsion to drink or use illegal drugs should preclude their loss of eligibility. They claim that their "involuntary" alcohol or drug use should not be considered "willful" misconduct. Most courts, however, have refused to accept this argument. Nonetheless, when workers with drinking problems have made good faith efforts to obtain treatment for their alcoholism, some courts have been willing to sustain their right to receive unemployment benefits.[25] Few have been willing to do so with respect to illegal drug users.[26]

An increasing number of firms require employees to submit to specific or random drug tests. **When company drug testing policies are reasonably applied, particularly when test requests are based on circumstances that objectively suggest drug abuse, people who refuse to comply may be found to have engaged in disqualifying misconduct.** On the other hand, if the employer cannot demonstrate an objective basis for believing that particular workers have been adversely affected by illegal drug use, their refusal to submit to requested tests would be unlikely to be considered disqualifying.

Employees are sometimes terminated when they refuse to work on Saturdays or Sundays or on the production of armaments because of their sincerely held religious convictions. If state unemployment administrators were to deny benefits to these persons based on their alleged "misconduct," this treatment would violate their First Amendment right to exercise their religious beliefs.[27] Even if states generally prohibit the use of controlled substances, they may not constitutionally apply misconduct disqualification provisions to people who are terminated because of their sacramental use of proscribed drugs. The Religious Freedom Restoration Act of 1993[28] requires the states to show a "compelling interest" to justify any policies that substantially burden the free exercise of religion.

Employers often claim that employees who have been discharged because of off-duty conduct should be denied unemployment benefits. Workers who misuse or misappropriate company property during their off-duty hours or commit unprovoked physical attacks against fellow employees are normally found ineligible for benefits. On the other hand, employees who have committed relatively minor off-duty thefts that do not indicate that they could no longer be trusted at work would probably not be found disqualified.

---

[25]*See, e.g.,* Independent Sch. Dist. v. Hansen, 412 N.W.2d 320 (Minn. App. 1987).

[26]*See, e.g.,* Kaminski v. Texas Employment Comm'n, 848 S.W.2d 811 (Tex. App. 1993).

[27]*See* Hobbie v. Unemployment Appeals Comm'n, 480 U.S. 136 (1987); Thomas v. Review Bd., 450 U.S. 707 (1981); Sherbert v. Verner, 374 U.S. 398 (1963).

[28]Pub. L. 103-141, 103 Cong., 1st Sess. (1993), *overruling* Employment Div. v. Smith, 494 U.S. 872 (1990).

Persons who engage in unlawful conduct during their off-duty hours away from company premises may similarly be found ineligible for benefits, if their employer can establish that their actions would have a negative impact on their employment relationship. For example, workers who develop off-duty ties with company customers that might adversely affect firm interests may be found guilty of disqualifying misconduct. Employees who commit serious off-duty crimes may also forfeit their eligibility, if their employer can show a reasonable relationship between their convictions and valid company interests. Disqualification would be likely with respect to persons who engage in notorious criminal acts that would reflect negatively on the reputation of their employer, or off-duty misconduct that would undermine the capacity of the guilty persons to perform their job functions (e.g., truck drivers who lose their licenses due to drunk driving violations; security personnel who lose their ability to be bonded because of theft convictions).

Voluntary Termination of Employment

Unemployment compensation is basically intended to provide financial assistance to individuals who are out of work through no fault of their own. As a result, it might seem inappropriate to award benefits to employees who voluntarily sever their employment relationships. State legislatures have recognized, however, that workers occasionally resign because of valid considerations that should not cause them to forfeit their unemployment eligibility. The unemployment compensation laws in all 50 states and the District of Columbia have sought to balance the competing interests by expressly disqualifying only those individuals who voluntarily leave their employment without good cause. When claimants are rendered ineligible under the voluntary termination disqualification, 45 states and the District of Columbia treat them as ineligible for benefits for the duration of their resulting unemployment. In Alaska, Colorado, Maryland, Nebraska, and Wisconsin, however, they are merely disqualified for periods ranging from 5 to 10 weeks.

In 13 states,[29] individuals who voluntarily sever their employment relationship do not forfeit their right to unemployment benefits if they

---

[29]Alaska, California, Hawaii, Nebraska, Nevada, New York, Ohio, Oregon, Pennsylvania, Rhode Island, South Carolina, Utah, and Virginia.

can demonstrate that they did so for "good cause." In the other 37 states and the District of Columbia, the exception to disqualification is limited to good cause that is either attributable to the employer or connected with their work. In these states, workers who resign their jobs for wholly personal reasons generally lose benefit eligibility because the resignation has no connection with their work.

The rules governing the voluntary termination disqualification vary widely from state to state. In states with the general "good cause" exception, personal considerations may be accepted in some states that would be rejected in others. Even within the many states requiring good cause attributable to the employer or connected with work, different results are often reached in cases involving similar circumstances. It is thus impossible to provide a set of universally applicable principles. Nonetheless, certain common themes should be mentioned.

When the right of claimants to receive benefits is challenged under voluntary termination disqualification provisions, three basic questions must normally be considered. First, did the workers actually terminate their employment. If there is merely evidence that they have been away from work for prolonged periods with no indication that they do not intend to return, they would probably not be considered to have resigned.

Second, even when claimants have truly severed their employment, courts must decide whether they did so "voluntarily." The mere fact that they have not been discharged does not automatically mean that they have left voluntarily. The surrounding circumstances must be scrutinized to determine whether their departures were in fact volitional. Even though they have actually tendered their resignations, their ultimate loss of employment may not be found "voluntary." If they sought to withdraw their resignations before they became effective but were informed that they could not do so, courts would be likely to find that their separations were not "voluntary." The claimants may also have resigned because they were told they would be discharged if they refused to quit. Although a number of courts regard such resignations as involuntary terminations, others treat such employment decisions as voluntary separations.

Third, workers are sometimes forced to end employment relationships due to health difficulties. Courts have usually recognized that employees who are impelled by sickness or disease to terminate their employment are engaged in involuntary, rather than voluntary, separation. On the other hand, if their employer has sought to accommodate their condition and they do not appear to have been truly compelled to leave their current position, their resignation would probably be found voluntary.

When benefit applicants are found to have voluntarily terminated their employment, through normal resignation or volitional retirement, they may only avoid disqualification by establishing that they fall within the statutory exception. In the 37 states and the District of Columbia that have narrow exceptions, they must show that their departure was generated by good cause that was either attributable to their employer or connected to their work. In the 13 states with general "good cause" exemptions, they may avoid disqualification by relying on valid employment-related reasons or acceptable personal considerations.

Good Cause Attributable to the Employer

In states that require claimants to establish that they terminated their employment for good cause attributable to their employer or connected with their work, it is clear that wholly personal reasons will be insufficient to prevent a loss of benefit eligibility. To avoid disqualification, they must convince unemployment compensation administrators that they had valid reasons for their actions and that the articulated justifications were related to their previous employment. Typical examples involve employees who quit when they learn that their wages are being reduced. If the reductions are "substantial"—20 to 25 percent or more—courts are likely to conclude that they terminated their employment for good cause associated with their employer. If the reductions are 15 percent or less, however, judges would probably find an absence of good cause. Employment-related good cause also may be found when individuals resign due to significantly increased workloads that are not accompanied by corresponding salary enhancements.

Some unemployment benefit applicants claim that they ended their employment because of work-related mistreatment or harassment. In these situations, courts ask whether the adverse circumstances in question were sufficient to have induced a reasonable employee to resign. A number of court decisions have indicated that individuals encountering such employment difficulties must initially notify management officials and provide their employer with the opportunity to correct the situation before they resort to termination.[30]

The mere fact that supervisors subject employees to abusive language is usually considered insufficient to provide good cause for resigning. Nonetheless, when the verbal abuse becomes extreme or is accompanied by other forms of harassment, good cause is normally found. When supervisors select their targets in a discriminatory manner, the victims of their demeaning tactics are likely to have good cause to quit. Typical cases involve gender or racial harassment that would violate applicable civil rights laws. Even when the harassment comes from co-workers instead of supervisory personnel, good cause attributable to the employer will usually be found if the offensive behavior is serious and management officials do not act promptly to correct the situation.

Some employees develop allergic reactions to substances found in their work environments. When their conditions become serious, they may be forced to resign. If these persons could show that they notified their employer of their problems but were unable to obtain corrective action or reassignment to more healthful positions, they would probably be found to have severed their employment due to good cause associated with their employer. Some decisions have found individuals who quit because of their inability to tolerate the cigarette smoke generated by co-workers to be still eligible for unemployment benefits.[31]

Employees occasionally decide to resign when their employer relocates to another community. If they can demonstrate that the distance to the new location is substantial or that adequate public transportation is unavailable, they may be able to avoid benefit disqualification. On the other hand, if the other location is not too far from their former place of work, they would most likely be found ineligible, particularly if adequate public transportation were available.

The unemployment statutes in 16 states[32] that disqualify employees who voluntarily terminate their employment without good cause

---

[30]*See, e.g.*, Smalls v. State Unemployment Appeals Comm'n, 485 So.2d 1 (Fla. App. 1985), *review denied*, 492 So.2d 1335 (Fla. 1985).

[31]*See, e.g.*, Alexander v. Unemployment Ins. Appeal Bd., 163 Cal. Rptr. 411 (Cal. App. 1980).

[32]Alabama, Connecticut, Florida, Illinois, Indiana, Kansas, Maine, Massachusetts, Michigan, Minnesota, Missouri, North Dakota, South Dakota, Washington, West Virginia, and Wisconsin.

associated with their employer provide an express exception for people who leave one firm to accept employment with another company. In Alabama, Florida, Missouri, South Dakota, and West Virginia, this exception is limited to situations in which workers on layoff from their regular employer give up interim positions to return to their usual jobs. In the other 11 states that have this statutory exception, disqualification may be avoided not only when people resign current jobs to return to former places of work, but also when they leave firms to accept more advantageous positions with other companies.

General Good Cause

The unemployment laws in 13 states[33] permit workers who voluntarily sever their employment to avoid benefit disqualification if they can establish that they left their job because of "good cause." Claimants in these states need not demonstrate cause associated with their employment. If unemployment administrators find that claimants offered personal reasons sufficiently compelling to justify their resignations, they continue to be eligible for benefits. Courts evaluating these cases usually ask whether the cited circumstances would have been likely to cause reasonable workers faced with the same situation to leave their employer. Due to the inherently subjective nature of this test, the judicial determinations vary greatly from state to state.

Many of the cases arising under general "good cause" provisions concern family-related considerations. For example, employees may terminate their present positions and relocate to other areas to become married, to follow their spouses, or to care for sick family members. They may also move to different geographical areas for health reasons or because of economic factors. While these individuals would almost always be found disqualified under statutes that only exempt persons who resign for good cause attributable to their employer, they may be able to retain their eligibility in states with general "good cause" exemptions.

Some states have elected to deal with these issues through express statutory provisions. These sections typically provide that employees who voluntarily terminate their employment to marry, to follow spouses

---

[33]Alaska, California, Hawaii, Nebraska, Nevada, New York, Ohio, Oregon, Pennsylvania, Rhode Island, South Carolina, Utah, and Virginia.

to new locations, or to satisfy other marital or family obligations will be considered ineligible for benefits. To survive constitutional challenge under the equal protection clause of the Fourteenth Amendment, these statutory provisions must apply equally to male and female claimants who resign to follow spouses or to satisfy other familial duties. In states with such provisions, claimants who resign from their employment because of family considerations can only obtain benefits if they can convince unemployment administrators that their family concerns were so substantial that their resignations should not be considered "volitional" acts. In most of these cases, the benefit applicants are found ineligible.

Unemployment laws in a few states have express provisions that treat claimants who resign because of family obligations quite differently. They specifically preserve the benefit eligibility of these individuals. As a result, people who quit for spousal or familial reasons may obtain benefits in these states, so long as their family duties do not render them unavailable for work and they actively attempt to locate suitable work.

In "good cause" states that do not have separate statutory sections dealing with the eligibility of people who resign because of marital or family considerations, it is not clear whether workers who quit for such reasons will be eligible for benefits. Many courts avoid disqualification by finding that significant family concerns constitute "good cause." Other courts, however, refuse to do so, unless the claimants can establish truly compelling circumstances. Employees who resign to get married are less likely to be found eligible than persons who quit to follow current spouses. Furthermore, people who leave their present jobs to follow nonmarital "loved ones" with whom they are merely cohabiting are rarely awarded benefits.

When individuals become divorced or widowed, they often encounter financial problems. Similar difficulties may arise when one of two gainfully employed spouses is laid off. If persons affected by such economic exigencies decide to relocate to less expensive geographical areas, they may retain their benefit eligibility if they can convince unemployment administrators that their situations were truly urgent. In the absence of clearly necessitous circumstances, however, they are likely to be found disqualified.

Workers occasionally move to other geographical areas when family members develop serious medical conditions and physicians recommend relocation to more healthful environments. If claimants who relocate for these reasons can show that their particular circumstances were extremely compelling, they may be found to have had "good cause" to terminate their former positions. In most cases of this kind, benefits are denied.

The employment of female workers is frequently affected by pregnancy and childbirth. Personal or medical considerations may cause workers to terminate their employment during portions of their pregnancy and/or the period immediately following childbirth. In 1976, Congress amended section 3304(a)(12) of the Federal Unemployment Tax Act (FUTA) to prohibit the disbursement of federal unemployment funds to any state that denies compensation to claimants "solely on the basis of pregnancy." Nonetheless, the United States Supreme Court has recognized that this section does not prevent states from disqualifying claimants who voluntarily terminate their employment for reasons that are unrelated to their employer.[34] Although this provision forbids states from singling out pregnancy for disadvantageous treatment, it does not require states to treat pregnancy in a preferential manner. As a result, states may continue to apply to pregnant employees regular statutory provisions disqualifying workers who voluntarily leave their jobs without good cause associated with their employment. In these states, claimants may only avoid the loss of benefit eligibility if they can establish that job-related circumstances adversely affected their pregnant conditions and forced them to resign.

Pregnant claimants who resign in states with general "good cause" exception provisions have a greater likelihood of obtaining benefits than workers who leave their employment in states that only exempt employees who quit for reasons attributable to their employer. Nonetheless, they must still overcome several obstacles before they can receive compensation. They must initially convince unemployment administrators that they had valid reasons for resigning that would have induced other similarly situated individuals to sever their employment. Even if they can satisfy this burden, they must still demonstrate that they remain able and available for work despite their pregnancy or postnatal condition. Doubts regarding their continued capacity to engage in gainful employment tend to be resolved against eligibility.

---

[34]*See* Wimberly v. Labor & Indus. Relations Comm'n, 479 U.S. 511 (1987).

Refusal to Accept Suitable Employment

The unemployment compensation statutes in all 50 states and the District of Columbia disqualify otherwise eligible claimants who refuse, without good cause, to accept "suitable employment" during the period of their unemployment. In three-fourths of the states and the District of Columbia, individuals who reject suitable employment render themselves ineligible for the duration of their unemployment. They can only reestablish their right to benefits through subsequent covered employment for a minimum period of time ranging from 4 weeks in Illinois and Minnesota to 16 weeks in Idaho and 17 weeks in Florida. Six state laws[35] limit the period of disqualification to from 3 to 20 weeks. The statutes in the remaining five states[36] provide variable periods of disqualification that depend on the circumstances involved.

Before claimants can be disqualified under this type of provision, there must be evidence that they refused without good cause to accept "suitable" employment that was offered to them. Mere knowledge of job openings is insufficient to cause a loss of benefit eligibility. Actual offers must normally have been made and rejected. The standards used to determine whether claimants have refused to accept "suitable" employment are similar to those applied to decide whether benefit applicants have initially made themselves "available" for appropriate work. Unemployment administrators review the relevant circumstances to determine whether the rejected job opportunities involved work that was commensurate with claimant skills, experience, and background. The administrators examine the employment environments, the job functions, the compensation levels, and other similar factors.

Section 3304(a)(5) of the FUTA specifically states that benefits shall not be denied to claimants who reject otherwise suitable work if: (1) the position is vacant due to a strike, lockout, or other labor dispute; (2) the wages, hours, or other conditions of work with respect to the offered position are substantially less beneficial than those prevailing for similar work in the geographical area; or (3) the person accepting the employment offer would be required to join a company union or to resign from or refrain from joining a bona fide labor organization.

---

[35]Alaska, Arkansas, Colorado, Massachusetts, Michigan, and New Jersey.
[36]Alabama, California, Maryland, Nebraska, and West Virginia.

Unemployed individuals who refuse to accept offered jobs frequently claim that the positions did not entail "suitable" work because of the substantially reduced skill levels involved, the increased commuting distance associated with the positions, or the lack of adequate public transportation. If unemployment administrators conclude that the offered positions were clearly not suited to people in claimant circumstances, they are likely to find no disqualification.

Unemployed persons often reject positions that have terms and conditions of employment that are not as beneficial as those associated with their previous employment. If the working conditions of the rejected jobs were substantially more onerous than those connected with their prior jobs, there is a good chance administrators would find the rejected positions unsuitable.

A number of cases have concluded that employment offers rejected by claimants did not involve suitable work as a result of their significantly reduced compensation levels. Most of these cases have concerned positions with wage rates 15 to 20 percent below those previously earned by the unemployed persons.[37] When less drastic reductions are involved, claims of a lack of suitability are likely to be rejected. Furthermore, as the duration of claimant unemployment increases, many states require those individuals to "lower their sights" and consider positions that have terms that are not as beneficial as those associated with their prior jobs. Although the decisions vary widely from state to state, because of the subjective factors involved, a number of cases have disqualified claimants who refused to accept jobs that paid 20 percent less than their previous positions after they had been unemployed for 15, 20, or 25 weeks.[38]

Claimants who are found to have rejected suitable employment offered to them may still avoid disqualification if they can establish that they had "good cause" for refusing those offers. For example, serious health considerations may have caused them to refuse work in environments that would probably have exacerbated their conditions. Such benefit applicants, however, would be obliged to show that they remained able to and available for other suitable work despite their health limitations, or they would lose their eligibility on that basis.

---

[37]See, e.g., Sproul v. Commonwealth, 322 A.2d 765 (Pa. Cmmw. 1974).

[38]See, e.g., Boeing Co. v. State Employment Sec. Bd. of Review, 496 P.2d 1376 (Kan. 1972).

Unemployment Caused by a Labor Dispute

When labor disputes arise between employers and unions, work stoppages may occur. The employees may decide to strike, or the company may decide to lock out the workers. The unemployment laws in all 50 states and the District of Columbia have disqualification provisions that relate to employees who are out of work because of labor-management controversies. Twenty-two states[39] disqualify individuals who are unemployed because of a "stoppage of work due to a labor dispute." Eleven states[40] and the District of Columbia disqualify people who are out of work due to a "labor dispute in active progress." In ten states,[41] workers are rendered ineligible during unemployment caused by the existence of labor disputes. The remaining seven states[42] employ somewhat different formulations to disqualify claimants who are out of work because of labor-management controversies.

States have historically denied unemployment benefits to striking employees because they consider those individuals to have severed their employment voluntarily. On the other hand, the "voluntariness" factor is absent when workers are locked out by their employer. Nonetheless, many states apply the labor dispute disqualification to both strikers and locked out personnel. This is primarily due to the belief that state governments should remain neutral during company-union conflicts. State legislatures do not want to provide government assistance to individuals involved in labor controversies. They also believe that it would be unfair to require companies to subsidize employees who are exerting economic pressure against them.

In most states, the period of disqualification only ends when the "stoppage of work due to a labor dispute" terminates or the unemployment is no longer caused by "a labor dispute in active progress."[43]

---

[39]Alaska, Delaware, Georgia, Hawaii, Illinois, Iowa, Kansas, Maine, Maryland, Massachusetts, Mississippi, Missouri, Nebraska, New Hampshire, New Jersey, Oklahoma, Pennsylvania, Texas, Utah, Vermont, West Virginia, and Wisconsin.

[40]Alabama, California, Florida, Kentucky, Louisiana, Minnesota, Nevada, Oregon, South Carolina, Tennessee, and Wisconsin.

[41]Arizona, Connecticut, Idaho, Montana, New Mexico, North Dakota, Ohio, Rhode Island, South Dakota, and Washington.

[42]Arkansas, Colorado, Indiana, Michigan, New York, North Carolina, and Virginia.

[43]In New York, the labor dispute disqualification continues for a maximum of seven weeks. After they have been out of work for more than seven weeks, New York claimants are thereafter entitled to benefits.

Nevertheless, if disqualified claimants find new employment with other firms, they may regain their benefit eligibility. In the vast majority of states, however, they cannot eliminate their ineligibility through mere interim employment. They must demonstrate that they have completely severed the relationship with their previous employer and have accepted "permanent" work with other companies.

Under the disqualification provisions set forth in most state laws, workers are only ineligible for benefits when they are totally or partially unemployed because of either a "stoppage of work" caused by a labor dispute or a "labor dispute in active progress." Application of these alternative formulations usually results in similar eligibility determinations. Nonetheless, there are occasions when persons who would be disqualified under one would remain eligible under the other, and vice versa.

States with "stoppage of work" language must initially determine whether a "stoppage of work" has occurred. It is generally recognized that this phrase concerns a meaningful reduction or cessation of employer operations. As a result, a slight decrease in production caused by a walkout by a few employees is usually not considered a "stoppage of work." The walkout must cause a "substantial curtailment" of operations. Furthermore, if a firm hires temporary or permanent replacements for striking individuals and resumes relatively normal operations or transfers the affected work to other nonstruck facilities, courts are likely to find no "stoppage of work." Such a conclusion would render the striking employees eligible for benefits, even though they continued to be unemployed due to a labor dispute.

Individuals are sometimes laid off by their employer because of a work stoppage by persons at another company facility or at a plant owned by an independent supplier or customer. **It is crucial to recognize that the disqualification provisions in most states only apply if the claimants are unemployed because of a labor dispute at the "factory, establishment or other premises at which [they are or were] last employed."** If their lack of work is caused by a labor-management controversy involving another company, including one closely related to their own employer, they will usually retain their benefit eligibility.

Even when workers are laid off due to a bargaining dispute involving people employed at another facility of the same company, the displaced personnel will not necessarily be disqualified. Courts examine the geographical proximity of the plants and the degree of functional integration between the two facilities to decide whether they should be considered a single "establishment" for disqualification purposes. When the operations being performed at the different facilities are not functionally interrelated or the plants are located some distance from one another, they are usually found to be separate "establishments."

Employees who voluntarily join a work stoppage by other company personnel or who willingly refuse to cross a picket line established by striking employees are usually found to be "participating in" that stoppage. If the picket line they honor is located at their place of employment, these "sympathy strikers" would be ineligible for benefits because they would be unemployed due to a labor dispute at the establishment at which they were last employed. On the other hand, if truck drivers or delivery people who are not employed by the firm directly involved in the labor-management conflict merely honor a picket line at the struck company's premises, they would be unlikely to lose their benefit eligibility since they would not be unemployed because of a labor dispute at *their* place of employment.

Employees who refuse to cross a picket line at their own place of employment can only retain their benefit eligibility if they can demonstrate that they did not honor the picket line voluntarily. They would have to show that they refused to go to work because they reasonably feared that meaningful physical harm would probably have resulted if they had attempted to pass through the picket line. Although threats of immediate physical injury may be sufficient to excuse their failure to report for work, mere verbal abuse or statements regarding possible future recriminations are normally found insufficient to preserve their benefit eligibility.

Compensation Procedures

State unemployment compensation laws are usually implemented by administrative agencies. Benefit claims are generally initiated in public employment offices. Unemployed individuals register for work with the local public employment service. If no suitable work is available, they may file claims for unemployment compensation. They must supply information regarding their recent past employment and the reason for their current unemployment. A claimant's immediate past employer will either have filed a form indicating the reason for the worker's loss of employment or it will be sent a form requesting such information. A claims examiner must then review the file to determine whether the claimant is eligible for benefits, is ready, willing, and able to work, and is not disqualified under one of the statutory disqualification provisions.

In the vast majority of cases, it is clear that the claimants are eligible for benefits and are not disqualified. The examiner calculates the amount and duration of their benefits, and they begin to receive their compensation. Only a few cases involve eligibility or disqualification questions. In these instances, the examiner reviews the relevant information and determines whether the claimants are entitled to benefits. Claimants who are denied benefits may request internal agency review, just as dissatisfied employers may appeal awards of compensation to individuals they think are ineligible. Relatively informal hearings are conducted by a single referee or a review board. The referee or board then decides whether the initial agency determination should be sustained, modified, or reversed. Parties dissatisfied by review board decisions may normally appeal those determinations to final administrative appeal bodies.

After final administrative decisions have been reached, losing parties may seek judicial review. In most states, only limited judicial review is permitted. Judges are required to accept agency fact-findings that are supported by substantial evidence. Although statutory interpretations are subject to closer judicial scrutiny, courts tend to defer to statutory constructions made by the administrative agency that was created to interpret and apply the state unemployment compensation law.

Interstate Benefit Payment Plan

On some occasions, unemployed individuals who are unable to find suitable employment within their home state move to another state where they think their job prospects will be better. If they do not locate new employment quickly, they may file for unemployment compensation in their new location. Under the universally followed Interstate Benefit Payment Plan, their new state acts as the agent for the state in which they earned their covered wages. The local unemployment examiners obtain the relevant information from the claimants and transfer that information to their former state, which elicits additional information from their prior employers. Administrators in the state in which they earned their qualifying wages then determine their benefit eligibility applying their own state law. If the claimants are found entitled to benefits, the compensation is provided by the agency in the state in which they currently reside, and that agency charges their former state for the benefits that are paid out.

Wage Combining Arrangement

Similar questions sometimes arise when claimants have earned qualifying wages in different states. These situations are governed by the Wage-Combining Arrangement. The state in which they file claims obtains information from the unemployment agencies in all of the states in which the claimants have recently been employed, and it determines, under its own law, whether they are entitled to benefits. If compensation is awarded, each state is charged a pro rata share based on the percentage of qualifying wages that were earned in those respective states.

Benefit Levels and Duration

When covered employees become unemployed, they may immediately apply for benefits. If they are found eligible and are not disqualified, they may receive compensation without any waiting period in 11 states.[44] The other 39 states and the District of Columbia usually require a one-week period of unemployment before claimants may begin to obtain benefits.

Individuals who are not totally unemployed but who suffer substantially reduced hours of work can apply for partial unemployment benefits. Twenty-five states[45] consider reduced-hour employees "partially unemployed" when their earnings are lower than the weekly unemployment benefit amounts for which they are eligible. Most of the remaining states use a definition that covers partially unemployed

---

[44]Alabama, Connecticut, Delaware, Georgia, Iowa, Kentucky, Maryland, Michigan, Nevada, New Hampshire, and Wisconsin.

[45]Alabama, Arizona, California, Colorado, Florida, Hawaii, Illinois, Indiana, Kansas, Louisiana, Michigan, Minnesota, Mississippi, Nebraska, Nevada, New Hampshire, New Mexico, North Dakota, Ohio, Oregon, South Carolina, South Dakota, Tennessee, Utah, and Virginia.

persons who have weekly earnings less than their weekly benefit amounts plus from $5 to $50 or below a specified multiple of their benefit amount ranging from 1.25 to 2.0.

Most states calculate weekly benefits as a percentage of the earnings received by claimants during the calendar quarter of the base period in which they had their greatest earnings. States usually set weekly benefit amounts as 1/23, 1/24, 1/25, or 1/26 of the earnings obtained by claimants during the relevant calendar quarter, resulting in benefit amounts ranging from 50 to 56 percent of their average weekly earnings. States also specify minimum and maximum weekly benefit amounts available to unemployed individuals.[46] The minimums range from $5 in Hawaii and $10 in Louisiana to $61 in New Jersey and $64 in Washington. The maximum amounts range from $150 in Alabama and $154 in South Dakota, to $356 in Rhode Island and $423 in Massachusetts. A few states provide weekly benefit supplements based on the number of dependent children being cared for. As a result of the Tax Reform Act of 1986, all unemployment benefits constitute taxable income.[47]

Totally unemployed claimants are entitled to the weekly benefit amounts available to persons with their prior earnings, subject to the maximum and minimum levels applicable to their state. Partially unemployed individuals are normally given their regular weekly benefit amounts reduced by the wages they actually earned during those weeks. Fully insured claimants are generally entitled to a maximum of 26 weeks of benefits. During recessionary periods, however, the federal government occasionally provides special funds to enable states to offer additional weeks of compensation to individuals who suffer prolonged unemployment. In most cases, claimants are provided with an extra 13 weeks of benefits. Congress frequently limits the availability of extended benefits to states with unemployment rates above the national average.

Benefit Reductions and Repayment

State unemployment administrators must occasionally decide whether claimant benefit eligibility should be affected by their receipt

---

[46]See U.S. Dep't of Labor, *Comparison of State Unemployment Insurance Laws* (updated semiannually), at 3-35 through 3-38, Table 304 (1993).

[47]See 26 U.S.C. §85 (1993).

of other forms of compensation, such as severance pay, vacation pay, supplemental unemployment benefits, workers' compensation, or retirement payments. Resolution of this issue depends upon the specific language contained in the applicable state unemployment statute. When statutory provisions cover such collateral income, they either require a commensurate reduction in weekly benefit amounts or cause the affected claimants to lose their unemployment benefit eligibility for the weeks in which they receive the extra income. Courts frequently disagree regarding the proper treatment of such things as severance pay and vacation pay. Some consider these payments forms of deferred compensation that were previously earned, and they do not allow current payments to affect unemployment benefit levels. Others, however, treat these payments as income when they are received and allow their receipt to cause a reduction in unemployment compensation.

Unemployment benefits are occasionally given to claimants who are not actually entitled to them, or excessive benefit amounts are erroneously granted to individuals. When benefits are improperly paid because of mistakes or misrepresentations made by claimants, state unemployment agencies may normally obtain court-ordered repayment of the sums involved. Individuals who make deliberate misrepresentations to unemployment agencies may also subject themselves to criminal liability. Most courts require repayment of benefits that were paid due to errors on the part of unemployment administrators, but they are less willing to order the repayment of excess benefits that were paid due to mistakes contained in reports prepared by employers.

10

Retirement

INTRODUCTION

Since World War II, pensions have been an important benefit of employment, but until 1974 there was no systematic regulation of the structure, funding, and activities of pension plans. Problems and abuses eventually surfaced as the first wave of workers under plans established during and after World War II began to retire and found that they had few, if any, rights to their pension benefits. For instance, many plans did not permit employees to participate until they had reached a certain age and had worked continuously for the company for a specified number of years. Breaks in employment because of events such as layoffs and disability often prevented workers from meeting the service requirement of their employer's plan. Similarly, many plans required a long period of continuous service, often as much as 20 or more years, before a worker's benefits would vest. In the early 1970s a Treasury Department study found that only one out of three workers participating in employer-sponsored plans had a 50 percent or greater vested right to his or her accrued benefits, and 54 percent of covered employees 60 years of age and older did not have vested rights to half of their accrued benefits.

In addition, although the concepts of using actuarial principles to predict future pension claims for defined benefit plans and funding those plans in advance were well established, there was no requirement

505

that plans be adequately funded. The most infamous plan failure involved the December 1963 closing of the Studebaker plant in South Bend, Indiana, and the termination of its pension plan with insufficient assets to pay all its liabilities. Over 4,000 workers with vested rights in the plan lost all or part of their pension benefits.[1] As one observer put it:

> In all too many cases the pension promise shrinks to this: 'If you remain in good health and stay with the same company until you are 68 years old, and if the company is still in business, and if your department has not been abolished, and if you haven't been laid off for too long a period, and if there is enough money in the fund, and if that money has been prudently managed, you will get a pension.'[2]

Interest in pension reform grew, and in 1974 Congress enacted the Employee Retirement Income Security Act (ERISA).[3] ERISA imposes minimum standards on employee benefit plans. All covered benefit plans, both pension plans and welfare plans, are subject to statutory structural requirements, reporting and disclosure obligations, fiduciary standards, preemption of state law, federal court enforcement, and civil and criminal remedies for violations. Pension plans, but not welfare plans, are also subject to participation, vesting, accrual, funding, and survivor's benefits requirements. In addition, ERISA regulates the termination of pension plans, provides for plan termination insurance, and imposes liability on employers that withdraw from multiemployer plans under certain circumstances. This chapter discusses the ERISA standards that apply only to pension plans and its fiduciary standards. Other ERISA requirements are discussed in chapter 3.

The passage of ERISA coincided with and probably contributed to the beginning of a second stage of pension plan development. Since the early 1970s, private pension plan coverage has remained stable at between 51 and 53 percent of full-time workers. At the same time, coverage under defined contribution plans has increased, while coverage under defined benefit plans has decreased. Observers have

---

[1]Michael S. Gordon, *Overview: Why Was ERISA Enacted?*, in U.S. Senate, Special Comm. on Aging, The Employee Retirement Income Security Act of 1974: The First Decade, S. Print. No. 221, 98th Cong., 2d Sess. (1984).

[2]Pension and Welfare Plans: Hearing Before the Subcom. on Labor, Comm. on Labor and Public Welfare, United States Senate, July 25, 1968, 90th Cong., 2d Sess. 217 (1968) (testimony of Assistant Secretary Thomas R. Donahue).

[3]29 U.S.C. §§1001–1461 (1992).

attributed these trends to a number of factors, including shifts in employment from large, heavily unionized, high-wage companies to smaller, nonunion, low-wage firms and the increasing costs and administrative burdens imposed by ERISA and its subsequent amendments.

COVERAGE OF PENSION PLANS

Under ERISA a pension benefit plan is "any plan, fund, or program" established or maintained by an employer, a union, or both, that "(i) provides retirement income to employees, or (ii) results in a deferral of income by employees for periods extending to the termination of covered employment or beyond," regardless of the method of calculating contributions or benefits or of distributing benefits.

Under ERISA there are two types of pension plans: individual account, or defined contribution plans, and defined benefit plans. A defined contribution plan is a plan in which a separate account is established for each participant, and retirement benefits are based on the amount in that account. Defined contribution plans include money purchase plans, as well as profit sharing plans and stock option plans. The employer makes annual contributions to each account in an amount established by the plan. The employer fulfills its funding obligation completely by making its annual contribution. The plan's trustees then manage the plan and invest its assets. Each account shares proportionately in the plan's investment gains or losses, and at retirement the employee's pension benefit depends solely on the amount in his or her account. Thus, the investment risk falls on the employee, not on the plan sponsor; if the plan performs poorly, the employee has less in his or her account and therefore a lower pension benefit. Of course, if the plan performs well, the employee benefits accordingly.

A defined benefit plan, on the other hand, is a plan that promises a certain retirement benefit. Most defined benefit plans provide for a benefit in the form of a life annuity, payable at the plan's normal retirement age (generally 65). The amount of the annuity is determined according to a formula, generally based on variables such as an employee's years of service and his or her average compensation for an entire career or a specified number of years before retirement. The employer must fund the plan so that the benefits fixed by the formula will be available to employees when they retire years in the future.

Basically, ERISA requires plan sponsors to contribute the present value of the future benefit obligations for each year of service. These contributions are determined actuarially, taking into account the age and mortality of employees and their spouses, employee turnover, projected wage increases, and economic assumptions about interest rates and rates of return on plan investments. In a defined benefit plan, unlike a defined contribution plan, the investment risk falls on the plan sponsor. If the plan's investments perform poorly and are not sufficient to fund promised benefit payments, the sponsor of a defined benefit plan must make up the difference through increased contributions. Conversely, if investments produce higher-than-expected returns, the employer's funding obligation is reduced.

ERISA also differentiates between single employer plans and multiemployer plans. A single employer plan is a plan sponsored by one employer, whether collectively bargained or not. Multiemployer plans, which are common in industries with patterns of multiemployer collective bargaining, such as trucking, building and construction, and entertainment, are collectively bargained plans to which more than one employer contributes. A major difference between the two kinds of plans is that multiemployer plans are also governed by section 302(c)(5) of the Taft-Hartley Act,[4] which requires jointly administered employee benefit plans to have an equal number of union-appointed and management-appointed trustees.

The Internal Revenue Code also regulates pension plans extensively. The favorable tax treatment received by plans meeting its requirements, or "qualified" plans, accounts in large part for the widespread growth of pension plans since World War II. Subject to certain limits, employer contributions to qualified plans are deductible when made, the employee is not taxed on contributions or earnings until benefits are paid, and the trust itself is tax-exempt. Although ERISA covers pension plans without regard to their tax-qualified status, most ERISA plans are also qualified plans.

Enforcement of ERISA's coverage of pension plans is divided among three government agencies. The Treasury Department has responsibility for administering and enforcing most of ERISA's participation, vesting, and funding requirements. The Department of Labor has responsibility for most of the fiduciary standards and prohibited

---

[4] 29 U.S.C. §186(c)(5) (1993).

transaction provisions. The Internal Revenue Service enforces the parts of the Tax Code that apply to qualified pension plans.

REQUIREMENTS FOR PENSION PLANS

One of ERISA's main purposes is protecting employees' expectations that they will actually receive the pension benefits their employers promised. To prevent harsh qualification and forfeiture rules and plan amendments limiting previously promised pension obligations, ERISA imposes minimum participation, vesting, and accrual requirements on most covered pension plans. To prevent employers from failing to set aside enough money to pay their future pension obligations, ERISA also imposes funding standards on defined benefit plans and money purchase plans. Welfare plans, discussed in chapter 3, are not subject to any of these requirements.

Years of Service

The basic measurement for participation, vesting, and accrual is years of service. ERISA has complicated rules of calculation, but basically a year of service is 1,000 hours of service during a 12-month period. Generally, all of an employee's years of service with the employer that sponsors the pension plan must be counted in determining periods of service.

Participation

An employee must be permitted to participate in a pension plan when he or she reaches the age of 21 or completes one year of service, whichever is later. A plan may delay participation until an employee has completed two years of service if it provides for 100 percent vesting after two years. Plans may not exclude employees from participation because they have reached a specified age.

Vesting

The concept of vesting and the requirement that vesting occur before retirement are key aspects of ERISA's reform of pension plan administration. An employee's right to participate in a pension plan matters only if at some point the employee vests in the plan. An accrued benefit is "vested" or "nonforfeitable" when the participant's claim to the benefit is unconditional and legally enforceable against the plan. Vested benefits cannot be lost through termination of employment.

ERISA establishes three minimum standards for vesting of accrued benefits. First, all pension plans must provide that employees' rights to their normal retirement benefits become nonforfeitable when they reach normal retirement age. This rule applies even if the employee does not have enough years of service to vest under one of the preretirement vesting schedules discussed below. Plans may define "normal retirement age" as the later of age 65 or the 10th anniversary of the beginning of an employee's participation in the plan.

Second, pension plans must provide that accrued benefits derived from employees' own contributions, if the plan requires or permits employee contributions, are nonforfeitable at all times.

Third, for accrued benefits derived from the employer's contributions, plans must provide one of three preretirement vesting schedules. Employees who satisfy the plan's preretirement vesting schedule have a nonforfeitable claim to their accrued benefits at retirement, even if they leave their jobs before reaching the plan's normal retirement age.

The first preretirement vesting option is five-year "cliff" vesting. Under this method, no vesting is required at all until the end of five years of service, but then the employee must be 100 percent vested. The second preretirement vesting schedule permits graduated vesting. Under this schedule, employees must be at least 20 percent vested after three years of service, with at least an additional 20 percent vesting in each successive year; the benefit must be 100 percent vested after seven years of service. Only multiemployer plans may use the third preretirement vesting schedule, which permits 10-year cliff vesting for employees covered by a collective bargaining agreement.

These preretirement vesting provisions were intended to prevent enforcement of so-called "bad boy" clauses, under which employees lose their otherwise vested pension benefits if they are fired for misconduct, or if they compete with the employer after leaving their jobs. Because plan documents may not contradict the statutory vesting and nonforfeitability requirements, plans may not apply bad boy clauses to benefits that have vested under one of the statutory schedules. Plans may, however, apply forfeiture provisions to benefits that are not subject to ERISA's accrual rules, such as welfare benefits, and to benefits that are vested under a more liberal schedule than the statute requires.

ERISA does contain some exceptions to the basic rule of nonforfeiture of vested accrued benefits. For instance, the participant's death can cause the loss of otherwise nonforfeitable accrued benefits, unless there is a survivor's benefit, as discussed later in this chapter.

Accrual

Vesting does not guarantee any particular amount or method of calculating a benefit; it merely allows the participant to enforce his or her claim to a certain percentage of the benefit provided for by the plan. When a participant becomes 100 percent vested, he or she has an enforceable right to 100 percent of the benefits accrued to date under the plan and to 100 percent of any additional benefits accrued in the future. Accrual rules determine the amount of the benefit to which a vested participant is entitled. Before the enactment of ERISA, a common plan practice was to "backload" benefits by providing for very little accrual in the early years of employment, with accelerated accrual only as the employee neared retirement age. An employee who did not continue in employment until the plan's normal retirement age might be 100 percent vested, but have virtually no accrued benefits. Another of ERISA's reforms was to prevent an employer from avoiding the impact of the statutory preretirement vesting requirements through delayed accrual of this kind.

Under ERISA benefits must begin to accrue when an employee becomes a participant in the plan. The rules for defined contribution plans are simple. Contributions to the plan must be made annually as required by the plan and allocated to individual accounts for each participant. Gains or losses on the contributions are also allocated to the individual accounts. A participant's accrued benefit in a defined contribution plan is the balance in his or her account.

Defined benefit plans must accrue part of the normal retirement benefit for each year of an employee's participation. Plans must use one of three accrual methods set out in the statute. The first accrual method is the 3 percent method, which requires that the benefits accrued for each year of participation, up to 33⅓ years, must be at least 3 percent of the normal retirement benefit. The second method is the 133⅓ percent method. It requires that the benefit accrued for any year be not more than 133⅓ percent of the benefit accrued in earlier years. The third method is the fractional method. It permits the accrued benefit to be determined by multiplying the normal retirement benefit by the fraction of the participant's years of participation over the total number of years of participation he or she would have if he or she had worked to normal retirement age. Defined benefit plans may not reduce accrued benefits because of the participant's age or years of service, and all plans, both defined benefit and defined contribution, must credit years of service after normal retirement age.

Commencement of Benefits

Unless the participant chooses to wait, payments of vested benefits must begin within 60 days after the end of the plan year in which the participant (1) reaches normal retirement age; (2) has participated in the plan for 10 years; or (3) terminates service with the employer, whichever is later. Plans must continue benefit accruals for participants who continue working past normal retirement age. ERISA does not have rules on how long an eligible participant may defer receipt of benefits, but the Internal Revenue Code requires the commencement of benefits no later than April 1 following the calendar year in which the participant reaches age 70½.

ERISA does not require a plan to offer early retirement benefits. If a plan does offer early retirement benefits conditioned on the satisfaction of age and service requirements, actuarially reduced benefits must be paid to a participant who satisfied the service requirement but left employment before reaching the required age when that individual does reach the plan's early retirement age.

SURVIVOR'S BENEFITS

Plans may stop payments of vested pension benefits when the participant dies, unless the plan is required to pay a survivor's annuity. ERISA creates two kinds of survivor's annuities, the "qualified joint and survivor annuity" (QJSA) and the "qualified preretirement survivor annuity" (QPSA). The purpose of these annuities is to give an employee's spouse rights in the employee's pension and to provide a source of retirement income for the surviving spouse if the participant dies first.

Qualified Joint and Survivor Annuity

The QJSA is an annuity for the life of the participant, with a survivor's annuity for the life of the participant's spouse. The survivor's annuity must be at least half of the amount payable during the couple's joint lives. Plans *must* pay a QJSA when the employee-participant retires, unless the nonemployee spouse waives the right to receive the pension benefit in that form. This is an important change from pre-ERISA law, which gave the choice of retirement benefit to the employee-participant alone. Under ERISA, the nonemployee spouse must affirmatively consent to a retirement benefit in any form other than a QJSA.

Qualified Preretirement Survivor Annuity

The QPSA is an annuity for the life of the surviving spouse of a vested participant who dies before retirement. As with the QJSA, a plan must pay a QPSA unless the nonemployee spouse waives the right to receive the benefit. All plans must begin QPSA benefit payments no later than the first month in which the participant could have taken early retirement.

Length of Marriage Requirement

With two exceptions, plans may require as a condition of paying survivor's benefits that the participant and his or her spouse have been married for at least a year before the date of retirement or the date of the participant's death, whichever is earlier. Under the first exception, if the couple was married less than a year before the annuity starting date and remains married for at least one year before the participant dies, the plan must pay survivor's benefits. Under the second exception, a "qualified domestic relations order," discussed later in this chapter, may require that a former spouse be treated as the surviving spouse for purposes of the survivor's annuity. In that case the one-year marriage rule is satisfied by one year of marriage at any time.

Waiver of Survivor's Annuities

Plans must pay survivor's annuities unless the nonemployee spouse waives them according to precise rules contained in the statute. The survivor's annuities may be waived or any previous election revoked only during the "applicable election period." For the QJSA the election period is the 90-day period ending on the annuity starting date. For the QPSA the period begins on the first day of the plan year in which the participant reaches age 35 and ends on the earlier of the date of the participant's death or the annuity starting date. A waiver at any time other than the applicable election period is not effective.

The spouse's waiver of the right to a survivor's annuity must be in writing and either notarized or witnessed by a plan representative. A consent by one spouse affects only that spouse and does not waive the rights of any later spouse of the same participant. Spousal consent to a waiver is obviously not necessary if the participant is not married, nor is it necessary if the participant establishes to the satisfaction of the plan that his or her spouse cannot be located. Prenuptial agreements in which one spouse waives survivor's rights in the other's pension do not satisfy the statutory consent requirements. Among other reasons, ERISA requires that the spouse be married to the participant at the time of the waiver, and by definition a prenuptial agreement is signed before the marriage.[5]

Spousal consent is also required if a participant wants to use any of his or her accrued benefit as security for a loan. Consent is also required for the cash-out of benefits after the annuity starting date or at any time if the present value of the survivor's benefits is more than $3,500. Plans may involuntarily cash out a survivor's benefit with a present value of less than $3,500.

Disclosure of Information

To enable participants to understand their rights and options, plans must give each participant a written explanation of the terms and conditions of the QJSA and the QPSA, the right of the participant's

---

[5]Hurwitz v. Sher, 982 F.2d 778, 16 EB Cases 1528 (2d Cir. 1992), *cert. denied*, 113 S. Ct. 2345, 16 EB Cases 2120 (1993).

spouse to waive these annuities, the financial and other effects of that waiver, and the right to revoke a waiver and its effect. For the QJSA, this explanation must be provided "within a reasonable period of time before the annuity starting date," which Treasury Department regulations define as the nine-month period before the participant reaches the earliest retirement age under the plan.

Plans must provide information concerning the QPSA before the latest of (1) the period beginning with the first day of the plan year in which the participant turns 32 and ending with the close of the plan year preceding the plan year in which the participant reaches 35, (2) a reasonable period after the person becomes a participant, or (3) a reasonable period after the survivor's benefit requirements become applicable to the participant. If a participant separates from service before reaching age 35, the QPSA notice must be provided within a reasonable period after separation.

Plan Liability

The plan is protected from liability for benefits paid if the fiduciary acts in accordance with ERISA's fiduciary standards in relying on a spouse's consent or in determining that the spouse's consent cannot be obtained, but later learns that someone other than the spouse signed the consent or that the spouse could in fact have been located and consent obtained. In the absence of actual knowledge of fraud or coercion in obtaining a spousal consent or actual knowledge of the invalidity of a consent, a plan fiduciary may rely on a waiver that on its face complies with the statutory requirements.

ERISA's fiduciary standards may, however, require a plan to do more than merely accept a participant's assertions that he or she is not married or cannot locate his or her spouse. The difference between a signed, notarized document in which the spouse waives his or her rights and the participant's attempt to waive the spouse's rights by declaring that he or she cannot be found may require the fiduciary to conduct an independent investigation of the participant's representations as part of its duty of prudence.[6]

---

[6]Lester v. Reagan Equip. Co. Profit Sharing Plan, 1992 U.S. Dist. LEXIS 12872 (E.D. La. 1992).

ALIENATION OR ASSIGNMENT OF BENEFITS

ERISA requires pension plans to provide that "benefits provided under the plan may not be assigned or alienated." This antialienation provision protects participants from losing their benefits through garnishment, attachment, or other legal process. A participant's creditors may not reach his or her pension benefits to satisfy their liens, even if the participant has a right to withdraw funds immediately or is awaiting a lump-sum distribution. This protection lasts only until the participant receives the benefits; after the funds are deposited in the participant's bank account, they are subject to legal process.

A plan may permit a participant to assign the right to future benefit payments if the assignment is voluntary and revocable and is not more than 10 percent of any benefit payment. A participant may also use nonforfeitable benefits as security for a loan from the plan under certain conditions.

Criminal Misconduct

In *Guidry v. Sheet Metal Workers National Pension Fund*,[7] the United States Supreme Court refused to create an exception to the antialienation rule for criminal activity against the employer or union that sponsors the plan. Guidry was a union officer and a trustee of a union pension fund who was convicted of embezzling funds from the union. After his conviction the lower courts ordered his pension benefits paid to the union as partial restitution of the money he had embezzled. The Supreme Court held that this order violated ERISA's antialienation requirement. The Court found that Congress made a considered choice to protect a participant's stream of retirement income, and it refused to approve any generalized exceptions for employee misconduct.

Qualified Domestic Relations Orders

ERISA does contain one exception to its antialienation rule for a "qualified domestic relations order" (QDRO). A QDRO is a judgment,

---

[7]493 U.S. 365, 11 EB Cases 2337 (1990).

decree, or order (including approval of a property settlement agreement) entered under state domestic relations law that relates to child support, alimony, or marital property rights of a participant's spouse, former spouse, child, or other dependent. The order must clearly state the name and last known mailing address of the participant and each person to whom payments must be made, the amount or percent of the participant's benefits to be paid to each of these people, the number of payments or the period of time covered by the order, and each plan to which the order applies. The plan is protected from multiple QDROs that exceed the amount of the participant's benefits.

With two exceptions, a QDRO may not require a plan to provide any type or form of benefit or option not otherwise provided under the plan, nor may it require a plan to increase benefits beyond those provided in the plan. The first exception is that a QDRO may require the plan to begin payments to the person named in the order when the participant reaches the age for early retirement under the plan, even if the participant does not actually retire at that time. Second, the QDRO may provide that the participant's former spouse is to be considered the surviving spouse for purposes of ERISA's survivor's benefits provisions, discussed earlier in this chapter. Thus, a plan can be required to pay an ex-spouse the survivor's benefits that would otherwise go to the participant's current spouse, or, if the participant did not remarry, would otherwise not have to be paid at all.

State court orders that do not meet the QDRO standards are unenforceable, and plans may not pay any benefits required by them. If there is a dispute about whether a state court order is a QDRO, the plan administrator may suspend payments ordered by the state court for up to 18 months while the question is resolved.

Bankruptcy

In *Patterson v. Shumate*,[8] the United States Supreme Court held that the Bankruptcy Code permits funds in an ERISA-covered pension plan to be excluded from the debtor's property. These funds, which could be substantial, thus may not be used to pay the bankrupt's debts.

---

[8]112 S. Ct. 2242, 15 EB Cases 1481 (1992).

Taxes

Under Treasury Department regulations the antialienation rule does not apply to federal tax levies, to the collection of a judgment for unpaid federal taxes, or to withholding for federal, state, or local taxes. State tax levies, however, are prohibited.[9]

FIDUCIARY PROVISIONS

The fiduciary provisions of ERISA apply to virtually all employee benefit plans covered by the Act. Thus, the fiduciary requirements apply to pension plans and to both funded and unfunded welfare plans. While most lawsuits for breach of ERISA's fiduciary duties involve challenges to the management of pension fund assets, the actions of the fiduciaries of even unfunded welfare plans can also violate the statutory requirements.

Fiduciary Status

ERISA requires each plan to have one or more fiduciaries. A person is a fiduciary if he or she (1) exercises any discretionary authority or discretionary control concerning management of the plan or exercises any authority or control with respect to management or disposition of plan assets, (2) gives investment advice about plan assets for a fee or other compensation, or (3) has any discretionary authority or discretionary responsibility in the administration of the plan.

In keeping with ERISA's remedial nature, courts have interpreted the term fiduciary broadly to include not only the fiduciary named in the plan documents, but also anyone who possesses or performs any of the three basic fiduciary functions—plan administration, asset management, or investment advice for a fee—even if that person has no formal relationship with the plan. Thus, while individuals who hold certain plan positions, such as a trustee, clearly have fiduciary status, a person who has no position with a plan may nevertheless be a fiduciary if he or

---

[9]Plumbing Indus. Retirement Trust v. Franchise Tax Bd., 909 F.2d 1266, 12 EB Cases 1993 (9th Cir. 1990).

she actually performs or controls the performance of a fiduciary function.

On the other hand, a person who operates within a preestablished framework of policies and procedures and who has no power to make any independent decisions about the management of the plan or the disposition of plan assets does not satisfy the statutory definition. Thus, a person is not a fiduciary if his or her sole function is to apply a formula contained in the plan documents to calculate the amount of benefits to which a plan participant is entitled.

A related concept is that some decisions that seriously affect the structure of the plan and the expectations of participants are simply not fiduciary in nature. By specifically permitting employer representatives to serve as fiduciaries, ERISA contemplates that employers will often wear two hats with respect to benefit plans. Accordingly, the courts have distinguished between decisions that are employer functions, to which the fiduciary standards do not apply, and those that are fiduciary functions. Day-to-day corporate business decisions involving the work force or the direction of the company, such as whether to keep employees on the payroll following the sale of a plant or whether the early retirement of a particular employee would be in the company's interest, are not subject to ERISA's fiduciary standards.

Employer functions generally are the "design" decisions, such as whether to establish a plan, what level and type of benefits to offer, whether to amend the plan to reduce or eliminate nonvested benefits, and whether to terminate the plan. ERISA's vesting and accrual requirements prevent the reduction or elimination of vested benefits and nonvested accrued benefits, but courts have found that the statutory fiduciary standards do not control employers' decisions to reduce or eliminate welfare benefits, to which the vesting and accrual requirements do not apply. Promises in the plan documents, in collective bargaining agreements, or in other statements may obligate an employer to continue to provide a welfare benefit, but ERISA's fiduciary standards do not.

Finally, firms or individuals who give professional advice to plans are generally not fiduciaries, as long as they do not cross the line between advising plan fiduciaries and actually exercising control over the plan. Thus, attorneys, accountants, and actuaries who advise plans in their professional capacities are not liable for breach of ERISA's fiduciary standards.

Fiduciary Duties

ERISA embodies strict principles of fiduciary duty developed by the law of trusts. There are four basic interrelated statutory standards. The first is the exclusive benefit rule. Fiduciaries must discharge their duties "solely in the interest of the participants and beneficiaries" of the plan and "for the exclusive purpose" of providing benefits and defraying reasonable administrative expenses. The second fiduciary standard is the "prudence" standard of care for administration and investment decisions. The third requires diversification of plan investments, and the fourth commands fiduciaries to act in accordance with plan documents to the extent they are consistent with the terms of the statute.

Under the exclusive benefit rule fiduciaries must act with complete and undivided loyalty to the beneficiaries of the trust. They may not act in their own personal interests or in the interest of some third party. As discussed above, however, ERISA does permit employees of the employer that sponsors the plan to serve as plan fiduciaries, and it also allows as much as 10 percent of the trust's assets to be invested in the stock of the employer that sponsors the plan. In the leading case of *Donovan v. Bierwirth*,[10] the Second Circuit Court of Appeals said that fiduciaries do not violate their statutory duties merely because an action that benefits the plan also benefits the plan sponsor or even the fiduciaries themselves. The fiduciaries must be extremely careful, however, to concentrate on the interests of the participants and beneficiaries. *Bierwirth* involved the actions of the trustees of the Grumman Corporation's pension fund, who were also officers of Grumman, in causing the fund to purchase large quantities of Grumman stock during the 1981 Grumman-LTV takeover battle. In finding a breach of ERISA's exclusive benefit rule, the court said that the trustees were obligated to engage in an intensive and scrupulous independent investigation of their options and "to take every feasible precaution to see that they had carefully considered the other side."

The prudence standard requires fiduciaries to act "with the care, skill, prudence, and diligence under the circumstances then prevailing that a prudent man acting in a like capacity and familiar with such matters would use in the conduct of an enterprise of a like character and

---

[10]680 F.2d 263, 3 EB Cases 1417 (2d Cir.), *cert. denied*, 459 U.S. 1069, 3 EB Cases 2490 (1982).

with like aims." Although most of the ERISA prudence cases involve investment decisions, courts have applied the standard to other fiduciary actions. For instance, in *Central States, Southeast & Southwest Areas Pension Fund v. Central Transport, Inc.*,[11] the United States Supreme Court found that the duty of prudence applied to the collection of employer contributions. In an influential early case, *Freund v. Marshall & Ilsley Bank*,[12] a federal district court found that a fiduciary's duty of prudence extends to his or her resignation, so that resignation without making adequate provision for the continued prudent management of the plan is a breach of fiduciary duty.

The fourth fiduciary duty is the duty to act in accordance with plan documents to the extent they are consistent with ERISA. Although this requirement has the potential to convert every individual claim for benefits into a claim for breach of fiduciary duty, the courts have generally measured a fiduciary's decision to deny a claim for benefits under the standards of review set forth in the Supreme Court's opinion in *Firestone Tire & Rubber Co. v. Bruch*.[13] Breaches of the duty to comply with plan documents can be found if the plan imposes specific requirements and the fiduciary fails to follow them, although these cases often involve breaches of one or more of the other fiduciary duties as well. The importance of the duty to follow plan documents is that it makes clear that although a fiduciary's actions are controlled primarily by the plan documents, they may be followed only if they are consistent with the statute's requirements.

Prohibited Transactions

ERISA's prohibited transactions provisions forbid fiduciary self-dealing and other transactions with the potential for misuse of fund assets. These transactions are defined by the relationship between the plan and the other parties to the arrangement. Subject to certain exceptions, ERISA prohibits fiduciaries from engaging in various transactions with a "party in interest," which includes fiduciaries, counsel, or employees of the plan, persons providing services to the plan, employers whose employees are covered by the plan, unions

---

[11]472 U.S. 559, 6 EB Cases 1665 (1985).
[12]485 F. Supp. 629, 1 EB Cases 1898 (W.D. Wis. 1979).
[13]489 U.S. 101, 10 EB Cases 1873 (1989). See chapter 3.

whose members are covered by the plan, and other related individuals or entities. Prohibited are the sale, exchange, or lease of property, loans and extensions of credit, furnishing of goods or services, transfer of assets, or the acquisition of employer securities or property beyond limits permitted by the statute. Fiduciaries are also prohibited from dealing with plan assets for their own accounts and from acting in a transaction involving the plan on behalf of a party whose interests are adverse to those of the plan, its participants, or beneficiaries. Kickbacks to fiduciaries are also prohibited.

Fiduciary Liability

ERISA imposes personal liability on a fiduciary to make good any losses to the plan resulting from a breach of statutory duties and to restore to the plan any profits the fiduciary made through the misuse of plan assets, even if the plan did not suffer any loss.

ERISA also imposes liability on a fiduciary for the breach of a co-fiduciary in three situations: (1) if the fiduciary knowingly participates in or tries to conceal a breach by a co-fiduciary; (2) if, by failing to comply with his or her own fiduciary duties, a fiduciary enables a co-fiduciary to commit a breach; and (3) if a fiduciary knows that a breach has taken place and fails to make reasonable efforts to remedy it. Although a fiduciary is not liable for breaches committed before he or she became a fiduciary, new fiduciaries have a duty to review prior investment decisions and to take reasonable actions to correct any breaches discovered in that review.

Although ERISA expressly establishes co-fiduciary liability, in *Mertens v. Hewitt Associates*,[14] the United States Supreme Court held that the statute does not permit the imposition of liability on nonfiduciaries in connection with a fiduciary's breach.

AGE DISCRIMINATION AND EMPLOYEE BENEFITS

The Age Discrimination in Employment Act (ADEA)[15] prohibits discrimination in employment on the basis of age against individuals

---

[14]113 S. Ct. 2063, 16 EB Cases 2169 (1993).
[15]29 U.S.C. §§621–34 (1993). See also chapter 2.

aged 40 and over. In 1990, Congress enacted the Older Workers Benefit Protection Act (OWBPA),[16] which amended the ADEA to make it clear that the prohibition on age discrimination includes discrimination in pension plans and other fringe benefits. The OWBPA contains an equal benefit or equal cost standard. Employee benefit plans must provide equal benefits to all workers regardless of age, or they must spend approximately the same amount on all workers. With certain exceptions, "the *only* justification for age discrimination in an employee benefit is the increased cost in providing the particular benefit to older individuals."

Exceptions for Some Pension Plan Practices

The OWBPA excepts some practices of defined benefit plans that may not comply with the equal benefit or equal cost rule. Pension plans may establish a minimum age as a condition of eligibility for normal or early retirement benefits. Defined benefit plans may subsidize early retirement benefits and may make Social Security bridge payments intended to substitute for Social Security benefits that will become available at age 62 or 65. To qualify for protection, these provisions must be permanent plan features, subject to amendment on a prospective basis through the plan amendment process, and continually available to employees who meet the eligibility requirements.

Coordination of Severance Benefits

In enacting the OWBPA Congress wanted to confirm that severance pay and pension benefits are not fungible. Ordinarily, an employer may not reduce the amount of severance pay it would otherwise owe an employee merely because the employee is eligible for pension benefits.

The OWBPA does, however, authorize coordination of severance benefits in certain narrowly defined circumstances. If a contingent event unrelated to age, such as a plant closing or layoff, entitles employees to severance pay, employers may deduct from the severance pay the value of any retiree health benefits received by an individual eligible for an immediate pension. If the pension is actuarially reduced, the severance

---

[16]Pub. L. No. 101-433, 104 Stat. 987 (1991).

pay deduction must be reduced by the same percentage as the reduction in pension benefits. For instance, if an employee receives a pension benefit that is actuarially reduced by 10 percent, the value of any retiree health benefits the employee receives must also be reduced by ten percent before the employer may set them off against the severance pay.

Employers may also deduct from severance pay the value of any additional pension benefits provided to the worker solely because of the contingent event, but only if the worker is eligible for not less than an immediate and unreduced pension.

Employers may reduce long-term disability benefits by any pension benefits that the individual voluntarily elects to receive or by any pension benefits for which an individual who has reached the later of age 62 or normal retirement age is eligible.

Early Retirement Incentives

During the restructuring and downsizing of U.S. industries in the 1980s, many employers adopted programs intended to encourage workers to retire before the pension plan's normal retirement age. Although these programs were linked to an employee's age, the courts held that the mere offer of an early retirement incentive was not unlawful age discrimination. Rather, early retirement programs were seen as favoring older workers by offering them extra benefits, as long as acceptance of an early retirement offer was truly voluntary. The OWBPA affirms this case law by permitting employers to maintain voluntary early retirement incentive plans that are consistent with the purposes of the ADEA. A voluntary early retirement incentive plan must give employees enough time to consider their choices, particularly if the employer has not previously offered retirement counseling, and provide complete and accurate information about the benefits available under the plan. In addition, the background must be free from threats, intimidation, and coercion. As a practical matter, many of Congress' concerns about the voluntariness of a decision to retire early may be allayed by the new requirements for waivers of age discrimination claims, discussed below.

Early retirement programs may offer incentives such as payment of a flat dollar amount, service-based benefits, a percentage of salary, flat dollar or percentage increases in pension benefits, and imputation of years of service and/or age. Early retirement plans that deny or reduce benefits to workers above a certain age while providing them to younger workers, and plans that exclude older workers based on age-related stereotypes may be unlawful because they conflict with the purposes of the ADEA.

Waivers

Employers often condition payment of benefits under an early retirement incentive program, as well as payments under individually tailored separation agreements, on the employee's signing of a release of claims against the company. Although the courts have developed a "knowing and voluntary" standard to measure the validity of releases under Title VII of the Civil Rights Act of 1964,[17] there was a question whether that body of law could be used for the ADEA. The ADEA uses many of the enforcement provisions of the Fair Labor Standards Act, which does not permit unsupervised waivers.[18] Therefore, the argument went, a release of age discrimination claims would not be valid unless approved by the EEOC. Most courts rejected this contention and applied some form of a knowing and voluntary test to ADEA releases, but the issue remained controversial.

The OWBPA resolves the issue of waivers of ADEA claims by adopting the general rule that a waiver will not be valid unless it is knowing and voluntary. The statute goes beyond the case law, however, by establishing seven minimum standards that any waiver of claims under the ADEA must meet.

- The waiver must be part of an agreement between the employee and the employer that is written in a manner that the employee or the average eligible individual can understand.

- The waiver must specifically refer to rights or claims arising under the ADEA.

- The waiver must not include rights or claims arising after the date it is signed.

---

[17]42 U.S.C. §2000e et seq. (1993). See chapter 2.
[18]See chapter 3.

- The employee must receive a payment or something of value in addition to any benefits to which he or she is already entitled.

- The employee must be advised in writing to consult with an attorney before signing the agreement.

- The employee must be given at least 21 days in which to consider the agreement.

- The agreement must provide for at least a seven-day grace period after signing, within which the employee may revoke it. The agreement may not become effective or enforceable until after the revocation period has expired.

If the waiver is sought as part of an exit incentive or other termination program offered to a group of employees, the waiting period is extended from 21 to 45 days. In addition, at the beginning of the 45-day period, the employer must inform the employee in writing of the group of employees covered by the program, any eligibility factors and time limits for the program, the job titles and ages of all employees who are eligible or selected for the program, and the ages of all employees in the same job classification or unit who are not eligible or selected for the program.

Waivers given in settlement of an EEOC charge or a lawsuit satisfy the knowing and voluntary requirement if they meet the first five tests described above and if the employee has a reasonable period of time within which to consider the settlement agreement. No waiver agreement may affect the EEOC's right to enforce the ADEA, or interfere with an employee's right to file a charge or participate in an EEOC investigation or proceeding.

Benefit Accruals After Normal Retirement Age

ERISA permits pension plans to specify a normal retirement age, usually 65, and it defines the concept of accrued benefits under a defined benefit plan in terms of the plan's normal retirement age. The ADEA, however, prohibits employers from requiring most employees to retire because of their age or from discriminating against them in any other manner because of their age. In 1986, Congress amended the ADEA and ERISA to make it clear that pension plans may not exclude employees from participation on the basis of age and that neither benefit accruals under a defined benefit plan nor allocations to an employee's account under a defined contribution plan may be stopped or reduced because the employee has reached the plan's normal retirement age.

SEX DISCRIMINATION IN PENSIONS

Because women as a group live longer than men as a group, from an actuarial standpoint employee benefits tied to life expectancy, such as life annuities, cost more for women than for men. In *City of Los Angeles Department of Water & Power v. Manhart*,[19] the employer maintained an unusual kind of pension plan, a defined benefit plan that required unequal employee contributions. The plan used sex-based mortality assumptions, and it required higher contributions from female employees so that both men and women would receive the same monthly benefit payments upon retirement. The United States Supreme Court held that this plan discriminated against women workers in violation of Title VII. Title VII requires that employees be treated as individuals, not as members of groups, and the use of actuarial tables based on group characteristics violates that principle.

In *Arizona Governing Committee v. Norris*,[20] the Supreme Court found that pension plans that require equal contributions on behalf of men and women workers but pay smaller pension benefits to women violate Title VII as well. The State of Arizona maintained a defined contribution plan under which the state used the employee's contribution to buy an annuity contract from an insurance company chosen by the employee from an approved list. When the employee retired, he or she could choose among different payment options. For one of these options, a life annuity, all of the companies used sex-based mortality assumptions. Thus, in converting her individual account to a life annuity, a female employee would receive a smaller monthly payment than would a man with an identical employment history. The Court found that discriminatory benefit payments were just as unlawful as discriminatory contributions. The Court rejected the state's arguments that its conduct was lawful because it offered other, nondiscriminatory payment options from which employees could choose or because it was

---

[19]435 U.S. 702, 17 FEP Cases 395 (1978).
[20]463 U.S. 1073, 32 FEP Cases 233 (1983).

merely offering the equivalent of what workers could buy on the open insurance market.

Although the plaintiffs in *Manhart* and *Norris* were women, abandoning the use of sex-based mortality assumptions often benefits men as a class. For instance, in converting a single life annuity to a joint and survivor annuity, a plan may not reduce a male participant's annuity more to take into account his wife's assumed longer life expectancy than it does for a female participant who elects a survivor's benefit for her husband.

Table of Cases

Cases are referenced to chapter and footnote number(s): e.g., **9:** 31 indicates the case is cited in chapter 9, footnote 31.

Q

R

S

Index

N

About the Authors

MARK A. ROTHSTEIN is Law Foundation Professor of Law at the University of Houston. A graduate of Georgetown University Law Center, Professor Rothstein has taught a range of employment law subjects for 20 years. Professor Rothstein is best known for his work in employment testing, workplace privacy, and occupational safety and health law. He is the author of nine books on employment law.

CHARLES B. CRAVER is Merrifield Research Professor of Law at George Washington University. After graduating from the University of Michigan Law School and practicing employment law, Professor Craver has been teaching labor and employment law for 20 years. A prolific author, Professor Craver has written leading books on labor relations, employment discrimination, and other topics.

ELINOR P. SCHROEDER is Professor of Law at the University of Kansas. After graduating from the University of Michigan Law School, Professor Schroeder practiced employment law before becoming a law professor. Professor Schroeder is a recognized expert in the fields of employee benefits and wrongful discharge.

ELAINE W. SHOBEN is Edward W. Cleary Professor of Law at the University of Illinois. A graduate of the University of California-Hastings College of the Law, Professor Shoben has been teaching employment law for 20 years. Her books on employment discrimination law and remedies are widely used in legal education.

LEA S. VANDERVELDE is Professor of Law at the University of Iowa. After graduating from the University of Wisconsin Law School, Professor Vandervelde clerked for a member of the Wisconsin Supreme Court and a U.S. district court judge in Iowa. She is known for her work on the history of employment law and the development of the common law of employment.